T0255096

Lecture Notes in Computer Science 10802

Commenced Publication in 1973
Founding and Former Series Editors:
Gerhard Goos, Juris Hartmanis, and Jan van Leeuwen

Advanced Research in Computing and Software Science
Subline of Lecture Notes in Computer Science

More information about this series at http://www.springer.com/series/7407

Alessandra Russo · Andy Schürr (Eds.)

Fundamental Approaches to Software Engineering

21st International Conference, FASE 2018
Held as Part of the European Joint Conferences
on Theory and Practice of Software, ETAPS 2018
Thessaloniki, Greece, April 14–20, 2018
Proceedings

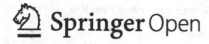

Editors
Alessandra Russo
Imperial College London
London
UK

Andy Schürr
TU Darmstadt
Darmstadt
Germany

ISSN 0302-9743   ISSN 1611-3349 (electronic)
Lecture Notes in Computer Science
ISBN 978-3-319-89362-4   ISBN 978-3-319-89363-1 (eBook)
https://doi.org/10.1007/978-3-319-89363-1

Library of Congress Control Number: 2018937400

LNCS Sublibrary: SL1 – Theoretical Computer Science and General Issues

ETAPS Foreword

Welcome to the proceedings of ETAPS 2018! After a somewhat coldish ETAPS 2017 in Uppsala in the north, ETAPS this year took place in Thessaloniki, Greece. I am happy to announce that this is the first ETAPS with gold open access proceedings. This means that all papers are accessible by anyone for free.

ETAPS 2018 was the 21st instance of the European Joint Conferences on Theory and Practice of Software. ETAPS is an annual federated conference established in 1998, and consists of five conferences: ESOP, FASE, FoSSaCS, TACAS, and POST. Each conference has its own Program Committee (PC) and its own Steering Committee. The conferences cover various aspects of software systems, ranging from theoretical computer science to foundations to programming language developments, analysis tools, formal approaches to software engineering, and security. Organizing these conferences in a coherent, highly synchronized conference program facilitates participation in an exciting event, offering attendees the possibility to meet many researchers working in different directions in the field, and to easily attend talks of different conferences. Before and after the main conference, numerous satellite workshops take place and attract many researchers from all over the globe.

ETAPS 2018 received 479 submissions in total, 144 of which were accepted, yielding an overall acceptance rate of 30%. I thank all the authors for their interest in ETAPS, all the reviewers for their peer reviewing efforts, the PC members for their contributions, and in particular the PC (co-)chairs for their hard work in running this entire intensive process. Last but not least, my congratulations to all authors of the accepted papers!

ETAPS 2018 was enriched by the unifying invited speaker Martin Abadi (Google Brain, USA) and the conference-specific invited speakers (FASE) Pamela Zave (AT & T Labs, USA), (POST) Benjamin C. Pierce (University of Pennsylvania, USA), and (ESOP) Derek Dreyer (Max Planck Institute for Software Systems, Germany). Invited tutorials were provided by Armin Biere (Johannes Kepler University, Linz, Austria) on modern SAT solving and Fabio Somenzi (University of Colorado, Boulder, USA) on hardware verification. My sincere thanks to all these speakers for their inspiring and interesting talks!

ETAPS 2018 took place in Thessaloniki, Greece, and was organised by the Department of Informatics of the Aristotle University of Thessaloniki. The university was founded in 1925 and currently has around 75,000 students; it is the largest university in Greece. ETAPS 2018 was further supported by the following associations and societies: ETAPS e.V., EATCS (European Association for Theoretical Computer Science), EAPLS (European Association for Programming Languages and Systems), and EASST (European Association of Software Science and Technology). The local organization team consisted of Panagiotis Katsaros (general chair), Ioannis Stamelos,

Lefteris Angelis, George Rahonis, Nick Bassiliades, Alexander Chatzigeorgiou, Ezio Bartocci, Simon Bliudze, Emmanouela Stachtiari, Kyriakos Georgiadis, and Petros Stratis (EasyConferences).

The overall planning for ETAPS is the main responsibility of the Steering Committee, and in particular of its Executive Board. The ETAPS Steering Committee consists of an Executive Board and representatives of the individual ETAPS conferences, as well as representatives of EATCS, EAPLS, and EASST. The Executive Board consists of Gilles Barthe (Madrid), Holger Hermanns (Saarbrücken), Joost-Pieter Katoen (chair, Aachen and Twente), Gerald Lüttgen (Bamberg), Vladimiro Sassone (Southampton), Tarmo Uustalu (Tallinn), and Lenore Zuck (Chicago). Other members of the Steering Committee are: Wil van der Aalst (Aachen), Parosh Abdulla (Uppsala), Amal Ahmed (Boston), Christel Baier (Dresden), Lujo Bauer (Pittsburgh), Dirk Beyer (Munich), Mikolaj Bojanczyk (Warsaw), Luis Caires (Lisbon), Jurriaan Hage (Utrecht), Rainer Hähnle (Darmstadt), Reiko Heckel (Leicester), Marieke Huisman (Twente), Panagiotis Katsaros (Thessaloniki), Ralf Küsters (Stuttgart), Ugo Dal Lago (Bologna), Kim G. Larsen (Aalborg), Matteo Maffei (Vienna), Tiziana Margaria (Limerick), Flemming Nielson (Copenhagen), Catuscia Palamidessi (Palaiseau), Andrew M. Pitts (Cambridge), Alessandra Russo (London), Dave Sands (Göteborg), Don Sannella (Edinburgh), Andy Schürr (Darmstadt), Alex Simpson (Ljubljana), Gabriele Taentzer (Marburg), Peter Thiemann (Freiburg), Jan Vitek (Prague), Tomas Vojnar (Brno), and Lijun Zhang (Beijing).

I would like to take this opportunity to thank all speakers, attendees, organizers of the satellite workshops, and Springer for their support. I hope you all enjoy the proceedings of ETAPS 2018. Finally, a big thanks to Panagiotis and his local organization team for all their enormous efforts that led to a fantastic ETAPS in Thessaloniki!

February 2018   Joost-Pieter Katoen

Preface

This book contains the proceedings of FASE 2018, the 21th International Conference on Fundamental Approaches to Software Engineering, held in Thessaloniki, Greece, in April 2018, as part of the annual European Joint Conferences on Theory and Practice of Software (ETAPS 2018).

As usual for FASE, the contributions combine the development of conceptual and methodological advances with their formal foundations, tool support, and evaluation on realistic or pragmatic cases. As a result, the volume contains regular research papers that cover a wide range of topics, such as program and system analysis, model transformations, configuration and synthesis, graph modeling and transformation, software product lines, test selection, as well as learning and inference. We hope that the community will find this volume engaging and worth reading.

The contributions included have been carefully selected. For the third time, FASE used a double-blind review process, as the past two years' experiments were considered valuable by authors and worth the additional effort of anonymizing the papers. We received 77 abstract submissions from 24 different countries, from which 63 full-paper submissions materialized. All papers were reviewed by three experts in the field, and after intense discussion, only 19 were accepted, giving an acceptance rate of 30%.

We thank the ETAPS 2018 general chair Katsaros Panagiotis, the ETAPS organizers, Ioannis Stamelos, Lefteris Angelis, and George Rahonis, the ETAPS publicity chairs, Ezio Bartocci and Simon Bliudze, as well as the ETAPS SC chair, Joost-Pieter Katoen, for their support during the whole process. We thank all the authors for their hard work and willingness to contribute. Last but not least, we thank all the Program Committee members and external reviewers, who invested time and effort in the selection process to ensure the scientific quality of the program.

February 2018

Alessandra Russo
Andy Schürr

Organization

Program Committee

Ruth Breu	Universität Innsbruck, Austria
Yuanfang Cai	Drexel University, USA
Sagar Chaki	Carnegie Mellon University, USA
Hana Chockler	King's College London, UK
Ewen Denney	NASA Ames, USA
Stefania Gnesi	ISTI-CNR, Italy
Dilian Gurov	Royal Institute of Technology (KTH), Sweden
Zhenjiang Hu	National Institute for Informatics, Japan
Reiner Hähnle	Darmstadt University of Technology, Germany
Valerie Issarny	Inria, France
Einar Broch Johnsen	University of Oslo, Norway
Gerti Kappel	Vienna University of Technology, Austria
Ekkart Kindler	Technical University of Denmark, Denmark
Kim Mens	Université catholique de Louvain, Belgium
Fernando Orejas	Universitat Politècnica de Catalunya, Spain
Fabrizio Pastore	University of Luxembourg, Luxembourg
Arend Rensink	Universiteit Twente, The Netherlands
Leila Ribeiro	Universidade Federal do Rio Grande do Sul, Brazil
Julia Rubin	The University of British Columbia, USA
Bernhard Rumpe	RWTH Aachen, Germany
Alessandra Russo	Imperial College London, UK
Rick Salay	University of Toronto, Canada
Ina Schaefer	Technische Universität Braunschweig, Germany
Andy Schürr	Darmstadt University of Technology, Germany
Marjan Sirjani	Reykjavik University, Iceland
Wil Van der Aalst	RWTH Aachen, Germany
Daniel Varro	Budapest University of Technology and Economics, Hungary
Virginie Wiels	ONERA/DTIM, France
Yingfei Xiong	Peking University, China
Didar Zowghi	University of Technology Sydney, Australia

Additional Reviewers

Adam, Kai
Ahmed, Khaled E.
Alrajeh, Dalal
Auer, Florian
Basile, Davide
Bergmann, Gábor
Bill, Robert
Bubel, Richard
Búr, Márton
Chen, Yifan
Cicchetti, Antonio
de Vink, Erik
Dulay, Naranker
Feng, Qiong
Guimaraes, Everton
Haeusler, Martin
Haglund, Jonas
Haubrich, Olga
Herda, Mihai
Hillemacher, Steffen
Huber, Michael
Jafari, Ali
Jiang, Jiajun
Johansen, Christian
Joosten, Sebastiaan
Kamburjan, Eduard
Kautz, Oliver
Khamespanah, Ehsan
Knüppel, Alexander
Laurent, Nicolas
Leblebici, Erhan
Liang, Jingjing
Lindner, Andreas
Lity, Sascha

Lochau, Malte
Markthaler, Matthias
Mauro, Jacopo
Melgratti, Hernan
Micskei, Zoltan
Mohaqeqi, Morteza
Mousavi, Mohamad
Nesic, Damir
Nieke, Michael
Pun, Ka I.
Saake, Gunter
Sauerwein, Clemens
Schlatte, Rudolf
Schuster, Sven
Seidl, Martina
Semeráth, Oszkár
Shaver, Chris
Shumeiko, Igor
Steffen, Martin
Steinebach, Martin
Steinhöfel, Dominic
Stolz, Volker
Tapia Tarifa, Silvia Lizeth
Ter Beek, Maurice H.
Tiezzi, Francesco
Varga, Simon
Wally, Bernhard
Wang, Bo
Weckesser, Markus
Whiteside, Iain
Wimmer, Manuel
Wolny, Sabine
Xiao, Lu
Yue, Ruru

Contents

Model-Based Software Development

A Formal Framework for Incremental Model Slicing

Gabriele Taentzer[1], Timo Kehrer[2], Christopher Pietsch[3(✉)],
and Udo Kelter[3]

[1] Philipps-Universität Marburg, Marburg, Germany
[2] Humboldt-Universität zu Berlin, Berlin, Germany
[3] University of Siegen, Siegen, Germany
cpietsch@informatik.uni-siegen.de

Abstract. Program slicing is a technique which can determine the simplest program possible that maintains the meaning of the original program w.r.t. a slicing criterion. The concept of slicing has been transferred to models, in particular to statecharts. In addition to the classical use cases of slicing adopted from the field of program understanding, model slicing is also motivated by specifying submodels of interest to be further processed more efficiently, thus dealing with scalability issues when working with very large models. Slices are often updated throughout specific software development tasks. Such a slice update can be performed by creating the new slice from scratch or by incrementally updating the existing slice. In this paper, we present a formal framework for defining model slicers that support incremental slice updates. This framework abstracts from the behavior of concrete slicers as well as from the concrete model modification approach. It forms a guideline for defining incremental model slicers independent of the underlying slicer's semantics. Incremental slice updates are shown to be equivalent to non-incremental ones. Furthermore, we present a framework instantiation based on the concept of edit scripts defining application sequences of model transformation rules. We implemented two concrete model slicers for this instantiation based on the Eclipse Modeling Framework.

1 Introduction

Program slicing as introduced by Weiser [1] is a technique which determines those parts of a program (the *slice*) which may affect the values of a set of (user-)selected variables at a specific point (the *slicing criterion*). Since the seminal work of Weiser, which calculates a slice by utilizing static data and control flow analysis and which primarily focuses on assisting developers in debugging, a plethora of program slicing techniques addressing a broad range of use cases have been proposed [2].

With the advent of Model-Driven Engineering (MDE) [3], models rather than source code play the role of primary software development artifacts. Similar use

© The Author(s) 2018
A. Russo and A. Schürr (Eds.): FASE 2018, LNCS 10802, pp. 3–20, 2018.
https://doi.org/10.1007/978-3-319-89363-1_1

cases as known from program slicing must be supported for model slicing [4–6]. In addition to classical use cases adopted from the field of program understanding, model slicing is often motivated by scalability issues when working with very large models [7,8], which has often been mentioned as one of the biggest obstacles in applying MDE in practice [9,10]. Modeling frameworks such as the Eclipse Modeling Framework (EMF) and widely-used model management tools do not scale beyond a few tens of thousands of model elements [11], while large-scale industrial models are considerably larger [12]. As a consequence, such models cannot even be edited in standard model editors. Thus, the *extraction of editable submodels from a larger model* is the only viable solution to support an efficient yet independent editing of huge monolithic models [8]. Further example scenarios in which model slices may be constructed for the sake of efficiency include model checkers, test suite generators, etc., in order to reduce runtimes and memory consumption.

Slice criteria are often modified during software development tasks. This leads to corresponding *slice updates* (also called slice *adaptations* in [8]). During a debugging session, e.g., the slicing criterion might need to be modified in order to closer inspect different debugging hypotheses. The independent editing of submodels is another example of this. Here, a slice created for an initial slicing criterion can turn out to be inappropriate, most typically because additional model elements are desired or because the slice is still too large. These *slice update* scenarios have in common that the original slicing criterion is modified and that the existing slice must be updated w.r.t. the new slicing criterion.

Model slicing is faced with two challenging requirements which do not exist or which are of minor importance for traditional program slicers. First, the increasing importance and prevalence of domain-specific modeling languages (DSMLs) as well as a considerable number of different use cases lead to a huge number of different concrete slicers, examples will be presented in Sect. 2. Thus, methods for developing model slicers should abstract from a slicer's concrete behavior (and thus from concrete modeling languages) as far as possible. Ideally, model slicers should be generic in the sense that the behavior of a slicer is *adaptable* with moderate configuration effort [7]. Second, rather than creating a new slice from scratch for a modified slicing criterion, slices must often be updated *incrementally*. This is indispensable for all use cases where slices are edited by developers since otherwise these slice edits would be blindly overwritten [8]. In addition, incremental slice updating is a desirable feature when it is more efficient than creating the slice from scratch. To date, both requirements have been insufficiently addressed in the literature.

In this paper, we present a fundamental methodology for developing model slicers which abstract from the behavior of a concrete slicer and which support incremental model slicing. To be independent of a concrete DSML and use cases, we restrict ourselves to static slicing in order to support both executable and non-executable models. We make the following contributions:

1. A formal framework for incremental model slicing which can function as a guideline for defining adaptable and incremental model slicers (s. Sect. 3).

This framework is based on graph-based models and model modifications and abstracts from the behavior of concrete slicers as well as from the concrete model modification approach. Within this framework we show that incremental slice updates are equivalent to non-incremental ones.

2. An instantiation of this formal framework where incremental model slicers are specified by model patches. Two concrete model slicers.

2   Motivating Example

In this section we introduce a running example to illustrate two use cases of model slicing and to motivate incremental slice updates.

Figure 1 shows an excerpt of the system model of the *Barbados Car Crash Crisis Management System (bCMS)* [13]. It describes the operations of a police and a fire department in case of a crisis situation.

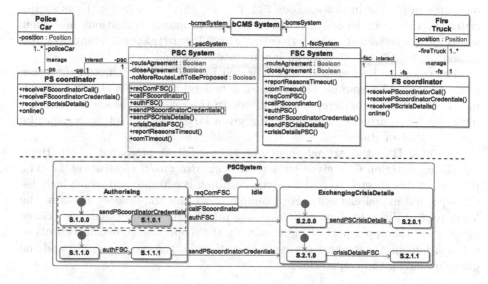

Fig. 1. Excerpt of the system model of the bCMS case study [13].

The system is modeled from different viewpoints. The class diagram models the key entities and their relationships from a static point of view. A police station coordinator (`PS coordinator`) and a fire station coordinator (`FS coordinator`) are responsible for coordinating and synchronizing the activities on the police and fire station during a crisis. The interaction of both coordinators is managed by the respective system classes `PSC System` and `FSC System` which contain several operations for, e.g., establishing the communication between the coordinators and exchanging crisis details. The state machine diagram models the dynamic view of the class `PSC System`, i.e., its runtime behavior, for sending and receiving authorization credentials and crisis details to and from a `FSC System`. Initially, the `PSC System` is in the state `Idle`. The establishment of the communication can be triggered by calling the operation `callFScoordinator` or `reqComFSC`. In the composite state `Authorising` the system waits for exchanging the credentials of the `PS` and `FS coordinator` by calling the operation `sendPScoordinatorCredentials` and `authFSC`, or vice versa. On entering the composite state `ExchangingCrisisDetails`, details can be sent by the operation call `sendPSCrisisDetails` or details can be received by the operation call `crisisDetailsFSC`.

Model Slicing. Model slicers are used to find parts of interest in a given model M. These parts of M are specified by a *slicing criterion*, which is basically a set of model elements or, more formally, a submodel C of M. A slicer extends C with further model elements of M according to the purpose of the slicer.

We illustrate this with two use cases. Use case **A** is known as *backward slicing* in state-based models [4]. Given a set of states C in a statechart M as slicing criterion, the slicer determines all model elements which may have an effect on states in C. For instance, using `S.1.0.1` (s. gray state in Fig. 1) as slicing criterion, the slicer recursively determines all incoming transitions and their sources, e.g., the transition with the event `sendPScoordinatorCredentials` and its source state `S.1.0.0`, until an initial state is reached.

The complete backward slice is indicated by the blue elements in the lower part of Fig. 1. The example shows that our general notion of a slicing criterion may be restricted by concrete model slicers. In this use case, the slicing criterion must not be an arbitrary submodel of a given larger model, but a very specific one, i.e., a set of states.

Use case **B** is the *extraction of editable models* as presented in [8]. Here, the slicing criterion C is given by a set of *requested model elements* of M. The purpose of this slicer is to find a submodel which is editable and which includes all requested model elements. For example, if we use the blue elements in the lower part of Fig. 1 as slicing criterion, the model slice also contains the orange elements in the upper part of Fig. 1, namely three operations, because events of a transitions in a statechart represent operations in the class diagram, and the class containing these operations.

Slice Update. The slicing criterion might be updated during a development task in order to obtain an updated slice. It is often desirable to update the slice rather than creating the new slice from scratch, e.g., because this is more efficient. Let us assume in use case **A** that the slicing criterion changes from `S.1.0.1` to `S.1.1.1`. The resulting model slice only differs in the contained regions of the composite state `Authorising`. The upper region and its contained elements would be removed, while the lower region and its contained elements would be added. Next we could use the updated model slice from use case **A** as slicing criterion in use case **B**. In the related resulting model slice, the operation `sendPScoordinatorCredentials` would then be replaced by the operation `authFSC`.

3 Formal Framework

We have seen in the motivating example that model slicers can differ considerably in their intended purpose. The formal framework we present in the following defines the fundamental concepts for model slicing and slice updates. This framework uses graph-based models and model modifications [14]. It shall serve as a guideline how to define model slicers that support incremental slice updates.

3.1 Models as Graphs

Considering models, especially visual models, their concrete syntax is distinguished from their abstract one. In Fig. 1, a UML model is shown in its concrete representation. In the following, we will reason about their underlying structure, i.e., their abstract syntax, which can be considered as graph. The abstract syntax of a modeling language is usually defined by a meta-model which contains the type information about nodes and edges as well as additional constraints. We assume that a meta-model is formalized by an attributed graph; model graphs are defined as attributed graphs being typed over the meta-model. This typing can be characterized by an attributed graph morphism [15]. In addition, graph constraints [16] may be used to specify additional requirements. Due to space limitations, we do not formalize constraints in this paper.

Definition 1 (Typed model graph and morphism). *Given two attributed graphs M and MM, called* model *and* meta-model, *the typed model (graph) of M is defined as $M^T = (M, type^M)$ with $type^M : M \to MM$ being an attributed graph morphism, called* typing morphism[1]. *Given two typed models M and N, an attributed graph morphism $f : M \to N$ is called* typed model morphism *if $type^N \circ f = type^M$.*

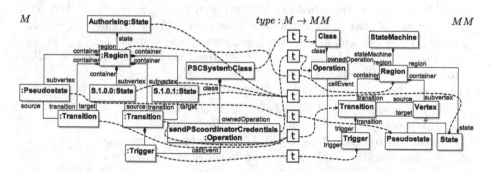

Fig. 2. Excerpt of a typed model graph.

Example 1 (Typed model graph). The left-hand side of Fig. 2 shows the model graph of an excerpt from the model depicted in Fig. 1. The model graph is

---

[1] In the following, we usually omit the adjective "attributed".

typed over the meta-model depicted on the right-hand side of Fig. 2. It shows a simplified excerpt of the UML meta-model. Every node (and edge) of the model graph is mapped onto a node or edge of the type graph by the graph morphism $type : M \rightarrow MM$.

Typed models and morphisms as defined above form the category $\mathbf{AGraphs}_{ATG}$ in [15]. It has various properties since it is an adhesive HLR category using a class $\mathcal{M}$ of injective graph morphisms with isomorphic data mapping, it has pushouts and pullbacks where at least one morphism is in $\mathcal{M}$. These constructions can be considered as generalized union and intersection of models being defined component-wise on nodes and edges such that they are structure-compatible. These constructions are used to define the formal framework.

3.2 Model Modifications

If we do not want to go into any details of model transformation approaches, the temporal change of models is roughly specified by model modifications. Each model modification describes the original model, an intermediate one after having performed all intended element deletions, and the resulting model after having performed all element additions.

Definition 2 (Model modification). *Given two models M_1 and M_2, a (direct) model modification $M_1 \Longrightarrow M_2$ is a span of injective morphisms $M_1 \xleftarrow{m_1} M_s \xrightarrow{m_2} M_2$.*

1. *Two model modifications $M_1 \xleftarrow{m_{11}} M_{12} \xrightarrow{m_{12}} M_2$ and $M_2 \xleftarrow{m_{22}} M_{23} \xrightarrow{m_{23}} M_3$ are concatenated to model modification $M_1 \xleftarrow{m_{13}} M_{13} \xrightarrow{m_{33}} M_3$ with (m_{13}, m_{33}) being the pullback of m_{12} and m_{22} (intersecting M_{12} and M_{23}).*
2. *Given two direct model modifications $m : M_1 \xleftarrow{m_1} M_s \xrightarrow{m_2} M_2$ and $p : P_1 \xleftarrow{p_1} P_s \xrightarrow{p_2} P_2$, p can be embedded into m, written $e : p \rightarrow m$, if there are injective morphisms (also called embeddings) $e_1 : P_1 \rightarrow M_1$, $e_s : P_s \rightarrow M_s$, and $e_2 : P_2 \rightarrow M_2$ with $e_1 \circ p_1 = m_1 \circ e_s$ and $e_2 \circ p_2 = m_2 \circ e_s$.*
3. *A sequence $M_0 \Longrightarrow M_1 \Longrightarrow \ldots \Longrightarrow M_n$ of direct model modifications is called model modification and is denoted by $M_0 \overset{*}{\Longrightarrow} M_n$.*
4. *There are five special kinds of model modifications:*
    (a) Model modification $M \xleftarrow{id_M} M \xrightarrow{id_M} M$ is called identical.
    (b) Model modification $\emptyset \longleftarrow \emptyset \longrightarrow \emptyset$ is called empty.
    (c) Model modification $\emptyset \longleftarrow \emptyset \longrightarrow M$ is called model creation.
    (d) Model modification $M \longleftarrow \emptyset \longrightarrow \emptyset$ is called model deletion.
    (e) $M_2 \xleftarrow{m_2} M_s \xrightarrow{m_1} M_1$ is called inverse modification to $M_1 \xleftarrow{m_1} M_s \xrightarrow{m_2} M_2$.

In a direct model modification, model M_s characterizes an intermediate model where all deletion actions have been performed but nothing has been added yet. To this end, M_s is the intersection of M_1 and M_2.

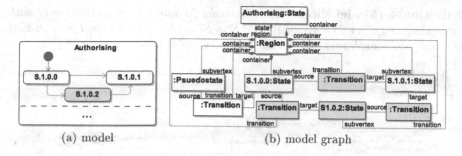

| (a) model | (b) model graph |

Fig. 3. Excerpt of a model modification

Example 2 (Direct model modification). Figure 3 shows a model modification using our running example. While Fig. 3(a) focuses on the concrete model syntax, Fig. 3(b) shows the changing abstract syntax graph. Figure 3(a) depicts an excerpt of the composite state `Authorising`. The red transition is deleted while the green state and transitions are created. The model modification $m : M_1 \xleftarrow{m_1} M_s \xrightarrow{m_2} M_2$ is illustrated in Fig. 3(b). The red elements represent the set of nodes (and edges) $M_1 \setminus m_1(M_s)$ to be deleted. The set $M_2 \setminus m_2(M_s)$ describing the nodes (and edges) to be created is illustrated by the green elements. All other nodes (and edges) represent the intermediate model M_s.

The *double pushout* approach to graph transformation [15] is a special kind of model modification:

Definition 3 (Rule application). *Given a model G and a model modification $r : L \xleftarrow{l} K \xrightarrow{r} R$, called* rule, *with injective morphism $m : L \to G$, called* match, *the rule application $G \Longrightarrow_{r,m} H$ is defined by the following two pushouts:*

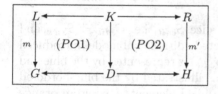

Model H is constructed in two passes: (1) $D := G \setminus m(L \setminus l(K))$, i.e., erase all model elements that are to be deleted; (2) $H := D \cup m'(R \setminus r(K))$ such that a new copy of all model elements that are to be created is added.

Note that the first pushout above exists if $G \setminus m(L \setminus l(K))$ does not yield dangling edges [15]. It is obvious that the result of a rule application $G \Longrightarrow_r H$ is a direct model modification $G \xleftarrow{g} D \xrightarrow{h} H$.

3.3 Model Slicing

In general, a model slice is an interesting part of a model comprising a given slicing criterion. It is up to a concrete slicing definition to specify which model parts are of interest.

Definition 4 (Model slice). *Given a model M and a slicing criterion C with a morphism $c : C \to M$. A model slice $S = Slice(M, c)$ is a model S such that there are two morphisms $m : S \to M$ and $e : C \to S$ with $m \circ e = c$.*

Note that each model slice $S = Slice(M, c)$ induces a model modification $C \xleftarrow{id_C} C \xrightarrow{e} S$.

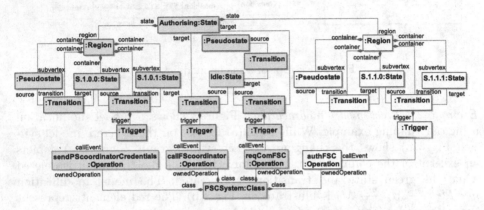

Fig. 4. Excerpt of two model slices

Example 3 (Model slice). Figure 4 depicts an excerpt of the model graph of M depicted in Fig. 1 and the two slices $S_{back} = Slice(M, c_{back})$ and $S_{edit} = Slice(M, c_{edit})$. S_{back} is the backward slice as informally described in Sect. 2. $C_{back} = \{S.1.0.1\}$ is the first slice criterion. The embedding $c_{back}(C_{back})$ is represented by the gray-filled element while embedding $m_{back}(S_{back})$ is represented by the blue-bordered elements. Model $e_{back}(C_{back})$ is illustrated by the gray-filled state having a blue border and $S_{back} \setminus e_{back}(C_{back})$ by the green-filled elements having a blue border.

Let S_{back} be the slicing criterion for the slice S_{edit}, i.e. $C_{edit} = S_{back}$ and $c_{edit}(C_{edit}) = m_{back}(S_{back})$. S_{edit} is the extracted editable submodel introduced in Sect. 2 by use case **B**. Its embedding $m_{edit}(S_{edit})$ is represented by the blue and orange-bordered elements. Model $e_{edit}(C_{edit})$ is illustrated by the blue-bordered elements and $S_{edit} \setminus e_{edit}(C_{edit})$ by the green-filled elements having an orange border.

3.4   Incremental Slice Update

Throughout working with a model slice, it might happen that the slice criterion has to be modified. The update of the corresponding model slice can be performed incrementally. Actually, modifying slice criteria can happen rather frequently in practice by, e.g., editing independent submodels of a large model in cooperative work.

Definition 5 (Slice update construction). *Given a model slice $S_1 = Slice(M, C_1 \rightarrow M)$ and a direct model modification $c = C_1 \xleftarrow{c_1} C_s \xrightarrow{c_2} C_2$, slice $S_2 = Slice(M, C_2 \rightarrow M)$ can be constructed as follows:*

1. *Given slice S_1 we deduce the model modification $C_1 \xleftarrow{id_{C_1}} C_1 \xrightarrow{e_1} S_1$ and take its inverse modification: $S_1 \xleftarrow{e_1} C_1 \xrightarrow{id_{C_1}} C_1$.*
2. *Then we take the given model modification c for the slice criterion.*
3. *And finally we take the model modification $C_2 \xleftarrow{id_{C_2}} C_2 \xrightarrow{e_2} S_2$ induced by slice S_2.*

All model modifications are concatenated yielding the direct model modification $S_1 \xleftarrow{e_1 \circ c_1} C_s \xrightarrow{e_2 \circ c_2} S_2$ called slice update construction *(see also Fig. 6).*

Example 4 (Slice update example). Figure 5 illustrates a slice update construction with $S_{edit} = Slice(M, C_{edit} \rightarrow M)$ being the extracted submodel of our previous example illustrated by the red-dashed box. The modification $c : C_{edit} \xleftarrow{c_{edit}} C_s \xrightarrow{c_{edit'}} C_{edit'}$ of the slicing criterion is depicted by the gray-filled elements. The red-bordered elements represent the set $C_s \setminus c_{edit}(C_{edit})$ of elements removed from the slicing criterion. The green-bordered elements form the set $C_s \setminus c_{edit'}(C_{edit'})$ of elements added to the slicing criterion. $S_{edit'} = Slice(M, C_{edit'} \rightarrow M)$ is the extracted submodel represented by the green-dashed box. Consequently, the slice is updated by deleting all elements in $S_{edit} \setminus e_{edit}(c_{edit}(C_s))$, represented by the red-bordered and red- and white-filled elements, and adding all elements in $S_{edit'} \setminus e_{edit'}(c_{edit'}(C_s))$, represented by the green-bordered and green- and white-filled elements. Note that the white-filled elements are removed and added again. This motivated us to consider incremental slice updates defined below.

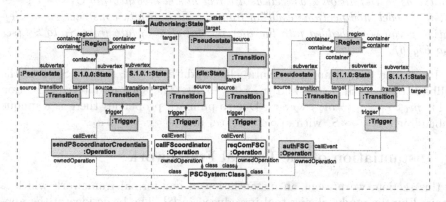

Fig. 5. Excerpt of an (incremental) slice update.

Definition 6 (Incremental slice update). *Given M and $C_1 \to M_1$ as in Definition 4 as well as a direct model modification $C_1 \xleftarrow{c_1} C_s \xrightarrow{c_2} C_2$, model slice $S_1 = Slice(M, C_1 \to M)$ is incrementally updated to model slice $S_2 = Slice(M, C_2 \to M)$ yielding a direct model modification $S_1 \xleftarrow{s_1} S_s \xrightarrow{s_2} S_2$, called incremental slice update from S_1 to S_2, with s_1 and s_2 being the pullback of $m_1 : S_1 \to M$ and $m_2 : S_2 \to M$ (see also Fig. 6).*

Example 5 (Incremental slice update example). Given S_{edit} and $S_{edit'}$ of our previous example. Furthermore, given the model modification $S_{edit} \xleftarrow{s_{edit}} S_s \xrightarrow{s_{edit'}} S_{edit'}$ whereby S_s is isomorphic to the intersection of S_{edit} and $S_{edit'}$ in M, i.e. $m_s : S_s \to m_{edit}(S_{edit}) \cap m_{edit'}(S_{edit'})$ with m_s being an isomorphism due to the pullback construction. S_s is illustrated by the elements contained in the intersection of the red- and green-dashed box in Fig. 5. In contrast to the slice update construction of the previous example the white-filled elements are not affected by the incremental slice update.

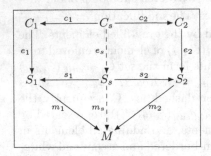

Fig. 6. Incremental slice update

Ideally, the slice update construction in Definition 5 should not yield a different update than the incremental one. However, this is not the case in general since the incremental update keeps as many model elements as possible in contrast to the update construction in Definition 5 In any case, both update constructions should be compatible with each other, i.e., should be in an embedding relation, as stated on the following proposition.

Proposition 1 (Compatibility of slice update constructions). *Given M and C_1 as in Definition 4 as well as a direct model modification $C_1 \xleftarrow{c_1} C_s \xrightarrow{c_2} C_2$, the model modification resulting from the slice update construction in Definition 5 can be embedded into the incremental slice update from S_1 to S_2 (see also Fig. 6).*

Proof idea: Given an incremental slice update $S_1 \xleftarrow{s_1} S_s \xrightarrow{s_2} S_2$, it is the pullback of $m_1 : S_1 \to M$ and $m_2 : S_2 \to M$. The slice update construction yields $m_1 \circ e_1 \circ c_1 = m_2 \circ e_2 \circ c_2$. Due to pullback properties there is a unique embedding $e : C_s \to S_s$ with $s_1 \circ e = e_1 \circ c_1$ and $s_2 \circ e = e_2 \circ c_2$.[2]

4 Instantiation of the Formal Framework

In this section, we present an instantiation of our formal framework which is inspired by the model slicing tool introduced in [8]. The basic idea of the approach is to create and incrementally update model slices by calculating and applying a special form of model patches, introduced and referred to as edit script in [17].

---

[2] This proof idea can be elaborated to a full proof in a straight forward manner.

4.1   Edit Scripts as Refinements of Model Modifications

An *edit script* $\Delta_{M_1 \Rightarrow M_2}$ specifies how to transform a model M_1 into a model M_2 in a stepwise manner. Technically, this is a data structure which comprises a set of rule applications, partially ordered by an acyclic dependency graph. Its nodes are rule applications and its edges are dependencies between them [17]. Models are represented as typed graphs as in Definition 1, rule applications are defined as in Definition 3. Hence, the semantics of an edit script is a set of rule application sequences taking all possible orderings of rule applications into account. Each sequence can be condensed into the application of one rule following the concurrent rule construction in, e.g., [15]. Hence, an edit script $\Delta_{M_1 \Rightarrow M_2}$ induces a set of model modifications of the form $M_1 \xleftarrow{m_1} M_s \xrightarrow{m_2} M_2$.

Given two models M_1 and M_2 as well as a set R of transformation rules for this type of models, edit scripts are calculated in two basic steps [17]:

First, the corresponding elements in M_1 and M_2 are calculated using a model matcher [18]. A basic requirement is that such a matching can be formally represented as a (partial) injective morphism $c : M_1 \rightarrow M_2$. If so, the matching morphism c yields a unique model modification $m : M_1 \xleftarrow{\supseteq} M_s \xrightarrow{m_2} M_2$ (up to isomorphism) with $m_2 = c|_{M_s}$. This means that M_s always has to be a graph.

Second, an edit script is derived. Elementary model changes can be directly derived from a model matching; elements in M_1 and M_2 which are not involved in a correspondence can be considered as deleted and added, respectively [19]. The approach presented in [17] partitions the set of elementary changes such that each partition represents the application of a transformation rule of the given set R of transformation rules [20], and subsequently calculates the dependencies between these rule applications [17], yielding an edit script $\Delta_{M_1 \Rightarrow M_2}$. Sequences of rule applications of an edit script do not contain transient effects [17], i.e., pairs of change actions which cancel out each other (such as creating and later deleting one and the same element). Thus, no change actions are factored out by an edit script.

4.2   Model Slicing Through Slice-Creating Edit Scripts

Edit scripts are also used to construct new model slices. Given a model M and a slicing criterion C, a *slice-creating edit script* $\Delta_{\epsilon \Rightarrow S}$ is calculated which, when applied to the empty model ϵ, yields the resulting slice S. The basic idea to construct $\Delta_{\epsilon \Rightarrow S}$ is to consider the model M as created by an edit script $\Delta_{\epsilon \Rightarrow M}$ applied to the empty model ϵ and to identify a sub-script of $\Delta_{\epsilon \Rightarrow M}$ which (at least) creates all elements of C. The slice creating edit script $\Delta_{\epsilon \Rightarrow S}$ consists of the subgraph of the dependency graph of the model-creating edit script $\Delta_{\epsilon \Rightarrow M}$ containing (i) all nodes which create at least one model element in C, and (ii) all required nodes and connecting edges according to the transitive closure of the "required" relation, which is implied by dependencies between rule applications.

Since the construction of edit scripts depends on a given set R of transformation rules, *a basic applicability condition is that all possible models and all possible slices can be created by rules available in R*. Given that this condition is satisfied, model slicing through slice-creating edit scripts indeed behaves according to Definition 4, i.e., a slice $S = Slice(M, C \to M)$ is obtained by applying $\Delta_{\epsilon \Rightarrow S}$ to the empty model: The resulting slice S is a submodel of M and a supermodel of C. As we will see in Sect. 5, the behavior of a concrete model slicer and thus its intended purpose is configured by the transformation rule set R.

4.3   Incremental Slicing Through Slice-Updating Edit Scripts

To incrementally update a slice $S_1 = Slice(M, C_1 \to M)$ to become slice $S_2 = Slice(M, C_2 \to M)$, we show that the approach presented in [8] constructs a *slice-updating edit script* $\Delta_{S_1 \Rightarrow S_2}$ which, if applied to the current slice S_1, yields S_2 in an incremental way.

Similar to the construction of slice-creating edit scripts, the basic idea is to consider the model M as model-creating edit script $\Delta_{\epsilon \Rightarrow M}$. The slice-updating edit script must delete all elements in the set $S_1 \setminus S_2$ from the current slice S_1, while adding all model elements in $S_2 \setminus S_1$. It is constructed as follows: Let P_{S_1} and P_{S_2} be the sets of rule applications which create all the elements in S_1 and S_2, respectively. Next, the sets P_{rem} and P_{add} of rule applications in $\Delta_{\epsilon \Rightarrow M}$ are determined with $P_{rem} = P_{S_1} \setminus P_{S_2}$ and $P_{add} = P_{S_2} \setminus P_{S_1}$. Finally, the resulting edit script $\Delta_{S_1 \Rightarrow S_2}$ contains (1) the rule applications in set P_{add}, with the same dependencies as in $\Delta_{\epsilon \Rightarrow M}$, and (2) for each rule application in P_{rem}, its inverse rule application with reversed dependencies as in $\Delta_{\epsilon \Rightarrow M}$. By construction, there cannot be dependencies between rule applications in both sets, so they can be executed in arbitrary order.

In addition to the completeness of the set R of transformation rules for a given modeling language (s. Sect. 4.2), *a second applicability condition is that, for each rule r in R, there must be an inverse rule r^{-1} which reverts the effect of r*. Given that these conditions are satisfied and a slice-updating edit script $\Delta_{S_1 \Rightarrow S_2}$ can be created, its application to S_1 indeed behaves according to the incremental slice update as in Definition 6. This is so because, by construction, none of the model elements in the intersection of S_1 and S_2 in M is deleted by the edit script $\Delta_{S_1 \Rightarrow S_2}$. Consequently, none of the elements in the intersection of C_1 and C_2 in M, which is a subset of $S_1 \cap S_2$, is deleted.

4.4   Implementation

The framework instantiation has been implemented using a set of standard MDE technologies on top of the widely used Eclipse Modeling Framework (EMF), which employs an object-oriented implementation of graph-based models in which nodes and edges are represented as objects and references, respectively. Edit scripts are calculated using the model differencing framework SiLift [21], which uses EMF Compare [22] in order to determine the corresponding elements in a pair of models being compared with each other. A matching determined by EMF Compare fulfills the requirements presented in Sect. 4.1 since EMF Compare (a) delivers 1:1-correspondences between elements, thus yielding an injective mapping, and (b) implicitly matches edges if their respective source and target nodes are matched and if they have the same type (because EMF does not support parallel edges of the same type in general), thus yielding an edge-preserving mapping. Finally, transformation rules are implemented using the model transformation language and framework Henshin [23,24] which is based on graph transformation concepts.

5   Solving the Motivating Examples

In this section, we outline the configurations of two concrete model slicers which are based on the framework instantiation presented in Sect. 4, and which are capable of solving the motivating examples introduced in Sect. 2. Each of these slicers is configured by a set of Henshin transformation rules which are used for the calculation of model-creating, and thus for the construction of slice-creating and slice-updating, edit scripts. The complete rule sets can be found at the accompanying website of this paper [25].

5.1   A State-Based Model Slicer

Two of the creation rules which are used to configure a state-based model slicer as described in our first example of Sect. 2 are shown in Fig. 7. The rules are depicted in an integrated form: the left- and right-hand sides of a rule are merged into a unified model graph following the visual syntax of the Henshin model transformation language [23].

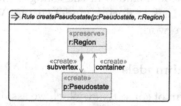 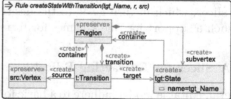

Fig. 7. Subset of the creation rules for configuring a state-based model slicer

Most of the creation rules are of a similar form as the creation rule *createPseudostate*, which simply creates a pseudostate and connects it with an existing container. The key idea of this slicer configuration, however, is the special creation rule *createStateWithTransition*, which creates a state together with an incoming transition in a

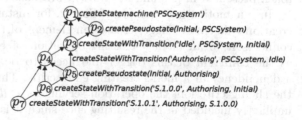

Fig. 8. Slice-creating edit script.

single step. To support the incremental updating of slices, for each creation rule an inverse deletion rule is included in the overall set of transformation rules. Parts of the resulting model-creating edit script using these rules are shown in Fig. 8. For example, rule application *p3* creates the state *Idle* in the top-level region of the state machine *PSCSystem*, together with an incoming transition having the initial state of the state machine, created by rule application *p2*, as source state. Thus, *p3* depends on *p2* since the initial state must be created first. Similar dependency relationships arise for the creation of other states which are created together with an incoming transition.

The effect of this configuration on the behavior of the model slicer is as follows (illustrated here for the creation of a new slice): If state *S.1.0.1* is selected as slicing criterion, as in our motivating example, rule application *p7* is included in the slice-creating edit script since it creates that state. Implicitly, all rule applications on which *p7* transitively depends on, i.e., all rule applications *p1* to *p6*, are also included in the slice-creating edit script. Consequently, the slice resulting from applying the slice-creating edit script to an empty model creates a submodel of the state machine of Fig. 1 which contains a transition path from its initial state to state *S.1.0.1*, according to the desired behavior of the slicer.

A current limitation of our solution is that, for each state *s* of the slicing criterion, only a single transition path from the initial state to state *s* is sliced. This path is determined non-deterministically from the set of all possible paths from the initial state to state *s*. To overcome this limitation, rule schemes comprising a kernel rule and a set of multi-rules (see, e.g., [26,27]) would have to be supported by our approach. Then, a rule scheme for creating a state with an arbitrary number of incoming transitions could be included in the configuration of our slicer, which in turn leads to the desired effect during model slicing. We leave such a support for rule schemes for future work.

5.2   A Slicer for Extracting Editable Submodels

In general, editable models adhere to a basic form of consistency which we assume to be defined by the effective meta-model of a given model editor [28]. The basic idea of configuring a model slicer for extracting editable submodels, adopted from [8], is that all creation and deletion rules preserve this level of consistency. Given an effective meta-model, such a rule set can be generated using the approach presented in [28] and its EMF-/UML-based implementation [29,30].

In our motivating example of Sect. 2, for instance, a consistency-preserving creation rule *createTrigger* creates an element of type *Trigger* and immediately connects it to an already existing operation of a class. The operation serves as the *callEvent* of this trigger and needs to be created first, which leads to a dependency in a model-creating edit script. Thus, if a trigger is included in the slicing criterion, the operation serving as *callEvent* of that trigger will be implicitly included in the resulting slice since it is created by the slice-creating edit script.

6   Related Work

A large number of model slicers has been developed. Most of them work only with one specific type of models, notably state machines [4] and other types of behavioral models such as MATLAB/Simulink block diagrams [5]. Other supported model types include UML class diagrams [31], architectural models [32] or system models defined using the SysML modeling language [33]. None of these approaches can be transferred to other (domain-specific) modeling languages, and they do not abstract from concrete slicing specifications.

The only well-known more generally usable technique which is adaptable to a given modeling language and slicing specification is Kompren [7]. In contrast to our formal framework, however, Kompren does not abstract from the concrete model modification approach and implementation technologies. It offers a domain-specific language based on the Kermeta model transformation language [34] to specify the behavior of a model slicer, and a generator which generates a fully functioning model slicer from such a specification. When Kompren is used in the so-called active mode, slices are incrementally updated when the input model changes, according to the principle of incremental model transformation [35]. In our approach, slices are incrementally updated when the slicing criterion is modified. As long as endogenous model transformations for constructing slices are used only, Kompren could be easily extended to become an instantiation of our formal framework.

Incremental slicing has also been addressed in [36], however, using a notion of incrementality which fundamentally differs from ours. The technique has been developed in the context of testing model-based delta-oriented software product lines [37]. Rather than incrementally updating an existing slice, the approach incrementally processes the product space of a product line, where each "product" is specified by a state machine model. As in software regression testing, the goal is to obtain retest information by utilizing differences between state machine slices obtained from different products.

In a broader sense, related work can be found in the area of model splitting and model decomposition. The technique presented in [38] aims at splitting a model into submodels according to linguistic heuristics and using information retrieval techniques. The model decomposition approach presented in [39] considers models as graphs and first determines strongly connected graph components from which the space of possible decompositions is derived in a second step. Both approaches are different from ours in that they produce a partitioning of an input model instead of a single slice. None of them supports the incremental updating of a model partitioning.

7   Conclusion

We presented a formal framework for defining model slicers that support incremental slice updates based on a general concept of model modifications. Incremental slice updates were shown to be equivalent to non-incremental ones. Furthermore, we presented a framework instantiation based on the concept of edit scripts defining application sequences of model transformation rules. This instantiation was implemented by two concrete model slicers based on the Eclipse Modeling Framework and the model differencing framework SiLift.

As future work, we plan to investigate incremental updates of both the underlying model and the slicing criterion. It is also worthwhile to examine the extent to which further concrete model slicers fit into our formal framework of incremental model slicing. For our own instantiation of this framework, we plan to cover further model transformation features such as rule schemes and application conditions, which will make the configuration of concrete model slicers more flexible and enable us to support further use cases and purposes.

Acknowledgments. This work was partially supported by the DFG (German Research Foundation) under the Priority Programme SPP1593: Design For Future - Managed Software Evolution.

References

1. Weiser, M.: Program slicing. In: Proceedings of ICSE 1981. IEEE Press (1981)
2. Xu, B., Qian, J., Zhang, X., Wu, Z., Chen, L.: A brief survey of program slicing. ACM SIGSOFT Softw. Eng. Notes **30**(2), 1–36 (2005)
3. Brambilla, M., Cabot, J., Wimmer, M.: Model-driven software engineering in practice. Synth. Lect. Softw. Eng. **1**(1), 1–182 (2012)
4. Androutsopoulos, K., Clark, D., Harman, M., Krinke, J., Tratt, L.: State-based model slicing: A survey. ACM Comput. Surv. **45**(4), 36 (2013). https://doi.org/10.1145/2501654.2501667. Article 53
5. Gerlitz, T., Kowalewski, S.: Flow sensitive slicing for matlab/simulink models. In: Proceedings of WICSA 2016. IEEE (2016)
6. Samuel, P., Mall, R.: A novel test case design technique using dynamic slicing of UML sequence diagrams. e-Informatica **2**(1), 71–92 (2008)
7. Blouin, A., Combemale, B., Baudry, B., Beaudoux, O.: Kompren: modeling and generating model slicers. SoSyM **14**(1), 321–337 (2015)
8. Pietsch, C., Ohrndorf, M., Kelter, U., Kehrer, T.: Incrementally slicing editable submodels. In: Proceedings of ASE 2017. IEEE Press (2017)
9. Baker, P., Loh, S., Weil, F.: Model-driven engineering in a large industrial context— Motorola case study. In: Briand, L., Williams, C. (eds.) MODELS 2005. LNCS, vol. 3713, pp. 476–491. Springer, Heidelberg (2005). https://doi.org/10.1007/11557432_36
10. Hutchinson, J., Whittle, J., Rouncefield, M., Kristoffersen, S.: Empirical assessment of MDE in industry. In: Proceedings of ICSE 2011. IEEE (2011)
11. Kolovos, D.S., Paige, R.F., Polack, F.A.C.: The grand challenge of scalability for model driven engineering. In: Chaudron, M.R.V. (ed.) MODELS 2008. LNCS, vol. 5421, pp. 48–53. Springer, Heidelberg (2009). https://doi.org/10.1007/978-3-642-01648-6_5
12. Kolovos, D.S., Rose, L.M., Matragkas, N., Paige, R.F., Guerra, E., Cuadrado, J.S., De Lara, J., Ráth, I., Varró, D., Tisi, M., et al.: A research roadmap towards achieving scalability in model driven engineering. In: Proceedings of BigMDE @ STAF 2013. ACM (2013)
13. Capozucca, A., Cheng, B., Guelfi, N., Istoan, P.: OO-SPL modelling of the focused case study. In: Proceedings of CMA @ MoDELS 2011 (2011)

14. Taentzer, G., Ermel, C., Langer, P., Wimmer, M.: Conflict detection for model versioning based on graph modifications. In: Ehrig, H., Rensink, A., Rozenberg, G., Schürr, A. (eds.) ICGT 2010. LNCS, vol. 6372, pp. 171–186. Springer, Heidelberg (2010). https://doi.org/10.1007/978-3-642-15928-2_12

15. Ehrig, H., Ehrig, K., Prange, U., Taentzer, G.: Fundamentals of Algebraic Graph Transformation. Springer, Heidelberg (2006). https://doi.org/10.1007/3-540-31188-2

16. Habel, A., Pennemann, K.: Correctness of high-level transformation systems relative to nested conditions. Math. Struct. Comput. Sci. **19**(2), 245–296 (2009)

17. Kehrer, T., Kelter, U., Taentzer, G.: Consistency-preserving edit scripts in model versioning. In: Proceedings of ASE 2013. IEEE (2013)

18. Kolovos, D.S., Di Ruscio, D., Pierantonio, A., Paige, R.F.: Different models for model matching: an analysis of approaches to support model differencing. In: Proceedings of CVSM @ ICSE 2009. IEEE (2009)

19. Kehrer, T., Kelter, U., Pietsch, P., Schmidt, M.: Adaptability of model comparison tools. In: Proceedings of ASE 2011. ACM (2012)

20. Kehrer, T., Kelter, U., Taentzer, G.: A rule-based approach to the semantic lifting of model differences in the context of model versioning. In: Proceedings of ASE 2011. IEEE (2011)

21. Kehrer, T., Kelter, U., Ohrndorf, M., Sollbach, T.: Understanding model evolution through semantically lifting model differences with SiLift. In: Proceedings of ICSM 2012. IEEE Computer Society (2012)

22. Brun, C., Pierantonio, A.: Model differences in the eclipse modeling framework. UPGRADE Eur. J. Inform. Prof. **9**(2), 29–34 (2008)

23. Arendt, T., Biermann, E., Jurack, S., Krause, C., Taentzer, G.: Henshin: advanced concepts and tools for in-place EMF model transformations. In: Petriu, D.C., Rouquette, N., Haugen, Ø. (eds.) MODELS 2010. LNCS, vol. 6394, pp. 121–135. Springer, Heidelberg (2010). https://doi.org/10.1007/978-3-642-16145-2_9

24. Strüber, D., Born, K., Gill, K.D., Groner, R., Kehrer, T., Ohrndorf, M., Tichy, M.: Henshin: a usability-focused framework for EMF model transformation development. In: de Lara, J., Plump, D. (eds.) ICGT 2017. LNCS, vol. 10373, pp. 196–208. Springer, Cham (2017). https://doi.org/10.1007/978-3-319-61470-0_12

25. Taentzer, G., Kehrer, T., Pietsch, C., Kelter, U.: Accompanying website for this paper (2017). http://pi.informatik.uni-siegen.de/projects/SiLift/fase2018/

26. Rozenberg, G. (ed.): Handbook of Graph Grammars and Computing by Graph Transformation. Foundations, vol. I. World Scientific Publishing Co., Inc., River Edge (1997)

27. Biermann, E., Ermel, C., Taentzer, G.: Lifting parallel graph transformation concepts to model transformation based on the eclipse modeling framework. Electron. Commun. EASST **26** (2010)

28. Kehrer, T., Taentzer, G., Rindt, M., Kelter, U.: Automatically deriving the specification of model editing operations from meta-models. In: Van Van Gorp, P., Engels, G. (eds.) ICMT 2016. LNCS, vol. 9765, pp. 173–188. Springer, Cham (2016). https://doi.org/10.1007/978-3-319-42064-6_12

29. Rindt, M., Kehrer, T., Kelter, U.: Automatic generation of consistency-preserving edit operations for MDE tools. In: Proceedings of Demos @ MoDELS 2014. CEUR Workshop Proceedings, vol. 1255 (2014)

30. Kehrer, T., Rindt, M., Pietsch, P., Kelter, U.: Generating edit operations for profiled UML models. In: Proceedings ME @ MoDELS 2013. CEUR Workshop Proceedings, vol. 1090 (2013)

31. Kagdi, H., Maletic, J.I., Sutton, A.: Context-free slicing of UML class models. In: Proceedings of ICSM 2005. IEEE (2005)
32. Lallchandani, J.T., Mall, R.: A dynamic slicing technique for UML architectural models. IEEE Trans. Softw. Eng. **37**(6), 737–771 (2011)
33. Nejati, S., Sabetzadeh, M., Falessi, D., Briand, L., Coq, T.: A SysML-based approach to traceability management and design slicing in support of safety certification: framework, tool support, and case studies. Inf. Softw. Technol. **54**(6), 569–590 (2012)
34. Jézéquel, J.-M., Barais, O., Fleurey, F.: Model driven language engineering with Kermeta. In: Fernandes, J.M., Lämmel, R., Visser, J., Saraiva, J. (eds.) GTTSE 2009. LNCS, vol. 6491, pp. 201–221. Springer, Heidelberg (2011). https://doi.org/10.1007/978-3-642-18023-1_5
35. Etzlstorfer, J., Kusel, A., Kapsammer, E., Langer, P., Retschitzegger, W., Schoenboeck, J., Schwinger, W., Wimmer, M.: A survey on incremental model transformation approaches. In: Pierantonio, A., Schätz, B. (eds.) Proceedings of the Workshop on Models and Evolution. CEUR Workshop Proceedings, vol. 1090, pp. 4–13 (2013)
36. Lity, S., Morbach, T., Thüm, T., Schaefer, I.: Applying incremental model slicing to product-line regression testing. In: Kapitsaki, G.M., Santana de Almeida, E. (eds.) ICSR 2016. LNCS, vol. 9679, pp. 3–19. Springer, Cham (2016). https://doi.org/10.1007/978-3-319-35122-3_1
37. Schaefer, I., Bettini, L., Bono, V., Damiani, F., Tanzarella, N.: Delta-oriented programming of software product lines. In: Bosch, J., Lee, J. (eds.) SPLC 2010. LNCS, vol. 6287, pp. 77–91. Springer, Heidelberg (2010). https://doi.org/10.1007/978-3-642-15579-6_6
38. Struber, D., Rubin, J., Taentzer, G., Chechik, M.: Splitting models using information retrieval and model crawling techniques. In: Gnesi, S., Rensink, A. (eds.) FASE 2014. LNCS, vol. 8411, pp. 47–62. Springer, Heidelberg (2014). https://doi.org/10.1007/978-3-642-54804-8_4
39. Ma, Q., Kelsen, P., Glodt, C.: A generic model decomposition technique and its application to the eclipse modeling framework. SoSyM **14**(2), 921–952 (2015)

Multiple Model Synchronization
with Multiary Delta Lenses

Zinovy Diskin[1]($\boxtimes$)(ID), Harald König[2](ID), and Mark Lawford[1](ID)

[1] McMaster University, Hamilton, Canada
{diskinz,lawford}@mcmaster.ca
[2] University of Applied Sciences FHDW Hannover, Hannover, Germany
harald.koenig@fhdw.de

Abstract. Multiple (more than 2) model synchronization is ubiquitous and important for MDE, but its theoretical underpinning gained much less attention than the binary case. Specifically, the latter was extensively studied by the bx community in the framework of algebraic models for update propagation called *lenses*. Now we make a step to restore the balance and propose a notion of multiary delta lens. Besides multiarity, our lenses feature *reflective* updates, when consistency restoration requires some amendment of the update that violated consistency. We emphasize the importance of various ways of lens composition for practical applications of the framework, and prove several composition results.

1 Introduction

Modelling normally results in a set of inter-related models presenting different views of the system. If one of the models changes and their joint consistency is violated, the related models should also be changed to restore consistency. This task is obviously of paramount importance for MDE, but its theoretical underpinning is inherently difficult and reliable practical solutions are rare. There are working solutions for file synchronization in systems like Git, but they are not applicable in the UML/EMF world of diagrammatic models. For the latter, much work has been done for the binary case (synchronizing two models) by the bidirectional transformation community (bx) [15], specifically, in the framework of so called *delta lenses* [3], but the multiary case (the number of models to be synchronized is $n \geq 2$) gained much less attention—cf. the energetic call to the community in a recent Stevens' paper [16].

The context underlying bx is model transformation, in which one model in the pair is considered as a transform of the other even though updates are propagated in both directions (so called round-tripping). Once we go beyond $n = 2$, we at once switch to a more general context of models inter-relations beyond model-to-model transformations. Such situations have been studied in the context of multiview system consistency, but rarely in the context of an accurate formal basis for update propagation. The present paper can be seen as an adaptation of the (delta) lens-based update propagation framework for the multiview

A. Russo and A. Schürr (Eds.): FASE 2018, LNCS 10802, pp. 21–37, 2018.
https://doi.org/10.1007/978-3-319-89363-1_2

consistency problem. We will call it multi-directional update propagation or *mx* following the bx-pattern. Our contributions to mx are as follows.

We show with a simple example (Sect. 2) an important special feature of mx: consistency restoration may require not only update propagation to other models but the very update created inconsistency should itself be amended (even for the case of a two-view system!); thus, update propagation should, in general, be *reflective*. Moreover, if even consistency can be restored without a reflective amendment, there are cases when such reflection is still reasonable. It means that *Hippocraticness* [15]—a major requirement for the classical bx, may have less weight in the mx world. In Sect. 3, we provide a formal definition of *multiary* (symmetric) lenses with reflection, and define (Sect. 4) several operations of such lens composition producing complex lenses from simple ones. Specifically, we show how n-ary lenses can be composed from n-tuples of asymmetric binary lenses (Theorems 1 and 2), thus giving a partial solution to the challenging issue of building mx synchronization via bx discussed by Stevens in [16]. We consider lens composition results important for practical application of the framework. If the tool builder has implemented a library of elementary synchronization modules based on lenses and, hence, ensuring basic laws for change propagation, then a complex module assembled from elementary lenses will automatically be a lens and thus also enjoys the basic laws.

2   Example

We will consider a simple example motivating our framework. Many formal constructs below will be illustrated with the example (or its fragments) and referred to as *Running example*.

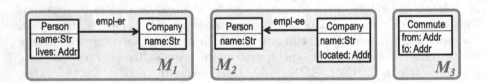

Fig. 1. Multi-metamodel in UML

2.1   A Multimodel to Play With

Suppose two data sources, whose schemas (we say metamodels) are shown in Fig. 1 as class diagrams M_1 and M_2 that record employment. The first source is interested in employment of people living in downtown, the second one is focused on software companies and their recently graduated employees. In general, population of classes Person and Company in the two sources can be different – they can even be disjoint, but if a recently graduated downtowner works for a software company, her appearance in both databases is very likely. Now suppose there is an agency investigating traffic problems, which maintains its own data on commuting between addresses (see schema M_3) computable by an obvious relational join over M_1 and M_2. In addition, the agency supervises consistency of the two sources and requires that if they both know a person p and a company c, then they must agree on the employment record (p, c): it is either stored by both or by neither of the sources. For this synchronization, it is assumed that persons and companies are globally identified by their names. Thus, a triple of data sets (we will say models) A_1, A_2, A_3, instantiating the respective metamodels, can be either consistent (if the constraints described above are satisfied) or inconsistent (if they aren't). In the latter case, we normally want to change some or all models to restore consistency. We will call a collection of models to be kept in sync a *multimodel*.

To talk about constraints for multimodels, we need an accurate notation. If A is a model instantiating metamodel M and X is a class in M, we write X^A for the set of objects instantiating X in A. Similarly, if $r : X_1 \leftrightarrow X_2$ is an association in M, we write r^A for the corresponding binary relation over $X_1^A \times X_2^A$. For example, Fig. 2 presents a simple model A_1 instantiating M_1 with $\mathsf{Person}^{A_1} = \{p_1, p_1'\}$, $\mathsf{Company}^{A_1} = \{c_1\}$, $\mathsf{empl\text{-}er}^{A_1} = \{(p_1, c_1)\}$, and similarly for attributes, e.g.,

$$\mathsf{lives}^{A_1} = \{(p_1, a1), (p_1', a1)\} \subset \mathsf{Person}^{A_1} \times \mathsf{Addr}$$

(lives^{A_1} and also name^{A_1} are assumed to be functions and Addr is the (model-independent) set of all possible addresses). The triple (A_1, A_2, A_3) is a (state of a) multimodel over the multimetamodel (M_1, M_2, M_3), and we say it is *consistent* if the two constraints specified below are satisfied. Constraint (C1) specifies mutual consistency of models A_1 and A_2 in the sense described above; constraint (C2) specifies consistency between the agency's view of data and the two data sources:

(C1)   if $p \in \mathsf{Person}^{A_1} \cap \mathsf{Person}^{A_2}$ and $c \in \mathsf{Company}^{A_1} \cap \mathsf{Company}^{A_2}$
         then $(p, c) \in \mathsf{empl\text{-}er}^{A_1}$ iff $(c, p) \in \mathsf{empl\text{-}ee}^{A_2}$

(C2) $\left(\mathsf{lives}^{A_1}\right)^{-1} \bowtie \left(\mathsf{empl\text{-}er}^{A_1} \cup (\mathsf{empl\text{-}ee}^{A_2})^{-1}\right) \bowtie \mathsf{located}^{A_2} \subseteq \mathsf{Commute}^{A_3}$

where $^{-1}$ refers to the inverse relations and $\bowtie$ denotes relational join (composition); using subsetting rather than equality in (C2) assumes that there are other data sources the agency can use. Note that constraint (C1) inter-relates two component models of the multimodel, while (C2) involves all three components and forces synchronization to be 3-ary.

It is easy to see that multimodel $A_{1,2,3}$ in Fig. 2 is "two-times" inconsistent: (C1) is violated as both A_1 and A_2 know Mary and IBM, and (IBM, Mary) $\in \mathsf{empl\text{-}ee}^{A_2}$ but (Mary, IBM) $\notin \mathsf{empl\text{-}er}^{A_1}$; (C2) is violated as A_1 and A_2 show a commuting pair (a1, a15) not recorded in A_3. We will discuss consistency restoration in the next subsection, but first we need to discuss an important part of the multimodel – traceability or correspondence mappings – held implicit so far.

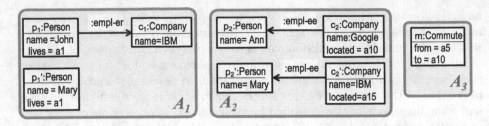

Fig. 2. A(n inconsistent) multimodel $\mathcal{A}^{\dagger}$ over the multi-metamodel in Fig. 1

Indeed, classes Person^{A_1} and Person^{A_2} are interrelated by a correspondence relation linking persons with the same name, and similarly for $\mathsf{Company}$. These correspondence links (we will write corr-links) may be implicit as they can always be restored. More important is to maintain corr-links between $\mathsf{Commute}^{A_3}$ and $\mathsf{empl\text{-}er}^{A_1} \cup \mathsf{empl\text{-}ee}^{A_2}$. Indeed, class $\mathsf{Commute}$ together with its two attributes can be seen as a relation, and this relation can be instantiated by a multirelation as people living at the same address can work for companies located at the same address. If some of such $\mathsf{Commute}$-objects is deleted, and this delete is to be propagated to models $A_{1,2}$, we need corr-links to know which employment links are to be deleted. Hence, it makes sense to establish such links when objects are added to $\mathsf{Commute}^{A_3}$, and use them later for deletion propagation.

Importantly, for given models $A_{1,2,3}$, there may be several different correspondence mappings: the same $\mathsf{Commute}$-object can correspond to different commute-links over A_1 and A_2. In fact, multiplicity of possible corr-specifications is a general story that can only be avoided if absolutely reliable keys are available, e.g., if we suppose that persons and companies can always be uniquely identified by names, then corrs between these classes are unique. But if keys (e.g., person names) are not absolutely reliable, we need a separate procedure of model matching or alignment that has to establish whether objects $p_1' \in \mathsf{Person}^{A_1}$ and $p_2' \in \mathsf{Person}^{A_2}$ both named Mary represent the same real world object. Constraints we declared above implicitly involve corr-links, e.g., formula for (C1) is a syntactic sugar for the following formal statement: if there are corr-links $p = (p_1, p_2)$ and $c = (c_1, c_2)$ with $p_i \in \mathsf{Person}^{A_i}$, $c_i \in \mathsf{Company}^{A_i}$ ($i = 1, 2$) then the following holds: $(p_1, c_1) \in \mathsf{empl\text{-}er}^{A_1}$ iff $(c_2, p_2) \in \mathsf{empl\text{-}ee}^{A_2}$. A precise formal account of this discussion can be found in [10].

Thus, a multimodel is actually a tuple $\mathcal{A} = (A_1, A_2, A_3, R)$ where R is a collection of correspondence relations over sets involved. This R is implicit in Fig. 2 since in this very special case it can be restored. Consistency of a multimodel is a property of the entire 4-tuple $\mathcal{A}$ rather than its 3-tuple carrier (A_1, A_2, A_3).

2.2   Synchronization via Update Propagation

There are several ways to restore consistency of the multimodel in Fig. 2 w.r.t. constraint (C1). We may delete Mary from A_1, or delete its employment with IBM from A_2, or even delete IBM from A_2. We can also change Mary's employment from IBM to Google, which will restore (C1) as A_1 does not know Google. Similarly, we can delete John's record from A_1 and then Mary's employment with IBM in A_2 would not violate (C1). As the number of constraints and the elements they involve increase, the number of consistency restoration variants grows fast.

The range of possibilities can be essentially decreased if we take into account the history of creating inconsistency and consider not only an inconsistent state $\mathcal{A}^\dagger$ but update $u: \mathcal{A} \rightarrow \mathcal{A}^\dagger$ that created it (assuming that $\mathcal{A}$ is consistent). For example, suppose that initially model A_1 contained record (Mary, IBM) (and A_3 contained (a1, a15)-commute), and the inconsistency appears after Mary's employment with IBM was deleted in A_1. Then it's reasonable to restore consistency by deleting this employment record in A_2 too; we say that deletion was propagated from A_1 to A_2 (where we assume that initially A_3 contained the commute (a1, a15)). If the inconsistency appears after adding (IBM, Mary)-employment to A_2, then it's reasonable to restore consistency by adding such a record to A_1. Although propagating deletions/additions to deletions/additions is typical, there are non-monotonic cases too. Let us assume that Mary and John are spouses (they live at the same address), and that IBM follows an exotic policy prohibiting spouses to work together. Then we can interpret addition of (IBM, Mary)-record to A_2 as swapping of the family member working for IBM, and then (John, IBM) is to be deleted from A_1.

Now let's consider how updates to and from model A_3 may be propagated. As mentioned above, traceability/correspondence links play a crucial role here. If additions to A_1 or A_2 or both create a new commute, the latter has to be added to A_3 (together with its corr-links) due to constraint (C2). In contrast, if a new commute is added to A_3, we change nothing in $A_{1,2}$ as (C2) only requires inclusion. If a commute is deleted from A_3, and it is traced to a corresponding employment in empl-er^{A_1} ∪ empl-ee^{A_2}, then this employment is deleted. (Of course, there are other ways to remove a commute derivable over A_1 and A_2.) Finally, if a commute-generating employment in empl-er^{A_1} ∪empl-ee^{A_2} is deleted, the respective commute in A_3 is deleted too. Clearly, many of the propagation policies above although formally correct, may contradict the real world changes and hence should be corrected, but this is a common problem of a majority of automatic synchronization approaches, which have to make guesses in order to resolve non-determinism inherent in consistency restoration.

2.3   Reflective Update Propagation

An important feature of update propagation scenarios above is that consistency could be restored without changing the model whose update caused inconsistency. However, this is not always desirable. Suppose again that violation of constraint (C1) in multimodel in Fig. 2 was caused by adding a new person Mary to A_1, e.g., as a result of Mary's moving to downtown. Now both models know both Mary and IBM, and thus either employment record (Mary, IBM) is to be added to A_1, or record (IBM, Mary) is to be removed from A_2. Either of the variants is possible, but in our context, adding (Mary, IBM) to A_1 seems more likely and less specific than deletion (IBM, Mary) from A_2. Indeed, if Mary has just moved to downtown, the data source A_1 simply may not have completed her record yet. Deletion (IBM, Mary) from A_2 seems to be a different event unless there are strong causal dependencies between moving to downtown and working for IBM. Thus, an update policy that would keep A_2 unchanged but amend addition of Mary to A_1 with further automatic adding her employment for IBM (as per model A_2) seems reasonable. This means that updates can be reflectively propagated (we also say self-propagated).

Of course, self-propagation does not necessarily mean non-propagation to other directions. Consider the following case: model A_1 initially only contains (John, IBM) record and is consistent with A_2 shown in Fig. 2. Then record (Mary, Google) was added to A_1, which thus became inconsistent with A_2. To restore consistency, (Mary, Google) is to be added to A_2 (the update is propagated from A_1 to A_2) and (Mary, IBM) is to be added to A_1 as discussed above (i.e., addition of (Mary, Google) is amended or self-propagated).

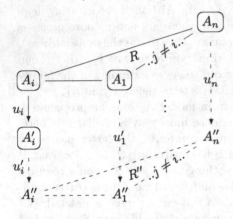

A general schema of update propagation including reflection is shown in Fig. 3. We begin with a consistent multi-model $(A_1...A_n, R)$[1] one of which members is updated $u_i\colon A_i \to A_i'$. The propagation operation, based on a priori defined propagation policies as sketched above, produces:

(a) updates on all other models $u_j'\colon A_j \to A_j''$, $1 \le j \ne i \le n$;
(b) a reflective update $u_i'\colon A_i' \to A_i''$;
(c) a new correspondence specification R'' such that the updated multimodel $(A_1''...A_n'', R'')$ is consistent.

Fig. 3. Update propagation pattern

To distinguish given data from those produced by the operation, the former are shown with framed nodes and solid lines in Fig. 3 while the latter are non-framed and dashed. Below we introduce an algebraic model encompassing several operations and algebraic laws formally modelling situations considered so far.

3   Multidirectional Update Propagation and Delta Lenses

A delta-based mathematical model for bx is well-known under the name of delta lenses; below we will say just *lens*. There are two main variants: asymmetric lenses, when one model is a view of the other and hence does not have any private information, and symmetric lenses, when both sides have their private data not visible on the other side [2,3,6]. In this section we will develop a framework for generalizing the idea for any $n \ge 2$ and including reflective updates.

---

[1] Here we first abbreviate $(A_1,\dots,A_n)$ by $(A_1...A_n)$, and then write $(A_1...A_n, R)$ for $((A_1...A_n), R)$. We will apply this style in other similar cases, and write, e.g., $i \in 1...n$ for $i \in \{1, ..., n\}$ (this will also be written as $i \le n$).

3.1   Background: Graphs and Categories

We reproduce well-known definitions to fix our notation. A *(directed multi-)graph* G consists of a set $G^\bullet$ of *nodes* and a set $G^\blacktriangleright$ of *arrows* equipped with two functions $\mathsf{s}, \mathsf{t} \colon G^\blacktriangleright \to G^\bullet$ that give arrow a its *source* $\mathsf{s}(a)$ and *target* $\mathsf{t}(a)$ nodes. We write $a \colon N \to N'$ if $\mathsf{s}(a) = N$ and $\mathsf{t}(a) = N'$, and $a \colon N \to \_$ or $a \colon \_ \to N'$ if only one of this conditions is given. Correspondingly, expressions $G^\blacktriangleright(N, N')$, $G^\blacktriangleright(N, \_)$, $G^\blacktriangleright(\_, N')$ denote sets of, resp., all arrows from N to N', all arrows from N, and all arrows into N'.

A (small) *category* is a graph, whose arrows are associatively composable and every node has a special *identity* loop, which is the unit of the composition. In more detail, given two consecutive arrows $a_1 \colon \_ \to N$ and $a_2 \colon N \to \_$, we denote the composed arrow by $a_1; a_2$. The identity loop of node N is denoted by id_N, and equations $a_1; \mathsf{id}_N = a_1$ and $\mathsf{id}_N; a_2 = a_2$ are to hold. A *functor* is a mapping of nodes and arrows from one category to another, which respects sources and targets. Having a tuple of categories $(\mathbf{A}_1...\mathbf{A}_n)$, their *product* is a category $\mathbf{A}_1 \times ... \times \mathbf{A}_n$ whose objects are tuples $(A_1...A_n) \in \mathbf{A}_1^\bullet \times ... \times \mathbf{A}_n^\bullet$, and arrows from $(A_1...A_n)$ to $(A'_1...A'_n)$ are tuples of arrows $(u_1...u_n)$ with $u_i \colon A_i \to A'_i$ for all $i \in 1...n$.

3.2   Model Spaces and Correspondences

Basically, a *model space* is a category, whose nodes are called *model states* or just *models*, and arrows are *(directed) deltas* or *updates*. For an arrow $u \colon A \to A'$, we treat A as the state of the model before update u, A' as the state after the update, and u as an update specification. Structurally, it is a specification of correspondences between A and A'. Operationally, it is an edit sequence (edit log) that changed A to A'. The formalism does not prescribe what updates are, but assumes that they form a category, i.e., there may be different updates from state A to state A'; updates are composable; and idle updates $\mathsf{id}_A \colon A \to A$ (doing nothing) are the units of the composition.

In addition, we require every model space $\mathbf{A}$ to be endowed with a family $(\mathsf{K}_A^{\blacktriangleright\blacktriangleright})_{A \in \mathbf{A}^\bullet}$ of binary relations $\mathsf{K}_A^{\blacktriangleright\blacktriangleright} \subset \mathbf{A}^\blacktriangleright(\_, A) \times \mathbf{A}^\blacktriangleright(A, \_)$ indexed by objects of $\mathbf{A}$, and specifying *non-conflicting* or *compatible* consecutive updates. Intuitively, an update u into A is compatible with update u' from A, if u' does not revert/undo anything done by u, e.g., it does not delete/create objects created/deleted by u, or re-modify attributes modified by u (see [14] for a detailed discussion). Formally, we only require $(u, \mathsf{id}_A) \in \mathsf{K}_A^{\blacktriangleright\blacktriangleright}$ and $(\mathsf{id}_A, u') \in \mathsf{K}_A^{\blacktriangleright\blacktriangleright}$ for all $A \in \mathbf{A}^\bullet$, $u \in \mathbf{A}^\blacktriangleright(\_, A)$ and $u' \in \mathbf{A}^\blacktriangleright(A, \_)$.

Definition 1 (Model spaces). *A model space is a pair* $\mathbf{A} = (|\mathbf{A}|, \mathsf{K}_A^{\blacktriangleright\blacktriangleright})$ *with* $|\mathbf{A}|$ *a category (the* carrier*) of models and updates and* $\mathsf{K}_A^{\blacktriangleright\blacktriangleright}$ *a family as specified above. A model space functor from* $\mathbf{A}$ *to* $\mathbf{B}$ *is a functor* $F \colon |\mathbf{A}| \to |\mathbf{B}|$, *such that* $(u, u') \in \mathsf{K}_A^{\blacktriangleright\blacktriangleright}$ *implies* $(F(u), F(u')) \in \mathsf{K}_B^{\blacktriangleright\blacktriangleright}$. *We will denote model spaces and their carriers by the same symbol and often omit explicit mentioning of* $\mathsf{K}^{\blacktriangleright\blacktriangleright}$. □

In the sequel, we will work with families of model spaces indexed by a finite set I, whose elements can be seen as space *names*. To simplify notation, we will assume that $I = \{1, \ldots, n\}$ although ordering will not play any role in our framework. Given a tuple of model spaces $\mathbf{A}_1, \ldots, \mathbf{A}_n$, we will refer to objects and arrows of the product category $\mathbf{A}_1 \times \cdots \times \mathbf{A}_n$ as *model tuples* and *update tuples* or, sometimes, as *discrete multimodels/multiupdates*.

Definition 2 (Multispace/Multimodels). *Let $n \geq 2$ be a natural number.*

(i) *An n-ary multimodel space or just an n-ary multispace $\mathcal{A}$ is given by a family of model spaces $\partial\mathcal{A} = (\mathbf{A}_1, \ldots, \mathbf{A}_n)$ called the boundary of $\mathcal{A}$, and a set $\mathcal{A}^\star$ of elements called corrs along with a family of functions $(\partial_i : \mathcal{A}^\star \to \mathbf{A}_i^\bullet)_{i \leq n}$ providing every corr R with its boundary $\partial R = (\partial_1 R \ldots \partial_n R)$, i.e., a tuple of models taken from the multispace boundary one model per space. Intuitively, a corr is understood as a consistent correspondence specification interrelating models from its boundary (and for this paper, all corrs are assumed consistent).*
Given a model tuple $(A_1 \ldots A_n)$, we write $\mathcal{A}^\star(A_1 \ldots A_n)$ for the set of all corrs R with $\partial R = (A_1 \ldots A_n)$; we call models A_i feet of R. Respectively, spaces $\mathbf{A}_i$ are feet of $\mathcal{A}$ and we write $\partial_i \mathcal{A}$ for $\mathbf{A}_i$.

(ii) *An (aligned consistent) multimodel over a multispace $\mathcal{A}$ is a model tuple $(A_1 \ldots A_n)$ along with a corr $R \in \mathcal{A}^\star(A_1 \ldots A_n)$ relating the models. A multimodel update $u : (A_1 \ldots A_n, R) \to (A_1' \ldots A_n', R')$ is a tuple of updates $(u_1 : A_1 \to A_1', \ldots, u_n : A_n \to A_n')$.* □

Note that any corr R uniquely defines a multimodel via the corr's boundary function ∂. We will also need to identify the set of all corrs for some fixed $A \in \mathbf{A}_i^\bullet$ for a given i: $\mathcal{A}_i^\star(A, \_) \overset{\text{def}}{=} \left\{ \; \middle| \; R \in \mathcal{A}^\star \right\} \partial_i R = A$.

The *Running example* of Sect. 2 gives rise to a 3-ary multimodel space. For $i \leq 3$, space $\mathbf{A}_i$ consists of all models instantiating metamodel M_i in Fig. 1 and their updates. To get a consistent multimodel $(A_1 A_2 A_3, R)$ from that one shown in Fig. 2, we can add to A_1 an empl-er-link connecting Mary to IBM, add to A_3 a commute with from $= a1$ and to $= a15$, and form a corr-set $R = \{(p_1', p_2'), (c_1, c_2')\}$ (all other corr-links are derivable from this data).

3.3 Update Propagation and Multiary (Delta) Lenses

Update policies described in Sect. 2 can be extended to cover propagation of all updates u_i, $i \in 1 \ldots 3$ according to the pattern in Fig. 3. This is a non-trivial task, but after it is accomplished, we have the following synchronization structure.

Definition 3 (Symmetric lenses). *An n-ary symmetric lens is a pair $\ell = (\mathcal{A}, \mathsf{ppg})$ with $\mathcal{A}$ an n-ary multispace called the carrier of ℓ, and $(\mathsf{ppg}_i)_{i \leq n}$ an n-tuple of operations of the following arities. Operation ppg_i takes a corr R (in fact, a multimodel) with boundary $\partial R = (A_1 \ldots A_n)$, and an update $u_i : A_i \to A_i'$ as its input, and returns*

(a) an $(n-1)$-tuple of updates u'_j: $A_j \to A''_j$ with $1 \leq j \neq i \leq n$;
(b) a reflective *update* u'_i: $A'_i \to A''_i$ also called an amendment *of* u_i,
(c) a new consistent corr $R'' \in \mathcal{A}^{\star}(A''_1...A''_n)$.

In fact, operations ppg_i complete a local update u_i to an entire multimodel update with components $(u'_j)_{j \neq i}$ and u_i; u'_i (see Fig. 3).   □

Notation. If the first argument R of operation ppg_i is fixed, the corresponding family of unary operations (whose only argument is u_i) will be denoted by ppg_i^R. By taking the jth component of the multi-element result, we obtain single-valued unary operations ppg_{ij}^R producing, resp. updates $u'_j = \mathsf{ppg}_{ij}^R(u_i)$: $A'_j \to A''_j$. Note that $A'_j = A_j$ for all $j \neq i$ (see clause (a) of the definition) while ppg_{ii}^R is the reflective update (b). We also have operation $\mathsf{ppg}_{i\star}^R$ returning a new consistent corr $R'' = \mathsf{ppg}_{i\star}^R(u_i)$ according to (c).

Definition 4 (Closed updates). *Given a lens $\ell = (\mathcal{A}, \mathsf{ppg})$ and a corr $R \in \mathcal{A}^{\star}(A_1...A_n)$, we call an update u_i: $A_i \to A'_i$ R-closed, if $\mathsf{ppg}_{ii}^R(u_i) = \mathrm{id}_{A'_i}$. An update is ℓ-closed if it is R-closed for all R. Lens ℓ is called non-reflective at foot A_i, if all updates in $\mathbf{A}_i^\blacktriangleright$ are ℓ-closed.*   □

For the *Running example*, update propagation policies described in Sect. 2 give rise to a lens non-reflective at space $\mathbf{A}_3$.

Definition 5 (Well-behavedness). *A lens $\ell = (\mathcal{A}, \mathsf{ppg})$ is called* well-behaved (wb) *if the following laws hold for all $i \leq n$, $A_i \in \mathbf{A}_i^\bullet$, $R \in \mathcal{A}_i^{\star}(A_i, \_)$ and u_i: $A_i \to A'_i$, cf. Fig. 3.*

(Stability)$_i$ $\forall j \in \{1...n\} : \mathsf{ppg}_{ij}^R(\mathrm{id}_{A_i}) = \mathrm{id}_{A_j}$ and $\mathsf{ppg}_{i\star}^R(\mathrm{id}_{A_i}) = R$
(Reflect1)$_i$ $(u_i, u'_i) \in \mathsf{K}_{A'_i}^{\blacktriangleright\blacktriangleright}$
(Reflect2)$_i$ $\forall j \neq i : \mathsf{ppg}_{ij}^R(u_i; u'_i) = \mathsf{ppg}_{ij}^R(u_i)$
(Reflect3)$_i$ $\mathsf{ppg}_{ii}^R(u_i; u'_i) = \mathrm{id}_{A''_i}$
where $u'_i = \mathsf{ppg}_{ii}^R(u_i)$ as in Definition 3.   □

Stability says that lenses do nothing voluntarily. Reflect1 says that amendment works towards "completion" rather than "undoing", and Reflect2-3 are idempotency conditions to ensure the completion indeed done.

Definition 6 (Invertibility). *A wb lens is called* (weakly) invertible, *if it satisfies the following law for any i, update u_i: $A_i \to A'_i$ and $R \in \mathcal{A}_i^{\star}(A_i, \_)$:*
(Invert)$_i$ *for all $j \neq i$:* $\mathsf{ppg}_{ij}^R(\mathsf{ppg}_{ji}^R(\mathsf{ppg}_{ij}^R(u_i))) = \mathsf{ppg}_{ij}^R(u_i)$ □

This law deals with "round-tripping": operation ppg_{ji}^R applied to update $u_j = \mathsf{ppg}_{ij}^R(u_i)$ results in update $\hat{u}_i$ equivalent to u_i in the sense that $\mathsf{ppg}_{ij}^R(\hat{u}_i) = \mathsf{ppg}_{ij}^R(u_i)$ (see [3] for a motivating discussion).

Example 1 (Identity Lens $\ell(n\mathbf{A})$). Let $\mathbf{A}$ be an arbitrary model space. It generates an n-ary lens $\ell(n\mathbf{A})$ as follows: The carrier $\mathcal{A}$ has n identical model spaces: $\mathbf{A}_i = \mathbf{A}$ for all $i \in \{1,..,n\}$, it has $\mathcal{A}^{\star} = \mathbf{A}^\bullet$, and boundary functions are identities. All updates are propagated to themselves (hence the name of $\ell(n\mathbf{A})$). Obviously, $\ell(n\mathbf{A})$ is a wb, invertible lens non-reflective at all its feet.   □

4 Compositionality of Update Propagation: Playing Lego with Lenses

We study how lenses can be composed. Parallel constructions are easy to manage and excluded from the paper to save space (they can be found in the long version [1, Sect. 4.1]). More challenging are sequential constructs, in which different lenses share some of their feet, and updates propagated by one lens are taken and propagated further by one or several other lenses. In Sect. 4.1, we consider a rich example of such—*star* composition of lenses. In Sect. 4.2, we study how (symmetric) lenses can be assembled from asymmetric ones.

Since we now work with several lenses, we need a notation for lens' components. Given a lens $\ell = (\mathcal{A}, \mathsf{ppg})$, we write $\ell^\star \overset{\text{def}}{=} \mathcal{A}^\star$ for its set of corrs. Feet are written ∂_i^ℓ (i-th boundary space) and $\partial_i^\ell R$ for the i-th boundary of a corr $R \in \ell^\star$. Propagation operations of the lens ℓ are denoted by $\ell.\mathsf{ppg}_{ij}^R$, $\ell.\mathsf{ppg}_{i\star}^R$.

4.1 Star Composition

Running Example Continued. Diagram in Fig. 4 presents a refinement of our example, which explicitly includes relational storage models $B_{1,2}$ for the two data sources. We assume that object models $A_{1,2}$ are simple projective views of databases $B_{1,2}$: data in A_i are copied from B_i without any transformation, while additional tables and attributes that B_i-data may have are excluded from the view A_i; the traceability mappings $R_i : A_i \leftrightarrow B_i$ are thus embeddings.

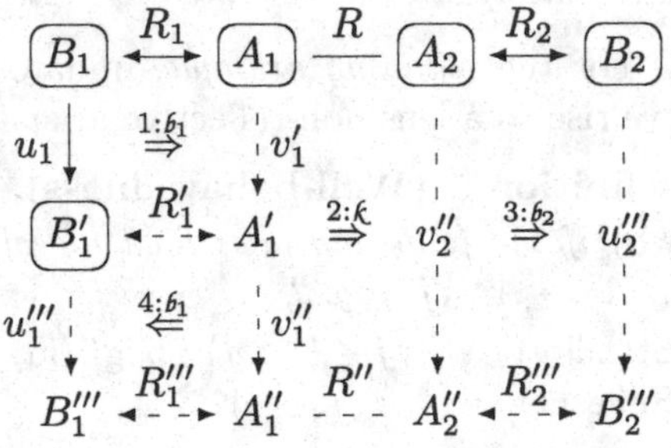

Fig. 4. Running example via lenses

We further assume that synchronization of bases B_i and their views A_i is realized by simple *constant-complement* lenses b_i, $i = 1, 2$ (see, e.g., [9]). Finally, let k be a lens synchronizing models A_1, A_2, A_3 as described in Sect. 2, and $R \in k^\star(A_1, A_2, A_3)$ be a corr for some A_3 not shown in the figure.

Consider the following update propagation scenario. Suppose that at some moment we have consistency (R_1, R, R_2) of all five models, and then B_1 is updated with $u_1 : B_1 \to B_1'$ that, say, adds to B_1 a record of Mary working for Google as discussed in Sect. 2. Consistency is restored with a four-step propagation procedure shown by double-arrows labeled by $x : y$ with x the step number and y the lens doing the propagation. **Step 1:** lens b_1 propagates update u_1 to v_1' that adds (Mary, Google) to view A_1 with no amendment to u_1 as v_1' is just a projection of u_1, thus, $B_1' = B_1''$. Note also the updated traceability mapping $R_1' : B_1' \leftrightarrow A_1'$. **Step 2:** lens k propagates v_1' to v_2'' that adds (Google, Mary) to A_2, and amends v_1' with v_1'' that adds (Mary, IBM) to A_1'; a new consistent corr R'' is also computed. **Step 3:** lens b_2 propagates v_2'' to u_2''' that adds Mary's employment by Google to B_2 with, perhaps, some other specific relational storage changes not visible in A_2. We assume no amendment to v_2'' as otherwise access to relational storage would amend application data, and thus we have a consistent corr R_2''' as shown. **Step 4:** lens b_1 maps update v_1'' (see above in Step 2) backward to u_1''' that adds (Mary, IBM) to B_1' so that B_1''' includes both (Mary, Google) and (Mary, IBM) and a respective consistent corr R_1''' is provided. There is no amendment for v_1'' by the same reason as in Step 3.

Thus, all five models in the bottom line of Fig. 4 (A_3'' is not shown) are mutually consistent and all show that Mary is employed by IBM and Google. Synchronization is restored, and we can consider the entire scenario as propagation of u_1 to u_2''' and its amendment with u_1''' so that finally we have a consistent corr (R_1''', R'', R_2''') interrelating B_1''', A_3'', B_2'''. Amendment u_1''' is compatible with u_1 as nothing is undone and condition $(u_1, u_1''') \in \mathsf{K}_{B_1'}^{\blacktriangleright\blacktriangleright}$ holds; the other two equations required by Reflect2-3 for the pair (u_1, u_1''') also hold. For our simple projection views, these conditions will hold for other updates too, and we have a well-behaved propagation from B_1 to B_2 (and trivially to A_3). Similarly, we have a wb propagation from B_2 to B_1 and A_3. Propagation from A_3 to $B_{1,2}$ is non-reflective and done in two steps: first lens k works, then lenses b_i work as described above (and updates produced by k are b_i-closed). Thus, we have built a wb ternary lens synchronizing spaces $\mathbf{B}_1, \mathbf{B}_2$ and $\mathbf{A}_3$ by joining lenses b_1 and b_2 to the central lens k.

Discussion. Reflection is a crucial aspect of lens composition. The inset figure describes the scenario above as a transition system and shows that Steps 3 and 4 can go concurrently. It is the non-trivial amendment created in Step 2 that causes the necessity of Step 4, otherwise Step 3 would finish consis- 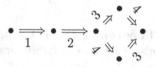 tency restoration (with Step 4 being an idle transition). On the other hand, if update v_2'' in Fig. 4 would not be closed for lens b_2, we'd have yet another concurrent step complicating the scenario. Fortunately for our example with simple projective views, Step 4 is simple and provides a non-conflicting amendment, but the case of more complex views beyond the constant-complement class needs care and investigation. Below we specify a simple situation of lens composition with reflection a priori excluded, and leave more complex cases for future work.

Formal Definition. Suppose we have an n-ary lens $k = (\mathcal{A}, \mathsf{ppg})$, and for every $i \le n$, a binary lens $b_i = (\mathbf{A}_i, \mathbf{B}_i, b_i.\mathsf{ppg})$, with the first model space $\mathbf{A}_i$ being the ith model space of k (see Fig. 5, where k is depicted in the center and b_i are shown as ellipses adjoint to k's feet). We also assume the following *Junction conditions:* For any $i \le n$, all updates propagated to $\mathbf{A}_i$ by lens b_i are k-closed, and all updates propagated to $\mathbf{A}_i$ by lens k are b_i-closed.

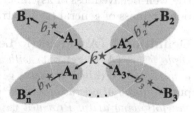

Fig. 5. Star composition

Below we will write a corr $R_i \in \mathcal{b}_i^\star(A_i, B_i)$ as $R_i: A_i \leftrightarrow B_i$, and the sixtuple of operations $\mathcal{b}_i.\mathsf{ppg}^{R_i}$ as the family $\left(\mathcal{b}_i.\mathsf{ppg}_{xy}^{R_i} \mid x \in \{\mathbf{A}, \mathbf{B}\}, y \in \{\mathbf{A}, \mathbf{B}, \star\}\right)$. Likewise we write $\partial_x^{\mathcal{b}_i}$ with $x \in \{\mathbf{A}, \mathbf{B}\}$ for the boundary functions of lenses $\mathcal{b}_i$.

The above configuration gives rise to the following n-ary lens ℓ. The carrier is the tuple of model spaces $\mathbf{B}_1...\mathbf{B}_n$ and corrs are tuples $(R, R_1...R_n)$ with $R \in \mathcal{k}^\star$ and $R_i \in \mathcal{b}_i^\star$, such that $\partial_i^{\mathcal{k}} R = \partial_{\mathbf{A}}^{\mathcal{b}_i} R_i$ for all $i \in 1..n$. Moreover, we define $\partial_i^\ell(R, R_1...R_n) \overset{\text{def}}{=} \partial_{\mathbf{B}}^{\mathcal{b}_i} R_i$ (see Fig. 5). Operations are defined as compositions of consecutive lens' executions as described below (we will use the dot notation for operation application and write $x.\mathsf{op}$ for $\mathsf{op}(x)$, where x is an argument).

Given a model tuple $(B_1...B_n) \in \mathbf{B}_1 \times ... \times \mathbf{B}_n$, a corr $(R, R_1...R_n)$, and update $v_i: B_i \to B_i'$ in $\mathbf{B}_i^\blacktriangleright$, we define, first for $j \neq i$,

$$v_i.\,\ell.\mathsf{ppg}_{ij}^{(R, R_1...R_n)} \overset{\text{def}}{=} v_i.(\mathcal{b}_i.\mathsf{ppg}_{\mathbf{BA}}^{R_i}).(\mathcal{k}.\mathsf{ppg}_{ij}^{R}).(\mathcal{b}_j.\mathsf{ppg}_{\mathbf{AB}}^{R_j}),$$

and $v_i.\,\ell.\mathsf{ppg}_{ii}^{(R, R_1...R_n)} \overset{\text{def}}{=} v_i.\mathcal{b}_i.\mathsf{ppg}_{\mathbf{BB}}^{R_i}$ for $j = i$. Note that all internal amendments to $u_i = v_i.(\mathcal{b}_i.\mathsf{ppg}_{\mathbf{BA}}^{R_i})$ produced by $\mathcal{k}$, and to $u_j' = u_i.(\mathcal{k}.\mathsf{ppg}_{ij}^{R})$ produced by $\mathcal{b}_j$, are identities due to the Junction conditions. This allows us to set corrs properly and finish propagation with the three steps above: $v_i.\,\ell.\mathsf{ppg}_{i\star}^{(R, R_1...R_n)} \overset{\text{def}}{=} (R', R_1'...R_n')$ where $R' = u_i.\mathcal{k}.\mathsf{ppg}_{i\star}^{R}$, $R_j' = u_j'.\mathcal{b}_j.\mathsf{ppg}_{\mathbf{A}\star}^{R_j}$ for $j \neq i$, and $R_i' = v_i.\mathcal{b}_i.\mathsf{ppg}_{\mathbf{B}\star}^{R_i}$. We thus have a lens ℓ denoted by $\mathcal{k}^\star(\mathcal{b}_1, \ldots, \mathcal{b}_n)$. □

Theorem 1 (Star Composition). *Given a star configuration of lenses as above, if lens $\mathcal{k}$ fulfills Stability, all lenses $\mathcal{b}_i$ are wb, and Junction conditions hold, then the composed lens $\mathcal{k}^\star(\mathcal{b}_1, \ldots, \mathcal{b}_n)$ defined above is wb, too.*

Proof. Laws Stability and Reflect1 for the composed lens are straightforward. Reflect2-3 also follow immediately, since the first step of the above propagation procedure already enjoys idempotency by Reflect2-3 for $\mathcal{b}_i$. □

4.2 Assembling n-ary Lenses from Binary Lenses

This section shows how to assemble n-ary (symmetric) lenses from binary asymmetric lenses modelling view computation [2]. As the latter is a typical bx, the well-behavedness of asymmetric lenses has important distinctions from well-behavedness of general (symmetric mx-tailored) lenses.

Definition 7 (Asymmetric Lens, cf. [2]). *An asymmetric lens (a-lens) is a tuple $\mathcal{b}^\leq = (\mathbf{A}, \mathbf{B}, \mathsf{get}, \mathsf{put})$ with $\mathbf{A}$ a model space called the (abstract) view, $\mathbf{B}$ a model space called the base, $\mathsf{get}: \mathbf{A} \leftarrow \mathbf{B}$ a functor (read "get the view"), and put a family of operations $(\mathsf{put}^B \mid B \in \mathbf{B}^\bullet)$ (read "put the view update back") of the following arity. Provided with a view update $v: \mathsf{get}(B) \to A'$ at the input, operation put^B outputs a base update $\mathsf{put}_b^B(v) = u': B \to B''$ and a reflected view update $\mathsf{put}_v^B(v) = v': A' \to A''$ such that $A'' = \mathsf{get}(B'')$. A view update $v: \mathsf{get}(B) \to A'$ is called closed if $\mathsf{put}_v^B(v) = \mathsf{id}_{A'}$.* □

The following is a specialization of Definition 5.

Definition 8 (Well-behavedness). *An a-lens is* well-behaved (wb) *if it satisfies the following laws for all* $B \in \mathbf{B}^\bullet$ *and* $v \colon \mathsf{get}(B) \to A'$

(Stability)	$\mathsf{put}_b^B(\mathsf{id}_{\mathsf{get}(B)}) = \mathsf{id}_B$
(Reflect0)	$\mathsf{put}_v^B(v) \neq \mathsf{id}_{A'}$ *implies* $A' \neq \mathsf{get}(X)$ *for all* $X \in \mathbf{B}^\bullet$
(Reflect1)	$(v, v') \in \mathsf{K}_{A'}^{\blacktriangleright\blacktriangleright}$
(Reflect2)	$\mathsf{put}_b^B(v; \mathsf{put}_v^B(v)) = \mathsf{put}_b^B(v)$
(PutGet)	$v; \mathsf{put}_v^B(v) = \mathsf{get}(\mathsf{put}_b^B(v))$

In contrast to the general lens case, a wb a-lens features Reflect0—a sort of self-Hippocraticness important for bx. Another distinction is inclusion of a strong invertibility law PutGet into the definition of well-behavedness: Put-Get together with Reflect2 provide (weak) invertibility: $\mathsf{put}_b^B(\mathsf{get}(\mathsf{put}_b^B(v))) = \mathsf{put}_b^B(v)$. Reflect3 is omitted as it is implied by Reflect0 and PutGet.

Any a-lens $b^\preceq = (\mathbf{A}, \mathbf{B}, \mathsf{get}, \mathsf{put})$ gives rise to a binary symmetric lens b. Its carrier consists of model spaces $\mathbf{A}$ and $\mathbf{B}$. Furthermore $b^\star = \mathbf{B}^\bullet$ with boundary mappings defined as follows: for $R \in b^\star = \mathbf{B}^\bullet$, $\partial_\mathbf{A}^b R = \mathsf{get}(R)$ and $\partial_\mathbf{B}^b R = R$. Thus, the set of corrs $b^\star(A, B)$ is $\{B\}$ if $A = \mathsf{get}(B)$, and is empty otherwise.

For a corr B, we need to define six operations $b.\mathsf{ppg}^B$. If $v \colon A \to A'$ is a view update, then $\mathsf{ppg}_{\mathbf{AB}}^B(v) = \mathsf{put}_b^B(v) : B \to B''$, $\mathsf{ppg}_{\mathbf{AA}}^B(\overline{v}) = \mathsf{put}_v^B(v) : A' \to A''$, and $\mathsf{ppg}_{\mathbf{A}\star}^B(v) = B''$. The condition $A'' = \mathsf{get}(B'')$ for $b^\preceq$ means that B'' is again a consistent corr with the desired boundaries. For a base update $u \colon B \to B'$ and corr B, $\mathsf{ppg}_{\mathbf{BA}}^B(u) = \mathsf{get}(u)$, $\mathsf{ppg}_{\mathbf{BB}}^B(u) = \mathsf{id}_{B'}$, and $\mathsf{ppg}_{\mathbf{B}\star}^B(u) = B'$. Functoriality of get yields consistency of B'.

Lemma 1. *Let* $b^\preceq$ *be a wb a-lens and* b *the corresponding symmetric lens. Then all base updates of* b *are closed, and* b *is wb and invertible.*

Proof. Base updates are closed by the definition of $\mathsf{ppg}_{\mathbf{BB}}$. Well-behavedness follows from wb-ness of $b^\preceq$. Invertibility has to be proved in two directions: $\mathsf{ppg}_{\mathbf{BA}}; \mathsf{ppg}_{\mathbf{AB}}; \mathsf{ppg}_{\mathbf{BA}} = \mathsf{ppg}_{\mathbf{BA}}$ follows from (PutGet) and (Reflect0), the other direction follows from (PutGet) and (Reflect2), see the remark after Definition 8. $\square$

Theorem 2 (Lenses from Spans). *An* n-ary span of wb a-lenses $b_i^\preceq = (\mathbf{A}_i, \mathbf{B}, \mathsf{get}_i, \mathsf{put}_i)$, $i = 1..n$ *with common base* $\mathbf{B}$ *of all* $b_i^\preceq$ *gives rise to a wb (symmetric) lens denoted by* $\Sigma_{i=1}^n b_i^\preceq$.

Proof. An n-ary span of a-lenses $b_i^\preceq$ (all of them interpreted as symmetric lenses b_i as explained above) is a construct equivalent to the star-composition of Definition 4.1.3, in which lens $k = \ell(n\mathbf{B})$ (cf. Example 1) and peripheral lenses are lenses b_i. The junction condition is satisfied as all base updates are b_i-closed for all i by Lemma 1, and also trivially closed for any identity lens. The theorem thus follows from Theorem 1. Note that a corr in $(\Sigma_{i=1}^n b_i^\preceq)^\star$ is nothing but a single model $B \in \mathbf{B}^\bullet$ with boundaries being the respective get_i-images. $\square$

The theorem shows that combining a-lenses in this way yields an n-ary symmetric lens, whose properties can automatically be inferred from the binary a-lenses.

Running example. Figure 6 shows a metamodel M^+ obtained by merging the three metamodels $M_{1,2,3}$ from Fig. 1 without loss and duplication of information. In addition, for persons and companies, the identifiers of model spaces, in which a given person or company occurs, can be traced back via attribute "spaces" (Commute-objects are known to appear in space $\mathbf{A}_3$ and hence do not need such an attribute). As shown in [10], any consistent multimodel $(A_1...A_n, R)$ can be merged into a comprehensive model A^+ instantiating M^+. Let $\mathbf{B}$ be the space of such together with their comprehensive updates $u^+ \colon A^+ \to A'^+$.

For a given $i \le 3$, we can define the following a-lens $\mathfrak{b}_i^{\rightleftarrows} = (\mathbf{A}_i, \mathbf{B}, \mathsf{get}_i, \mathsf{put}_i)$: get_i takes update u^+ as above and outputs its restriction to the model containing only objects recorded in space $\mathbf{A}_i$. Operation put_i takes an update $v_i \colon A_i \to A'_i$ and first propagates it to all directions as discussed in Sect. 2, then merges these propagated local updates into a comprehensive

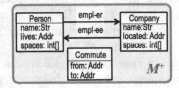

Fig. 6. Merged metamodel

$\mathbf{B}$-update between comprehensive models. This yields a span of a-lenses that implements the same synchronization behaviour as the symmetric lens discussed in Sect. 2.

From lenses to spans. There is also a backward transformation of (symmetric) lenses to spans of a-lenses. Let $\ell = (\mathcal{A}, \mathsf{ppg})$ be a wb lens. It gives rise to the following span of wb a-lenses $\ell_i^{\rightleftarrows} = (\partial_i(\mathcal{A}), \mathbf{B}, \mathsf{get}_i, \mathsf{put}_i)$ where space $\mathbf{B}$ is built from consistent multimodels and their updates, and functors $\mathsf{get}_i \colon \mathbf{B} \to \mathbf{A}_i$ are projection functors. Given $B = (A_1...A_n, R)$ and update $u_i \colon A_i \to A'_i$, let

$$\mathsf{put}_{ib}^B(u_i) \stackrel{\text{def}}{=} (u'_1, .., u'_{i-1}, (u_i; u'_i), u'_{i+1}, .., u'_n) \colon (A_1...A_n, R) \to (A''_1...A''_n, R'')$$

where $u'_j \stackrel{\text{def}}{=} \mathsf{ppg}_{ij}^R(u_i)$ (all j) and $R'' = \mathsf{ppg}_{i\star}^R(u_i)$. Finally, $\mathsf{put}_{iv}^B(v_i) \stackrel{\text{def}}{=} \mathsf{ppg}_{ii}^R(u_i)$. Validity of Stability, Reflect0-2, PutGet directly follows from the above definitions.

An open question is whether the span-to-lens transformation in Theorem 2 and the lens-to-span transformation described above are mutually inverse. The results for the binary case in [8] show that this is only the case modulo certain equivalence relations. These equivalences may be different for our reflective multiary lenses, and we leave this important question for future research.

5   Related Work

For state-based lenses, the work closest in spirit is Stevens' paper [16]. Her and our goals are similar, but the technical realisations are different even besides the state- vs. delta-based opposition. Stevens works with restorers, which take a multimodel (in the state-based setting, just a tuple of models) presumably *inconsistent*, and restores consistency by changing some models in the tuple while keeping other models (from the *authority set*) unchanged. In contrast, lenses take a *consistent* multimodel *and* updates, and return a consistent multimodel and updates. Also, update amendments are not considered in [16] – models in the authority set are intact.

Another distinction is how the multiary vs. binary issue is treated. Stevens provides several results for decomposing an n-ary relation $\mathcal{A}^\star$ into binary relations $\mathcal{A}^\star_{ij} \subseteq \mathbf{A}_i \times \mathbf{A}_j$ between the components. For us, a relation is a span, i.e., a set $\mathcal{A}^\star$ endowed with an n-tuple of projections $\partial_i \colon \mathcal{A}^\star \to \mathbf{A}_i$ uniquely identifying elements in $\mathcal{A}^\star$. Thus, while Stevens considers "binarisation" of a relation R over its boundary $A_1...A_n$, we "binarise" it via the corresponding span (the UML would call it reification). Our (de)composition results demonstrate advantages of the span view. Discussion of several other works in the state-based world, notably by Macedo *et al.* [12] can be found in [16].

Compositionality as a fundamental principle for building synchronization tools was proposed by Pierce and his coauthors, and realized for several types of binary lenses in [4,6,7]. In the delta-lens world, a fundamental theory of equivalence of symmetric lenses and spans of a-lenses (for the binary case) is developed by Johnson and Rosebrugh [8], but they do not consider reflective updates. The PutGetPut law has been discussed (in a different context of state-based asymmetric injective editing) in several early bx work from Tokyo, e.g., [13]. A notion close to our update compatibility was proposed by Orejas *et al* in [14]. We are not aware of multiary update propagation work in the delta-lens world. Considering amendment and its laws in the delta lens setting is also new.

In [11], Königs and Schürr introduced multigraph grammars (MGGs) as a multiary version of well-known triple graph grammar (TGG). Their multi-domain-integration rules specify how all involved graphs evolve simultaneously. The idea of an additional correspondence graph is close to our consistent corrs. However, their scenarios are specialized towards (1) directed graphs, (2) MOF-compliant artifacts like QVT, and (3) the global consistency view on a multimodel rather than update propagation.

6   Conclusions and Future Work

We have considered multiple model synchronization via multi-directional update propagation, and argued that reflective propagation to the model whose change originated inconsistency is a reasonable feature of the scenario. We presented a mathematical framework for such synchronization based on a multiary generalisation of binary symmetric delta lenses introduced earlier in [3], and enriched it with reflective propagation. Our lens composition results make the framework interesting for practical applications, but so far it has an essential limitation: we consider consistency violation caused by only one model change, and thus consistency is restored by propagating only one update, while in practice we often deal with several models changing concurrently. If these updates are in conflict, consistency restoration needs conflict resolution, and hence an essential development of the framework.

There are also several open issues for the non-concurrent case considered in the paper (and its future concurrent generalisation). First, our pool of lens composition constructs is far incomplete (because of both space limitations and the necessity of further research). We need to enrich it with (i) sequential composition of (reflective) a-lenses so that a category of a-lenses could be built, and (ii) a relational composition of symmetric lenses sharing several of their feet (similar to relational join). It is also important to investigate composition with weaker junction conditions than we considered. Another important issue is invertibility, which nicely fits in some but not all of our results, which shows the necessity of further investigation. It is a sign that we do not well understand the nature of invertibility. We conjecture that while invertibility is essential for bx, its role for mx may be less important. The (in)famous PutPut law is also awaiting its exploration in the case of multiary reflective propagation. And the last but not the least is the (in)famous PutPut law: how well our update propagation operations are compatible with update composition is a very important issue to explore. Finally, paper [5] shows how binary delta lenses can be implemented with TGG, and we expect that MGG could play a similar role for multiary delta lenses.

References

1. Diskin, Z., König, H., Lawford, M.: Multiple model synchronization with multiary delta lenses. Technical report. McMaster Centre for Software Certification, McSCert-2017-10-01, McMaster University (2017). http://www.mcscert.ca/projects/mcscert/wp-content/uploads/2017/10/Multiple-Model-Synchronization-with-Multiary-Delta-Lenses-ZD.pdf
2. Diskin, Z., Xiong, Y., Czarnecki, K.: From state- to delta-based bidirectional model transformations: the asymmetric case. J. Object Technol. **10**(6), 1–25 (2011)
3. Diskin, Z., Xiong, Y., Czarnecki, K., Ehrig, H., Hermann, F., Orejas, F.: From state- to delta-based bidirectional model transformations: the symmetric case. In: Whittle, J., Clark, T., Kühne, T. (eds.) MODELS 2011. LNCS, vol. 6981, pp. 304–318. Springer, Heidelberg (2011). https://doi.org/10.1007/978-3-642-24485-8_22
4. Foster, J.N., Greenwald, M.B., Moore, J.T., Pierce, B.C., Schmitt, A.: Combinators for bi-directional tree transformations: a linguistic approach to the view update problem. In: Palsberg, J., Abadi, M. (eds.) Proceedings of the 32nd ACM SIGPLAN-SIGACT Symposium on Principles of Programming Languages, POPL 2005, 12–14 January 2005, Long Beach, California, USA, pp. 233–246. ACM (2005). https://doi.org/10.1145/1040305.1040325
5. Hermann, F., Ehrig, H., Orejas, F., Czarnecki, K., Diskin, Z., Xiong, Y.: Correctness of model synchronization based on triple graph grammars. In: Whittle, J., Clark, T., Kühne, T. (eds.) MODELS 2011. LNCS, vol. 6981, pp. 668–682. Springer, Heidelberg (2011). https://doi.org/10.1007/978-3-642-24485-8_49
6. Hofmann, M., Pierce, B.C., Wagner, D.: Symmetric lenses. In: Ball, T., Sagiv, M. (eds.) Proceedings of the 38th ACM SIGPLAN-SIGACT Symposium on Principles of Programming Languages, POPL 2011, 26–28 January 2011, Austin, TX, USA, pp. 371–384. ACM (2011). https://doi.org/10.1145/1926385.1926428

7. Hofmann, M., Pierce, B.C., Wagner, D.: Edit lenses. In: Field, J., Hicks, M. (eds.) Proceedings of the 39th ACM SIGPLAN-SIGACT Symposium on Principles of Programming Languages, POPL 2012, 22–28 January 2012, Philadelphia, Pennsylvania, USA, pp. 495–508. ACM (2012). https://doi.org/10.1145/2103656.2103715
8. Johnson, M., Rosebrugh, R.D.: Symmetric delta lenses and spans of asymmetric delta lenses. J. Object Technol. **16**(1), 2:1–2:32 (2017). https://doi.org/10.5381/jot.2017.16.1.a2
9. Johnson, M., Rosebrugh, R.D., Wood, R.J.: Lenses, fibrations and universal translations. Math. Struct. Comput. Sci. **22**(1), 25–42 (2012). https://doi.org/10.1017/S0960129511000442
10. König, H., Diskin, Z.: Efficient consistency checking of interrelated models. In: Anjorin, A., Espinoza, H. (eds.) ECMFA 2017. LNCS, vol. 10376, pp. 161–178. Springer, Cham (2017). https://doi.org/10.1007/978-3-319-61482-3_10
11. Königs, A., Schürr, A.: MDI: a rule-based multi-document and tool integration approach. Softw. Syst. Model. **5**(4), 349–368 (2006). https://doi.org/10.1007/s10270-006-0016-x
12. Macedo, N., Cunha, A., Pacheco, H.: Towards a framework for multidirectional model transformations. In: Proceedings of the Workshops of the EDBT/ICDT 2014 Joint Conference (EDBT/ICDT 2014), 28 March 2014, Athens, Greece, pp. 71–74 (2014). http://ceur-ws.org/Vol-1133/paper-11.pdf
13. Mu, S.-C., Hu, Z., Takeichi, M.: An algebraic approach to bi-directional updating. In: Chin, W.-N. (ed.) APLAS 2004. LNCS, vol. 3302, pp. 2–20. Springer, Heidelberg (2004). https://doi.org/10.1007/978-3-540-30477-7_2
14. Orejas, F., Boronat, A., Ehrig, H., Hermann, F., Schölzel, H.: On propagation-based concurrent model synchronization. ECEASST **57**, 1–19 (2013). http://journal.ub.tu-berlin.de/eceasst/article/view/871
15. Stevens, P.: Bidirectional model transformations in QVT: semantic issues and open questions. Softw. Syst. Model. **9**(1), 7–20 (2010)
16. Stevens, P.: Bidirectional transformations in the large. In: 20th ACM/IEEE International Conference on Model Driven Engineering Languages and Systems, MODELS 2017, 17–22 September 2017, Austin, TX, USA, pp. 1–11 (2017). https://doi.org/10.1109/MODELS.2017.8

Controlling the Attack Surface
of Object-Oriented Refactorings

Sebastian Ruland[1]([✉]) [iD], Géza Kulcsár[1] [iD], Erhan Leblebici[1] [iD],
Sven Peldszus[2] [iD], and Malte Lochau[1] [iD]

[1] Real-Time Systems Lab, TU Darmstadt, Darmstadt, Germany
{sebastian.ruland,geza.kulcsar,erhan.leblebici,
malte.lochau}@es.tu-darmstadt.de
[2] Institute for Software Technology, University of Koblenz-Landau,
Koblenz, Germany
speldszus@uni-koblenz.de

Abstract. Refactorings constitute an effective means to improve quality and maintainability of evolving object-oriented programs. Search-based techniques have shown promising results in finding optimal sequences of behavior-preserving program transformations that (1) maximize code-quality metrics and (2) minimize the number of changes. However, the impact of refactorings on extra-functional properties like security has received little attention so far. To this end, we propose as a further objective to minimize the attack surface of programs (i.e., to maximize strictness of declared accessibility of class members). Minimizing the attack surface naturally competes with applicability of established *MoveMethod* refactorings for improving coupling/cohesion metrics. Our tool implementation is based on an EMF meta-model for Java-like programs and utilizes MOMoT, a search-based model-transformation framework. Our experimental results gained from a collection of real-world Java programs show the impact of attack surface minimization on design-improving refactorings by using different accessibility-control strategies. We further compare the results to those of existing refactoring tools.

1 Introduction

The essential activity in designing object-oriented programs is to identify class candidates and to assign *responsibility* (i.e., data and operations) to them. An appropriate solution to this *Class-Responsibility-Assignment (CRA)* problem, on the one hand, intuitively reflects the problem domain and, on the other hand, exhibits acceptable quality measures [4]. In this context, *refactoring* has become a key technique for agile software development: productive program-evolution phases are interleaved with behavior-preserving code transformations for updating CRA decisions, to proactively maintain, or even improve, code-quality metrics [13,29]. Each refactoring pursues a trade-off between two major, and generally contradicting, objectives: (1) maximizing code-quality metrics, including fine-grained coupling/cohesion measures as well as coarse-grained anti-pattern

© The Author(s) 2018
A. Russo and A. Schürr (Eds.): FASE 2018, LNCS 10802, pp. 38–55, 2018.
https://doi.org/10.1007/978-3-319-89363-1_3

avoidance, and (2) minimizing the number of changes to preserve the initial program design as much as possible [8]. Manual search for refactorings sufficiently meeting both objectives becomes impracticable already for medium-size programs, as it requires to find optimal sequences of interdependent code transformations with complex constraints [10]. The very large search space and multiple competing objectives make the underlying optimization problem well-suited for search-based optimization [15] for which various semi-automated approaches for recommending refactorings have been recently proposed [18,27,28,30,34].

The validity of proposed refactorings is mostly concerned with purely *functional* behavior preservation [24], whereas their impact on *extra-functional* properties like program security has received little attention so far [22]. However, applying elaborated information-flow metrics for identifying security-preserving refactorings is computationally too expensive in practice [36]. As an alternative, we consider *attack-surface metrics* as a sufficiently reliable, yet easy-to-compute indicator for preservation of program security [20,41]. *Attack surfaces* of programs comprise all conventional ways of entering a software by users/attackers (e.g., invoking API methods or inheriting from super-classes) such that an unnecessarily large surface increases the danger of exploiting vulnerabilities. Hence, the goal of a secure program design should be to grant least privileges to class members to reduce the extent to which data and operations are exposed to the world [41]. In JAVA-like languages, accessibility constraints by means of modifiers `public`, `private` and `protected` provide a built-in low-level mechanism for controlling and restricting information flow within and across classes, sub-classes and packages [38]. Accessibility constraints introduce compile-time security barriers protecting trusted system code from untrusted mobile code [19]. As a downside, restricted accessibility privileges naturally obstruct possibilities for refactorings, as CRA updates (e.g., moving members [34]) may be either rejected by those constraints, or they require to relax accessibility privileges, thus increasing the attack surface [35].

In this paper, we present a search-based technique to find optimal sequences of refactorings for object-oriented JAVA-like programs, by explicitly taking accessibility constraints into account. To this end, we do not propose novel refactoring operations, but rather apply established ones and control their impact on attack-surface metrics. We focus on *MoveMethod* refactorings which have been proven effective for improving CRA metrics [34], in combination with operations for on-demand strengthening and relaxing of accessibility declarations [38]. As objectives, we consider (**O1**) *elimination of design flaws*, particularly, (**O1a**) optimization of object-oriented coupling/cohesion metrics [5,6] and (**O1b**) avoidance of anti-patterns, namely *The Blob*, (**O2**) *preservation of original program design* (i.e., minimizing the number of change operations), and (**O3**) *attack-surface minimization*. Our model-based tool implementation, called GOBLIN, represents individuals (i.e., intermediate refactoring results) as program-model instances complying to an EMF meta-model for JAVA-like programs [33]. Hence, instead of regenerating source code after every single refactoring step, we apply and evaluate sequences of refactoring operations, specified as model-transformation rules in HENSHIN [2], on the program model. To this end,

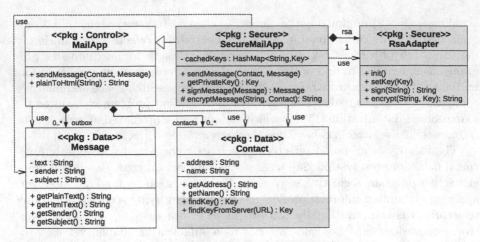

Fig. 1. UML class diagram of MAILAPP

we apply MOMoT [11], a generic framework for search-based model transformations. Our experimental evaluation results gained from applying GOBLIN as well as the recent tools JDEODORANT [12] and CODE-IMP [27] to a collection of real-world JAVA programs provide us with in-depth insights into the subtle interplay between traditional code-quality metrics and attack-surface metrics. Our tool and all experiment results are available on the GitHub site of the project[1].

2   Background and Motivation

We first introduce a running example to provide the necessary background and to motivate the proposed refactoring methodology.

Running Example. We consider a (simplified) e-mail client, called MAILAPP, implemented in JAVA. Figure 1 shows the UML class diagram of MAILAPP, where security-critical extensions (in gray) will be described below. We use stereotype ⟨⟨pkg : name⟩⟩ to annotate classes with package declarations. Central class MailApp is responsible for handling objects of classes Message and Contact both encapsulating application data and operations to access those attributes. The text of a message may be formatted as plain String, or it may be converted into HTML using method plainToHtml().

Design Flaws in Object-Oriented Programs. The over-centralized architectural design of MAILAPP, consisting of a predominant *controller class* (MailApp) intensively accessing inactive *data classes* (Message and Contact), is frequently referred to as *The Blob* anti-pattern [7]. As a consequence, method plainToHtml() in class MailApp frequently calls method getPlainText() in class Message across

---

[1]   https://github.com/Echtzeitsysteme/goblin.

class- and even package-boundaries. *The Blob* and other *design flaws* are widely considered harmful with respect to software quality in general and program maintainability in particular [7]. For instance, assume a developer to extend MailApp by (1) adding further classes SecureMailApp and RsaAdapter for encrypting and signing messages, and by (2) extending class Contact with public RSA key handling: method findKey() searches for public RSA keys of contacts by repeatedly calling method findKeyFromServer() with the URL of available key servers. This *program evolution* further decays the already flawed design of MAILAPP as class SecureMailApp may be considered as a second instance of *The Blob* anti-pattern: method encryptMessage() of class SecureMailApp intensively calls method findKey() in class Contact. This example illustrates a well-known dilemma of agile program development in an object-oriented world: *Class-Responsibility Assignment* decisions may become unbalanced over time, due to unforeseen changes crosscutting the initial program design [31]. As a result, a majority of object-oriented design flaws like *The Blob* anti-pattern is mainly caused by low cohesion/high coupling ratios within/among classes and their members [5,6].

Refactoring of Object-Oriented Programs. Object-oriented *refactorings* constitute an emerging and widely used counter-measure against design flaws [13]. Refactorings impose systematic, semantic-preserving program transformations for continuously improving code-quality measures of evolving source code. For instance, the *MoveMethod* refactoring is frequently used to update CRA decisions after program changes, by moving method implementations between classes [34]. Applied to our example, a developer may (manually) conduct two refactorings, **R1** and **R2**, to counteract the aforementioned design flaws:

(R1) move method plainToHtml() from class MailApp to class Message, and
(R2) move method encryptMessage() from class SecureMailApp to class Contact.

However, concerning programs of realistic size and complexity, tool support for (semi-)automated program refactorings becomes more and more inevitable. The major challenges in finding effective sequences of object-oriented refactoring operations consists in *detecting* flawed program parts to be refactored, as well as in *recommending* program transformations applied to those parts to obtain an improved, yet behaviorally equivalent program design. The complicated nature of the underlying optimization problem stems from several phenomena.

- **Very large search-space** due to the combinatorial explosion resulting from the many possible sequences of (potentially interdependent) refactoring-operation applications.
- **Multiple objectives** including various (inherently contradicting) refactoring goals (e.g., **O1−O3**).
- **Many invalid solutions** due to (generally very complicated) constraints to be imposed for ensuring behavior preservation.

Further research especially on the last phenomenon is required to understand to what extent a refactoring actually alters (in a potentially critical way) the original program. For instance, for refactoring **R2** to yield a correct result, it requires to relax declared *accessibility constraints*: method encryptMessage() has to become public instead of protected after being moved into class Contact to remain accessible for method sendMessage, and, conversely, method getPrivateKey() has to become public instead of private to remain accessible for encryptMessage(). Although these small changes do not affect the functionality of the original program, it may have a negative impact on extra-functional properties like program security. Therefore, the amount of invalid solutions highly depends on the interaction between constraints and repair mechanisms.

Attack Surface of Object-Oriented Programs. The *attack surface* of a program comprises all conventional ways of entering a software from outside such that a larger surface increases the danger of exploiting vulnerabilities (either unintentionally by some user, or intentionally by an attacker) [20]. Concerning JAVA-like programs in particular, explicit restrictions of accessibility of class members provide an essential mechanism to control the attack surface. Hence, refactoring **R2** should be definitely blamed as harmful as the enforced relaxations of accessibility constraints, especially those of the indeed security-critical method getPrivateKey(), unnecessarily widen the attack surface of the original program. In contrast, refactoring **R1** should be appreciated as it even narrows the attack surface by setting method plainToHtml() from public to private.

Challenges. As illustrated by our example, the attack surface of a program is a crucial, but yet unexplored, factor when searching for reasonable object-oriented program refactorings. However, if not treated with special care, accessibility constraints may seriously obstruct program maintenance by eagerly suppressing any refactoring opportunity in advance. We therefore pursue a model-based methodology for automating the search for optimal sequences of program refactorings by explicitly taking accessibility constraints into account. We formulate the underlying problem as constrained multi-objective optimization problem (MOOP) incorporating explicit control and minimization of attack-surface metrics. This framework allows us to facilitate search-based model transformation capabilities for approximating optimal solutions.

3 Search-Based Program Refactorings with Attack-Surface Control

We now describe our model-based framework for identifying (presumably) optimal sequences of object-oriented refactoring operations. To explicitly control (and minimize) the impact of recommended refactorings on the attack surface, we extend an existing EMF meta-model for representing JAVA-like programs with accessibility information and respective constraints. Based on this model, refactoring operations are defined as model-transformation rules which allow us to apply search-based model-transformation techniques to effectively explore candidate solutions of the resulting MOOP.

3.1   Program Model

In the context of model-based program transformation, a *program model* serves as unified program representation (1) constituting an appropriate level of abstraction comprising only (syntactic) program entities being relevant for a given task, and (2) including additional (static semantic) information required for a given task [24]. Concerning program models for model-based object-oriented program refactorings in particular, the corresponding model-transformation operations are mostly applied at the level of classes and members, whereas more fine-grained source code details can be neglected. Instead, program elements are augmented with additional (static semantic) dependencies to other entities being crucial for refactoring operations to yield correct results [24–26]. Here, we employ and enhance the program model proposed by Peldszus et al. [33] for automatically detecting structural anti-patterns (cf. **O1b**) in JAVA programs. Their incremental detection process also includes evaluation of coupling and cohesion metrics (cf. **O1a**), and both metric values and the detected anti-patterns are added as additional information into the program model.

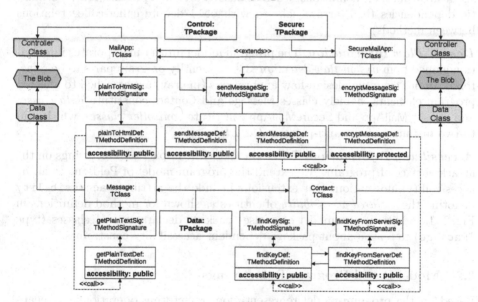

Fig. 2. Excerpt of the program-model representation of MailApp

Figure 2 shows an excerpt of the program-model representation for MailApp including the classes MailApp, Message, SecureMailApp, and Contact together with a selection of their method definitions. Each program element is represented by a white rectangle labeled with **name : type**. The available types of program entities and possible (syntactic and semantic) dependencies (represented by arrows) between respective program elements are defined by a *program meta-model*, serving as a template for valid program models [26,37]. The program model comprises as first-class entities the classes (type TClass)

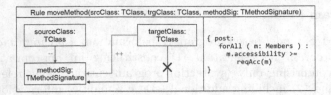

Fig. 3. Model-transformation rule for *MoveMethod* refactoring

together with their members as declared in the program. The representation of methods is split into signatures (type `TMethodSignature`) and definitions (type `TMethodDefinition`) to capture overloading/overriding dependencies among method declarations (e.g., overriding of method `sendMessage()` imposes one shared method signature, but two different method definitions). Solid arrows correspond to syntactic dependencies between program elements such as aggregation (unlabeled) and inheritance (label `extends`) and relations between method signatures and their definitions, whereas dashed arrows represent (static) semantic dependencies (e.g., arrows labeled with `call` denote caller-callee relations between methods).

Design-Flaw Information. The program model further incorporates information gained from *design-flaw detection* [33], to identify program parts to be refactored. In our example, design-flaw annotations (in gray) are attached to affected program elements, namely classes Message and Contact constitute *data classes* and classes MailApp and SecureMailApp constitute *controller classes*, which lead to two instances of the anti-pattern *The Blob*.

Accessibility Information. To reason about the impact of refactorings on the attack surface of programs, we extend the program model of Peldszus et al. by accessibility information. Our extensions include the attribute `accessibility` denoting the *declared accessibility* of entities as shown for method definitions in Fig. 2. In addition, our model comprises package declarations of classes (type `TPackage`) to reason about package-dependent accessibility constraints.

3.2   Model-Based Program Refactorings

Based on the program-model representation, refactoring operations by means of semantic-preserving program transformations can be concisely formalized in a declarative manner in terms of *model-transformation rules* [26]. A *model-transformation rule* specifies a generic change pattern consisting of a *left-hand side* pattern to be matched in an input model for applying the rule, and a *right-hand side* replacing the occurrence of the left-hand side to yield an output model. Here, we focus on (sequences of) *MoveMethod* refactorings as it has been shown in recent research that *MoveMethod* refactorings are considerably effective in improving CRA measures in flawed object-oriented program designs [34]. Figure 3 shows a (simplified) rule for *MoveMethod* refactorings defined on our program metamodel, using a compact visual notation superimposing the left- and right-hand side. The rule takes a source class srcClass, a target class trgClass and a method signature methodSig as parameters, *deletes* the containment arrow between source class and signature (red arrow annotated with --) and *creates* a new containment arrow from the target class (green arrow annotated with ++), only if such an arrow not already exists before rule application. The latter *(pre-)condition* is expressed by a *forbidden* (crossed-out) arrow. For a comprehensive list of all necessary pre-conditions (or, *pre-constraints*), we refer to [38].

Accessibility Post-constraints. Besides pre-constraints, for refactoring operations to yield correct results, it must satisfy further *post-constraints* to be evaluated after rule application, especially concerning accessibility constraints as declared in the original program (i.e., member accesses like method calls in the original program must be preserved after refactoring [24]). As an example, a (simplified) post-constraint for the *MoveMethod* rule is shown on the right of Fig. 3 using OCL-like notation. Members refers to the collection of all class members in the program. The post-constraint utilizes helper-function reqAcc(m) to compute the *required access modifier* of class member m and checks whether the declared accessibility of m is at least as generous as required (based on the canonical ordering `private` < `default` < `protected` < `public`) [38].

For instance, if refactoring **R2** is applied to MAILAPP, method encryptMessage() violates this post-constraint, as the call from sendMessage() from another package requires accessibility `public`, whereas the declared accessibility is `protected`. Instead of immediately rejecting refactorings like **R2**, we introduce an *accessibility-repair operation* of the form m.accessibility := reqAcc(m) for each member violating the post-constraint which therefore causes a *relaxation* of the attack surface. However, this repair is not always possible as relaxations may lead to incorrect refactorings altering the original program semantics (e.g., due to method overriding/overloading [38]). In contrast, refactoring **R1** (i.e., moving plainToHtml() to class Message) satisfies the post-constraint as the required accessibility of plainToHtml() becomes `private`, whereas its declared accessibility is `public`. In those cases, we may also apply the operation m.accessibility := reqAcc(m), now leading to a *reduction* of the attack surface. Different strategies for attack-surface reduction will be investigated in Sect. 4.

3.3 Optimization Objectives

We now describe the evaluation of objectives **(O1)–(O3)** on the program model, to serve as fitness values in a search-based setting.

Coupling/Cohesion. Concerning **(O1a)**, coupling and cohesion metrics are well-established quality measures for CRA decisions in object-oriented program design [4]. In our program model, *coupling* (**COU**) is related to the overall number of member accesses (e.g., *call*-arrows) across class boundaries [5], and for measuring *cohesion*, we adopt the well-known **LCOM5** metric to quantify *lack* of cohesion among members within classes [17]. While there are other metrics which indicate good CRA decisions, such as **Number of Children**, these metrics are not modifiable using *MoveMethod* refactorings and are therefore not used in this paper [9]. Consequently, good CRA decisions exhibit low values for both **COU** and **LCOM5**. Hence, refactorings **R1** and **R2** both improve values of **COU** (i.e., by eliminating inter-class *call*-arrows) and **LCOM5** (i.e., by moving methods into classes where they are called).

Anti-patterns. Concerning **(O1b)**, we limit our considerations to occurrences of *The Blob* anti-pattern for convenience. We employ the detection-approach of Peldszus et al. [33] and consider as objective to minimize the number of *The Blob* instances (denoted **#BLOB**). For instance, for the original MailApp program (white parts in Fig. 1), we have **#BLOB** = 1, while for the extended version (white and gray parts), we have **#BLOB** = 2. Refactoring **R1** may help to remove the first occurrence and **R2** potentially removes the second one.

Changes. Concerning **(O2)**, real-life studies show that refactoring recommendations to be accepted by users must avoid a too large deviation from the original design [8]. Here, we consider the *number* of *MoveMethod* refactorings (denoted **#REF**) to be performed in a recommendation, as a further objective to be minimized. For example, solely applying **R1** results in **#REF** = 1, whereas a sequence of **R1** followed by **R2** most likely imposes more design changes (i.e., **#REF** = 2). In contrast, accessibility-repair operations do not affect the value **#REF**, but rather impact objective **(O3)**.

Attack Surface. Concerning **(O3)**, the guidelines for secure object-oriented programming encourages developers to grant as least access privileges as possible to any accessible program element to minimize the attack surface [19]. In our program model, the attack-surface metric (denoted **AS**) is measured as

$$\mathbf{AS} = \sum\nolimits_{m \in \text{Members}} \omega(m.accessibility), \tag{1}$$

where weighting function $\omega : Mod \to \mathbb{N}_0$ on the set Mod of accessibility modifiers may be, for instance, defined as $\omega(\texttt{private}) = 0$, $\omega(\texttt{default}) = 1$, $\omega(\texttt{protected}) = 2$, $\omega(\texttt{public}) = 3$. Hence, a lower value corresponds to a smaller attack surface. For example, **R1** enables an attack-surface reduction by setting plainToHtml() from `public` to `private` which decreases **AS** by 3. In contrast, **R2** involves a repair step setting encryptMessage() from `protected` to `public` which increases **AS** by 1. Whether such negative impacts of refactorings on **(O3)** are outweighed by simultaneous improvements gained for other objectives depends, among others, on the actual weighting ω applied. For instance, each further modifier `public` considerably opens the attack surface and should therefore be blamed by a higher weighting value, as compared to the other modifiers (cf. Sect. 4).

3.4   Search-Based Optimization Process

Our tool for recommending optimized object-oriented refactoring sequences, called GOBLIN[2], is based on a combination of search-based multi-objective

---

[2] Goblin is supervillain and Head of National *Security* in the Marvel universe [3]. GOBLIN also means *G*eneric *O*bjective-*B*ased *L*ayout *I*mprovements for *N*on-designs.

optimization techniques using genetic algorithms and model-transformations on the basis of the MOMoT framework [11]. Figure 4 shows an overview on GOB-LIN. First, the input JAVA program is translated into our program model [33]. This *original program model* together with its objective values for **(O1)−(O3)** (i.e., its *fitness* values) serves as a baseline for evaluating the improvements obtained by candidate refactorings. The built-in genetic algorithm (NSGA-III) of MOMoT is initialized by an *initial population* of a fixed number of *individuals* serving as *generation* 0, where each individual constitutes a *sequence* of at least 1 up to a maximum number of *MoveMethod* rule applications (cf. Fig. 3) to the original program model. Thus, each individual corresponds to a refactored version of the original program model on which the resulting fitness values are evaluated. The refactored program model is obtained by applying the given sequence of refactorings to the original program model. Steps within a sequence not being applicable to an intermediate model (e.g., due to unsatisfied pre-conditions) are skipped, whereas steps producing infeasible results (e.g., due to unsatisfied and non-repairable post-conditions) cause the entire individual to become invalid (thus being removed from the population).

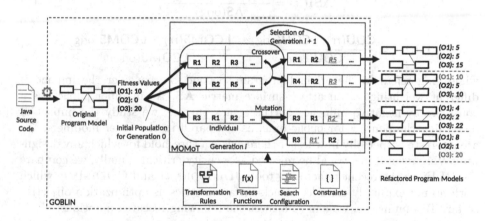

Fig. 4. Architecture of the GOBLIN tool

For deriving generation $i + 1$ from generation i, NSGA-III first creates a set of new individuals using random *crossover* and *mutation* operators. As indicated in Fig. 4, a crossover splits and recombines two individuals into a new one, while a mutation generates a new individual by injecting small changes into an existing one. Afterwards, in the *selection* phase, individuals from the overall population (the original and newly created individuals) are selected into the next generation, depending on their *fitness* values. For more details on NSGA-III, we refer to [15,28]. The search-process terminates when a maximum number of generations (or, individuals, respectively) has been reached, resulting in a Pareto-front of non-dominated individuals, each constituting a refactoring recommendation [11].

4   Experimental Evaluation

We now present experimental evaluation results gained from applying GOB-
LIN to a collection of JAVA programs. First, to investigate the impact of *attack-
surface reduction* on the resulting refactoring recommendations, we consider the
following *reduction strategies*, differing in when to perform attack-surface reduction during search-space exploration (where step means a refactoring step):

- **Strategy 1: *A priori* reduction.** Before the first and after the last step.
- **Strategy 2: *A posteriori* reduction.** Only after the last step.
- **Strategy 3: *Continuous* reduction.** After every refactoring step.

We are interested in the impact of each strategy on the trade-off between *attack-
surface* metrics and design-quality metrics (i.e., do the recommended refactoring sequences tend to optimize more the attack surface aspect or the program
design?). We quantify *attack-surface impact* (**ASI**) and *design impact* (**DI**) of a
refactoring recommendation rr as follows:

$$\mathbf{ASI}(\mathsf{rr}) = \frac{\mathbf{AS}(\mathsf{rr}) - \mathbf{AS}(\mathsf{orig})}{\mathbf{AS}(\mathsf{orig})} \tag{2}$$

$$\mathbf{DI}(\mathsf{rr}) = \frac{\mathbf{COU}(\mathsf{rr}) - \mathbf{COU}(\mathsf{orig})}{\mathbf{COU}(\mathsf{orig})} + \frac{\mathbf{LCOM5}(\mathsf{rr}) - \mathbf{LCOM5}(\mathsf{orig})}{\mathbf{LCOM5}(\mathsf{orig})} \tag{3}$$

where orig refers to the original program. Second, we consider the impact of
different weightings ω on attack-surface metric **AS**. As modifier public has a
considerably negative influence on the attack surface, we study the impact of
increasing the penalty for public in ω, as compared to the other modifiers. We
are interested especially in whether there exists a threshold for which any design-
improving refactoring would be rejected as security-critical. Finally, we compare
GOBLIN to the recent refactoring tools JDEODORANT and CODE-IMP, which
both do not explicitly consider attack-surface metrics as optimization objective
so far. To summarize, we aim to answer the following research questions:

- **(RQ1: Objective Trade-Off)** Which attack-surface reduction strategy
  offers the best trade-off between attack-surface impact and design impact
  when taking the original program as a baseline?
- **(RQ2: Weighting of Attack Surface)** Which weighting of public in the
  attack-surface metric constitutes a critical threshold obstructing any design-
  improving refactorings?
- **(RQ3: Tool Comparison)** Which tool provides the best trade-off between
  attack-surface impact and design impact in refactoring recommendations?

4.1   Experiment Setup and Results

We conducted our experiments on an established corpus of real-life open-source
JAVA programs of various size [33,39] as listed in Table 1 (with lines of code

LOC, number of packages $\#P$, number of classes $\#C$ and number of methods $\#M$). For a compact presentation, we divide the corpus into three program-size categories (*small, mid-sized, large*), indicated by horizontal lines in Table 1. All experiments have been executed on a Windows-Server-2016 machine with a 2.4 GHz quad-core CPU, 32 GB RAM and JRE 1.8. We used the default genetic-algorithm configuration of MOMoT in all our experiments [11]: termination after 10,000 individual evaluations, population size of 100, and each individual consisting of at most 10 refactorings. We applied the metrics for **(O1)–(O3)** (cf. Sect. 3.3) to compute fitness values. GOBLIN requires 25 min to compute a set of refactoring recommendations for the smallest program, up to several hours in the case of large programs, which is acceptable for a search-based (off-line) optimization approach. We selected a representative set of computed recommendations which were manually checked for program correctness and impact.

For **(RQ1)**, we measured **ASI** and **DI** values for two runs of GOBLIN (cf. Figs. 6a, b, c, d, e and f). Figures 6a and b (first row, side by side) show a box-plot for each Strategy (1–3) for *small* programs of our corpus (*#iSj* referring to the program number i in Table 1 and Strategy j). The box-plots show the distribution of **ASI** (Fig. 6a) and **DI** (Fig. 6b) values for each refactoring recommendation of GOBLIN. The figure-pairs 6c–6d and 6e–6f show the same data for *mid-sized* and *large programs*, respectively. For **(RQ2)**, we used Strategy 3 from **(RQ2)** and varied function ω to study different penalties for modifier public. Figure 5 plots the (minimal) values of **ASI** and **DI** depending on ω(public) (from 3 up to 100). Regarding **(RQ3)**, we compare the results of GOBLIN to those of state-of-the-art refactoring recommender tools, JDEODORANT [12] and CODE-IMP [27]. Refactorings proposed by JDEODORANT have as singleton optimization objective to eliminate specific anti-patterns through heuristic refactoring strategies. In particular, JDEODORANT employs *ExtractClass* [13] to eliminate *The Blob* (also called *GodClass*), by separating parts from the controller-class into a freshly created class. Thus, each recommendation of JDEODORANT subsumes multiple *MoveMethod* refactorings (into the fresh target class). In contrast, CODE-IMP pursues a search-based approach, including a variety of

Program	Version	LOC	#P	#C	#M
1: QuickUML	2001	2,667	1	19	175
2: JSciCalc	2.1.0	5,437	3	121	563
3: JUnit	3.8.2	5,780	11	105	841
4: Gantt	1.10.2	21,331	28	256	1,925
5: Nutch	0.9	21,437	24	273	1,750
6: Lucene	1.4.3	25,472	15	276	1,750
7: log4j	1.2.17	31,429	35	394	3,240
8: JHotDraw	7.6	31,434	24	312	3,781

Table 1. Evaluation corpus

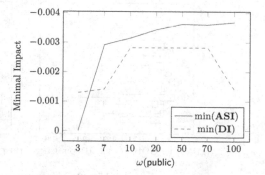

Fig. 5. Minimal **ASI** and **DI** values for different weightings of public

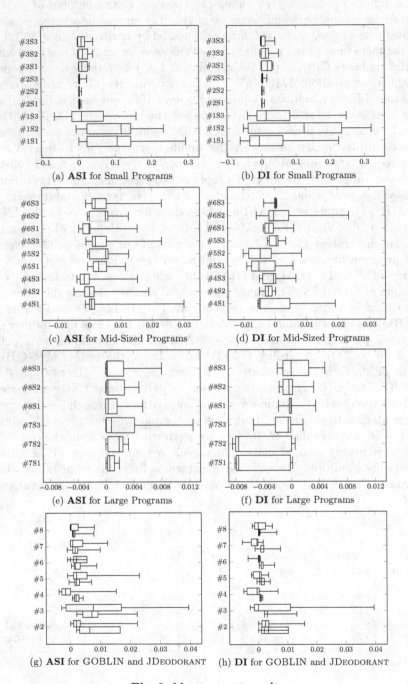

(a) **ASI** for Small Programs

(b) **DI** for Small Programs

(c) **ASI** for Mid-Sized Programs

(d) **DI** for Mid-Sized Programs

(e) **ASI** for Large Programs

(f) **DI** for Large Programs

(g) **ASI** for GOBLIN and JDEODORANT

(h) **DI** for GOBLIN and JDEODORANT

Fig. 6. Measurement results

refactoring operations and design-quality metrics. For a comparison to GOB-LIN, we used the *MoveMethod* refactoring of CODE-IMP which produces one sequence of *MoveMethod* refactorings per run. Figures 6g and h contain comparisons of **ASI** and **DI** values, respectively, for our corpus (excluding QUICKUML due to relatively very high variations). For each program, the upper box-plot shows the results for GOBLIN and the lower one for JDEODORANT, respectively. CODE-IMP only successfully produced results for QUICKUML and JUNIT (10 runs each) while terminating without any result for the others.

4.2 Discussion

Concerning **(RQ1)**, Strategy 3 leads to the best attack-surface impact for *small* programs (under neglectible execution-time overhead), while even slightly improving the design impact. Although this clear advantage dissolves for *mid-sized* and *large* programs, it still contributes to a reasonable trade-off, while attack-surface reductions tend to hamper design improvements as expected. Calculating the Pearson correlation [32] between **ASI** and **DI** shows that (1) the strategy does not influence the correlation and (2) for *small* programs, GOBLIN finds refactorings which are beneficial for both attack surface and program design.

Concerning **(RQ2)**, Fig. 5 shows that a higher value for ω(public) leads to a better attack-surface impact, as attack-surface-critical refactorings are less likely to survive throughout generations. The increase in **ASI** is remarkably steep from ω(public) = 3 to ω(public) = 7, but exhibits slow linear growth for higher values. Regarding the design impact, up to ω(public) = 10, the best achieved **DI** also grows linearly, but afterwards, no more **DI** improvements emerge. In higher value ranges (>70), **DI** reaches a threshold, and degrades afterwards.

Regarding **(RQ3)**, the *The Blob* elimination strategy of JDEODORANT necessarily increases attack surfaces, as calls to extracted methods have to access the new class, thus necessarily increasing accessibility at least up to `default`. As also shown in Fig. 6g, there are almost no refactorings proposed by JDEODORANT with a positive attack-surface impact. Surprisingly, JDEODORANT also achieves a less beneficial design impact than GOBLIN, with a strong correlation between **ASI** and **DI**. Our unfortunately very limited set of observations for CODE-IMP shows that, due to the similar search technique, the refactorings found by CODE-IMP and GOBLIN are quite similar. Nevertheless, due to the different focus of objectives, CODE-IMP tends to increase attack surfaces. Although, the differences in metrics definitions forbid any definite conclusions, however, CODE-IMP does not achieve any design improvements according to our metrics.

To summarize, our experimental results demonstrate that attack-surface impacts of refactorings clearly deserve more attention in the context of refactoring recommendations, revealing a practically relevant trade-off (or, even contradiction) between traditional design-improvement efforts and extra-functional (particularly, security) aspects. Our experiments further uncover that existing tools are mostly unaware of attack-surface impacts of recommended refactorings.

5   Related Work

Automating Design-Flaw Detection and Refactorings. Marinescu proposes a metric-based design-flaw detection approach similar to Peldszus et al. in [33], which is used in our work. However, both works do not deal with elimination of detected flaws [21]. In contrast, the DECOR framework also includes recommendations for eliminating anti-patterns, whereas, in contrast to our work, those recommendations remain rather atomic and local. More related to our approach, Fokaefs et al. [12] and Tsantalis et al. [40] consider (semi-)automatic refactorings to eliminate anti-patterns like *The Blob* in the tool JDEODORANT. Nevertheless, they focus on optimizing one single objective and do not consider multiple, esp. extra-functional, aspects like security metrics as in our approach.

Multi-objective Search-Based Refactorings. O'Keeffe and Ó Cinnéide use search-based refactorings in their tool CODE-IMP [28] including various standard refactoring operations and different quality metrics as objectives [27]. Seng et al. consider a search-based setting, where, similar to our approach, compound refactoring recommendations comprise atomic *MoveMethod* operations. Harman and Tratt also investigate a Pareto-front of refactoring recommendations including various design objectives [16], and more recently, Ouni et al. conducted a large-scale real-world study on multi-objective search-based refactoring recommendations [30]. However, neither of the approaches investigates the impact of refactorings on security-relevant metrics as in our approach.

Security-Aware Refactorings. Steimann and Thies were the first to propose a comprehensive set of accessibility constraints for refactorings covering full JAVA [38]. Although their constraints are formally founded, they do not consider software metrics to quantify the attack surface impact of (sequences of) refactorings. Alshammari et al. propose an extensive catalogue of software metrics for evaluating the impact of refactorings on program security of object-oriented programs [1]. Similarly, Maruyama and Omori propose a technique [22] and tool [23] for checking if a refactoring operation raises security issues. However, all these approaches are concerned with security and accessibility constraints of specific refactorings, but they do not investigate those aspects in a multi-objective program optimization setting. The problem of measuring attack surfaces serving as a metric for evaluating secure object-oriented programming policies has been investigated by Zoller and Schmolitzky [41] and Manadhata and Wing [20], respectively. Nevertheless, those and similar metrics have not yet been utilized as optimization objective for program refactoring. Finally, Ghaith and Ó Cinnéide consider a catalogue of security-relevant metrics to recommend refactorings using CODE-IMP, but they also consider security as single objective [14].

6 Conclusion

We presented a search-based approach to recommend sequences of refactorings for object-oriented JAVA-like programs by taking the attack surface as additional optimization objective into account. Our model-based methodology, implemented in the tool GOBLIN, utilizes the MOMoT framework including the genetic algorithm NSGA-III for search-space exploration. Our experimental results gained from applying GOBLIN to real-world Java programs provides us with detailed insights into the impact of attack-surface metrics on fitness values of refactorings and the resulting trade-off with competing design-quality objectives. As a future work, we plan to incorporate additional domain knowledge about critical code parts to further control security-aware refactorings.

Acknowledgements. This work was partially funded by the Hessian LOEWE initiative within the Software-Factory 4.0 project as well as by the German Research Foundation (DFG) in the Priority Programme SPP 1593: Design For Future - Managed Software Evolution (LO 2198/2-1, JU 2734/2-1).

References

1. Alshammari, B., Fidge, C., Corney, D.: Assessing the impact of refactoring on security-critical object-oriented designs. In: Proceedings of APSEC, pp. 186–195 (2010)
2. Arendt, T., Biermann, E., Jurack, S., Krause, C., Taentzer, G.: Henshin: advanced concepts and tools for in-place EMF model transformations. In: Petriu, D.C., Rouquette, N., Haugen, Ø. (eds.) MODELS 2010. LNCS, vol. 6394, pp. 121–135. Springer, Heidelberg (2010). https://doi.org/10.1007/978-3-642-16145-2_9
3. Bendis, B.M.: Secret Invasion, vol. 1-8. Marvel, New York (2009)
4. Bowman, M., Briand, L.C., Labiche, Y.: Solving the class responsibility assignment problem in object-oriented analysis with multi-objective genetic algorithms. IEEE Trans. Softw. Eng. **36**(6), 817–837 (2010)
5. Briand, L.C., Daly, J.W., Wust, J.K.: A unified framework for coupling measurement in object-oriented systems. IEEE Trans. Softw. Eng. **25**(1), 91–121 (1999)
6. Briand, L.C., Daly, J.W., Wüst, J.: A unified framework for cohesion measurement in object-oriented systems. Empir. Softw. Eng. **3**(1), 65–117 (1998)
7. Brown, W.J., Malveau, R.C., McCormick III, H.W., Mowbray, T.J.: AntiPatterns: Refactoring Software, Architectures, and Projects in Crisis. Wiley, New York (1998)
8. Candela, I., Bavota, G., Russo, B., Oliveto, R.: Using cohesion and coupling for software remodularization: is it enough? ACM Trans. Softw. Eng. Methodol. **25**(3), 24:1–24:28 (2016)
9. Chidamber, S., Kemerer, C.: A metrics suite for object oriented design. IEEE Trans. Softw. Eng. **20**(6), 476–493 (1994)
10. Van Eetvelde, N., Janssens, D.: Extending graph rewriting for refactoring. In: Ehrig, H., Engels, G., Parisi-Presicce, F., Rozenberg, G. (eds.) ICGT 2004. LNCS, vol. 3256, pp. 399–415. Springer, Heidelberg (2004). https://doi.org/10.1007/978-3-540-30203-2_28

11. Fleck, M., Troya, J., Wimmer, M.: Search-based model transformations with MOMoT. In: Van Gorp, P., Engels, G. (eds.) ICMT 2016. LNCS, vol. 9765, pp. 79–87. Springer, Cham (2016). https://doi.org/10.1007/978-3-319-42064-6_6

12. Fokaefs, M., Tsantalis, N., Stroulia, E., Chatzigeorgiou, A.: JDeodorant: identification and application of extract class refactorings. In: Proceedings of ICSE, pp. 1037–1039 (2011)

13. Fowler, R.: Refactoring: Improving the Design of Existing Code. Addison-Wesley, Reading (2000)

14. Ghaith, S., Ó Cinnéide, M.: Improving software security using search-based refactoring. In: Fraser, G., Teixeira de Souza, J. (eds.) SSBSE 2012. LNCS, vol. 7515, pp. 121–135. Springer, Heidelberg (2012). https://doi.org/10.1007/978-3-642-33119-0_10

15. Harman, M., Mansouri, S.A., Zhang, Y.: Search based software engineering: a comprehensive analysis and review of trends techniques and applications (2009)

16. Harman, M., Tratt, L.: Pareto optimal search based refactoring at the design level. In: Proceedings of GECCO, pp. 1106–1113. ACM (2007)

17. Henderson-Sellers, B.: Object-Oriented Metrics: Measures of Complexity. Prentice-Hall Inc., Upper Saddle River (1996)

18. Kessentini, M., Sahraoui, H., Boukadoum, M., Wimmer, M.: Search-based design defects detection by example. In: Giannakopoulou, D., Orejas, F. (eds.) FASE 2011. LNCS, vol. 6603, pp. 401–415. Springer, Heidelberg (2011). https://doi.org/10.1007/978-3-642-19811-3_28

19. Long, F., Mohindra, D., Seacord, R.C., Sutherland, D.F., Svoboda, D.: The CERT Oracle Secure Coding Standard for Java. Addison-Wesley Professional, Boston (2011)

20. Manadhata, P.K., Wing, J.M.: An attack surface metric. IEEE Trans. Softw. Eng. **37**(3), 371–386 (2011)

21. Marinescu, R.: Detection strategies: metrics-based rules for detecting design flaws, pp. 350–359. IEEE (2004)

22. Maruyama, K., Omori, T.: Security-aware refactoring alerting its impact on code vulnerabilities. In: APSEC, pp. 445–451. IEEE (2008)

23. Maruyama, K., Omori, T.: A security-aware refactoring tool for Java programs. In: Proceedings of WRT, pp. 22–28. ACM (2011)

24. Mens, T., Demeyer, S., Janssens, D.: Formalising behaviour preserving program transformations. In: Corradini, A., Ehrig, H., Kreowski, H.-J., Rozenberg, G. (eds.) ICGT 2002. LNCS, vol. 2505, pp. 286–301. Springer, Heidelberg (2002). https://doi.org/10.1007/3-540-45832-8_22

25. Mens, T., Taentzer, G., Runge, O.: Analysing refactoring dependencies using graph transformation. SOSYM **6**(3), 269–285 (2007)

26. Mens, T., Van Eetvelde, N., Demeyer, S., Janssens, D.: Formalizing refactorings with graph transformations. J. Softw. Evol. Process **17**(4), 247–276 (2005)

27. Moghadam, I.H., Ó Cinnéide, M.: Code-Imp: a tool for automated search-based refactoring. In: Proceedings of WRT, pp. 41–44. ACM (2011)

28. O'Keeffe, M., Ó Cinnéide, M.: Search-based refactoring: an empirical study. J. Softw. Maint. Evol. Res. Pract. **20**(5), 345–364 (2008)

29. Opdyke, W.: Refactoring Object-Oriented Frameworks. Ph.D. thesis, University of Illinois (1992)

30. Ouni, A., Kessentini, M., Sahraoui, H.A., Inoue, K., Deb, K.: Multi-criteria code refactoring using search-based software engineering: an industrial case study. ACM Trans. Softw. Eng. Methodol. **25**(3), 23:1–23:53 (2016)

31. Parnas, D.L.: Software aging, pp. 279–287. IEEE (1994)
32. Pearson, K.: VII. Mathematical contributions to the theory of evolution.—III. regression, heredity, and panmixia. Philos. Trans. R. Soc. Lond. Math. Phys. Eng. Sci. **187**, 253–318 (1896)
33. Peldszus, S., Kulcsár, G., Lochau, M., Schulze, S.: Continuous detection of design flaws in evolving object-oriented programs using incremental multi-pattern matching. In: Proceedings of ASE, pp. 578–589 (2016)
34. Seng, O., Stammel, J., Burkhart, D.: Search-based determination of refactorings for improving the class structure of object-oriented systems. In: Proceedings of GECCO, pp. 1909–1916 (2006)
35. Shin, Y., Williams, L.: Is complexity really the enemy of software security? In: QoP, pp. 47–50 (2008)
36. Smith, S.F., Thober, M.: Refactoring programs to secure information flows, pp. 75–83. ACM (2006)
37. Stahl, T., Völter, M.: Model-Driven Software Development: Technology, Engineering, Management. Wiley, Chichester (2006)
38. Steimann, F., Thies, A.: From public to private to absent: refactoring JAVA programs under constrained accessibility. In: Drossopoulou, S. (ed.) ECOOP 2009. LNCS, vol. 5653, pp. 419–443. Springer, Heidelberg (2009). https://doi.org/10.1007/978-3-642-03013-0_19
39. Tempero, E., Anslow, C., Dietrich, J., Han, T., Li, J., Lumpe, M., Melton, H., Noble, J.: The Qualitas Corpus: a curated collection of Java code for empirical studies. In: Asia Pacific Software Engineering Conference, pp. 336–345 (2010)
40. Tsantalis, N., Chatzigeorgiou, A.: Identification of move method refactoring opportunities. IEEE Trans. Softw. Eng. **35**(3), 347–367 (2009)
41. Zoller, C., Schmolitzky, A.: Measuring inappropriate generosity with access modifiers in Java systems. In: Proceedings of IWSM-MENSURA, pp. 43–52 (2012)

Effective Analysis of Attack Trees:
A Model-Driven Approach

Rajesh Kumar[1]([✉]), Stefano Schivo[1], Enno Ruijters[1],
Buğra Mehmet Yildiz[1], David Huistra[1], Jacco Brandt[1], Arend Rensink[1],
and Mariëlle Stoelinga[1,2]

[1] Formal Methods and Tools, University of Twente, Enschede, The Netherlands
{r.kumar,s.schivo,e.j.j.ruijters,b.m.yildiz,d.j.huistra,
a.rensink,m.i.a.stoelinga}@utwente.nl, j.h.brandt@student.utwente.nl
[2] Department of Software Science, Radboud University, Nijmegen, The Netherlands

Abstract. Attack trees (ATs) are a popular formalism for security analysis, and numerous variations and tools have been developed around them. These were mostly developed independently, and offer little interoperability or ability to combine various AT features.

We present ATTop, a software bridging tool that enables automated analysis of ATs using a model-driven engineering approach. ATTop fulfills two purposes: 1. It facilitates interoperation between several AT analysis methodologies and resulting tools (e.g., ATE, ATCalc, ADTool 2.0), 2. it can perform a comprehensive analysis of attack trees by translating them into timed automata and analyzing them using the popular model checker UPPAAL, and translating the analysis results back to the original ATs. Technically, our approach uses various metamodels to provide a unified description of AT variants. Based on these metamodels, we perform model transformations that allow to apply various analysis methods to an AT and trace the results back to the AT domain. We illustrate our approach on the basis of a case study from the AT literature.

1   Introduction

Formal methods are often employed to support software engineers in particularly complex tasks: model-based testing, type checking and extended static checking are typical examples that help in developing better software faster. This paper is about the reverse direction: showing how software engineering can assist formal methods in developing complex analysis tools.

More specifically, we reap the benefits of model-driven engineering (MDE) to design and build a tool for analyzing attack trees (ATs). ATs [25,31] are a popular formalism for security analysis, allowing convenient modeling and analysis of complex attack scenarios. ATs have become part of various system engineering frameworks, such as UMLsec [16] and SysMLsec [27].

Attack trees come in a large number of variations, employing different security attributes (e.g., attack time, costs, resources, etc.) as well as modeling constructs (e.g., sequential vs. parallel execution of scenarios). Each of these variations comes with its own tooling; examples include ADTool [12], ATCalc [2],

© The Author(s) 2018
A. Russo and A. Schürr (Eds.): FASE 2018, LNCS 10802, pp. 56–73, 2018.
https://doi.org/10.1007/978-3-319-89363-1_4

and Attack Tree Evaluator [5]. This "jungle of attack trees" seriously hampers the applicability of ATs, since it is impossible or very difficult to combine different features and tooling. This paper addresses these challenges and presents ATTop[1], a software tool that overarches existing tooling in the AT domain.

In particular, the main features of ATTop are (see Fig. 1):

1. *A unified input format that encompasses the known AT features.* We have collected these features in one comprehensive metamodel. Following MDE best practices, this metamodel is extensible to easily accommodate future needs.
2. *Systematic model transformations.* Many AT analysis methods are based on converting the AT into a mathematical model that can be analyzed with existing formal techniques, such as timed automata [11,23], Bayesian networks [13], Petri nets [8], etc. An important contribution of our work is to make these translations more systematic, and therefore more extensible, maintainable, reusable, and less error-prone.
   To do so, we again refer to the concepts of MDE and deploy *model transformations*. We deploy two categories here: so-called *horizontal* transformations achieve interoperability between existing tools. *Vertical* transformations interpret a model via a set of semantic rules to produce a mathematical model to be analyzed with formal methods.
3. *Bringing the results back to the original domain.* When a mathematical model is analyzed, the analysis result is computed in terms of the mathematical model, and not in terms of the original AT. For example, if AT analysis is done via model checking, a trace in the underlying model (i.e., transition system) can be produced to show that, say, the cheapest attack costs $100. What security practitioners need, however, is a path or attack vector in the original AT. This interpretation in terms of the original model is achieved by a vertical model transformation in the inverse direction, from the results as obtained in the analysis model back into the AT domain.

These features make ATTop a *software bridging tool*, acting as a bridge between existing AT languages, and between ATs and formal languages.

Our Contributions. The contributions of this paper include:

- a full-fledged tool based on MDE, which allows for high maintainability and extensibility;
- a unified input format, enabling interoperability between different AT dialects;
- systematic use of model transformations; which increases reusability while reducing error likelihood;
- a complete cycle from AT to formal model and back, allowing domain experts to profit from formal methods without requiring specific knowledge.

Overview of Our Approach. Figure 1 depicts the general workflow of our approach. It shows how ATTop acts as a bridge between different languages and

[1] Available at https://github.com/utwente-fmt/attop.

formalisms. In particular, thanks to horizontal transformations, ATTop makes it possible to use ATs described in different formats, both as an input to other tools and as an input to ATTop itself. In the latter case, vertical transformations are used in order to deal with UPPAAL as a back-end tool without exposing ATTop's users to the formal language of timed automata.

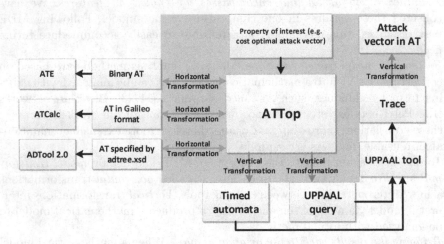

Fig. 1. Overview of our approach, showing the contributions of the paper in the gray rectangle. Here ATE, ATCalc, ADTool 2.0 are different attack tree analysis tools, each with its own input format. ATTop allows these tools to be interoperable (horizontal model transformations, see Sect. 4.1). ATTop also provides a much more comprehensive AT analysis by automatic translation of attack trees into timed automata and using UPPAAL as the back-end analysis tool (vertical transformations, see Sect. 4.2).

Related Work. A large number of AT analysis frameworks have been developed, based on lattice theory [18], timed automata [11,21,23], I/O-IMCs [3,22], Bayesian networks [13], Petri nets [8], stochastic games [4,15], etc. We refer to [20] for an overview of AT formalisms. Surprisingly, little effort has been made to provide a security practitioner with a generic tool that integrates the benefits of all these analysis tools.

The use of model transformations with UPPAAL was explored in [29] for a range of different formalisms; the UPPAAL metamodel that was presented there is the one we use in ATTop. A related approach for fault trees was proposed in [28]. In [14], the authors manually translate UML sequence diagrams into timed automata models to analyze timeliness properties of embedded systems. In [1], the OpenMADS tool is proposed that takes the input of SysML diagrams and UML/MARTE annotations and automatically translates these into deterministic and stochastic Petri nets (DSPNs); however, no model-driven engineering technique was applied.

Organization of the Paper. In Sect. 2, we describe the background. Section 3 presents the metamodels we use in ATTop, while the model transformations are described in Sect. 4. Section 5 describes the features of ATTop, and in Sect. 6 we show the results of our case study using ATTop. Finally, we conclude the paper in Sect. 7.

2   Background

2.1   Attack Trees in the Security Domain

Modern enterprises are ever growing complex socio-technical systems comprised of multiple actors, physical infrastructures, and IT systems. Adversaries can take advantage of this complexity, by exploiting multiple security vulnerabilities simultaneously. Risk managers, therefore, need to predict possible attack vectors, in order to combat them. For this purpose, attack trees are a widely-used formalism to identify, model, and quantify complex attack scenarios.

Attack trees (ATs) were popularized by Schneier through his seminal paper in [31] and were later formalized by Mauw in [25]. ATs show how different attack steps combine into a multi-stage attack scenario leading to a security breach. Due to the intuitive representation of attack scenarios, this formalism has been used in both academia and industry to model practical case studies such as ATMs [10], SCADA communication systems [7], etc. Furthermore, the attack tree formalism has also been advocated in the Security Quality Requirements Engineering (SQUARE) [26] methodology for security requirements.

Example 1. Figure 2 shows an example AT (adapted from [36]) modeling the compromise of an Internet of Things (IoT) device.

At the top of the tree is the event `compromise_IoT_device`, which is refined using *gates* until we reach the atomic steps where no further refinement is desired (the leaves of the tree). The top gate in Fig. 2 is a SAND (*sequential AND*)-gate denoting that, in order for the attack to be successful, the children of this gate must be executed sequentially from left to right. In the example, the attacker first needs to successfully perform `access_home_network`, then `exploit_software_vulnerability_in_IoT_device`, and then `run_malicious_script`. The AND-gate at `access_home_network` represents that both `gain_access_to_private_networks` and `get_credentials` must be performed, but these can be performed in any order, possibly in parallel. Similarly, the OR gate at `gain_access_to_private_networks` denotes that its children `access_LAN` and `access_WLAN` can be attempted in parallel, but only one needs to succeed for a successful attack.

Traditionally, each leaf of an attack tree is decorated with a single attribute, e.g., the probability of successfully executing the step, or the cost incurred when taking this step. The attributes are then combined in the analysis to obtain metrics, such as the probability or required cost of a successful attack [19].

Over the years, the AT formalism has been enriched both structurally (e.g., adding more logical gates, countermeasures, ordering relationships; see [20] for

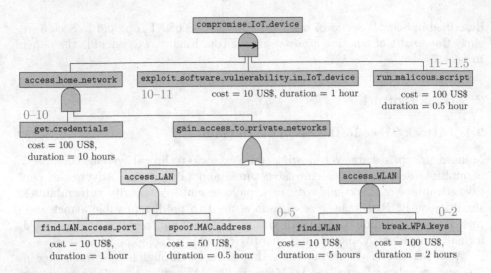

Fig. 2. Attack tree modeling the compromise of an IoT device. Leaves are equipped with the cost and time required to execute the corresponding step. The parts of the tree attacked in the cheapest successful attack are indicated by a darker color, with start and end times for the steps in this cheapest attack denoted in red (times correspond to the scenario in Fig. 11). (Color figure online)

an overview) and analytically (e.g., multi-attribute analysis, time- and cost-optimal analysis). This has resulted in a large number of tools (ADTool 2.0 [12], ATCalc [5], ATE [2], etc.), each with their own analysis technique.

Such a wide range of tools can be useful for a security practitioner to perform different kinds of analyses of attack trees. However, this requires preparing the AT for each tool, as each one has its own input format. To overcome the difficulty of orchestrating all these different tools, we propose one tool—ATTop—to allow specification of ATs combining features of multiple formalisms and to support analysis of such ATs by different tools without duplicating it for each tool.

2.2 Model-Driven Engineering

Model-driven engineering (MDE) is a software engineering methodology that treats models not only as documentation, but also as first-class citizens, to be directly used in the engineering processes [32]. In MDE, a *metamodel* (also referred to as a *domain-specific language*, DSL) is specified as a model at a more abstract level to serve as a language for models [33]. A metamodel captures the concepts of a particular domain with the permitted structure and behavior, to which models must adhere. Typically, metamodels are specified in class diagram-like structures.

MDE provides interoperability between domains (and tools and technologies in these domains) via *model transformations*. The concept of model transformation is shown in Fig. 3. Model transformations map the elements of a source

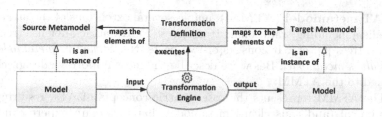

Fig. 3. The concept of *model transformation*

metamodel to the elements of a target metamodel. This mapping is described as a transformation definition, using a language specifically designed for this purpose. The transformation engine executes the transformation definition on the input model and generates an output model.

Adaptation of MDE provides various benefits [30,34,37], specifically:

1. *Empowering domain experts with abstraction:* With the introduction of metamodels and related tooling, domain experts can focus on modeling in the domain; while the technical problems below the modeling level, such as low-level implementation details are abstracted away from the domain experts.
2. *Higher level of reusability:* The models, metamodels and the tools based on them are high-level artifacts that can be reused by many projects targeting similar domains. Such reuse increases productivity and quality of the final product since the reused units are maintained and improved continuously.
3. *Interoperability:* There can be various tools and technologies used in a domain, each having its own I/O formats. Model transformations provide interoperability between these tools and technologies.

There are a number of tools available for realizing MDE. In this paper, we have used the Eclipse Modeling Framework (EMF) [35], which is a state-of-the-art tool developed to this aim. EMF provides the *Ecore* format for defining the metamodels and has many plug-ins to support the various functionalities related to MDE. The model transformations we present in this paper were implemented using the Epsilon Transformation Language (ETL) [17], which is one of the domain-specific languages provided by the Epsilon framework. We have chosen ETL since it is an easy-to-use language and allows users to inherit, import and reuse other Epsilon modules, which increases reusability. We use Java to select and execute the ETL transformations.

3   Metamodels for Attack Tree Analysis

ATTop uses three different metamodels to represent the attack tree domain concepts, all defined in the Ecore format. These are shown in Figs. 4, 5 and 6, in a notation similar to that of UML class diagrams. They show the domain classes and edges representing associations between classes. Edges denote references ($\rightarrow$), containment ($\rightarrow\!\!\bullet$), or supertype ($\longrightarrow$) relations. Multiplicities are denoted between square brackets (e.g., [0..*] for unrestricted multiplicity).

1. The **AT metamodel (ATMM)**, unifies several extensions of the attack tree formalism including traditional attack trees [25,31], attack-defense trees [18], defense trees [6], etc. It consists of two parts: the *Structure metamodel* and the *Values metamodel*. Below we describe the most important design choices that led to the ATMM:
   - The ATMM represents the core, generic concepts of ATs, resulting in a minimal (and thus clean) metamodel that a domain expert can easily read, understand and use to create models.
   - The ATMM provides a lot of flexibility in specifying the relevant concepts by using string names and generic values. Concepts such as the Connector and the Edge are specified as abstract entities with a set of concrete instances. Therefore, new connectors and edges can easily be added to the metamodel without breaking existing model instances. The metamodel is designed to have good support for model operations, such as traversal of the AT models. From a node, any other node can be reached directly or indirectly following references.
   - The ATMM node and tree attributes offer convenient and generic methods for supporting the results of analysis tools. This allows us to translate results from a formal tool back into the AT domain and associate them to the original AT model (see Sect. 4.4).
2. The **query metamodel** formalizes the security queries to be analyzed over attack trees. We support both qualitative queries (i.e., properties such as feasibility of attack) and quantitative queries (i.e., security metrics such as probability of successful attack, cheapest attack, etc.).
3. The **scenario metamodel** represents attack scenarios (a.k.a. attack vectors) consisting of the steps leading to, e.g., the cheapest, fastest, or most damaging security breaches.

Below we discuss these metamodels in more detail.

1. AT Metamodel (ATMM). The ATMM metamodel is a combination of two separate metamodels, one representing the attack tree structure (*Structure metamodel*, Fig. 4 left) and the other representing the attack tree attributes (*Values metamodel*, Fig. 4 right). This separation allows us to consider different attack scenarios modeled via the same attack tree, but decorated with different attributes. For example, it is easy to define attribute values based on the attacker type: script kiddie, malicious insider, etc. may be all be interested in the same asset, but each of them possesses different access privileges and is equipped with different resources.

Structure Metamodel. The structure model, depicted in Fig. 4 on the left, represents the structure of the attack tree. Its main class AttackTree contains a set of one or more Nodes, as indicated by the containment arrow between AttackTree and Node. One of these nodes is designated as the root of the tree, denoted by the root reference. Each Node is equipped with an id, used as a reference during transformation processes. Furthermore, each node has a (possibly empty) list of its parents and children, which allows to easily traverse the AT. A node may have a connector, i.e., a *gate* such as AND, OR, SAND (sequential-AND), etc.

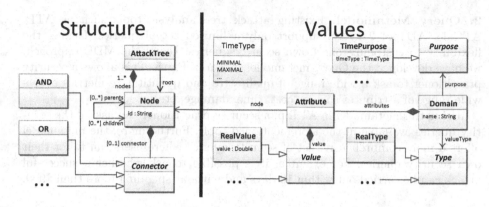

Fig. 4. The ATMM metamodel separated into the structure and values metamodels. Some connectors, types, and purposes are omitted for clarity and denoted by ellipses.

In addition to the structure specified by the metamodel, some constraints can be used to ensure that a model is a valid attack tree. For example, the tree cannot contain cycles, the nodes must form a connected graph, etc. These constraints are separately formulated in the Epsilon Validation Language (EVL [17]). An example of such a constraint is shown in Listing 1.

Values Metamodel. The Values metamodel (Fig. 4, right side) describes how values are attributed to nodes (arrow from **Attribute** on the right to **Node** on the left). Each **Attribute** contains exactly one **Value**, which can be of various (basic or complex) types: For example, **RealValue** is a type of Value that contains real (Double) numbers. A **Domain** groups all those attributes that have the same **Purpose**. By separating the purpose of attributes from their data type, we can use basic data types (integer, boolean, real number) for different purposes: For example, a real number (**RealType**) can be used in a **Domain** named "Maximum Duration", where the **purpose** is a TimePurpose with timeType = MAXIMAL. A RealType number could also be used in a different Domain, say "Likelihood of attack" with the purpose to represent a probability (ProbabilityPurpose, not shown in the diagram). Thanks to the flexibility of this construct, the set of available domains is easily extensible.

```
1   context ATMM!AttackTree {
2       constraint OneAndOnlyOneChildWithoutParents {
3           check : ATMM!Node.allInstances.select(n|n.parents.size() == 0).size() = 1
4           and self.root = ATMM!Node.allInstances.select(n|n.parents.size() == 0).first()
5       }
6   }
```

Listing 1. Constraint specifying that the root node is the only node in an ATMM AT with no parents.

2. Query Metamodel. Existing attack tree analysis tools such as ATE, ATCalc, ADTool 2.0, etc. support only a limited set of queries, lacking the flexibility to customize one's own security queries. Using the MDE approach, we have developed the Query metamodel shown in Fig. 5. This allows a security practitioner to ask a wide range of qualitative and quantitative metrics over a wide range of attributes such as cost, time, damage, etc.

Using this metamodel in ATTop, a security practitioner can ask all the security queries available in the aforementioned tools. Furthermore, the metamodel offers a more comprehensive set of security queries where users can tailor their own security queries. For example, it is possible to ask whether a successful attack can be carried out within 10 days and without spending more than $900.

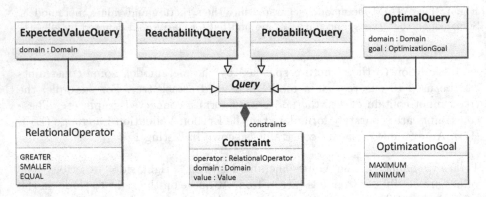

Fig. 5. The query metamodel. The types 'Domain' and 'Value' refer to the classes of the ATMM metamodel (Fig. 4).

The main component of the query metamodel is the element named Query. A query can be one of the following:

- Reachability, i.e., Is it feasible to reach the top node of an attack tree? Supported by every tool.
- Probability, i.e., What is the probability that a successful attack occurs? Supported by every tool.
- ExpectedValue, i.e., What is the expected (average) value of a given quantity over all possible attacks? Supported by ATTop.
- Optimality, i.e., Which is the attack that is optimal w.r.t. a given attribute (e.g., time or cost)? Supported by ATE, ADTool 2.0, ATTop.

Furthermore, a query can be framed by combining one of the above query types with a set of Constraints over the AT attributes. A Constraint is made of a RelationalOperator, a Value and its Domain. For example, the constraint "within 10 days" is expressed with the SMALLER RelationalOperator, a Value of 10, and the Domain of "Maximum Duration".

3. Scenario Metamodel. ATTop is geared to provide different results: some of which are numeric, like the probability to execute attack, the maximum cost to execute an attack, etc. Other results contain qualitative information such as an attack vector, which is a partially ordered set of basic attack steps resulting in the compromise of an asset under a given set of constraints (for example, incurring minimum cost). In order to properly trace back the qualitative output to the original attack tree, we use the Scenario metamodel (see Fig. 6).

The Scenario metamodel is used to represent attack vectors. In our context, we consider an attack vector to be a Schedule where there is only one Executor, which we name "Attacker". The sequence of Tasks appearing in a Scenario are then interpreted as the sequence of the attack steps the Attacker needs to carry out in order to reach their objective. Each attack step is actually a node of the original AT, and is represented as an Executable whose name corresponds to the id of the original Node. Timing information contained in each Task describes the start (startTime) and end (endTime) time points for each attack step. Note that an attack can start but not end before the objective is reached (multiplicity "1" for startTime and "0..1" for endTime).

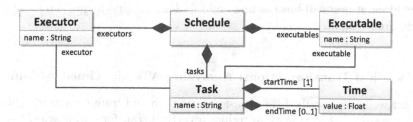

Fig. 6. The Scenario metamodel from [29]. In the context of ATs, all instances of this metamodel will have only one Executor, the Attacker; Executables represent attack steps (i.e. Nodes from the AT), while a Scenario is known as an attack vector.

4 Model Transformations

ATTop supports *horizontal* and *vertical* model transformations. Figure 7 illustrates the difference between these. *Horizontal transformations* convert one model into another that conforms to the same metamodel, e.g., a transformation from one AT analysis tool to another (where the models of both tools are represented in the ATMM metamodel). *Vertical transformations* transform a model into another that conforms to a different metamodel, e.g., the transformation from an AT into a timed automaton. A key feature of ATTop is that it also provides vertical transformations in the reverse direction: analysis results (e.g., traces produced by UPPAAL) are interpreted in terms of the original attack tree model.

4.1   Horizontal Transformations: Unifying Dialects of Attack Trees

One of the goals of applying the model-driven approach is to facilitate interoperation between different tools. To this end, we provide transformations to and from the file formats of ADTool 2.0 [12], Attack Tree Evaluator (ATE) [5], and ATCalc [2].

Due to the different features supported by the various tools, not all input formalisms can be converted to any other format preserving all semantics. For example, ATCalc performs only timing analysis, while ADTool can also perform cost analysis of untimed attack trees. In such cases, the transformations convert whatever information is supported by their output format, omitting unsupported features. As the ATMM metamodel unifies the features of all the listed tools, transformations into this metamodel are lossless.

Example 2. ATE Transformation. The Attack Tree Evaluator [5] tool can only process binary trees. Using a simple transformation, we can transform any instance of the ATMM into a binary tree. A simplified version of this transformation, written in ETL, is given in Listing 2. This transformation is based on a recursive method that traverses the tree. For every node with more than two children, it nests all but the first child under a new node until no more than two children remain.

4.2   Vertical Transformations: Analyzing ATs via Timed Automata

Thus far we have described the transformations to and from dedicated tools for attack trees. In this section we introduce a vertical transformation which we use in ATTop to translate attack trees into the more general-purpose formalism of timed automata (TA). Specifically, we provide model transformations to TAs that can be analyzed by the UPPAAL tool to obtain the wide range of qualitative and quantitative properties supported by the query metamodel.

Our transformation targets the UPPAAL metamodel described in [29]. It transforms each element of the attack tree (i.e., each gate and basic attack step)

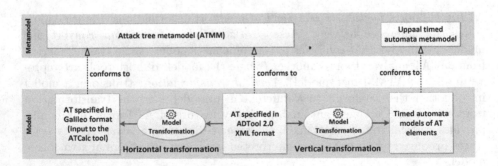

Fig. 7. Examples of *horizontal* and *vertical* model transformations.

```
1   var structure := AttackTree.all. first ();
2   structure.Root.NodeToBinary();
3
4   operation Node NodeToBinary(){
5       if(self.Children.size()>2){
6           var newNode = new Node();
7           newNode.Parents.add(self);
8           structure.Nodes.add(newNode);
9
10          var replaceNodes := self.Children.excluding(self.Children. first ());
11          newNode.Children := replaceNodes;
12          self.Children.removeAll(replaceNodes);
13          self.Children.add(newNode);
14      }
15   ·  for(child in self.Children)
16          child.NodeToBinary();
17  }
```

Listing 2. Transformation of an ATMM attack tree to a binary AT

into a timed automaton. These automata communicate via signals and together describe the behavior of the entire tree. For example, Fig. 8 shows the timed automaton obtained by transforming an attack step with a deterministic time to execute of 5 units.

Depending on the features of the model and the desired property to be analyzed, the output of the transformation can be analyzed by different extensions of UPPAAL. For example, UPPAAL CORA supports the analysis of cost-optimal queries, such as "What is the lowest cost an attacker needs to incur in order to complete an attack",

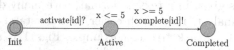

Fig. 8. Example of a timed automaton modeling a basic attack step with a fixed time to execute of 5 units.

while UPPAAL-SMC supports statistical model checking, allowing the analysis of models with stochastic times and probabilistic attack steps with queries such as "What is the probability that an attacker successfully completes an attack within one hour". The advantages of UPPAAL CORA's exact results come at the cost of state space explosion, which limits the applicability of this approach for larger problems. On the other hand, the speed and scalability of the simulation-based UPPAAL-SMC are countered by approximated results and the unavailability of (counter-)example traces.

4.3   Query Transformation: From Domain-Specific to Tool-Specific

ATTop aims to enable the analysis of ATs also by users that are less familiar with the underlying tools. One challenge for such a user is that every tool has its own method to specify what property of the AT should be computed.

Section 3 describes our metamodel for expressing a wide range of possible queries, and we now transform such queries to a tool-specific format. Many tools support only a single query (e.g., ATE [5] only supports Pareto curves of cost vs. probability), in which case no transformation is performed but ATTop only allows that single query as input.

The UPPAAL tool is an example of a tool supporting many different queries. After transforming the AT to a timed automaton (cf. Sect. 4.2), we transform the query into the textual formula supported by UPPAAL. The basic form of this formula is determined by the query type (e.g., a ReachabilityQuery will be translated as "E<> toplevel.completed", which asks for the existence of a trace that reaches the top level event), while constraints add additional terms limiting the permitted behavior of the model. By using an UPPAAL-specific metamodel for its query language linked to the TA metamodel, our transformation can easily refer to the TA elements that correspond to converted AT elements.

4.4   Result Transformation: From Tool-Specific to Domain-Specific

Analyses done with a back-end tool produce results that may only be immediately understandable to an expert in that tool. An important feature of ATTop to ease its use by non-experts, is that it provides interpretations of these results in terms of the original AT.

For example, given an attack tree whose leaves are annotated with (time-dependent) costs, UPPAAL can produce a trace showing the cheapest way to reach a security breach (optionally within a specified time bound). This trace is given in a textual format, with many details that are irrelevant to a security analyst. It is much easier to understand this scenario when shown in terms of the attack tree (for example, Fig. 11 is a scenario described by several pages of UPPAAL output). This is exactly the purpose of having reverse transformations: UPPAAL's textual traces are automatically parsed by ATTop, generating instances of the Trace metamodel described in [29]. To do so, the transformation from ATMM to UPPAAL retains enough information to trace identifiers in the UPPAAL model back to the elements of the AT. When parsing the trace, ATTop extracts only the relevant events (e.g., the starts and ends of attack steps) and related information (e.g., time). This information is then stored as an instance of the Scenario metamodel described in Sect. 3.

In the generated Schedule, attack steps are represented as Executables, while Tasks indicate the start and finish time of each attack step, thus describing the attack vector. Only one Executor is present in any attack vector produced by this transformation, and that is the Attacker. An example of such a generated schedule can be seen in Fig. 11.

5   Tool Support

We have developed the tool ATTop to enable users to easily use the transformations described in this paper, without requiring knowledge of the underlying techniques or formalisms. ATTop automatically selects which transformations to apply based on the available inputs and desired outputs. For example, if the user provides an ADTool input and requests an UPPAAL output,

ATTop will automatically first execute the transformation from ADTool to the ATMM, and then the transformation from ATMM to UPPAAL.

Users operate the tool by specifying input files and their corresponding languages, and the desired output files and languages. ATTop then performs a search for the shortest sequence of transformations achieving the desired outputs from the inputs. For example, Fig. 9 shown the tool's main screen, where the user has provided an input AT in Galileo format. The

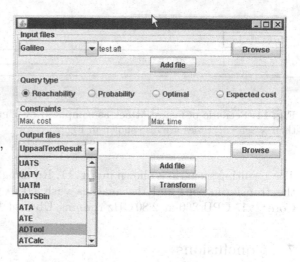

Fig. 9. Screenshot of ATTop's main screen, allowing input file selection, query specification, and output selection.

user can now choose between different queries and analysis engines.

6 Case Study

As a case study we use the example annotated attack tree given in Fig. 2. We apply ATTop to automatically compute several qualitative and quantitative security metrics. Specifically, we apply a horizontal transformation to convert the model from the ATCalc format to that accepted by ADTool 2.0, and a vertical transformation to analyze the model using UPPAAL.

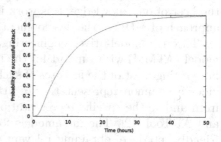

Fig. 10. ATCalc plot showing probability of successful attack over time

We specify the AT in the Galileo format as accepted by ATCalc. Analysis with ATCalc yields a graph of the probability of a successful attack over time, as shown in Fig. 10. Next, we would like to determine the minimal cost of a successful attack, which ATCalc cannot provide. Therefore, we use ATTop to transform the AT to the ADTool 2.0 format, and use ADTool 2.0 to compute the minimal cost (yielding \$270).

Next, we perform a more comprehensive timing analysis using the vertical transformation described in Sect. 4.2. We use ATTop to transform the AT to a timed automaton that can be analyzed using the UPPAAL tool. We also transform a query (OptimalityQuery asking for minimal time) to the corresponding UPPAAL query. Combining these, we obtain a trace for the fastest successful attack, which ATTop transforms into a scenario in terms of the AT as described in Sect. 4.3.

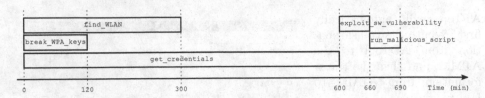

Fig. 11. Scenario of fastest attack as computed by UPPAAL . The executed steps and their start–end times are also shown in Fig. 2.

The resulting scenario is shown in Fig. 11. Running the whole process, including the transformations and the analysis with UPPAAL, took 6.5 s on an Intel® Core™ i7 CPU 860 at 2.80 GHz running Ubuntu 16.04 LTS.

7   Conclusions

We have presented a model-driven approach to the analysis of attack trees and a software bridging tool—ATTop—implementing this approach. We support interoperability between different existing analysis tools, as well as our own analysis using the popular tool UPPAAL as a back-end engine.

Formal methods have the advantage of being precise, unambiguous and systematic. A lot of effort is spent on their correctness proofs. However, these benefits are only reaped if the tools supporting formal analysis are also correct. To the best of our knowledge, this work is among the first to apply the systematic approach of MDE to the development of formal analysis tools.

Through model-driven engineering, we have developed the attack tree metamodel (ATMM) with support for the many extended formalisms of attack trees, integrating most of the features of such extensions. This unified metamodel provides a common representation of attack trees, allowing easy transformations from and to the specific representations of individual tools such as ATCalc [2] and ADTool [12]. The metamodels for queries and schedules facilitate a user-friendly interface, obtaining relevant questions and presenting results without needing expert knowledge of the underlying analysis tool.

We have presented our approach specifically for attack trees, but we believe it can be equally fruitful for different formalisms and tools as well (e.g. PRISM [24], STORM [9]) by using different metamodels and model transformations. We thus expect our approach to be useful in the development of other tools that bridge specialized domains and formal methods.

Acknowledgments. This research was partially funded by STW and ProRail under the project ArRangeer (grant 12238), STW, TNO-ESI, Océ and PANalytical under the project SUMBAT (13859), STW project SEQUOIA (15474), NWO projects BEAT (612001303) and SamSam (628.005.015), and EU project SUCCESS (102112).

References

1. Andrade, E.C., Alves, M., Matos, R., Silva, B., Maciel, P.: OpenMADS: an open source tool for modeling and analysis of distributed systems. In: Bitsch, F., Guiochet, J., Kaâniche, M. (eds.) SAFECOMP 2013. LNCS, vol. 8153, pp. 277–284. Springer, Heidelberg (2013). https://doi.org/10.1007/978-3-642-40793-2_25
2. Arnold, F., Belinfante, A., Van der Berg, F., Guck, D., Stoelinga, M.: DFTCALC: a tool for efficient fault tree analysis. In: Bitsch, F., Guiochet, J., Kaâniche, M. (eds.) SAFECOMP 2013. LNCS, vol. 8153, pp. 293–301. Springer, Heidelberg (2013). https://doi.org/10.1007/978-3-642-40793-2_27
3. Arnold, F., Guck, D., Kumar, R., Stoelinga, M.: Sequential and parallel attack tree modelling. In: Koornneef, F., van Gulijk, C. (eds.) SAFECOMP 2015. LNCS, vol. 9338, pp. 291–299. Springer, Cham (2015). https://doi.org/10.1007/978-3-319-24249-1_25
4. Aslanyan, Z., Nielson, F., Parker, D.: Quantitative verification and synthesis of attack-defence scenarios. In: Computer Security Foundations (CSF), pp. 105–119 (2016). https://doi.org/10.1109/CSF.2016.15
5. Aslanyan, Z.: Attack Tree Evaluator, developed for EU project TREsPASS, Technical University of Denmark. https://vimeo.com/145070436
6. Bistarelli, S., Fioravanti, F., Peretti, P., Santini, F.: Evaluation of complex security scenarios using defense trees and economic indexes. J. Exp. Theor. Artif. Intell. 24(2), 161–192 (2012). https://doi.org/10.1080/13623079.2011.587206
7. Byres, E.J., Franz, M., Miller, D.: The use of attack trees in assessing vulnerabilities in SCADA systems. In: Proceedings of Infrastructure Survivability Workshop. IEEE (2004)
8. Dalton, G.C.I., Mills, R.F., Colombi, J.M., Raines, R.A.: Analyzing attack trees using generalized stochastic petri nets. In: 2006 IEEE Information Assurance Workshop, pp. 116–123, June 2006. https://doi.org/10.1109/IAW.2006.1652085
9. Dehnert, C., Junges, S., Katoen, J.-P., Volk, M.: A STORM is coming: a modern probabilistic model checker. In: Majumdar, R., Kunčak, V. (eds.) CAV 2017. LNCS, vol. 10427, pp. 592–600. Springer, Cham (2017). https://doi.org/10.1007/978-3-319-63390-9_31
10. Fraile, M., Ford, M., Gadyatskaya, O., Kumar, R., Stoelinga, M., Trujillo-Rasua, R.: Using attack-defense trees to analyze threats and countermeasures in an ATM: a case study. In: Horkoff, J., Jeusfeld, M.A., Persson, A. (eds.) PoEM 2016. LNBIP, vol. 267, pp. 326–334. Springer, Cham (2016). https://doi.org/10.1007/978-3-319-48393-1_24
11. Gadyatskaya, O., Hansen, R.R., Larsen, K.G., Legay, A., Olesen, M.C., Poulsen, D.B.: Modelling attack-defense trees using timed automata. In: Fränzle, M., Markey, N. (eds.) FORMATS 2016. LNCS, vol. 9884, pp. 35–50. Springer, Cham (2016). https://doi.org/10.1007/978-3-319-44878-7_3
12. Gadyatskaya, O., Jhawar, R., Kordy, P., Lounis, K., Mauw, S., Trujillo-Rasua, R.: Attack trees for practical security assessment: ranking of attack scenarios with ADTool 2.0. In: Agha, G., Van Houdt, B. (eds.) QEST 2016. LNCS, vol. 9826, pp. 159–162. Springer, Cham (2016). https://doi.org/10.1007/978-3-319-43425-4_10
13. Gribaudo, M., Iacono, M., Marrone, S.: Exploiting Bayesian networks for the analysis of combined attack trees. In: Proceedings of PASM. ENTCS, vol. 310, pp. 91–111 (2015). https://doi.org/10.1016/j.entcs.2014.12.014

14. Hendriks, M., Verhoef, M.: Timed automata based analysis of embedded system architectures. In: Proceedings of 20th International Conference on Parallel and Distributed Processing (IPDPS), p. 179. IEEE (2006). https://doi.org/10.1109/IPDPS.2006.1639422

15. Hermanns, H., Krämer, J., Krčál, J., Stoelinga, M.: The value of attack-defence diagrams. In: Piessens, F., Viganò, L. (eds.) POST 2016. LNCS, vol. 9635, pp. 163–185. Springer, Heidelberg (2016). https://doi.org/10.1007/978-3-662-49635-0_9

16. Jürjens, J.: UMLsec: extending UML for secure systems development. In: Jézéquel, J.-M., Hussmann, H., Cook, S. (eds.) UML 2002. LNCS, vol. 2460, pp. 412–425. Springer, Heidelberg (2002). https://doi.org/10.1007/3-540-45800-X_32

17. Kolovos, D., Rose, L., García-Domńguez, A., Paige, R.: The Epsilon Book (2016). http://www.eclipse.org/epsilon/doc/book

18. Kordy, B., Mauw, S., Radomirović, S., Schweitzer, P.: Foundations of attack–defense trees. In: Degano, P., Etalle, S., Guttman, J. (eds.) FAST 2010. LNCS, vol. 6561, pp. 80–95. Springer, Heidelberg (2011). https://doi.org/10.1007/978-3-642-19751-2_6

19. Kordy, B., Mauw, S., Schweitzer, P.: Quantitative questions on attack–defense trees. In: Kwon, T., Lee, M.-K., Kwon, D. (eds.) ICISC 2012. LNCS, vol. 7839, pp. 49–64. Springer, Heidelberg (2013). https://doi.org/10.1007/978-3-642-37682-5_5

20. Kordy, B., Piètre-Cambacédès, L., Schweitzer, P.: DAG-based attack and defense modeling: don't miss the forest for the attack trees. Comput. Sci. Rev. **13–14**, 1–38 (2014). https://doi.org/10.1016/j.cosrev.2014.07.001

21. Kumar, R., Stoelinga, M.: Quantitative security and safety analysis with attack-fault trees. In: Proceedings of IEEE 18th International Symposium on High Assurance Systems Engineering (HASE), pp. 25–32, January 2017. https://doi.org/10.1109/HASE.2017.12

22. Kumar, R., Guck, D., Stoelinga, M.: Time dependent analysis with dynamic counter measure trees. In: Proceedings of 13th Workshop on Quantitative Aspects of Programming Languages (QAPL) (2015). http://arxiv.org/abs/1510.00050

23. Kumar, R., Ruijters, E., Stoelinga, M.: Quantitative attack tree analysis via priced timed automata. In: Sankaranarayanan, S., Vicario, E. (eds.) FORMATS 2015. LNCS, vol. 9268, pp. 156–171. Springer, Cham (2015). https://doi.org/10.1007/978-3-319-22975-1_11

24. Kwiatkowska, M., Norman, G., Parker, D.: PRISM 4.0: verification of probabilistic real-time systems. In: Gopalakrishnan, G., Qadeer, S. (eds.) CAV 2011. LNCS, vol. 6806, pp. 585–591. Springer, Heidelberg (2011). https://doi.org/10.1007/978-3-642-22110-1_47

25. Mauw, S., Oostdijk, M.: Foundations of attack trees. In: Won, D.H., Kim, S. (eds.) ICISC 2005. LNCS, vol. 3935, pp. 186–198. Springer, Heidelberg (2006). https://doi.org/10.1007/11734727_17

26. Mead, N.: SQUARE Process (2013). https://buildsecurityin.us-cert.gov/articles/best-practices/requirements-engineering/square-process

27. Roudier, Y., Apvrille, L.: SysML-Sec: a model driven approach for designing safe and secure systems. In: Proceedings of 3rd International Conference on Model-Driven Engineering and Software Development (MODELSWARD), pp. 655–664 (2015)

28. Ruijters, E., Schivo, S., Stoelinga, M.I.A., Rensink, A.: Uniform analysis of fault trees through model transformations. In: Proceedings of IEEE 63rd Annual Reliability and Maintainability Symposium (RAMS), January 2017. https://doi.org/10.1109/RAM.2017.7889759

29. Schivo, S., Yildiz, B.M., Ruijters, E., Gerking, C., Kumar, R., Dziwok, S., Rensink, A., Stoelinga, M.: How to efficiently build a front-end tool for UPPAAL: a model-driven approach. In: Larsen, K.G., Sokolsky, O., Wang, J. (eds.) SETTA 2017. LNCS, vol. 10606, pp. 319–336. Springer, Cham (2017). https://doi.org/10.1007/978-3-319-69483-2_19

30. Schmidt, D.C.: Guest editor's introduction: model-driven engineering. Computer **39**(2), 25–31 (2006). https://doi.org/10.1109/MC.2006.58

31. Schneier, B.: Attack trees. Dr. Dobb's J. **24**(12), 21–29 (1999)

32. da Silva, A.R.: Model-driven engineering: a survey supported by the unified conceptual model. Comput. Lang. Syst. Struct. **43**, 139–155 (2015). https://doi.org/10.1016/j.cl.2015.06.001

33. Sprinkle, J., Rumpe, B., Vangheluwe, H., Karsai, G.: Chapter 3: Metamodelling. In: Giese, H., Karsai, G., Lee, E., Rumpe, B., Schätz, B. (eds.) MBEERTS 2007. LNCS, vol. 6100, pp. 57–76. Springer, Heidelberg (2010). https://doi.org/10.1007/978-3-642-16277-0_3

34. Stahl, T., Voelter, M., Czarnecki, K.: Model-Driven Software Development: Technology, Engineering, Management. Wiley, Chichester (2006)

35. Steinberg, D., Budinsky, F., Paternostro, M., Merks, E.: EMF: Eclipse Modeling Framework 2.0, 2nd edn. Addison-Wesley Professional, Reading (2009)

36. Steiner, M., Liggesmeyer, P.: Qualitative and quantitative analysis of CFTs taking security causes into account. In: Koornneef, F., van Gulijk, C. (eds.) SAFECOMP 2015. LNCS, vol. 9338, pp. 109–120. Springer, Cham (2015). https://doi.org/10.1007/978-3-319-24249-1_10

37. Völter, M., Stahl, T., Bettin, J., Haase, A., Helsen, S.: Model-Driven Software Development: Technology, Engineering, Management. Wiley, Chichester (2006)

Distributed Program and System Analysis

ROLA: A New Distributed Transaction Protocol and Its Formal Analysis

Si Liu[1]([✉]) [iD], Peter Csaba Ölveczky[2] [iD], Keshav Santhanam[1] [iD], Qi Wang[1] [iD],
Indranil Gupta[1] [iD], and José Meseguer[1] [iD]

[1] University of Illinois, Urbana-Champaign, USA
siliu3@illinois.edu
[2] University of Oslo, Oslo, Norway

Abstract. Designers of distributed database systems face the choice between stronger consistency guarantees and better performance. A number of applications only require *read atomicity* (RA) and *prevention of lost updates* (PLU). Existing distributed database systems that meet these requirements also provide additional stronger consistency guarantees (such as *causal consistency*), and therefore incur lower performance. In this paper we define a new distributed transaction protocol, ROLA, that targets applications where only RA and PLU are needed. We formally model ROLA in Maude. We then perform model checking to analyze both the correctness and the performance of ROLA. For *correctness*, we use standard model checking to analyze ROLA's satisfaction of RA and PLU. To analyze *performance* we: (a) use statistical model checking to analyze key performance properties; and (b) compare these performance results with those obtained by analyzing in Maude the well-known protocol Walter. Our results show that ROLA outperforms Walter.

1 Introduction

Distributed transaction protocols are complex distributed systems whose design is quite challenging because: (i) validating correctness is very hard to achieve by testing alone; (ii) the high performance requirements needed in many applications are hard to measure before implementation; and (iii) there is an unavoidable tension between the *degree of consistency* needed for the intended applications and the *high performance* required of the transaction protocol for such applications: balancing well these two requirements is essential.

In this work, we present our results on how to use formal modeling and analysis as early as possible in the design process to arrive at a mature design of a *new* distributed transaction protocol, called ROLA, meeting specific correctness and performance requirements *before* such a protocol is implemented. In this way, the above-mentioned design challenges (i)–(iii) can be adequately met. We also show how using this formal design approach it is relatively easy to *compare* ROLA with other existing transaction protocols.

© The Author(s) 2018
A. Russo and A. Schürr (Eds.): FASE 2018, LNCS 10802, pp. 77–93, 2018.
https://doi.org/10.1007/978-3-319-89363-1_5

ROLA in a Nutshell. Different applications require negotiating the consistency vs. performance trade-offs in different ways. The key issue is the application's required *degree of consistency*, and how to meet such requirements with *high performance*. Cerone *et al.* [4] survey a *hierarchy of consistency models* for distributed transaction protocols including (in increasing order of strength):

- *read atomicity* (RA): either *all* or *none* of a distributed transaction's updates are visible to another transaction (that is, there are no "fractured reads");
- *causal consistency* (CC): if transaction T_2 is *causally dependent* on transaction T_1, then if another transaction sees the updates by T_2, it must also see the updates of T_1 (e.g., if A posts something on a social media, and C sees B's comment on A's post, then C must also see A's original post);
- *parallel snapshot isolation* (PSI): like CC but without lost updates;
- and so on, all the way up to the well-known *serializability* guarantees.

A key property of transaction protocols is the *prevention of lost updates* (PLU). The weakest consistency model in [4] satisfying both RA and PLU is PSI. However, PSI, and the well-known protocol Walter [20] implementing PSI, also guarantee CC. Cerone *et al.* conjecture that a system guaranteeing RA and PLU *without* guaranteeing CC should be useful, but up to now we are not aware of any such protocol. The point of ROLA is exactly to fill this gap: guaranteeing RA and PLU, but not CC. Two key questions are then: (a) are there *applications* needing high performance where RA plus PLU provide a sufficient degree of consistency? and (b) can a new design meeting RA plus PLU *outperform* existing designs, like Walter, meeting PSI?

Regarding question (a), an example of a transaction that requires RA and PLU but not CC is the "becoming friends" transaction on social media. Bailis *et al.* [3] point out that RA is crucial for this operation: If Edinson and Neymar become friends, then Unai should not see a *fractured read* where Edinson is a friend of Neymar, but Neymar is not a friend of Edinson. An implementation of "becoming friends" must obviously guarantee PLU: the new friendship between Edinson and Neymar should not be lost. Finally, CC could be sacrificed for the sake of performance: Assume that Dani is a friend of Neymar. When Edinson becomes Neymar's friend, he sees that Dani is Neymar's friend, and therefore also becomes friend with Dani. The second friendship therefore causally depends on the first one. However, it does not seem crucial that others are aware of this causality: If Unai sees that Edinson and Dani are friends, then it is not necessary that he knows that (this happened *because*) Edinson and Neymar are friends.

Regarding question (b), Sect. 6 shows that ROLA clearly outperforms Walter in all performance requirements for all read/write transaction rates.

Maude-Based Formal Modeling and Analysis. In rewriting logic [16], distributed systems are specified as *rewrite theories*. Maude [5] is a high-performance language implementing rewriting logic and supporting various model checking analyses. To model time and performance issues, ROLA is specified in Maude as a *probabilistic rewrite theory* [1,5]. ROLA's RA and PLU requirements are then analyzed by standard model checking, where we disregard time issues. To estimate ROLA's performance, and to compare it with that of Walter, we have also specified Walter in Maude, and subject the Maude models of both ROLA and Walter to *statistical model checking* analysis using the PVESTA [2] tool.

Main Contributions include: (1) the design, formal modeling, and model checking analysis of ROLA, a new transaction protocol having useful applications and meeting RA and PLU consistency properties with competitive performance; (2) a detailed performance comparison by statistical model checking between ROLA and the Walter protocol showing that ROLA outperforms Walter in all such comparisons; (3) to the best of our knowledge the first demonstration that, by a suitable use of formal methods, a completely new distributed transaction protocol can be designed and thoroughly analyzed, as well as be compared with other designs, very early on, *before* its implementation.

2   Preliminaries

Read-Atomic Multi-Partition (RAMP) Transactions. To deal with ever-increasing amounts of data, large cloud systems *partition* their data across multiple data centers. However, guaranteeing strong consistency properties for multi-partition transactions leads to high latency. Therefore, trade-offs that combine efficiency with weaker transactional guarantees for such transactions are needed.

In [3], Bailis *et al.* propose an isolation model, *read atomic* isolation, and *Read Atomic Multi-Partition* (RAMP) transactions, that together provide efficient multi-partition operations that guarantee read atomicity (RA).

RAMP uses multi-versioning and attaches metadata to each write. Reads use this metadata to get the correct version. There are three versions of RAMP; in this paper we build on RAMP-Fast. To guarantee that all partitions perform a transaction successfully or that none do, RAMP performs two-phase writes using the two-phase commit protocol (2PC). In the *prepare* phase, each time-stamped write is sent to its partition, which adds the write to its local database.[1] In the *commit* phase, each such partition updates an index which contains the highest-timestamped committed version of each item stored at the partition.

RAMP assumes that there is no data *replication*: a data item is only stored at one partition. The timestamps generated by a partition P are unique identifiers but are sequentially increasing only with respect to P. A partition has access to methods GET_ALL(I : set of items) and PUT_ALL(W : set of ⟨item, value⟩ pairs).

PUT_ALL uses two-phase commit for each w in W. The first phase initiates a *prepare* operation on the partition storing $w.item$, and the second phase completes the commit if each write partition agrees to commit. In the first phase, the client (i.e., the partition executing the transaction) passes a *version* v : ⟨item, value, ts_v, md⟩ to the partition, where ts_v is a timestamp generated for the transaction and md is metadata containing all other items modified in the same transaction. Upon receiving this version v, the partition adds it to a set *versions*.

---

[1] RAMP does not consider write-write conflicts, so that writes are always prepared successfully (which is why RAMP does not prevent lost updates).

When a client initiates a GET_ALL operation, then for each $i \in I$ the client will first request the latest version vector stored on the server for i. It will then look at the metadata in the version vector returned by the server, iterating over each item in the metadata set. If it finds an item in the metadata that has a later timestamp than the ts_v in the returned vector, this means the value for i is out of date. The client can then request the RA-consistent version of i.

Rewriting Logic and Maude. In rewriting logic [16] a concurrent system is specified a as *rewrite theory* $(\Sigma, E \cup A, R)$, where $(\Sigma, E \cup A)$ is a *membership equational logic theory* [5], with Σ an algebraic signature declaring sorts, subsorts, and function symbols, E a set of conditional equations, and A a set of equational axioms. It specifies the system's state space as an algebraic data type. R is a set of *labeled conditional rewrite rules*, specifying the system's local transitions, of the form $[l] : t \longrightarrow t'$ **if** *cond*, where *cond* is a condition and l is a label. Such a rule specifies a transition from an instance of t to the corresponding instance of t', provided the condition holds.

Maude [5] is a language and tool for specifying, simulating, and model checking rewrite theories. The distributed state of an object-oriented system is formalized as a *multiset* of objects and messages. A class C with attributes att_1 to att_n of sorts s_1 to s_n is declared class $C \mid att_1 : s_1, \ldots, att_n : s_n$. An object of class C is modeled as a term < $o : C \mid att_1 : v_1, \ldots, att_n : v_n$ >, with o its object identifier, and where the attributes att_1 to att_n have the current values v_1 to v_n, respectively. Upon receiving a message, an object can change its state and/or send messages to other objects. For example, the rewrite rule

```
rl [1] :   m(O,z) < O : C | a1 : x, a2 : O' >
      =>          < O : C | a1 : x + z, a2 : O' >  m'(O',x + z) .
```

defines a transition where an incoming message m, with parameters O and z, is consumed by the target object O of class C, the attribute a1 is updated to x + z, and an outgoing message m'(O',x + z) is generated.

Statistical Model Checking and PVESTA. Probabilistic distributed systems can be modeled as *probabilistic rewrite theories* [1] with rules of the form

$$[l] : t(\overrightarrow{x}) \longrightarrow t'(\overrightarrow{x}, \overrightarrow{y}) \quad \textbf{if} \quad cond(\overrightarrow{x}) \quad \textit{with probability} \quad \overrightarrow{y} := \pi(\overrightarrow{x})$$

where the term t' has new variables $\overrightarrow{y}$ disjoint from the variables $\overrightarrow{x}$ in the term t. The concrete values of the new variables $\overrightarrow{y}$ in $t'(\overrightarrow{x}, \overrightarrow{y})$ are chosen probabilistically according to the probability distribution $\pi(\overrightarrow{x})$.

Statistical model checking [18,21] is an attractive formal approach to analyzing (purely) probabilistic systems. Instead of offering a yes/no answer, it can verify a property up to a user-specified level of confidence by running Monte-Carlo simulations of the system model. We then use PVESTA [2], a parallelization of the tool VESTA [19], to statistically model check purely probabilistic systems against properties expressed as QUATEX expressions [1]. The expected value of a QUATEX expression is iteratively evaluated w.r.t. two parameters α

and δ by sampling, until we obtain a value v so that with $(1-\alpha)100\%$ statistical confidence, the expected value is in the interval $[v - \frac{\delta}{2}, v + \frac{\delta}{2}]$.

3   The ROLA Multi-Partition Transaction Algorithm

Our new algorithm for distributed multi-partition transactions, ROLA, extends RAMP-Fast. RAMP-Fast guarantees RA, but it does not guarantee PLU since it allows a write to overwrite conflicting writes: When a partition commits a write, it only compares the write's timestamp t_1 with the local latest-committed timestamp t_2, and updates the latest-committed timestamp with t_1 or t_2. If the two timestamps are from two conflicting writes, then one of the writes is lost.

ROLA's key idea to prevent lost updates is to sequentially order writes on the same key from a partition's perspective by adding to each partition a data structure which maps each incoming version to an incremental sequence number. For write-only transactions the mapping can always be built; for a read-write transaction the mapping can only be built if there has not been a mapping built since the transaction fetched the value. This can be checked by comparing the last prepared version's timestamp's mapping on the partition with the fetched version's timestamp's mapping. In this way, ROLA prevents lost updates by allowing versions to be prepared only if no conflicting prepares occur concurrently.

More specifically, ROLA adds two partition-side data structures: sqn, denoting the local sequence counter, and $seq[ts]$, that maps a timestamp to a local sequence number. ROLA also changes the data structure of *versions* in RAMP from a set to a list. ROLA then adds two methods: the coordinator-side[2] method UPDATE(I : set of items, OP : set of operations) and the partition-side method PREPARE_UPDATE(v : version, ts_{prev} : timestamp) for read-write transactions. Furthermore, ROLA changes two partition-side methods in RAMP: PREPARE, besides adding the version to the local store, maps its timestamp to the increased local sequence number; and COMMIT marks versions as committed and updates an index containing the highest-sequenced-timestamped committed version of each item. These two partition-side methods apply to both write-only and read-write transactions. ROLA invokes RAMP-Fast's PUT_ALL, GET_ALL and GET methods (see [3,14]) to deal with read-only and write-only transactions.

ROLA starts a read-write transaction with the UPDATE procedure. It invokes RAMP-Fast's GET_ALL method to retrieve the values of the items the client wants to update, as well as their corresponding timestamps. ROLA writes then proceed in two phases: a first round of communication places each timestamped write on its respective partition. The timestamp of each version obtained previously from the GET_ALL call is also packaged in this *prepare* message. A second round of communication marks versions as committed.

At the partition-side, the partition begins the PREPARE_UPDATE routine by retrieving the last version in its *versions* list with the same item as the received version. If such a version is not found, or if the version's timestamp ts_v matches

---

[2] The *coordinator*, or *client*, is the partition executing the transaction.

Algorithm 1. ROLA

Server-side Data Structures
1: *versions*: list of versions ⟨item, value, timestamp ts_v, metadata md⟩
2: *latestCommit*[i]: last committed timestamp for item i
3: *seq*[ts]: local sequence number mapped to timestamp ts
4: *sqn*: local sequence counter

Server-side Methods
GET same as in RAMP-Fast

5: **procedure** PREPARE_UPDATE(v : version, ts_{prev} : timestamp)
6:     $latest \leftarrow$ last $w \in versions : w.item = v.item$
7:     **if** $latest =$ NULL **or** $ts_{prev} = latest.ts_v$ **then**
8:         $sqn \leftarrow sqn + 1$; $seq[v.ts_v] \leftarrow sqn$; $versions.add(v)$
9:         **return** ACK
10:    **else return** $latest$

11: **procedure** PREPARE(v : version)
12:    $sqn \leftarrow sqn + 1$; $seq[v.ts_v] \leftarrow sqn$; $versions.add(v)$

13: **procedure** COMMIT(ts_c : timestamp)
14:    $I_{ts} \leftarrow \{w.item \mid w \in versions \wedge w.ts_v = ts_c\}$
15:    **for** $i \in I_{ts}$ **do**
16:        **if** $seq[ts_c] > seq[latestCommit[i]]$ **then** $latestCommit[i] \leftarrow ts_c$

Coordinator-side Methods
PUT_ALL, GET_ALL same as in RAMP-Fast

17: **procedure** UPDATE(I : set of items, OP : set of operations)
18:    $ret \leftarrow$ GET_ALL(I); $ts_{tx} \leftarrow$ generate new timestamp
19:    **parallel-for** $i \in I$ **do**
20:        $ts_{prev} \leftarrow ret[i].ts_v$; $v \leftarrow ret[i].value$
21:        $w \leftarrow \langle item = i, value = op_i(v), ts_v = ts_{tx}, md = (I - \{i\})\rangle$
22:        $p \leftarrow$ PREPARE_UPDATE(w, ts_{prev})
23:        **if** $p = latest$ **then**
24:            invoke application logic to, e.g., abort and/or retry the transaction
25:    **end parallel-for**
26:    **parallel-for** server $s : s$ contains an item in I **do**
27:        invoke COMMIT(ts_{tx}) on s
28:    **end parallel-for**

the passed-in timestamp ts_{prev}, then the version is deemed prepared. The partition keeps a record of this locally by incrementing a local sequence counter and mapping the received version's timestamp ts_v to the current value of the sequence counter. Finally the partition returns an ACK to the client. If ts_{prev}

does not match the timestamp of the last version in *versions* with the same item, then this *latest* timestamp is simply returned to the coordinator.

If the coordinator receives an ACK from PREPARE_UPDATE, it immediately commits the version with the generated timestamp ts_{tx}. If the returned value is instead a timestamp, the transaction is aborted.

4 A Probabilistic Model of ROLA

This section defines a formal executable probabilistic model of ROLA. The whole model is given at https://sites.google.com/site/fase18submission/.

As mentioned in Sect. 2, statistical model checking assumes that the system is *fully probabilistic*; that is, has no unquantified nondeterminism. We follow the techniques in [6] to obtain such a model. The key idea is that message delays are sampled probabilistically from dense/continuous time intervals. The probability that two messages will have the same delay is therefore 0. If events only take place when a message arrives, then two events will not happen at the same time, and therefore unquantified nondeterminism is eliminated.

We are also interested in correctness analysis of a model that captures all possible behaviors from a given initial configuration. We obtain such a nondeterministic untimed model, that can be subjected to standard model checking analysis, by just removing all message delays from our probabilistic timed model.

4.1 Probabilistic Sampling

Nodes send messages of the form [Δ, *rcvr* <- *msg*], where Δ is the message delay, *rcvr* is the recipient, and *msg* is the message content. When time Δ has elapsed, this message becomes a *ripe* message {T, *rcvr* <- *msg*}, where T is the "current global time" (used for analysis purposes only).

To sample message delays from different distributions, we use the following functionality provided by Maude: The function random, where random(k) returns the k-th pseudo-random number as a number between 0 and $2^{32} - 1$, and the built-in constant counter with an (implicit) rewrite rule counter => N:Nat. The first time counter is rewritten, it rewrites to 0, the next time it rewrites to 1, and so on. Therefore, each time random(counter) rewrites, it rewrites to the next random number. Since Maude does not rewrite counter when it appears in the condition of a rewrite rule, we encode a probabilistic rewrite rule $t(\overrightarrow{x}) \longrightarrow t'(\overrightarrow{x}, \overrightarrow{y})$ if $cond(\overrightarrow{x})$ *with probability* $\overrightarrow{y} := \pi(\overrightarrow{x})$ in Maude as the rule $t(\overrightarrow{x}) \longrightarrow t'(\overrightarrow{x}, sample(\pi(\overrightarrow{x})))$ if $cond(\overrightarrow{x})$. The following operator sampleLogNormal is used to sample a value from a lognormal distribution with mean MEAN and standard deviation SD:

```
op sampleLogNormal : Float Float -> [Float] .
eq sampleLogNormal(MEAN,SD) = exp(MEAN + SD * sampleNormal) .

op sampleNormal : -> [Float] .    op sampleNormal : Float -> [Float] .
eq sampleNormal = sampleNormal(float(random(counter) / 4294967296)) .
eq sampleNormal(RAND) = sqrt(- 2.0 * log(RAND)) * cos(2.0 * pi * RAND) .
```

random(counter)/4294967296 rewrites to a different "random" number between 0 and 1 each time it is rewritten, and this is used to define the sampling function. For example, the message delay rd to a remote site can be sampled from a lognormal distribution with mean 3 and standard deviation 2 as follows:

```
eq rd = sampleLogNormal(3.0, 2.0) .
```

4.2 Data Types, Classes, and Messages

We formalize ROLA in an object-oriented style, where the state consists of a number of *partition* objects, each modeling a partition of the database, and a number of messages traveling between the objects. A *transaction* is formalized as an object which resides inside the partition object that executes the transaction.

Data Types. A *version* is a timestamped version of a data item (or key) and is modeled as a 4-tuple version(*key, value, timestamp, metadata*). A timestamp is modeled as a pair ts(*addr, sqn*) consisting of a partition's identifier *addr* and a local sequence number *sqn*. Metadata are modeled as a set of keys, denoting, for each key, the other keys that are written in the same transaction.

The sort OperationList represents lists of read and write operations as terms such as (x := read $k1$) (y := read $k2$) write($k1, x + y$), where LocalVar denotes the "local variable" that stores the value of the key read by the operation, and Expression is an expression involving the transaction's local variables:

```
op write : Key Expression -> Operation [ctor] .
op _:=read_ : LocalVar Key -> Operation [ctor] .
pr LIST{Operation} * (sort List{Operation} to OperationList) .
```

Classes. A *transaction* is modeled as an object of the following class Txn:

```
class Txn | operations : OperationList,  readSet : Versions,
            localVars : LocalVars,       latest : KeyTimestamps .
```

The operations attribute denotes the transaction's operations. The readSet attribute denotes the versions read by the read operations. localVars maps the transaction's local variables to their current values. latest stores the local view as a mapping from keys to their respective latest committed timestamps.

A *partition* (or *site*) stores parts of the database, and executes the transactions for which it is the coordinator/server. A partition is formalized as an object instance of the following class Partition:

```
class Partition | datastore : Versions,      sqn : Nat,
                  gotTxns : ObjectList,       executing : Object,
                  committed : ObjectList,     aborted : ObjectList,
                  tsSqn : TimestampSqn,       latestCommit : KeyTimestamps,
                  votes : Vote,               voteSites : TxnAddrSet,
                  1stGetSites : TxnAddrSet,   2ndGetSites : TxnAddrSet,
                  commitSites : TxnAddrSet .
```

The `datastore` attribute represents the partition's local database as a list of versions for each key stored at the partition. The attribute `latestCommit` maps to each key the timestamp of its last committed version. `tsSqn` maps each version's timestamp to a local sequence number `sqn`. The attributes `gotTxns`, `executing`, `committed` and `aborted` denote the transaction(s) which are, respectively, waiting to be executed, currently executing, committed, and aborted.

The attribute `votes` stores the votes in the two-phase commit. The remaining attributes denote the partitions from which the executing partition is awaiting votes, committed acks, first-round get replies, and second-round get replies.

The following shows an initial state (with some parts replaced by '...') with two partitions, `p1` and `p2`, that are coordinators for, respectively, transactions `t1`, and `t2` and `t3`. `p1` stores the data items `x` and `z`, and `p2` stores `y`. Transaction `t1` is the read-only transaction `(x1 := read x) (y1 := read y)`, transaction `t2` is a write-only transaction `write(y, 3) write(z, 8)`, while transaction `t3` is a read-write transaction on data item `x`. The states also include a buffer of messages in transit and the global clock value, and a table which assigns to each data item the site storing the item. Initially, the value of each item is `[0]`; the version's timestamp is empty (`eptTS`), and metadata is an empty set.

```
eq init = { 0.0 | nil}
< tb : Table | table : [sites(x, p1) ;; sites(y, p2) ;; sites(z, p1)] >
< p1 : Partition |
      gotTxns: < t1 : Txn | operations: ((x1 :=read x) (y1 :=read y)),
                            readSet: empty, latest: empty,
                            localVars: (x1 |-> [0], y1 |-> [0]) >,
         datastore: (version(x, [0], eptTS, empty)
                     version(z, [0], eptTS, empty)),
         sqn: 1,  ... >
< p2 : Partition |
      gotTxns: < t2 : Txn | operations: (write(y, 3) write(z, 8)), ... >
               < t3 : Txn | operations: ((x1 := read x)
                                         write(x, x1 plus 1)),  ... >
         datastore: version(y, [0], eptTS, empty), ... > .
```

Messages. The message **prepare**(*txn, version, sender*) sends a version from a write-only transaction to its partition, and **prepare**(*txn, version, ts, sender*) does the same thing for other transactions, with *ts* the timestamp of the version it read. The partition replies with a message **prepare-reply**(*txn, vote, sender*), where *vote* tells whether this partition can commit the transaction. A message **commit**(*txn, ts, sender*) marks the versions with timestamp *ts* as committed. **get**(*txn, key, ts, sender*) asks for the highest-timestamped committed version or a missing version for *key* by timestamp *ts*, and **response1**(*txn, version, sender*) and **response2**(*txn, version, sender*) respond to first/second-round **get** requests.

4.3   Formalizing ROLA's Behaviors

This section formalizes the dynamic behaviors of ROLA using rewrite rules, referring to the corresponding lines in Algorithm 1. We only show 2 of the 15 rewrite rules in our model, and refer to the report [14] for further details.[3]

Receiving prepare *Messages (lines 5–10).* When a partition receives a prepare message for a read-write transaction, the partition first determines whether the timestamp of the last version (VERSION) in its local version list VS matches the incoming timestamp TS' (which is the timestamp of the version read by the transaction). If so, the incoming version is added to the local store, the map tsSqn is updated, and a positive reply (true) to the prepare message is sent ("**return** *ack*" in our pseudo-code); otherwise, a negative reply (false, or "**return** *latest*" in the pseudo-code) is sent. Depending on whether the sender PID' of the *prepare* message happens to be PID itself, the reply is equipped with a local message delay ld or a remote message delay rd, both of which are sampled probabilistically from distributions with different parameters:[4]

```
crl [receive-prepare-rw] :
  {T, PID <- prepare(TID, version(K, V, TS, MD), TS', PID')}
  < PID : Partition | datastore: VS,   sqn: SQN,   tsSqn: TSSQN,   AS' >
  =>
  if VERSION == eptVersion or tstamp(VERSION) == TS'
  then < PID : Partition | datastore: (VS version(K,V,TS,MD)), sqn: SQN',
                          tsSqn: insert(TS,SQN',TSSQN), AS' >
       [if PID == PID' then ld else rd fi,
           PID' <- prepare-reply(TID, true, PID)]
  else < PID : Partition | datastore: VS,  sqn: SQN,  tsSqn: TSSQN, AS' >
       [if PID == PID' then ld else rd fi,
           PID' <- prepare-reply(TID, false, PID)]  fi
  if SQN' := SQN + 1 /\ VERSION := latestPrepared(K,VS) .
```

Receiving Negative Replies (lines 23–24). When a site receives a prepare-reply message with vote false, it aborts the transaction by moving it to the aborted list, and removes PID' from the "vote waiting list" for this transaction:

```
rl [receive-prepare-reply-false-executing] :
  {T, PID <- prepare-reply(TID, false, PID')}
  < PID : Partition | executing: < TID : Txn | AS >,   aborted: TXNS,
                      voteSites: VSTS addrs(TID, (PID', PIDS)), AS' >
  =>
  < PID : Partition | executing: noTxn,
                      aborted: (TXNS ;; < TID : Txn | AS >),
                      voteSites: VSTS addrs(TID, PIDS), AS' > .
```

---

[3] We do not give variable declarations, but follow the convention that variables are written in (all) capital letters.

[4] The variable AS' denotes the "remaining" attributes in the object.

5 Correctness Analysis of ROLA

In this section we use reachability analysis to analyze whether ROLA guarantees read atomicity and prevents lost updates.

For both correctness and performance analysis, we add to the state an object

```
< m : Monitor | log: log >
```

which stores crucial information about each transaction. The *log* is a list of records record(*tid, issueTime, finishTime, reads, writes, committed*), with *tid* the transaction's ID, *issueTime* its issue time, *finishTime* its commit/abort time, *reads* the versions read, *writes* the versions written, and *committed* a flag that is true if the transaction is committed.

We modify our model by updating the Monitor when needed. For example, when the coordinator has received all committed messages, the monitor records the commit time (T) for that transaction, and sets the "committed" flag to true[5]:

```
crl [receive-committed] :
    {T, PID <- committed(TID, PID')}
    < M : Monitor | log: (LOG record(TID, T', T'', RS, WS, false) LOG') >
    < PID : Partition | executing: < TID : Txn | AS >,
                        committed: TXNS, commitSites: CMTS,  AS' >
    =>
    if CMTS'[TID] == empty  --- all "committed" received
    then < M : Monitor | log: (LOG record(TID, T', T, RS, WS, true) LOG') >
         < PID : Partition | executing: noTxn,  commitSites: CMTS',
                        committed: (TXNS ;; < TID : Txn | AS >, AS' >
    else < M : Monitor | log: (LOG record(TID, T', T'', RS, WS, false) LOG') >
         < PID : Partition | executing: < TID : Txn | AS >,
                        committed: TXNS, commitSites: CMTS', AS' > fi
    if CMTS' := remove(TID, PID', CMTS) .
```

Since ROLA is terminating if a finite number of transactions are issued, we analyze the different (correctness and performance) properties by inspecting this monitor object in the final states, when all transactions are finished.

Read Atomicity. A system guarantees RA if it prevents fractured reads, and also prevents transactions from reading uncommitted, aborted, or intermediate data [3], where a transaction T_j exhibits *fractured reads* if transaction T_i writes version x_m and y_n, T_j reads version x_m and version y_k, and $k < n$ [3].

We analyze this property by searching for a reachable *final* state (arrow =>!) where the property does *not* hold:

```
search [1] initConfig =>! C:Config < M:Address : Monitor | log: LOG:Record >
    such that fracRead(LOG) or abortedRead(LOG) .
```

---

[5] The additions to the original rule are written in italics.

The function `fracRead` checks whether there are fractured reads in the execution log. There is a fractured read if a transaction TID2 reads X and Y, transaction TID1 writes X and Y, TID2 reads the version TSX of X written by TID1, and reads a version TSY' of Y written *before* TSY (TSY' < TSY). Since the transactions in the log are ordered according to start time, TID2 could appear *before* or *after* TID1 in the log. We spell out the case when TID1 comes before TID2:

```
op fracRead : Record -> Bool .
ceq fracRead(LOG ;
    record(TID1,T1,T1',RS1,(version(X,VX,TSX,MDX), version(Y,VY,TSY,MDY)),true) ; LOG' ;
    record(TID2,T2,T2',(version(X,VX,TSX,MDX), version(Y,VY',TSY',MDY')), WS2,true) ; LOG'')
  = true if TSY' < TSY .
ceq fracRead(LOG ; record(TID2,...) ; LOG' ; record(TID1,...) ; LOG'') = true if TSY' < TSY .
eq fracRead(LOG) = false [owise] .
```

The function `abortedRead` checks whether a transaction TID2 reads a version TSX that was written by an aborted (flag `false`) transaction TID1:

```
op abortedRead : Record -> Bool .
eq abortedRead(LOG ;
    record(TID1,T1,T1',RS1,(version(X,VX,TSX,MDX),VS),false) ; LOG' ;
    record(TID2,T2,T2',(version(X,VX,TSX,MDX),VS),WS2,true) ; LOG'') = true .
eq abortedRead(LOG ; record(TID2,...) ; LOG' ; record(TID1,...) ; LOG'') = true.
eq abortedRead(LOG) = false [owise] .
```

No Lost Updates. We analyze the PLU property by searching for a final state in which the monitor shows that an update was lost:

```
search [1] initConfig =>! C:Config < M:Address : Monitor | log: LOG:Record >
    such that lu(LOG) .
```

The function `lu`, described in [14], checks whether there are lost updates in LOG.

We have performed our analysis with 4 different initial states, with up to 8 transactions, 2 data items and 4 partitions, without finding a violation of RA or PLU. We have also model checked the causal consistency (CC) property with the same initial states, and found a counterexample showing that ROLA does *not* satisfy CC. (This might imply that our initial states are large enough so that violations of RA or PLU could have been found by model checking.) Each analysis command took about 30 seconds to execute on a 2.9 GHz Intel 4-Core i7-3520M CPU with 3.7 GB memory.

6 Statistical Model Checking of ROLA and Walter

The weakest consistency model in [4] guaranteeing RA and PLU is PSI, and the main system providing PSI is Walter [20]. ROLA must therefore outperform Walter to be an attractive design. To quickly check whether ROLA does so, we have also modeled Walter—without its data replication features—in Maude (see [11] and https://sites.google.com/site/fase18submission/maude-spec), and use statistical model checking with PVESTA to compare the performance of ROLA and Walter in terms of throughput and average transaction latency.

Extracting Performance Measures from Executions. PVeStA estimates the expected (average) value of an expression on a run, up to a desired statistical confidence. The key to perform statistical model checking is therefore to define a measure on runs. Using the monitor in Sect. 5 we can define a number of functions on (states with) such a monitor that extract different performance metrics from this "system execution log."

The function `throughput` computes the number of committed transactions per time unit. `committedNumber` computes the number of committed transactions in `LOG`, and `totalRunTime` returns the time when all transactions are finished (i.e., the largest *finishTime* in `LOG`):

```
op throughput : Config -> Float [frozen] .
eq throughput(< M : Monitor | log: LOG > REST)
 = committedNumber(LOG) / totalRunTime(LOG) .
```

The function `avgLatency` computes the average transaction latency by dividing the sum of the latencies of all committed transactions by the number of such transactions:

```
op avgLatency : Config -> Float [frozen] .
eq avgLatency(< M : Monitor | log: LOG > REST)
 = totalLatency(LOG) / committedNumber(LOG) .
```

where `totalLatency` computes the sum of all transaction latencies (time between the issue time and the finish time of a committed transaction).

Generating Initial States. We use an operator `init` to *probabilistically* generate initial states: `init`(*rtx*, *wtx*, *rwtx*, *part*, *keys*, *rops*, *wops*, *rwops*, *distr*) generates an initial state with *rtx* read-only transactions, *wtx* write-only transactions, *rwtx* read-write transactions, *part* partitions, *keys* data items, *rops* operations per read-only transaction, *wops* operations per write-only transaction, *rwops* operations per read-write transactions, and *distr* the key access distribution (the probability that an operation accesses a certain data item). To capture the fact that some data items may be accessed more frequently than others, we also use Zipfian distributions in our experiments.

Statistical Model Checking Results. We performed our experiments under different configurations, with 200 transactions, 2–4 operations per transaction, up to 200 data items and 50 partitions, with lognormal message delay distributions, and with uniform and Zipfian data item access distributions.

The plots in Fig. 1 show the *throughput* as a function of the percentage of read-only transactions, number of partitions, and number of keys (data items), sometimes with both uniform and Zipfian distributions. The plots show that ROLA outperforms Walter for all parameter combinations. More partitions gives ROLA higher throughput (since concurrency increases), as opposed to Walter (since Walter has to propagate transactions to more partitions to advance the vector timestamp). We only plot the results under uniform key access distribution, which are consistent with the results using Zipfian distributions.

The plots in Fig. 2 show the *average transaction latency* as a function of the same parameters as the plots for throughput. Again, we see that ROLA outperforms Walter in all settings. In particular, this difference is quite large for write-heavy workloads; the reason is that Walter incurs more and more overhead for providing causality, which requires background propagation to advance the vector timestamp. The latency tends to converge under read-heavy workload (because reads in both ROLA and Walter can commit locally without certification), but ROLA still has noticeable lower latency than Walter.

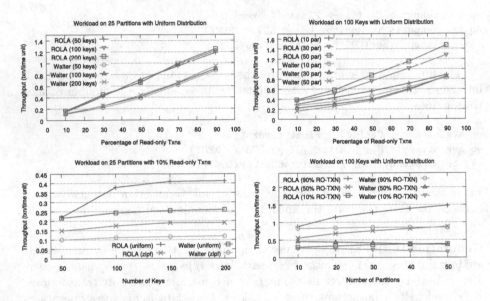

Fig. 1. Throughput comparison under different workload conditions.

Computing the probabilities took 6 hours (worst case) on 10 servers, each with a 64-bit Intel Quad Core Xeon E5530 CPU with 12 GB memory. Each point in the plots represents the average of three statistical model checking results.

7   Related Work

Maude and PVeStA have been used to model and analyze the correctness and performance of a number of distributed data stores: the Cassandra key-value store [12,15], different versions of RAMP [10,13], and Google's Megastore [7,8]. In contrast to these papers, our paper uses formal methods to develop and validate an entirely new design, ROLA, for a new consistency model.

Concerning formal methods for distributed data stores, engineers at Amazon have used TLA+ and its model checker TLC to model and analyze the correctness of key parts of Amazon's celebrated cloud computing infrastructure [17].

In contrast to our work, they only use formal methods for correctness analysis; indeed, one of their complaints is that they cannot use their formal method for performance estimation. The designers of the TAPIR transaction protocol for distributed storage systems have also specified and model checked correctness (but not performance) properties of their design using TLA+ [22].

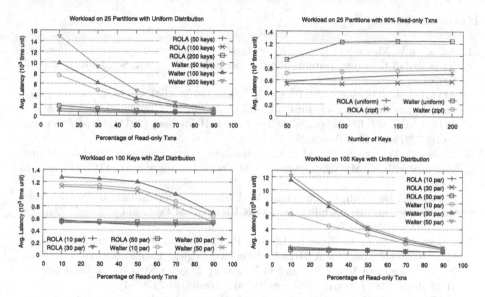

Fig. 2. Average latency comparison across varying workload conditions.

8   Conclusions

We have presented the formal design and analysis of ROLA, a distributed transaction protocol that supports a new consistency model not present in the survey by Cerone *et al.* [4]. Using formal modeling and both standard and statistical model checking analyses we have: (i) validated ROLA's RA and PLU consistency requirements; and (ii) analyzed its performance requirements, showing that ROLA outperforms Walter in all performance measures.

This work has shown, to the best of our knowledge for the first time, that the design and validation of a *new* distributed transaction protocol can be achieved relatively quickly *before* its implementation by the use of formal methods. Our next planned step is to implement ROLA, evaluate it experimentally, and compare the experimental results with the formal analysis ones. In previous work on existing systems such as Cassandra [9] and RAMP [3], the performance estimates obtained by formal analysis and those obtained by experimenting with the real system were basically in agreement with each other [10,12]. This confirmed the useful predictive power of the formal analyses. Our future research will investigate the existence of a similar agreement for ROLA.

Acknowledgments. We thank Andrea Cerone, Alexey Gotsman, Jatin Ganhotra, and Rohit Mukerji for helpful early discussions on this work, and the anonymous reviewers for useful comments. This work was supported in part by the following grants: NSF CNS 1409416, NSF CNS 1319527, AFOSR/AFRL FA8750-11-2-0084, and a generous gift from Microsoft.

References

1. Agha, G.A., Meseguer, J., Sen, K.: PMaude: rewrite-based specification language for probabilistic object systems. Electr. Notes Theor. Comput. Sci. **153**(2), 213–239 (2006)
2. AlTurki, M., Meseguer, J.: PVeStA: a parallel statistical model checking and quantitative analysis tool. In: Corradini, A., Klin, B., Cîrstea, C. (eds.) CALCO 2011. LNCS, vol. 6859, pp. 386–392. Springer, Heidelberg (2011). https://doi.org/10.1007/978-3-642-22944-2_28
3. Bailis, P., Fekete, A., Ghodsi, A., Hellerstein, J.M., Stoica, I.: Scalable atomic visibility with RAMP transactions. ACM Trans. Database Syst. **41**(3), 15:1–15:45 (2016)
4. Cerone, A., Bernardi, G., Gotsman, A.: A framework for transactional consistency models with atomic visibility. In: CONCUR. Schloss Dagstuhl - Leibniz-Zentrum fuer Informatik (2015)
5. Clavel, M., Durán, F., Eker, S., Lincoln, P., Martí-Oliet, N., Meseguer, J., Talcott, C.: All About Maude - A High-Performance Logical Framework: How to Specify, Program, and Verify Systems in Rewriting Logic. LNCS, vol. 4350. Springer, Heidelberg (2007). https://doi.org/10.1007/978-3-540-71999-1
6. Eckhardt, J., Mühlbauer, T., Meseguer, J., Wirsing, M.: Statistical model checking for composite actor systems. In: Martí-Oliet, N., Palomino, M. (eds.) WADT 2012. LNCS, vol. 7841, pp. 143–160. Springer, Heidelberg (2013). https://doi.org/10.1007/978-3-642-37635-1_9
7. Grov, J., Ölveczky, P.C.: Formal modeling and analysis of Google's Megastore in Real-Time Maude. In: Iida, S., Meseguer, J., Ogata, K. (eds.) Specification, Algebra, and Software. LNCS, vol. 8373, pp. 494–519. Springer, Heidelberg (2014). https://doi.org/10.1007/978-3-642-54624-2_25
8. Grov, J., Ölveczky, P.C.: Increasing consistency in multi-site data stores: Megastore-CGC and its formal analysis. In: Giannakopoulou, D., Salaün, G. (eds.) SEFM 2014. LNCS, vol. 8702, pp. 159–174. Springer, Cham (2014). https://doi.org/10.1007/978-3-319-10431-7_12
9. Hewitt, E.: Cassandra: The Definitive Guide. O'Reilly Media, Sebastopol (2010)
10. Liu, S., Ölveczky, P.C., Ganhotra, J., Gupta, I., Meseguer, J.: Exploring design alternatives for RAMP transactions through statistical model checking. In: Duan, Z., Ong, L. (eds.) ICFEM 2017. LNCS, vol. 10610, pp. 298–314. Springer, Cham (2017). https://doi.org/10.1007/978-3-319-68690-5_18
11. Liu, S., Ölveczky, P.C., Wang, Q., Meseguer, J.: Formal modeling and analysis of the Walter transactional data store. In: Proceedings of WRLA 2018. LNCS. Springer (2018, to appear). https://sites.google.com/site/siliunobi/walter
12. Liu, S., Ganhotra, J., Rahman, M., Nguyen, S., Gupta, I., Meseguer, J.: Quantitative analysis of consistency in NoSQL key-value stores. Leibniz Trans. Embed. Syst. **4**(1), 03:1–03:26 (2017)

13. Liu, S., Ölveczky, P.C., Rahman, M.R., Ganhotra, J., Gupta, I., Meseguer, J.: Formal modeling and analysis of RAMP transaction systems. In: SAC 2016. ACM (2016)
14. Liu, S., Ölveczky, P.C., Santhanam, K., Wang, Q., Gupta, I., Meseguer, J.: ROLA: a new distributed transaction protocol and its formal analysis (2017). https://sites. google.com/site/fase18submission/tech-report
15. Liu, S., Rahman, M.R., Skeirik, S., Gupta, I., Meseguer, J.: Formal modeling and analysis of Cassandra in Maude. In: Merz, S., Pang, J. (eds.) ICFEM 2014. LNCS, vol. 8829, pp. 332–347. Springer, Cham (2014). https://doi.org/10.1007/978-3-319-11737-9_22
16. Meseguer, J.: Conditional rewriting logic as a unified model of concurrency. Theor. Comput. Sci. **96**(1), 73–155 (1992)
17. Newcombe, C., Rath, T., Zhang, F., Munteanu, B., Brooker, M., Deardeuff, M.: How Amazon Web Services uses formal methods. Commun. ACM **58**(4), 66–73 (2015)
18. Sen, K., Viswanathan, M., Agha, G.: On statistical model checking of stochastic systems. In: Etessami, K., Rajamani, S.K. (eds.) CAV 2005. LNCS, vol. 3576, pp. 266–280. Springer, Heidelberg (2005). https://doi.org/10.1007/11513988_26
19. Sen, K., Viswanathan, M., Agha, G.A.: VESTA: a statistical model-checker and analyzer for probabilistic systems. In: QEST 2005. IEEE Computer Society (2005)
20. Sovran, Y., Power, R., Aguilera, M.K., Li, J.: Transactional storage for geo-replicated systems. In: SOSP 2011. ACM (2011)
21. Younes, H.L.S., Simmons, R.G.: Statistical probabilistic model checking with a focus on time-bounded properties. Inf. Comput. **204**(9), 1368–1409 (2006)
22. Zhang, I., Sharma, N.K., Szekeres, A., Krishnamurthy, A., Ports, D.R.K.: Building consistent transactions with inconsistent replication. In: Proceedings of Symposium on Operating Systems Principles, SOSP 2015. ACM (2015)

A Process Network Model for Reactive Streaming Software with Deterministic Task Parallelism

Fotios Gioulekas[1], Peter Poplavko[2], Panagiotis Katsaros[1,5(✉)],
Saddek Bensalem[3], and Pedro Palomo[4]

[1] Aristotle University of Thessaloniki, Thessaloniki, Greece
{gioulekas,katsaros}@csd.auth.gr
[2] Mentor®, A Siemens Business, Montbonnot, France
petro.poplavko@siemens.com
[3] Université Grenoble Alpes (UGA), VERIMAG, Grenoble, France
Saddek.Bensalem@univ-grenoble-alpes.fr
[4] Deimos Space®, Madrid, Spain
pedro.palomo@deimos-space.com
[5] Information Technology Institute, Centre of Research and Technology,
Thessaloniki, Greece

Abstract. A formal semantics is introduced for a Process Network model, which combines streaming and reactive control processing with task parallelism properties suitable to exploit multi-cores. Applications that react to environment stimuli are implemented by communicating sporadic and periodic tasks, programmed independently from an execution platform. Two functionally equivalent semantics are defined, one for sequential execution and one real-time. The former ensures functional determinism by implying precedence constraints between jobs (task executions), hence, the program outputs are independent from the task scheduling. The latter specifies concurrent execution on a real-time platform, guaranteeing all model's constraints; it has been implemented in an executable formal specification language. The model's implementation runs on multi-core embedded systems, and supports integration of run-time managers for shared HW/SW resources (e.g. for controlling QoS, resource interference or power consumption). Finally, a model transformation approach has been developed, which allowed to port and statically schedule a real spacecraft on-board application on an industrial multi-core platform.

Keywords: Process network · Stream processing · Reactive control
Real-time

The research leading to these results has received funding from the European Space Agency project MoSaTT-CMP, Contract No. 4000111814/14/NL/MH.

A. Russo and A. Schürr (Eds.): FASE 2018, LNCS 10802, pp. 94–110, 2018.
https://doi.org/10.1007/978-3-319-89363-1_6

1   Introduction

The proliferation of multi-cores in timing-critical embedded systems requires a
programming paradigm that addresses the challenge of ensuring predictable timing. Two prominent paradigms and a variety of associated languages are widely
used today. For streaming signal processing, synchronous dataflow languages [18]
allow writing programs in the form of directed graphs with nodes for their functions and arcs for the data flows between functions. Such programs can exploit
concurrency when they are deployed to multi-cores [15], while their functions
can be statically scheduled [17] to ensure a predictable timing behavior.

On the other hand, the reactive-control synchronous languages [12] are used
for reactive systems (*e.g.,* flight control systems) expected to react to stimuli
from the environment within strict time bounds. The synchronicity abstraction
eliminates the non-determinism from the interleaving of concurrent behaviors.

The synchronous languages lack appropriate concepts for task parallelism
and timing-predictable scheduling on multiprocessors, whereas the streaming
models do not support reactive behavior. The *Fixed Priority Process Network*
(FPPN) model of computation has been proposed as a trade-off between streaming and reactive control processing, for task parallel programs. In FPPNs, task
invocations depend on a combination of periodic data availability (similar to
streaming models) and sporadic control events. Static scheduling methods for
FPPNs [20] have demonstrated a predictable timing on multi-cores. A first implementation of the model [22] in an executable formal specification language called
BIP (Behavior, Interaction, Priority) exists, more specifically in its real-time
dialect [3] extended to tasks [10]. In [21], the FPPN scheduling was studied by
taking into account resource interference; an approach for incrementally plugging online schedulers for HW/SW resource sharing (*e.g.,* for QoS management)
was proposed.

This article presents the first comprehensive FPPN semantics definition, at
two levels: semantics for sequential execution, which ensures functional determinism, and a real-time semantics for concurrent task execution while adhering
to the constraints of the former semantics. Our definition is related to a new
model transformation framework, which enables programming at a high level by
embedding FPPNs into the architecture description, and allows an incremental
refinement in terms of task interactions and scheduling[1]. Our approach is demonstrated with a real spacecraft on-board application ported onto the European
Space Agency's quad-core Next Generation Microprocessor (NGMP).

2   Related Work

Design frameworks for embedded applications, like Ptolemy II [6] and
PeaCE [11], allow designing systems through refining high-level models. They
are based on various models of computation (MoC), but we focus mainly on
those that support task scheduling with timing constraints. Dataflow MoCs that

---

[1] The framework is online at [2].

stem from the Kahn Process Networks [16] have been adapted for the timing constraints of signal processing applications and design frameworks like Comp-SoC [13] have been introduced; these MoCs do not support reactive behavior and sporadic tasks as in the FPPN MoC that can be seen as an extension in that direction. DOL Critical [10] ensures predictable timing, but its functional behavior depends on scheduling. Another timing-aware reactive MoC that does not guarantee functional determinism is the DPML [4]. The Prelude design framework [5] specifies applications in a synchronous reactive MoC, but due to its expressive power it is hard to derive scheduling analyses, unless restricting its semantics. Last but not the least, though the reactive process networks (RPN) [8] do not support scheduling with timing constraints, they lay an important foundation for combining the streaming and reactive control behaviors. In the FPPN semantics we reuse an important principle of RPN semantics, namely, performing the *maximal execution run* of a dataflow network in response to a control event.

3   A PN Model for Streaming and Reactive Control

An FPPN model is composed of *Processes*, *Data Channels* and *Event Generators*.

A *Process* represents a software subroutine that operates with internal variables and input/output channels connected to it through ports. The *functional code* of the application is defined in processes, whereas the necessary *middleware* elements of the FPPN are channels, event generators, and *functional priorities*, which define a relation between the processes to ensure deterministic execution.

An example process is shown in Fig. 1. This process performs a check on the internal variables, if the check succeeds then it reads from the input channel, and, if the value read *is valid* (refer to the channel definition below) its square is computed. The write operation on an output channel is then performed. A call to the process subroutine is referred to as a *job*. Like the real-time jobs, the subroutine should have a bounded execution time subject to WCET (worst-case execution time) analysis.

```
struct SQ_Inititialize(){
   SQ_index = 0;
   SQ_length = 200;
}

void SQ_PeriodicJob() {
   float x, y;
   bool x_valid;
   if (SQ_index < SQ_length) {
      XIF_Read(&x, &x_valid);
      if(x_valid == true)  {
         y = x * x;
         y_valid = true;
         YIF_Write(&y);
      }
   }
SQ_index++;
}
```

Fig. 1. Example code for "Square" process

An FPPN is defined by two directed graphs. The first is a (possibly cyclic) graph (P, C), whose nodes P are processes and edges C are channels for pairs of communicating processes with a dataflow direction, *i.e.,* from the writer to the reader (there are also external channels interacting with the environment).

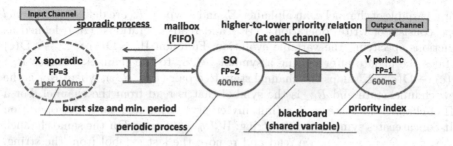

Fig. 2. Example Fixed Priority Process Network

A channel is denoted by a $c \in C$ or a pair (p_1, p_2) of writer and reader. For p_1 the channel is said to be an output and for p_2 an input. The second graph $(P, \mathcal{FP})$ is the functional priority directed acyclic graph (DAG) defining a functional priority relation between processes. For any two communicating processes we require,

$$(p_1, p_2) \in C \implies (p_1, p_2) \in \mathcal{FP} \lor (p_2, p_1) \in \mathcal{FP}$$

i.e., a functional priority either follows the direction of dataflow or the opposite. Given a $(p_1, p_2) \in \mathcal{FP}$, p_1 is said to have a *higher priority* than p_2.

The FPPN in Fig. 2, represents an imaginary data processing application, where the "X" sporadic process generates values, "Square" calculates the square of the received value and the "Y" periodic process serves as sink for the squared value. A sporadic event (command from the environment) invokes "X", which is annotated by its minimal inter-arrival time. The periodic processes are annotated by their periods. The two types of non-blocking channels are also illustrated. The FIFO (or mailbox) has a semantics of a queue. The blackboard remembers the last written value that can be read multiple times. The arc depicted above the channels indicates the functional priority relation $\mathcal{FP}$. Additionally, the external input/output channels are shown. In this example, the dataflow in the channels go in the opposite direction of the functional priority order. Note that, by analogy to the scheduling priorities, a convenient method to define priority is to assign a unique priority index to every process, the smaller the index the higher the priority. This method is demonstrated in Fig. 2. In this case the minimal required $\mathcal{FP}$ relation would be defined by joining each pair of communicating processes by an arc going from the higher-priority process to the lower-priority one.

Let us denote by *Var* the set of all variables. For a variable x or an ordered set (vector) X of variables we denote by $\mathbf{D}(x)$ (resp. $\mathbf{D}(X)$) its domain (or vector of domains), *i.e.*, the set(s) of values that the variable(s) may take. Valuations of variables X are shown as $X^0, X^1 \ldots$, or simply as X, dropping the superscript. Each variable is assumed to have a unique initial valuation. From the software point of view, this means that all variables are initialized by a default value.

Var includes all *process state* variables X_p and the *channel state* variables γ_c. The current valuation of a state variable is often referred to simply as *state*.

For a variable of channel c, an alphabet Σ_c and a type CT_c are defined; a *channel type* consists of write 'operations' (W_c) and read 'operations' (R_c) defined as functions specifying the variable evolution. Function $W_c : \mathbf{D}(c) \times \Sigma_c \to \mathbf{D}(c)$ defines the update after writing a symbol $s \in \Sigma_c$ to the channel, whereas $R_c : \mathbf{D}(c) \to \mathbf{D}(c) \times \Sigma_c$ maps the channel state to a pair (Rc_1, Rc_2), where Rc_1 is the new channel state and Rc_2 is the symbol that is read from the channel. For a FIFO channel, its state γ_c is a (initially empty) string and the write operation left-concatenates symbol s to the string: $W_c(\gamma_c, s) = s \circ \gamma_c$. For the same channel, $R_c(\gamma_c \circ s) = (\gamma_c, s)$, *i.e.*, we read and remove the last symbol from the string. The write and read functions are defined for each possible channel state, thus rendering the channels non-blocking. This is implemented by including $\bot$ in the alphabet, in order to define the read operation when the channel does not contain any 'meaningful' data. Thus, reading from an empty FIFO is defined by: $R_c(\epsilon) = (\epsilon, \bot)$, where ϵ denotes an empty string. For blackboard channel, its state is a (initially empty) string that contains at most one symbol – the last symbol written to the channel: $W_c(\gamma_c, s) = s$, $R_c(\gamma_c) = (\gamma_c, \gamma_c)$, $R_c(\epsilon) = (\epsilon, \bot)$.

An *external channel*'s state is an infinite sequence of samples, *i.e.*, variables $c[1], c[2], c[3], \ldots$ with the same domain. For a sample $c[k]$, k is the *sample index*. Though the sequence is infinite, no infinite memory is required, because each sample can be accessed (as will be shown) within a limited time interval. If c is an external output, the channel type defines the sample write operation in the form $W_c' : \mathbf{D}'(c) \times \mathbb{N}_+ \times \Sigma_c \to \mathbf{D}'(c)$, where $\mathbf{D}'(c)$ is the sample domain, the second argument is the sample index and the result is the new sample value. For an external input, we have the sample read operation $R_c' : \mathbf{D}'(c) \times \mathbb{N}_+ \to \mathbf{D}'(c) \times \Sigma_c$. The set of outputs is denoted by O and the set of inputs by I.

The program expressions involve variables. Let us call Act the set of all possible *actions* that represent operations on variables. An assignment is an action written as $Y := f(X)$. For the channels, two types of actions are defined, $x!c$ for writing a variable x, and $x?c$ for reading from the channel, where $\mathbf{D}(x) = \Sigma_c$. For external channels, we have $x!_{[k]}c$, $c \in O$ and $y?_{[k]}c$, $c \in I$, where $[k]$ is the sample index. Actions are defined by a function $Effect : Act \times \mathbf{D}(Var) \to \mathbf{D}(Var)$, which for every action a states how the new values of all variables are calculated from their previous values. The *actions are assumed to have zero delay*. The physical time is modeled by a special action for waiting until time stamp τ, $\mathbf{w}(\tau)$.

An *execution trace* $\alpha \in Act^*$ is a sequence of actions, *e.g.*,

$$\alpha = \mathbf{w}(0),\ x?_{[1]}I_1,\ x := x^2,\ x!c_1, \mathbf{w}(100),\ y?c_1,\ O_1!_{[2]}y$$

The time stamps in the execution are non-decreasing, and denote the time until the next time stamp, at which the following actions occur. In the example, at time 0 we read sample [1] from I_1 and we compute its square. Then we write to channel c_1. At time 100, we read from c_1 and write the sample [2] to O_1.

A process models a subroutine with a set of locations (code line numbers), variables (data) and operators that define a guard on variables ('if' condition), the action (operator body) and the transfer of control to the next location.

Definition 1 (Process). *Each process p is associated with a deterministic transition system $(\ell_p{}^0, L_p, X_p, X_p{}^0, \mathcal{I}_p, \mathcal{O}_p, A_p, \mathcal{T}_p)$, with L_p a set of locations, $\ell_p{}^0 \in L_p$ an initial location, and X_p the set of state variables with initial values $X_p{}^0$. $\mathcal{I}_p, \mathcal{O}_p$ are (internal and external) input/output channels. A_p is a set actions with variable assignments for X_p, reads from $\mathcal{I}_p$, and writes to $\mathcal{O}_p$. $\mathcal{T}_p$ is transition relation $\mathcal{T}_p : L_p \times G_p \times A_p \times L_p$, where G_p is the set of predicates (guarding conditions) defined on the variables from X_p.*

One *execution step* $(\ell_1, X^1, \gamma^1) \xrightarrow{g:a} (\ell_2, X^2, \gamma^2)$ for the valuations X^1, X^2 of variables in X_p and the valuations γ^1, γ^2 of channels in $\mathcal{I}_p \cup \mathcal{O}_p$, implies that there is transition $(\ell_1, g, a, \ell_2) \in \mathcal{T}_p$, such that X^1 satisfies guarding condition g (i.e., $g(X^1) = True$) and $(X^2, \gamma^2) = \mathit{Effect}(a, (X^1, \gamma^1))$.

Definition 1 prescribes a deterministic transition system: for each location ℓ_1 the guarding conditions enable for each possible valuation X^i a single execution step.

Definition 2 (Process job execution). *A job execution $(X^1, \gamma^1) \xrightarrow{\alpha}_p (X^2, \gamma^2)$ is a non-empty sequence of process p execution steps starting and ending in p's initial location ℓ_0, without intermediate occurrences of ℓ^0:*

$$(\ell^0, X^1, \gamma^1) \xrightarrow{g_1:\alpha_1} (\ell_1, X_1, \gamma_1) \ldots \xrightarrow{g_n:\alpha_n} (\ell^0, X^2, \gamma^2), \text{ for } n \geq 1, \ell_i \neq \ell^0$$

From a software point of view, a job execution is seen as a subroutine run from a caller location that returns control back to the caller. We assume that at k-th job execution, external channels I_p, O_p are read/written at sample index $[k]$.

In an FPPN, there is a one-to-one mapping between every process p and the respective event generator e that defines the constraints of interaction with the environment. Every e is associated with (possibly empty) subsets I_e, O_e of the external input/output (I/O) channels. Those are the external channels that the process p can access: $I_e \subseteq \mathcal{I}_p$, $O_e \subseteq \mathcal{O}_p$. The I/O sets of different event generators are disjoint, so different processes cannot share external channels.

Every e defines the set of possible sequences of time stamps τ_k for the 'event' of k-th invocation of process p and a relative deadline $d_e \in \mathbb{Q}_+$. The intervals $[\tau_k, \tau_k + d_e]$ determine when the k-th job execution can occur. This timing constraint has two important reasons. First, if the subsets I_e or O_e are not empty then these intervals should indicate the timing windows when the environment opens the k-th sample in the external I/O channels for read or write access at the k-th job execution. Secondly, τ_k defines the order in which the k-th job should execute, the earlier it is invoked the earlier it should execute. Concerning the τ_k sequences, two event generator types are considered, namely *multi-periodic* and *sporadic*. Both are parameterized by a burst size m_e and a period T_e. Bursts of m_e periodic events occur at 0, T_e, $2T_e$, etc. For sporadic events, at most m_e events can occur in any half-closed interval of length T_e. In the sequel we associate the attributes of an event generator with the corresponding process, e.g., T_p and d_p.

Definition 3 (FPPN). *An FPPN is a tuple* $\mathcal{PN} = (P, C, \mathcal{FP}, e_p, I_e, O_e,$
$d_e, \Sigma_c, CT_c)$, *where* P *is a set of processes and* $C \subseteq P \times P$ *is a set of internal channels, with* (P, C) *defining a (possibly cyclic) directed graph. An acyclic directed graph* $(P, \mathcal{FP})$ *is also defined, with* $\mathcal{FP} \subset P \times P$ *a functional priority relation (if* $(p_1, p_2) \in \mathcal{FP}$, *we also write* $p_1 \to p_2$). *This relation should be defined at least for processes accessing the same channel, i.e.,* $(p_1, p_2) \in C \Rightarrow p_1 \to p_2 \lor p_2 \to p_1$. e_p *maps every process* p *to a unique event generator, whereas* I_e *and* O_e *map each event generator to (possibly empty) partitions of the global set of external input channels* I *and output channels* O, *resp.* d_e *defines the relative deadline for accessing the I/O channels of generator* e, Σ_c *defines alphabets for internal and external I/O channels and* CT_c *specifies the channel types.*

The priority $\mathcal{FP}$ defines the order in which two processes are executed *when invoked at the same time*. It is not necessarily a transitive relation. For example, if $(p_1, p_2) \in \mathcal{FP}$, $(p_2, p_3) \in \mathcal{FP}$, and both p_1 and p_3 get invoked simultaneously then $\mathcal{FP}$ does not imply any execution-order constraint between them unless p_2 is also invoked at the same time. The functional priorities differ from the scheduling priorities. The former disambiguate the order of read/write accesses to internal channels, whereas the latter ensure satisfaction of timing constraints.

4   Zero-Delay Semantics for the FPPN Model

The functional determinism requirement prescribes that the data sequences and time stamps at the outputs are a well-defined function of the data sequences and time stamps at the inputs. This is ensured by the so-called functional priorities. In essence, functional priorities control the process job execution order, which is equivalent to the effect of fixed priorities on a set of tasks under uniprocessor fixed-priority scheduling with zero task execution times. A distinct feature of the FPPN model is that priorities are not used directly in scheduling, but rather in the definition of model's semantics. From now on, the term 'task' will refer to an FPPN process. Following the usual real-time systems terminology, invoking a task implies generation of a job which has to be executed before the task's deadline. The so-called *precedence constraints, i.e.,* the semantical restrictions of FPPN job execution order are implied firstly from the time stamps when the tasks are invoked and secondly from the functional priorities. In this section, we define these constraints in terms of a sequential order (an execution trace).

The FPPN model requires that *all simultaneous process invocations should be signaled synchronously*. This can be realized by introducing a periodic clock with sufficiently small period (the *gcd* of all T_p), such that invocations events can only occur at clock ticks, synchronously. Two variant semantics are then defined, namely the *zero-delay* and the *real-time* semantics.

The *zero-delay semantics* imposes an ordering of the job executions assuming that they have zero delay and that they are never postponed to the future. Since in this case the deadlines are always met even without exploiting parallelism, a sequential execution of processes is considered for simplicity. The semantics is defined in terms of the rules for constructing the execution trace of the FPPN for a given sequence $(t_1, \mathbf{P}^1)$, $(t_2, \mathbf{P}^2)$ ..., where $t_1 < t_2 < \ldots$ are time stamps and $\mathbf{P}^i$ is the multiset of processes invoked at time t_i. For convenience, we associate each 'invoked process' p in $\mathbf{P}^i$ with respective invocation event, e_p. The execution trace has the form:

$$Trace(\mathcal{PN}) = \mathbf{w}(t_1) \circ \alpha^1 \circ \mathbf{w}(t_2) \circ \alpha^2 \ldots$$

where α^i is a concatenation of job executions of processes in $\mathbf{P}^i$ included in an order, such that if $p_1 \rightarrow p_2$ then the job(s) of p_1 execute earlier than those of p_2.

Definition 4 (Configuration). *An FPPN configuration $(\pi, \gamma, \mathbf{P})$ consists of:*

- *a process configuration π, a function that assigns to every process a state $\pi(p) \in \mathbf{D}(X_p)$*
- *a channel configuration γ, i.e., the states of internal and external channels*
- *a set of pending events $\mathbf{P}$*

Executing one job in a process network:

$$\frac{(\pi(p), \gamma) \xrightarrow{\alpha}_p (X', \gamma') \wedge e_p \in \mathbf{P} \\ \wedge \\ \nexists p' : e_{p'} \in \mathbf{P} \wedge (p', p) \in \mathcal{FP}}{(\pi, \gamma, \mathbf{P}) \xrightarrow{\alpha}_{\mathcal{PN}} (\pi\{X'/p\}, \gamma', \mathbf{P} \setminus \{e_p\})}$$

where $\pi\{X'/p\}$ is obtained from π by replacing the state of p by X'.

Given a non-empty set of events $\mathbf{P}$ invoked at time t, a *maximal execution run* of a process network is defined by a sequence of job executions that continues until the set of pending events is empty.

$$\frac{(\pi^0, \gamma^0, \mathbf{P}) \xrightarrow{\alpha_1}_{\mathcal{PN}} (\pi_1, \gamma_1, \mathbf{P} \setminus \{e_{p_1}\}) \xrightarrow{\alpha_2}_{\mathcal{PN}} \ldots (\pi^1, \gamma^1, \emptyset)}{(\pi^0, \gamma^0) \xmapsto{\mathbf{w}(t) \circ \alpha_1 \circ \alpha_2 \circ \ldots}_{\mathcal{PN}(\mathbf{P})} (\pi^1, \gamma^1)}$$

Given an initial configuration (π^0, γ^0) and a sequence $(t_1, \mathbf{P}^1)$, $(t_2, \mathbf{P}^2)$ ... of events invoked at times $t_1 < t_2 < \ldots$, the run of process network is defined by a sequence of maximal runs that occur at the specified time stamps.

$$Run(\mathcal{PN}) = (\pi^0, \gamma^0) \xmapsto{\alpha^1}_{\mathcal{PN}(\mathbf{P}^1)} (\pi^1, \gamma^1) \xmapsto{\alpha^2}_{\mathcal{PN}(\mathbf{P}^2)} \ldots$$

The execution trace of a process network is a projection of the process network run to actions:

$$Trace(\mathcal{PN}) = \alpha^1 \circ \alpha^2 \ldots$$

This trace represents the time stamps $(\mathbf{w}(t_1), \mathbf{w}(t_2) \ldots)$ and the data processing actions executed at every time stamp. From the effect of these actions it is possible to determine the sequence of values written to the internal and external channels. These values depend on the states of the processes and internal channels. The concurrent activities – the job executions – that modify each process/channel states are deterministic themselves and are ordered relatively to each other in a way which is completely determined by the time stamps and the $\mathcal{FP}$ relation. Therefore we can make the following claim.

Proposition 1 (Functional determinism). *The sequences of values written at all external and internal channels are functionally dependent on the time stamps of the event generators and on the data samples at the external inputs.*

Basically, this property means that the outputs calculated by FPPN depend only on the event invocation times and the input data sequences, but not on the scheduling. To exploit task parallelism, in the real-time semantics of Sect. 5 the sequential order of execution and the zero-delay assumption are relaxed.

5 Real-Time Semantics for the FPPN Model

In the real-time semantics, job executions last for some physical time and can start concurrently with each other at any time after their invocation. Certain precedence constraints are respected which for certain jobs impose the same relative order of execution as in the zero-delay semantics, so that non-deterministic updates of the states of processes and channels are excluded. To ensure timeliness, the jobs should complete their execution within the deadline after their invocation. The semantics specifies the entities for communication, synchronization, scheduling and is defined by compilation to an *executable* formal specification language.

Our approach is based on (real-time) 'BIP' [3] for modeling networks of connected timed automata components [24]. We adopt the extension in [10], which introduces the concept of *continuous* (asynchronous) automata transitions, which, unlike the default (discrete) transitions take a certain physical time. Next to support of tasks (via continuous transitions), BIP supports the urgency in timing constraints, and those are timed-automata features required for adequate modeling and timing verification of dataflow languages [9]. An important BIP language feature for implementing the functional code of tasks is the possibility to specify data actions in imperative programming language (C/C++).

Figure 3 illustrates how an FPPN process is compiled to a BIP component. The source code is parsed, searching for primitives that are relevant for the interactions of the process with other components. The relevant primitives are the reads and writes from/to the data channels. For those primitives the generated BIP component gets ports, *e.g.*, 'XIF_Read(IN x,IN valid)', through which the respective transitions inside the component synchronize and exchange data with other components. In line with Definition 1, every job execution corresponds to a sequence of transitions that starts and ends in an initial location. The first transition in this sequence, 'Start', is synchronized with the event generator component, which enables this transition only after the process has been invoked. The event generator shown in Fig. 3 is a simplified variant for periodic tasks whose deadline is equal to the period. In [22] it is also described how we model internal channels and give more details on event generator modelling.

To ensure a functional behavior equivalent to zero-delay semantics, the job executions have to satisfy precedence constraints between subsequent jobs of the same process, and the jobs of process pairs connected by a channel. In both

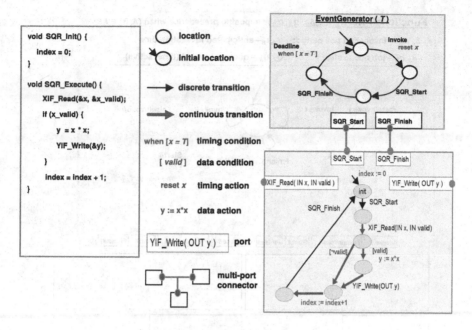

Fig. 3. Compilation of functional code to BIP

cases, the relative execution order of these subsets of jobs is dictated by zero-delay semantics, whereby the jobs are executed in the invocation order and the simultaneously invoked jobs follow the functional priority order. In this way, we ensure deterministic updates in both cases: (i) for the states of processes by *excluding auto-concurrency*, and (ii) for the data shared between the processes by *excluding data races* on the channels. The precedence constraints for (i) are satisfied by construction, because BIP components for processes never start a new job execution until the previous job of the same process has finished. For the precedence constraints in (ii), an appropriate component is generated for each pair of communicating processes and plugged incrementally into the network of BIP components.

Figure 4 shows such a component generated a given pair of processes "A" and "B", assuming $(A, B) \in \mathcal{FP}$. We saw in Fig. 3 that the evolution of a job execution goes through three steps: 'invoke', 'start' and 'finish'. The component handles the three steps of both processes in almost symmetrical way, except in the method that determines whether the job is ready to start: if two jobs are simultaneously invoked, then first the job of process "A" gets ready and then, after it has executed, the job of "B" becomes ready. The "Functional Priority"

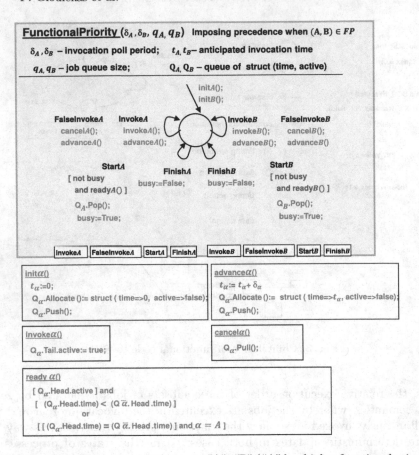

Fig. 4. Imposing precedence order between "A", "B" ("A" has higher functional priority)

component maintains two job queues[2] denoted Q_α where $\alpha \in \{A, B\}$ indicates a process selection. In our notation, $\overline{\alpha}$ means 'other than α', *i.e.*, if $\alpha = A$ then $\overline{\alpha} = B$ and if $\alpha = B$ then $\overline{\alpha} = A$.

The component receives from the event generator of process 'α' at regular intervals with period δ_α either 'Invoke α' or 'FalseInvoke α'. In the latter case (*i.e.*, no invocation), the job in the tail of the queue is 'pulled' away[3].

---

[2] Queues are implemented by a circular buffer with the following operations:
- **Allocate()** picks an available (statically allocated) cell and gives reference to it
- **Push()** push the last allocated cell into the *tail*
- **Pull()** undo the push
- **Pop()** retrieve the data from the *head* of the queue.

[3] Thanks to 'init α' and 'advance α', the queue tail always contains the next anticipated job, which is conservatively marked as non-active until 'Invoke α' transition.

6   Model Transformation Framework

The model-based design philosophy for embedded systems which we follow [14] is grounded on the evolutionary design using models, which support the gradual refinement (refined models are more accurate than those refined) and the setting of real-time attributes that ensure predictable timing. Such a process allows considering various design scenarios and promotes the late binding to design decisions. Our approach to refinement is based on *incremental component-based* models, where the system is evolved by incrementally plugging new components and transforming existing ones.

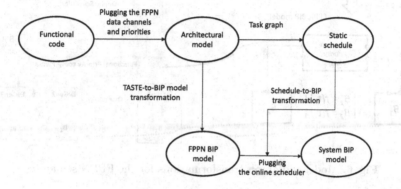

Fig. 5. Evolutionary design of time-critical systems using FPPNs

We propose such a design approach (Fig. 5), in which we take as a starting point a set of tasks defined by their *functional code* and real-time attributes (*e.g.,* periods, deadlines, WCET, job queue capacity). We assume that these tasks are encapsulated into software-architecture functional blocks, corresponding to FPPN processes. Before being integrated into a single *architectural model* they can be compiled and tested separately by functional simulation or by running on embedded platform.

The high-level architecture description framework of our choice is the TASTE toolset [14,19], whose front-end tools are based on the AADL (Architecture Analysis & Design Language) syntax [7]. An *architecture model* in TASTE consists of functional blocks – so-called 'functions' – which interact with each other via pairs of interfaces (IF) 'required IF'/'provided IF', where the first performs a procedure call in the second one. In TASTE, the provided interfaces can be explicitly used for task invocations, *i.e.,* they may get attributes like 'periodic'/'sporadic', 'deadline' and 'period'. The FPPN processes are represented by TASTE 'functions' that 'provide' such interfaces, implementing job execution of the respective task in C/C++. Our TASTE-to-BIP framework is available for download at [2].

The first refinement step is plugging the data channels for explicit communication between the processes. The data channels are also modeled as TASTE functions, whereas reads and writes are implemented via interfaces. We have

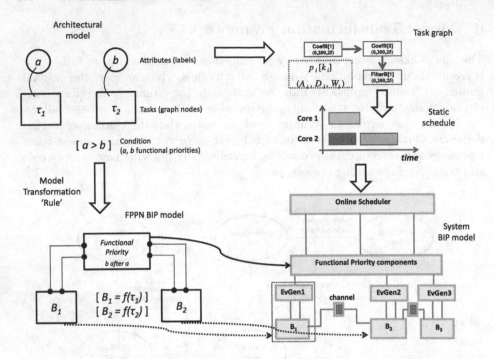

Fig. 6. Model and graph transformations for the FPPN semantics

amended the attributes of TASTE functions to reflect the priority index of processes and the parameters of FPPN channels, such as capacity of FIFO channels. The resulting model can be compiled and simulated in TASTE.

The second and final refinement step is scheduling. To schedule on multi-cores while respecting the real-time semantics of FPPN this step is preceded by transformation from TASTE architectural model into BIP FPPN model. The transformation process implements the FPPN-to-BIP 'compilation' sketched in the previous section, and we believe it could be formalized by a set of *transformation rules*. For example, as illustrated in Fig. 6, one of the rules could say that if there are two tasks τ_1 and τ_2 related by $\mathcal{FP}$ relation then their respective BIP components B_1 and B_2 are connected (via 'Start' and 'Finish' ports) to a functional priority component.

The scheduling is done offline, by first deriving a task graph from the architectural model, taking into account the periods, functional priorities and WCET of processes. The task graph represents a maximal set of jobs invoked in a hyper-period and their precedence constraints; it defines the invocation and the deadline of jobs relatively to the hyperperiod start time. The task graph derivation algorithm is detailed in [20].

Definition 5 (Task Graph). *A directed acyclic graph* $\mathcal{TG}(\mathcal{J}, \mathcal{E})$ *whose nodes* $\mathcal{J} = \{J_i\}$ *are jobs defined by tuples* $J_i = (p_i, k_i, A_i, D_i, W_i)$, *where* p_i *is the job's process,* k_i *is the job's invocation count,* $A_i \in \mathbb{Q}_{\geq 0}$ *is the invocation time,* $D_i \in \mathbb{Q}_+$ *is the absolute deadline and* $W_i \in \mathbb{Q}_+$ *is the WCET. The k-th job of process p is denoted by* $p[k]$. *The edges* $\mathcal{E}$ *represent the precedence constraints.*

The task graph is given as input to a static scheduler. The schedule obtained from the static scheduler is translated into parameters for the *online-scheduler* (cf. Fig. 6), which, on top of the functional priority components, further constraints the job execution order and timing, with the purpose of ensuring deadline satisfaction. The joint application/scheduler BIP model is called System Model. This model is eventually compiled and linked with the BIP-RTE, which ensures correct BIP semantics of all components online [23].

7   Case Study: Guidance, Navigation and Control Application

Our design flow was applied to a Guidance Navigation & Control (GNC) onboard spacecraft application that was ported onto ESA's NGMP, more specifically the quad-core LEON4FT processor [1]. In the space industry, multi-cores provide a means for integrating more software functions onto a single platform, which contributes to reducing size, weight, cost, and power consumption. Onboard software has to efficiently utilize the processor resources, while retaining predictability.

A GNC application affects the movement of the vehicle by reading the sensors and controlling the actuators. We estimated the WCETs of all tasks, W_p, by measurements. There are four tasks: the Guidance Navigation Task ($T_p = 500\,\text{ms}$, $d_p = 500\,\text{ms}$, $W_p = 22\,\text{ms}$), the Control Output Task ($T_p = 50\,\text{ms}$, $d_p = 50\,\text{ms}$, $W_p = 3\text{ms}$) that sends the outputs to the appropriate spacecraft unit, the Control FM Task ($T_p = 50\,\text{ms}$, $d_p = 50\,\text{ms}$, $W_p = 8\,\text{ms}$) which runs the control and flight management algorithms, and the Data Input Dispatcher Task ($T_p = 50\,\text{ms}$, $d_p = 50\,\text{ms}$, $W_p = 6\,\text{ms}$), which reads, decodes and dispatches data to the right destination whenever new data from the spacecraft's sensors are available. The hyperperiod of the system was therefore 500 ms, and it includes one execution of the Guidance Navigation Task and ten executions of each other task, which results in 31 jobs. The Guidance Navigation and Control Output tasks were invoked with relative time offsets 450 ms and 30 ms, respectively. Fig. 7 shows the GNC FPPN, where the functional priorities impose precedence from the numerically smaller FP index (*i.e.*, higher-priority) to the numerically larger ones, we defined them based on analysis of the specification documents and the original implementation of task interactions by inter-thread signalling.

The architectural model in TASTE format was automatically transformed into a BIP model and the task-graph model of the hyperperiod was derived. The task graph was passed to the static scheduler, which calculated the system load to be 112% (*i.e.*, at least two cores required, taking into account precedences [20] and interference [21]) and generated the static schedule.

The BIP model was compiled and linked with the BIP RTE and the executables were loaded and ran on the LEON4FT board. Figure 8 shows the measured Gantt chart of a hyper-period (500 ms) plus 100 ms. We label the process executions as 'P<id>', where '<id>' is a numeric process identifier. Label 'P20' is an exception, it indicates the execution of the BIP RTE engine and all discrete-event controllers – event generators, functional priority controllers, and the online

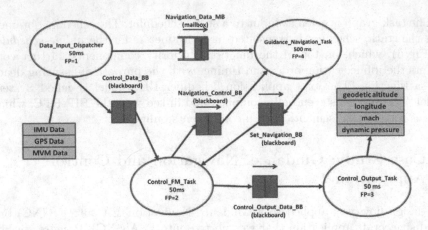

Fig. 7. The GNC FPPN model

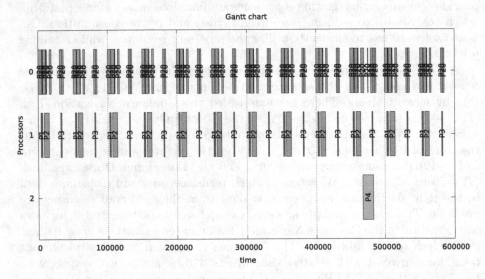

Fig. 8. Execution of the GNC application on LEON4FT (in microseconds).

scheduler. Since there are four discrete transitions per one job execution and 31 jobs per hyperperiod, $31 \times 4 = 124$ discrete transitions are executed by BIP RTE per hyperperiod. The P20 activities were mapped to Core 0, whereas the jobs of tasks (P1, P2, P3, P4) were mapped to Core 1 and Core 2. P1 stands for the Data Input Dispatcher, P2 for the Control FM, P3 for the Control Output and P4 for the Guidance Navigation task. Right after 10 consecutive jobs of P1, P2, P3 the job on P4 is executed. The job of P4 is delayed due to the 450 ms invocation offset and the least functional priority. Since P3 and P4 do not communicate via the channels, in our framework $(P3, P4) \notin \mathcal{FP}$ and they can execute in parallel, which was actually programmed in our static schedule. Due to more than 100% system load this was necessary for deadline satisfaction.

8 Conclusion

We presented the formal semantics of the FPPN model, at two levels: zero-delay semantics with precedence constraints on the job execution order to ensure functional determinism, and real-time semantics for scheduling. The semantics was implemented by a model transformational framework. Our approach was validated through a spacecraft on-board application running on a multi-core. In future work we consider it important to improve the efficiency of code generation, formal proofs of equivalence of the scheduling constraints (like the task graph) and the generated BIP model. The offline and online schedulers need to be enhanced to a wider spectrum of online policies and a better awareness of resource interference.

References

1. GR-CPCI-LEON4-N2X: Quad-core LEON4 next generation microprocessor evaluation board. http://www.gaisler.com/index.php/products/boards/gr-cpci-leon4-n2x
2. Multicore code generation for time-critical applications. http://www-verimag.imag.fr/Multicore-Time-Critical-Code,470.html
3. Abdellatif, T., Combaz, J., Sifakis, J.: Model-based implementation of real-time applications. In: EMSOFT 2010 (2010)
4. Chaki, S., Kyle, D.: DMPL: programming and verifying distributed mixed-synchrony and mixed-critical software. Technical report, Carnegie Mellon University (2016). http://www.andrew.cmu.edu/user/schaki/misc/dmpl-extended.pdf
5. Cordovilla, M., Boniol, F., Forget, J., Noulard, E., Pagetti, C.: Developing critical embedded systems on multicore architectures: the Prelude-SchedMCore toolset. In: RTNS (2011)
6. Eker, J., Janneck, J.W., Lee, E.A., Liu, J., Liu, X., Ludvig, J., Neuendorffer, S., Sachs, S., Xiong, Y.: Taming heterogeneity - the Ptolemy approach. Proc. IEEE 91(1), 127–144 (2003)
7. Feiler, P., Gluch, D., Hudak, J.: The architecture analysis & design language (AADL): an introduction. Technical report CMU/SEI-2006-TN-011, Software Engineering Institute, Carnegie Mellon University, Pittsburgh, PA (2006). http://resources.sei.cmu.edu/library/asset-view.cfm?AssetID=7879
8. Geilen, M., Basten, T.: Reactive process networks. In: EMSOFT 2004, pp. 137–146. ACM (2004)
9. Ghamarian, A.H.: Timing analysis of synchronous dataflow graphs. Ph.D. thesis, Eindhoven University of Technology (2008)
10. Giannopoulou, G., Poplavko, P., Socci, D., Huang, P., Stoimenov, N., Bourgos, P., Thiele, L., Bozga, M., Bensalem, S., Girbal, S., Faugere, M., Soulat, R., Dinechin, B.D.d.: DOL-BIP-Critical: a tool chain for rigorous design and implementation of mixed-criticality multi-core systems. Technical report (2016)
11. Ha, S., Kim, S., Lee, C., Yi, Y., Kwon, S., Joo, Y.P.: PeaCE: a hardware-software codesign environment for multimedia embedded systems. ACM Trans. Des. Autom. Electron. Syst. 12(3), 24:1–24:25 (2008)
12. Halbwachs, N.: Synchronous Programming of Reactive Systems. Springer, Berlin (2010). https://doi.org/10.1007/978-1-4757-2231-4

13. Hansson, A., Goossens, K., Bekooij, M., Huisken, J.: CoMPSoC: a template for composable and predictable multi-processor system on chips. ACM Trans. Des. Autom. Electron. Syst. (TODAES) **14**(1), 2 (2009)
14. Hugues, J., Zalila, B., Pautet, L., Kordon, F.: From the prototype to the final embedded system using the Ocarina AADL tool suite. ACM Trans. Embed. Comput. Syst. **7**(4), 42:1–42:25 (2008)
15. Johnston, W.M., Hanna, J.R.P., Millar, R.J.: Advances in dataflow programming languages. ACM Comput. Surv. **36**(1), 1–34 (2004)
16. Kahn, G.: The semantics of a simple language for parallel programming. In: Rosenfeld, J.L. (ed.) Information Processing 1974: Proceedings of the IFIP Congress, pp. 471–475. North-Holland, New York (1974)
17. Lee, E.A., Messerschmitt, D.G.: Static scheduling of synchronous data flow programs for digital signal processing. IEEE Trans. Comput. **C–36**(1), 24–35 (1987)
18. Lee, E.A., Messerschmitt, D.G.: Synchronous data flow. Proc. IEEE **75**(9), 1235–1245 (1987)
19. Perrotin, M., Conquet, E., Delange, J., Schiele, A., Tsiodras, T.: TASTE: a real-time software engineering tool-chain overview, status, and future. In: Ober, I., Ober, I. (eds.) SDL 2011. LNCS, vol. 7083, pp. 26–37. Springer, Heidelberg (2011). https://doi.org/10.1007/978-3-642-25264-8_4
20. Poplavko, P., Socci, D., Bourgos, P., Bensalem, S., Bozga, M.: Models for deterministic execution of real-time multiprocessor applications. In: DATE 2015, pp. 1665–1670. IEEE, March 2015
21. Poplavko, P., Kahil, R., Socci, D., Bensalem, S., Bozga, M.: Mixed-critical systems design with coarse-grained multi-core interference. In: Margaria, T., Steffen, B. (eds.) ISoLA 2016. LNCS, vol. 9952, pp. 605–621. Springer, Cham (2016). https://doi.org/10.1007/978-3-319-47166-2_42
22. Socci, D., Poplavko, P., Bensalem, S., Bozga, M.: A timed-automata based middleware for time-critical multicore applications. In: SEUS 2015, pp. 1–8. IEEE (2015)
23. Triki, A., Combaz, J., Bensalem, S., Sifakis, J.: Model-based implementation of parallel real-time systems. In: Cortellessa, V., Varró, D. (eds.) FASE 2013. LNCS, vol. 7793, pp. 235–249. Springer, Heidelberg (2013). https://doi.org/10.1007/978-3-642-37057-1_18
24. Waez, M.T.B., Dingel, J., Rudie, K.: A survey of timed automata for the development of real-time systems. Comput. Sci. Rev. **9**, 1–26 (2013)

Distributed Graph Queries for Runtime Monitoring of Cyber-Physical Systems

Márton Búr[1,3(✉)] Ⓘ, Gábor Szilágyi[2], András Vörös[1,2] Ⓘ,
and Dániel Varró[1,2,3] Ⓘ

[1] MTA-BME Lendület Cyber-Physical Systems Research Group, Budapest, Hungary
{bur,vori,varro}@mit.bme.hu
[2] Department of Measurement and Information Systems,
Budapest University of Technology and Economics, Budapest, Hungary
[3] Department of Electrical and Computer Engineering,
McGill University, Montreal, Canada

Abstract. In safety-critical cyber-physical systems (CPS), a service failure may result in severe financial loss or damage in human life. Smart CPSs have complex interaction with their environment which is rarely known in advance, and they heavily depend on intelligent data processing carried out over a heterogeneous computation platform and provide autonomous behavior. This complexity makes design time verification infeasible in practice, and many CPSs need advanced runtime monitoring techniques to ensure safe operation. While graph queries are a powerful technique used in many industrial design tools of CPSs, in this paper, we propose to use them to specify safety properties for runtime monitors on a high-level of abstraction. Distributed runtime monitoring is carried out by evaluating graph queries over a distributed runtime model of the system which incorporates domain concepts and platform information. We provide a semantic treatment of distributed graph queries using 3-valued logic. Our approach is illustrated and an initial evaluation is carried out using the MoDeS3 educational demonstrator of CPSs.

1 Introduction

A smart and safe cyber-physical system (CPS) [23,30,36] heavily depends on intelligent data processing carried out over a heterogeneous computation platform to provide autonomous behavior with complex interactions with an environment which is rarely known in advance. Such a complexity frequently makes design time verification be infeasible in practice, thus CPSs need to rely on run-time verification (RV) techniques to ensure safe operation by monitoring.

Traditionally, RV techniques have evolved from formal methods [24,26], which provide a high level of precision, but offer a low-level specification language (with simple atomic predicates to capture information about the system) which hinders their use in every day engineering practice. Recent RV approaches [17] started to exploit rule-based approaches over a richer information model.

A. Russo and A. Schürr (Eds.): FASE 2018, LNCS 10802, pp. 111–128, 2018.
https://doi.org/10.1007/978-3-319-89363-1_7

In this paper, we aim to address runtime monitoring of distributed systems from a different perspective by using runtime models (aka models@ runtime [8,38]) which have been promoted for the assurance of self-adaptive systems in [10,44]. The idea is that runtime models serve as a rich knowledge base for the system by capturing the runtime status of the domain, services and platforms as a graph model, which serves as a common basis for executing various analysis algorithms. Offering centralized runtime models accessible via the network, the Kevoree Modeling Framework [28] has been successfully applied in numerous Internet-of-Things applications over the Java platform. However, the use of such run-time models for analysis purposes in *resource-constrained* smart devices or critical CPS components is problematic due to the lack of control over the actual deployment of the model elements to the execution units of the platform.

Graph queries have already been applied in various design and analysis tools for CPSs thanks to their highly expressive declarative language, and their scalability to large industrial models [40]. Distributed graph query evaluation techniques have been proposed in [22,34], but all of these approaches use a cloud-based execution environment, and the techniques are not directly applicable for a heterogeneous execution platform with low-memory computation units.

As a *novelty* in our paper, we specify *safety criteria for runtime monitoring by graph queries* formulated over runtime models (with domain concepts, platform elements, and allocation as runtime information) where graph query results highlight model elements that violate a safety criterion. Graph queries are evaluated over a distributed runtime model where each model element is managed by a dedicated computing unit of the platform while relevant contextual information is communicated to neighboring computing units periodically via asynchronous messages. We provide a *semantic description for the distributed runtime model using 3-valued logic* to uniformly capture contextual uncertainty or message loss. Then we discuss how *graph queries can be deployed as a service to the computing units* (i.e., low-memory embedded devices) of the execution platform of the system in a distributed way, and provide precise *semantics of distributed graph query evaluation over our distributed runtime model*. We provide an *initial performance evaluation* of our distributed query technique over the MoDeS3 CPS demonstrator [45], which is an open source educational platform, and also compare its performance to an open graph query benchmark [35].

2   Overview of Distributed Runtime Monitoring

Figure 1 is an overview of distributed runtime monitoring of CPSs deployed over heterogeneous computing platform using runtime models and graph queries.

Our approach reuses a *high-level graph query language* [41] *for specifying safety properties of runtime monitors*, which language is widely used in various design tools of CPS [37]. Graph queries can capture safety properties with rich structural dependencies between system entities which is unprecedented in most temporal logic formalisms used for runtime monitoring. Similarly, OCL has been used in [20] for related purposes. While graph queries can be extended to express

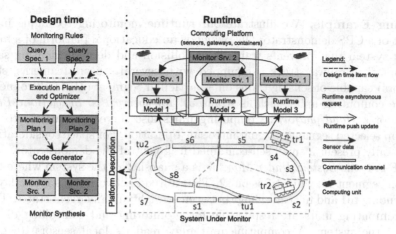

Fig. 1. Distributed runtime monitoring by graph queries

temporal behavior [11], our current work is restricted to (structural) safety properties where the violation of a property is expressible by graph queries.

These queries will be *evaluated over a runtime model which reflects the current state of the monitored system*, e.g. data received from different sensors, the services allocated to computing units, or the health information of computing infrastructure. In accordance with the models@ runtime paradigm [8,38], observable changes of the real system gets updated—either periodically with a certain frequency, or in an event-driven way upon certain triggers.

Runtime monitor programs are *deployed to a distributed heterogeneous computation platform*, which may include various types of computing units ranging from ultra-low-power microcontroller units, through smart devices to high-end cloud-based servers. These computation units primarily process the data provided by sensors and they are able to perform edge- or cloud-based computations based on the acquired information. The monitoring programs are deployed and executed on them exactly as the primary services of the system, thus resource restrictions (CPU, memory) need to be respected during allocation.

Runtime monitors are synthesized by *transforming high-level query specifications into deployable, platform dependent source code* for each computation unit used as part of a monitoring service. The synthesis includes a query optimization step and a code generation step to produce platform-dependent C++ source code ready to be compiled into an executable for the platform. Due to space restrictions, this component of our framework is not detailed in this paper.

Our system-level monitoring framework is hierarchical and distributed. Monitors may observe the local runtime model of the their own computing unit, and they can collect information from runtime models of different devices, hence providing a distributed monitoring architecture. Moreover, one monitor may rely on information computed by other monitors, thus yielding a hierarchical network.

Running Example. We illustrate our runtime monitoring technique in the context of a CPS demonstrator [45], which is an educational platform of a model railway system that prevents trains from collision and derailment using safety monitors. The railway track is equipped with several sensors (cameras, shunt detectors) capable of sensing trains on a particular segment of a track connected to some computing units, such as *Arduinos*, *Raspberry Pis*, *BeagleBone Blacks* (BBB), or a *cloud platform*. Computing units also serve as actuators to stop trains on selected segments to guarantee safe operation. For space considerations, we will only present a small self-contained fragment of the demonstrator.

In Fig. 1, the *System Under Monitor* is a snapshot of the system where train tr1 is on segment s4, while tr2 is on s2. The railroad network has a static layout, but turnouts tu1 and tu2 can change between straight and divergent states. Three BBB computing units are responsible for monitoring and controlling disjoint parts of the system. A computing unit may read its local sensors, (e.g. the occupancy of a segment, or the status of a turnout), collect information from other units during monitoring, and it can operate actuators accordingly (e.g. change turnout state) for the designated segment. All this information is reflected in the (distributed) runtime model which is deployed on the three computing units and available for the runtime monitors.

3   Towards Distributed Runtime Models

3.1   Runtime Models

Many industrial modeling tools used for engineering CPS [3,31,47] build on the concepts of domain-specific (modeling) languages (DSLs) where a domain is typically defined by a *metamodel* and a set of well-formedness constraints. A metamodel captures the main concepts in a domain as classes with attributes, their relations as references, and specifies the basic structure of graph models.

A metamodel can be formalized as a vocabulary $\Sigma = \{C_1, \ldots, C_{n_1}, A_1, \ldots, A_{n_2}, R_1, \ldots, R_{n_3}\}$ with a unary predicate symbol C_i for each class, a binary predicate symbol A_j for each attribute, and a binary predicate symbol R_k for each relation.

Example 1. Figure 2 shows a metamodel for the CPS demonstrator with Computing Units (identified on the network by hostID attribute) which host Domain Elements and communicate with other Computing Units. A Domain Element is either a Train or Railroad Element where the latter is either a Turnout or a Segment. A Train is situated on a Railroad Element which is connected to at most two other Railroad Elements. Furthermore, a Turnout refers to Railroad Elements connecting to its straight and divergent exits. A Train also knows its speed.

Objects, their attributes, and links between them constitute a runtime model [8,38] of the underlying system in operation. Changes to the system and its environment are reflected in the runtime model (in an event-driven or time-triggered way) and operations executed on the runtime model (e.g. setting values of controllable attributes or relations between objects) are reflected in the system

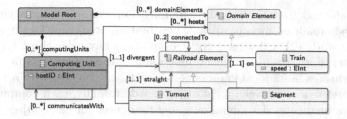

Fig. 2. Metamodel for CPS demonstrator

itself (e.g. by executing scripts or calling services). We assume that this runtime model is self-descriptive in the sense that it contains information about the computation platform and the allocation of services to platform elements, which is a key enabler for self-adaptive systems [10,44].

A *runtime model* $M = \langle Dom_M, \mathcal{I}_M \rangle$ can be formalized as a 2-valued logic structure over Σ where $Dom_M = Obj_M \sqcup Data_M$ where Obj_M is a finite set of objects, while $Data_M$ is the set of (built-in) data values (integers, strings, etc.). $\mathcal{I}_M$ is a 2-valued interpretation of predicate symbols in Σ defined as follows:

- **Class predicates:** If object o_p is an instance of class C_i then the 2-valued interpretation of C_i in M denoted by $[\![C_i(o_p)]\!]^M = 1$, otherwise 0.
- **Attribute predicates:** If there exists an attribute of type A_j in o_p with value a_r in M then $[\![A_j(o_p, a_r)]\!]^M = 1$, and otherwise 0.
- **Reference predicates:** If there is a link of type R_k from o_p to o_q in M then $[\![R_k(o_p, o_q)]\!]^M = 1$, otherwise 0.

3.2   Distributed Runtime Models

Our framework addresses decentralized systems where each computing unit periodically communicates a part of its internal state to its neighbors in an *update phase*. We abstract from the technical details of communication, but we assume approximate synchrony [13] between the clocks of computing units, thus all update messages regarded lost that does not arrive within given timeframe T_{update}.

As such, a centralized runtime model is not a realistic assumption for mixed synchronous systems. First, each computing unit has only incomplete knowledge about the system: it fully observes and controls a fragment of the runtime model (to enforce the single source of truth principle), while it is unaware of the internal state of objects hosted by other computing units. Moreover, uncertainty may arise in the runtime model due to sensing or communication issues.

Semantics of Distributed Runtime Models. We extend the concept of runtime models to a distributed setting with heterogeneous computing units which periodically communicate certain model elements with each other via messages. We introduce a semantic representation for *distributed runtime models* (DRMs) which can abstract from the actual communication semantics (e.g. asynchronous messages vs. broadcast messages) by (1) evaluating predicates locally at a computing unit with (2) a 3-valued truth evaluation having a third $1/2$ value in case of uncertainty. Each computing unit maintains a set of facts described by atomic predicates in its local knowledge base wrt. the objects with attributes it hosts, and references between local objects. Additionally, each computing unit incorporates predicates describing outgoing references for each object it hosts.

The 3-valued truth evaluation of a predicate $P(v_1, \ldots, v_n)$ on a computing unit cu is denoted by $[\![P(v_1, \ldots, v_n)]\!]@cu$. The DRM of the system is constituted from the truth evaluation of all predicates on all computing units. For the current paper, we assume the single source of truth principle, i.e. each model element is always faithfully observed and controlled by its host computing unit, thus the local truth evaluation of the corresponding predicate P is always 1 or 0. However, 3-valued evaluation could be extended to handle such local uncertainties.

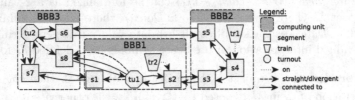

Fig. 3. Distributed runtime model for CPS demonstrator

Example 2. Figure 3 shows a DRM snapshot for the CPS demonstrator (bottom part of Fig. 1). Computing units BBB1–BBB3 manage different parts of the system, e.g. BBB1 hosts objects s1, s2, tu1 and tr2 and the links between them. We illustrate the local knowledge bases of computing units.

Since computing unit BBB1 hosts train tr2, thus $[\![\texttt{Train(tr2)}]\!]@\text{BBB1} = 1$. However, according to computing module BBB2, $[\![\texttt{Train(tr2)}]\!]@\text{BBB2} = 1/2$ as there is no train tr2 hosted on BBB2, but it may exist on a different one.

Similarly, $[\![\texttt{ConnectedTo(s1, s7)}]\!]@\text{BBB1} = 1$, as BBB1 is the host of s1, the source of the reference. This means BBB1 knows that there is a (directed) reference of type connectedTo from s1 to s7. However, the knowledge base on BBB3 may have uncertain information about this link, thus $[\![\texttt{ConnectedTo(s1, s7)}]\!]@\text{BBB3} = 1/2$, i.e. there may be a corresponding link from s1 to s7, but it cannot be deduced using exclusively the predicates evaluated at BBB3.

4   Distributed Runtime Monitoring

4.1   Graph Queries for Specifying Safety Monitors

To capture the safety properties to be monitored, we rely on the VIATRA Query Language (VQL) [7]. VIATRA has been intensively used in various design tools of CPSs to provide scalable queries over large system models. The current paper aims to reuse this declarative graph query language for runtime verification purposes, which is a novel idea. The main benefit is that safety properties can be captured on a high level of abstraction over the runtime model, which eases the definition and comprehension of safety monitors for engineers. Moreover, this specification is free from any platform-specific or deployment details.

The expressiveness of the VQL language converges to first-order logic with transitive closure, thus it provides a rich language for capturing a variety of complex structural conditions and dependencies. Technically, a graph query captures the erroneous case, when evaluating the query over a runtime model. Thus any match (result) of a query highlights a violation of the safety property at runtime.

Example 3. In the railway domain, safety standards prescribe a minimum distance between trains on track [1,14]. Query closeTrains captures a (simplified) description of the minimum headway distance to identify violating situations where trains have only limited space between each other. Technically, one needs to detect if there are two different trains on two different railroad elements, which are connected by a third railroad element. Any match of this pattern highlights track elements where passing trains need to be stopped immediately. Figure 4a shows the graph query closeTrains in a textual syntax, Fig. 4b displays it as a graph formula, and Fig. 4c is a graphical illustration as a graph pattern.

Syntax. Formally, a graph pattern (or query) is a first order logic (FOL) formula $\varphi(v_1, \ldots, v_n)$ over variables [42]. A graph pattern φ can be inductively constructed (see Table 1) by using atomic predicates of runtime models $C(v)$, $A(v_1, v_2)$, $R(v_1, v_2)$, $C, A, R \in \Sigma$, equality between variables $v_1 = v_2$, FOL connectives $\vee, \wedge$, quantifiers $\exists, \forall$, and positive (*call*) or negative (*neg*) pattern calls.

```
pattern closeTrains (
  St  : RailroadElement ,
  End : RailroadElement)
{
  Train.on(T,St);
  Train.on(OT,End);
  T != OT;
  RailroadElement.connectedTo(St, Mid);

  RailroadElement.connectedTo(Mid, End);
  St != End;
}
```

$$CloseTrains(St, End) =$$
$$RailroadElement(St) \wedge$$
$$RailroadElement(End) \wedge$$
$$\exists T : Train(T) \wedge On(T, St) \wedge$$
$$\exists OT : Train(OT) \wedge On(OT, End) \wedge$$
$$\neg (T = OT) \wedge$$
$$\exists Mid : RailroadElement(Mid) \wedge$$
$$ConnectedTo(St, Mid) \wedge$$
$$ConnectedTo(Mid, End) \wedge$$
$$\neg (St = End)$$

(a) Graph query in the VIATRA Query Language   (b) Query as formula

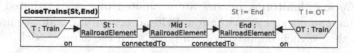

(c) Graphical query representation

Fig. 4. Safety monitoring objective closeTrains specified as graph pattern

Table 1. Semantics of graph patterns (predicates)

---

1. $[\![\texttt{C}(v)]\!]^M_Z \mathcal{I}_M(\texttt{C})(Z(v))$

2. $[\![\texttt{A}(v_1, v_2)]\!]^M_Z \mathcal{I}_M(\texttt{A})(Z(v_1), Z(v_2))$

3. $[\![\texttt{R}(v_1, v_2)]\!]^M_Z \mathcal{I}_M(\texttt{R})(Z(v_1), Z(v_2))$

4. $[\![\exists v : \varphi]\!]^M_Z \max\{[\![\varphi]\!]^M_{Z,v \mapsto x} : x \in Obj_M\}$

5. $[\![\forall v : \varphi]\!]^M_Z \min\{[\![\varphi]\!]^M_{Z,v \mapsto x} : x \in Obj_M\}$

6. $[\![v_1 = v_2]\!]^M_Z 1$ iff $Z(v_1) = Z(v_2)$

7. $[\![\varphi_1 \wedge \varphi_2]\!]^M_Z \min([\![\varphi_1]\!]^M_Z, [\![\varphi_2]\!]^M_Z)$

8. $[\![\varphi_1 \vee \varphi_2]\!]^M_Z \max([\![\varphi_1]\!]^M_Z, [\![\varphi_2]\!]^M_Z)$

9. $[\![\neg\varphi]\!]^M_Z 1 - [\![\varphi]\!]^M_Z$

10. $[\![call(\varphi(v_1, \ldots, v_n))]\!]^M_Z \begin{cases} \exists Z' : Z \subseteq Z' \wedge \forall_{i \in 1..n} : \\ Z'(v_i^c) = Z(v_i) : [\![\varphi(v_1^c, \ldots, v_n^c)]\!]^M_{Z'} \end{cases}$

11. $[\![neg(\varphi(v_1, \ldots, v_n))]\!]^M_Z 1 - [\![call(\varphi(v_1, \ldots, v_n))]\!]^M_Z$

This language enables to specify a hierarchy of runtime monitors as a query may explicitly use results of other queries (along pattern calls). Furthermore, distributed evaluation will exploit a spatial hierarchy between computing units.

Semantics. A graph pattern $\varphi(v_1, \ldots, v_n)$ can be evaluated over a (centralized) runtime model M (denoted by $[\![\varphi(v_1, \ldots, v_n)]\!]^M_Z$) along a variable binding $Z : \{v_1, \ldots, v_n\} \to Dom_M$ from variables to objects and data values in M in accordance with the semantic rules defined in Table 1 [42].

A variable binding Z is called a *match* if pattern φ is evaluated to 1 over M, i.e. $[\![\varphi(v_1, \ldots, v_n)]\!]^M_Z = 1$. Below, we may use $[\![\varphi(v_1, \ldots, v_n)]\!]$ as a shorthand for $[\![\varphi(v_1, \ldots, v_n)]\!]^M_Z$ when M and Z are clear from context. Note that min and max take the numeric minimum and maximum values of 0, $1/2$ and 1 with $0 \leq 1/2 \leq 1$.

4.2 Execution of Distributed Runtime Monitors

To evaluate graph queries of runtime monitors in a distributed setting, we propose to deploy queries to the same target platform in a way that is compliant with the distributed runtime model and the potential resource restrictions of computation units. If a graph query engine is deployed as a service on a computing unit, it can serve as a *local monitor* over the runtime model. However, such local monitors are usable only when all graph nodes traversed and retrieved during query evaluation are deployed on the same computing unit, which is not the general case. Therefore, a *distributed monitor* needs to gather information from other model fragments and monitors stored at different computing units.

A Query Cycle. Monitoring queries are evaluated over a distributed runtime model during the *query cycle*, where individual computing units communicate with each other asynchronously in accordance with the actor model [18].

- A monitoring service can be initiated (or scheduled) at a designated computing unit cu by requesting the evaluation of a graph query with at least one unbound variable denoted as $[\![\varphi(v_1, \ldots, v_n)]\!]@cu =?$.
- A computing unit attempts to evaluate a query over its local runtime model.

- If any links of its local runtime model point to a fragment stored at a neighboring computing unit, or if a subpattern call is initiated, corresponding query $R(v_1, v_2)$, $call(\varphi)$ or $neg(\varphi)$ needs to be evaluated at all neighbors cu_i.
- Such calls to distributed monitors are carried out by sending asynchronous messages to each other thus graph queries are evaluated in a distributed way along the computing platform. First, the requester cu_r sends a message of the form "$[\![\varphi(v_1,\ldots,v_n)]\!]@cu_p =?$". The provider cu_p needs to send back a reply which contains further information about the internal state or previous monitoring results of the provider which contains all *potential* matches known by cu_p, i.e. all bindings $[\![\varphi(o_1,\ldots,o_n)]\!]@cu_p \geq 1/2$ (where we abbreviated the binding $v_i \mapsto o_i$ into the predicate as a notational shortcut).
- Matches of predicates sent as a reply to a computing unit can be cached.
- Messages may get delayed due to network traffic and they are considered to be lost by the requester if no reply arrives within a deadline. Such a case introduces uncertainty in the truth evaluation of predicates, i.e. the requestor cu_r stores $[\![\varphi]\!]@cu_p = 1/2$ in its cache, if the reply of the provider cu_p is lost.
- After acquiring truth values of predicates from its neighbors, a computing unit needs to decide on a single truth value for each predicate evaluated along different variable bindings. This local decision will be detailed below.
- At the end of the query cycle, each computing unit resets its cache to remove information acquired within the last cycle.

Example 4. Figure 5 shows the beginning of a query evaluation sequence for monitor closeTrains initiated at computing unit BBB3. Calls are asynchronous (cf. actor model), while diagonal lines illustrate the latency of network communication. Message numbers represent the order between timestamps of messages.

When the query is initiated (message 1, shortly, m1), and the first predicate Train of the query is sent to the other two computing unit as requests with a free variable parameter T (m2 and m3). In the reply messages, BBB2 reports tr1 as an object satisfying the predicate (m4), while BBB1 answers that tr2 is a suitable binding to T (m5). Next BBB3 is requesting facts about outgoing

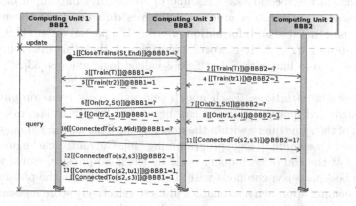

Fig. 5. Beginning of distributed query execution for monitor closeTrains

references of type On leading from objects tr2 and tr1 to objects stored in BBB1 and BBB2, respectively (m6 and m7). As the answer, each computing unit sends back facts stating outgoing references from the objects (m8 and m9).

The next message (m10) asks for outgoing references of type ConnectedTo from object s2. To send a reply, first BBB1 asks BBB2 to ensure that a reference from s2 to s3 exists, since s3 is hosted by BBB2 (m11). This check adds tolerance against lost messages during model update. After BBB1 receives the answer from BBB2 (m12), it replies to BBB3 containing all facts maintained on this node.

Semantics of Distributed Query Evaluation. Each query is initiated at a designated computing unit which will be responsible for calculating query results by aggregating the partial results retrieved from its neighbors. This aggregation has two different dimensions: (1) adding new matches to the result set calculated by the provider, and (2) making a potential match more precise. While the first case is a consequence of the distributed runtime model and query evaluation, the second case is caused by uncertain information caused by message loss/delay.

Fortunately, the 3-valued semantics of graph queries (see Table 1) already handles the first case: any match reported to the requester by any neighboring provider will be included in the query results if its truth evaluation is 1 or $1/2$. As such, any potential violation of a safety property will be detected, which may result in false positive alerts but critical situations would not be missed.

However, the second case necessitates extra care since query matches coming from different sources (e.g. local cache, reply messages from providers) need to be fused in a consistent way. This match fusion is carried out at cu as follows:

- If a match is obtained exclusively from the local runtime model of cu, then it is a certain match, formally $[\![\varphi(o_1, \ldots, o_n)]\!]@cu = 1$.
- If a match is sent as a reply by multiple neighboring computing units cu_i (with $cu_i \in nbr(cu)$), then we take the most certain result at cu, formally, $[\![\varphi(o_1, \ldots, o_n)]\!]@cu := \underline{\max}\{[\![\varphi(o_1, \ldots, o_n)]\!]@cu_i | cu_i \in nbr(cu)\}$.
- Otherwise, tuple $o_1, \ldots, o_n$ is surely not a match: $[\![\varphi(o_1, \ldots, o_n)]\!]@cu = 0$.

Note that in the second case uses $\underline{\max}\{\}$ to assign a maximum of 3-valued logic values wrt. *information ordering* (which is different from the numerical maximum used in Table 1). Information ordering is a partial order $(\{1/2, 0, 1\}, \sqsubseteq)$ with $1/2 \sqsubseteq 0$ and $1/2 \sqsubseteq 1$. It is worth pointing out that this distributed truth evaluation is also in line with Sobociński 3-valued logic axioms [33].

Performance Optimizations. Each match sent as a reply to a computing unit during distributed query evaluation can be cached locally to speed up the re-evaluation of the same query within the query cycle. This *caching of query results* is analogous to *memoing* in logic programming [46]. Currently, cache invalidation is triggered at the end of each query cycle by the local physical clock, which we assume to be (quasi-)synchronous with high precision across the platform.

This memoing approach also enables units to selectively store messages in the local cache depending on their specific needs. Furthermore, this can incorporate to deploy query services to computing units with limited amount of memory and prevent memory overflow due to the several messages sent over the network.

A graph query is evaluated according to a *search plan* [43], which is a list of predicates ordered in a way that matches of predicates can be found efficiently. During query evaluation, free variables of the predicates are bound to a value following the search plan. The evaluation terminates when all matches in the model are found. An in-depth discussion of query optimization is out of scope for this paper, but Sect. 5 will provide an initial investigation.

Semantic Guarantees and Limitations. Our construction ensures that (1) the execution will surely terminate upon reaching the end of the query time window, potentially yielding uncertain matches, (2) each local model serves as a single source of truth which cannot be overridden by calls to other computing units, and (3) matches obtained from multiple computing units will be fused by preserving information ordering. The over- and under approximation properties of 3-valued logic show that the truth values fused this way will provide a sound result (Theorem 1 in [42]). Despite the lack of total consistency, our approach still has safety guarantees by detecting all *potentially* unsafe situations.

There are also several assumptions and limitations of our approach. We use asynchronous communication without broadcast messages. We only assumed faults of communication links, but not the failures of computing units. We also excluded the case when computing units maliciously send false information. Instead of refreshing local caches in each cycle, the runtime model could incorporate information aging which may enable to handle other sources of uncertainty (which is currently limited to consequences of message loss). Finally, in case of longer cycles, the runtime model may no longer provide up-to-date information at query evaluation time.

Implementation Details. The concepts presented in the paper are implemented in a prototype software, which has three main components: (i) an EMF-based tool [39] for data modeling and code generation for the runtime model, (ii) an Eclipse-based tool for defining and compiling monitoring rules built on top of the VIATRA framework [41], and (iii) the runtime environment to evaluate queries.

The design tools are dominantly implemented in Java. We used EMF metamodels for data modeling, but created a code generator to derive lightweight C++ classes as representations of the runtime model. The query definition environment was extended to automatically compile queries into C++ monitors.

The runtime monitoring libraries and the runtime framework is available in C++. Our choice of C++ is motivated by its low runtime and memory overhead on almost any type of platforms, ranging from low-energy embedded microcontrollers to large-scale cloud environments. Technically, a generic *query service* can start *query runners* for each monitoring objective on each node. While query runners execute the query-specific search plan generated compile time, the network communication is handled by a query service if needed. To serialize the data between different nodes, we used the lightweight Protocol Buffers [16].

5   Evaluation

We conducted measurements to evaluate and address two research questions:

Q1: How does distributed graph query execution perform compared to executing the queries on a single computing unit?

Q2: Is query evaluation performance affected by alternative allocation of model objects to host computing units?

5.1   Measurement Setup

Computation Platform. We used the real distributed (physical) platform of the CPS demonstrator to answer these research questions (instead of setting up a virtual environment). It consists of 6 interconnected BBB devices (all running embedded Debian Jessie with PREEMPT-RT patch) connected to the railway track itself. This arrangement represents a distributed CPS with several computing units having only limited computation and communication resources. We used these units to maintain the distributed runtime model, and evaluate monitoring queries. This way we are able to provide a realistic evaluation, however, due to the fixed number of embedded devices built into the platform, we cannot evaluate the scalability of the approach wrt. the number of computing units.

CPS Monitoring Benchmark. To assess the distributed runtime verification framework, we used the MoDeS3 railway CPS demonstrator where multiple *safety properties* are monitored. They are all based on important aspects of the domain, and they have been integrated into the real monitoring components. Our properties of interest (in increasing complexity of queries) are the following:

- *Train locations*: gets all trains and the segments on which trains are located.
- *Close trains*: this pattern is the one introduced in Fig. 4.
- *Derailment*: detects the train when approaching a turnout, but the turnout is set to the other direction (causing the train to run off from the track).
- *End of siding*: detects trains approaching an end of the track.

Since the original runtime model of the CPS demonstrator has only a total of 49 objects, we scaled up the model by replicating the original elements (except for the computing units). This way we obtained models with 49–43006 objects and 114–109015 links, having similar structural properties as the original one.

Query Evaluation Benchmark. In order to provide an independent evaluation for our model query-based monitoring approach, we adapted the open-source Train Benchmark [35] that aims at comparing query evaluation performance of various tools. This benchmark defines several queries describing violations of well-formedness constraints with different complexity over graph models. Moreover, it also provides a model generator to support scalability assessment.

5.2 Measurement Results

Execution Times. The query execution times over models deployed to a single BBB were first measured to obtain a *baseline evaluation time of monitoring* for each rule (referred to as *local* evaluation). Then the execution times of system-level distributed queries were measured over the platform with 6 BBBs, evaluating two different allocations of objects (*standard* and *alternative* evaluations).

In Fig. 6 each result captures the times of 29 consecutive evaluations of queries excluding the warm-up effect of an initial run which loads the model and creates necessary auxiliary objects. A query execution starts when a node initiates evaluation, and terminates when all nodes have finished collecting matches and sent back their results to the initiator.

Overhead of Distributed Evaluation. On the positive side, the performance of graph query evaluation on a single unit is comparable to other graph query techniques reported in [35] for models with over 100 K objects, which shows a certain level of maturity of our prototype. Furthermore, the CPS demonstrator showed that distributed query evaluation yielded significantly better result than local-only execution for the *Derailment* query on medium size models (with 4K–43K objects reaching $2.23\times - 2.45\times$ average speed-up) and comparable runtime for *Close trains* and *Train locations* queries on these models (with the greatest average difference being 30 ms across all model sizes). However, distributed query evaluation had problems for *End of siding*, which is a complex query with negative application conditions, which provides clear directions for future research. Anyhow, the parallelism

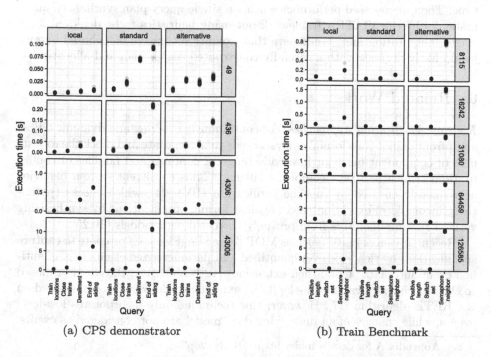

(a) CPS demonstrator   (b) Train Benchmark

Fig. 6. Query evaluations times over different model sizes

of even a small execution platform with only 6 computing units could suppress the communication overhead between units in case of several distributed queries, which is certainly a promising outcome.

Impact of Allocation on Query Evaluation. We synthesized different allocations of model elements to computing units to investigate the impact of allocation of model objects on query evaluation. With the CPS demonstrator model in particular, we chose to allocate all Trains to BBB1, and assigned every other node stored previously on BBB1 to the rest of the computing units. Similarly, for the Train Benchmark models, we followed this pattern with selected types, in addition to experimenting with fully random allocation of objects.

The two right-most columns of Fig. 6a and 6b show results of two alternate allocations for the same search plan with a peak difference of 2.06× (*Derailment*) and 19.92× (*Semaphore neighbor*) in the two cases. However, both of these allocations were manually optimized to exploit locality of model elements. In case of random allocations, difference in runtime may reach an order of magnitude[1]. Therefore it is worth investigating new allocation strategies and search plans for distributed queries for future work.

Threats to Validity. The generalizability of our experimental results is limited by certain factors. First, to measure the performance of our approach, the platform devices (1) executed only query services and (2) connected to an isolated local area network via Ethernet. Performance on a real network with a busy channel would likely have longer delays and message losses thus increasing execution time. Then we assessed performance using a single query plan synthesized automatically by the VIATRA framework but using heuristics to be deployed for a single computation unit. We believe that execution times of distributed queries would likely decrease with a carefully constructed search plan and allocation.

6   Related Work

Runtime Verification Approaches. For continuously evolving and dynamic CPSs, an upfront design-time formal analysis needs to incorporate and check the robustness of component behavior in a wide range of contexts and families of configurations, which is a very complex challenge. Thus consistent system behavior is frequently ensured by runtime verification (RV) [24], which checks (potentially incomplete) execution traces against formal specifications by synthesizing verified runtime monitors from provenly correct design models [21,26].

Recent advances in RV (such as MOP [25] or LogFire [17]) promote to capture specifications by rich logic over quantified and parameterized events (e.g. quantified event automata [4] and their extensions [12]). Moreover, Havelund proposed to check such specifications on-the-fly by exploiting rule-based systems based on the RETE algorithm [17]. However, this technique only incorporates low-level events; while changes of an underlying data model are not considered as events.

---

[1] See Appendix A for details under http://bit.ly/2op3tdy.

Traditional RV approaches use variants of temporal logics to capture the requirements [6]. Recently, novel combinations of temporal logics with context-aware behaviour description [15,19] (developed within the R3-COP and R5-COP FP7 projects) for the runtime verification of autonomous CPS appeared and provide a rich language to define correctness properties of evolving systems.

Runtime Verification of Distributed Systems. While there are several existing techniques for runtime verification of sequential programs available, the authors of [29] claim that much less research was done in this area for distributed systems. Furthermore, they provide the first sound and complete algorithm for runtime monitoring of distributed systems based on the 3-valued semantics of LTL.

The recently introduced Brace framework [49] supports RV in distributed resource-constrained environments by incorporating dedicated units in the system to support global evaluation of monitoring goals. There is also focus on evaluating LTL formulae in a fully distributed manner in [5] for components communicating on a synchronous bus in a real-time system. Additionally, machine learning-based solution for scalable fault detection and diagnosis system is presented in [2] that builds on correlation between observable system properties.

Distributed Graph Queries. Highly efficient techniques for local-search based [9] and incremental model queries [40] as part of the VIATRA framework were developed, which mainly builds on RETE networks as baseline technology. In [34], a distributed incremental graph query layer deployed over a cloud infrastructure with numerous optimizations was developed. Distributed graph query evaluation techniques were reported in [22,27,32], but none of these techniques considered an execution environment with resource-constrained computation units.

Runtime Models. The models@ runtime paradigm [8] serves as the conceptual basis for the Kevoree framework [28] (developed within the HEADS FP7 project). Other recent distributed, data-driven solutions include the Global Data Plane [48] and executable metamodels at runtime [44]. However, these frameworks currently offer very limited support for efficiently evaluating queries over a distributed runtime platform, which is the main focus of our current work.

7   Conclusions

In this paper, we proposed a runtime verification technique for smart and safe CPSs by using a high-level graph query language to capture safety properties for runtime monitoring and runtime models as a rich knowledge representation to capture the current state of the running system. A distributed query evaluation technique was introduced where none of the computing units has a global view of the complete system. The approach was implemented and evaluated on the physical system of MoDeS3 CPS demonstrator. Our first results show that it scales for medium-size runtime models, and the actual deployment of the query components to the underlying platform has significant impact on execution time. In the future, we plan to investigate how to characterize effective search plans and allocations in the context of distributed queries used for runtime monitoring.

Acknowledgements. This paper is partially supported by MTA-BME Lendület Cyber-Physical Systems Research Group, the NSERC RGPIN-04573-16 project, the Werner Graupe International Fellowship in Engineering (as part of the MEDA program), and the ÚNKP-17-2-I New National Excellence Program of the Ministry of Human Capacities. We are grateful for Oszkár Semeráth for helping with the semantics of 3-valued logic, Gábor Szárnyas for the help with setting up Train Benchmark, the contributors of MoDeS3 for setting up the evaluation platform, and the feedback from anonymous reviewers and Gábor Bergmann.

References

1. Abril, M., et al.: An assessment of railway capacity. Transp. Res. Part E Logist. Transp. Rev. **44**(5), 774–806 (2008)
2. Alippi, C., et al.: Model-free fault detection and isolation in large-scale cyber-physical systems. IEEE Trans. Emerg. Top. Comput. Intell. **1**(1), 61–71 (2017)
3. AUTOSAR Tool Platform: Artop. https://www.artop.org/
4. Barringer, H., Falcone, Y., Havelund, K., Reger, G., Rydeheard, D.: Quantified event automata: towards expressive and efficient runtime monitors. In: Giannakopoulou, D., Méry, D. (eds.) FM 2012. LNCS, vol. 7436, pp. 68–84. Springer, Heidelberg (2012). https://doi.org/10.1007/978-3-642-32759-9_9
5. Bauer, A., Falcone, Y.: Decentralised LTL monitoring. Formal Methods Syst. Des. **48**(1–2), 46–93 (2016)
6. Bauer, A., Leucker, M., Schallhart, C.: Runtime verification for LTL and TLTL. ACM Trans. Softw. Eng. Methodol. **20**(4), 14 (2011)
7. Bergmann, G., Ujhelyi, Z., Ráth, I., Varró, D.: A graph query language for EMF models. In: Cabot, J., Visser, E. (eds.) ICMT 2011. LNCS, vol. 6707, pp. 167–182. Springer, Heidelberg (2011). https://doi.org/10.1007/978-3-642-21732-6_12
8. Blair, G.S., et al.: Models@run.time. IEEE Comput. **42**(10), 22–27 (2009)
9. Búr, M., Ujhelyi, Z., Horváth, Á., Varró, D.: Local search-based pattern matching features in EMF-INCQUERY. In: Parisi-Presicce, F., Westfechtel, B. (eds.) ICGT 2015. LNCS, vol. 9151, pp. 275–282. Springer, Cham (2015). https://doi.org/10.1007/978-3-319-21145-9_18
10. Cheng, B.H.C., et al.: Using models at runtime to address assurance for self-adaptive systems. In: Bencomo, N., France, R., Cheng, B.H.C., Aßmann, U. (eds.) Models@run.time. LNCS, vol. 8378, pp. 101–136. Springer, Cham (2014). https://doi.org/10.1007/978-3-319-08915-7_4
11. Dávid, I., Ráth, I., Varró, D.: Foundations for streaming model transformations by complex event processing. Softw. Syst. Model. **17**, 1–28 (2016). https://doi.org/10.1007/s10270-016-0533-1
12. Decker, N., Leucker, M., Thoma, D.: Monitoring modulo theories. Int. J. Softw. Tools Technol. Transf. **18**(2), 205–225 (2015)
13. Desai, A., Seshia, S.A., Qadeer, S., Broman, D., Eidson, J.C.: Approximate synchrony: an abstraction for distributed almost-synchronous systems. In: Kroening, D., Păsăreanu, C.S. (eds.) CAV 2015. LNCS, vol. 9207, pp. 429–448. Springer, Cham (2015). https://doi.org/10.1007/978-3-319-21668-3_25
14. Emery, D.: Headways on high speed lines. In: 9th World Congress on Railway Research, pp. 22–26 (2011)
15. Gönczy, L., et al.: MDD-based design, configuration, and monitoring of resilient cyber-physical systems. Trustworthy Cyber-Physical Systems Engineering (2016)
16. Google: Protocol buffers. https://github.com/google/protobuf

17. Havelund, K.: Rule-based runtime verification revisited. Int. J. Softw. Tools Technol. Transf. **17**(2), 143–170 (2015)
18. Hewitt, C., et al.: A universal modular ACTOR formalism for artificial intelligence. In: International Joint Conference on Artificial Intelligence, pp. 235–245 (1973)
19. Horányi, G., Micskei, Z., Majzik, I.: Scenario-based automated evaluation of test traces of autonomous systems. In: DECS workshop at SAFECOMP (2013)
20. Iqbal, M.Z., et al.: Applying UML/MARTE on industrial projects: challenges, experiences, and guidelines. Softw. Syst. Model. **14**(4), 1367–1385 (2015)
21. Joshi, Y., et al.: Runtime verification of LTL on lossy traces. In: Proceedings of the Symposium on Applied Computing - SAC 2017, pp. 1379–1386. ACM Press (2017)
22. Krause, C., Tichy, M., Giese, H.: Implementing graph transformations in the bulk synchronous parallel model. In: Gnesi, S., Rensink, A. (eds.) FASE 2014. LNCS, vol. 8411, pp. 325–339. Springer, Heidelberg (2014). https://doi.org/10.1007/978-3-642-54804-8_23
23. Krupitzer, C., et al.: A survey on engineering approaches for self-adaptive systems. Perv. Mob. Comput. **17**, 184–206 (2015)
24. Leucker, M., Schallhart, C.: A brief account of runtime verification. J. Log. Algebr. Program. **78**(5), 293–303 (2009)
25. Meredith, P.O., et al.: An overview of the MOP runtime verification framework. Int. J. Softw. Tools Technol. Transf. **14**(3), 249–289 (2012)
26. Mitsch, S., Platzer, A.: ModelPlex: verified runtime validation of verified cyber-physical system models. In: Bonakdarpour, B., Smolka, S.A. (eds.) RV 2014. LNCS, vol. 8734, pp. 199–214. Springer, Cham (2014). https://doi.org/10.1007/978-3-319-11164-3_17
27. Mitschke, R., Erdweg, S., Köhler, M., Mezini, M., Salvaneschi, G.: i3QL: Language-integrated live data views. ACM SIGPLAN Not. **49**(10), 417–432 (2014)
28. Morin, B., et al.: Kevoree Modeling Framework (KMF): efficient modeling techniques for runtime use. University of Luxembourg, Technical report (2014)
29. Mostafa, M., Bonakdarpour, B.: Decentralized runtime verification of LTL specifications in distributed systems. In: 2015 IEEE International Parallel and Distributed Processing Symposium, pp. 494–503, May 2015
30. Nielsen, C.B., et al.: Systems of systems engineering: Basic concepts, model-based techniques, and research directions. ACM Comput. Surv. **48**(2), 18 (2015)
31. No Magic: MagicDraw. https://www.nomagic.com/products/magicdraw
32. Peters, M., Brink, C., Sachweh, S., Zündorf, A.: Scaling parallel rule-based reasoning. In: Presutti, V., d'Amato, C., Gandon, F., d'Aquin, M., Staab, S., Tordai, A. (eds.) ESWC 2014. LNCS, vol. 8465, pp. 270–285. Springer, Cham (2014). https://doi.org/10.1007/978-3-319-07443-6_19
33. Sobociński, B.: Axiomatization of a Partial System of Three-Value Calculus of Propositions. Institute of Applied Logic (1952)
34. Szárnyas, G., Izsó, B., Ráth, I., Harmath, D., Bergmann, G., Varró, D.: IncQuery-D: a distributed incremental model query framework in the cloud. In: Dingel, J., Schulte, W., Ramos, I., Abrahão, S., Insfran, E. (eds.) MODELS 2014. LNCS, vol. 8767, pp. 653–669. Springer, Cham (2014). https://doi.org/10.1007/978-3-319-11653-2_40
35. Szárnyas, G., et al.: The Train Benchmark: cross-technology performance evaluation of continuous model queries. Softw. Syst. Model., 1–29 (2017). https://doi.org/10.1007/s10270-016-0571-8
36. Sztipanovits, J., et al.: Toward a science of cyber-physical system integration. Proc. IEEE **100**(1), 29–44 (2012)

37. Sztipanovits, J., Bapty, T., Neema, S., Howard, L., Jackson, E.: OpenMETA: a model- and component-based design tool chain for cyber-physical systems. In: Bensalem, S., Lakhneck, Y., Legay, A. (eds.) ETAPS 2014. LNCS, vol. 8415, pp. 235–248. Springer, Heidelberg (2014). https://doi.org/10.1007/978-3-642-54848-2_16

38. Szvetits, M., Zdun, U.: Systematic literature review of the objectives, techniques, kinds, and architectures of models at runtime. Softw. Syst. Model. 15(1), 31–69 (2013)

39. The Eclipse Project: Eclipse Modeling Framework. http://www.eclipse.org/emf

40. Ujhelyi, Z., et al.: EMF-IncQuery: an integrated development environment for live model queries. Sci. Comput. Program. 98, 80–99 (2015)

41. Varró, D., et al.: Road to a reactive and incremental model transformation platform: three generations of the VIATRA framework. Softw. Syst. Model 15(3), 609–629 (2016)

42. Varró, D., Semeráth, O., Szárnyas, G., Horváth, Á.: Towards the automated generation of consistent, diverse, scalable and realistic graph models. In: Heckel, R., Taentzer, G. (eds.) Graph Transformation, Specifications, and Nets. LNCS, vol. 10800, pp. 285–312. Springer, Cham (2018). https://doi.org/10.1007/978-3-319-75396-6_16

43. Varró, G., et al.: An algorithm for generating model-sensitive search plans for pattern matching on EMF models. Softw. Syst. Model 14(2), 597–621 (2015)

44. Vogel, T., Giese, H.: Model-driven engineering of self-adaptive software with EUREMA. ACM Trans. Auton. Adapt. Syst. 8(4), 18 (2014)

45. Vörös, A., et al.: MoDeS3: model-based demonstrator for smart and safe cyber-physical systems. In: NASA Formal Methods Symposium (2018, accepted)

46. Warren, D.S.: Memoing for logic programs. Commun. ACM 35(3), 93–111 (1992)

47. Yakindu Statechart Tools: Yakindu. http://statecharts.org/

48. Zhang, B., et al.: The cloud is not enough: saving IoT from the cloud. In: 7th USENIX Workshop on Hot Topics in Cloud Computing (2015)

49. Zheng, X., et al.: Efficient and scalable runtime monitoring for cyber-physical system. IEEE Syst. J. PP, 1–12 (2016)

EventHandler-Based Analysis Framework for Web Apps Using Dynamically Collected States

Joonyoung Park[1]([⊠])⬤, Kwangwon Sun[2]⬤, and Sukyoung Ryu[1]([⊠])⬤

[1] KAIST, Daejeon, Republic of Korea
{gmb55,sryu.cs}@kaist.ac.kr
[2] Samsung Electronics, Seoul, Republic of Korea
kwangwon.sun@samsung.com

Abstract. JavaScript web applications (apps) are prevalent these days, and quality assurance of web apps gets even more important. Even though researchers have studied various analysis techniques and software industries have developed code analyzers for their own code repositories, statically analyzing web apps in a sound and scalable manner is challenging. On top of dynamic features of JavaScript, abundant execution flows triggered by user events make a sound static analysis difficult.

In this paper, we propose a novel *EventHandler* (*EH*)-based static analysis for web apps using dynamically collected state information. Unlike traditional whole-program analyses, the *EH*-based analysis intentionally analyzes partial execution flows using concrete user events. Such analyses surely miss execution flows in the entire program, but they analyze less infeasible flows reporting less false positives. Moreover, they can finish analyzing partial flows of web apps that whole-program analyses often fail to finish analyzing, and produce partial bug reports. Our experimental results show that the *EH*-based analysis improves the precision dramatically compared with a state-of-the-art JavaScript whole-program analyzer, and it can finish analysis of partial execution flows in web apps that the whole-program analyzer fails to analyze within a timeout.

Keywords: JavaScript · Web applications · Event analysis
Static analysis

1 Introduction

Web applications (apps) written in HTML, CSS, and JavaScript have become prevalent, and JavaScript is now the 7th most popular programming language [22]. Because web apps can run on any platforms and devices that provide any browsers, they are being used widely. The overall structure of web apps is specified in HTML, which is represented as a tree structure via Document Object Model (DOM) APIs. CSS describes visual effects like colors, positions, and animation of contents of the web app, and JavaScript handles events triggered by user interaction. JavaScript code can change the status of the web app

© The Author(s) 2018
A. Russo and A. Schürr (Eds.): FASE 2018, LNCS 10802, pp. 129–145, 2018.
https://doi.org/10.1007/978-3-319-89363-1_8

by interoperation with HTML and CSS, load other JavaScript code dynamically, and access device-specific features via APIs provided by underlying platforms. JavaScript is the *de facto* standard language for web programming these days.

To help developers build high-quality web apps, researchers have studied various analysis techniques and software industries have developed in-house static analyzers. Static analyzers such as SAFE [12,15], TAJS [2,10], and WALA [19] analyze JavaScript web apps without concretely executing them, and dynamic analyzers such as Jalangi [20] utilize concrete values obtained by actually executing the apps. Thus, static analysis results aim to cover all the possible execution flows but they often contain infeasible execution flows, and dynamic analysis results contain only real execution flows but they often struggle to cover abundant execution flows. Such different analysis results are meaningful for different purposes: *sound* static analysis results are critical for verifying absence of bugs and *complete* dynamic analysis results are useful for detecting genuine bugs. In order to enhance the quality of their own software, IT companies develop in-house static analyzers like Infer from Facebook [4] and Tricorder from Google [18].

However, statically analyzing web apps in a sound and scalable manner is extremely challenging. Especially because JavaScript, the language that handles controls of web apps, is totally dynamic, purely static analysis has various limitations. While JavaScript can generate code to execute from string literals during evaluation, such code is not available for static analyzers before run time. In addition, dynamically adding and deleting object properties, and treating property names as values make statically analyzing them difficult [17]. Moreover, since execution flows triggered by user events are abundant, statically analyzing them often incurs analysis performance degradation [16].

Among many challenges in statically analyzing JavaScript web apps, we focus on analysis of event-driven execution flows in this paper. Most existing JavaScript static analyzers are focusing on analysis of web apps at loading time and they over-approximate event-driven execution flows to be sound. In order to consider all possible event sequences soundly, they abstract the event-driven semantics in a way that any events can happen in any order. Such a sound event modeling contains many infeasible event sequences, which lead to unnecessary operations computing imprecise analysis results. Thus, the state-of-the-art JavaScript static analyzers often fail to analyze event flows in web apps.

In this paper, we propose a novel *EventHandler-based (EH-based) static analysis* for web apps using *dynamically collected state information*. First, we present a new analysis unit, an *EH*. While traditional static analyzers perform whole-program analysis covering all possible execution flows, the *EH*-based analysis aims to analyze *partial* execution flows triggered by user events more precisely. In other words, unlike the whole-program analysis that starts analyzing from a single entry point of a given program, the *EH*-based analysis considers each event function call triggered by a user event as an entry point. Because the *EH*-based analysis enables a subset of the entire execution flows to be analyzed at a time, it can analyze less infeasible execution flows than the whole-program analysis, which balances soundness and precision. Moreover, since it considers a smaller set of execution flows, it may finish analysis of web apps that the whole-program analysis fails to analyze within a reasonable timeout. Second, in order to analyze each event function call in arbitrary call contexts, we present a hybrid approach to construct an abstract heap for the event function call. More specifically, to analyze each event function body, the analyzer should have information about non-local variables. Thus, for each event function, we construct a conservative abstract initial heap that holds abstract values of non-local variables by abstraction of dynamically collected states.

We formally present the mechanism as a framework, EHA, parameterized by a dynamic event generator and a static whole-program analyzer. After describing the high-level structure of EHA, we present its prototype implementation, EHA_{SAFE}^{man}, instantiated with manual event generation and a state-of-the-art JavaScript static analyzer SAFE. Our experimental results show that EHA_{SAFE}^{man} indeed reports less false positives than SAFE, and it can finish analysis of parts of web apps that SAFE fails to analyze within the timeout of 72 h.

Our paper makes the following contributions:

- We propose EHA, a bug detection framework that performs static analysis for each event handler as an entry point using an abstraction of dynamically collected states as an initial heap.
- We present EHA_{SAFE}^{man}, an instantiation of EHA with manual event generation and SAFE, which is applicable to real-world web apps.
- We evaluate EHA_{SAFE}^{man} in terms of analysis coverage and precision.

The remainder of this paper is organized as follows. We first explain the concrete semantics of event handlers in web apps, describe how existing whole-program analyzers handle events in a sound but unscalable manner, and present an overview of our approach using concrete code examples in Sect. 2. We describe EHA and its prototype implementation in Sect. 3 and Sect. 4, respectively. We evaluate the EHA instance using real-world web apps in Sect. 5, discuss related work in Sect. 6, and conclude in Sect. 7 with future work.

2 Analyses of Event Handlers

2.1 Event Handlers in Web Apps

Web apps may receive *events* from their execution environments like browsers or from users[1]. When a web app receives an event, it reacts to the event by executing JavaScript code registered as a handler (or a listener) of the event. An *event handler* consists of three components: an event target, an event type, and a callback function. An event target may be any DOM object like `Element`, `window`, and `XMLHttpRequest`. An event type is a string representation of the event action type such as `"load"`, `"click"`, and `"keydown"`. Finally, a callback function is a JavaScript function to be executed when its corresponding event occurs.

---

[1] http://www.w3schools.com/js/js_events.asp.

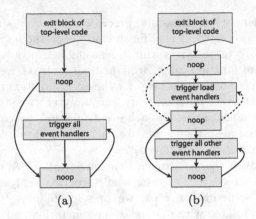

Fig. 1. (a) A conservative modeling of event control flows (b) Modeling in TAJS [9]

Users execute web apps by triggering various events, thus we consider sequences of events triggered by users as user inputs to web apps. During execution, a set of event handlers that can be executed by a user may vary. First, because event handlers are dynamically registered to and removed from DOM objects, executable event handlers for an event change at run time. For example, when a DOM object has only the following event handler registered:

```
(A, "click", function f(){ B.addEventListener("click", function g(){}); })
```

if a user clicks the target A, a new event handler becomes registered, which makes two handlers executable. Second, changes in DOM states of a web app also change a set of executable event handlers for an event. For instance, an event target may be removed from document via DOM API calls, which makes the detached event target inaccessible from users. Also, events may not be captured depending on their capturing/bubbling options and CSS style settings of visibility or display. In addition, it is a common practice to manipulate CSS styles like the following:

- HTMLElement.style.opacity = 0;
- HTMLElement.style.zIndex = n;

to hide an element such as a button under another element, making it inaccessible from users. These various features affect event sequences that users can trigger and event handlers that are executed accordingly.

2.2 Analysis of Event Handlers in Whole-Program Analyzers

Most existing whole-program JavaScript analyzers handle event handlers in a sound but unscalable manner as illustrated in Fig. 1(a). They first analyze top-level code that is statically available in a given web app; event handlers may be registered during the analysis of top-level code. Then, after the "exit block of top-level code" node, they analyze code initiated by event handlers in any order as denoted by the "trigger all event handlers" node in any number of times. According to this modeling of event control flows, all possible event sequences that occur after loading the top-level code are soundly analyzed. Note that even though whole-program analyzers use this sound event modeling, the analyzers themselves may not be sound because of other features like dynamic code generation. However, because registered event handlers may be removed during evaluation and they may be even inaccessible due to some CSS styles as discussed in Sect. 2.1, the event modeling in Fig. 1(a) may contain too many infeasible event sequences that are impossible in concrete executions. Analysis with lots of infeasible event sequences involves unnecessary computation that wastes analysis time, and often results in imprecise analysis results. Such a conservative modeling of event control flows indeed reports many false positives [16].

To reduce the amount of infeasible event sequences to analyze, TAJS uses a refined modeling of event control flows as shown in Fig. 1(b). Among various event handlers, this modeling distinguishes "load event handlers" and analyzes them before all the other event handlers. While this modeling is technically unsound because non-load events may precede load events [15], most web apps satisfy this modeling in practice. Moreover, because load event handlers often initialize top-level variables, the event modeling in Fig. 1(a) often produces false positives by analyzing non-load event functions before load event functions initialize top-level variables. On the contrary, the TAJS modeling reduces such false positives by analyzing load event handlers before non-load event handlers. Although the TAJS modeling distinguishes a load event, the over-approximation of the other event handler calls still brings analysis precision and scalability issues.

2.3 Analysis of Event Handlers in *EH*-Based Analyzers

To alleviate the analysis precision and scalability problem due to event modeling, we propose the EHA framework, which aims to analyze a subset of execution flows within a limited time budget to detect bugs in partial execution flows rather than to analyze all execution flows. EHA presents two key points to achieve the goal. First, it slices the entire execution flows by using each event handler as an individual entry point, which amounts to consider a given web app as a collection of smaller web apps. This slicing brings the effect of breaking the loop structures in existing event modelings shown in Fig. 1. Second, in order to analyze sliced event control flows in various contexts, EHA constructs an initial abstract heap of each entry point that contains necessary information to analyze a given event control flow by abstracting dynamically collected states. More specifically, EHA takes two components—a *dynamic event generator* and a *static analyzer*—and collects concrete values of non-local variables of event functions via the dynamic event generator, and abstracts the collected values using the static analyzer.

Let us compare static, dynamic, and *EH*-based analyses with an example. We assume that a top-level code registers three event handlers: *l*, *a*, and *b* where *l* denotes a load event handler, which precedes the others and runs once. In addition, a and b simulate a pop-up and its close button, respectively. Thus, we can represent possible event sequences as a regular expression: $l(ab)^*a?$. For a given event sequence $lababa$, Fig. 2 represents the event flows analyzed by each analysis technique. A conservative static analysis contains infeasible event sequences like the ones starting with a or b, whereas a dynamic analysis covers only short prefixes out of infinitely many flows. The EH-based analysis slices the web app into three handler units: l, a, and b. Hence, there is no loop in the event modeling; each handler considers every prefix of the given event sequence that ends with itself. For example, the handler a considers la, $laba$, and $lababa$ as possible event sequences. Moreover, instead of abstracting the evaluation result of each sequence separately and merging them, it first merges the evaluation result of each sequence just before the handler a—l, lab, and $labab$—and uses its abstraction as the initial heap of analyzing a, which analyzes more event flows.

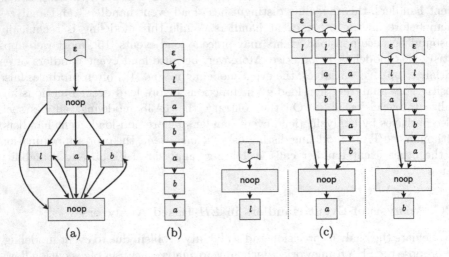

Fig. 2. Event flows analyzed by (a) static, (b) dynamic, and (c) EH-based analyses.

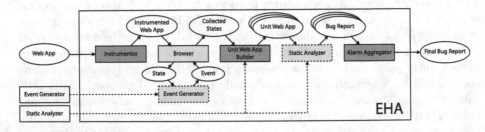

Fig. 3. Overall structure of EHA

3   Technical Details

This section discusses the EHA framework, which composes of five phases as shown in Fig. 3. Boxes denote modules and ellipses denote data. EHA takes three inputs: a web app (Web App) to analyze and find bugs in it, and two modules to use as its components—a dynamic event sequence generator (Event Generator) and a static analyzer (Static Analyzer). During the first *instrumentation* phase, Instrumentor inserts code that dynamically collects states into the input web app. Then, during the *execution* phase, the Instrumented Web App runs on a browser producing Collected States. One of the input module Event Generator repeatedly receives states of the running web app and sends user events to it during this phase. In the third *unit building* phase, Unit Web App Builder constructs a small Unit Web App for each event handler from Collected States. After analyzing the set of Unit Web Apps by another input module Static Analyzer in the *static analysis* phase, Alarm Aggregator summarizes the resulting set of Bug Reports and generates a Final Bug Report for the original input Web App in the final *alarm aggregation* phase. We now describe each phase in more detail.

$$
\begin{aligned}
&Inst\ (h \equiv \texttt{<head>}) &&=\ h.\texttt{addChildFront(<script src="helper" />)}\\
&Inst\ (\texttt{function } f(\cdots)\ b) &&=\ \texttt{function } f(\cdots)\{\\
&\qquad\qquad \texttt{var envId = getNewEnvId(); var nonlocals = } \{x'_1\!:\!x_1 \cdots\};\\
&\qquad\qquad \texttt{pushCallStack(); collectState(nonlocals); } b;\ \texttt{popCallStack(); }\}\\
&Inst\ (\texttt{return } x;) &&=\ \{\ \texttt{var retVal = } x;\ \texttt{popCallStack(); return retVal; }\}\\
&Inst\ (\texttt{catch}(e)\{\ b\ \}) &&=\ \{\ \texttt{popCallStack(); } b\ \}\\
&Inst\ (x = e) &&=\ x = e;\ \texttt{update(}x',x\texttt{)}\\
&Inst\ (x \oplus) &&=\ x \oplus;\ \texttt{update(}x',x,\oplus\texttt{)}\\
&Inst\ (\oplus\ x) &&=\ \oplus\ x;\ \texttt{update(}x',x\texttt{)}
\end{aligned}
$$

Fig. 4. Instrumentation rules (partial)

Instrumentation Phase. The first phase instruments a given web app so that the instrumented web app can record dynamically collected states during execution. Figure 4 presents the instrumentation rules for the most important cases where the unary operator $\oplus$ is either ++ or --. For presentation brevity, we abuse the notation and write x' to denote the string representation of a variable name x. The *Inst* function converts necessary JavaScript language constructs to others that perform dynamic logging. For example, for each function declaration of f, *Inst* inserts four statements before the function body and one statement after the function body to keep track of non-local variables of the function f.

Execution Phase. The execution phase runs an instrumented web app on a browser using events generated by Event Generator. Because EHA is parameterized by the input Event Generator, it may be an automated testing tool or manual efforts. The following definitions formally specify the concepts being used in the execution phase and the rest of this section:

Execution $\sigma \in \mathbb{S}^*$	State $\quad s \in \mathbb{S} = \mathbb{P} \times \mathbb{H}$	ProgramPoint $\; p \in \mathbb{P}$
Heap $\quad h \in \mathbb{H} = \mathbb{A} \to \mathbb{O}$	Address $@x \in \mathbb{A}$	Object $\qquad \mathbb{O} = \mathbb{F} \to \mathbb{V}$
Field $\quad x \in \mathbb{F}$	Value $\quad \mathbb{V} = \mathbb{V}_b \uplus \mathbb{A}$	PrimitiveValue $\mathbb{V}_b$

An execution of a web app σ is a sequence of states that are results of evaluation of the web app code. We omit how states change according to the evaluation of different language constructs, but focus on which states are collected during execution. A state s is a pair of a program point p denoting the source location of the code being evaluated and a heap h denoting a memory status. A heap is a map from addresses to objects. An address is a unique identifier assigned whenever an object is created, and an object is a map from fields to values. A field is an object property name and a value is either a primitive value or an address that denotes an object. For presentation brevity, we abuse *Object* to represent *Environment* as well, which is a map from variables to values. Then, EHA collects states at event callback entries during execution:

$$Collected \; States(\sigma) = \{s \mid s \in \sigma \; \text{s.t.} \; s \text{ is at an event callback entry}\}$$

the program points of which are function entries and the call stack depths are 1.

Unit Building Phase. As shown in Fig. 3, this phase constructs a set of sliced unit web apps using dynamically collected states. More specifically, it divides the collected states into *EH* units, and then for each *EH* unit u, it constructs an *initial summary* $\hat{s}_I^u$ that contains merged values about non-local variables from the states in u. As discussed in Sect. 2.1, an event handler consists of three components: an event target, an event type, and a callback function. Thus, we design an *EH* unit u with an abstract event target ϕ, an event type τ, and a program point p:

$$u \in \mathbb{U} \qquad\qquad = AbsEventTarget \times EventType \times \mathbb{P}$$
$$\phi \in AbsEventTarget = DOMTreePosition \uplus \mathbb{A}$$
$$\tau \in EventType$$

While we use the same concrete event types and program points for *EH*s, we abstract concrete event targets to maintain a modest number of event targets. We assume the static analyzer expresses analysis results as summaries. A summary $\hat{s}$ is a map from a pair of a program point and a context to an abstract heap:

$$\hat{s} \in \hat{S} = \mathbb{P} \times Context \to \hat{\mathbb{H}} \qquad\qquad c \in Context$$

where *Context* is parameterized by an input static analyzer of EHA.

For each dynamically collected state $s = (p, h)$ with an event target o and an event type τ both contained in h, Unit Web App Builder calculates an *EH* unit u as follows:

$$u = \alpha_s(s) = (\alpha_o(o), \; \tau, \; p)$$
$$\text{where } \alpha_o(o) = \begin{cases} DOMTreePosition(o) & \text{if } o \text{ is attached on DOM} \\ o & \text{otherwise} \end{cases}$$

where $DOMTreePosition(o)$ represents the DOM tree position of o in terms of sequences of child indices from the root node of DOM. Then, it constructs an initial summary for each unit u, $\hat{s}_I^u$, as follows:

$$\hat{s}_I^u(p, c) = \begin{cases} \widehat{h}_u^{\text{init}} & \text{if } p \text{ is the global entry point} \wedge c = \epsilon \\ \bot_{\mathbb{H}} & \text{otherwise} \end{cases}$$

The initial summary maps all pairs of program points and contexts to the heap bottom $\bot_{\mathbb{H}}$ denoting no information, but it keeps a single map from a pair of the global entry program point and the empty context ϵ to the initial abstract heap $\widehat{h}_u^{\text{init}} = \bigsqcup_i \alpha_h(h_i)$ where $s_i \in$ Collected States $\wedge \; \alpha_s(s_i) = u \wedge s_i = (p_i, h_i)$. The initial abstract heap for a unit u is a join of all abstraction results of the heaps in the collected states that are mapped to the same u. The heap abstraction α_h and the abstract heap join $\bigsqcup$ are parameterized by the input static analyzer.

Static Analysis Phase. Now, the static analysis phase analyzes each sliced unit web app one by one, and detects any bugs in it. Let us call the static analyzer that EHA takes as its input SA. Without loss of generality, let us assume that SA performs a whole-program analysis to compute the analysis result $\hat{s}_{\text{final}}$ with the initial summary $\hat{s}_I$ by computing the least fixpoint of a semantics transfer function $\hat{F}$: $\hat{s}_{\text{final}} = \texttt{leastFix } \lambda\hat{s}.(\hat{s}_I \sqcup_{\hat{S}} \hat{F}(\hat{s}))$ and then reports alarms for possible bugs in it. We call an instance of EHA that takes SA as its input static analyzer EHA$_{\text{SA}}$. Then, for each EH unit u, EHA$_{\text{SA}}$ performs an EH-based analysis to compute its analysis result $\hat{s}_{\text{final}}^u$ with the initial summary $\hat{s}_I^u$ constructed during the unit building phase by computing the least fixpoint of the same semantics transfer function $\hat{F}$: $\hat{s}_{\text{final}}^u = \texttt{leastFix } \lambda\hat{s}.(\hat{s}_I^u \sqcup_{\hat{S}} \hat{F}(\hat{s}))$. It also reports alarms for possible bugs in each unit u.

Alarm Aggregation Phase. The final phase combines all bug reports from sliced unit web apps and constructs a final bug report. Because source locations of bugs in a bug report from a unit web app are different from those in an original input web app, Alarm Aggregator resolves such differences. Since a single source location in the original web app may appear multiple times in differently sliced unit web apps, Alarm Aggregator also merges bug reports for the same source locations.

4   Implementation

This section describes how we implemented concrete data representation and each module in dark boxes in Fig. 3 in our prototype implementation.

Instrumentor. The main idea of instrumentor is similar to that of Jalangi [20], a JavaScript dynamic analysis framework, and we implemented the rules (partially) shown in Fig. 4. An instrumented web app collects states during execution by stringifying them and writing them on files. Dynamically collected information may be ordinary JavaScript values or built-in objects of JavaScript engines or browsers, which are often implemented in non-JavaScript, native languages. Because such built-in values are inaccessible from JavaScript code, we omit their values in the collected states. On the contrary, ordinary JavaScript values are stringified in JSON format. A primitive value is stringified by JSON.stringify and stored in ValueMap. An object value is stored in two places—its pointer in Storage and its pointer identifier in ValueMap—and its property values are also recursively stringified and stored in StorageMap. The stringified document, ValueMap, and StorageMap are written in files at the end of execution, and Unit Web App Builder converts them to states in the unit building phase.

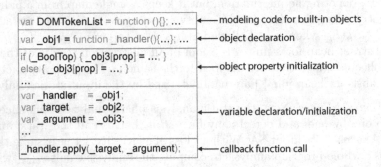

Fig. 5. Contents in a JavaScript file of a unit web app

Unit Web App Builder. In our prototype implementation, the unit web app builder parses the collected states as in JSON format and constructs a unit web app as multiple HTML files and one JavaScript file. A single JavaScript file contains all the information to build an initial abstract heap as Fig. 5. It contains modeling code for built-in objects on the top, declares objects recorded in StorageMap and initializes their properties, and then declares and initializes nonlocal variables, which are all the information needed to build an initial abstract heap. At the bottom, the handler function is being called.

Starting from the above 3 variables—_handler, _target, and _arguments— we can fill in contents of a unit web app using the collected states. For each variable, we get its value from the collected states and construct a corresponding JavaScript code. When the value of a variable is a primitive value, create a corresponding code fragment as a string literal. For an object value, get the value from StorageMap using its pointer id, and repeat the process for its property values. For a function object value, repeat the process for its non-local variables.

Alarm Aggregator. The alarm aggregator maintains a mapping between different source locations and eliminates duplicated alarms. It should map between locations in the original web app and in sliced unit web apps. Our implementation keeps track of corresponding AST nodes in different web apps, and utilizes the information for mapping locations. It identifies duplicated alarms by string comparison of their bug messages and locations after mapping the source locations.

5 Experimental Evaluation

In this section, we evaluate EHA_{SAFE}^{man}, an instantiation of EHA with manual event generation and SAFE [12], to answer the following research questions:

In the case of providing dynamic events as many as possible,

- RQ1. **Full Coverage**: How many event flows does the *EH*-based analysis cover compared with the whole-program analysis?
- RQ2. **Precision**: How precise is the *EH*-based analysis compared with the whole-program analysis?
- RQ3. **Scalability**: What is the execution time of each phase in the analyses?
- RQ4. **Partial Coverage**: How many event flows does the *EH*-based analysis cover for timeout analyses?

5.1 Experimental Setup

We studied 8 open-source game web apps [8], which were used in the evaluation of SAFE. They have various buttons and show event-dependent behaviors. The first two columns of Table 1 show the names and lines of code of the apps, respectively. The first four apps do not use any JavaScript libraries, and the remaining apps use the jQuery library version 2.0.3. They are all cross-platform apps that can run on Chrome, Chrome-extension, and Tizen environments.

To perform experiments, we instantiated EHA with two inputs. As an Event Generator input, we chose manual event generation by one undergraduate researcher who was ignorant of EHA. He was instructed to explore behaviors of web apps as much as possible, and he could check the number of functions being called during execution as a guidance. In order to make execution environments simple enough to reproduce multiple times, we collected dynamic states from a browser without any cached data. As a Static Analyzer input, we use SAFE

Table 1. Analysis coverage of SAFE and EHA_{SAFE}^{man}.

App	LoC	#Analyzed Handler Ftn			#Analyzed Ftn			Total
(Id) App name		Both	SAFE only	EHA_{SAFE}^{man} only	Both	SAFE only	EHA_{SAFE}^{man} only	
(01) HangOnMan	1326	20	0	11	67	3	19	89
(02) MakeAMonster	1405	22	0	5	63	5	7	75
(03) Mancala	1546	28	0	4	67	4	5	76
(04) Rabbit	1403	34	0	2	76	22	2	100
(05) Bubblewrap	7220	-	-	8	-	-	10	10
(06) CountingBeads	6949	-	-	9	-	-	11	11
(07) MemoryGameForOlderKids	6955	-	-	7	-	-	9	9
(08) WordsSwarm	7557	-	-	9	-	-	48	48
Total	34363	104	0	55	273	34	111	418

because it can analyze the most JavaScript web apps among existing analyzers via the state-of-the-art DOM tree abstraction [14,15] and it supports a bug detector [16]. We ran the apps with Chrome on a 2.9 GHz quad-core Intel Core i7 with 16 GB memory in the execution phase. The other phases are conducted on Ubuntu 16.04.1 with intel Core i7 and 32 GB memory.

5.2   Answers to RQs

Answer to RQ1. For the analysis coverage, we measured the numbers of analyzed functions and true positives by SAFE and EHA_{SAFE}^{man}. Because SAFE could not analyze 4 apps that use jQuery within the timeout of 72 h, we considered only the other apps for SAFE.

Table 1 summarizes the result of analyzed functions. The 3rd to the 5th columns show the numbers of registered event handler functions analyzed by both, SAFE only, and EHA_{SAFE}^{man} only, respectively. Similarly, the 6th to the 8th columns show the numbers of functions analyzed by both, SAFE only, and EHA_{SAFE}^{man} only, respectively. When we compare only the registered event handler functions among all the analyzed functions, EHA_{SAFE}^{man} outperforms SAFE. Even though SAFE was designed to be sound, it missed some behaviors. Our investigation showed that the causes of the unsoundness were due to incomplete DOM modeling. For the numbers of analyzed functions, the analyses covered more than 75% of the functions in common. EHA_{SAFE}^{man} analyzed more functions for the first 3 subjects than SAFE due to missing event registrations caused by incomplete DOM modeling in SAFE. On the other hand, SAFE analyzed more functions for the 4th subject because EHA_{SAFE}^{man} missed flows during the execution phase. We studied the analysis result of the 4th subject in more detail, and found flows that resume previously suspended execution by using cached data in a `localStorage` object. EHA_{SAFE}^{man} could not analyze the flows because it does not contain cached data, while SAFE could use a sound modeling of `localStorage`. Lastly, EHA_{SAFE}^{man} did not miss any true positives that SAFE detected, and EHA_{SAFE}^{man} could detect four more true positives in common functions as shown in Table 2, which implies that EHA_{SAFE}^{man} analyzed execution flows in those functions that SAFE missed. We explain Table 2 in more detail in the next answer.

Answer to RQ2. To compare the analysis precision, we measured the numbers of false positives (FPs) in alarm reports by SAFE and EHA_{SAFE}^{man}. Note that true positives (TPs) may not be considered as "bugs" by app developers. For example, while SAFE reports a warning when the `undefined` value is implicitly converted to a number because it is a well-known error-prone pattern, it may be an intentional behavior of a developer. Thus, TPs denote they are reproducible in concrete executions while FPs denote it is impossible to reproduce them in feasible executions. Similarly for RQ1, we compare the analysis precision for four apps that do not use jQuery.

Tables 2 and 3 categorize alarms in three categories: alarms reported by both SAFE and EHA_{SAFE}^{man}, alarms in functions commonly analyzed by both, and alarms in functions that are analyzed by only one. Table 2 shows numbers of TPs and

Table 2. Alarms reported by SAFE and EHA_{SAFE}^{man}.

App Id	Common alarms		Different alarms							
			Common functions				Different functions			
			SAFE		EHA_{SAFE}^{man}		SAFE		EHA_{SAFE}^{man}	
	#TP	#FP	#TP	#FP	#TP	#FP	#TP	#FP	#TP	#FP
01	1	3	0	10	3	2	0	0	0	2
02	1	2	0	0	1	8	0	5	0	1
03	1	3	0	30	0	6	0	0	0	2
04	3	7	0	1	0	0	0	0	0	0
05	-	-	-	-	-	-	-	-	0	1
06	-	-	-	-	-	-	-	-	0	3
07	-	-	-	-	-	-	-	-	0	1
08	-	-	-	-	-	-	-	-	0	1
Total	6	15	0	41	4	16	0	5	0	11

Table 3. False alarms categorized by causes

Cause	Common alarms	Different alarms			
		Common functions		Different functions	
		SAFE	EHA_{SAFE}^{man}	SAFE	EHA_{SAFE}^{man}
Infeasible event flow	-	40	-	0	-
ECMAScript 5	1	0	0	0	0
Object join	0	0	3	0	0
Handler unit abstraction	-	-	3	-	0
Omitted property	-	-	0	-	2
Absence of DOM model	14	1	10	5	9
Total	15	41	16	5	11

FPs for each app, and Table 3 further categorizes alarms in terms of their causes. Out of 21 common alarms, 6 are TPs and 15 are FPs. Among 15 common FPs, 14 are due to absence of DOM modeling and 1 is due to the unsupported getter and setter semantics. For the functions commonly analyzed by both, they may report different alarms because they are based on different abstract heaps. We observed that 40 FPs from SAFE are due to the over-approximated event system modeling. Especially, the causes of FPs in the 01 and 03 apps are because top-level variables are initialized when non-load event handler functions are called, which implies that the event modeling of Fig. 1(b) would have a similar imprecision problem. On the contrary, EHA_{SAFE}^{man} reported only 16 FPs mostly (10 FPs) due to absence of DOM modeling. The remaining three FPs from object joins and three FPs by handler unit abstraction are due to inherent problems of static analysis that merges multiple values losing precision. Finally, for the functions analyzed by only one analyzer, all the reported alarms are FPs due to absence of DOM modeling and omitted properties in the EHA^{man}_{SAFE} implementation. In short, EHA^{man}_{SAFE} could partially analyze more subjects than SAFE, and it improved the analysis precision by finding four TPs and less FPs for commonly analyzed functions. Especially, its *handler unit abstraction* produced three FPs which are considerably fewer than 40 FPs from over-approximated event modeling in SAFE without missing any TPs.

Answer to RQ3. To compare the analysis scalability, we measured the execution time of each phase for the both analyzers as summarized in Table 4.

Table 4. Execution time (seconds) of each phase for SAFE and EHA^{man}_{SAFE}

Id	SAFE			EHA^{man}_{SAFE}							
	Total	Top-Level	Event Loop	Execution			Unit build	Static analysis			
				Total	#Call	Ave.		Total	#EH	#TO	Ave.
01	375.7	8.9	366.8	465.41	682	0.68	10.0	33038.4	130	9	96.6
02	282.0	8.2	273.8	252.86	135	1.87	6.0	6379.7	33	0	70.4
03	850.2	15.5	834.7	82.70	168	0.49	2.0	7894.1	43	3	68.8
04	1276.6	325.3	951.3	302.36	589	0.51	2.1	16223.9	95	7	54.2
05	✗	137.3	✗	1713.61	151	11.35	287.2	66238.5	63	55	10.4
06	✗	86.9	✗	383.08	85	4.51	221.5	17257.1	27	9	146.5
07	✗	119.3	✗	2836.05	242	11.72	348.2	104583.5	94	87	7.7
08	✗	82.4	✗	1074.73	146	7.36	1158.5	39506.3	41	32	33.5
Ave.	696.1	98.0	606.6	888.85	275	3.24	254.4	3076.5	66	25	76.0

For SAFE, we measured the time took for analyses of the entire code, top-level code, and event loops: Total = Top-Level + Event Loop. For four subjects that do not use any JavaScript libraries, the total analysis took at most 1276.6 s among which 951.3 s took for analyzing event loops. While SAFE finished analyzing the top-level code of the other subjects that use jQuery in 137.3 s at the maximum, it could not finish analyzing their entire code within the time of 72 h (259,200 s).

For EHA^{man}_{SAFE}, because the maximum execution time of the instrumentation phase and the alarm aggregation phase are 10.3 s and 4.9 s, respectively, much smaller than the other phases, the table shows only the other phases. For the execution phase, we present the overhead to collect states:

EHA^{man}_{SAFE} (Execution Phase): Total = #Call × Ave.

The 6th column presents the numbers of event handler function calls that Event Generator executed; each event handler function pauses for 3.24 s on average. In order to understand the performance overhead due to the instrumentation, we measured its slowdown effect by replacing all the instrumented helper functions with a function with the empty body. With the Sunspider benchmark, Jalangi showed x30 slowdown and EHA^{man}_{SAFE} showed x178 slowdown on average. We observed that collecting non-local variables for each function incurs much performance overhead, and more function calls make more overhead.

The unit building phase takes time to generate unit web app code. Our investigation showed that the time heavily depends on the size of collected data. For the static analysis phase, we measured the analysis time of unit web apps except timeout (TO):

$$\text{EHA}_{\text{SAFE}}^{\text{man}} \text{ (Static Analysis Phase): Total} = (\#\text{EH} - \#\text{TO}) \times \text{Ave.} + 1200 \times \#\text{TO}$$

We analyzed each unit web app with the timeout of 1200 s. While the 02 app has no timeout, the 07 app has 87 timeouts out of 94 unit web apps. On average, analysis of 38% (25/66) of the unit web apps was timeout. Note that even for the first four apps that SAFE finished analysis, $\text{EHA}_{\text{SAFE}}^{\text{man}}$ had some timeouts. We conjecture that SAFE finished analysis quickly since it missed some flows because of unsupported DOM modeling. By contrast, because $\text{EHA}_{\text{SAFE}}^{\text{man}}$ analyzes more flows using dynamically collected data, it had several timeouts.

Answer to RQ4. To see how many event flows $\text{EHA}_{\text{SAFE}}^{\text{man}}$ covers with a limited time budget, let us consider four apps that SAFE did not finish in 72 h from Tables 1 and 4. $\text{EHA}_{\text{SAFE}}^{\text{man}}$ finished 19% (42/225) of the units within the timeout of 1200 s as shown in Table 4, and the average analysis time excluding timeouts was 76.0 s. Because it implies that web apps have event flows that can be analyzed in about 76 s, it may be meaningful to analyze such simple event flows quickly first to find bugs in them. Starting with 42 units, $\text{EHA}_{\text{SAFE}}^{\text{man}}$ covered 78 functions as shown in Table 1. While SAFE could not provide any bug reports for four apps using jQuery, $\text{EHA}_{\text{SAFE}}^{\text{man}}$ reported 6 alarms from the analzyed functions.

6 Related Work

Researchers have studied event dependencies to analyze event flows more precisely. Madsen *et al.* [13] proposed event-based call graphs, which extend traditional call graphs with behaviors of event handlers such as registration and trigger of events. While they do not consider analysis of DOM state changes and event capturing/bubbling behaviors, EHA addresses them by utilizing dynamically collected states. Sung *et al.* [21] introduced DOM event dependency and exploited it to test JavaScript web apps. Their tool improved the efficiency of event testing but it has not yet been applied for static analysis of event loops.

Taking advantage of both static analysis and dynamic analysis is not a new idea [5]. For JavaScript analysis, researches tried to analyze dynamic features of JavaScript [7] and DOM values of web apps [23,24] precisely. Alimadadi *et al.* [1] proposed a DOM-sensitive change impact analysis for JavaScript web apps. JavaScript Blended Analysis Framework (JSBAF) [26] collects dynamic traces of a given app, specializes dynamic features of JavaScript like eval calls and reflective property accesses utilizing the collected traces. JSBAF analyzes each trace separately and combines the results, but EHA abstracts the collected states on each *EH* first and then analyzes the units to get generalized contexts. Finally, Ko *et al.* [11] proposed a tunable static analysis framework that utilizes a light-weight pre-analysis. Similarly, our work builds an approximation of selected executions by constructing an initial abstract heap utilizing dynamic information, which enables to analyze complex event flows although partially.

7   Conclusion and Future Work

Because existing JavaScript static analyzers conservatively approximate event-driven flows, even state-of-the-art analyzers often fail to analyze event flows in web apps within a timeout of several hours. We present EHA, a bug detection framework that performs a novel EH-based static analysis using dynamically collected state information. As a general framework, EHA is parameterized by a way to generate event sequences and a JavaScript static analyzer. We present $\mathrm{EHA^{man}_{SAFE}}$, an instantiation of EHA with manual event generation and the SAFE JavaScript static analyzer. Our experimental evaluation shows that the EH-based analysis ($\mathrm{EHA^{man}_{SAFE}}$) reduced false positives reported by the whole-program analysis (SAFE) due to its over-approximation of the event system modeling. Moreover, $\mathrm{EHA^{man}_{SAFE}}$ finished analyzing partial execution flows of the web apps that SAFE failed to analyze within the timeout of 72 h. We plan to inspect the soundness issues due to the lack of DOM modeling in whole-program analyzers with systematic ways via dynamic analyses [3,6,25], and to use an automated testing tool as a dynamic event generator instead of the manual generation.

Acknowledgment. The research leading to these results has received funding from National Research Foundation of Korea (NRF) (Grants NRF-2017R1A2B3012020 and 2017M3C4A7068177).

References

1. Alimadadi, S., Mesbah, A., Pattabiraman, K.: Hybrid DOM-sensitive change impact analysis for JavaScript. In: ECOOP 2015 (2015)
2. Andreasen, E., Møller, A.: Determinacy in static analysis for jQuery. In: OOPSLA 2014 (2014)
3. Andreasen, E.S., Møller, A., Nielsen, B.B.: Systematic approaches for increasing soundness and precision of static analyzers. In: SOAP 2017 (2017)
4. Calcagno, C., et al.: Moving fast with software verification. In: Havelund, K., Holzmann, G., Joshi, R. (eds.) NFM 2015. LNCS, vol. 9058, pp. 3–11. Springer, Cham (2015). https://doi.org/10.1007/978-3-319-17524-9_1
5. Ernst, M.D.: Static and dynamic analysis: synergy and duality. In: PASTE 2004 (2004)
6. Grech, N., Fourtounis, G., Francalanza, A., Smaragdakis, Y.: Heaps don't lie: countering unsoundness with heap snapshots. In: OOPSLA 2017 (2017)
7. Guarnieri, S., Livshits, B.: GATEKEEPER: mostly static enforcement of security and reliability policies for JavasSript code. In: SSYM 2009 (2009)
8. Intel: HTML5 web apps (2017). https://01.org/html5webapps/webapps
9. Jensen, S.H., Madsen, M., Møller, A.: Modeling the HTML DOM and browser API in static analysis of JavaScript web applications. In: ESEC/FSE 2011 (2011)
10. Jensen, S.H., Møller, A., Thiemann, P.: Type analysis for JavaScript. In: Palsberg, J., Su, Z. (eds.) SAS 2009. LNCS, vol. 5673, pp. 238–255. Springer, Heidelberg (2009). https://doi.org/10.1007/978-3-642-03237-0_17
11. Ko, Y., Lee, H., Dolby, J., Ryu, S.: Practically tunable static analysis framework for large-scale JavaScript applications. In: ASE 2015 (2015)

12. Lee, H., Won, S., Jin, J., Cho, J., Ryu, S.: SAFE: formal specification and implementation of a scalable analysis framework for ECMAScript. In: FOOL 2012 (2012)
13. Madsen, M., Tip, F., Lhoták, O.: Static analysis of event-driven Node.js JavaScript applications. In: OOPSLA 2015 (2015)
14. Park, C., Ryu, S.: Scalable and precise static analysis of JavaScript applications via loop-sensitivity. In: ECOOP 2015 (2015)
15. Park, C., Won, S., Jin, J., Ryu, S.: Static analysis of JavaScript web applications in the wild via practical DOM modeling. In: ASE 2015 (2015)
16. Park, J., Lim, I., Ryu, S.: Battles with false positives in static analysis of JavaScript web applications in the wild. In: ICSE-SEIP 2016 (2016)
17. Richards, G., Lebresne, S., Burg, B., Vitek, J.: An analysis of the dynamic behavior of JavaScript programs. In: PLDI 2010 (2010)
18. Sadowski, C., Van Gogh, J., Jaspan, C., Söderberg, E., Winter, C.: Tricorder: building a program analysis ecosystem. In: ICSE 2015 (2015)
19. Schäfer, M., Sridharan, M., Dolby, J., Tip, F.: Dynamic determinacy analysis. In: PLDI 2013 (2013)
20. Sen, K., Kalasapur, S., Brutch, T., Gibbs, S.: Jalangi: a selective record-replay and dynamic analysis framework for JavaScript. In: ESEC/FSE 2013 (2013)
21. Sung, C., Kusano, M., Sinha, N., Wang, C.: Static DOM event dependency analysis for testing web applications. In: FSE 2016 (2016)
22. TIOBE: TIOBE Index for September 2017. http://www.tiobe.com/tiobe-index
23. Tripp, O., Ferrara, P., Pistoia, M.: Hybrid security analysis of web JavaScript code via dynamic partial evaluation. In: ISSTA 2014 (2014)
24. Tripp, O., Weisman, O.: Hybrid analysis for JavaScript security assessment. In: ESEC/FSE 2011 (2011)
25. Wang, Y., Zhang, H., Rountev, A.: On the unsoundness of static analysis for android GUIs. In: SOAP 2016 (2016)
26. Wei, S., Ryder, B.G.: Practical blended taint analysis for JavaScript. In: ISSTA 2013 (2013)

Software Design and Verification

Hierarchical Specification and Verification of Architectural Design Patterns

Diego Marmsoler(✉)

Technische Universität München, Munich, Germany
diego.marmsoler@tum.de

Abstract. Architectural design patterns capture architectural design experience and provide abstract solutions to recurring architectural design problems. Their description is usually expressed informally and it is not verified whether the proposed specification indeed solves the original design problem. As a consequence, an architect cannot fully rely on the specification when implementing a pattern to solve a certain problem. To address this issue, we propose an approach for the specification and verification of architectural design patterns. Our approach is based on interactive theorem proving and leverages the hierarchical nature of patterns to foster reuse of verification results. The following paper presents FACTum, a methodology and corresponding specification techniques to support the formal specification of patterns. Moreover, it describes an algorithm to map a given FACTum specification to a corresponding Isabelle/HOL theory and shows its soundness. Finally, the paper demonstrates the approach by verifying versions of three widely used patterns: the singleton, the publisher-subscriber, and the blackboard pattern.

Keywords: Architectural design patterns
Interactive theorem proving · Dynamic architectures
Algebraic specification · Configuration traces

1 Introduction

Architectural design patterns capture architectural design experience and provide abstract solutions to recurring architectural design problems. They are an important concept in software engineering and regarded as one of the major tools to support an architect in the conceptualization and analysis of software systems [1]. The importance of patterns resulted in a panoply of pattern descriptions in literature [1–3]. They usually consist of a description of some key architectural constraints imposed by the pattern, such as involved data types, types of components, and assertions about the activation/deactivation of components as well as connections between component ports. These descriptions are usually highly informal and the claim that they indeed solve a certain design problem remains unverified. As a consequence, an architect cannot fully rely on a pattern's specification to solve a design problem faced during the development of a

© The Author(s) 2018
A. Russo and A. Schürr (Eds.): FASE 2018, LNCS 10802, pp. 149–168, 2018.
https://doi.org/10.1007/978-3-319-89363-1_9

new architecture. Moreover, verified pattern descriptions are a necessary precondition for automatic pattern conformance analyses, since missing assertions in a pattern's specification renders their detection impossible. Compared to concrete architectures, architectural design patterns pose several new challenges to the specification as well as the verification:

- C1: *Axiomatic Specifications*. Compared to traditional architectural specifications, specifications of patterns are usually axiomatic, focusing on a few, but important properties.
- C2: *Dynamic Aspects*: Pattern specifications usually involve the specification of dynamic aspects, such as instantiation of components and reconfiguration of connections.
- C3: *Hierarchical Specifications*: Pattern specifications usually build on each other, i.e., the specification of a pattern may instantiate the specification of another pattern.

This is why traditional techniques for the specification and verification of concrete architectures are not well-suited to be applied for the specification and verification of patterns.

Therefore, we propose an approach for the formal specification and verification of architectural design patterns which is based on interactive theorem proving [4]. Our approach is built on top of a pre-existing model of dynamic architectures [5,6] and its formalization in Isabelle/HOL [7] which comes with a calculus to support reasoning about such architectures [8]. Our approach provides techniques to specify patterns and corresponding design problems and allows to map a specification to a corresponding Isabelle/HOL theory [9]. The theory and the corresponding calculus can then be used to verify that a specification indeed solves the design problem the pattern claims to solve.

With this paper, we elaborate on our previous work by providing the following contributions: First, we present FACTum, a novel approach for the formal specification of architecture design patterns. Second, we provide an improved version of the algorithm to map a given FACTum specification to a corresponding Isabelle/HOL theory and show soundness of the mapping. Third, we demonstrate the approach by specifying and verifying versions of three architectural design patterns: the singleton pattern, the publisher subscriber pattern, and the blackboard pattern.

The remainder of the paper is structured as follows: In Sect. 2, we provide necessary background on interactive theorem proving and configuration traces (our model of dynamic architectures). We then describe our approach to specify patterns in Sect. 3. To this end, we define the notion of (hierarchical) pattern specification and demonstrate it by specifying three architectural design patterns. In Sect. 4, we first define the semantics of a pattern specification in terms of configuration traces. Then, we provide an algorithm to map a given specification to a corresponding Isabelle/HOL theory and show its soundness, i.e., that the semantics of a specification is indeed preserved by the algorithm. We proceed with an overview of related work in Sect. 5 and conclude the paper in Sect. 6 with a brief discussion about how the approach addresses the challenges C1–C3 identified above.

2   Background

In the following, we provide some background on which our work is build.

2.1   Interactive Theorem Proving

Interactive theorem proving (ITP) is a semi-automatic approach for the development of formal theories. Therefore, a set of proof assistants [4] have been developed to support a human in the development of formal proofs. Since our approach is based on Isabelle/HOL [9], in the following we describe some relevant features about this specific prover.

In general, Isabelle is an LCF-style [10] theorem prover based on Standard ML. It provides a so-called meta-logic on which different object logics are based. Isabelle/HOL is one of them, implementing higher-order logic for Isabelle. It integrates a prover IDE and comes with an extensive library of theories from various domains. New theories are then developed by defining terms of a certain type and deriving theorems from these definitions. Data types can be specified in Isabelle/HOL in terms of freely generated, inductive data type definitions [11]. Axiomatic specification of data types is also supported in terms of type classes [12]. To support the specification of theories over the data types, Isabelle/HOL provides tools for inductive definitions and recursive function definitions. Moreover, Isabelle/HOL provides a structured proof language called Isabelle/Isar [13] and a set of logical reasoners to support the verification of theorems. Modularization of theories is achieved through the notion of locales [14] in which an interface is specified in terms of sets of functions (called parameters) with corresponding assumptions about their behavior. Locales can extend other locales and may be instantiated by concrete definitions of the corresponding parameters.

2.2   A Model of Dynamic Architectures

Since architectures implementing an ADP may be dynamic as well (in the sense that components of a certain type can be instantiated over time), our approach is based on a model of dynamic architectures. One way to model such architectures is in terms of *sets* of configuration traces [5,6], i.e., streams [15,16] over architecture configurations. Thereby, architecture configurations can be thought of as snapshots of the architecture during execution. Thus, they consist of a set of (active) components with their ports valuated by messages and connections between the ports of the components. Moreover, components of a certain type may be parametrized by a set of messages.

Example 1 (Configuration trace). Assuming that $A, \ldots, Z$ and $1, \ldots, 9$ are messages. Figure 1 depicts a configuration trace t with corresponding architecture configurations $t(0) = k_0$, $t(1) = k_1$, and $t(2) = k_2$. Architecture configuration k_1, for example, consists of two active components named c_1 and c_2. Thereby, component c_1 is parametrized by $\{A\}$, has one input port i_0 valuated with $\{8\}$, and three output ports o_0, o_1, o_2, valuated with $\{1\}$, $\{G\}$, and $\{7\}$. □

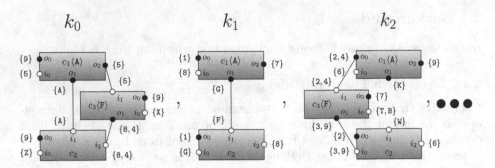

Fig. 1. Configuration trace with its first three architecture configurations.

Note that the model allows components to be valuated by a set of messages, rather than just a single message, at each point in time. To evaluate the behavior of a single component, the model comes with an operator $\Pi_c(t)$ to extract the behavior of a single component c out of a given configuration trace t.

The model of configuration traces is also implemented by a corresponding Isabelle/HOL theory which is available through the archive of formal proofs [7]. The implementation formalizes a configuration trace as a function $trace = nat \rightarrow cnf$ and provides an interface to the model in terms of a locale "dynamic_component". The locale can be instantiated with components of a dynamic architecture by providing definitions for two parameters:

- $tCMP: id \times cnf \rightarrow cmp$: an operator to obtain a component cmp with a certain identifier id from an architecture configuration cnf, and
- $active: id \times cnf \rightarrow bool$: a predicate to assert whether a certain component with identifier id is activated within an architecture configuration cnf.

For each dynamic component instantiating the locale, a set of definitions is provided to support the specification of its behavior [17]. Moreover, a calculus to reason about the behavior of the component in a dynamic context is provided [8].

3   Specifying Architectural Design Patterns

In the following, we describe FACTum, an approach to specify architectural design patterns. Therefore, we first provide a definition of the different parts of a pattern specification and then we explain each part in more detail. We conclude the section with an exemplary specification of three patterns: the singleton, the publisher subscriber, and the blackboard pattern. Thereby, the publisher component is modeled as an instance of the singleton and the blackboard pattern is specified as an instance of the publisher subscriber pattern.

Definition 1 (Pattern specification). *A pattern specification is a 5-tuple* (VAR, DS, IS, CT, AS), *consisting of:*

- *Variables $VAR = (V, V', C, C')$ with*
  - *data type variables V and so-called* rigid *data type variables V' (variables with a fixed interpretation during execution) and*
  - *component variables C and* rigid *component variables C'.*
- *A* datatype specification $DS = (\Sigma, DA, Gen)$ *with*
  - *a signature $\Sigma = (S, F, B)$, containing sorts S and function/predicate symbols F/B for a pattern's data types,*
  - *a set of data type assertions DA specifying the meaning of the signature symbols in terms of a set of axioms, and*
  - *a set of generator clauses Gen to construct data types.*
- *An* interface specification $IS = (P, tp, IF)$ *with*
  - *a set of ports P and corresponding type function $tp\colon P \to S$ which assigns a sort to each port,*
  - *a set of interfaces $(CP, IP, OP) \in IF$ with input ports $IP \subseteq P$ and output ports $OP \subseteq P$, as well as a set of configuration parameters $CP \subseteq P$.*
- *A* component type specification $(CT_{if})_{if \in IF}$ *which assigns assertions CT_{if} about the behavior of a component to each interface if $\in IF$.*
- *A set of* architectural assertions AS, *which specify activation and deactivation of components and connections between the component's ports.*

Since a pattern specification may also instantiate other pattern specifications, we require that for each instantiated pattern $(VAR', DS', IS', CT', AS')$, the specification contains an additional *port instantiation* $(\eta_{i'})_{i' \in IF'}$, with *injective* functions $\eta_{i'}\colon CP' \cup IP' \cup OP' \to CP \cup IP \cup OP$, such that $\eta_{i'}(CP') \subseteq CP$, $\eta_{i'}(IP') \subseteq IP$, and $\eta_{i'}(OP') \subseteq OP$, for some $(CP, IP, OP) \in IF$. Thereby, we require that for each $(CP', IP', OP') \in IF'$ and $p' \in CP' \cup IP' \cup OP'$ the corresponding data type refines the type of p', i.e., that $tp(\eta_{i'}(p'))$ refines $(tp'(p'))$.

In the following, we explain the different parts of a FACTum specification in more detail.

3.1   Specifying Data Types

The data types involved in a pattern specification can be specified using *algebraic specification techniques* [18,19]. Algebraic specifications usually consist of two parts: First, a signature $\Sigma = (S, F, B)$, specifying a set of sorts S and function/predicate symbols F/B, typed by a list of sorts. In addition, an algebraic specification provides a set of axioms DA to assign meaning to the symbols of Σ. These axioms specify the characteristic properties of the data types used by a pattern specification and are formulated over the symbols of F and B, respectively. Finally, a data type specification may require that all elements of the corresponding type are constructed by corresponding constructor terms Gen, i.e., that each element of the corresponding type is build up from symbols of Gen.

3.2   Specifying Interfaces

The specification of interfaces proceeds then in two steps: First, ports are specified by providing a set of ports P and a corresponding mapping $tp\colon P \to S$ to specify which types of data may be exchanged through each port. Then, a set of interfaces (CP, IP, OP) is specified by declaring input ports $IP \subseteq P$, output ports $OP \subseteq P$, and a set of configuration parameters $CP \subseteq P$. Thereby, configuration parameters are a way to parametrize components of a certain type and they can be thought of as ports with a predefined value which is fixed for each component.

Interfaces can then be specified using so-called *configuration diagrams* consisting of a graphical depiction of the involved interfaces (see Sect. 3.6 for examples). Thereby, each interface consists of two parts: A name followed by a list of configuration parameters (enclosed between '⟨' and '⟩'). Input and output ports are represented by empty and filled circles, respectively.

3.3   Specifying Component Types

Component types are specified by assigning assertions about the input/output behavior to the interfaces. Thereby, configuration parameters can be used to distinguish between different components of a certain type.

The assertions are expressed in terms of linear temporal logic equations [20] formulated over the signature Σ by using port names as free variables. For example, the term "$\Box(c.p = \text{POS} \longrightarrow c.o \geq 1)$" denotes an assertion that port o of component c, for which configuration parameter p has the value POS (for positive), is guaranteed to be greater or equal to 1 for the whole execution of the system.

3.4   Specifying Activation and Connection Assertions

Finally, a set of assertions about the activation and deactivation of components as well as assertions about connections between component ports are specified. Both types of assertions may be expressed in terms of so called *configuration trace assertions*, i.e, linear temporal logic formulæ with special predicates to denote activation of components and port connections. Thereby, $c.p$ denotes the valuation of port p of a component c (where $\widehat{c.p}$ denotes that port p of component c is valuated, at all), $\|c\|$ denotes that a component c is currently active, and $c.p \rightsquigarrow c'.p'$ denotes that output port p of component c is connected to input port p' of component c'.

3.5   Specifying Pattern Instantiations

As described above, pattern specifications may be built on top of other pattern specifications by instantiating their component types. Such instantiations can be directly specified in a pattern's configuration diagram by annotating the

Diagram Singleton	**ASpec** Singleton	**for** Singleton

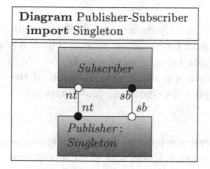

var	c:	*Singleton*
rig	c':	*Singleton*

$$\square(\exists c: \|c\|) \tag{1}$$

$$\exists c': \Big(\square(\forall c: (\|c\| \longrightarrow c = c'))\Big) \tag{2}$$

(a) Configuration diagram.   (b) Activation specification.

Fig. 2. Specification of the singleton pattern.

Diagram Publisher-Subscriber **import** Singleton

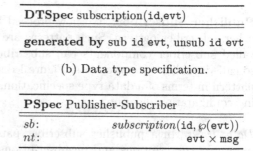

DTSpec subscription(id,evt)

generated by sub id evt, unsub id evt

(b) Data type specification.

PSpec Publisher-Subscriber

sb:	$subscription(\mathbf{id}, \wp(\mathbf{evt}))$
nt:	$\mathbf{evt} \times \mathbf{msg}$

(a) Configuration diagram.   (c) Port specification.

Fig. 3. Specification of the publisher subscriber pattern.

corresponding interfaces. To denote that a certain component type t of the specification is an instance of component type t' (from the instantiated pattern), we simply write $t : t'$ followed by a corresponding *port mapping* $[p'_i, p'_o \mapsto p_i, p_o]$, which assigns a port of t to each port of t'.

3.6   Example: An Initial Pattern Hierarchy

In the following, we demonstrate the FACTum approach by specifying variants of three well-known patterns: the singleton pattern, the publisher subscriber pattern, and the blackboard pattern. Thereby, the publisher component of the publisher subscriber pattern is modeled as an instance of the singleton, whereas the blackboard pattern is specified by instantiating the publisher subscriber pattern.

Singleton. The singleton pattern is a pattern for dynamic architectures in which, for a certain type of component, it is desired to have only one active instance at all points in time. Figure 2 depicts a possible specification of the pattern in terms of a configuration diagram and a corresponding activation specification. Since the pattern is only concerned with activation of components, we do neither have data types, nor port specifications for that pattern.

Interfaces. The interface is specified by the configuration diagram in Fig. 2a: It consists of a single interface *Singleton* and does not require any special ports.

Architectural Assertions. Activation assertions are formalized by the specification depicted in Fig. 2b: With Eq. 1 we require that there exists a component c which is always activated and with Eq. 2 we require the component to be unique. In our version of the singleton, we require that the singleton component is not allowed to change over time. This is why variable c is declared to be rigid in Fig. 2b. Indeed, other versions of the singleton are possible in which the singleton may change over time.

Publisher Subscriber. We now proceed by specifying a version of the publisher subscriber pattern. Such patterns are used for architectures in which so-called subscriber components can subscribe for certain messages from other, so-called publisher components. Figure 3 depicts a possible specification of the pattern in terms of a data type specification, port specification, and corresponding configuration diagram.

Data Types. In a publisher subscriber pattern we usually have two types of messages: subscriptions and unsubscriptions. Figure 3b depicts the corresponding data type specification. Subscriptions are modeled as *parametric* data types over two type parameters: a type `id` for component identifiers and some type `evt` denoting events to subscribe for. The data type is freely generated by the constructor terms "sub `id` `evt`" and "unsub `id` `evt`", meaning that every element of the type has the form "sub `id` `evt`" or "sub `id` `evt`".

Ports. Two port types are specified over these data types by the specification given in Fig. 3c: a type `sb` which allows to exchange subscriptions to a specific event and type `nt` which allows to exchange messages associated to any event.

Interfaces. The configuration diagram depicted in Fig. 3a depicts the specification of the interfaces of the two types of components: An interface *Publisher* is defined with an input port `sb` to receive subscriptions and an output port `nt` to send out notifications. Moreover, an interface *Subsciber* is defined with an input port `nt` receiving notifications and an output port `sb` to send out subscriptions. As stated in the beginning, we want a publisher to be unique and activated which is why it is specified as *Publisher:Singleton*, meaning that it is considered to be an instance of the *Singleton* type of the specification of the singleton pattern.

Architectural Assertions. Activation assertions for publisher subscriber architectures are mainly inherited from the singleton pattern: since a publisher is specified to be a singleton, a publisher component is unique and always activated. Moreover, two connection assertions for publisher subscriber architectures are specified in Fig. 4: Eq. (3) requires a publisher's input port `sb` to be connected to the corresponding output port of every active subscriber which sends some

ASpec Publisher-Subscriber		for Publisher-Subscriber
var	s:	*Subscriber*
	p:	*Publisher*
	m:	msg
	E:	$\wp(\text{evt})$
rig	s':	*Subscriber*
	e:	evt

$$\square\left(\|p\| \wedge \|s\| \wedge \widehat{s.sb} \longrightarrow p.sb \rightsquigarrow s.sb\right) \tag{3}$$

$$\square\left(\|s'\| \wedge (\exists E: \text{sub } s' \ E \in s'.sb \wedge e \in E)\right. \tag{4}$$

$$\left.\longrightarrow\left(\left(\|p\|\wedge\|s'\|\wedge(e,m)\in p.nt \longrightarrow s'.nt \rightsquigarrow p.nt\right) \ \mathcal{W} \ \left(\|s'\|\wedge(\exists E: \text{unsub } s' \ E \in s'.sb \wedge e \in E)\right)\right)\right)$$

Fig. 4. Architectural constraints for the blackboard pattern.

message. Equation (4), on the other hand, requires a subscriber's input port nt to be connected to the corresponding output port of the publisher, whenever the latter sends a message for which the subscriber is subscribed.

Blackboard. We conclude our example by specifying a dynamic version of the blackboard pattern. A blackboard architecture is usually used for the task of collaborative problem solving, i.e., a set of components work together to solve an overall, complex problem. Our specification of the pattern is depicted in Fig. 5 and consists of a data type specification, port specification, and corresponding configuration diagram.

Data Types. Blackboard architectures usually work with *problems* and *solutions* for them. Figure 5b provides a specification of the corresponding data types. We denote by PROB the set of all problems and by SOL the set of all solutions. Complex problems consist of *subproblems* which can be complex themselves. To solve a problem, its subproblems have to be solved first. Therefore, we assume the existence of a *subproblem relation* $\prec \ \subseteq$ PROB $\times$ PROB. For complex problems, the *details* of the relation may not be known in advance. Indeed, one of the benefits of a blackboard architecture is that a problem can be solved even without knowing the exact nature of this relation in advance. However, the subproblem relation has to be well-founded (Eq. (5)) for a problem to be solvable. In particular, we do not allow for cycles in the transitive closure of $\prec$. While there may be different approaches to solve a problem (i.e., several ways to split a problem into subproblems), we assume, without loss of generality, that the final solution for a problem is always unique. Thus, we assume the existence of a function *solve*: PROB $\to$ SOL which assigns the *correct* solution to each problem. Note, however, that it is not known in advance *how* to compute this function and it is indeed one of the reasons for using this pattern to calculate this function.

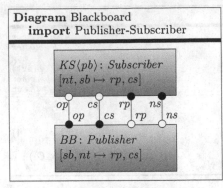

(a) Configuration diagram.

DTSpec ProbSol	imports SET
$\prec$:	PROB $\times$ PROB
$solve$:	PROB $\rightarrow$ SOL
$well\text{-}founded(\prec)$	(5)

(b) Data type specification.

PSpec BPort	
rp:	PROB $\times$ $\wp$(PROB)
ns, cs:	PROB $\times$ SOL
$op, prob$:	PROB

(c) Port specification.

Fig. 5. Specification of the blackboard pattern.

Ports. In Fig. 5c, we specify 4 ports for the pattern:

- rp is used to exchange a problem $p \in$ PROB which a knowledge source is able to solve, together with a set of subproblems $P \subseteq$ PROB the knowledge source requires to be solved first.
- ns is used to exchange a problem $p \in$ PROB solved by a knowledge source, together with the corresponding solution $s \in$ SOL.
- op is used to exchange a set $P \subseteq$ PROB of all the problems which still need to be solved.
- cs is used to exchange solutions $s \in$ SOL for problems $p \in$ PROB.

Moreover a configuration parameter *prob* is specified to parametrize knowledge source according to the problems $p \in$ PROB they can solve.

Interfaces. A blackboard pattern usually involves two types of components: blackboards and knowledge sources. The corresponding interfaces are specified by the configuration diagram in Fig. 5a. Since our version of the blackboard pattern is specified to be an instance of the publisher subscriber pattern, we import the corresponding pattern specification in the header of the diagram. We then specify two interfaces. The blackboard interface is denoted *BB* and is declared to be an instance of a *Publisher* component in a publisher subscriber pattern. It consists of two input ports rp and ns to receive required subproblems and new solutions. Moreover, it specifies two output ports op and cs to communicate currently open problems and solutions for all currently solved problems. Thereby, port rp is specified to be an instance of port sb of a publisher and port cs to be an instance of a publisher's nt port.

The interface for knowledge sources is denoted *KS* and is declared to be an instance of a *Subscriber* component in a publisher subscriber pattern. Note that each knowledge source can only solve certain problems, which is why a knowledge source is parameterized by a problem "*prob*". The specification of ports actually mirrors the corresponding specification of the blackboard interface. Thus, a knowledge source is required to have two input ports op and cs to

BSpec Blackboard	for BB of Blackboard
var p:	PROB
P:	PROB SET
rig p':	PROB
s':	SOL

$$\Box\big((p',s') \in ns \longrightarrow \Diamond((p',s') \in cs)\big) \tag{6}$$

$$\Box\big((p,P) \in rp \longrightarrow (\forall p' \in P: \ (\Diamond(p' \in op)))\big) \tag{7}$$

$$\Box\big(p' \in op \longrightarrow (p' \in op \ \mathcal{W} \ (p',solve(p')) \in cs \tag{8}$$

Fig. 6. Specification of behavior for blackboard components.

receive currently open problems and solutions for all currently solved problems, and two output ports rp and ns to communicate required subproblems and new solutions. Thereby, port rp is specified to be an instance of a subscribers nt port and port cs to be an instance of a subscribers sb port, respectively.

Component Types. A blackboard provides the *current state* towards solving the original problem and forwards problems and solutions from knowledge sources. Figure 6 provides a specification of the blackboard's behavior in terms of three behavior assertions:

- If a solution s' to a subproblem p' is received on its input port ns, then it is eventually provided at its output port cs (Eq. 6).
- If, on its input port rp, it gets notified that solutions for some subproblems P are required in order to solve a certain problem p, these problems are eventually provided at its output port op (Eq. (7)).
- A problem p' is provided at its output port op as long as it is not solved (Eq. (8)).

Note that the last assertion (Eq. (8)) is formulated using a *weak* until operator which is defined as follows: $\gamma' \ \mathcal{W} \ \gamma \ \overset{\text{def}}{=} \ \Box(\gamma') \vee (\gamma' \ \mathcal{U} \ \gamma)$.

A knowledge source receives open problems via op and provides solutions for other problems via cs. It might contribute to the solution of the original problem by solving currently open subproblems. Figure 7 provides a specification of the knowledge sources's behavior in terms of four behavior assertions:

- If a knowledge source (able to solve a problem pp) requires some subproblems P to be solved in order to solve pp and it gets solutions for all these subproblems p' on its input port cs, then it eventually solves pp and provides the solution on its output port ns (Eq. (9)).
- To solve a problem pp, a knowledge source requires solutions only for smaller problems $p \in P$ (Eq. (10)).
- A knowledge source will eventually communicate its ability to solve an open problem pp via its output port rp (Eq. (11)).
- A knowledge source does not unsubscribe from receiving solutions for subproblems it required until it indeed received these solutions (Eq. (12)).

BSpec Knowledge Source	**for** $ks = KS\langle pp \rangle$ **of** Blackboard
var p:	PROB
P:	$\wp(\text{PROB})$
rig p':	PROB

$$\square\Big(\forall(pp, P) \in rp\colon \big((\forall p' \in P\colon \Diamond(p', solve(p')) \in cs\big) \longrightarrow \Diamond(pp, solve(pp)) \in ns\big)\Big) \tag{9}$$

$$\square\Big(\forall(pp, P) \in rp\colon \forall p \in P\colon p \prec pp\Big) \tag{10}$$

$$\square\Big(pp \in op \longrightarrow \Diamond(\exists P\colon (pp, P) \in rp)\Big) \tag{11}$$

$$\square\Big(\textbf{sub } ks\ P = rp \longrightarrow \big(\neg \exists P'\colon p \in P' \wedge \textbf{unsub } ks\ P' = rp\ \mathcal{W}\ (p, solvep) \in cs\big)\Big) \tag{12}$$

Fig. 7. Specification of behavior for knowledge source components.

ASpec Blackboard	**for** Blackboard
var ks:	$KS\langle pp \rangle$
bb:	BB
rig ks':	$KS\langle pp \rangle$

$$\square\Big(\|ks'\| \wedge pp \in ks'.op \longrightarrow \big(\|ks'\|\ \mathcal{W}\ \|ks'\| \wedge (pp, solve(pp)) \in ks'.ns\big)\Big) \tag{13}$$

$$\square\Big(\|ks\| \wedge \|bb\| \wedge \widehat{bb.op} \longrightarrow ks.op \rightsquigarrow bb.op\Big) \tag{14}$$

$$\square\Big(\|bb\| \wedge \|ks\| \wedge \widehat{ks.ns} \longrightarrow bb.ns \rightsquigarrow ks.ns\Big) \tag{15}$$

Fig. 8. Specification of activation constraints for blackboard architectures.

Architectural Assertions. Activation constraint for blackboards are mainly inherited from the singleton pattern: since a blackboard is specified to be an instance of a publisher which is again an instance of a singleton, a blackboard component is unique and always activated. Activation constraint for knowledge sources are provided in Fig. 8 by Eq. (13): Whenever a knowledge source (able to solve a problem pp) gets notified about a request to solve pp, it stays active until pp is indeed solved. Connection assertions for the blackboard pattern are mainly inherited from the corresponding specification of the publisher subscriber pattern (for ports rp and cs, respectively). Two additional assertions, however, are provided in Fig. 8: with Eq. 14 we require input ports op of active blackboard components to be connected to the corresponding output ports of knowledge sources and with Eq. 15 we require a similar property for port ns.

4   Verifying Architectural Design Patterns

In the last section we presented FACTum, a methodology and corresponding techniques to specify architectural design pattern. Thereby, we relied on an intuitive understanding of the semantics of the techniques. In the following, we first provide a more formal definition of the semantics of a FACTum specification. Then, we describe an algorithm to map a given specification to a corresponding Isabelle/HOL theory and we show soundness of the algorithm.

4.1   Semantics of Pattern Specifications

The semantics of a pattern specification is given in terms of sets of configuration traces introduced in Sect. 2.

Definition 2 (Semantics of Pattern Specification). *The semantics of a pattern specification* (VAR, DS, IS, CT, AS) *is given by a 5-tuple* $(\mathcal{A}, \mathcal{P}, \mathcal{T}, \mathcal{C}, AT)$, *consisting of:*

- *an algebra* $\mathcal{A} = ((A_s)_{s \in S}, (f^{\mathcal{A}})_{f \in F}, (p^{\mathcal{A}})_{p \in B})$ *for* Σ,
- *a set of ports* $\mathcal{P}$ *with cardinality greater or equal to the cardinality of* P,
- *port typing* $\mathcal{T} \colon \mathcal{P} \to \wp(\mathcal{M})$ *with* $\mathcal{M} = \bigcup_{s \in S}(A_s)$,
- *a nonempty set of component identifiers* $\mathcal{C}_{if}$ *for each component interface* $if \in CI_{\mathcal{T}}^{P}$, *and*
- *an architecture* $AT \in DA_{\mathcal{T}}^{\mathcal{C}}$;

such that for all port interpretations $\delta \colon P \to \mathcal{P}$ *(injective mappings which respect tp and* $\mathcal{T}$*), variable interpretations* $\iota \colon V \to A$ *and* $\iota' \colon V' \to A$, *and component variable interpretations* $\kappa \colon C \to \mathcal{C}$ *and* $\kappa' \colon C' \to \mathcal{C}$ *(respecting interface types) the following conditions hold:*

- A *is an algebra for the data type specification:* $A, \iota \models DS$,
- *the projection to the behavior of a component* c *for every configuration trace* t *of the architecture satisfies the corresponding behavior specification:* $\forall c \in C_{\mathcal{T}}^{\mathcal{C}}, t \in AT \colon \Pi_c(t) \frown b \models CT_c$, *and*
- *all configuration traces* t *of the architecture satisfy the architectural assertions:* $\forall t \in AT \colon t, \iota', \kappa' \models AS$.

4.2   Mapping to Isabelle/HOL

Algorithm 1 describes how to systematically transfer a pattern specification to a corresponding Isabelle/HOL theory. In general, the transformation is done in 4 main steps: (i) The specified data types are transferred to corresponding Isabelle/HOL data type specifications (ii) An Isabelle locale is created for the corresponding pattern which imports other locales for each instantiated pattern. (iii) Specifications of component behavior are added as assumptions. (iv) Activation and connection assertions are provided as assumptions.

The following soundness criterion guarantees that Algorithm 1 indeed preserves the semantics of a pattern specification.

Theorem 1 (Soundness of Algorithm 1). *For every pattern specification* PT, *and model* T *of the Isabelle/HOL locale (as specified in* [21]*) generated by Algorithm 1, there exists a* T' *such that* $T' \models PT$ *(as defined by Definition 2) and* T' *is isomorphic to* T; *and vice versa.*

Note that the generated theory is based on Isabelle/HOLs implementation of configuration traces [7]. Thus, a calculus is instantiated for each component type which provides a set of rules to reason about the specification of the behavior of components of that type.

Algorithm 1. Mapping a pattern specification to an Isabelle/HOL Theory.

Input: (VAR, DS, IS, CT, AS) {pattern specification according to Definition 1}
Output: An Isabelle/HOL theory for the specification
  1: create Isabelle/HOL data type specification for DS
  2: create Isabelle/HOL locale for the pattern
  3: **for all** Interfaces $i = (CP, IP, OP) \in IF$ **do**
  4:     **if** i instantiates a component of another pattern **then**
  5:         import the corresponding locale
  6:         create instance of ports according to δ_i
  7:     **else**
  8:         import locale "dynamic_component" of theory "Configuration_Traces" [8]
  9:     **end if**
 10:     create instance of locale parameters $tCMP$ and $active$
 11:     **for all** configuration parameters $p \in CP$ which are not instances **do**
 12:         create locale parameter p of type $tp(p)$
 13:         create locale assumption "$\forall x.\ \exists c.\ x = p(c)$"
 14:     **end for**
 15:     **for all** ports $p \in IP \cup OP$ which are not instances **do**
 16:         create locale parameter p of type $tp(p)$
 17:     **end for**
 18:     **for all** behavior assertions $b \in CT_i$ **do**
 19:         create locale assumption for b using def. of theory "Configuration_Traces" [8]
 20:     **end for**
 21: **end for**
 22: **for all** activation/connection assertions $c \in AS$ **do**
 23:     create locale assertion for c
 24: **end for**

4.3   Example: Pattern Hierarchy

Algorithm 1 can be used to transfer a given pattern specification to a corresponding Isabelle/HOL theory where it is subject to formal verification. This is demonstrated by applying it to the specification of the singleton, publisher subscriber, and blackboard pattern presented in Sect. 3.6. To demonstrate the verification capabilities, we then proof one characteristic property for each pattern. The corresponding Isabelle/HOL theory files are provided online [22].

Singleton. We first come up with a basic property for singleton components which ensures that there exists indeed a *unique* component of the corresponding type which is always activated:

$$\exists! c \colon \square\,(\|c\|)\,. \tag{16}$$

Publisher Subscriber. Lets now turn to the publisher subscriber pattern. First of all, remember that the publisher component was specified to be an instance of the singleton pattern which is why all results from the verification of the singleton pattern are lifted to the publisher component. Thus, we get an equivalent result as Eq. (16) for free. Moreover, we can use the additional assertions imposed by the specification to come up with another property for the publisher subscriber pattern which guarantees that a subscriber indeed receives all the messages for which he is subscribed:

$$\square\Big(\|c\| \wedge \text{sub } c\ E \in c.sb \longrightarrow$$ (17)

$$((e,m) \in p.nt \wedge e \in E \longrightarrow (e,m) \in c.sb)\ \mathcal{W}\ (\text{unsub } c\ E' \in c.sb \wedge e \in E')\Big).$$

Note that the proof of the above property is based on Eq. (16) inherited from the singleton pattern. Indeed, the hierarchical nature of FACTum allows for reuse of verification results from instantiated patterns.

Blackboard. Again, the properties verified for singletons (Eq. (16)) as well as the properties verified for publisher subscriber architectures (Eq. (17)) are inherited for the blackboard specification. In the following, we use these properties to verify another property for blackboard architectures: A blackboard pattern guarantees that if for each open (sub-)problem, there exists a knowledge source which is able to solve the corresponding problem:

$$\square\Big(\forall p' \in bb'.op \colon \Diamond(\|ks_{p'}\|)\Big),$$ (18)

then, it is guaranteed, that the architecture will eventually solve an overall problem, even if no single knowledge source is able to solve the problem on its own:

$$\square\Big(p' \in bb'.rp \longrightarrow \Diamond(p', solve(p')) \in bb'.cs\Big).$$ (19)

5 Related Work

Related work can be found in three different areas.

Formal Specification of Architectural Styles. Over the last years, several approaches emerged to support the formal specification of architectural design patterns. One of the first attempts in this direction was Wright [23] which provided the possibility to specify architectural styles which is similar to our notion of architectural design pattern. More recent approaches to specify styles are based on the BIP framework [24] and provide logics [25] as well as graphical notation [26] to specify styles. There are, however, two differences of these approaches to the work presented in this paper: One difference concerns the expressive power of the specification techniques. While the above approaches focus mainly on the specification of patterns for static architectures, we allow for the specification of static as well as dynamic architectures. Another difference arises from the scope of the work. While the above approaches focus mainly on the specification of patterns, our focus is more on the verification of such specifications.

Verification of Architectural Styles and Patterns. Recently, some approaches emerged which focus on the verification of architectural styles and patterns. Kim and Garlan [27], for example, apply the Alloy [28] analyzer to automatically verify architectural styles specified in ACME [29]. A similar approach comes from Wong et al. [30] which applies Alloy to the verification of architectural models. Zhang et al. [31] applied model checking techniques to verify architectural styles formulated in Wright#, an extension of Wright. Similarly, Marmsoler and Degenhardt [32] also apply model checking for the verification of design patterns. Another approach comes from Wirsing et al. [33] where the authors apply rewriting logic to specify and verify cloud-based architectures. While all these approaches focus on the verification of architectures and architectural patterns, they all apply automatic verification techniques. While this has many advantages, verification is limited to properties subject to automatic verification. Indeed, with our work we actually complement these approaches by providing an alternative approach based on, rather than automatic verification techniques.

Interactive Theorem Proving for Software Architectures. Another area of related work can be found in applications of to software architectures in general. Fensel and Schnogge [34], for example, apply the KIV interactive theorem prover to verify concrete architectures in the area of knowledge-based systems. Their work differs from our work in two main aspects. (i) While they focus on the verification of concrete architectures, we propose an approach to verify architectural patterns. (ii) While they focus on the verification of static architecture, our approach allows for the verification of dynamic architectures. Thus, we complement their work by providing a more general approach. More recently, some attempts were made to apply to the verification of architectural connectors. Li and Sun [35], for example, apply the Coq proof assistant to verify connectors specified in Reo [36]. With our work we complement their approach since we focus on the verification of patterns, rather than connectors.

To summarize, to the best of our knowledge, this is the first attempt applying to the verification of architectural design patterns.

6   Conclusion

With this paper we presented a novel approach for the specification and verification of architecture design patterns. Therefore, we provide a methodology and corresponding specification techniques for the specification of patterns in terms of configuration traces. Then, we describe an algorithm to map a given specification to a corresponding Isabelle/HOL theory and show soundness of the algorithm. Our approach can be used to formally specify patterns in a hierarchical way. Using the algorithm, the specification can then be mapped to a corresponding Isabelle/HOL theory where the pattern can be verified using a pre-existing calculus. This is demonstrated by specifying and verifying versions of three architecture patterns: the singleton, the publisher subscriber, and the blackboard. Thereby, patterns were specified hierarchical and verification results for lower level patterns were reused for the verification of higher level patterns.

The proposed approach addresses the challenges for pattern verification identified in the introduction as follows:

	C1 Axiomatic specifications	C2 Dynamic aspects	C3 Hierarchical specifications
Specification	Model-theoretic semantics	Model of dynamic architectures	Structured specifications
Verification	Axiomatic reasoning	A calculus to support verification	Import of verification results

In order to achieve our overall vision of interactive, hierarchical pattern verification [37], future work is needed in two directions: We are currently working on an implementation of the approach for the eclipse modeling framework [38] where a pattern can be specified and a corresponding Isabelle/HOL theory can be generated using the algorithm presented in the paper. In a second step, we want to lift the verification to the architecture level, hiding the complexity of an interactive theorem prover and interpreting its output at the architecture level.

Acknowledgments. We would like to thank Veronika Bauer, Maximilian Junker, and all the anonymous reviewers of FASE 2018 for their comments and helpful suggestions on earlier versions of this paper. Parts of the work on which we report in this paper was funded by the German Federal Ministry of Education and Research (BMBF) under grant no. 01Is16043A.

References

1. Taylor, R.N., Medvidovic, N., Dashofy, E.M.: Software Architecture: Foundations, Theory, and Practice. Wiley Publishing, Chichester (2009)
2. Buschmann, F., Meunier, R., Rohnert, H., Sommerlad, P., Stal, M.: Pattern-Oriented Software Architecture: A System of Patterns. Wiley, West Sussex (1996)
3. Shaw, M., Garlan, D.: Software Architecture: Perspectives on an Emerging Discipline, vol. 1. Prentice Hall, Englewood Cliffs (1996)
4. Wiedijk, F. (ed.): The Seventeen Provers of the World. LNCS (LNAI), vol. 3600. Springer, Heidelberg (2006). https://doi.org/10.1007/11542384
5. Marmsoler, D., Gleirscher, M.: On activation, connection, and behavior in dynamic architectures. Sci. Ann. Comput. Sci. **26**(2), 187–248 (2016)
6. Marmsoler, D., Gleirscher, M.: Specifying properties of dynamic architectures using configuration traces. In: Sampaio, A., Wang, F. (eds.) ICTAC 2016. LNCS, vol. 9965, pp. 235–254. Springer, Cham (2016). https://doi.org/10.1007/978-3-319-46750-4_14
7. Marmsoler, D.: Dynamic architectures. Archive of Formal Proofs, pp. 1–65. Formal proof development, July 2017
8. Marmsoler, D.: Towards a calculus for dynamic architectures. In: Hung, D., Kapur, D. (eds.) ICTAC 2017. LNCS, vol. 10580. Springer, Cham (2017). https://doi.org/10.1007/978-3-319-67729-3_6

9. Nipkow, T., Wenzel, M., Paulson, L.C. (eds.): Isabelle/HOL: A Proof Assistant for Higher-Order Logic. LNCS, vol. 2283. Springer, Heidelberg (2002). https://doi.org/10.1007/3-540-45949-9

10. Gordon, M.J., Milner, A.J., Wadsworth, C.P.: Edinburgh LCF: A Mechanised Logic of Computation. LNCS, vol. 78. Springer, Heidelberg (1979). https://doi.org/10.1007/3-540-09724-4

11. Berghofer, S., Wenzel, M.: Inductive datatypes in HOL — lessons learned in formal-logic engineering. In: Bertot, Y., Dowek, G., Théry, L., Hirschowitz, A., Paulin, C. (eds.) TPHOLs 1999. LNCS, vol. 1690, pp. 19–36. Springer, Heidelberg (1999). https://doi.org/10.1007/3-540-48256-3_3

12. Wenzel, M.: Type classes and overloading in higher-order logic. In: Gunter, E.L., Felty, A. (eds.) TPHOLs 1997. LNCS, vol. 1275, pp. 307–322. Springer, Heidelberg (1997). https://doi.org/10.1007/BFb0028402

13. Wenzel, M.: Isabelle/Isar - a generic framework for human-readable proof documents. In: From Insight to Proof - Festschrift in Honour of Andrzej Trybulec vol. 10, no. 23, pp. 277–298 (2007)

14. Ballarin, C.: Locales and locale expressions in Isabelle/Isar. In: Berardi, S., Coppo, M., Damiani, F. (eds.) TYPES 2003. LNCS, vol. 3085, pp. 34–50. Springer, Heidelberg (2004). https://doi.org/10.1007/978-3-540-24849-1_3

15. Broy, M.: A logical basis for component-oriented software and systems engineering. Comput. J. **53**(10), 1758–1782 (2010)

16. Broy, M.: A model of dynamic systems. In: Bensalem, S., Lakhneck, Y., Legay, A. (eds.) ETAPS 2014. LNCS, vol. 8415, pp. 39–53. Springer, Heidelberg (2014). https://doi.org/10.1007/978-3-642-54848-2_3

17. Marmsoler, D.: On the semantics of temporal specifications of component-behavior for dynamic architectures. In: Eleventh International Symposium on Theoretical Aspects of Software Engineering. Springer (2017)

18. Broy, M.: Algebraic specification of reactive systems. In: Wirsing, M., Nivat, M. (eds.) AMAST 1996. LNCS, vol. 1101, pp. 487–503. Springer, Heidelberg (1996). https://doi.org/10.1007/BFb0014335

19. Wirsing, M.: Algebraic specification. In: van Leeuwen, J. (ed.) Handbook of Theoretical Computer Science, pp. 675–788. MIT Press, Cambridge (1990)

20. Manna, Z., Pnueli, A.: The Temporal Logic of Reactive and Concurrent Systems. Springer, New York (1992). https://doi.org/10.1007/978-1-4612-0931-7

21. Wenzel, M., et al.: The Isabelle/Isar reference manual (2004)

22. Marmsoler, D.: Isabelle/HOL theories for the singleton, publisher subscriber, and blackboard pattern. http://www.marmsoler.com/docs/FASE18

23. Allen, R.J.: A formal approach to software architecture. Technical report, DTIC Document (1997)

24. Attie, P., Baranov, E., Bliudze, S., Jaber, M., Sifakis, J.: A general framework for architecture composability. Form. Asp. Comput. **28**(2), 207–231 (2016)

25. Mavridou, A., Baranov, E., Bliudze, S., Sifakis, J.: Architecture diagrams: a graphical language for architecture style specification. In: Bartoletti, M., Henrio, L., Knight, S., Vieira, H.T. (eds.) Proceedings of the 9th Interaction and Concurrency Experience. ICE 2016, Heraklion, 8–9 June 2016. EPTCS, vol. 223, pp. 83–97 (2016)

26. Mavridou, A., Baranov, E., Bliudze, S., Sifakis, J.: Configuration logics: modelling architecture styles. In: Braga, C., Ölveczky, P.C. (eds.) FACS 2015. LNCS, vol. 9539, pp. 256–274. Springer, Cham (2016). https://doi.org/10.1007/978-3-319-28934-2_14

27. Kim, J.S., Garlan, D.: Analyzing architectural styles with alloy. In: Proceedings of the ISSTA 2006 Workshop on Role of Software Architecture for Testing and Analysis, pp. 70–80. ACM (2006)
28. Jackson, D.: Alloy: a lightweight object modelling notation. ACM Trans. Softw. Eng. Methodol. (TOSEM) 11(2), 256–290 (2002)
29. Garlan, D.: Formal modeling and analysis of software architecture: components, connectors, and events. In: Bernardo, M., Inverardi, P. (eds.) SFM 2003. LNCS, vol. 2804, pp. 1–24. Springer, Heidelberg (2003). https://doi.org/10.1007/978-3-540-39800-4_1
30. Wong, S., Sun, J., Warren, I., Sun, J.: A scalable approach to multi-style architectural modeling and verification. In: Engineering of Complex Computer Systems, pp. 25–34. IEEE (2008)
31. Zhang, J., Liu, Y., Sun, J., Dong, J.S., Sun, J.: Model checking software architecture design. In: High-Assurance Systems Engineering, pp. 193–200. IEEE (2012)
32. Marmsoler, D., Degenhardt, S.: Verifying patterns of dynamic architectures using model checking. In: Proceedings of the International Workshop on Formal Engineering approaches to Software Components and Architectures, FESCA@ETAPS 2017, Uppsala, Sweden, 22 April 2017, pp. 16–30 (2017)
33. Wirsing, M., Eckhardt, J., Mühlbauer, T., Meseguer, J.: Design and analysis of cloud-based architectures with KLAIM and Maude. In: Durán, F. (ed.) WRLA 2012. LNCS, vol. 7571, pp. 54–82. Springer, Heidelberg (2012). https://doi.org/10.1007/978-3-642-34005-5_4
34. Fensel, D., Schnogge, A.: Using KIV to specify and verify architectures of knowledge-based systems. In: Automated Software Engineering, pp. 71–80, November 1997
35. Li, Y., Sun, M.: Modeling and analysis of component connectors in Coq. In: Fiadeiro, J.L., Liu, Z., Xue, J. (eds.) FACS 2013. LNCS, vol. 8348, pp. 273–290. Springer, Cham (2014). https://doi.org/10.1007/978-3-319-07602-7_17
36. Arbab, F.: Reo: a channel-based coordination model for component composition. Math. Struct. Comput. Sci. 14(03), 329–366 (2004)
37. Marmsoler, D.: Towards a theory of architectural styles. In: Proceedings of the 22nd ACM SIGSOFT International Symposium on Foundations of Software Engineering - FSE 2014, pp. 823–825. ACM Press (2014)
38. Steinberg, D., Budinsky, F., Merks, E., Paternostro, M.: EMF: Eclipse Modeling Framework. Pearson Education, London (2008)

Supporting Verification-Driven Incremental Distributed Design of Components

Claudio Menghi[1]([⊠]) [iD], Paola Spoletini[2] [iD], Marsha Chechik[3] [iD],
and Carlo Ghezzi[4] [iD]

[1] Chalmers | University of Gothenburg, Gothenburg, Sweden
`claudio.menghi@gu.se`
[2] Kennesaw State University, Marietta, USA
`pspoleti@kennesaw.edu`
[3] University of Toronto, Toronto, Canada
`chechik@cs.toronto.edu`
[4] Politecnico di Milano, Milan, Italy
`carlo.ghezzi@polimi.it`

Abstract. Software systems are usually formed by multiple components which interact with one another. In large systems, components themselves can be complex systems that need to be decomposed into multiple sub-components. Hence, system design must follow a systematic approach, based on a recursive decomposition strategy. This paper proposes a comprehensive verification-driven framework which provides support for designers during development. The framework supports hierarchical decomposition of components into sub-components through formal specification in terms of pre- and post-conditions as well as independent development, reuse and verification of sub-components.

1 Introduction

Software is usually not a monolithic product: it is often comprised of multiple components that interact with each other to provide the desired functionality. Components themselves can be complex, requiring their own decomposition into sub-components. Hence, system design, must follow a systematic approach, based on a recursive decomposition strategy that yields a modular structure. A good decomposition and a careful specification should allow components and sub-components to be developed in isolation by different development teams, delegated to third parties [32], or reused off-the-shelf.

In this context, guaranteeing correctness of the system under development becomes particularly challenging because of the intrinsic tension between two main requirements. On the one hand, to handle complexity, we need to enable development of sub-components where only a partial view of the system is available [28]. On the other hand, we must ensure that independently developed and verified (sub-)components can be composed to guarantee global correctness of

© The Author(s) 2018
A. Russo and A. Schürr (Eds.): FASE 2018, LNCS 10802, pp. 169–188, 2018.
https://doi.org/10.1007/978-3-319-89363-1_10

The **p&d** running example. The p&d system supports furniture purchase and delivery. It uses two existing web services, which implement furniture-sale and delivery, as well as a component that implements the user interface. These are modeled by the labeled transition systems shown in Fig. 1a-1c. The p&d component under design is responsible for interaction with these components, which form its execution environment. The overall system must ensure satisfaction of the properties informally described in Fig. 1d.

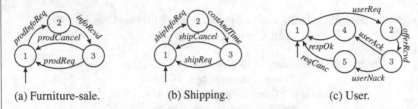

(a) Furniture-sale.   (b) Shipping.   (c) User.

P1: ship and product info are provided only if a request has been received.
P2: when user requests are processed, offers are considered only after users received information about the desired product.
P3: the furniture service is activated only if the user has decided to purchase.
P4: when a user request is cancelled by the p&d system, no user ack precedes the cancellation.

(d) Properties of the p&d system.

Fig. 1. The p&d running example.

the resulting system. Thus, we believe that component development should be supported by a process that (1) is intrinsically iterative; (2) supports decentralized development; and (3) guarantees correctness at each development stage.

The need for supporting incremental development of components has been widely recognized. Some approaches [15,37] synthesize a partial model of components from properties and scenarios and facilitate an iterative development of this model through refinement. Others [7,8,10,26,27] provide support for checking and refining partial models, with the goal of preserving correctness when such systems get refined. However, while these techniques guarantee correctness at each development stage, they do not address the problem of decentralized development.

In this paper, we describe a unified framework called FIDDle (a Framework for Iterative and Distributed Design of components) which supports decentralized top-down development. FIDDle supports a formal specification of global properties, a decomposition process and specification of component interfaces by providing a set of tools to guarantee correctness of the different artifacts produced during the process. The main contribution of the paper is a method for supporting an iterative and distributed verification-driven component development process through a coherent set of tools. Specific novel contributions are (1) a new formalism, called *Interface Partial Labelled Transition System (IPLTS)*, for specifying components through a decomposition that encapsulates sub-components into unspecified black-box states; (2) an approach to specify *the expected behavior of black-box states* via pre- and post-conditions expressed in Fluent Linear Time Temporal Logic; and (3) a notion of *component correctness*

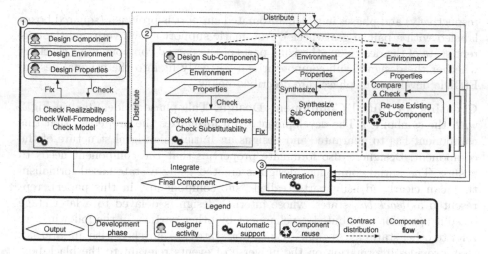

Fig. 2. Overview of the application of FIDDle for developing a component. Thick-bordered components are implemented in FIDDle. Thick-dashed bordered components are currently supported by the theory presented in this paper, but they are still not fully implemented. Thin-dashed bordered components are not discussed in this work.

and a *local verification procedure* that *guarantees preservation of global properties* once the components are composed.

We illustrate FIDDle using a simple example: the *purchase&delivery* (p&d) example [14, 29] – see Fig. 1. We evaluate FIDDle on a realistic case study obtained by reverse-engineering the executive module of the Mars Rover developed at NASA [12,17,18]. Scalability is evaluated by considering randomly-generated examples.

Organization. Sect. 2 provides an overview of FIDDle. Section 3 gives the necessary background. Section 4 presents Interface Partial Labelled Transition Systems (IPLTS). Section 5 defines a set of algorithms for reasoning on partial components and describes their implementation. Section 6 reports on an evaluation of the proposed approach. Section 7 compares FIDDle with related approaches, and Sect. 8 concludes. Proofs for the theorems in the paper can be found in the Appendix available at http://ksuweb.kennesaw.edu/~pspoleti/fase-appendix.pdf; source code and video of the tool and a complete replication package can be found at https://github.com/claudiomenghi/FIDDLE.

2 Overview

FIDDle is a verification-driven environment supporting incremental and distributed component development. A high-level view of FIDDle is shown in Fig. 2. FIDDle allows incrementally developing a component through a set of development phases in which the human insight and experience are exploited (rounded boxes labeled with a designer icon or a recycle symbol, to indicate design or reuse, respectively) and phases in which automated support is provided (squared boxes labeled with a pair of gearwheels). Automatic support allows verifying the current state of the design, synthesizing parts of the partial component, or checking whether the designed sub-component can correctly fit into the original design. FIDDle development phases are described below.

Creating an Initial Component Design. This phase is identified in Fig. 2 with the symbol ①. The development team formalizes the properties that this component has to guarantee and designs an initial, high-level structure of the component. Designers also formulate properties that the component needs to ensure. The initial component design is created using a state-based formalism that can clearly identify parts (called "sub-components" in this paper), represented as *black-box* states, whose internal design is delayed to a later stage or split apart for distributed development by other parties. In the following, we refer to other states as "regular". Black-box states are enriched with an *interface* that provides information on the universe of events relevant to the black-box. They are also decorated with via pre- and post-conditions that allow distributed teams to develop sub-components without the need to know about the rest of the system. The *contract* of a black box state consists of its interface and pre- and post-conditions.

In the p&d example, the environment (assumed as given) in which the p&d component will be deployed is composed by the furniture-sale component (Fig. 1a), the shipping component (Fig. 1b) and the user (Fig. 1c). A possible initial design for the p&d component is shown in Fig. 3c. It contains the regular states 1 and 3 and black-box states 2 and 4. The initial state is state 1. Whenever a *userReq* event is detected, the component moves from the initial state 1 into the black-box state 2, which represents a sub-component in charge of managing the user request. An event *offerRcvd* which indicates that an offer is provided to the user labels the transition to state 3. The pre- and post- conditions for black-box states 2 and 4 are shown in Fig. 3b. Events *prodInfoReq*, *infoRcvd*, *shipInfoReq* and *costAndTime* can occur while the component is in the black-box state 2. The pre-condition requires that there is a user request that has not yet been handled, while the post-condition ensures that the furniture-sale and the shipping services provided info on the product and on delivery cost and time. FIDDle supports the developer in checking properties of the initial component design.

The *realizability checker* confirms the existence of an integration that completes the partially specified component and ensures the satisfaction of the properties of interest. If such a component does not exist, the designer needs to redesign the partially-specified component. The *well-formedness checker* verifies that both the pre- and the post-conditions of black-box states are satisfiable. Finally, the *model checker* verifies whether the (partial) component (together with its contract) guarantees satisfaction of the properties of interest.

In the p&d example, the model checker identifies a problem with the partial solution sketched in Fig. 3c. No matter how the black-box state 2 is to be defined, the p&d component cannot satisfy property $P4$ since every time *reqCanc* occurs

$$P1 = (\neg((\neg F\_UserReq)\,\mathcal{U}\,(F\_ShipInfoReq \lor F\_ProdInfoReq)))$$
$$P2 = \Box(F\_UserReq \to (\neg((\neg F\_InfoRcvd)\,\mathcal{U}\,F\_OfferRcvd)))$$
$$P3 = \Box(F\_UsrReq \to ((\neg((\neg F\_UserAck)\,\mathcal{W}\,F\_ShipReq))$$
$$P4 = \Box((F\_UsrReq \land ((\neg F\_UsrReq)\,\mathcal{U}\,F\_ReqCanc)) \to ((\neg F\_UserAck)\,\mathcal{U}\,F\_ReqCanc))$$

(a) FLTL formulation of the p&d properties.

	State 2
interface	{ prodInfoReq, infoRcvd, shipInfoReq, costAndTime }
pre	$\Diamond(F\_UserReq \land \neg\Diamond(F\_RespOk \lor F\_ReqCanc))$
post	$(\Diamond F\_InfoRcvd) \land (\Diamond F\_CostAndTime)$
	State 4
interface	{ prodReq, shipReq }
pre	$\Box(F\_UserReq \to \Diamond F\_InfoRcvd)$
post	$(\Diamond(F\_ProdReq) \land \Diamond(F\_ShipReq))$
	State 5
interface	{ prodCancel, shipCancel }
pre	$\Box(F\_UserReq \to \Diamond F\_InfoRcvd)$
post	$(\Diamond(F\_ProdCancel) \land \Diamond(F\_ShipCancel))$

(b) Contracts for black-box states of Figs. 3c-3g.

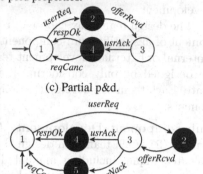

(c) Partial p&d.

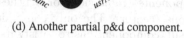

(d) Another partial p&d component.

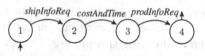

(e) A sub-component for black-box state 2.   (f) Another sub-component for black-box state 2.

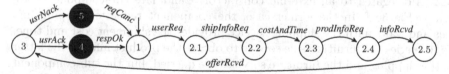

(g) Integration of the sub-component of Fig. 3e and the component of Fig. 3d.

Fig. 3. The p&d running example: artifacts produced by FIDDle.

it is preceded by *usrAck*. This suggests a re-design of the p&d component, which may lead to a new model, shown in Fig. 3d. This model includes two regular states: state 1, in which the component waits for a new user request, and state 3, in which the component has provided the user with an offer and is waiting for an answer. The user might accept (*userAck*) or reject (*userNack*) an offer and, depending on this choice, either state 4 or 5 is entered. States 2, 4 and 5 are black-box states, to be refined later. The designer also provides pre- and post-conditions for the black-box states. Pre- and post-conditions of the black-box state 2 specify that there is a pending user request, and that cost, time and product information are collected. Pre- and post-conditions of the black-box state 4 specify that *infoRcvd* has occurred after the user request, and both a product and shipping requests are performed. Finally, pre- and post-conditions of the black-box state 5 specify that *infoRcvd* has occurred after the user request and before entering the state, and both the product and the shipping requests are cancelled when leaving the state. This model is checked using the provided tools; since it passes all the checks, it can be used in the next phase of the development.

The design team may choose to refine the component or *distribute* the development of unspecified sub-components (represented by black box states) to other (internal or external) development teams. In both cases, the sub-component can be designed by only considering the contract of the corresponding black-box state. Each team can develop the assigned sub-component or reuse existing components.

Sub-component Development. This phase is identified in Fig. 2 with the symbol ②. Each team can design the assigned sub-component using any available technique, including manual design (left side), reusing of existing sub-components (right side) or synthesizing new ones from the provided specifications (center). The only constraints are (1) given the stated pre-condition, the sub-component has to satisfy its post-condition, and (2) the sub-component should operate in the same environment as the overall partially specified component. Sub-component development can itself be an iterative process, but neither the model of the environment nor the overall properties of the system can be changed during this process. Otherwise, the resulting sub-component cannot be automatically integrated into the overall system.

In the p&d example, development of the sub-component for the black-box state 2 is delegated to an external contractor. Candidate sub-components are shown in Fig. 3e–f. In the former case, the component requests shipping info details and waits until the shipping service provides the shipment cost and time. Then it queries the furniture-sale service to obtain the product info. In the latter case, the shipping and the furniture services are queried, but the sub-component does not wait for an answer from the furniture-sale. Since these candidates are fully defined, the well-formedness check is not needed. Yet, the *substitutability checking* confirms that of these, only the sub-component in Fig. 3e satisfies the post-condition in Fig. 3b.

Sub-component Integration. This phase is identified in Fig. 2 with the symbol ③. FIDDle guarantees that if each sub-component is developed correctly w.r.t. the contract of the corresponding black-box state, the component obtained by integrating the sub-components is also correct. In the p&d example, the sub-component in Fig. 3e passes the substitutability check and can be a valid implementation of the black-box state 2 in Fig. 3d. Their integration is showed in Fig. 3g.

3   Preliminaries

The model of the environment and the properties of interest are expressed using Labelled Transition Systems and Fluent Linear Time Temporal Logic.

Model of the Environment. Let Act be the universal set of observable events and let $Act_\tau = Act \cup \{\tau\}$, where τ denotes an unobservable local event. A *Labeled Transition System (LTS)* [20] is a tuple $A = \langle Q, q_0, \alpha A, \Delta \rangle$, where Q is the set of states, $q_0 \in Q$ is the initial state, $\alpha A \subseteq Act$ is a finite set of events, and $\Delta \subseteq Q \times \alpha A \cup \{\tau\} \times Q$ is the transition relation. The parallel composition operation is defined as usual (see for example [14]).

Properties. A fluent [33] Fl is a tuple $\langle I_{Fl}, T_{Fl}, Init_{Fl} \rangle$, where $I_{Fl} \subset Act$, $T_{Fl} \subset Act$, $I_{Fl} \cap T_{Fl} = \emptyset$ and $Init_{Fl} \in \{true, false\}$. A fluent may be *true* or *false*. A fluent is *true* if it has been initialized by an event $i \in I_{Fl}$ at an earlier time point (or if it was initially *true*, that is, $Init_{Fl} = true$) and has not yet been terminated by another event $t \in T_{Fl}$; otherwise, it is *false*. For example, consider the LTS in Fig. 1c and the fluent $F\_ReqPend = \langle \{userReq\}, \{respOk, reqCanc\}, false \rangle$. $F\_ReqPend$ holds in a trace of the LTS from the moment at which *userReq* occurs and until a transition labeled with *respOk* or *reqCanc* is fired. In the following, we use the notation F_Event to indicate a fluent that is *true* when the event with label *event* occurs.

An FLTL formula is obtained by composing fluents with standard LTL operators: $\bigcirc$ (next), $\Diamond$ (eventually), $\Box$ (always), $\mathcal{U}$ (until) and $\mathcal{W}$ (weak until). For example, FLTL encodings of the properties *P1*, *P2*, *P3* and *P4* are shown in Fig. 3a.

Satisfaction of FLTL formulae can be evaluated over *finite* and *infinite* traces, by first constructing and FLTL interpretation of the infinite and finite trace and then by evaluating the FLTL formulae over this interpretation The FLTL interpretation of a finite trace is obtained by slightly changing the interpretation of infinite traces. The evaluation of the FLTL formulae on the finite trace is obtained by considering the standard interpretation of LTL operator over finite traces (see [13]). In the following, we assume that Definitions 5 and 4 (available in the Appendix) are considered to evaluate whether an FLTL formula is satisfied on finite and infinite traces, respectively.

4 Modeling and Refining Components

This section introduces a novel formalism for modeling and refining components. We define the notion of a partial LTS and then extend it with pre- and post-conditions.

Partial LTS. A *partial LTS* is an LTS where some states are "regular" and others are "black-box". Black-box states model portions of the component whose behavior still has to be specified. Each black-box state is augmented with an interface that specifies the universe of events that can occur in the black-box. A *Partial LTS (PLTS)* is a structure $P = \langle A, R, B, \sigma \rangle$, where: $A = \langle Q, q_0, \alpha A, \Delta \rangle$ is an LTS; Q is the set of states, s.t. $Q = R \cup B$ and $R \cap B = \emptyset$; R is the set of *regular* states; B is the set of *black-box* states; $\sigma : B \to 2^{\alpha A}$ is the *interface*. An LTS is a PLTS where the set of black-box states is empty. The PLTS in Fig. 3d is defined over the regular states 1 and 3, and the black-box states 2,

4 and 5. The interface specifies that events *prodInfoReq, infoRcvd, shipInfoReq* and *costAndTime* can occur in the black-box state 2.

Definition 1. *Given a PLTS* $P = \langle A, R, B, \sigma \rangle$ *defined over the LTS* $A = \langle Q^A, q_0^A, \alpha A, \Delta^A \rangle$ *and an LTS* $D = \langle Q^D, q_0^D, \alpha D, \Delta^D \rangle$, *the parallel composition* $P \parallel D$ *is an LTS* $S = \langle Q^S, q_0^S, \alpha S, \Delta^S \rangle$ *such that* $Q^S = Q^A \times Q^D$; $q_0^S = (q_0^A, q_0^D)$; $\alpha S = \alpha A \cup \alpha D$; *and the set of transitions* Δ^S *is defined as follows:*

- $\dfrac{(s,l,s') \in \Delta^A}{(\langle s,t \rangle, l, \langle s',t \rangle) \in \Delta^S}$, *and* $l \in \alpha A \setminus \alpha D$ *or* $l = \tau$;
- $\dfrac{(t,l,t') \in \Delta^D}{(\langle s,t \rangle, l, \langle s,t' \rangle) \in \Delta^S}$, *and one of the following is satisfied: (1)* $l \in \alpha D \setminus \alpha A$, *(2)* $l = \tau$, *or (3)* $(s \in B$ *and* $l \in \sigma(s))$;
- $\dfrac{(s,l,s') \in \Delta^A, (t,l,t') \in \Delta^D}{(\langle s,t \rangle, l, \langle s',t' \rangle) \in \Delta^S}$ *and* $l \in \alpha A \cap \alpha D, l \neq \tau$.

Given P, A, D defined above, the system $S = P \parallel D$ and a state q of P, we say that a finite trace $l_0, l_1, \ldots l_n$ of S *reaches* q if there exists a sequence $\langle s_0, t_0 \rangle, l_0, \langle s_1, t_1 \rangle, \ldots l_n, \langle q, t_{n+1} \rangle$, where for every $0 \leq i \leq n$, we have $(\langle s_i, t_i \rangle, l_i, \langle s_{i+1}, t_{i+1} \rangle) \in \Delta^S$. For example, considering the PLTS in Fig. 3d and the LTS in Fig. 1c, the finite trace obtained by performing a *userReq* event reaches the black-box state 2 of the PLTS.

Given a finite trace $\pi = l_0, l_1, \ldots l_n$ (or an infinite trace $l_0, l_1, \ldots$) of S, we say that its sub-trace $l_i, l_{i+1} \ldots l_k$ is *inside* the black-box state b if one of the sub-sequences associated with π is in the form $\langle b, t_i \rangle, l_i, \langle b, t_{i+1} \rangle, \ldots, l_k, \langle b, t_k \rangle$, where $l_i, l_{i+1}, \ldots, l_k \in \sigma(b)$. Note that a sub-trace is a *finite* trace. For example, considering the parallel composition of the PLTS in Fig. 3d and the LTSs in Fig. 1c and b, and the finite trace associated with events *userReq, shipInfoReq, offerRcvd*, the sub-trace associated with *shipInfoReq* is inside the black-box state 2. This means that *shipInfoReq* must occur in the sub-component replacing the black-box state 2.

Adding Pre- and Post-conditions. The intended behavior of a sub-component refining a black-box state can be captured using pre- and post-conditions. The *contract* for the sub-component associated with a box consists of the box interface and its pre- and post-conditions. Given the universal set *FLTL* of the FLTL formulae, an *Interface PLTS* (IPLTS) I is a structure $\langle A, R, B, \sigma, pre, post \rangle$, where $\langle A, R, B, \sigma \rangle$ is a PLTS, $pre : B \rightarrow FLTL$ and $post : B \rightarrow FLTL$.

For each black-box state b, the function *pre* specifies a constraint that must be satisfied by all *finite* traces of P that reach b. For example, the FLTL-expressed pre-condition for the black-box state 4 of the IPLTS in Fig. 3d requires that any trace of the composition between the IPLTS and an LTS that reaches the black-box state 4 provides info on the product to the user after his/her request.

For each black-box state b, the function *post* specifies *a post-condition* that constrains the behavior of the system in any sub-trace performed inside b. For example, the post-condition of the black-box state 4 of the IPLTS in Fig. 3d ensures that whenever this IPLTS is composed with an LTS, a product request and a shipping request are performed by the furniture-sale service while the system is inside the black-box state.

Given an IPLTS I and an LTS D, the *parallel composition* S between I and D is obtained by considering the PLTS P associated with I and the LTS D as specified in Definition 1. Given an IPLTS I, an LTS D and the *parallel composition* S between I and D, trace π of S is *valid* iff it is infinite and for every black-box state b, the post-condition $post(b)$ holds in any sub-trace of π performed inside b.

Definition 2. *Given an LTS D, an IPLTS I is* well-formed *(over D) iff every valid trace of $S = I \parallel D$ satisfies all the pre-conditions of black-box states of I.*

We say that $S = I \parallel D$ *satisfies* an FLTL property ϕ if and only if ϕ is satisfied by every valid trace of S. In the p&d example, the post-condition $\diamondsuit$ $(F\_ProdReq)$ $\wedge \diamondsuit$ $(F\_ShipReq)$ of the black-box 4 ensures that the parallel composition of the component in Fig. 3d and its environment satisfies *P3*.

Sub-components and Their Integration. Integration aims to replace black-box states of a given IPLTS with the corresponding sub-components. Given an IPLTS I, one of its black-box states b and its interface $\sigma(b)$, a *sub-component for b* is an IPLTS R defined over the set of events $\sigma(b)$. One state q_f^R of R is defined as the *final state* of R. Given a sub-component R, an LTS of its environment E, and a trace in the form $\pi_i; \pi_e$ such that $\pi_i = l_0, l_1 \ldots l_n$ and $\pi_e = l_{n+1}, l_{n+2}, \ldots l_k$, we say that $\pi_i; \pi_e$ is *a trace of the parallel composition between R and E* if and only if (1) there exists a sequence $q_0, l_0, q_1, l_1 \ldots l_n, q_n$ in the environment such that for all i, where $0 \le i < n$, (q_i, l_i, q_{i+1}) is a transition of E; (2) π_e is obtained by $R \parallel E$ considering q_n as the initial state for the environment, (3) π_e reaches q_f^R. A sub-component is *valid* if it ensures that the traces of the parallel composition satisfy its post-conditions. Intuitively, a trace of the parallel composition between a sub-component R and the environment E is obtained by concatenating two sub-traces: π_i and π_e. The sub-trace π_i corresponds to a set of transitions performed by the environment before the sub-component is activated, while π_e is a trace the system generates while it is in the sub-component R.

Definition 3. *Given an IPLTS I with a black-box state b, the environment E and a sub-component R for b, R is a* substitutable *sub-component iff every trace $\pi_i; \pi_e$ of the parallel composition between R and E is such that if π_i satisfies $pre(b)$ then π_e guarantees $post(b)$.*

Intuitively, whenever the sub-component is entered and the pre-condition $pre(b)$ is satisfied (i.e., the trace π_i satisfies $pre(b)$), then a trace of the parallel composition between the sub-component and the environment that reaches the final state of the sub-component must satisfy the post-condition $post(b)$.

A black-box state of an IPLTS C can be replaced by a substitutable sub-component R though an integration procedure. The resulting IPLTS C' is called *integration*. Intuitively, the integration procedure connects every incoming and outgoing transition of the considered black-box state to the initial and final state of the substitutable sub-component R, respectively. Integrating the sub-component R for black-box state 2 in Fig. 3e into the component in Fig. 3d produces the IPLTS in Fig. 3g. The prefix "2." is used to identify the states obtained from R. The contracts of black-box states 4 and 5 are the same as those in Fig. 3b.

Theorem 1. *Given a well-formed IPLTS C and a substitutable sub-component R for a black-box state b of C, if C satisfies an FLTL property ϕ, then the integration C' obtained by substituting b with R also satisfies ϕ.*

The sub-component R from Fig. 3e is substitutable; thus, integrating it into the partial component C shown in Fig. 3g ensures that the resulting integrated component C' preserves properties *P1-P4*.

5 Verification Algorithms

In this section, we describe the algorithms for the analysis of partial components, which we have implemented on top of LTSA [25].

Checking Realizability. Realizability of a property ϕ is checked via the following procedure. Let E be the environment of the partial component C, and C^B be the LTS resulting from removing all black-box states and their incoming and outgoing transitions from C. Check $C^B \parallel E \models \phi$. If ϕ is not satisfied, the component is not realizable: no matter how the black-box states are specified, there will be a behavior of the system that does not satisfy ϕ. Otherwise, compute $C \parallel E$ (as specified in Definition 1) and model-check it against $\neg \phi$. If the property $\neg \phi$ is satisfied, the component is not realizable. Indeed, all the behaviors of $C \parallel E$ satisfy $\neg \phi$, i.e., there is no behavior that the component can exhibit to satisfy ϕ. Otherwise, the component may be realizable. For example, the realizability checker shows that it is possible to realize a component refining the one shown in Fig. 3c while satisfying property *P2*. Specifically, it returns a trace that ensures that after a *userReq* event, the offer is provided to the user (the event *offerRcvd*) only if the furniture service has confirmed the availability of the requested product (the event *inforRcvd*).

Theorem 2. *Given a component specified using an IPLTS C, its environment E, and a property of interest ϕ, the realizability checker returns "not realizable" if there is no component C' obtained from C by integrating sub-components, s.t. $(C' \parallel E) \models \phi$.*

Checking Well-Formedness. Given a partial component C with a black-box state b annotated with a pre-condition *pre(b)* and its environment E, the well-formedness checks whether *pre(b)* is satisfied in C as follows.

(1) *Transform post-conditions into LTSs.* Transform every FLTL post-condition $post(b_i)$ of every black-box state b_i of C, including b, into an FLTL formula $post(b_i)'$ as specified in [13]. This transformation ensures that the *infinite* traces that satisfy $post(b_i)'$ have the form $\pi, \{end\}^\omega$, where π satisfies $post(b_i)$. For each black-box state b_i, the corresponding post-condition

$post(b_i)'$ is transformed into an equivalent LTS, called LTS_{b_i}, using the procedure in [37]. Since LTS_{b_i} has traces in the form $\pi, \{end\}^\omega$, it has a state s with an end-labelled self-loop. This self-loop is removed, and s is considered as final state of LTS_{b_i}. All other end-labeled transitions are replaced by τ-transitions. Each automaton LTS_{b_i} contains all the traces that do not violate the corresponding post-condition.

(2) *Integrate the LTSs of all the black-box states $b_i \neq b$.* For every black-box state $b_i \neq b$, eliminate b_i and add LTS_{b_i} to C by replacing every incoming transition of b_i with a transition whose destination is the initial state of LTS_{b_i}, and every outgoing transition of b_i with a transition whose source is the final state of LTS_{b_i}. This step creates an LTS which encodes all the traces of the component that do not violate any post-conditions of its black-box states.

(3) *Integrate the LTS of the black-box state b.* Integrate LTS_b into C together with two additional states, q_1 and q_2, calling the resulting model C'. Replace every incoming transition of b by a transition with destination q_1. Replace every outgoing transition of b by a transition whose source is the final state of LTS_b. Add a transition labeled with τ from q_1 to the initial state of LTS_b. Add a self-loop labeled with an event end to q_2. Add a τ-transition from q_1 to q_2. The obtained LTS C' encodes all the valid traces of the system. When a valid trace reaches the black-box state b, C' can enter state q_2 from which only the end-labelled self-loop is available.

(4) *Verify.* Recall that the precondition $pre(b)$ of b is defined over finite traces, i.e., those that reach the initial state of the sub-component to be substituted for b. To use standard verification procedures, we transform $pre(b)$ into an equivalent formula, $pre(b)'$, over infinite traces. This transformation, specified in [13], ensures that every trace of the form $\pi, \{end\}^\omega$ satisfies $pre(b)'$ iff π satisfies $pre(b)$. By construction in step 3 above, $C' \parallel E$ has a valid trace of this form which is generated when $C \parallel E$ reaches the initial state of the LTS LTS_b associated with the black-box state b of C. To check the pre-condition, we verify whether $C' \parallel E \models pre(b)'$ using traditional model checking.

In the p&d example, if we remove the clause $\Diamond F\_InfoRcvd$ from the post-condition of the black-box state 2, the p&d component is not well-formed since the pre-condition of state 4 is violated. The counterexample shows a trace that reaches the black-box state 4 in which an event $userReq$ is not followed by $infoRcvd$. Adding $\Diamond F\_InfoRcvd$ to the post-condition of state 2 solves the problem.

Theorem 3. *Given a partial component C with a black-box state b annotated with a pre-condition $pre(b)$ and its environment E, the well-formedness procedure returns true iff the valid traces of C satisfy the pre-condition $pre(b)$.*

Model Checking. To check whether $C \parallel E$ satisfies ϕ, we first construct an LTS C' that generates only valid traces, by plugging into C the LTSs corresponding to all of its black-box states (as done in steps 1 and 2 of the well-formedness check) and use a classical FLTL model-checker to verify $C' \parallel E \models \phi$. If we consider the design of Fig. 3d and assume that the black-box state 2 is not associated with any post-condition, the model checker returns the counterexample *userReq,τ, offerRcvd* for property *P2*, since the sub-component that will replace the black-box state 2 is not forced to ask to book the furniture service. Adding the post-condition in Fig. 3b solves the problem.

Theorem 4. *The model checking procedure returns* true *iff every valid trace of* $C \parallel E$ *satisfies* ϕ.

Checking Substitutability. Given the environment E, a component C with a black-box state b and pre- and post-conditions *pre(b)* and *post(b)*, and a sub-component R, this procedure checks whether R can be used in C in place of b. We first present a procedure assuming that R has no black-box states.

(1) *Transform the pre-condition pre(b) into an LTS, called* LTS_b, *using Step (1) of the well-formedness procedure.*
(2) *Compute the sequential composition* $(LTS_b.R)$ *between the* LTS_b *and* R. This is done by connecting the final state q_1 of LTS_b with the initial state of R by a transition labelled with a fresh event *init*. Then, the final state of R is connected to an additional state q_2 through a τ-labeled transition. A self-loop labeled with a fresh event *end* is added to q_2. Performing these steps ensures that the prefix π of every infinite trace in the form $\pi, \{end\}^\omega$ is comprised of two parts: $\pi = \pi_1; \pi_2$, where π_1 satisfies *pre(b)* and π_2 is generated by the LTS R.
(3) *Verify the result.* The formula $\lambda = \textit{init} \rightarrow \bigcirc(\textit{post(b)})$ must hold on any trace that reaches the final state of R, e.g., on any trace of the form $\pi; \{end\}^\omega$, where λ' is the result of applying the finite- to infinite-trace FLTL transformation [13] to λ. This transformation ensures that π satisfies λ iff a trace of the form $\pi; \{end\}^\omega$ satisfies λ'. And that, in turn, can be verified by checking $((LTS_b.R) \parallel E) \models \lambda'$ using a classical model-checker.

If R contains black-box states, checking R requires performing Steps (1) and (2) of the well-formedness check before running the substitutability procedure.

In the p&d example, the substitutability checker does not return any counterexample for the sub-component in Fig. 3e. Thus, the post-condition is satisfied and the sub-component can be integrated in place of the black-box state 2.

Theorem 5. *Let a component C with a black-box state b, its pre- and post-conditions pre(b) and post(b), a sub-component R, and C's environment E be given. The substitutability checker returns* true, *indicating that R can be used in C in place of b, iff for every trace $\pi = \pi_i; \pi_e$ of $R \parallel E$, if π_i is the finite prefix of E satisfying pre(b) and π_e is obtained by $R \parallel E$ considering the final state of π_i as the initial state of the environment, then π_e satisfies post(b).*

6   Evaluation

We aim to answer two questions: **RQ.1**: How effective is FIDDle w.r.t. supporting an iterative, distributed development of correct components? (Sect. 6.1) and **RQ.2**: How scalable is the automated part of the proposed approach? (Sect. 6.2).

6.1   Assessing Effectiveness

We simulated development of a complex component and analyzed FIDDle-provided support along the steps described in Sect. 2.

Experimental Setup. We chose the executive module of the K9 Mars Rover developed at NASA Ames [12,17,18] and specified using LTSs. The overall size of the LTS is $\sim 10^7$ states. The executive module was made by several components: *Executive, ExecCondChecker, ActionExecution* and *Database. ExecCondChecker* was further decomposed into *db-monitor* and *internal*. Each of these components was associated with a shared variable (*exec, conditionList, action* and *db*, respectively) used to communicate with the other components, e.g., the *exec* variable was used by *ExecCondChecker* to communicate with *Executive*. The access of each shared variable was regulated through a condition variable and a lock. The complete model of the *Executive* component comprised of 11 states, each further decomposed as an LTS. The final model of the *Executive* component was obtained by replacing these states with the corresponding LTSs. This model had about 100 states which is a realistic component of a medium size [5,6,24]. We considered two properties: ($\mathcal{P}1$): *Executive* performed an action only after a new plan was read from *Database*; ($\mathcal{P}2$): *Executive* got the lock over the *condList* variable only after obtaining the *exec* lock.

Creating an Initial Component Design. We considered the existing model ($D3$) of the *Executive* and abstracted portions of the complete model into black-box states to create two partial components $D1$ and $D2$ representing partial designs. To generate $D2$ we encapsulated three states that receive plans and prepare for plan execution into the black-box state *Read_Plans*. To generate $D1$, we also set one of the 10 states of the *Executive* whose corresponding LTS is in charge of executing a plan, i.e., state *ExecuteTaskAction*, as a black-box state. By following this procedure, $D3$ and $D2$ can be obtained from $D2$ and $D1$, respectively, by integrating the abstracted sub-components.

We considered the (partial) components $D1$, $D2$ and $D3$ and used FIDDle to iteratively develop and check their contracts. For $D1$, the steps were as follows: (1) The *realizability checker* confirmed the existence of a model that refined $D1$ and satisfied the properties of interest. (2) The *model checker* returned a counterexample for both properties of interest. For $\mathcal{P}1$, the model checker returned a counterexample in which no plan was read and yet an action was performed. For $\mathcal{P}2$, the counterexample was where *Executive* got the *condList* lock without possessing the *exec* lock. To guarantee the satisfaction of $\mathcal{P}1$, we specified a post-condition to the black-box state *Read_Plans* that ensures that a plan was read. We also added a pre-condition requiring that an action was not under execution when the black-box state *Read_Plans* was entered. (3) The *well-formedness checker* returned a counterexample trace that reached the black-box state *Read_Plans* while an action was under execution. (4) To ensure well-formedness, we added a postcondition to the black-box state *ExecuteTaskAction* ensuring that an action was not under execution when the system exited the black-box state. (5) The *model checker* confirmed that $\mathcal{P}1$ held. (6) To guarantee the satisfaction of $P2$, we added a post-condition to the black-box state *Read_Plans* ensuring that when the control left the black-box, $P2$ remained *true* and the *Executive* had the *exec* lock.

For design $D2$, the steps were as follows: (1) The *realizability checker* confirmed the existence of a model that refined $D2$ and satisfied the properties of interest. (2) We ran the model checker that returned a counterexample for both properties of interest. (3) We added to the black-box state *Read_Plans* the same pre- and post-conditions of as those developed for design $D1$ and ran the *well-formedness* and the *model checker*. (4) The *well-formedness checker* confirmed that $D2$ satisfied the pre-condition of the black-box *Read_Plans*; the *model checker* certified the satisfaction of $P1$ and $P2$.

Since the model of *Executive* was complete, we ran only the *model checker* to check $D3$. Properties $P1$ and $P2$ were satisfied.

Sub-component Development. We simulated a refinement process in which pre- and post-conditions were given to third parties for sub-component development. We considered the sub-components *SUB1* and *SUB2* containing the portion of the *Executive* component abstracted by the black-box states *ExecuteTaskAction* and *Read_Plans*, respectively. We run the *substitutability checker* to verify, affirmatively, whether *SUB1* and *SUB2* ensured the post-condition of the black-box states *ExecuteTaskAction* and *Read_Plans* given their pre-conditions.

Sub-component Integration. We then plugged in the designed sub-components into their corresponding black-box states. We integrated each sub-component into design $D1$ and used the *model checker* to verify the resulting (partial) components w.r.t. properties $P1$-$P2$. The properties were satisfied, as intended.

Results. FIDDle was effective in analyzing partial components and helping change their design to ensure the satisfaction of the properties of interest. The experiment confirmed the possibility of distributing the design of sub-components for the black-box states. As expected, no rework at the integration level was required, i.e., integration produced components that satisfied the properties of interest. This confirmed that FIDDle supports verification-driven iterative and distributed development of components.

Threats to Validity. A threat to construct validity concerns the (manual) construction of intermediate model produced during development by abstracting an existing component model and the design of the properties to be considered. However, the intermediate partial designs and the selected properties were based on original developer comments present in the model. A threat to internal validity concerns the design of the contracts (pre- and post- conditions and interfaces) for the black-box states chosen along the process. However, pre- and post- conditions were chosen and designed by consulting property specification patterns proposed in literature [16]. The fact that a single example has been considered is a threat to external validity. However, the considered example is a medium-size complex real case study [6,22,35].

Table 1. Results of experiments $E1$ and $E2$.

	#CompStates												
	$E1 : (T_w)/(T_m)$							$E2 : (T_s)/(T_m)$					
#EnvStates	10	50	100	250	500	750	1000	10	50	100	250	500	750	1000
10	1.45	1.26	1.51	1.29	1.42	1.43	1.31	2.20	4.37	2.18	1.50	2.19	1.62	1.62
100	1.15	1.25	1.50	1.08	0.88	1.02	2.33	3.51	4.66	3.61	2.80	3.18	1.96	2.73
1000	1.39	1.23	0.60	1.44	4.90	1.00	2.83	13.98	8.12	3.84	2.64	2.83	2.91	2.00

6.2   Assessing Scalability

We set up two experiments ($E1$ and $E2$) comparing performance of the *well-formedness* and the *substitutability checkers* w.r.t. classical model checking as the size of the partial components under development and their environments grew. Our experiments were based on a set of *randomly-generated* models.

E1. To evaluate the *well-formedness checker*, we generated an LTS model of the environment and a complete model for the component. We checked the parallel composition between the component and the environment w.r.t. a property of interest using a standard model checker. Then, we generated a partial component by marking one of the states of the complete component as a black-box, defining pre- and post- conditions for it and ran the well-formedness checker, comparing performance of the two.

E2. To evaluate the *substitutability checker*, we generated a complete component as in the previous experiment. Then, we extracted a sub-component by selecting half of the component states and the transitions between them. States q_0 and q_f were added to the sub-component as the initial and final state, respectively. State q_0 (q_f) was connected with all the states of the sub-component that had, in the original component, at least one incoming (resp., outgoing) transition from (resp., to) a state that was not added to the sub-component. We defined the pre- and post-conditions for the sub-component and ran the substitutability checker comparing its performance with model-checking.

Experimental Setup. We implemented a *random model generator* to create LTSs with a specified number of states, transition density (transitions per state) and number of events. We generated environments with an increasing number of states: 10, 100 and 1000. We have chosen 10 as a fixed value for the transition density and 50 as the cardinality of the set of events. We considered components with 10, 50, 100, 250, 500, 750 and 1000 states. The components were generated using the same transition density and number of events as in the produced environment. To produce the partial component, we considered one of the states of the component obtained previously as a black-box, and randomly selected 25% of the events of the component as the interface of the partial component. To produce the sub-component, we randomly extracted half of the component states and the transitions between them.

Properties of Interest, Pre- and Post-conditions. We considered properties $\mathcal{K}1 = \Box(Q \rightarrow P)$, $\mathcal{K}2 = \Diamond Q \rightarrow (\neg P \mathcal{U} Q)$, $\mathcal{K}3 = \Box(Q \rightarrow \Box(\neg P))$), which correspond to commonly used property patterns [16], and where Q and P are appropriately defined fluents. We considered $\mathcal{K}1$, $\mathcal{K}2$ and $\mathcal{K}3$ as pre- and post-conditions for the black-box.

Methodology and Results. We ran each experiment 5 times on a 2 GHz Intel Core i7, with 8 GB 1600 MHz DDR3 disk. For each combination of values of the #EnvStates and #ContStates we computed the average between the time required by the well-formedness checker (T_w) and by the model checker (T_m), for the experiment $E1$, and the average between the time required by the substitutability checker (T_s) and by the model checker (T_m), for the experiment $E2$ (see Table 1). The results show that the well-formedness and the substitutability checker scale as the classical model checker.

Threats to Validity. The procedure employed to randomly generate models is a threat to construct validity. However, the transition density of the components was chosen based on the Mars Rover example. Furthermore, the number of states of the sub-component was chosen such that the ratio between the sizes of the component and the sub-component was approximately the same of the Mars Rover. The properties considered in the experiment are a threat to internal validity. However, they were chosen by consulting property specification patterns proposed in literature [16]. Considering a single black-box state is a threat to external validity. However, our goal was to evaluate how FIDDle scales with respect to the component and the environment sizes and not w.r.t. the number of black-box states and the size of the post-conditions. Considering multiple black-box states reduces to the case of considering a single black-box with a more complex post-condition.

7   Related Work

We discuss approaches for developing incrementally correct components.

Modeling Partiality. Modal Transition Systems [21], Partial Kripke Structures [8], and LTS† [17] support the specification of incomplete concurrent systems and can be used in an iterative development process. Other formalisms, such as Hierarchical State Machines (HSMs) [4], are used to model sequential processes via a top-down development process but can only be analyzed when a fully-specified model is available.

Checking Partial Models. Approaches to analyze partial models (e.g., [8,10]) are not applicable to the problem considered in this paper where missing sub-components are specified using contracts and their development is distributed across different development teams. The assumption generation problem for LTSs [17] is complementary to the one considered in this paper and concerns the computation of an assumption that describes how the system model interacts with the environment.

Substitutability Checking. The goal of substitutability checking is to verify whether a possibly partial sub-component can be plugged into a higher level structure without affecting its correctness. Problems such as "compositional reasoning" [1,19,30], "component substitutability" [9], and "hierarchical model checking" [4] are related to this part of our work. Our work differs because we first guarantee that the properties of interest are satisfied in the initially-defined partial component and then check that the provided sub-components can be plugged into the initial component.

Synthesis. Program synthesis [14,31] aims at computing a model of the system that satisfies the properties of interest. Moreover, synthesis can be used to generate assumptions on a system's environment to make its specification relizable (e.g., [23]). Sketch [36] supports programmers in describing an initial structure of the program that can be completed using synthesis techniques, but does not explicitly consider models. Many techniques for synthesizing components have been proposed, e.g., [14,37], and a fully automated synthesis of highly non-trivial components of over 2000 states big is becoming possible [11] for special cases, by limiting the types of synthesizable goals and using heuristics. However, such cases might not be applicable in general. Recent work has been done in the direction of compositional [2,3] and distributed [34] synthesis. We do not consider our approach to be an alternative to synthesis, but instead a way to combine synthesis techniques with the human design.

8 Conclusion

We presented a verification-driven methodology, called FIDDle, to support iterative distributed development of components. It enables recursively decomposing a component into a set of sub-components so that the correctness of the overall component is ensured. Development of sub-components that satisfy their specifications can then be done independently, via distributed development. We have evaluated FIDDle on a realistic Mars Rover case study. Scalability was evaluated using randomly generated examples.

Acknowledgments. Research partly supported from the EU H2020 Research and Innovation Programme under GA No. 731869 (Co4Robots).

References

1. Alur, R., Henzinger, T.A.: Reactive modules. Formal Meth. Softw. Des. **15**(1), 7–48 (1999)
2. Alur, R., Moarref, S., Topcu, U.: Pattern-Based Refinement of Assume-Guarantee Specifications in Reactive Synthesis. In: Baier, C., Tinelli, C. (eds.) TACAS 2015. LNCS, vol. 9035, pp. 501–516. Springer, Heidelberg (2015). https://doi.org/10.1007/978-3-662-46681-0_49

3. Alur, R., Moarref, S., Topcu, U.: Compositional synthesis of reactive controllers for multi-agent systems. In: Chaudhuri, S., Farzan, A. (eds.) CAV 2016. LNCS, vol. 9780, pp. 251–269. Springer, Cham (2016). https://doi.org/10.1007/978-3-319-41540-6_14
4. Alur, R., Yannakakis, M.: Model checking of hierarchical state machines. ACM SIGSOFT Softw. Eng. Notes **23**(6), 175–188 (1998)
5. Amalfitano, D., Fasolino, A.R., Tramontana, P.: Reverse engineering finite state machines from rich internet applications. In: Proceedings of the 15th Working Conference on Reverse Engineering, pp. 69–73 (2008)
6. Bensalem, S., Bozga, M., Krichen, M., Tripakis, S.: Testing conformance of real-time applications by automatic generation of observer. In: Proceedings of RV, Electronic Notes in Theoretical Computer Science, pp. 23–43 (2004)
7. Bernasconi, A., Menghi, C., Spoletini, P., Zuck, L.D., Ghezzi, C.: From model checking to a temporal proof for partial models. In: Cimatti, A., Sirjani, M. (eds.) SEFM 2017. LNCS, vol. 10469, pp. 54–69. Springer, Cham (2017). https://doi.org/10.1007/978-3-319-66197-1_4
8. Bruns, G., Godefroid, P.: Model checking partial state spaces with 3-valued temporal logics. In: Halbwachs, N., Peled, D. (eds.) CAV 1999. LNCS, vol. 1633, pp. 274–287. Springer, Heidelberg (1999). https://doi.org/10.1007/3-540-48683-6_25
9. Chaki, S., Clarke, E.M., Sharygina, N., Sinha, N.: Verification of evolving software via component substitutability analysis. Formal Methods Softw. Des. **32**(3), 235–266 (2008)
10. Chechik, M., Devereux, B., Easterbrook, S., Gurfinkel, A.: Multi-valued symbolic model-checking. ACM Trans. Softw. Eng. Methodol. **12**(4), 371–408 (2003)
11. Ciolek, D., Braberman, V.A., D'Ippolito, N., Uchitel, S.: Technical Report: Directed Controller Synthesis of Discrete Event Systems. CoRR, abs/1605.09772 (2016)
12. Cobleigh, J.M., Giannakopoulou, D., PÅsÅreanu, C.S.: Learning assumptions for compositional verification. In: Garavel, H., Hatcliff, J. (eds.) TACAS 2003. LNCS, vol. 2619, pp. 331–346. Springer, Heidelberg (2003). https://doi.org/10.1007/3-540-36577-X_24
13. De Giacomo, G., De Masellis, R., Montali, M.: Reasoning on LTL on finite traces: insensitivity to infiniteness. In: Proceedings of AAAI, pp. 1027–1033 (2014)
14. D'Ippolito, N., Braberman, V., Piterman, N., Uchitel, U.: Synthesising non-anomalous event-based controllers for liveness goals. ACM Tran. Softw. Eng. Methodol. **22**, 9 (2013)
15. D'Ippolito, N., Braberman, V., Piterman, N., Uchitel, S.: Controllability in partial and uncertain environments. In: Proceedings of ACSD, pp. 52–61. IEEE (2014)
16. Dwyer, M.B., Avrunin, G.S., Corbett, J.C.: Property specification patterns for finite-state verification. In: Proceedings of FMSP, pp. 7–15. ACM (1998)
17. Giannakopoulou, D., Pasareanu, C.S., Barringer, H.: Assumption generation for software component verification. In: Proceedings of ASE, pp. 3–12. IEEE (2002)
18. Giannakopoulou, D., Păsăreanu, C.S., Barringer, H.: Component verification with automatically generated assumptions. J. Autom. Softw. Eng. **12**(3), 297–320 (2005)
19. Jones, C.B.: Tentative steps toward a development method for interfering programs. ACM Trans. Program. Lang. Syst. **5**(4), 596–619 (1983)
20. Keller, R.M.: Formal verification of parallel programs. Commun. ACM **19**(7), 371–384 (1976)
21. Larsen, K.G., Thomsen, B.: A modal process logic. In: Proceedings of LICS, pp. 203–210. IEEE (1988)

22. Levy, L.S.: Taming the Tiger: Software Engineering and Software Economics. Springer Books on Professional Computing Series. Springer-Verlag, New York (1987). https://doi.org/10.1007/978-1-4612-4718-0

23. Li, W., Dworkin, L., Seshia, S.A.: Mining assumptions for synthesis. In: Proceedings of ACM/IEEE MEMPCODE, pp. 43–50 (2011)

24. Lorenzoli, D., Mariani, L., Pezzè, M.: Automatic generation of software behavioral models. In: Proceedings of ICSE, pp. 501–510 (2008)

25. Magee, J., Kramer, J.: State Models and Java Programs. Wiley, New York (1999)

26. Menghi, C., Spoletini, P., Ghezzi, C.: Dealing with incompleteness in automata-based model checking. In: Fitzgerald, J., Heitmeyer, C., Gnesi, S., Philippou, A. (eds.) FM 2016. LNCS, vol. 9995, pp. 531–550. Springer, Cham (2016). https://doi.org/10.1007/978-3-319-48989-6_32

27. Menghi, C., Spoletini, P., Ghezzi, C.: Integrating goal model analysis with iterative design. In: Grünbacher, P., Perini, A. (eds.) REFSQ 2017. LNCS, vol. 10153, pp. 112–128. Springer, Cham (2017). https://doi.org/10.1007/978-3-319-54045-0_9

28. Nivoit, J.-B.: Issues in strategic management of large-scale software product line development. Master's thesis, MIT, USA (2013)

29. Pistore, M., Barbon, F., Bertoli, P., Shaparau, D., Traverso, P.: Planning and monitoring web service composition. In: Bussler, C., Fensel, D. (eds.) AIMSA 2004. LNCS (LNAI), vol. 3192, pp. 106–115. Springer, Heidelberg (2004). https://doi.org/10.1007/978-3-540-30106-6_11

30. Pnueli, A.: In transition from global to modular temporal reasoning about programs. In: Apt, K.R. (ed.) Logics and Models of Concurrent Systems. NATO ASI Series, pp. 123–144. Springer-Verlag, New York Inc (1985). https://doi.org/10.1007/978-3-642-82453-1_5

31. Pnueli, A., Rosner, R.: On the synthesis of a reactive module. In: Proceedings of POPL, pp. 179–190. ACM (1989)

32. Pretschner, A., Broy, M., Kruger, I.H., Stauner, T.: Software engineering for automotive systems: a roadmap. In: Proceedings of FOSE, pp. 55–71. IEEE Computer Society (2007)

33. Sandewall, E.: Features and Fluents (Vol. 1): The Representation of Knowledge about Dynamical Systems. Oxford University Press Inc, New York (1995)

34. Sibay, G.E., Uchitel, S., Braberman, V., Kramer, J.: Distribution of modal transition systems. In: Giannakopoulou, D., Méry, D. (eds.) FM 2012. LNCS, vol. 7436, pp. 403–417. Springer, Heidelberg (2012). https://doi.org/10.1007/978-3-642-32759-9_33

35. Software Measurement Services Ltd. "small project", "medium-size project", and "large project": What do these terms mean? (2004). http://www.totalmetrics.com/function-points-downloads/Function-Point-Scale-Project-Size.pdf

36. Solar-Lezama, A.: Program synthesis by sketching. Ph.D. thesis. University of California, Berkeley (2008)

37. Uchitel, S., Brunet, G., Chechik, M.: Synthesis of partial behavior models from properties and scenarios. IEEE Trans.Softw. Eng. 35(3), 384–406 (2009)

Summarizing Software API Usage Examples Using Clustering Techniques

Nikolaos Katirtzis[1,2](✉)(iD), Themistoklis Diamantopoulos[3](iD),
and Charles Sutton[2](iD)

[1] Hotels.com, London, UK
nkatirtzis@ed-alumni.net
[2] School of Informatics, University of Edinburgh, Edinburgh, UK
csutton@ed.ac.uk
[3] Electrical and Computer Engineering Department,
Aristotle University of Thessaloniki, Thessaloniki, Greece
thdiaman@issel.ee.auth.gr

Abstract. As developers often use third-party libraries to facilitate
software development, the lack of proper API documentation for
these libraries undermines their reuse potential. And although several
approaches extract usage examples for libraries, they are usually tied
to specific language implementations, while their produced examples are
often redundant and are not presented as concise and readable snippets. In this work, we propose a novel approach that extracts API
call sequences from client source code and clusters them to produce a
diverse set of source code snippets that effectively covers the target API.
We further construct a summarization algorithm to present concise and
readable snippets to the users. Upon evaluating our system on software
libraries, we indicate that it achieves high coverage in API methods, while
the produced snippets are of high quality and closely match handwritten
examples.

Keywords: API usage mining · Documentation · Source code reuse
Code summarization · Mining software repositories

1 Introduction

Third-party libraries and frameworks are an integral part of current software
systems. Access to the functionality of a library is typically offered by its API,
which may consist of numerous classes and methods. However, as noted by multiple studies [24,30], APIs often lack proper examples and documentation and,
in general, sufficient explanation on how to be used. Thus, developers often
use general-purpose or specialized code search engines (CSEs), and Question-
Answering (QA) communities, such as Stack Overflow, in order to find possible
API usages. However, the search process in these services can be time consuming

A. Russo and A. Schürr (Eds.): FASE 2018, LNCS 10802, pp. 189–206, 2018.
https://doi.org/10.1007/978-3-319-89363-1_11

[13], while the source code snippets provided in web sites and QA communities might be difficult to recognise, ambiguous, or incomplete [28,29].

As a result, several researchers have studied the problem of API usage mining, which can be described as automatically identifying a set of patterns that characterize how an API is typically used from a corpus of client code [11]. There are two main types of API mining methods. First are methods that return API call sequences, using techniques such as frequent sequence mining [31–33], clustering [25,31,33], and probabilistic modeling [9]. Though interesting, API call sequences do not always describe important information like method arguments and control flow, and their output cannot be directly included in one's code.

A second class of approaches automatically produces source code snippets which, compared to API call sequences, provide more information to the developer, and are more similar to human-written examples. Methods for mining snippets, however, tend to rely on detailed semantic analysis, including program slicing [5,13–15] and symbolic execution [5], which can make them more difficult to deploy to new languages. Furthermore, certain approaches do not use any clustering techniques, thus resulting to a redundant and non-diverse set of API soure code snippets [20], which is not representative as it only uses a few API methods as noted by Fowkes and Sutton [9]. On the other hand, approaches that do use clustering techniques are usually limited to their choice of clustering algorithms [34] and/or use feature sets that are language-specific [13–15].

In this paper, we propose *CLAMS (Clustering for API Mining of Snippets)*, an approach for mining API usage examples that lies between snippet and sequence mining methods, which ensures lower complexity and thus could apply more readily to other languages. The basic idea is to cluster a large set of usage examples based on their API calls, generate summarized versions for the top snippets of each cluster, and then select the most representative snippet from each cluster, using a tree edit distance metric on the ASTs. This results in a diverse set of examples in the form of concise and readable source code snippets. Our method is entirely data-driven, requiring only syntactic information from the source code, and so could be easily applied to other programming languages. We evaluate CLAMS on a set of popular libraries, where we illustrate how its results are more diverse in terms of API methods than those of other approaches, and assess to what extent the snippets match human-written examples.

2   Related Work

Several studies have pointed out the importance of API documentation in the form of examples when investigating API usability [18,22] and API adoption in cases of highly evolving APIs [16]. Different approaches have thus been presented to find or create such examples; from systems that search for examples on web pages [28], to ones that mine such examples from client code located in source code repositories [5], or even from video tutorials [23]. Mining examples from client source code has been a typical approach for Source Code-Based Recommendation Systems *(SCoReS)* [19]. Such methods are distinguished according to their output which can be either source code snippets or API call sequences.

2.1   Systems that Output API Call Sequences

One of the first systems to mine API usage patterns is *MAPO* [32] which employs *frequent sequence mining* [10] to identify common usage patterns. Although the latest version of the system outputs the API call sequences along with their associated snippets [33], it is still more of a sequence-based approach, as it presents the code of the client method without performing any summarization, while it also does not consider the structure of the source code snippets.

Wang et al. [31] argue that MAPO outputs a large number of usage patterns, many of which are redundant. The authors therefore define *scalability*, *succinctness* and *high-coverage* as the required characteristics of an API miner and construct UP-Miner, a system that mines probabilistic graphs of API method calls and extracts more useful patterns than MAPO. However, the presentation of such graphs can be overwhelming when compared to ranked lists.

Recently, Fowkes and Sutton [9] proposed a method for mining API usage patterns called PAM, which uses probabilistic machine learning to mine a less redundant and more representative set of patterns than MAPO or UP-Miner. This paper also introduced an automated evaluation framework, using handwritten library usage examples from Github, which we adapt in the present work.

2.2   Systems that Output Source Code Snippets

A typical snippet mining system is *eXoaDocs* [13–15] that employs slicing techniques to summarize snippets retrieved from online sources into useful documentation examples, which are further organized using clustering techniques. However, clustering is performed using semantic feature vectors approximated by the Deckard tool [12], and such features are not straightforward to get extracted for different programming languages. Furthermore, eXoaDocs only targets usage examples of single API methods, as its feature vectors do not include information for mining frequent patterns with multiple API method calls.

APIMiner [20] introduces a summarization algorithm that uses slicing to preserve only the API-relevant statements of the source code. Further work by the same authors [4] incorporates association rule techniques, and employs an improved version of the summarization algorithm, with the aim of resolving variable types and adding descriptive comments. Yet the system does not cluster similar examples, while most examples show the usage of a single API method.

Even when slicing is employed in the aforementioned systems, the examples often contain extraneous statements (i.e. statements that could be removed as they are not related to the API), as noted by Buse and Weimer [5]. Hence, the authors introduce a system that synthesizes representative and well-typed usage examples using path-sensitive data flow analysis, clustering, and pattern abstraction. The snippets are complete and abstract, including abstract naming and helpful code, such as try/catch statements. However, the sophistication of their program analysis makes the system more complex [31], and increases the required effort for applying it to new programming languages.

Allamanis and Sutton [1] present a system for mining syntactic idioms, which are syntactic patterns that recur frequently and are closely related to snippets, and thus many of their mined patterns are API snippets. That method is language agnostic, as it relies only on ASTs, but uses a sophisticated statistical method based on Bayesian probabilistic grammars, which limits its scalability.

Although the aforementioned approaches can be effective in certain scenarios, they also have several drawbacks. First, most systems output API call sequences or other representations (e.g. call graphs), which may not be as helpful as snippets, both in terms of understanding and from a reuse perspective (e.g. adapting an example to fit one's own code). Several of the systems that output snippets do not group them into clusters and thus they do not provide a diverse set of usage examples, and even when clustering is employed, the set of features may not allow extending the approaches in other programming languages. Finally, certain systems do not provide concise and readable snippets as their source code summarization capabilities are limited.

In this work, we present a novel API usage mining system, CLAMS, to overcome the above limitations. CLAMS employs clustering to group similar snippets and the output examples are subsequently improved using a summarization algorithm. The algorithm performs heuristic transformations, such as variable type resolution and replacement of literals, while it also removes non-API statements, in order to output concise and readable snippets. Finally, the snippets are ranked in descending order of support and given along with comprehensive comments.

3 Methodology

3.1 System Overview

The architecture of the system is shown in Fig. 1. The input for each library is a set of *Client Files* and the API of the library. The *API Call Extractor* generates a list of API call sequences from each method. The *Clustering Preprocessor* computes a distance matrix of the sequences, which is used by the *Clustering Engine* to cluster them. After that, the top (most representative) sequences from

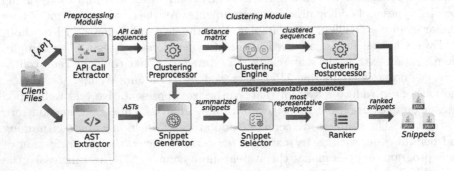

Fig. 1. Overview of the proposed system.

each cluster are selected (*Clustering Postprocessor*). The source code and the ASTs (from the *AST Extractor*) of these top snippets are given to the *Snippet Generator* that generates a summarized snippet for each of them. Finally, the *Snippet Selector* selects a single snippet from each cluster, and the output is given by the *Ranker* that ranks the examples in descending order of support.

3.2   Preprocessing Module

The Preprocessing Module receives as input the client source code files and extracts their ASTs and their API call sequences. The *AST Extractor* employs srcML [8] to convert source code to an XML AST format, while the *API Call Extractor* extracts the API call sequences using the extractor provided by Fowkes and Sutton [9] which uses the Eclipse JDT parser to extract method calls using depth-first AST traversal.

3.3   Clustering Module

We perform clustering at sequence-level, instead of source code-level, this way considering all useful API information contained in the snippets. As an example, the snippets in Figs. 2a and b, would be clustered together by our Clustering Engine as they contain the same API call sequence. Given the large number and the diversity of the files, our approach is more effective than a clustering that would consider the structure of the client code, while such a decision makes the deployment to new languages easier. Note however that we take into consideration the structure of clustered snippets at a later stage (see Sect. 3.5).

```
editor.putString("", tkn.getToken());           if (token != null) {
editor.putString("", tkn.getTokenSecret());        editor.putString("", token.getToken());
                                                   editor.putString("", token.getTokenSecret());
                                                }
```

(a)   (b)

Fig. 2. The sample client code on the left side contains the same API calls with the client code on the right side, which are encircled in both snippets.

Our clustering methodology involves first generating a distance matrix and then clustering the sequences using this matrix. The *Clustering Preprocessor* uses the *Longest Common Subsequence (LCS)* between any two sequences in order to compute their distance and then create the distance matrix. Given two sequences S_1 and S_2, their LCS distance is defined as:

$$LCS\_dist\,(S_1, S_2) = 1 - 2 \cdot \frac{|LCS\,(S_1, S_2)|}{|S_1| + |S_2|} \qquad (1)$$

where $|S_1|$ and $|S_2|$ are the lengths of S_1 and S_2, and $|LCS\,(S_1, S_2)|$ is the length of their LCS. Given the distance matrix, the *Clustering Engine* explores the k-medoids algorithm which is based on the implementation provided by Bauckhage [3], and the hierarchical version of DBSCAN, known as *HDBSCAN* [7], which makes use of the implementation provided by McInnes et al. [17].

The next step is to retrieve the source code associated with the most representative sequence of each cluster (*Clustering Postprocessor*). Given, however, that each cluster may contain several snippets that are identical with respect to their sequences, we select multiple snippets for each cluster, this way retaining source code structure information, which shall be useful for selecting a single snippet (see Sect. 3.5). Our analysis showed that selecting all possible snippets did not further improve the results, thus we select n snippets and set n to 5 for our experiments, as trying higher values would not affect the results.

3.4 Snippet Generator

The *Snippet Generator* generates a summarized version for the top snippets. Our summarization method, a static, flow-insensitive, intra-procedural slicing approach, is presented in Fig. 3. The input (Fig. 3, top left) is the snippet source code, the list of its invoked API calls and a set of variables defined in its outer scope (encircled and highlighted in bold respectively).

At first, any comments are removed and literals are replaced by their srcML type, i.e. string, char, number or boolean (*Step 1*). In *Step 2*, the algorithm creates two lists, one for API and one for non-API statements (highlighted in bold), based on whether an API method is invoked or not in each statement. Any *control flow statements* that include API statements in their code block are also retained (e.g. the else statement in Fig. 3). In *Step 3*, the algorithm creates a list with all the variables that reside in the local scope of the snippet (highlighted in bold). This is followed by the removal of all non-API statements (*Step 4*), by traversing the AST in reverse (bottom-up) order.

In *Step 5*, the list of declared variables is filtered, and only those used in the summarized tree are retained (highlighted in bold). Moreover, the algorithm creates a list with all the variables that are declared in API statements and used only in non-API statements (encircled). In *Step 6*, the algorithm adds declarations (encircled) for the variables retrieved in Step 5. Furthermore, descriptive comments of the form "Do something with variable" (highlighted in bold) are added for the variables that are declared in API statements and used in non-API statements (retrieved also in Step 5). Finally, the algorithm adds "Do something" comments in any empty blocks (highlighted in italics).

Finally, note that our approach is quite simpler than static, syntax preserving slicing. E.g., static slicing would not remove any of the statements inside the else block, as the call to the getFromUser API method is assigned to a variable (userName), which is then used in the assignment of user. Our approach, on the other hand, performs a single pass over the AST, thus ensuring lower complexity, which in its turn reduces the overall complexity of our system.

Summarizer Input
```
if (t.getCreatedAt().getTime() + 1000 < mTime) {
  breakPaging = 'y';
  //TODO
} else {
  userName = t.getFromUser().toLowerCase();
  JUser user = userMap.get(userName);
  if (user == null) {
    user = new JUser(userName).init(t);
    userMap.put(userName, user);
  }
}
```

Step 1: Preprocess comments and literals
```
if (t.getCreatedAt().getTime() + number < mTime) {
  breakPaging = char;
} else {
  userName = t.getFromUser().toLowerCase();
  JUser user = userMap.get(userName);
  if (user == null) {
    user = new JUser(userName).init(t);
    userMap.put(userName, user);
  }
}
```

Step 2: Identify API statements
```
if (t.getCreatedAt().getTime() + number < mTime) {
  breakPaging = char;
} else {
  userName = t.getFromUser().toLowerCase();
  JUser user = userMap.get(userName);
  if (user == null) {
    user = new JUser(userName).init(t);
    userMap.put(userName, user);
  }
}
```

Step 3: Retrieve local scope variables
```
if (t.getCreatedAt().getTime() + number < mTime) {
  breakPaging = char;
} else {
  userName = t.getFromUser().toLowerCase();
  JUser user = userMap.get(userName);
  if (user == null) {
    user = new JUser(userName).init(t);
    userMap.put(userName, user);
  }
}
```

Step 4: Remove non-API statements
```
if (t.getCreatedAt().getTime() + number < mTime) {
} else {
  userName = t.getFromUser().toLowerCase();
}
```

Step 5: Filtering variables
```
if (t.getCreatedAt().getTime() + number < mTime) {
} else {
  userName = t.getFromUser().toLowerCase();
}
```

Step 6: Add declaration statements and comments
```
long mTime;
Tweet t;
String userName;

if (t.getCreatedAt().getTime() + number < mTime) {
  // Do something
} else {
  userName = t.getFromUser().toLowerCase();
  // Do something with userName
}
```

Fig. 3. Example summarization of source code snippet.

3.5 Snippet Selector

The next step is to select a single snippet for each cluster. Given that the selected snippet has to be the most representative of the cluster, we select the one that is most similar to the other top snippets. The score between any two snippets is defined as the tree edit distance between their ASTs, computed using the AP-TED algorithm [21]. Given this metric, we create a matrix for each cluster, which contains the distance between any two top snippets of the cluster. Finally, we select the snippet with the minimum sum of distances in each cluster's matrix.

3.6 Ranker

We rank the snippets according to the support of their API call sequences, as in [9]. In specific, if the API call sequence of a snippet is a subsequence of the sequence of a file in the repository, then we claim that the file supports the snippet. For example, the snippet with API call sequence [twitter4j.Status.getUser, twitter4j.Status.getText], is supported by a file with sequence [twitter4j.Paging.<init>,

twitter4j.Status.getUser, twitter4j.Status.getId, twitter4j.Status.getText, twitter4j.
Status.getUser]. In this way, we compute the support for each snippet and create
a complete ordering. Upon ordering the snippets, the AStyle formatter [2] is also
used to fix the indentation and spacing.

3.7 Deploying to New Languages

Our methodology can be easily applied on different programming languages. The
Preprocessing Module and the Snippet Selector make use of the source code's
AST, which is straightforward to extract in different languages. The Clustering
Module and the Ranker use API call sequences and not any semantic features
that are language-specific, while our summarization algorithm relies on statements and their control flow, a fundamental concept of imperative languages.
Thus, extending our methodology to additional programming languages requires
only the extraction of the AST of the source code, which can be done using appropriate tools (e.g. srcML), and possibly a minor adjustment on our summarization
algorithm to conform to the AST schema extracted from different tools.

4 Evaluation

4.1 Evaluation Framework

We evaluate CLAMS on the APIs (all public methods) of 6 popular Java libraries,
which were selected as they are popular (based on their GitHub stars and forks),
cover various domains, and have handwritten examples to compare our snippets
with. The libraries are shown in Table 1, along with certain statistics concerning
the lines of code of their examples' directories (Example LOC) and the lines of
code considered from GitHub as using their API methods (Client LOC).

Table 1. Summary of the evaluation dataset.

Project	Package Name	Client LOC	Example LOC
Apache Camel	org.apache.camel	141,454	15,256
Drools	org.drools	187,809	15,390
Restlet Framework	org.restlet	208,395	41,078
Twitter4j	twitter4j	96,020	6,560
Project Wonder	com.webobjects	375,064	37,181
Apache Wicket	org.apache.wicket	564,418	33,025

To further strengthen our hypothesis, we also employ an automated method
for evaluating our system, to allow quantitative comparison of its different variants. To assess whether the snippets of CLAMS are representative, we look for
"gold standard" examples online, as writing our own examples would be time-
consuming and lead to subjective results.

We focus our evaluation on the 4 research questions of Fig. 4. RQ1 and RQ2 refer to summarization and clustering respectively and will be evaluated with respect to handwritten examples. For RQ3 we assess the API coverage achieved by CLAMS versus the ones achieved by the API mining systems MAPO [32,33] and UP-Miner [31]. RQ4 will determine whether the extra information of source code snippets when compared to API call sequences is useful to developers.

RQ1: How much more concise, readable, and precise with respect to handwritten examples are the snippets after summarization?

RQ2: Do more powerful clustering techniques, that cluster similar rather than identical sequences, lead to snippets that more closely match handwritten examples?

RQ3: Does our tool mine more diverse patterns than other existing approaches?

RQ4: Do snippets match handwritten examples more than API call sequences?

Fig. 4. Research Questions (RQs) to be evaluated.

We consider four configurations for our system: *NaiveNoSum*, *NaiveSum*, *KMedoidsSum*, and *HDBSCANSum*. To reveal the effect of clustering sequences, the first two configurations do not use any clustering and only group identical sequences together, while the last two use the k-medoids and the *HDBSCAN* algorithms, respectively. Also the first configuration (*NaiveNoSum*) does not employ our summarizer, while all others do, so that we can measure its effect.

We define metrics to assess the *readability, conciseness*, and *quality* of the returned snippets. For readability, we use the metric defined by Buse and Weimer [6] which is based on human studies and agrees with a large set of human annotators. Given a Java source code file, the tool provided by Buse and Weimer [27] outputs a value in the range [0.0, 1.0], where a higher value indicates a more readable snippet. For conciseness, we use the number of *Physical Lines of Code* (*PLOCs*). Both metrics have already been used for the evaluation of similar systems [5]. For quality, as a proxy measure we use the similarity of the set of returned snippets to a set of handwritten examples from the module's developers.

We define the similarity of a snippet s given a set of examples E as *snippet precision*. First, we define a set E_s with all the examples in E that have exactly the same API calls with snippet s. After that, we compute the similarity of s with all matching examples $e \in E_s$ by splitting the code into sets of tokens and applying set similarity metrics[1]. Tokenization is performed using a Java code tokenizer and the tokens are cleaned by removing symbols (e.g. brackets, etc.) and comments, and by replacing literals (i.e. numbers, etc.) with their respective types. The precision of s is the maximum of its similarities with all $e \in E_s$:

---

[1] Our decision to apply set similarity metrics instead of an edit distance metric is based on the fact that the latter one is heavily affected and can be easily skewed by the order of the statements in the source code (e.g. nested levels, etc.), while it would not provide a fair comparison between snippets and sequences.

$$Prec(s) = max_{e \in E_s} \left\{ \frac{|T_s \cap T_e|}{|T_s|} \right\} \tag{2}$$

where T_s and T_e are the set of tokens of the snippet s and of the example e, respectively. Finally, if no example has exactly the same API calls as the snippet (i.e. $E_s = \varnothing$), then snippet precision is set to zero. Given the snippet precision, we also define the average snippet precision for n snippets $s_1, s_2, \ldots, s_n$ as:

$$AvgPrec(n) = \frac{1}{n} \sum_{i=1}^{n} Prec(s_i) \tag{3}$$

Similarly, average snippet precision at top k can be defined as:

$$AvgPrec@k = \frac{1}{k} \sum_{j=1}^{k} Prec@j \text{ where } Prec@j = \frac{1}{j} \sum_{i=1}^{j} Prec(s_i) \tag{4}$$

This metric is useful for evaluating our system which outputs ordered results, as it allows us to illustrate and draw conclusions for precision at different levels.

We also define coverage at k as the number of unique API methods contained in the top k snippets. This metric has already been defined in a similar manner by Fowkes and Sutton [9], who claim that a list of patterns with identical methods would be redundant, non-diverse, and thus not representative of the target API.

Finally, we measure additional information provided in source code snippets when compared with API call sequences. For each snippet we extract its *snippet-tokens* T_s, as defined in (2), and its *sequence-tokens* $T_s{}'$, which are extracted by the underlying API call sequence of the snippet, where each token is the name of an API method. Based on these sets, we define the *additional info* metric as:

$$AdditInfo = \frac{1}{m} \sum_{i=1}^{m} \frac{\max_{e \in E_s}\{|T_{s_i} \cap T_e|\}}{\max_{e \in E_s}\{|T_{s_i}{}' \cap T_e|\}} \tag{5}$$

where m is the number of snippets that match to at least one example.

4.2   Evaluation Results

RQ1: How much more concise, readable, and precise with respect to handwritten examples are the snippets after summarization? We evaluate how much reduction in the size of the snippets is achieved by the summarization algorithm, and the effect of summarization on the precision with respect to handwritten examples. If snippets have high or higher precision after summarization, then this indicates that the tokens removed by summarization are ones that do not typically appear in handwritten examples, and thus are possibly less relevant. For this purpose, we use the first two versions of our system, namely the *NaiveSum* and the *NaiveNoSum* versions. Both of them use the naive clustering technique, where only identical sequences are clustered together. Figures 5a and b depict the average readability of the snippets mined for each library and the

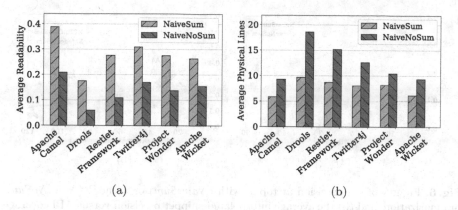

Fig. 5. Figures of (a) the average readability, and (b) the average PLOCs of the snippets, for each library, with (*NaiveSum*) and without (*NaiveNoSum*) summarization.

average PLOCs, respectively. The readability of the mined snippets is almost doubled when performing summarization, while the snippets generated by the *NaiveSum* version are clearly smaller than those mined by *NaiveNoSum*. In fact, the majority of the snippets of *NaiveSum* contain less than 10 PLOCs, owing mainly to the non-API statements removal of the algorithm. On average, the summarization algorithm leads to 40% fewer PLOCS. Thus, we may argue that the snippets provided by our summarizer are readable and concise.

Apart from readability and conciseness, which are both regarded as highly desirable features [26], we further assess whether the summarizer produces snippets that closely match handwritten examples. Therefore, we plot the snippet precision at top k, in Fig. 6a. The plot indicates a downward trend in precision for both configurations, which is explained by the fact that the snippets of lower positions are more complex, as they normally contain a large number of API calls. In any case, it is clear that the version that uses the summarizer mines more precise snippets than the one not using it, for any value of k. E.g., for $k = 10$, the summarizer increases snippet precision from 0.27 to 0.35, indicating that no useful statements are removed and no irrelevant statements are added.

RQ2: Do more powerful clustering techniques, that cluster similar rather than identical sequences, lead to snippets that more closely match handwritten examples? In this experiment we compare *NaiveSum*, *KMedoidsSum*, and *HDBSCANSum* to assess the effect of applying different clustering techniques on the snippets. In order for the comparison to be fair, we use the same number of clusters for both k-medoids and HDBSCAN. Therefore, we first run HDBSCAN (setting its *min_cluster_size* parameter to 2), and then use the number of clusters generated by the algorithm for k-medoids. After that, we consider the top k results of the three versions, so that the comparison with the Naive method (that cannot be tuned) is also fair. Hence, we plot precision against coverage, in a similar manner to precision versus recall graphs. For this

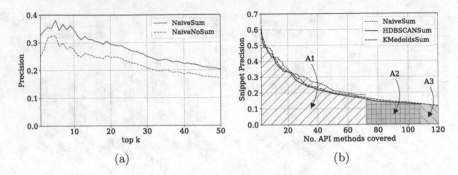

Fig. 6. Figures of (a) precision at top k, with (*NaiveSum*) or without (*NaiveNoSum*) summarization, and (b) the average interpolated snippet precision versus API coverage for three system versions (clustering algorithms), using the top 100 mined snippets.

we use the snippet precision at k and coverage at k, while we make use of an *interpolated* version of the curve, where the precision value at each point is the maximum for the corresponding coverage value. Figure 6b depicts the curve for the top 100 snippets, where the areas under the curves are shaded. Area *A2* reveals the additional coverage in API methods achieved by *HDBSCANSum*, when compared to *NaiveSum* (*A1*), while *A3* shows the corresponding additional coverage of *KMedoidsSum*, when compared to *HDBSCANSum* (*A2*).

NaiveSum achieves slightly better precision than the versions using clustering, which is expected as most of its top snippets use the same API calls, and contain only a few API methods. As a consequence, however, its coverage is quite low, due to the fact that only identical sequences are grouped together. Given that coverage is considered quite important when mining API usage examples [31], and that precision among all three configurations is similar, we may argue that *KMedoidsSum* and *HDBSCANSum* produce sufficiently precise and also more varying results for the developer. The differences between these two methods are mostly related to the separation among the clusters; the clusters created by *KMedoidsSum* are more separated and thus it achieves higher coverage, whereas *HDBSCANSum* has slightly higher precision. To achieve a trade-off between precision and coverage, we select *HDBSCANSum* for the last two RQs.

RQ3: Does our tool mine more diverse patterns than other existing approaches? For this research question, we evaluate the diversity of the examples of CLAMS to that of two API mining approaches, MAPO [32,33] and UP-Miner [31], which were deemed most similar to our approach from a mining perspective (as it also works at sequence level)[2]. We measure diversity using the coverage at k. Figure 7a depicts the coverage in API methods for each approach and each library, while Fig. 7b shows the average number of API methods covered at top k, using the top 100 examples of each approach.

---

[2] Comparing with other tools was also hard, as most are unavailable, such as, e.g., the eXoaDocs web app (http://exoa.postech.ac.kr/) or the APIMiner website (http://java.labsoft.dcc.ufmg.br/apimineride/resources/docs/reference/).

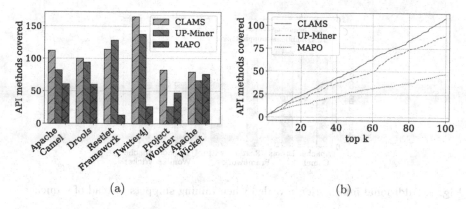

(a)   (b)

Fig. 7. Graphs of the coverage in API methods achieved by CLAMS, MAPO, and UP-Miner, (a) for each project, and (b) on average, at top k, using the top 100 examples.

The coverage by MAPO and UP-Miner is quite low, which is expected since both tools perform frequent sequence mining, thus generating several redundant patterns, a limitation noted also by Fowkes and Sutton [9]. On the other hand, our system integrates clustering techniques to reduce redundancy which is further eliminated by the fact that we select a single snippet from each cluster (Snippet Selector). Finally, the average coverage trend (Fig. 7b) indicates that our tool mines more diverse sequences than the other two tools, regardless of the number of examples.

RQ4: Do source code snippets match handwritten examples more than API call sequences? Obviously source code snippets contain more tokens than API call sequences, but the additional tokens might not be useful. Therefore, we measure specifically whether the additional tokens that appear in snippets rather than sequences also appear in handwritten examples. Computing the average of the *additional info* metric for each library, we find that the average ratio between snippets-tokens and sequence-tokens, that are shared between snippets and corresponding examples, is 2.75. This means that presenting snippets instead of sequences leads to 2.75 times more information. By further plotting the additional information of the snippets for each library in Fig. 8, we observe that snippets almost always provide at least twice as much valuable information. To further illustrate the contrast between snippets and sequences, we present an indicative snippet mined by CLAMS in Fig. 9. Note, e.g., how the try/catch tokens are important, however not included in the sequence tokens.

Finally, we present the top 5 usage examples mined by CLAMS, MAPO and UP-Miner, in Fig. 10. As one may observe, snippets provide useful information that is missing from sequences, including identifiers (e.g. String secret), control flow statements (e.g. if-then-else statements), etc. Moreover, snippets are easier to integrate into the source code of the developer, and thus facilitate reuse.

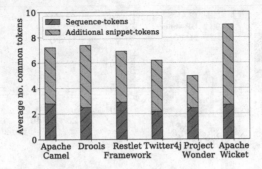

Fig. 8. Additional information revealed when mining snippets instead of sequences.

```
AccessToken accessToken;
String oauthToken;
String oAuthVerifier;
Twitter twitter;
try {
    accessToken = twitter.getOAuthAccessToken(oauthToken,oAuthVerifier);
    // Do something with accessToken
} catch (TwitterException e) {
    e.printStackTrace();
}
```

Fig. 9. Example snippet matched to handwritten example. Sequence-tokens are encircled and additional snippet-tokens are highlighted in bold.

```
Twitter mTwitter;
mTwitter = new TwitterFactory().getInstance();
// Do something with mTwitter

Twitter mTwitter;
final String CONSUMER_KEY;
final String CONSUMER_SECRET;
mTwitter = new TwitterFactory().getInstance();
mTwitter.setOAuthConsumer(CONSUMER_KEY,
    CONSUMER_SECRET);

BasicDBObject tweet;
Status status;
tweet.put(string, status.getUser().getScreenName());
tweet.put(string, status.getText());

String mConsumerKey;
Twitter mTwitter;
AccessToken mAccessToken;
String mSecretKey;
if (mAccessToken != null) {
    mTwitter.setOAuthConsumer(mConsumerKey, mSecretKey);
    mTwitter.setOAuthAccessToken(mAccessToken);
}

Twitter mTwitter;
String token;
String secret;
AccessToken at = new AccessToken(token, secret);
mTwitter.setOAuthAccessToken(at);
```
(a)

```
TwitterFactory.<init>
TwitterFactory.getInstance

Status.getUser
Status.getText

ConfigurationBuilder.<init>
ConfiguratiorBuilder.build

ConfigurationBuilder.<init>
TwitterFactory.<init>

ConfigurationBuilder.<init>
ConfigurationBuilder.setOAuthConsumerKey
```
(b)

```
TwitterFactory.getInstance
Twitter.setOAuthConsumer

TwitterFactory.<init>
TwitterFactory.getInstance
Twitter.setOAuthConsumer

Status.getUser
Status.getUser

ConfigurationBuilder.<init>
ConfigurationBuilder.build
TwitterFactory.<init>

ConfigurationBuilder.<init>
ConfigurationBuilder.build
TwitterFactory.<init>
TwitterFactory.getInstance
```
(c)

Fig. 10. Top 5 usage examples mined by (a) CLAMS, (b) MAPO, and (c) UP-Miner. The API methods for the examples of our system are highlighted.

Interestingly, the snippet ranked second by CLAMS has not been matched to any handwritten example, although it has high support in the dataset. In fact, there is no example for the setOauthConsumer method of *Twitter4J*, which is one of its most popular methods. This illustrates how CLAMS can also extract snippets beyond those of the examples directory, which are valuable to developers.

5   Threats to Validity

The main threats to validity of our approach involve the choice of the evaluation metrics and the lack of comparison with snippet-based approaches. Concerning the metrics, snippet API coverage is typical when comparing API usage mining approaches. On the other hand, the choice of metrics for measuring snippet quality is indeed a subjective criterion. To address this threat, we have employed three metrics, for the conciseness (PLOCs), readability, and quality (similarity to real examples). Our evaluation indicates that CLAMS is effective on all of these axes. In addition, as these metrics are applied on snippets, computing them for sequence-based systems such as MAPO and UP-Miner was not possible. Finally, to evaluate whether CLAMS can be practically useful when developing software, we plan to conduct a developer survey. To this end, we have already performed a preliminary study on a team of 5 Java developers of Hotels.com, the results of which were encouraging. More details about the study can be found at https://mast-group.github.io/clams/user-survey/ (omitted here due to space limitations).

Concerning the comparison with current approaches, we chose to compare CLAMS against sequence-based approaches (MAPO and UP-Miner), as the mining methodology is actually performed at sequence level. Nevertheless, comparing with snippet-based approaches would also be useful, not only as a proof of concept but also because it would allow us to comparatively evaluate CLAMS with regard to the snippet quality metrics mentioned in the previous paragraph. However, such a comparison was troublesome, as most current tools (including e.g., eXoaDocs, APIMiner, etc.) are currently unavailable (see RQ3 of Sect. 4.2). We may however note this comparison as an important point for future work, while we also choose to upload our code and findings online (https://mast-group.github.io/clams/) to facilitate future researchers that may face similar challenges.

6   Conclusion

In this paper we have proposed a novel approach for mining API usage examples in the form of source code snippets, from client code. Our system uses clustering techniques, as well as a summarization algorithm to mine useful, concise, and readable snippets. Our evaluation shows that snippet clustering leads to better precision versus coverage rate, while the summarization algorithm effectively increases the readability and decreases the size of the snippets. Finally, our tool offers diverse snippets that match handwritten examples better than sequences.

204   N. Katirtzis et al.

In future work, we plan to extend the approach used to retrieve the top mined sequences from each cluster. We could use a two-stage clustering approach where, after clustering the API call sequences, we could further cluster the snippets of the formed clusters, using a tree edit distance metric. This would allow retrieving snippets that use the same API call sequence, but differ in their structure.

References

1. Allamanis, M., Sutton, C.: Mining idioms from source code. In: Proceedings of the 22nd ACM SIGSOFT International Symposium on Foundations of Software Engineering, FSE 2014, pp. 472–483. ACM, New York (2014)
2. Artistic Style 3.0: http://astyle.sourceforge.net/. Accessed Jan 2018
3. Bauckhage, C.: Numpy/scipy Recipes for Data Science: k-Medoids Clustering. Technical report. University of Bonn (2015)
4. Borges, H.S., Valente, M.T.: Mining usage patterns for the Android API. PeerJ Comput. Sci. 1, e12 (2015)
5. Buse, R.P.L., Weimer, W.: Synthesizing API usage examples. In: Proceedings of the 34th International Conference on Software Engineering, ICSE 2012, pp. 782–792. IEEE Press, Piscataway (2012)
6. Buse, R.P., Weimer, W.R.: A metric for software readability. In: Proceedings of the 2008 International Symposium on Software Testing and Analysis, ISSTA 2008, pp. 121–130. ACM, New York (2008)
7. Campello, R.J.G.B., Moulavi, D., Sander, J.: Density-based clustering based on hierarchical density estimates. In: Pei, J., Tseng, V.S., Cao, L., Motoda, H., Xu, G. (eds.) PAKDD 2013. LNCS (LNAI), vol. 7819, pp. 160–172. Springer, Heidelberg (2013). https://doi.org/10.1007/978-3-642-37456-2_14
8. Collard, M.L., Decker, M.J., Maletic, J.I.: srcML: an infrastructure for the exploration, analysis, and manipulation of source code: a tool demonstration. In: Proceedings of the 2013 IEEE International Conference on Software Maintenance, ICSM 2013, pp. 516–519. IEEE Computer Society, Washington, DC (2013)
9. Fowkes, J., Sutton, C.: Parameter-free probabilistic API mining across GitHub. In: Proceedings of the 24th ACM SIGSOFT International Symposium on Foundations of Software Engineering, FSE 2016, pp. 254–265. ACM, New York (2016)
10. Han, J., Kamber, M., Pei, J.: Data Mining: Concepts and Techniques, vol. 3, pp. 1–38. Morgan Kaufmann Publishers Inc., San Francisco (2011)
11. Ishag, M.I.M., Park, H.W., Li, D., Ryu, K.H.: Highlighting current issues in API usage mining to enhance software reusability. In: Proceedings of the 15th International Conference on Software Engineering, Parallel and Distributed Systems, SEPADS 2016, pp. 200–205. WSEAS (2016)
12. Jiang, L., Misherghi, G., Su, Z., Glondu, S.: DECKARD: scalable and accurate tree-based detection of code clones. In: Proceedings of the 29th International Conference on Software Engineering, ICSE 2007, pp. 96–105. IEEE Computer Society, Washington, DC (2007)
13. Kim, J., Lee, S., Hwang, S.W., Kim, S.: Adding examples into Java documents. In: Proceedings of the 2009 IEEE/ACM International Conference on Automated Software Engineering, ASE 2009, pp. 540–544. IEEE, Washington, DC (2009)
14. Kim, J., Lee, S., Hwang, S.W., Kim, S.: Towards an intelligent code search engine. In: Proceedings of the Twenty-Fourth AAAI Conference on Artificial Intelligence, AAAI 2010, pp. 1358–1363. AAAI Press (2010)

15. Kim, J., Lee, S., Hwang, S.W., Kim, S.: Enriching documents with examples: a corpus mining approach. ACM Trans. Inf. Syst. **31**(1), 1:1–1:27 (2013)
16. McDonnell, T., Ray, B., Kim, M.: An empirical study of API stability and adoption in the android ecosystem. In: Proceedings of the 2013 IEEE International Conference on Software Maintenance, ICSM 2013, pp. 70–79. IEEE Computer Society, Washington, DC (2013)
17. McInnes, L., Healy, J., Astels, S.: HDBSCAN: hierarchical density based clustering. J. Open Source Softw. **2**(11), 205 (2017)
18. McLellan, S.G., Roesler, A.W., Tempest, J.T., Spinuzzi, C.I.: Building more usable APIs. IEEE Softw. **15**(3), 78–86 (1998)
19. Mens, K., Lozano, A.: Source code-based recommendation systems. In: Robillard, M.P., Maalej, W., Walker, R.J., Zimmermann, T. (eds.) Recomm. Syst. Softw. Eng., pp. 93–130. Springer, Heidelberg (2014). https://doi.org/10.1007/978-3-642-45135-5_5
20. Montandon, J.E., Borges, H., Felix, D., Valente, M.T.: Documenting APIs with examples: lessons learned with the APIMiner platform. In: Proceedings of the 20th Working Conference on Reverse Engineering, WCRE 2013, pp. 401–408 (2013)
21. Pawlik, M., Augsten, N.: Tree edit distance: robust and memory-efficient. Inf. Syst. **56**(C), 157–173 (2016)
22. Piccioni, M., Furia, C.A., Meyer, B.: An empirical study of API usability. In: Proceedings of the 7th ACM/IEEE International Symposium on Empirical Software Engineering and Measurement, ESEM 2013, pp. 5–14 (2013)
23. Ponzanelli, L., Bavota, G., Mocci, A., Penta, M.D., Oliveto, R., Russo, B., Haiduc, S., Lanza, M.: CodeTube: extracting relevant fragments from software development video tutorials. In: Proceedings of the 38th International Conference on Software Engineering Companion, ICSE-C 2016, pp. 645–648 (2016)
24. Robillard, M.P.: What makes APIs hard to learn? answers from developers. IEEE Softw. **26**(6), 27–34 (2009)
25. Saied, M.A., Benomar, O., Abdeen, H., Sahraoui, H.: Mining multi-level API usage patterns. In: 2015 IEEE 22nd International Conference on Software Analysis, Evolution, and Reengineering (SANER), pp. 23–32 (2015)
26. Sillito, J., Maurer, F., Nasehi, S.M., Burns, C.: What makes a good code example?: a study of programming Q&A in stackoverflow. In: Proceedings of the 2012 IEEE International Conference on Software Maintenance, ICSM 2012, pp. 25–34. IEEE Computer Society, Washington, DC (2012)
27. Source Code Readability Metric. http://www.arrestedcomputing.com/readability. Accessed Jan 2018
28. Stylos, J., Faulring, A., Yang, Z., Myers, B.A.: Improving API documentation using API usage information. In: Proceedings of the 2009 IEEE Symposium on Visual Languages and Human-Centric Computing, VLHCC 2009, pp. 119–126 (2009)
29. Subramanian, S., Inozemtseva, L., Holmes, R.: Live API documentation. In: Proceedings of the 36th International Conference on Software Engineering, ICSE 2014, pp. 643–652. ACM, New York (2014)
30. Uddin, G., Robillard, M.P.: How API documentation fails. IEEE Softw. **32**(4), 68–75 (2015)
31. Wang, J., Dang, Y., Zhang, H., Chen, K., Xie, T., Zhang, D.: Mining succinct and high-coverage API usage patterns from source code. In: Proceedings of the 10th Working Conference on Mining Software Repositories, MSR 2013, pp. 319–328. IEEE Press, Piscataway (2013)

32. Xie, T., Pei, J.: MAPO: Mining API usages from open source repositories. In: Proceedings of the 2006 International Workshop on Mining Software Repositories, MSR 2006, pp. 54–57. ACM, New York (2006)

33. Zhong, H., Xie, T., Zhang, L., Pei, J., Mei, H.: MAPO: mining and recommending API usage patterns. In: Drossopoulou, S. (ed.) ECOOP 2009. LNCS, vol. 5653, pp. 318–343. Springer, Heidelberg (2009). https://doi.org/10.1007/978-3-642-03013-0_15

34. Zhu, Z., Zou, Y., Xie, B., Jin, Y., Lin, Z., Zhang, L.: Mining API usage examples from test code. In: Proceedings of the 2014 IEEE International Conference on Software Maintenance and Evolution, ICSME 2014, pp. 301–310. IEEE Computer Society, Washington, DC (2014)

Fast Computation of Arbitrary Control Dependencies

Jean-Christophe Léchenet[1,2](✉) , Nikolai Kosmatov[1] , and Pascale Le Gall[2]

[1] CEA, LIST, Software Reliability Laboratory, PC 174, 91191 Gif-sur-Yvette, France
{jean-christophe.lechenet,nikolai.kosmatov}@cea.fr
[2] Laboratoire de Mathématiques et Informatique pour la Complexité et les Systèmes
CentraleSupélec, Université Paris-Saclay, 91190 Gif-sur-Yvette, France
pascale.legall@centralesupelec.fr

Abstract. In 2011, Danicic et al. introduced an elegant generalization of the notion of control dependence for any directed graph. They also proposed an algorithm computing the weak control-closure of a subset of graph vertices and performed a paper-and-pencil proof of its correctness. We have performed its proof in the Coq proof assistant. This paper also presents a novel, more efficient algorithm to compute weak control-closure taking benefit of intermediate propagation results of previous iterations in order to accelerate the following ones. This optimization makes the design and proof of the algorithm more complex and requires subtle loop invariants. The new algorithm has been formalized and mechanically proven in the Why3 verification tool. Experiments on arbitrary generated graphs with up to thousands of vertices demonstrate that the proposed algorithm remains practical for real-life programs and significantly outperforms Danicic's initial technique.

1 Introduction

Context. *Control dependence* is a fundamental notion in software engineering and analysis (e.g. [6, 12, 13, 21, 22, 27]). It reflects structural relationships between different program statements and is intensively used in many software analysis techniques and tools, such as compilers, verification tools, test generators, program transformation tools, simulators, debuggers, etc. Along with data dependence, it is one of the key notions used in *program slicing* [25, 27], a program transformation technique allowing to decompose a given program into a simpler one, called a program slice.

In 2011, Danicic et al. [11] proposed an elegant generalization of the notions of closure under non-termination insensitive (*weak*) and non-termination sensitive (*strong*) control dependence. They introduced the notions of weak and strong control-closures, that can be defined on any directed graph, and no longer only on control flow graphs. They proved that weak and strong control-closures subsume the closures under all forms of control dependence previously known in the literature. In the present paper, we are interested in the non-termination insensitive form, i.e. *weak control-closure*.

© The Author(s) 2018
A. Russo and A. Schürr (Eds.): FASE 2018, LNCS 10802, pp. 207–224, 2018.
https://doi.org/10.1007/978-3-319-89363-1_12

Besides the definition of weak control-closure, Danicic et al. also provided an algorithm computing it for a given set of vertices in a directed graph. This algorithm was proved by paper-and-pencil. Under the assumption that the given graph is a CFG (or more generally, that the maximal out-degree of the graph vertices is bounded), the complexity of the algorithm can be expressed in terms of the number of vertices n of the graph, and was shown to be $O(n^3)$. Danicic et al. themselves suggested that it should be possible to improve its complexity. This may explain why this algorithm was not used until now.

Motivation. Danicic et al. introduced basic notions used to define weak control-closure and to justify the algorithm, and proved a few lemmas about them. While formalizing these concepts in the Coq proof assistant [5,24], we have discovered that, strictly speaking, the paper-and-pencil proof of one of them [11, Lemma 53] is inaccurate (a previously proven case is applied while its hypotheses are not satisfied), whereas the lemma itself is correct. Furthermore, Danicic's algorithm does not take advantage of its iterative nature and does not reuse the results of previous iterations in order to speed up the following ones.

Goals. First, we fully formalize Danicic's algorithm, its correctness proof and the underlying concepts in Coq. Our second objective is to design a more efficient algorithm sharing information between iterations to speed up the execution. Since our new algorithm is carefully optimized and more complex, its correctness proof relies on more subtle arguments than for Danicic's algorithm. To deal with them and to avoid any risk of error, we have decided again to use a mechanized verification tool – this time, the Why3 proof system [1,14] – to guarantee correctness of the optimized version. Finally, in order to evaluate the new algorithm with respect to Danicic's initial technique, we have implemented both algorithms in OCaml (using OCamlgraph library [9]) and tested them on a large set of randomly generated graphs with up to thousands of vertices. Experiments demonstrate that the proposed optimized algorithm is applicable to large graphs (and thus to CFGs of real-life programs) and significantly outperforms Danicic's original technique.

Contributions. The contributions of this paper include:

- A formalization of Danicic's algorithm and proof of its correctness in Coq;
- A new algorithm computing weak control-closure and taking benefit from preserving some intermediary results between iterations;
- A mechanized correctness proof of this new algorithm in the Why3 tool including a formalization of the basic concepts and results of Danicic et al.;
- An implementation of Danicic's and our algorithms in OCaml, their evaluation on random graphs and a comparison of their execution times.

The Coq, Why3 and OCaml implementations are all available in [17].

Outline. We present our motivation and a running example in Sect. 2. Then, we recall the definitions of some important concepts introduced by [11] in Sect. 3 and state two important lemmas in Sect. 4. Next, we describe Danicic's algorithm in Sect. 5 and our algorithm along with a sketch of the proof of its correctness in Sect. 6. Experiments are presented in Sect. 7. Finally, Sect. 8 presents some related work and concludes.

2   Motivation and Running Example

This section informally presents weak control-closure using a running example.

The inputs of our problem are a directed graph $G = (V, E)$ with set of vertices (or nodes) V and set of edges E, and a subset of vertices $V' \subseteq V$. The property of interest of such a subset is called *weakly control-closed* in [11] (cf. Definition 3). V' is said to be *weakly control-closed* if the nodes reachable from V' are V'-*weakly committing* (cf. Definition 2), i.e. always lead the flow to at most one node in V'. Since V' does not necessarily satisfy this property, we want to build a superset of V' satisfying it, and more particularly the smallest one, called the *weak control-closure* of V' in G (cf. Definition 5). For that, as it will be proved by Lemma 2, we need to add to V' the points of divergence closest to V', called

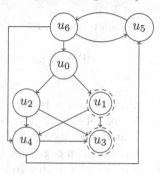

Fig. 1. Example graph G_0, with $V_0' = \{u_1, u_3\}$

the V'-*weakly deciding* vertices, that are reachable from V'. Formally, vertex u is V'-*weakly deciding* if there exist two non-trivial paths starting from u and reaching V' that have no common vertex except u (cf. Definition 4).

Let us illustrate these ideas on an example graph G_0 shown in Fig. 1. $V_0' = \{u_1, u_3\}$ is the subset of interest represented with dashed double circles ($\langle\!\langle u_i \rangle\!\rangle$) in Fig. 1. u_5 is reachable from V_0' and is not V_0'-weakly committing, since it is the origin of two paths u_5, u_6, u_0, u_1 and u_5, u_6, u_0, u_2, u_3 that can lead the flow to two different nodes u_1 and u_3 in V_0'. Therefore, V_0' is not weakly control-closed. To build the weak control-closure, we need to add to V_0' all V_0'-weakly deciding nodes reachable from V_0'. u_0 is such a node. Indeed, it is reachable from V_0' and we can build two non-trivial paths u_0, u_1 and u_0, u_2, u_3 starting from u_0, ending in V_0' (respectively in u_1 and u_3) and sharing no other vertex than u_0. Similarly, nodes u_2, u_4 and u_6 must be added as well. On the contrary, u_5 must not be added, since every non-empty path starting from u_5 has u_6 as second vertex. More generally, a node with only one child cannot be a "divergence point closest to V'" and must never be added to build the weak control-closure. The weak control-closure of V_0' in G_0 is thus $\{u_0, u_1, u_2, u_3, u_4, u_6\}$.

To build the closure, Danicic's algorithm, like the one we propose, does not directly try to build the two paths sharing only one node. Both algorithms rely on a concept called *observable vertex*. Given a vertex $u \in V$, the set of *observable vertices* in V' from u contains all nodes reachable from u in V' without using edges starting in V'. The important property about this object is that, as it will be proved by Lemma 4, if there exists an edge $(u, v) \in E$ such that u is not in V', u is reachable from V', v can reach V' and there exists a vertex w

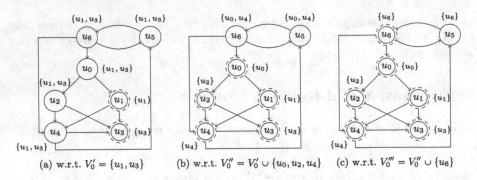

Fig. 2. Example graph G_0 annotated with observable sets

observable from u but not from v, then u must be added to V' to build the weak control-closure. Figure 2a shows our example graph G_0, each node being annotated with its set of observables in V_0'.

(u_0, u_1) is an edge such that u_0 is reachable from V_0', u_1 can reach V_0' and u_3 is an observable vertex from u_0 in V_0' but not from u_1. u_0 is thus a node to be added in the weak control-closure. Likewise, from the edges (u_2, u_3) and (u_4, u_3), we can deduce that u_2 and u_4 belong to the closure. However, we have seen that u_6 belongs to the closure, but it is not possible to apply the same reasoning to (u_6, u_0), (u_6, u_4) or (u_6, u_5). We need another technique. As Lemma 3 will establish, the technique is actually iterative. We can add to the initial V_0' the nodes that we have already detected and apply our technique to this new set V_0''. The vertices that will be detected this way will also be in the closure of the initial set V_0'. The observable sets w.r.t. to $V_0'' = V_0' \cup \{u_0, u_2, u_4\}$ are shown in Fig. 2b. This time, both edges (u_6, u_4) and (u_6, u_0) allow us to add u_6 to the closure. Applying again the technique with the augmented set $V_0''' = V_0'' \cup \{u_6\}$ (cf. Fig. 2c) does not reveal new vertices. This means that all the nodes have already been found. We obtain the same set as before for the weak control-closure of V_0', i.e. $\{u_0, u_1, u_2, u_3, u_4, u_6\}$.

3   Basic Concepts

This section introduces basic definitions and properties needed to define the notion of weak control-closure. They have been formalized in Coq [17], including in particular Property 3 whose proof in [11] was inaccurate.

From now on, let $G = (V, E)$ denote a directed graph, and V' a subset of V. We define a *path* in G in the usual way. We write $u \xrightarrow{path} v$ if there exists a path from u to v. Let $\mathsf{R}_G(V') = \{v \in V \mid \exists u \in V', u \xrightarrow{path} v\}$ be the set of nodes reachable from V'. In our example (cf. Fig. 1), u_6, u_0, u_1, u_3 is a (4-node) path in G_0, u_1 is a trivial one-node path in G_0 from u_1 to itself, and $\mathsf{R}_{G_0}(V_0') = V_0$.

Definition 1 (V'-disjoint, V'-path). *A path π in G is said to be V'-disjoint in G if all the vertices in π but the last one are not in V'. A V'-path in G is a V'-disjoint path whose last vertex is in V'. In particular, if $u \in V'$, the only V'-path starting from u is the trivial path u.*

We write $u \xrightarrow{V'-disjoint} v$ (resp. $u \xrightarrow{V'-path} v$) if there exists a V'-disjoint path (resp. a V'-path) from u to v.

Example. In G_0, u_3; u_2, u_3; u_0, u_1; u_0, u_2, u_3 are V_0'-paths and thus V_0'-disjoint paths. u_6, u_0 is a V_0'-disjoint path but not a V_0'-path.

Remark 1. Definition 1 and the following ones are slightly different from [11], where a V'-path must contain at least two vertices and there is no constraint on its first vertex, which can be in V' or not. Our definitions lead to the same notion of weak control-closure.

Definition 2 (V'-weakly committing vertex). *A vertex u in G is V'-weakly committing if all the V'-paths from u have the same end point (in V'). In particular, any vertex $u \in V'$ is V'-weakly committing.*

Example. In G_0, u_1 and u_3 are the only V_0'-weakly committing nodes.

Definition 3 (Weakly control-closed set). *A subset V' of V is weakly control-closed in G if every vertex reachable from V' is V'-weakly committing.*

Example. Since in particular u_2 is not V_0'-weakly committing and reachable from V_0', V_0' is not weakly control-closed in G_0. $\varnothing$, singletons and the set of all nodes V_0 are trivially weakly control-closed. Less trivial weakly control-closed sets include $\{u_0, u_1\}$, $\{u_4, u_5, u_6\}$ and $\{u_0, u_1, u_2, u_3, u_4, u_6\}$.

Definition 3 characterizes a weakly control-closed set, but does not explain how to build one. It would be particularly interesting to build the smallest weakly control-closed set containing a given set V'. The notion of *weakly deciding vertex* will help us to give an explicit expression to that set.

Definition 4 (V'-weakly deciding vertex). *A vertex u is V'-weakly deciding if there exist at least two non-trivial V'-paths from u that share no vertex except u. Let $\mathsf{WD}_G(V')$ denote the set of V'-weakly deciding vertices in G.*

Property 1. If $u \in V'$, then $u \notin \mathsf{WD}_G(V')$ (by Definitions 1, 4).

Example. In G_0, by Property 1, $u_1, u_3 \notin \mathsf{WD}_{G_0}(V_0')$. We have illustrated the definition for nodes u_0 and u_5 in Sect. 2. We have $\mathsf{WD}_{G_0}(V_0') = \{u_0, u_2, u_4, u_6\}$.

Lemma 1 (Characterization of being weakly control-closed). *V' is weakly control-closed in G if and only if there is no V'-weakly deciding vertex in G reachable from V'.*

Example. In G_0, u_2 is reachable from V_0' and is V_0'-weakly deciding. This gives another proof that V_0' is not weakly control-closed.

Here are two other useful properties of WD_G.

Property 2. $\forall\, V_1', V_2' \subseteq V,\ V_1' \subseteq V_2' \implies \mathsf{WD}_G(V_1') \subseteq V_2' \cup \mathsf{WD}_G(V_2')$

Property 3. $\mathsf{WD}_G(V' \cup \mathsf{WD}_G(V')) = \varnothing$.

We can prove that adding to a given set V' the V'-weakly deciding nodes that are reachable from V' gives a weakly control-closed set in G. This set is the smallest superset of V' weakly control-closed in G.

Lemma 2 (Existence of the weak control-closure). *Let $W = \mathsf{WD}_G(V') \cap R_G(V')$ denote the set of vertices in $\mathsf{WD}_G(V')$ that are reachable from V'. Then $V' \cup W$ is the smallest weakly control-closed set containing V'.*

Definition 5 (Weak control-closure). *We call* weak control-closure *of V', denoted $\mathsf{WCC}_G(V')$, the smallest weakly control-closed set containing V'.*

Property 4. Let V', V_1' and V_2' be subsets of V. Then

(a) $\mathsf{WCC}_G(V') = V' \cup (\mathsf{WD}_G(V') \cap R_G(V')) = (V' \cup \mathsf{WD}_G(V')) \cap R_G(V')$.
(b) If $V_1' \subseteq V_2'$, then $\mathsf{WCC}_G(V_1') \subseteq \mathsf{WCC}_G(V_2')$.
(c) If V' is weakly control-closed, then $\mathsf{WCC}_G(V') = V'$.
(d) $\mathsf{WCC}_G(\mathsf{WCC}_G(V')) = \mathsf{WCC}_G(V')$.

4   Main Lemmas

This section gives two lemmas used to justify both Danicic's algorithm and ours.

Lemma 3. *Let V' and W be two subsets of V. If $V' \subseteq W \subseteq V' \cup \mathsf{WD}_G(V')$, then $W \cup \mathsf{WD}_G(W) = V' \cup \mathsf{WD}_G(V')$. If moreover $V' \subseteq W \subseteq \mathsf{WCC}_G(V')$, then $\mathsf{WCC}_G(W) = \mathsf{WCC}_G(V')$.*

Proof. Assume $V' \subseteq W \subseteq V' \cup \mathsf{WD}_G(V')$. Since $V' \subseteq W$, we have by Property 2, $\mathsf{WD}_G(V') \subseteq W \cup \mathsf{WD}_G(W)$. Moreover, $W \subseteq V' \cup \mathsf{WD}_G(V')$, thus $\mathsf{WD}_G(W) \subseteq V' \cup \mathsf{WD}_G(V') \cup \mathsf{WD}_G(V' \cup \mathsf{WD}_G(V'))$ by Property 2, hence $\mathsf{WD}_G(W) \subseteq V' \cup \mathsf{WD}_G(V')$ by Property 3. These inclusions imply $W \cup \mathsf{WD}_G(W) = V' \cup \mathsf{WD}_G(V')$.

If now $V' \subseteq W \subseteq \mathsf{WCC}_G(V')$, we deduce $\mathsf{WCC}_G(W) = \mathsf{WCC}_G(V')$ from the previous result by intersecting with $R_G(V')$ by Property 4a.   □

Lemma 3 allows to design iterative algorithms to compute the closure. Indeed, assume that we have a procedure which, for any non-weakly control-closed set V', can return one or more elements of the weak control-closure of V' not in V'. If we apply such a procedure to V' once, we get a set W that satisfies $V' \subseteq W \subseteq \mathsf{WCC}_G(V')$. From Lemma 3, $\mathsf{WCC}_G(W) = \mathsf{WCC}_G(V')$. To compute the weak control-closure of V', it is thus sufficient to build the weak control-closure of W. We can apply our procedure again, this time to W, and repetitively on all the successively computed sets. Since each set is a strict superset of the previous one, this iterative procedure terminates because graph G is finite.

Before stating the second lemma, we introduce a key concept. It is called Θ in [11]. We use the name "observable" as in [26].

Definition 6 (Observable). *Let $u \in V$. The set of* observable vertices *from u in V', denoted $\mathsf{obs}_G(u, V')$, is the set of vertices u' in V' such that $u \xrightarrow{V'-path} u'$.*

Remark 2. A vertex $u \in V'$ is its unique observable: $\mathsf{obs}_G(u, V') = \{u\}$.

The concept of observable set was illustrated in Fig. 2 (cf. Sect. 2).

Lemma 4 (Sufficient condition for being V'-weakly deciding). *Let (u, v) be an edge in G such that $u \notin V'$, v can reach V' and there exists a vertex u' in V' such that $u' \in \mathsf{obs}_G(u, V')$ and $u' \notin \mathsf{obs}_G(v, V')$. Then $u \in \mathsf{WD}_G(V')$.*

Proof. We need to exhibit two V'-paths from u ending in V' that share no vertex except u. We take the V'-path from u to u' as the first one, and a V'-path connecting u to V' through v as the second one (we construct it by prepending u to the smallest prefix of the path from v ending in V' which is a V'-path). If these V'-paths intersected at a node y different from u, we would have a V'-path from v to u' by concatenating the paths from v to y and from y to u', which is contradictory. □

Example. In G_0, $\mathsf{obs}_{G_0}(u_0, V_0') = \{u_1, u_3\}$ and $\mathsf{obs}_{G_0}(u_1, V_0') = \{u_1\}$ (cf. Fig. 2a). Since u_1 is a child of u_0, we can apply Lemma 4, and deduce that u_0 is V_0'-weakly deciding. $\mathsf{obs}_{G_0}(u_5, V_0') = \{u_1, u_3\}$ and $\mathsf{obs}_{G_0}(u_6, V_0') = \{u_1, u_3\}$. We cannot apply Lemma 4 to u_5, and for good reason, since u_5 is not V_0'-weakly deciding. But we cannot apply Lemma 4 to u_6 either, since u_6 and all its children u_0, u_4 and u_5 have observable sets $\{u_1, u_3\}$ w.r.t. V_0', while u_6 is V_0'-weakly deciding. This shows that with Lemma 4, we have a sufficient condition, but not a necessary one, for proving that a vertex is weakly deciding.

Example. Let us apply Algorithm 1 to our running example G_0 (cf. Fig. 1). Initially, $W_0 = V_0' = \{u_1, u_3\}$.

1. $\mathsf{obs}_{G_0}(u_0, W_0) = \{u_1, u_3\}$ and $\mathsf{obs}_{G_0}(u_1, W_0) = \{u_1\}$, therefore (u_0, u_1) is a W_0-critical edge. Set $W_1 = \{u_0, u_1, u_3\}$.
2. $\mathsf{obs}_{G_0}(u_2, W_1) = \{u_0, u_3\}$ and $\mathsf{obs}_{G_0}(u_3, W_1) = \{u_3\}$, therefore (u_2, u_3) is a W_1-critical edge. Set $W_2 = \{u_0, u_1, u_2, u_3\}$.
3. $\mathsf{obs}_{G_0}(u_4, W_2) = \{u_0, u_3\}$ and $\mathsf{obs}_{G_0}(u_3, W_2) = \{u_3\}$, therefore (u_4, u_3) is a W_2-critical edge. Set $W_3 = \{u_0, u_1, u_2, u_3, u_4\}$.
4. $\mathsf{obs}_{G_0}(u_6, W_3) = \{u_0, u_4\}$ and $\mathsf{obs}_{G_0}(u_0, W_3) = \{u_0\}$, therefore (u_6, u_0) is a W_3-critical edge. Set $W_4 = \{u_0, u_1, u_2, u_3, u_4, u_6\}$.
5. There is no W_4-critical edge. $\mathsf{WCC}_{G_0}(V_0') = W_4 = \{u_0, u_1, u_2, u_3, u_4, u_6\}$.

Input: $G = (V, E)$ a directed graph
    $V' \subseteq V$
Output: $W \subseteq V$ the weak control-closure of V'
Ensures: $W = \mathsf{WCC}_G(V')$
1 **begin**
2 | $W \leftarrow V'$
3 | **while** *there exists a W-critical edge in E* **do**
4 | | choose such a W-critical edge (u, v)
5 | | $W \leftarrow W \cup \{u\}$
6 | **end**
7 | **return** W
8 **end**

Algorithm 1. Danicic's original algorithm for weak control-closure [11]

5 Danicic's Algorithm

We present here the algorithm described in [11]. This algorithm and a proof of its correctness have been formalized in Coq [17]. The algorithm is nearly completely justified by a following lemma (Lemma 5, equivalent to [11, Lemma 60]).

We first need to introduce a new concept, which captures edges that are of particular interest when searching for weakly deciding vertices. This concept is taken from [11], where it was not given a name. We call such edges *critical edges*.

Definition 7 (Critical edge). *An edge (u, v) in G is called V'-critical if:*

(1) $|\mathsf{obs}_G(u, V')| \geq 2$;
(2) $|\mathsf{obs}_G(v, V')| = 1$;
(3) u is reachable from V' in G.

Example. In G_0, (u_0, u_1), (u_2, u_3) and (u_4, u_3) are the V_0'-critical edges.

Lemma 5. *If V' is not weakly control-closed in G, then there exists a V'-critical edge (u, v) in G. Moreover, if (u, v) is such a V'-critical edge, then $u \in \mathsf{WD}_G(V') \cap \mathsf{R}_G(V')$, therefore $u \in \mathsf{WCC}_G(V')$.*

Proof. Let x be a vertex in $\mathsf{WD}_G(V')$ reachable from V'. There exists a V'-path π from x ending in $x' \in V'$. It follows that $|\mathsf{obs}_G(x, V')| \geq 2$ and $|\mathsf{obs}_G(x', V')| = 1$. Let u be the last vertex on π with at least two observable nodes in V' and v its successor on π. Then (u, v) is a V'-critical edge.

Assume there exists a V'-critical edge (u, v). Since $|\mathsf{obs}_G(u, V')| \geq 2$ and $|\mathsf{obs}_G(v, V')| = 1$, $u \notin V'$, v can reach V' and there exists u' in $\mathsf{obs}_G(u, V')$ but not in $\mathsf{obs}_G(v, V')$. By Lemma 4, $u \in \mathsf{WD}_G(V')$ and thus $u \in \mathsf{WCC}_G(V')$. □

Remark 3. We can see in the proof above that we do not need the exact values 2 and 1. We just need strictly more observable vertices for u than for v and at least one observable for v, to satisfy the hypotheses of Lemma 4.

As described in Sect. 4, we can build an iterative algorithm constructing the weak control-closure of V' by searching for critical edges on the intermediate sets built successively. This is the idea of Danicic's algorithm shown as Algorithm 1.

Proof of Algorithm 1. To establish the correction of the algorithm, we can prove that W_i, the value of W before iteration $i + 1$, satisfies both $V' \subseteq W_i$ and $W_i \subseteq \mathsf{WCC}_G(V')$ for any i by induction. If $i = 0$, $W_0 = V'$, and both relations trivially hold. Let i be a natural number such that $V' \subseteq W_i$, $W_i \subseteq \mathsf{WCC}_G(V')$ and there exists a W_i-critical edge (u, v). We have $W_{i+1} = W_i \cup \{u\}$. $V' \subseteq W_{i+1}$ is straightforward. By Lemma 5, $u \in \mathsf{WCC}_G(W_i)$. Therefore, by Lemma 3, $u \in \mathsf{WCC}_G(V')$, and thus, $W_{i+1} \subseteq \mathsf{WCC}_G(V')$. At the end of the algorithm, there is no W-critical edge, therefore W is weakly control-closed by Lemma 5. Since $V' \subseteq W$ and $W \subseteq \mathsf{WCC}_G(V')$, $W = \mathsf{WCC}_G(V')$ by Lemma 3. Termination follows from the fact that W strictly increases in the loop and is upper-bounded by $\mathsf{WCC}_G(V')$.   □

In terms of complexity, [11] shows that, assuming that the degree of each vertex is at most 2 (and thus that $O(|V|) = O(|E|)$), the complexity of the algorithm is $O(|V|^3)$. Indeed, the main loop of Algorithm 1 is run at most $O(|V|)$ times, and each loop body computes obs in $O(|V|)$ for at most $O(|V|)$ edges.

Remark 4. We propose two optimizations for Algorithm 1:

– at each step, consider all critical edges rather than only one;
– use the weaker definition of critical edge suggested in Remark 3.

Example. We can replay Algorithm 1 using the first optimization. This run corresponds to the steps shown in Fig. 2. Initially, $W_0 = V'_0 = \{u_1, u_3\}$.

1. (u_0, u_1), (u_2, u_3), (u_4, u_3) are W_0-critical edges. Set $W_1 = \{u_0, u_1, u_2, u_3, u_4\}$.
2. (u_6, u_0) is a W_1-critical edge. Set $W_2 = \{u_0, u_1, u_2, u_3, u_4, u_6\}$.
3. There is no W_2-critical edge in G_0.

The optimized version computes the weak control-closure of V'_0 in G_0 in only 2 iterations instead of 4. This run also demonstrates that the algorithm is necessarily iterative: even when considering all V'_0-critical edges in the first step, u_6 is not detected before the second step.

6   The Optimized Algorithm

Overview. A potential source of inefficiency in Danicic's algorithm is the fact that no information is shared between the iterations. The observable sets are recomputed at each iteration since the target set changes. This is the reason why the first optimization proposed in Remark 4 is interesting, because it allows to work longer on the same set and thus to reuse the observable sets.

We propose now to go even further: to store some information about the paths in the graph and reuse it in the *following* iterations. The main idea of the proposed algorithm is to label each processed node u with a node $v \in W$ observable from u in the resulting set W being progressively constructed by the algorithm. Labels survive through iterations and can be reused.

Unlike Danicic's algorithm, ours does not directly compute the weak control-closure. It actually computes the set $W = V' \cup \mathsf{WD}_G(V')$. To obtain the closure

$\mathrm{WCC}_G(V') = W \cap \mathrm{R}_G(V')$, W is then simply filtered to keep only vertices reachable from V' (cf. Property 4a).

In addition to speeding up the algorithm, the usage of labels brings another benefit: for each node of G, its label indicates its observable vertex in W (when it exists) at the end of the algorithm. Recall that since $\mathrm{WD}_G(W) = \varnothing$ (by Property 3), each node in the graph has at most one observable vertex in W.

One difficult point with this approach is that the labels of the nodes need to be refreshed with care at each iteration so that they remain up-to-date. Actually, our algorithm does not ensure that at each iteration the label of each node is an observable vertex from this node in W. This state is only ensured at the beginning and at the end of the algorithm. Meanwhile, some nodes are still in the worklist and some labels are wrong, but this does not prevent the algorithm from working.

Informal Description. Our algorithm is given a directed graph G and a subset of vertices V' in G. It manipulates three objects: a set W which is equal to V' initially, which grows during the algorithm and which at the end contains the result, $V' \cup \mathrm{WD}_G(V')$; a partial mapping obs associating at most one label $obs[u]$ to each node u in the graph, this label being a vertex in W reachable from this node (and which is the observable from u in $V' \cup \mathrm{WD}_G(V')$ at the end); a worklist L of nodes of the closure not processed yet. Each iteration proceeds as follows. If the worklist is not empty, a vertex u is extracted from it. All the vertices that transitively precede vertex u in the graph and that are not hidden by vertices in W are labeled with u. During the propagation, nodes that are good candidates to be V'-weakly deciding are accumulated. After the propagation, we filter them so that only true V'-weakly deciding nodes are kept. Each of these vertices is associated to itself in obs, and is added to W and L. If L is not empty, a new iteration begins. Otherwise, W is equal to $V' \cup \mathrm{WD}_G(V')$ and obs associates each node in the graph with its observable vertex in the closure (when it exists).

Note that each iteration consists in two steps: a complete backward propagation in the graph, which collects potential V'-weakly deciding vertices, and a filtering step. The set of predecessors of the propagated node are thus filtered twice: once during the propagation and once afterwards. We can try to filter as much as possible in the first step or, at the opposite, to avoid filtering during the first step and do all the work in the second step. For the sake of simplicity of mechanized proof, the version we chose does only simple filtering during the first step. We accumulate in our candidate V'-weakly deciding nodes all nodes that have at least two children and a label different from the one currently propagated, and we eliminate the false positives in the second step, once the propagation is done.

Example. Let us use our running example (cf. Fig. 1) to illustrate the algorithm. The successive steps are represented in Fig. 3. In the different figures, nodes in W already processed (that is, in $W \backslash L$) are represented using a solid double circle ($\textcircled{u_i}$), while nodes in W not already processed (that is, still in worklist L) are represented using a dashed double circle ($\textcircled{u_i}$). A label u_j next to a node u_i

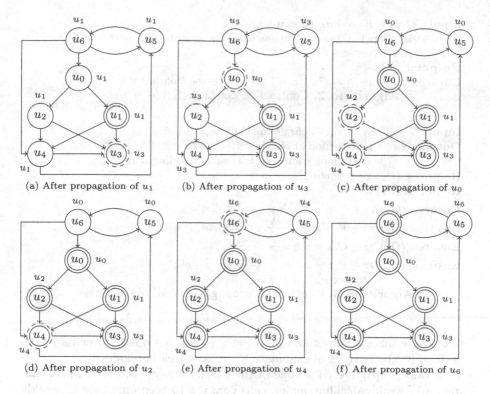

(a) After propagation of u_1 (b) After propagation of u_3 (c) After propagation of u_0

(d) After propagation of u_2 (e) After propagation of u_4 (f) After propagation of u_6

Fig. 3. The optimized algorithm applied on G_0, where $V' = \{u_1, u_3\}$

(u_i u_j) means that u_j is associated to u_i, i.e. $obs[u_i] = u_j$. Let us detail the first steps of the algorithm. Initially, $W_0 = V_0' = \{u_1, u_3\}$ (cf. Fig. 1).

1. u_1 is selected and is propagated backwards from u_1 (cf. Fig. 3a). We find no candidate, the first iteration is finished, $W_1 = \{u_1, u_3\}$.
2. u_3 is selected and is propagated backwards from u_3 (cf. Fig. 3b). u_0, u_2, u_4 and u_6 are candidates, but only u_0 is confirmed as a V_0'-weakly deciding node. It is stored in worklist L and its label is set to u_0. Now $W_2 = \{u_0, u_1, u_3\}$.
3–6. u_0, u_2, u_4 and u_6 are processed similarly (cf. Fig. 3c, d, e, f). At the end, we get $W_6 = \{u_0, u_1, u_2, u_3, u_4, u_6\} = V_0' \cup \mathsf{WD}_G(V_0')$.

As all nodes in W_6 are already reachable from V_0', $W_6 = \mathsf{WCC}_G(V_0')$.

We can make two remarks on this example. First, as we can see in Fig. 3f, each node is labeled with its observable in W at the end of the algorithm. Second, in Fig. 3e, we have the case of a node labeled with an obsolete label, since u_5 is labeled u_4 while its only observable node in W is u_6.

Detailed Description. Our algorithm is split into three functions:

– `confirm` is used to check if a given node is V'-weakly deciding by trying to find a child with a different label from its own label given as an argument.

Input: $G = (V, E)$ a directed graph
       $obs : \mathrm{Map}(V, V)$ associating at most one label to each vertex of G
       $u, v \in V$ vertices in G
Output: $b : bool$
Ensures: $b = true \iff \exists u', (u, u') \in E \wedge u' \in obs \wedge obs[u'] \neq v$
    Algorithm 2. Contract of $\mathtt{confirm}(G, obs, u, v)$

Input: $G = (V, E)$, $W \subseteq V$, $obs : \mathrm{Map}(V, V)$, $u, v \in V$
Output: obs', a new version of obs
       $C \subseteq V$ containing candidate W-weakly deciding nodes
Requires: $(\mathbf{P_1})$ $\forall z \in V, obs[z] = v \iff z = u$
Requires: $(\mathbf{P_2})$ $u \in W$
Ensures: $(\mathbf{Q_1})$ $\forall z \in V, z \xrightarrow{W-path} u \implies obs'[z] = v$
Ensures: $(\mathbf{Q_2})$ $\forall z \in V, \neg(z \xrightarrow{W-path} u) \implies obs'[z] = obs[z]$
Ensures: $(\mathbf{Q_3})$ $\forall z \in C, z \neq u \wedge z \xrightarrow{W-path} u$
Ensures: $(\mathbf{Q_4})$ $\forall z \in V, z \neq u \wedge z \xrightarrow{W-path} u \wedge z \in obs$
       $\wedge |\mathsf{succ}_G(z)| > 1 \implies z \in C$
    Algorithm 3. Contract of $\mathtt{propagate}(G, W, obs, u, v)$

- $\mathtt{propagate}$ takes a vertex and propagates backwards a label over its predecessors. It returns a set of candidate V'-weakly-deciding nodes.
- $\mathtt{main}$ calls $\mathtt{propagate}$ on a node of the closure not yet processed, gets candidate V'-weakly deciding nodes, calls $\mathtt{confirm}$ to keep only true V'-weakly deciding nodes, adds them to the closure and updates their labels, and loops until no more V'-weakly deciding nodes are found.

Function Confirm. A call to $\mathtt{confirm}(G, obs, u, v)$ takes four arguments: a graph G, a labeling of graph vertices obs, and two vertices u and v. It returns *true* if and only if at least one child u' of u in G has a label in obs different from v, which can be written $u' \in obs \wedge obs[u'] \neq v$. This simple function is left abstract here for lack of space. The Why3 formalization [17] contains a complete proof. Its contract is given as Algorithm 2.

Function Propagate. A call to $\mathtt{propagate}(G, W, obs, u, v)$ takes five arguments: a graph G, a subset W of nodes of G, a labeling of nodes obs, and two vertices u and v. It traverses G backwards from u (stopping at nodes in W) and updates obs so that all predecessors not hidden by vertices in W have label v at the end of the function. It returns a set of potential V'-weakly deciding vertices. Again, this function is left abstract here but is proved in the Why3 development [17]. Its contract is given as Algorithm 3.

$\mathtt{propagate}$ requires that, when called, only u is labeled with v (P_1) and that $u \in W$ (P_2). It ensures that, after the call, all the predecessors of u not hidden by a vertex in W are labeled v (Q_1), the labels of the other nodes are unchanged (Q_2), C contains only predecessors of u but not u itself (Q_3), and all the predecessors that had a label before the call (different from v due to P_1) and that have at least two children are in C (Q_4).

Input: $G = (V, E)$, a directed graph
$\qquad$ $V' \subseteq V$, the input subset
Output: $W \subseteq V$, the main result
$\qquad$ $obs : \mathrm{Map}(V, V)$, the final labeling
Variables: $L \subseteq V$, a worklist of nodes to be treated
$\qquad\quad$ $C \subseteq V$, a set of candidate V'-weakly deciding vertices
$\qquad\quad$ $\Delta \subseteq V$, a set of new V'-weakly deciding vertices
Ensures: $W = V' \cup \mathrm{WD}_G(V')$
Ensures: $\forall u, v \in V, obs[u] = v \iff v \in \mathrm{obs}_G(u, W)$

```
1  begin
2  |   W ← V' ; obs|_V' ← id_V' ; L ← V'                // initialization
3  |   while L ≠ ∅ do                                    // main loop
   |   |   // invariant: I₁ ∧ I₂ ∧ I₃ ∧ I₄ ∧ I₅ ∧ I₆
   |   |   // variant: cardinal(L ∪ V \ W)
4  |   |   u ← choose(L) ; L ← L \ {u}
5  |   |   C ← propagate (G, W, obs, u, u)              // propagation
6  |   |   Δ ← ∅
7  |   |   while C ≠ ∅ do                                // filtering
8  |   |   |   v ← choose(C) ; C ← C \ {v}
9  |   |   |   if confirm (G, obs, v, u) = true then  Δ ← Δ ∪ {v}
10 |   |   end
11 |   |   W ← W ∪ Δ ; obs|_Δ ← id_Δ ; L ← L ∪ Δ        // update
12 |   end
   |   // assert: A₁ ∧ A₂ ∧ A₃ ∧ A₄
13 |   return (W, obs)
14 end
```

$(\mathbf{I_1})$ $\forall z \in W, obs[z] = z$

$(\mathbf{I_2})$ $\forall y, z \in V, obs[y] = z \implies z \in W$

$(\mathbf{I_3})$ $\forall y, z \in V, obs[y] = z \wedge z \in L$
$\qquad \implies y = z$

$(\mathbf{I_4})$ $\forall y, z \in V, obs[y] = z \implies y \xrightarrow{path} z$

$(\mathbf{I_5})$ $V' \subseteq W \subseteq V' \cup \mathrm{WD}_G(V')$

$(\mathbf{I_6})$ $\forall y, z, z' \in V, y \xrightarrow{W-disjoint} z \wedge obs[z] = z'$
$\qquad \wedge z' \notin L \implies obs[y] = z'$

$(\mathbf{A_1})$ $\forall u, v \in V, v \in \mathrm{obs}_G(u, W)$
$\qquad\qquad \implies obs[u] = v$

$(\mathbf{A_2})$ $\mathrm{WD}_G(W) = \varnothing$

$(\mathbf{A_3})$ $V' \subseteq W \subseteq V' \cup \mathrm{WD}_G(V')$

$(\mathbf{A_4})$ $W = V' \cup \mathrm{WD}_G(V')$

Algorithm 4. Function **main** with annotations

Function Main. The main function of our algorithm is given as Algorithm 4. It takes two arguments: a graph G and a subset of vertices V'. It returns $V' \cup \mathrm{WD}_G(V')$ and a labeling associating to each node its observable vertex in this set if it exists. It maintains a worklist L of vertices that must be processed. L is initially set to V', and their labels to themselves (line 2). If L is not empty, a node u is taken from it and $\mathtt{propagate}(G, W, obs, u, u)$ is called (lines 3–5). It returns a set of candidate V'-weakly deciding nodes (C) that are not added to W yet. They are first filtered using $\mathtt{confirm}$ (lines 6–10). The confirmed nodes (Δ) are then added to W and to L, and the label of each of them is updated to itself (line 11). The iterations stop when L is empty (cf. lines 3, 13).

Proof of the Optimized Algorithm. We opted for Why3 instead of Coq for this proof to take advantage of Why3's automation. Indeed, most of the goals could be discharged in less than a minute using Alt-Ergo, CVC4, Z3 and E. Some of them still needed to be proved manually in Coq, resulting in 330 lines of Coq proof. The Why3 development [17] focuses on the proof of the algorithm, not on the concepts presented in Sects. 3 and 4. Most of the concepts are proved, one of them is assumed in Why3 but was proved in Coq previously. Due to lack of space, we detail here only the main invariants necessary to prove `main` (cf. Algorithm 4). The proofs of I_1, I_2, I_3, I_4 are rather simple. while those of I_5 and I_6 are more complex.

I_1 states that each node in W has itself as a label. It is true initially for all nodes in V' and is preserved by the updates.

I_2 states that all labels are in W. This is true initially since all labels are in V'. The preservation is verified, since all updates are realized using labels in W.

I_3 states that labels in L have not been already propagated. Given a node y in L, y is the only node whose label is y. It is true initially since every vertex in V' has itself as a label. After an update, the new nodes obey the same rule, so I_3 is preserved.

I_4 states that if label z is associated to a node y then there exists a path between y and z. Initially, there exist trivial paths from each node in V' to itself. When obs is updated, there exists a W-path, thus in particular a path.

I_5 states that W remains between V' and $V' \cup \mathsf{WD}_G(V')$ during the execution of the algorithm. The first part $V' \subseteq W$ is easy to prove, because it is true initially and W is growing. For the second part, we need to prove that after the filtering, $\Delta \subseteq \mathsf{WD}_G(V')$. For that, we will prove that $\Delta \subseteq \mathsf{WD}_G(W)$ thanks to Lemma 3. Let v be a node in Δ. Since $\Delta \subseteq C$, we know that $v \notin W$ and $u \in \mathsf{obs}_G(v, W)$. Moreover, we have $\mathtt{confirm}(G, obs, v, u) = true$, i.e. v has a child v' such that $v' \in obs$, hence v' can reach W by I_4, and $obs[v'] \neq u$, hence $u \notin \mathsf{obs}_G(v', W)$. We can apply Lemma 4 and deduce that $v \in \mathsf{WD}_G(W)$.

I_6 is the most complicated invariant. I_6 states that if there is a path between two vertices y and z that does not intersect W, and z has a label already processed, then y and z have the same label. Let us give a sketch of the proof of preservation of I_6 after an iteration of the main loop. Let us note obs' the map at the end of the iteration. Let $y, z, z' \in V$ such that $y \xrightarrow{(W \cup \Delta) - disjoint} z$, $obs'[z] = z'$ and $z' \notin (L \setminus \{u\}) \cup \Delta$. Let us show that $obs'[y] = z'$. First, observe that neither y nor z can be in Δ, otherwise z' would be in Δ, which would be contradictory. We examine four cases depending on whether the conditions $z \xrightarrow{W-path} u$ (H_1) and $y \xrightarrow{W-path} u$ (H_2) hold.

- $H_1 \wedge H_2$: Both z and y were given the label u during the last iteration, thus $obs'[z] = obs'[y] = u$ as expected.
- $H_1 \wedge (\neg H_2)$: This case is impossible, since $y \xrightarrow{(W \cup \Delta) - disjoint} z$.
- $(\neg H_1) \wedge (\neg H_2)$: Both z and y have the same label as before the iteration. We can therefore conclude by I_6 at the beginning of the iteration.
- $(\neg H_1) \wedge H_2$: This is the only complicated case. We show that it is contradictory. For that, we introduce v_1 as the last vertex on the $(W \cup \Delta)$-disjoint

path connecting y and z which is also the origin of a W-path to u, and v_2 as its successor on this $(W \cup \Delta)$-disjoint path. We can show that $v_1 \in \Delta$, which contradicts the fact that it lives on a $(W \cup \Delta)$-disjoint path.

We can now prove the assertions A_1, A_2, A_3 and A_4 at the end of main. A_1 is a direct consequence of I_6 since at the end $L = \varnothing$. A_1 implies that each vertex u has at most one observable in W: $obs[u]$ if $u \in obs$. A W-weakly deciding vertex would have two observables, thus $\mathsf{WD}_G(W) = \varnothing$. A_3 is a direct consequence of I_5. A_4 can be deduced from A_2 and Lemma 3 applied to A_3. This proves that at the end $W = V' \cup \mathsf{WD}_G(V')$. To prove the other post-condition, we must prove that if there are two nodes u, v such that $obs[u] = v$, then $v \in \mathsf{obs}_G(u, W)$. By I_4, there is a path from u to v. Let w be the first element in W on this path. Then $u \xrightarrow{W-path} w$. By A_1, $obs[u] = w$. Thus, $w = v$ and $u \xrightarrow{W-path} v$. This proves the second post-condition. $\qquad\square$

7   Experiments

We have implemented Danicic's algorithm (additionally improved by the two optimizations proposed in Remark 4) and ours in OCaml [17] using the OCamlgraph library [9], taking care to add a filtering step at the end of our algorithm to preserve only nodes reachable from the initial subset. To be confident in their correctness, we have tested both implementations on small examples w.r.t. a certified but slow Coq-extracted implementation as an oracle. We have also carefully checked that the results returned by both implementations were the same in all experiments.

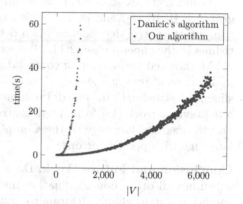

Fig. 4. Danicic's vs. our algorithm

We have experimentally evaluated both implementations on thousands of random graphs with up to thousands of vertices, generated by OCamlgraph. For every number of vertices between 10 and 1000 (resp. 6500) that is a multiple of 10, we generate 10 graphs with twice as many edges as vertices and randomly select three vertices to form the initial subset V' and run both algorithms (resp. only our algorithm) on them. Although the initial subsets are small, the resulting closures nearly always represent a significant part of the set of vertices of the graph. To avoid the trivial case, we have discarded the examples where the closure is restricted to the initial subset itself (where execution time is insignificant), and computed the average time of the remaining tests. Results are presented in Fig. 4. Experiments have been performed on an Intel Core i7 4810MQ with 8 cores at 2.80 GHz and 16 GB RAM.

We observe that Danicic's algorithm explodes for a few hundreds of vertices, while our algorithm remains efficient for graphs with thousands of nodes.

8   Related Work and Conclusion

Related Work. The last decades have seen various definitions of control dependence given for larger and larger classes of programs [6,12,13,21,22,27]. To consider programs with exceptions and potentially infinite loops, Ranganath et al. [23] and then Amtoft [2] introduced non-termination sensitive and non-termination insensitive control dependence on arbitrary program structures. Danicic et al. [11] further generalized control dependence to arbitrary directed graphs, by defining weak and strong control-closure, which subsume the previous non-termination insensitive and sensitive control dependence relations. They also gave a control dependence semantics in terms of projections of paths in the graph, allowing to define new control dependence relations as long as they are compatible with it. This elegant framework was reused for slicing extended finite state machines [3] and probabilistic programs [4]. In both works, an algorithm computing weak control-closure, working differently from ours, was designed and integrated in a rather efficient slicing algorithm.

While there exist efficient algorithms to compute the dominator tree in a graph [8,10,16,19], and even certified ones [15], and thus efficient algorithms computing control dependence when defined in terms of post-dominance, algorithms in the general case [2,11,23] are at least cubic.

Mechanized verification of control dependence computation was done in formalizations of program slicing. Wasserrab [26] formalized language-independent slicing in Isabelle/HOL, but did not provide an algorithm. Blazy et al. [7] and our previous work [18] formalized control dependence in Coq, respectively, for an intermediate language of the CompCert C compiler [20] and on a WHILE language with possible errors.

Conclusion and Future Work. Danicic et al. claim that weak control-closure subsumes all other non-termination insensitive variants. It was thus a natural candidate for mechanized formalization. We used the Coq proof assistant to formalize it. A certified implementation of the algorithm can be extracted from the Coq development. During formalization in Coq of the algorithm and its proof, we have detected an inconsistency in a secondary proof, which highlights how useful proof assistants are to detect otherwise overlooked cases. To the best of our knowledge, the present work is the first mechanized formalization of weak control-closure and of an algorithm to compute it. In addition to formalizing Danicic's algorithm in Coq, we have designed, formalized and proved a new one, that is experimentally shown to be faster than the original one. Short-term future work includes considering further optimizations. Long-term future work is to build a verified generic slicer. Indeed, generic control dependence is a first step towards it. Adding data dependence is the next step in this direction.

Acknowledgements. We thank the anonymous reviewers for helpful suggestions.

References

1. Why3, a tool for deductive program verification, GNU LGPL 2.1, development version, January 2018. http://why3.lri.fr
2. Amtoft, T.: Slicing for modern program structures: a theory for eliminating irrelevant loops. Inf. Process. Lett. **106**(2), 45–51 (2008)
3. Amtoft, T., Androutsopoulos, K., Clark, D.: Correctness of slicing finite state machines. Technical report RN/13/22. University College London, December 2013
4. Amtoft, T., Banerjee, A.: A theory of slicing for probabilistic control flow graphs. In: Jacobs, B., Löding, C. (eds.) FoSSaCS 2016. LNCS, vol. 9634, pp. 180–196. Springer, Heidelberg (2016). https://doi.org/10.1007/978-3-662-49630-5_11
5. Bertot, Y., Castéran, P.: Interactive Theorem Proving and Program Development. Springer, Heidelberg (2004). https://doi.org/10.1007/978-3-662-07964-5
6. Bilardi, G., Pingali, K.: Generalized dominance and control dependence. In: PLDI, pp. 291–300. ACM (1996)
7. Blazy, S., Maroneze, A., Pichardie, D.: Verified validation of program slicing. In: CPP 2015, pp. 109–117 (2015)
8. Buchsbaum, A.L., Georgiadis, L., Kaplan, H., Rogers, A., Tarjan, R.E., Westbrook, J.: Linear-time algorithms for dominators and other path-evaluation problems. SIAM J. Comput. **38**(4), 1533–1573 (2008)
9. Conchon, S., Filliâtre, J., Signoles, J.: Designing a generic graph library using ML functors. In: Morazán, M.T. (ed.) Trends in Functional Programming, vol. 8, pp. 124–140. Intellect, Bristol (2007)
10. Cooper, K.D., Harvey, T.J., Kennedy, K.: A simple, fast dominance algorithm. Softw. Pract. Exp. **4**(1–10), 1–8 (2001)
11. Danicic, S., Barraclough, R.W., Harman, M., Howroyd, J., Kiss, Á., Laurence, M.R.: A unifying theory of control dependence and its application to arbitrary program structures. Theor. Comput. Sci. **412**(49), 6809–6842 (2011)
12. Denning, D.E., Denning, P.J.: Certification of programs for secure information flow. Commun. ACM **20**(7), 504–513 (1977)
13. Ferrante, J., Ottenstein, K.J., Warren, J.D.: The program dependence graph and its use in optimization. ACM Trans. Program. Lang. Syst. **9**(3), 319–349 (1987)
14. Filliâtre, J.-C., Paskevich, A.: Why3 — where programs meet provers. In: Felleisen, M., Gardner, P. (eds.) ESOP 2013. LNCS, vol. 7792, pp. 125–128. Springer, Heidelberg (2013). https://doi.org/10.1007/978-3-642-37036-6_8
15. Georgiadis, L., Tarjan, R.E.: Dominator tree certification and divergent spanning trees. ACM Trans. Algorithms **12**(1), 11:1–11:42 (2016)
16. Georgiadis, L., Tarjan, R.E., Werneck, R.F.F.: Finding dominators in practice. J. Graph Algorithms Appl. **10**(1), 69–94 (2006)
17. Léchenet, J.-C.: Formalization of weak control dependence (2018). http://perso.ecp.fr/~lechenetjc/control/
18. Léchenet, J.-C., Kosmatov, N., Le Gall, P.: Cut branches before looking for bugs: sound verification on relaxed slices. In: Stevens, P., Wąsowski, A. (eds.) FASE 2016. LNCS, vol. 9633, pp. 179–196. Springer, Heidelberg (2016). https://doi.org/10.1007/978-3-662-49665-7_11
19. Lengauer, T., Tarjan, R.E.: A fast algorithm for finding dominators in a flowgraph. ACM Trans. Program. Lang. Syst. **1**(1), 121–141 (1979)
20. Leroy, X.: Formal verification of a realistic compiler. Commun. ACM **52**(7), 107–115 (2009)

21. Ottenstein, K.J., Ottenstein, L.M.: The program dependence graph in a software development environment. In: The First ACM SIGSOFT/SIGPLAN Software Engineering Symposium on Practical Software Development Environments (SDE 1984), pp. 177–184. ACM Press (1984)
22. Podgurski, A., Clarke, L.A.: A formal model of program dependences and its implications for software testing, debugging, and maintenance. IEEE Trans. Softw. Eng. **16**(9), 965–979 (1990)
23. Ranganath, V.P., Amtoft, T., Banerjee, A., Hatcliff, J., Dwyer, M.B.: A new foundation for control dependence and slicing for modern program structures. ACM Trans. Program. Lang. Syst. **29**(5) (2007). Article No. 27
24. The Coq Development Team: The Coq proof assistant, v8.6 (2017). http://coq.inria.fr/
25. Tip, F.: A survey of program slicing techniques. J. Prog. Lang. **3**(3), 121–189 (1995)
26. Wasserrab, D.: From formal semantics to verified slicing: a modular framework with applications in language based security. Ph.D. thesis, Karlsruhe Inst. of Techn. (2011)
27. Weiser, M.: Program slicing. In: ICSE 1981 (1981)

Specification and Program Testing

Iterative Generation of Diverse Models for Testing Specifications of DSL Tools

Oszkár Semeráth[1,2]([⊠]) [iD] and Dániel Varró[1,2,3] [iD]

[1] MTA-BME Lendület Cyber-Physical Systems Research Group, Budapest, Hungary
{semerath,varro}@mit.bme.hu
[2] Department of Measurement and Information Systems,
Budapest University of Technology and Economics, Budapest, Hungary
[3] Department of Electrical and Computer Engineering,
McGill University, Montreal, Canada

Abstract. The validation of modeling tools of custom domain-specific languages (DSLs) frequently relies upon an automatically generated set of models as a test suite. While many software testing approaches recommend that this test suite should be diverse, model diversity has not been studied systematically for graph models. In the paper, we propose diversity metrics for models by exploiting neighborhood shapes as abstraction. Furthermore, we propose an iterative model generation technique to synthesize a diverse set of models where each model is taken from a different equivalence class as defined by neighborhood shapes. We evaluate our diversity metrics in the context of mutation testing for an industrial DSL and compare our model generation technique with the popular model generator Alloy.

1 Introduction

Motivation. Domain-Specific Language (DSL) based modeling tools are gaining an increasing role in the software development processes. Advanced DSL frameworks such as Xtext, or Sirius built on top of model management frameworks such as Eclipse Modeling Framework (EMF) [37] significantly improve productivity of domain experts by automating the production of rich editor features.

Modelling environments may provide validation for the system under design from an early stage of development with efficient tool support for checking well-formedness (WF) constraints and design rules over large model instances of the DSL using tools like Eclipse OCL [24] or graph queries [41]. Model generation techniques [16,19,35,39] are able to automatically provide a range of solution candidates for allocation problems [19], model refactoring or context generation [21]. Finally, models can be processed by query-based transformations or code generators to automatically synthesize source code or other artifacts.

The design of complex DSLs tools is a challenging task. As the complexity of DSL tools increases, special attention is needed to validate the modeling tools themselves (e.g. for tool qualification purposes) to ensure that WF constraints

A. Russo and A. Schürr (Eds.): FASE 2018, LNCS 10802, pp. 227–245, 2018.
https://doi.org/10.1007/978-3-319-89363-1_13

and the preconditions of model transformation and code generation functionality [4,32,35] are correctly implemented in the tool.

Problem Statement. There are many approaches aiming to address the testing of DSL tools (or transformations) [1,6,42] which necessitate *the automated synthesis of graph models* to serve as test inputs. Many best practices of testing (such as equivalence partitioning [26], mutation testing [18]) recommends the synthesis of *diverse* graph models where any pairs of models are structurally different from each other to achieve high coverage or a diverse solution space.

While software diversity is widely studied [5], existing diversity metrics for graph models are much less elaborate [43]. Model comparison techniques [38] frequently rely upon the existence of node identifiers, which can easily lead to many isomorphic models. Moreover, checking graph isomorphism is computationally very costly. Therefore practical solutions tend to use approximate techniques to achieve certain diversity by random sampling [17], incremental generation [19,35], or using symmetry breaking predicates [39]. Unlike equivalence partitions which capture diversity of inputs in a customizable way for testing traditional software, a similar diversity concept is still missing for graph models.

Contribution. In this paper, we propose *diversity metrics* to characterize a single model and a set of models. For that purpose, we innovatively reuse neighborhood graph shapes [28], which provide a fine-grained typing for each object based on the structure (e.g. incoming and outgoing edges) of its neighborhood. Moreover, we propose an *iterative model generation technique* to automatically synthesize a diverse set of models for a DSL where each model is taken from a different equivalence class wrt. graph shapes as an equivalence relation.

We evaluate our diversity metrics and model generator in the context of mutation-based testing [22] of WF constraints in an industrial DSL tool. We evaluate and compare the *mutation score* and *our diversity metrics* of test suites obtained by (1) an Alloy based model generator (using symmetry breaking predicates to ensure diversity), (2) an iterative graph solver based generator using neighborhood shapes, and (3) from real models created by humans. Our finding is that a diverse set of models derived along different neighborhood shapes has better mutation score. Furthermore, based on a test suite with 4850 models, we found that high correlation between mutation score and our diversity metrics, which indicates that our metrics may be good predictors in practice for testing.

Added Value. Up to our best knowledge, our paper is one of the first studies on (software) model diversity. From a testing perspective, our diversity metrics provide a stronger characterization of a test suite of models than traditional metamodel coverage which is used in many research papers. Furthermore, model generators using neighborhood graph shapes (that keep models only if they are surely non-isomorphic) provide increased diversity compared to symmetry breaking predicates (which exclude models if they are surely isomorphic).

2   Preliminaries

Core modeling concepts and testing challenges of DSL tools will be illustrated in the context of Yakindu Statecharts [46], which is an industrial DSL for developing reactive, event-driven systems, and supports validation and code generation.

2.1   Metamodels and Instance Models

Metamodels define the main concepts, relations and attributes of a domain to specify the basic graph structure of models. A simplified metamodel for Yakindu state machines is illustrated in Fig. 1 using the popular Eclipse Modeling Framework (EMF) [37] is used for domain modeling. A state machine consists of `Regions`, which in turn contain states (called `Vertexes`) and `Transitions`. An abstract state `Vertex` is further refined into `RegularStates` (like `State` or `FinalState`) and `PseudoStates` (like `Entry`, `Exit` or `Choice`).

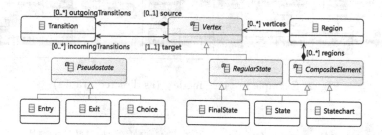

Fig. 1. Metamodel extract from Yakindu state machines

Formally [32,34], a metamodel defines a vocabulary of type and relation symbols $\Sigma = \{C_1, \ldots, C_n, R_1, \ldots, R_m\}$ where a unary predicate symbol C_i is defined for each *EClass*, and a binary predicate symbol R_j is derived for each *EReference*. For space considerations, we omit the precise handling of attributes.

An *instance model* can be represented as a logic structure $M = \langle Obj_M, \mathcal{I}_M \rangle$ where Obj_M is the finite set of objects (the size of the model is $|M| = |Obj_M|$), and $\mathcal{I}_M$ provides interpretation for all predicate symbols in Σ as follows:

- the interpretation of a unary predicate symbol C_i is defined in accordance with the types of the EMF model: $\mathcal{I}_M(C_i) : Obj_M \to \{1, 0\}$ An object $o \in Obj_M$ is an instance of a class C_i in a model M if $\mathcal{I}_M(C_i)(o) = 1$.
- the interpretation of a binary predicate symbol R_j is defined in accordance withe the links in the EMF model: $\mathcal{I}_M(R_j) : Obj_M \times Obj_M \to \{1, 0\}$. There is a reference R_j between $o_1, o_2 \in Obj_M$ in model M if $\mathcal{I}_M(R_j)(o_1, o_2) = 1$.

A metamodel also specifies extra structural constraints (type hierarchy, multiplicities, etc.) that need to be satisfied in each valid instance model [32].

Example 1. Figure 2 shows graph representations of three (partial) instance models. For the sake of clarity, `Regions` and inverse relations `incomingTransitions` and `outgoingTransitions` are excluded from the diagram. In M_1 there are two `States` ($s1$ and $s2$), which are connected to a loop via `Transitions` $t2$ and $t3$. The initial state is marked by a `Transition` $t1$ from an entry $e1$ to state $s1$. M_2 describes a similar statechart with three states in loop ($s3$, $s4$ and $s5$ connected via $t5$, $t6$ and $t7$). Finally, in M_3 there are two main differences: there is an incoming `Transition` $t11$ to an `Entry` state ($e3$), and there is a `State` $s7$ that does not have outgoing transition. While all these $M1$ and $M2$ are non-isomorphic, later we illustrate why they are not diverse.

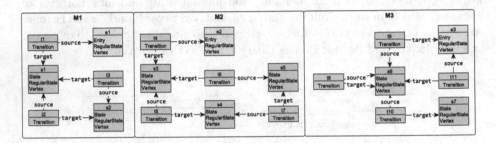

Fig. 2. Example instance models (as directed graphs)

$$\llbracket \mathtt{C}(v) \rrbracket_Z^M := \mathcal{I}_M(\mathtt{C})(Z(v)) \qquad \llbracket \varphi_1 \wedge \varphi_2 \rrbracket_Z^M := \llbracket \varphi_1 \rrbracket_Z^M \wedge \llbracket \varphi_2 \rrbracket_Z^M$$
$$\llbracket \mathtt{R}(v_1, v_2) \rrbracket_Z^M := \mathcal{I}_M(\mathtt{R})(Z(v_1), Z(v_2)) \llbracket \varphi_1 \vee \varphi_2 \rrbracket_Z^M := \llbracket \varphi_1 \rrbracket_Z^M \vee \llbracket \varphi_2 \rrbracket_Z^M$$
$$\llbracket v_1 = v_2 \rrbracket_Z^M := Z(v_1) = Z(v_2) \qquad \llbracket \neg \varphi \rrbracket_Z^M := \neg \llbracket \varphi \rrbracket_Z^M$$
$$\llbracket \forall v : \varphi \rrbracket_Z^M := \bigwedge_{x \in Obj_M} \llbracket \varphi \rrbracket_{Z, v \mapsto x}^M \qquad \llbracket \exists v : \varphi \rrbracket_Z^M := \bigvee_{x \in Obj_M} \llbracket \varphi \rrbracket_{Z, v \mapsto x}^M$$

Fig. 3. Inductive semantics of graph predicates

2.2   Well-Formedness Constraints as Logic Formulae

In many industrial modeling tools, WF constraints are captured either by OCL constraints [24] or graph patterns (GP) [41] where the latter captures structural conditions over an instance model as paths in a graph. To have a unified and precise handling of evaluating WF constraints, we use a tool-independent logic representation (which was influenced by [29,32,34]) that covers the key features of concrete graph pattern languages and a first-order fragment of OCL.

Syntax. A graph predicate is a first order logic predicate $\varphi(v_1, \ldots v_n)$ over (object) variables which can be inductively constructed by using class and relation predicates $\mathtt{C}(v)$ and $\mathtt{R}(v_1, v_2)$, equality check $=$, standard first order logic connectives $\neg$, $\vee$, $\wedge$, and quantifiers $\exists$ and $\forall$.

Semantics. A graph predicate $\varphi(v_1, \ldots, v_n)$ can be evaluated on model M along a variable binding $Z : \{v_1, \ldots, v_n\} \to Obj_M$ from variables to objects in M. The truth value of φ can be evaluated over model M along the mapping Z (denoted by $[\![\varphi(v_1, \ldots, v_n)]\!]_Z^M$) in accordance with the semantic rules defined in Fig. 3.

If there is a variable binding Z where the predicate φ is evaluated to 1 over M is often called a *pattern match*, formally $[\![\varphi]\!]_Z^M = 1$. Otherwise, if there are no bindings Z to satisfy a predicate, i.e. $[\![\varphi]\!]_Z^M = 0$ for all Z, then the predicate φ is evaluated to 0 over M. Graph query engines like [41] can retrieve (one or all) matches of a graph predicate over a model. When using graph patterns for validating WF constraints, a match of a pattern usually denotes a violation, thus the corresponding graph formula needs to capture the erroneous case.

2.3   Motivation: Testing of DSL Tools

A code generator would normally assume that the input models are well-formed, i.e. all WF constraints are validated prior to calling the code generator. However, there is no guarantee that the WF constraints actually checked by the DSL tool are exactly the same as the ones required by the code generator. For instance, if the validation forgets to check a subclause of a WF constraint, then runtime errors may occur during code generation. Moreover, the precondition of the transformation rule may also contain errors. For that purpose, WF constraints and model transformations of DSL tools can be systematically tested.Alternatively, model validation can be interpreted as a special case of model transformation, where precondition of the transformation rules are fault patterns, and the actions place error markers on the model [41].

A popular approach for testing DSL tools is mutation testing [22,36] which aims to reveal missing or extra predicates by (1) deriving a set of mutants (e.g. WF constraints in our case) by applying a set of mutation operators. Then (2) the test suite is executed for both the original and the mutant programs, and (3) their output are compared. (4) A mutant is killed by a test if different output is produced for the two cases (i.e. different match set). (5) The mutation score of a test suite is calculated as the ratio of mutants killed by some tests wrt. the total number of mutants. A test suite with better mutation score is preferred [18].

Fault Model and Detection. As a fault model, we consider omission faults in WF constraints of DSL tools where some subconstraints are not actually checked. In our fault model, a WF constraint is given in a conjunctive normal form $\varphi_e = \varphi_1 \wedge \cdots \wedge \varphi_k$, all unbound variables are quantified existentially ($\exists$), and may refer to other predicates specified in the same form. Note that this format is equivalent to first order logic, and does not reduce the range of supported graph predicates. We assume that in a faulty predicate (a mutant) the developer may forget to check one of the predicates φ_i (Constraint Omission, CO), i.e. $\varphi_e = [\varphi_1 \wedge \ldots \wedge \varphi_i \wedge \ldots \wedge \varphi_k]$ is rewritten to $\varphi_f = [\varphi_1 \wedge \cdots \wedge \varphi_{i-1} \wedge \varphi_{i+1} \wedge \cdots \wedge \varphi_k]$, or may forgot a negation (Negation Omission), i.e. $\varphi_e = [\varphi_1 \wedge \ldots \wedge (\neg\varphi_i) \wedge \ldots \wedge \varphi_k]$ is rewritten to $\varphi_f = [\varphi_1 \wedge \ldots \wedge \varphi_i \wedge \ldots \wedge \varphi_k]$. Given an instance model M, we assume that both $[\![\varphi_e]\!]^M$ and the faulty $[\![\varphi_f]\!]^M$ can be evaluated separately by the DSL tool. Now a test model M detects a fault if there is a variable binding Z, where the two evaluations differ, i.e. $[\![\varphi_e]\!]_Z^M \neq [\![\varphi_f]\!]_Z^M$.

Example 2. Two WF constraints checked by the Yakindu environment can be captured by graph predicates as follows:

– $\varphi : incomingToEntry(E) := \exists T : \texttt{Entry}(E) \wedge \texttt{target}(T, E)$
– $\phi : noOutgoingFromEntry(E) := \texttt{Entry}(E) \wedge \neg(\exists T : \texttt{source}(T, E))$

According to our fault model, we can derive two mutants for *incomingToEntry* as predicates $\varphi_{f_1} := \texttt{Entry}(E)$ and $\varphi_{f_2} := \exists t : \texttt{target}(T, E)$.

Constraints φ and ϕ are satisfied in model M_1 and M_2 as the corresponding graph predicates have no matches, thus $[\![\varphi]\!]_Z^{M_1} = 0$ and $[\![\phi]\!]_Z^{M_1} = 0$. As a test model, both M_1 and M_2 is able to detect the same omission fault both for φ_{f_1} as $[\![\varphi_{f_1}]\!]^{M_1} = 1$ (with $E \mapsto e1$ and $E \mapsto e2$) and similarly φ_{f_2} (with $s1$ and $s3$). However, M_3 is unable to kill mutant φ_{f_1} as (φ had a match $E \mapsto e3$ which remains in φ_{f_1}), but able to detect others.

3   Model Diversity Metrics for Testing DSL Tools

As a general best practice in testing, a good test suite should be diverse, but the interpretation of diversity may differ. For example, equivalence partitioning [26] partitions the input space of a program into equivalence classes based on observable output, and then select the different test cases of a test suite from different execution classes to achieve a diverse test suite. However, while software diversity has been studied extensively [5], model diversity is much less covered.

In existing approaches [6,7,9,10,31,42] for testing DSL and transformation tools, a test suite should provide full *metamodel coverage* [45], and it should also guarantee that any pairs of models in the test suite are non-isomorphic [17,39]. In [43], the diversity of a model M_i is defined as the number of (direct) types used from its MM, i.e. M_i is more diverse than M_j if more types of MM are used in M_i than in M_j. Furthermore, a model generator *Gen* deriving a set of models $\{M_i\}$ is diverse if there is a designated distance between each pairs of models M_i and M_j: $dist(M_i, M_j) > D$, but no concrete distance function is proposed.

Below, we propose diversity metrics for a single model, for pairs of models and for a set of models based on neighborhood shapes [28], a formal concept known from the state space exploration of graph transformation systems [27]. Our diversity metrics generalize both metamodel coverage and (graph) isomorphism tests, which are derived as two extremes of the proposed metric, and thus it defines a finer grained equivalence partitioning technique for graph models.

3.1   Neighborhood Shapes of Graphs

A neighborhood Nbh_i describes the local properties of an object in a graph model for a range of size $i \in \mathbb{N}$ [28]. The neighbourhood of an object o describes all unary (class) and binary (reference) relations of the objects within the given range. Informally, neighbourhoods can be interpreted as richer types, where the original classes are split into multiple subclasses based on the difference in the incoming and outgoing references. Formally, neighborhood descriptors are defined recursively with the set of class and reference symbols Σ:

- For range $i = 0$, Nbh_0 is a subset of class symbols: $Nbh_0 \subseteq 2^{\{C_1,\dots,C_n\}}$
- A neighbor Ref_i for $i > 0$ is defined by a reference symbol and a neighborhood: $Ref_i \subseteq \{R_1, \dots, R_m\} \times Nbh_{i-1}$.
- For a range $i > 0$ neighborhood Nbh_i is defined by a previous neighborhood and two sets of neighbor descriptors (for incoming and outgoing references separately): $Nbh_i \subseteq Nbh_{i-1} \times 2^{Ref_i} \times 2^{Ref_i}$.

Shaping function $nbh_i : Obj_M \to Nbh_i$ maps each object in a model M to a neighborhood with range i: (1) if $i = 0$, then $nbh_0(o) = \{C | [\![C(o)]\!]^M = 1\}$; (2) if $i > 0$, then $nbh_i(o) = \langle nbh_{i-1}(o), in, out \rangle$, where

$$in = \{\langle R, n \rangle | \exists o' \in Obj_M : [\![R(o', o)]\!]^M \wedge n = nbh_{i-1}(o')\}$$
$$out = \{\langle R, n \rangle | \exists o' \in Obj_M : [\![R(o, o')]\!]^M \wedge n = nbh_{i-1}(o')\}$$

A *(graph) shape* of a model M for range i (denoted as $S_i(M)$) is a set of neighborhood descriptors of the model: $S_i(M) = \{x | \exists o \in Obj_M : nbh_i(o) = x\}$. A shape can be interpreted and illustrated as a as a type graph: after calculating the neighborhood for each object, each neighborhood is represented as a node in the graph shape. Moreover, if there exist at least one link between objects in two different neighborhoods, the corresponding nodes in the shape will be connected by an edge. We will use the size of a shape $|S_i(M)|$ which is the number of shapes used in M.

Example 3. We illustrate the concept of graph shapes for model M_1. For range 0, objects are mapped to class names as neighborhood descriptors:

- $nbh_0(e) = \{\text{Entry}, \text{PseudoState}, \text{Vertex}\}$
- $nbh_0(t1) = nbh_0(t2) = nbh_0(t3) = \{\text{Transition}\}$
- $nbh_0(s1) = nbh_0(s2) = \{\text{State}, \text{RegularState}, \text{Vertex}\}$

For range 1, objects with different incoming or outgoing types are further split, e.g. the neighborhood of $t1$ is different from that of $t2$ and $t3$ as it is connected to an Entry along a source reference, while the source of $t2$ and $t3$ are States.

- $nbh_1(t1) = \langle\{\text{Transition}\}, \emptyset, \{\langle \text{source}, \{\text{Entry}, \text{PseudoState}, \text{Vertex}\}\rangle, \langle \text{target}, \{\text{State}, \text{RegularState}, \text{Vertex}\}\rangle$
- $nbh_1(t2) = \langle\{\text{Transition}\}, \emptyset, \{\langle \text{source}, \{\text{State}, \text{RegularState}, \text{Vertex}\}\rangle, \langle \text{target}, \{\text{State}, \text{RegularState}, \text{Vertex}\}\rangle = nbh_1(t3)$

For range 2, each object of M_1 would be mapped to a unique element. In Fig. 4, the neighborhood shapes of models M_1, M_2, and M_3 for range 1, are represented in a visual notation adapted from [28, 29] (without additional annotations e.g. multiplicities or predicates used for verification purposes). The trace of the

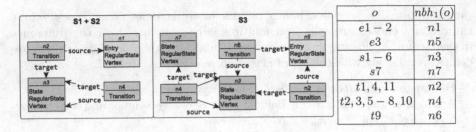

Fig. 4. Sample neighborhood shapes of M_1, M_2 and M_3

concrete graph nodes to neighbourhood is illustrated on the right. For instance, $e1$ and $e2$ in $M1$ and M_2 Entries are both mapped to the same neighbourhood $n1$, while $e3$ can be distinguished from them as it has incoming reference from a transition, thus creating a different neighbourhood $n5$.

Properties of Graph Shapes. The theoretical foundations of graph shapes [28,29] prove several key semantic properties which are exploited in this paper:

P1 There are only a *finite number of graph shapes in a certain range*, and a smaller range reduces the number of graph shapes, i.e. $|S_i(M)| \leq |S_{i+1}(M)|$.
P2 $|S_i(M_j)| + |S_i(M_k)| \geq |S_i(M_j \cup M_k)| \geq |S_i(M_j)|$ and $|S_i(M_k)|$.

3.2 Metrics for Model Diversity

We define two metrics for model diversity based upon neighborhood shapes. *Internal diversity* captures the diversity of a single model, i.e. it can be evaluated individually for each and every generated model. As neighborhood shapes introduce extra subtypes for objects, this model diversity metric measures the number of neighborhood types used in the model with respect to the size of the model. *External diversity* captures the distance between pairs of models. Informally, this diversity distance between two models will be proportional to the number of different neighborhoods covered in one model but not the other.

Definition 1 (Internal model diversity). *For a range i of neighborhood shapes for model M, the internal diversity of M is the number of shapes wrt. the size of the model: $d_i^{int}(M) = |S_i(M)|/|M|$.*

The range of this internal diversity metric $d_i^{int}(M)$ is $[0..1]$, and a model M with $d_1^{int}(M) = 1$ (and $|M| \geq |MM|$) *guarantees full metamodel coverage* [45], i.e. it surely contains all elements from a metamodel as types. As such, it is an appropriate diversity metric for a model in the sense of [43]. Furthermore, given a specific range i, the number of potential neighborhood shapes within that range is finite, but it grows superexponentially. Therefore, for a small range i, one can derive a model M_j with $d_i^{int}(M_j) = 1$, but for larger models M_k (with $|M_k| > |M_j|$) we will likely have $d_i^{int}(M_j) \geq d_i^{int}(M_k)$. However, due to the rapid growth of the number of shapes for increasing range i, for most practical cases, $d_i^{int}(M_j)$ will converge to 1 if M_j is sufficiently diverse.

Definition 2 (External model diversity). *Given a range i of neighborhood shapes, the external diversity of models M_j and M_k is the number of shapes contained exclusively in M_j or M_k but not in the other, formally, $d_i^{ext}(M_j, M_k) = |S_i(M_j) \oplus S_i(M_k)|$ where $\oplus$ denotes the symmetric difference of two sets.*

External model diversity allows to compare two models. One can show that this metric is a (pseudo)-distance in the mathematical sense [2], and thus, it can serve as a diversity metric for a model generator in accordance with [43].

Definition 3 (Pseudo-distance). *A function $d : \mathcal{M} \times \mathcal{M} \to \mathbb{R}$ is called a (pseudo-)distance, if it satisfies the following properties:*

- *d is non-negative: $d(M_j, M_k) \geq 0$*
- *d is symmetric $d(M_j, M_k) = d(M_k, M_j)$*
- *if M_j and M_k are isomorphic, then $d(M_j, M_k) = 0$*
- *triangle inequality: $d(M_j, M_l) \leq d(M_k, M_j) + d(M_j, M_l)$*

Corollary 1. *External model diversity $d_i^{ext}(M_j, M_k)$ is a (pseudo-)distance between models M_j and M_k for any i.*

During model generation, we will exclude a model M_k if $d_i^{ext}(M_j, M_k) = 0$ for a previously defined model M_j, but *it does not imply that they are isomorphic*. Thus our definition allows to avoid graph isomorphism checks between M_j and M_k which have high computation complexity. Note that external diversity is a dual of symmetry breaking predicates [39] used in the Alloy Analyzer where $d(M_j, M_k) = 0$ implies that M_j and M_k are isomorphic (and not vice versa).

Definition 4 (Coverage of model set). *Given a range i of neighborhood shapes and a set of models $MS = \{M_1, \ldots, M_k\}$, the coverage of this model set is defined as $cov_i\langle MS \rangle = |S_i(M_1) \cup \cdots \cup S_i(M_k)|$.*

The coverage of a model set is not normalised, but its value monotonously grows for any range i by adding new models. Thus it corresponds to our expectation that adding a new test case to a test suite should increase its coverage.

Example 4. Let us calculate the different diversity metrics for M_1, M_2 and M_3 of Fig. 2. For range 1, they have the shapes illustrated in Fig. 4. The internal diversity of those models are $d_1^{int}(M_1) = 4/6$, $d_1^{int}(M_2) = 4/8$ and $d_1^{int}(M_3) = 6/7$, thus M_3 is the most diverse model among them. As M_1 and M_2 has the same shape, the distance between them is $d_1^{ext}(M_1, M2) = 0$. The distance between M_1 and M_3 is $d_1^{ext}(M_1, M3) = 4$ as M_1 has 1 different neighbourhoods ($n1$), and M_3 has 3 ($n5$, $n6$ and $n7$). The set coverage of M_1, M_2 and M_3 is 7 altogether, as they have 7 different neighbourhoods ($n1$ to $n7$).

4 Iterative Generation of Diverse Models

Now we aim at generating a diverse set of models $MS = \{M_1, M_2, \ldots, M_k\}$ for a given metamodel MM (and potentially, a set of constraints WF). Our approach (see Fig. 5) intentionally reuses several components as building blocks obtained from existing research results aiming to derive consistent graph models. First, model generation is an iterative process where previous solutions serve as further constraints [35]. Second, it repeatedly calls a back-end graph solver [33,44] to automatically derive consistent instance models which satisfy WF.

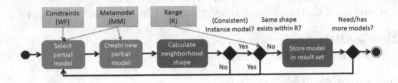

Fig. 5. Generation of diverse models

As a key conceptual novelty, we enforce the structural diversity of models during the generation process using neighborhood shapes at different stages. Most importantly, if the shape $S_i(M_n)$ of a new instance model M_n obtained as a candidate solution is identical to the shape $S_i(M_j)$ for a previously derived model M_j for a predefined (input) neighborhood range i, the solution candidate is discarded, and iterative generation continues towards a new candidate.

Internally, our tool operates over partial models [30,34] where instance models are derived along a refinement calculus [43]. The shapes of intermediate (partial) models found during model generation are continuously being computed. As such, they may help guide the search process of model generation by giving preference to refine (partial) model candidates that likely result in a different graph shape. Furthermore, this extra bookkeeping also pays off once a model candidate is found since comparing two neighborhood shapes is fast (conceptually similar to lexicographical ordering). However, our concepts could be adapted to postprocess the output of other (black-box) model generator tools.

Example 5. As an illustration of the iterative generation of diverse models, let us imagine that model M_1 (in Fig. 2) is retrieved first by a model generator. Shape $S_2(M_1)$ is then calculated (see Fig. 4), and since there are no other models with the same shape, M_1 is stored as a solution. If the model generator retrieves M_2 as the next solution candidate, it turns out that $S_2(M_2) = S_2(M_1)$, thus M_2 is excluded. Next, if model M_3 is generated, it will be stored as a solution since $S_2(M_3) \neq S_2(M_2)$. Note that we intentionally omitted the internal search procedure of the model generator to focus on the use of neighborhood shapes.

Finally, it is worth highlighting that graph shapes are conceptually different from other approaches aiming to achieve diversity. Approaches relying upon object identifiers (like [38]) may classify two graphs which are isomorphic to be different. Sampling-based approaches [17] attempt to derive non-isomorphic models on a statistical basis, but there is no formal guarantee that two models are non-isomorphic. The Alloy Analyzer [39] uses *symmetry breaking predicates as sufficient conditions* of isomorphism (i.e. two models are surely isomorphic). *Graph shapes provide a necessary condition* for isomorphism i.e. if a two non-isomorphic models have identical shape, one of them is discarded.

5   Evaluation

In this section, we provide an empirical evaluation of our diversity metrics and model generation technique to address the following research questions:

RQ1: How effective is our technique in creating diverse models for testing?
RQ2: How effective is our technique in creating diverse test suites?
RQ3: Is there correlation between diversity metrics and mutation score?

Target Domain. In order to answer those questions, we executed model generation campaigns on a DSL extracted from Yakindu Statecharts (as proposed in [35]). We used the partial metamodel describing the state hierarchy and transitions of statecharts (illustrated in Fig. 1, containing 12 classes and 6 references). Additionally, we formalized 10 WF constraints regulating the transitions as graph predicates, based on the built-in validation of Yakindu.

For mutation testing, we used a constraint or negation omission operator (CO and NO) to inject an error to the original WF constraint in every possible way, which yielded 51 mutants from the original 10 constraints (but some mutants may never have matches). We checked both the original and mutated versions of the constraints for each instance model, and a model kills a mutant if there is a difference in the match set of the two constraints. The mutation score for a test suite (i.e. a set of models) is the total number of mutants killed that way.

Compared Approaches. Our test input models were taken from three different sources. First, we generated models with our iterative approach using a graph solver (**GS**) with different neighborhoods for ranges $r = 1$ to $r = 3$.

Next, we generated models for the same DSL using **Alloy** [39], a well-known SAT-based relational model finder. For representing EMF metamodels we used traditional encoding techniques [8,32]. To enforce model diversity, Alloy was configured with three different setups for symmetry breaking predicates: $s = 0$, $s = 10$ and $s = 20$ (default value). For greater values the tool produced the same set of models. We used the latest 4.2 build for Alloy with the default Sat4j [20] as back-end solver. All other configuration options were set to default.

Finally, we included 1250 manually created statechart models in our analysis (marked by **Human**). The models were created by students as solutions for similar (but not identical) statechart modeling homework assignments [43] representing real models which were *not* prepared for testing purposes.

Measurement Setup. To address **RQ1–RQ3**, we created a two-step measurement setup. In **Step I.** a set of instance models is generated with all **GS** and **Alloy** configurations. Each tool in each configuration generated a sequence of 30 instance models produced by subsequent solver calls, and each sequence is repeated 20 times (so 1800 models are generated for both **GS** and **Alloy**). In

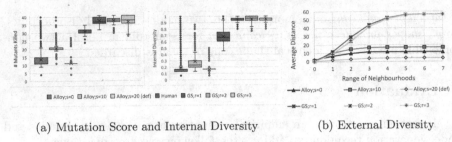

(a) Mutation Score and Internal Diversity   (b) External Diversity

Fig. 6. Mutation Scores and Diversity properties of models sets

case of **Alloy**, we prevented the deterministic run of the solver to enable statistical analysis. The model generators was to create metamodel-compliant instances compliant with the structural constraints of Subsect. 2.1 but ignoring the WF constraints. The target model size is set to 30 objects as Alloy did not scale with increasing size (the scalability and the details of the back-end solver is reported in [33]). The size of **Human** models ranges from 50 to 200 objects.

In **Step II.**, we evaluate and the mutation score for all the models (and for the entire sequence) by comparing results for the mutant and original predicates and record which mutant was killed by a model. We also calculate our diversity metrics for a neighborhood range where no more equivalence classes are produced by shapes (which turned out to be $r = 7$ in our case study). We calculated the internal diversity of each model, the external diversity (distance) between pairs of models in each model sequence, and the coverage of each model sequence.

RQ1: Measurement Results and Analysis. Figure 6a shows the distribution of the number of mutants killed by at least one model from a model sequence (left box plot), and the distribution of internal diversity (right box plot). For killing mutants, **GS** was the best performer (regardless of the **r** range): most models found 36–41 mutants out of 51. On the other hand, **Alloy** performance varied based on the value of symmetry: for $s = 0$, most models found 9–15 mutants (with a large number of positive outliers that found several errors). For $s = 10$, the average is increased over 20, but the number of positive outliers simultaneously dropped. Finally, in default settings ($s = 20$) **Alloy** generated similar models, and found only a low number of mutants. We also measured the efficiency of killing mutants by **Human**, which was between **GS** and **Alloy**. None of the instance models could find more than 41 mutants, which suggests that those mutants cannot be detected at all by metamodel-compliant instances.

The right side of Fig. 6a presents the internal diversity of models measured as shape nodes/graph nodes (for fixpoint range 7). The result are similar: the diversity was high with low variance in **GS** with slight differences between ranges. In case of **Alloy**, the diversity is similarly affected by the symmetry value: $s = 0$ produced low average diversity, but a high number of positive outliers. With $s = 10$, the average diversity increased with decreasing number of positive outliers. And finally, with the default $s = 20$ value the average diversity was low. The internal diversity of **Human** models are between **GS** and **Alloy**.

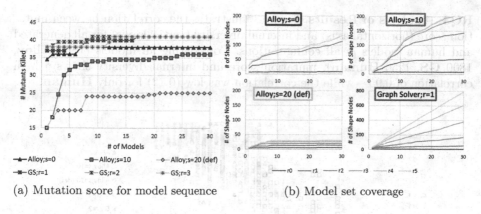

(a) Mutation score for model sequence   (b) Model set coverage

Fig. 7. Mutation score and set coverage for model sequences

Figure 6b illustrates the average distance between all model pairs generated in the same sequence (vertical axis) for range 7. The distribution of external diversity also shows similar characteristics as Fig. 6a: **GS** provided high diversity for all ranges (56 out of the maximum 60), while the diversity between models generated by **Alloy** varied based on the symmetry value.

As a summary, our model generation technique consistently outperformed Alloy wrt. both the diversity metrics and mutation score for individual models.

RQ2: Measurement Results and Analysis. Figure 7a shows the number of killed mutants (vertical axis) by an increasing set of models (with 1 to 30 elements; horizontal axis) generated by **GS** or **Alloy**. The diagram shows the *median* of 20 generation runs to exclude the outliers. **GS** found a large amount of mutants in the first model, and the number of killed mutants (36–37) increased to 41 by the 17th model, which after no further mutants were found. Again, our measurement showed little difference between ranges $r = 1$, 2 and 3. For **Alloy**, the result highly depends on the symmetry value: for $s = 0$ it found a large amount of mutants, but the value saturated early. Next, for $s = 10$, the first model found significantly less mutants, but the number increased rapidly in the for the first 5 models, but altogether, less mutants were killed than for $s = 0$. Finally, the default configuration ($s = 20$) found the least number of mutants.

In Fig. 7b, the average coverage of the model sets is calculated (vertical axis) for increasing model sets (horizontal axis). The neighborhood shapes are calculated for $r = 0$ to 5, which after no significant difference is shown. Again, configurations of symmetry breaking predicates resulted in different characteristics for **Alloy**. However, the number of shape nodes investigated by the test set was significantly higher in case of **GS** (791 vs. 200 equivalence classes) regardless of the range, and it was monotonously increasing by adding new models.

Altogether, both mutation score and equivalence class coverage of a model sequence was much better for our model generator approach compared to Alloy.

RQ3: Analysis of Results. Figure 8 illustrates the correlation between mutation score (horizontal axis) and internal diversity (vertical axis) for all generated
and human models in all configurations. Considering all models (1800 **Alloy**,
1800 **GS**, 1250 **Human**), mutation score and internal diversity shows a high
correlation of 0.95 – while the correlation was low (0.12) for only **Human**.

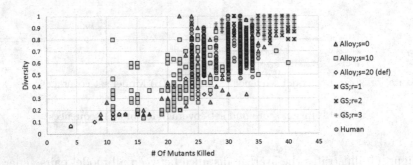

Fig. 8. Model diversity and mutation score correlation

*Our initial investigation suggests that a high internal diversity will provide
good mutation score, thus our metrics can potentially be good predictors in a
testing context, but we cannot generalize to full statistical correlation.*

Threats to Validity and Limitations. We evaluated more than 4850 test
inputs in our measurement, but all models were taken from a single domain
of Yakindu statecharts with a dedicated set of WF constraints. However, our
model generation approach did not use any special property of the metamodel
or the WF constraints, thus we believe that similar results would be obtained for
other domains. For mutation operations, we checked only omission of predicates,
as extra constraints could easily yield infeasible predicates due to inconsistency
with the metamodel, thus further reducing the number of mutants that can be
killed. Finally, although we detected a strong correlation between diversity and
mutation score with our test cases, this result cannot be generalized to statistical
causality, because the generated models were not random samples taken from
the universe of models. Thus additional investigations are needed to justify this
correlation, and we only state that if a model is generated by either **GS** or **Alloy**,
a higher diversity means a higher mutation score with high probability.

6   Related Work

Diverse model generation plays a key role in testing model transformations
code generators and complete developement environments [25]. Mutation-based
approaches [1,11,22] take existing models and make random changes on them
by applying mutation rules. A similar random model generator is used for exper-
imentation purposes in [3]. Other automated techniques [7,12] generate models
that only conform to the metamodel. While these techniques scale well for larger
models, there is no guarantee whether the mutated models are well-formed.

There is a wide set of model generation techniques which provide certain promises for test effectiveness. White-box approaches [1,6,14,15,31,32] rely on the implementation of the transformation and dominantly use back-end logic solvers, which lack scalability when deriving graph models.

Scalability and diversity of solver-based techniques can be improved by iteratively calling the underlying solver [19,35]. In each step a partial model is extended with additional elements as a result of a solver call. Higher diversity is achieved by avoiding the same partial solutions. As a downside, generation steps need to be specified manually, and higher diversity can be achieved only if the models are decomposable into separate well-defined partitions.

Black-box approaches [8,13,15,23] can only exploit the specification of the language or the transformation, so they frequently rely upon contracts or model fragments. As a common theme, these techniques may generate a set of simple models, and while certain diversity can be achieved by using symmetry-breaking predicates, they fail to scale for larger sizes. In fact, the effective diversity of models is also questionable since corresponding safety standards prescribe much stricter test coverage criteria for software certification and tool qualification than those currently offered by existing model transformation testing approaches.

Based on the logic-based Formula solver, the approach of [17] applies stochastic random sampling of output to achieve a diverse set of generated models by taking exactly one element from each equivalence class defined by graph isomorphism, which can be too restrictive for coverage purposes. Stochastic simulation is proposed for graph transformation systems in [40], where rule application is stochastic (and not the properties of models), but fulfillment of WF constraints can only be assured by a carefully constructed rule set.

7   Conclusion and Future Work

We proposed novel diversity metrics for models based on neighbourhood shapes [28], which are true generalizations of metamodel coverage and graph isomorphism used in many research papers. Moreover, we presented a model generation technique that to derive structurally diverse models by (i) calculating the shape of the previous solutions, and (ii) feeding back to an existing generator to avoid similar instances thus ensuring high diversity between the models. The proposed generator is available as an open source tool [44].

We evaluated our approach in a mutation testing scenario for Yakindu Statecharts, an industrial DSL tool. We compared the effectiveness (mutation score) and the diversity metrics of different test suites derived by our approach and an Alloy-based model generator. Our approach consistently outperformed the Alloy-based generator for both a single model and the entire test suite. Moreover, we found high (internal) diversity values normally result in high mutation score, thus highlighting the practical value of the proposed diversity metrics.

Conceptually, our approach can be adapted to an Alloy-based model generator by adding formulae obtained from previous shapes to the input specification. However, our initial investigations revealed that such an approach does not scale well with increasing model size. While Alloy has been used as a model generator for numerous testing scenarios of DSL tools and model transformations [6,8,35,36,42], our measurements strongly indicate that it is not a justified choice as (1) Alloy is very sensitive to configurations of symmetry breaking predicates and (2) the diversity and mutation score of generated models is problematic.

Acknowledgement. This paper is partially supported by the MTA-BME Lendület Cyber-Physical Systems Research Group, the NSERC RGPIN-04573-16 project and the UNKP-17-3-III New National Excellence Program of the Ministry of Human Capacities.

References

1. Aranega, V., Mottu, J.-M., Etien, A., Degueule, T., Baudry, B., Dekeyser, J.-L.: Towards an automation of the mutation analysis dedicated to model transformation. Softw. Test. Verif. Reliab. **25**(5–7), 653–683 (2015)
2. Arkhangel'Skii, A., Fedorchuk, V.: General Topolgy I: Basic Concepts and Constructions Dimension Theory, vol. 17. Springer, Heidelberg (2012). https://doi.org/10.1007/978-3-642-61265-7
3. Batot, E., Sahraoui, H.: A generic framework for model-set selection for the unification of testing and learning MDE tasks. In: MODELS, pp. 374–384 (2016)
4. Baudry, B., Dinh-Trong, T., Mottu, J.-M., Simmonds, D., France, R., Ghosh, S., Fleurey, F., Le Traon, Y.: Model transformation testing challenges. In: Integration of Model Driven Development and Model Driven Testing (2006)
5. Baudry, B., Monperrus, M., Mony, C., Chauvel, F., Fleurey, F., Clarke, S.: Diversify: ecology-inspired software evolution for diversity emergence. In: Software Maintenance, Reengineering and Reverse Engineering, pp. 395–398 (2014)
6. Bordbar, B., Anastasakis, K.: UML2ALLOY: a tool for lightweight modeling of discrete event systems. In: IADIS AC, pp. 209–216 (2005)
7. Brottier, E., Fleurey, F., Steel, J., Baudry, B., Le Traon, Y.: Metamodel-based test generation for model transformations: an algorithm and a tool. In: 17th International Symposium on Software Reliability Engineering, pp. 85–94 (2006)
8. Büttner, F., Egea, M., Cabot, J., Gogolla, M.: Verification of ATL transformations using transformation models and model finders. In: Aoki, T., Taguchi, K. (eds.) ICFEM 2012. LNCS, vol. 7635, pp. 198–213. Springer, Heidelberg (2012). https://doi.org/10.1007/978-3-642-34281-3_16
9. Cabot, J., Clarisó, R., Riera, D.: UMLtoCSP: a tool for the formal verification of UML/OCL models using constraint programming. In: ASE, pp. 547–548 (2007)
10. Cabot, J., Clariso, R., Riera, D.: Verification of UML/OCL class diagrams using constraint programming. In: ICSTW, pp. 73–80 (2008)
11. Darabos, A., Pataricza, A., Varró, D.: Towards testing the implementation of graph transformations. In: GTVMT, ENTCS. Elsevier (2006)
12. Ehrig, K., Küster, J.M., Taentzer, G.: Generating instance models from meta models. Softw. Syst. Model. **8**(4), 479–500 (2009)
13. Fleurey, F., Baudry, B., Muller, P.-A., Le Traon, Y.: Towards dependable model transformations: qualifying input test data. SoSyM, **8** (2007)
14. González, C.A., Cabot, J.: Test data generation for model transformations combining partition and constraint analysis. In: Di Ruscio, D., Varró, D. (eds.) ICMT 2014. LNCS, vol. 8568, pp. 25–41. Springer, Cham (2014). https://doi.org/10.1007/978-3-319-08789-4_3

15. Guerra, E., Soeken, M.: Specification-driven model transformation testing. Softw. Syst. Model. **14**(2), 623–644 (2015)
16. Jackson, D.: Alloy: a lightweight object modelling notation. ACM Trans. Softw. Eng. Methodol. **11**(2), 256–290 (2002)
17. Jackson, E.K., Simko, G., Sztipanovits, J.: Diversely enumerating system-level architectures. In: International Conference on Embedded Software, p. 11 (2013)
18. Jia, Y., Harman, M.: An analysis and survey of the development of mutation testing. IEEE Trans. Softw. Eng. **37**(5), 649–678 (2011)
19. Kang, E., Jackson, E., Schulte, W.: An approach for effective design space exploration. In: Calinescu, R., Jackson, E. (eds.) Monterey Workshop 2010. LNCS, vol. 6662, pp. 33–54. Springer, Heidelberg (2011). https://doi.org/10.1007/978-3-642-21292-5_3
20. Le Berre, D., Parrain, A.: The sat4j library. J. Satisf. Boolean Model. Comput. **7**, 59–64 (2010)
21. Micskei, Z., Szatmári, Z., Oláh, J., Majzik, I.: A concept for testing robustness and safety of the context-aware behaviour of autonomous systems. In: Jezic, G., Kusek, M., Nguyen, N.-T., Howlett, R.J., Jain, L.C. (eds.) KES-AMSTA 2012. LNCS (LNAI), vol. 7327, pp. 504–513. Springer, Heidelberg (2012). https://doi.org/10.1007/978-3-642-30947-2_55
22. Mottu, J.-M., Baudry, B., Le Traon, Y.: Mutation analysis testing for model transformations. In: Rensink, A., Warmer, J. (eds.) ECMDA-FA 2006. LNCS, vol. 4066, pp. 376–390. Springer, Heidelberg (2006). https://doi.org/10.1007/11787044_28
23. Mottu, J.-M., Simula, S.S., Cadavid, J., Baudry, B.: Discovering model transformation pre-conditions using automatically generated test models. In: ISSRE, pp. 88–99. IEEE, November 2015
24. The Object Management Group.: Object Constraint Language, v2.0, May 2006
25. Ratiu, D., Voelter, M.: Automated testing of DSL implementations: experiences from building mbeddr. In: AST@ICSE 2016, pp. 15–21 (2016)
26. Reid, S.C.: An empirical analysis of equivalence partitioning, boundary value analysis and random testing. In: Software Metrics Symposium, pp. 64–73 (1997)
27. Rensink, A.: Isomorphism checking in GROOVE. ECEASST **1** (2006)
28. Rensink, A., Distefano, D.: Abstract graph transformation. Electron. Notes Theor. Comput. Sci. **157**(1), 39–59 (2006)
29. Reps, T.W., Sagiv, M., Wilhelm, R.: Static program analysis via 3-valued logic. In: Alur, R., Peled, D.A. (eds.) CAV 2004. LNCS, vol. 3114, pp. 15–30. Springer, Heidelberg (2004). https://doi.org/10.1007/978-3-540-27813-9_2
30. Salay, R., Famelis, M., Chechik, M.: Language independent refinement using partial modeling. In: de Lara, J., Zisman, A. (eds.) FASE 2012. LNCS, vol. 7212, pp. 224–239. Springer, Heidelberg (2012). https://doi.org/10.1007/978-3-642-28872-2_16
31. Schonbock, J., Kappel, G., Wimmer, M., Kusel, A., Retschitzegger, W., Schwinger, W.: TETRABox - a generic white-box testing framework for model transformations. In: APSEC, pp. 75–82. IEEE, December 2013
32. Semeráth, O., Barta, Á., Horváth, Á., Szatmári, Z., Varró, D.: Formal validation of domain-specific languages with derived features and well-formedness constraints. Softw. Syst. Model. **16**(2), 357–392 (2017)
33. Semeráth, O., Nagy, A.S., Varró, D.: A graph solver for the automated generation of consistent domain-specific models. In: 40th International Conference on Software Engineering (ICSE 2018), Gothenburg, Sweden. ACM (2018)

34. Semeráth, O., Varró, D.: Graph constraint evaluation over partial models by constraint rewriting. In: Guerra, E., van den Brand, M. (eds.) ICMT 2017. LNCS, vol. 10374, pp. 138–154. Springer, Cham (2017). https://doi.org/10.1007/978-3-319-61473-1_10

35. Semeráth, O., Vörös, A., Varró, D.: Iterative and incremental model generation by logic solvers. In: Stevens, P., Wąsowski, A. (eds.) FASE 2016. LNCS, vol. 9633, pp. 87–103. Springer, Heidelberg (2016). https://doi.org/10.1007/978-3-662-49665-7_6

36. Sen, S., Baudry, B., Mottu, J.-M.: Automatic model generation strategies for model transformation testing. In: Paige, R.F. (ed.) ICMT 2009. LNCS, vol. 5563, pp. 148–164. Springer, Heidelberg (2009). https://doi.org/10.1007/978-3-642-02408-5_11

37. The Eclipse Project.: Eclipse Modeling Framework. https://www.eclipse.org/modeling/emf/

38. The Eclipse Project.: EMF DiffMerge. http://wiki.eclipse.org/EMF_DiffMerge

39. Torlak, E., Jackson, D.: Kodkod: a relational model finder. In: Grumberg, O., Huth, M. (eds.) TACAS 2007. LNCS, vol. 4424, pp. 632–647. Springer, Heidelberg (2007). https://doi.org/10.1007/978-3-540-71209-1_49

40. Torrini, P., Heckel, R., Ráth, I.: Stochastic simulation of graph transformation systems. In: Rosenblum, D.S., Taentzer, G. (eds.) FASE 2010. LNCS, vol. 6013, pp. 154–157. Springer, Heidelberg (2010). https://doi.org/10.1007/978-3-642-12029-9_11

41. Ujhelyi, Z., Bergmann, G., Hegedüs, Á., Horváth, Á., Izsó, B., Ráth, I., Szatmári, Z., Varró, D.: EMF-IncQuery: an integrated development environment for live model queries. Sci. Comput. Program. **98**, 80–99 (2015)

42. Vallecillo, A., Gogolla, M., Burgueño, L., Wimmer, M., Hamann, L.: Formal specification and testing of model transformations. In: Bernardo, M., Cortellessa, V., Pierantonio, A. (eds.) SFM 2012. LNCS, vol. 7320, pp. 399–437. Springer, Heidelberg (2012). https://doi.org/10.1007/978-3-642-30982-3_11

43. Varró, D., Semeráth, O., Szárnyas, G., Horváth, Á.: Towards the automated generation of consistent, diverse, scalable and realistic graph models. In: Heckel, R., Taentzer, G. (eds.) Graph Transformation, Specifications, and Nets. LNCS, vol. 10800, pp. 285–312. Springer, Cham (2018). https://doi.org/10.1007/978-3-319-75396-6_16

44. Viatra Solver Project (2018). https://github.com/viatra/VIATRA-Generator

45. Wang, J., Kim, S.-K., Carrington, D.: Verifying metamodel coverage of model transformations. In: Software Engineering Conference, p. 10 (2006)

46. Yakindu Statechart Tools.: Yakindu. http://statecharts.org/

Optimising Spectrum Based Fault Localisation for Single Fault Programs Using Specifications

David Landsberg$^{(\boxtimes)}$ (ORCID), Youcheng Sun (ORCID), and Daniel Kroening (ORCID)

Department of Computer Science, University of Oxford, Oxford, UK
david.landsberg@linacre.ox.ac.uk

Abstract. Spectrum based fault localisation determines how suspicious a line of code is with respect to being faulty as a function of a given test suite. Outstanding problems include identifying properties that the test suite should satisfy in order to improve fault localisation effectiveness subject to a given measure, and developing methods that generate these test suites efficiently.

We address these problems as follows. First, when single bug optimal measures are being used with a single-fault program, we identify a formal property that the test suite should satisfy in order to optimise fault localisation. Second, we introduce a new method which generates test data that satisfies this property. Finally, we empirically demonstrate the utility of our implementation at fault localisation on SV-COMP benchmarks and the `tcas` program, demonstrating that test suites can be generated in almost a second with a fault identified after inspecting under 1% of the program.

Keywords: Software quality · Spectrum based fault localisation
Debugging

1 Introduction

Faulty software is estimated to cost 60 billion dollars to the US economy per year [1] and has been single-handedly responsible for major newsworthy catastrophes[1]. This problem is exacerbated by the fact that debugging (defined as the process of finding and rectifying a fault) is complex and time consuming – estimated to consume 50–60% of the time a programmer spends in the maintenance and development cycle [2]. Consequently, the development of effective and efficient methods for software fault localisation has the potential to greatly reduce costs, wasted programmer time and the possibility of catastrophe.

In this paper, we advance the state of the art in lightweight fault localisation by building on research in spectrum-based fault localisation (SBFL). SBFL is one

---

This research was supported by the Innovate UK project 113099 SECT-AIR.
[1] https://www.newscientist.com/gallery/software-faults/.

A. Russo and A. Schürr (Eds.): FASE 2018, LNCS 10802, pp. 246–263, 2018.
https://doi.org/10.1007/978-3-319-89363-1_14

of the most prominent areas of software fault localisation research, estimated to make up 35% of published work in the field to date [3], and has been demonstrated to be efficient and effective at finding faults [4–12]. The effectiveness relies on two factors, (1) the quality of the measure used to identify the lines of code that are suspected to be faulty, and (2) the quality of the test suite used. Most research in the field has been focussed on finding improved measures [4–12], but there is a growing literature on how to improve the quality of test suites [13–20]. An outstanding problem in this field is to identify the properties that test suites should satisfy to improve fault localisation.

To address this problem, we focus our attention on improving the quality of test suites for the purposes of fault localisation on single-fault programs. Programs with a single fault are of special interest, as a recent study demonstrates that 82% of faulty programs could be repaired with a "single fix" [21], and that "when software is being developed, bugs arise one-at-a-time and therefore can be considered as single-faulted scenarios", suggesting that methods optimised for use with single-fault programs would be most helpful in practice. Accordingly, the contributions of this paper are as follows.

1. We identify a formal property that a test suite must satisfy in order to be optimal for fault localisation on a single-fault program when a single-fault optimal SBFL measure is being used.
2. We provide a novel algorithm which generates data that is formally shown to satisfy this property.
3. We integrate this algorithm into an implementation which leverages model checkers to generate small test suites, and empirically demonstrate its practical utility at fault localisation on our benchmarks.

The rest of this paper is organized as follows. In Sect. 2, we present the formal preliminaries for SBFL and our approach. In Sect. 3, we motivate and describe a property of single-fault optimality. In Sect. 4, we present an algorithm which generates data for a given faulty program, and prove that the data generated satisfies the property of single fault optimality, and in Sect. 5 discuss implementation details. In Sect. 6 we present our experimental results where we demonstrate the utility of an implementation of our algorithm on our benchmarks, and in Sect. 7 we present related work.

2 Preliminaries

In this section we formally present the preliminaries for understanding our fault localisation approach. In particular, we describe probands, proband models, and SBFL.

2.1 Probands

Following the terminology in Steimann et al. [22], a *proband* is a faulty program together with its test suite, and can be used for evaluating the performance of

```
int main() {
  int input1, input2, input3; // C1
  int least = input1;
  int most = input1;

  if (most < input2)
    most = input2;  // C2

  if (most < input3)
    most = input3;  // C3

  if (least > input2)
    most = input2;  // C4 (bug)

  if (least > input3)
    least = input3;  // C5

  assert(least <= most); // E
}
```

	C_1	C_2	C_3	C_4	C_5	E
t_1	1	0	1	1	0	1
t_2	1	0	0	1	1	1
t_3	1	0	0	1	0	1
t_4	1	1	0	0	0	0
t_5	1	0	1	0	0	0
t_6	1	0	0	0	1	0
t_7	1	0	0	1	1	0
t_8	1	0	0	0	0	0
t_9	1	1	0	0	1	0
t_{10}	1	1	1	0	0	0

Fig. 1. minmax.c   Fig. 2. Coverage matrix

a given fault localization method. A *faulty program* is a program that fails to always satisfy a *specification*, which is a property expressible in some formal language and describes the intended behaviour of some part of the program under test (PUT). When a specification fails to be satisfied for a given execution (i.e., an *error* occurs), it is assumed there exists some (incorrectly written) lines of code in the program which was the cause of the error, identified as a *fault* (aka *bug*).

Example 1. An example of a faulty C program is given in Fig. 1 (minmax.c, taken from Groce et al. [23]), and we shall use it as our running example throughout this paper. There are some executions of the program in which the assertion statement least <= most is violated, and thus the program fails to always satisfy the specification. The fault in this example is labelled C4, which should be an assignment to least instead of most.

A *test suite* is a collection of test cases whose result is independent of the order of their execution, where a *test case* is an execution of some part of a program. Each test case is associated with an input vector, where the n-th value of the vector is assigned to the n-th input of the given program for the purposes of a test (according to some given method of assigning values in the vector to inputs in the program). Each test suite is associated with a set of input vectors which can be used to generate the test cases. A test case *fails* (or is *failing*) if it violates a given specification, and *passes* (or is *passing*) otherwise.

Example 2. We give an example of a test case for the running example. The test case with associated input vector $\langle 0, 1, 2 \rangle$ is an execution in which input1 is assigned 0, input2 is assigned 1, and input3 is assigned 2, the statements labeled C1, C2 and C3 are executed, but C4 and C5 are not executed, and the assertion is not violated at termination, as least and most assume values of 0 and 2 respectively. Accordingly, we may associate a collection of test cases (a test suite) with a set of input vectors. For the running example the following ten input vectors are associated with a test suite of ten test cases: $\langle 1,0,2\rangle$, $\langle 2,0,1\rangle$, $\langle 2,0,2\rangle$, $\langle 0,1,0\rangle$, $\langle 0,0,1\rangle$, $\langle 1,1,0\rangle$, $\langle 2,0,0\rangle$, $\langle 2,2,2\rangle$, $\langle 1,2,0\rangle$, and $\langle 0,1,2\rangle$. Here, the first three input vectors result in error (and thus their associated test cases are failing), and the last seven do not (and thus their associated test cases are passing).

A *unit under test* UUT is a concrete artifact in a program which is a candidate for being at fault. Many types of UUTs have been defined and used in the literature, including methods [24], blocks [25,26], branches [16], and statements [27–29]. A UUT is said to be *covered* by a test case just in case that test case executes the UUT. For convenience, it will help to always think of UUTs as being labeled C1, C2, ... etc. in the program itself (as they are in the running example). Assertion statements are not considered to be UUTs, and we assume that each fault in the program has a corresponding UUT.

Example 3. To illustrate some UUTs for the running example (Fig. 1), we have chosen the units under test to be the statements labeled in comments marked C1, ..., C5. The assertion is labeled E, which is violated when an error occurs. To illustrate a proband, the faulty program minmax.c (described in Example 1), and the test suite associated with the input vectors described in Example 2, together form a proband.

2.2 Proband Models

In this section we define proband models, which are the principle formal objects used in SBFL. Informally, a proband model is a mathematical abstraction of a proband. We assume the existence of a given proband in which the UUTs have already been identified for the faulty program and appropriately labeled C1, ..., Cn, and assume a total of n UUTs. We begin as follows.

Definition 1. *A set of coverage vectors, denoted by* $\mathbf{T}$, *is a set* $\{t_1, \ldots, t_{|\mathbf{T}|}\}$ *in which each* $t_k \in \mathbf{T}$ *is a coverage vector defined* $t_k = \langle c_1^k, \ldots, c_{n+1}^k, k\rangle$, *where*

- *for all* $0 < i \leqslant n$, $c_i^k = 1$ *if the i-th UUT is covered by the test case associated with* t_k, *and 0 otherwise.*
- $c_{n+1}^k = 1$ *if the test case associated with* t_k *fails and 0 if it passes.*

We also call a set of coverage vectors $\mathbf{T}$ the fault localisation *data* or a *dataset*. Intuitively, each coverage vector can be thought of as a mathematical abstraction of an associated test case which describes which UUTs were executed/covered in that test case. We also use the following additional notation. If the last argument of a coverage vector in $\mathbf{T}$ is the number k it is denoted t_k where k uniquely identifies a coverage vector in $\mathbf{T}$ and the corresponding test case in the associated test suite. In general, for each $t_k \in \mathbf{T}$, c_i^k is a *coverage variable* and gives the value of the i-th argument in t_k. If $c_{n+1}^k = 1$, then t_k is called a *failing* coverage vector, and *passing* otherwise. The set of failing coverage vectors/the event of an error is denoted E (such that the set of passing vectors is then $\overline{E}$). Element c_{n+1}^k is also denoted e^k (as it describes whether the error occurred). For convenience, we may represent the set of coverage vectors $\mathbf{T}$ with a *coverage matrix*, where for all $0 < i \leqslant n$ and $t_k \in \mathbf{T}$ the cell intersecting the i-th column and k-th row is c_i^k and represents whether the i-th UUT was covered in the test case corresponding to t_k. The cell intersecting the last column and k-th row is e^k and represents whether t_k is a failing or passing test case. Fig. 2 is an example coverage matrix. In practice, given a program and an input vector, one can extract coverage information from an associated test case using established tools[2].

Example 4. For the test suite given in Example 2 we can devise a set of coverage vectors $\mathbf{T} = \{t_1, \ldots, t_{10}\}$ in which $t_1 = \langle 1, 0, 1, 1, 0, 1, 1 \rangle$, $t_2 = \langle 1, 0, 0, 1, 1, 1, 2 \rangle$, $t_3 = \langle 1, 0, 0, 1, 0, 1, 3 \rangle$, $t_4 = \langle 1, 1, 0, 0, 0, 0, 4 \rangle$, $t_5 = \langle 1, 1, 0, 0, 0, 0, 5 \rangle$, $t_6 = \langle 1, 0, 0, 0, 1, 0, 6 \rangle$, $t_7 = \langle 1, 0, 0, 1, 1, 0, 7 \rangle$, $t_8 = \langle 1, 0, 0, 0, 0, 0, 8 \rangle$, $t_9 = \langle 1, 1, 0, 0, 1, 0, 9 \rangle$, and $t_{10} = \langle 1, 1, 1, 0, 0, 0, 10 \rangle$. Here, coverage vector t_k is associated with the k-th input vector described in the list in Example 2. To illustrate how input and coverage vectors relate, we observe that t_{10} is associated with a test case with input vector $\langle 0, 1, 2 \rangle$ which executes the statements labeled C1, C2 and C3, does not execute the statements labeled C4 and C5, and does not result in error. Consequently $c_1^{10} = c_2^{10} = c_3^{10} = 1$, and $c_4^{10} = c_5^{10} = e^{10} = 0$, and $k = 10$ such that $t_{10} = \langle 1, 1, 1, 0, 0, 0, 10 \rangle$ (by the definition of coverage vectors). The coverage matrix representing $\mathbf{T}$ is given in Fig. 2.

Definition 2. *Let $\mathbf{T}$ be a non-empty set of coverage vectors, then $\mathbf{T}$'s program model $\mathbf{PM}$ is defined as the sequence $\langle C_1, \ldots, C_{|\mathbf{PM}|} \rangle$, where for each $C_i \in \mathbf{PM}$, $C_i = \{t_k \in \mathbf{T} | c_i^k = 1\}$.*

We often use the notation $\mathbf{PM_T}$ to denote the program model $\mathbf{PM}$ associated with $\mathbf{T}$. The final component $C_{|\mathbf{PM}|}$ is also denoted E (denoting the event of the error). Each member of a program model is called a *program component* or *event*, and if $c_i^k = 1$ we say C_i occurred in t_k, that t_k *covers* C_i, and say that C_i is *faulty* just in case its corresponding UUT is faulty. Following the definition above, each component C_i is the set of vectors in which C_i is covered, and obey set theoretic relationships. For instance, for all components C_i, $C_j \in \mathbf{PM}$, we have $\forall t_k \in C_j . c_i^k = 1$ just in case $C_j \subseteq C_i$. In general, we assume that E contains at least one coverage vector and each coverage vector covers at least one component. Members of E and $\overline{E}$ are called failing/passing vectors, respectively.

Example 5. We use the running example to illustrate a program model. For the set of coverage vectors $\mathbf{T} = \{t_1, \ldots, t_{10}\}$, we may define a program model

---

[2] For C programs Gcov can be used, available at http://www.gcovr.com.

$\mathbf{PM} = \langle C_1, C_2, C_3, C_4, C_5, E \rangle$, where $C_1 = \{t_1, \ldots, t_{10}\}$, $C_2 = \{t_4, t_9, t_{10}\}$, $C_3 = \{t_1, t_5, t_{10}\}$, $C_4 = \{t_1, t_2, t_3, t_7\}$, $C_5 = \{t_2, t_6, t_7, t_9\}$, $E = \{t_1, t_2, t_3\}$. Here, we may think of $C_1, \ldots, C_5$ as events which occur just in case a corresponding UUT (lines of code labeled C1, ...,C5 respectively) is executed, and E as an event which occurs just in case the assertion least <= most is violated. C_4 is identified as the faulty component.

Definition 3. *For a given proband we define a* proband model $\langle \mathbf{PM}, \mathbf{T} \rangle$, *consisting of the given faulty program's program model* $\mathbf{PM}$, *and an associated test suite's set of coverage vectors* $\mathbf{T}$.

Finally, we extend our setup to distinguish between samples and populations. The *population test suite* for a given program is a test suite consisting of all possible test cases for the program, a *sample test suite* is a test suite consisting of some (but not necessarily all) possible test cases for the program. All test suites are sample test suites drawn from a given population. Let $\langle \mathbf{PM}, \mathbf{T} \rangle$ be a given proband model for a given faulty program and sample test suite, we denote the *population vectors*, corresponding to the population test suite of the given faulty program, as $\mathbf{T}^*$ (and E^* and $\overline{E}^*$ as the population failing and passing vectors in $\mathbf{T}^*$ respectively). The *population program model* associated with the population test suite is denoted $\mathbf{PM}^*$ (aka $\mathbf{PM}^*_{\mathbf{T}^*}$). $\langle \mathbf{PM}^*, \mathbf{T}^* \rangle$ is called the *population proband model*. Finally, we extend the use of asterisks to make clear that the asterisked variable is associated with a given population. Accordingly, each component in the population program model is also superscripted with a $*$ to denote that it is a member of $\mathbf{PM}^*$ (e.g. C_1^*). Each vector in the population set of vectors $\mathbf{T}^*$ (e.g., t_1^*), and each coverage variable in each vector $t_k^* \in \mathbf{T}^*$ (e.g., c_1^{k*}).

It is assumed that for a given sample proband model $\langle \mathbf{PM}, \mathbf{T} \rangle$ and its population proband model $\langle \mathbf{PM}^*, \mathbf{T}^* \rangle$, we have $\mathbf{T} \subseteq \mathbf{T}^*$. Intuitively, this is because a sample test suite is drawn from the population. In addition, for each $i \in \mathbb{N}$ if $C_i \in \mathbf{PM}$ and $C_i^* \in \mathbf{PM}^*$, then $C_i \subseteq C_i^*$. Intuitively, this is because if the i-th UUT is executed by a test case in the sample then it is executed by that test case in the population.

2.3 Spectrum Based Fault Localisation

We first define what a program spectrum is, as it serves as the principle formal object used in spectrum based fault localization (SBFL).

Definition 4. *For each proband model* $\langle PM, \mathbf{T} \rangle$, *and each component* $C_i \in PM$, *a component's program spectrum is a vector* $\langle |C_i \cap E|, |\overline{C_i} \cap E|, |C_i \cap \overline{E}|, |\overline{C_i} \cap \overline{E}| \rangle$.

Informally, $|C_i \cap E|$ is the number of failing coverage vectors in $\mathbf{T}$ that cover C_i, $|\overline{C_i} \cap E|$ is the number of failing coverage vectors in $\mathbf{T}$ that do not cover C_i, $|C_i \cap \overline{E}|$ is the number of passing coverage vectors in $\mathbf{T}$ that cover C_i, and $|\overline{C_i} \cap \overline{E}|$ is the number of passing coverage vectors in $\mathbf{T}$ that do not cover C_i. $|C_i \cap E|, |\overline{C_i} \cap E|, |C_i \cap \overline{E}|$ and $|\overline{C_i} \cap \overline{E}|$ are often denoted a_{ef}^i, a_{nf}^i, a_{ep}^i, and a_{np}^i respectively in the literature [4, 7–12].

252 D. Landsberg et al.

Example 6. For the proband model of the running example $\langle \mathbf{PM}, \mathbf{T} \rangle$ (where $\mathbf{PM} = \langle C_1, \ldots, C_5, E \rangle$ and $\mathbf{T}$ is represented by the coverage matrix in Fig. 2), the spectra for $C_1, \ldots C_5$, and E are $\langle 3,0,7,0 \rangle$, $\langle 0,3,3,4 \rangle$, $\langle 1,2,2,5 \rangle$, $\langle 3,0,1,6 \rangle$, $\langle 1,2,3,4 \rangle$, and $\langle 3,0,0,7 \rangle$ respectively.

Following Naish et al. [7], we define a suspiciousness measure as follows.

Definition 5. *A suspiciousness measure w is a function with signature w : $\mathbf{PM} \to \mathbb{R}$, and maps each $C_i \in \mathbf{PM}$ to a real number as a function of C_i's program spectrum $\langle |C_i \cap E|, |\overline{C_i} \cap E|, |C_i \cap \overline{E}|, |\overline{C_i} \cap \overline{E}| \rangle$, where this number is called the component's degree of suspiciousness.*

The higher/lower the degree of suspiciousness the more/less suspicious C_i is assumed to be with respect to being a fault. A property of some SBFL measures is *single-fault optimality* [7,30]. Using our notation we can express this property as follows:

Definition 6. *A suspiciousness measure w is* single-fault optimal *if it satisfies the following. For every program model $\mathbf{PM}$ and every $C_i \in \mathbf{PM}$:*

1. *If $E \not\subseteq C_i$ and $E \subseteq C_j$, then $w(C_j) > w(C_i)$ and*
2. *if $E \subseteq C_i$, $E \subseteq C_j$, $|C_i \cap \overline{E}| = k$ and $|C_j \cap \overline{E}| < k$, then $w(C_j) > w(C_i)$.*

Under the assumption that there is a single fault in the program, Naish et al. argue that a measure must have this property to be optimal [7]. Informally, the first condition demands that UUTs covered by all failing test cases are more suspicious than anything else. The rationale here is that if there is only one faulty UUT in the program, then it must be executed by all failing test cases (otherwise there would be some failing test case which executes no fault – which is impossible given it is assumed that all errors are caused by the execution of some faulty UUT) [7,30]. The second demands that of two UUTs covered by all failing test cases, the one which is executed by fewer passing test cases is more suspicious.

An example of a single fault optimal measure is the Naish-I measure $w(C_i) = a_{ef}^i - \frac{a_{ep}^i}{a_{ep}^i + a_{np}^i + 1}$ [31]. A framework that optimises any given SBFL measure to being single fault optimal was first given by Naish [31]. For any suspiciousness measure w scaled from 0 to 1, we can construct the *single fault optimised* version for w (written Opt_w) as follows (here, we use the equivalent formulation of Landsberg et al. [4]): $Opt_w(C_i) = a_{np}^i + 2$ if $a_{ef}^i = |E|$, and $w(C_i)$ otherwise.

We now describe the established SBFL algorithm [4,7–12]. The method produces a list of program component indices ordered by suspiciousness, as a function of set of coverage vectors $\mathbf{T}$ (taken from a proband model $\langle \mathbf{PM}, \mathbf{T} \rangle$) and suspiciousness measure w. As the algorithm is simple, we informally describe the algorithm in three stages, as follows. First, the program spectrum for each program component is constructed as a function of $\mathbf{T}$. Second, the indices of program components are ordered in a *suspiciousness list* according to decreasing order of suspiciousness. Third, the suspiciousness list is returned to the user, who will inspect each UUT corresponding to each index in the suspiciousness list in decreasing order of suspiciousness until a fault is found. We assume that in the case of ties of suspiciousness, the UUT that comes earlier in the code is investigated first, and assume effectiveness of a SBFL measure on a proband is measured by the number of non-faulty UUTs a user has to investigate before a fault is found.

Example 7. We illustrate an instance of SBFL using our running `minmax.c` example of Fig. 1, and the Naish-I measure as an example suspiciousness measure. First, the program spectra (given in Example 6) are constructed as a function of the given coverage vectors (represented by the coverage matrix of Fig. 2). Second, the suspiciousness of each program component is computed (here, the suspiciousness of the five components are $2.125, -0.375, 0.75, 2.875, 0.625$ respectively), and the indices of components are ordered according to decreasing order of suspiciousness. Thus we get the list $\langle 4, 1, 3, 5, 2 \rangle$. Finally, the list is returned to the user, and the UUTs in the program are inspected according to this list in descending order of suspiciousness until a fault is found. In our running example, C4 (the fault) is investigated first.

3   A Property of Single-Fault Optimal Data

In this section, we identify a new property for the optimality of a given dataset $\mathbf{T}$ for use in fault localisation. Throughout we make two assumptions: Firstly that a single bug optimal measure w is being used and secondly that there is a single bug in a given faulty program (henceforth our *two assumptions*). Let $\langle \mathbf{PM}, \mathbf{T} \rangle$ be a given sample proband model, then we have the following:

Definition 7. A PROPERTY OF SINGLE FAULT OPTIMAL DATA. *If* $\mathbf{T}$ *is single bug optimal, then* $\forall C_i \in \mathbf{PM_T}.\ E \subseteq C_i \rightarrow E^* \subseteq C_i^*$.

If this condition holds, then we say the dataset $\mathbf{T}$ (and its associated test suite) satisfies this property of single fault optimality. Informally, the condition demands that if a UUT is covered by all failing test cases in the sample test suite then it is covered by all failing test cases in the population. If our two assumptions hold, we argue it is a desirable that a test suite satisfies this property. This is because the fault is assumed to be covered by all failing test cases in the population (similar to the rationale of Naish et al. [7]), and as UUTs executed by all failing test cases in the sample are investigated first when a single fault optimal measure is being used, it is desirable that UUTs not covered by all failing test cases in the population are less suspicious in order to guarantee the fault is found earlier. An additional desirable feature of knowing one's data satisfies this property, is that we do not have to add any more failing test cases to a test suite, given it is then impossible to improve fault localization effectiveness by adding more failing test cases under our two assumptions.

Algorithm 1. Single-fault optimal data generation algorithm

Data: E, E^* (pre-condition: $E \subseteq E^* \wedge E \neq \emptyset$)

1 **repeat**
2 $\quad\big|\quad T \leftarrow choose(\{t_k^* \in E^* | \exists i \in \mathbb{N}.\forall t_j \in E.c_i^j = 1 \wedge c_i^{k*} = 0\});$
3 $\quad\big|\quad E \leftarrow E \cup T;$
4 **until** $T = \emptyset$;
5 **return** E

---

4   Algorithm

In this section we present an algorithm which outputs single fault optimal data for a given faulty program. We assume several preconditions for our algorithm.

- For the given faulty program, at least one UUT is executed by all failing test cases (for C programs this could be a variable initialization in the main function).
- The population proband model is available (but as we shall see in the next section, practical implementations will not require this).
- We also assume that E is a mutable set, and shall make use of a $choose(X)$ subroutine which non-deterministically returns the set of a single a member of X (if one exists, otherwise it returns the empty set).

The algorithm is formally presented as Algorithm 1. We assume that an associated sample test suite will also be available as a by-product of the algorithm in addition to producing the data E. The intuition behind the algorithm is that failing vectors are iteratively accumulated in a set E one by one, where the next failing vector added does not cover some component which is covered by all vectors already in E (the algorithm terminates if no such vector exists). The resulting set is observed to be single-fault optimal. To illustrate the algorithm we give the example below. We then give a proof of partial correctness.

Example 8. We assume some population set of failing coverage vectors E^*, which we may identify with the set $\{t_1^*, t_2^*, t_3^*\} = \{\langle 1, 0, 1, 1, 0, 1, 1 \rangle, \langle 1, 0, 0, 1, 1, 1, 2 \rangle, \langle 1, 0, 0, 1, 0, 1, 3 \rangle\}$ described in the coverage matrix of Fig. 2. In reality, the population set of failing coverage vectors for this faulty program is much larger than this, but this will suffice for our example. The algorithm proceeds as follows. First, we assume E is a non-empty subset of E^*, and thus may assume $E = \{\langle 1, 0, 1, 1, 0, 1, 1 \rangle\}$. Now, to evaluate step 2, we first evaluate the set $\{t_k^* \in E^* | \exists i \in \mathbb{N}.\forall t_j \in E.c_i^j = 1 \wedge c_i^{k*} = 0\}$. Intuitively, this is the set of failing vectors in the population which do not cover some component which is covered by all vectors in E. We may find a member of this set as follows. First, we must evaluate the condition for when $E^* = \{t_1^*, t_2^*, t_3^*\}$. Given $c_3^1 = 1$ holds of t_1, and t_1 is the only member of E, and given $c_3^{2*} = 0$, we have the conclusion that t_2^* is a member of the set. Thus, for our example we may assume that *choose* returns t_2^* from this set such that $T = \{t_2^*\}$. So at step 3 the new version of E is

$E = \{\langle 1,0,1,1,0,1,1 \rangle, \langle 1,0,0,1,1,1,2 \rangle\}$. Consequently, on the next iteration of the loop the set condition will be unsatisfiable – this is because there is no index to a component i such that both $\forall t_j \in E . c_i^j = 1$ holds (i.e., $E \subseteq C_i$), and also $c_i^{k*} = 0$ holds for some vector t_k^* in the population (i.e., not $E^* \subseteq C_i$). Thus, *choose* will return the empty set, and the algorithm will terminate returning the dataset E to the user to be used in SBFL. Using the Naish-I measure with this dataset, we have the result that C1 and C4 are associated with the largest suspicious score of 2.0. Thus, with single-fault optimal data alone we can find a fault C4 reasonably effectively in our running example.

Proposition 1. *All datasets returned by Algorithm 1 are single-fault optimal.*

Proof. We show partial correctness as follows. Let $\langle \mathbf{PM}^*, \mathbf{T}^* \rangle$ be a given population proband model, where $E^* \subseteq \mathbf{T}^*$ is the population set of failing vectors, and let E be returned by the algorithm. We must show that for all $C_i \in \mathbf{PM}_E$, $E \subseteq C_i \rightarrow E^* \subseteq C_i^*$ (by def. of single fault optimality). We prove this by contradiction. Assume there is some $C_i \in \mathbf{PM}_E$ (without loss of generality we may assume $i = 1$), such that $E \subseteq C_1$ but not $E^* \subseteq C_1^*$. Given we assume E has been returned by the algorithm, we may assume $T = \emptyset$ (step 4), and thus *choose* returned $\emptyset$ at step 2 (by def. of *choose*). Accordingly, there is no $t_k^* \in E^*$ where $((\forall t_k \in E) c_1^j = 1) \wedge c_1^{k*} = 0$ (by the set condition at step 2). Thus, $(\forall t_k^* \in E^*)$ $((\forall t_j \in E) c_1^j = 1) \rightarrow c_1^{k*} = 1$. Now, $((\forall t_j \in E) c_1^j = 1)$ just in case $E \subseteq C_1$ (by def. of program models). So, $(\forall t_k^* \in E^*)$, if $E \subseteq C_1$ then $c_1^{k*} = 1$ (by substitution of equivalents). Equivalently, if $E \subseteq C_1$ then $(\forall t_k^* \in E^*) c_1^{k*} = 1$. Now, in general it holds that $((\forall t_k^* \in E^*) c_1^{k*} = 1)$ just in case $E^* \subseteq C_1^*$ (by def. of program models). Thus $E \subseteq C_1 \rightarrow E^* \subseteq C_1^*$ (by substitution of equivalents). This contradicts the initial assumption. $\qquad\square$

Finally, we informally observe that the maximum size of the E returned is the number of UUTs. In this case E is input to the algorithm with a failing vector that covers all components, and *choose* always returns a failing vector that covers 1 fewer UUTs than the failing vector covering the fewest UUTs already in E (noting that we assume at least one component will always be covered). The minimum is one. In this case E is input to the algorithm with a failing vector which covers some components and the post-condition is already fulfilled. In general, E can potentially be much smaller than E^*.

5   Implementation

We now discuss our implementation of the algorithm. In practice, we can leverage model checkers to compute members of E^* (the population set of failing vectors) on the fly, where computing E^* as a pre-condition would usually be intractable. This can be done by appeal to a SMT solving subroutine, which we describe as follows. Given a formal model of some code F_{code}, a formal specification ϕ, set of Booleans which are true just in case a corresponding UUT is executed in a given execution $\{C1, \ldots, Cn\}$, and a set $E \subseteq E^*$, we can use a SMT solver to return a satisfying assignment by calling $\text{SMT}(F_{code} \wedge \neg\phi \wedge \bigvee_{(\forall t_k \in E)c_i^k = 1} \text{Ci} = 0)$, and then extracting a coverage vector from that assignment. A subroutine which returns this coverage vector (or the empty set if one does not exist) can act as a substitute for the *choose* subroutine in Algorithm 1, and the generation of a static object E^* is no longer required as an input to the algorithm. Our implementation of this is called *sfo* (single fault optimal data generation tool).

We now discuss extensions of *sfo*. It is known that adding passing executions help in SBFL [4,5,7–12], thus to develop a more effective fault localisation procedure we developed a second implementation sfo_p (*sfo* with passing traces) that runs *sfo* and then adds passing test cases. To do this, after running *sfo* we call a SMT solver 20 times to find up to 20 new passing execution, where on each call if the vector found has new coverage properties (does not cover all the same UUTs as some passing vector already computed) it is added to a set of passing vectors.

Our implementations of *sfo* and sfo_p are integrated into a branch of the model checker CBMC [32]. Our branch of the tool is available for download at the URL given in the footnote[3]. Our implementations, along with generating fault localisation data, rank UUTs by degree of suspiciousness according to the Naish-I measure and report this fault localisation data to the user.

6   Experimentation

In this section we provide details of evaluation results for the use of *sfo* and sfo_p in fault localisation. The purpose of the experiment is to demonstrate that implementations of Algorithm 1 can be used to facilitate efficient and effective fault localisation in practice on small programs (≤ 2.5KLOC). We think generation of fault localisation information in a few seconds (≤ 2) is sufficient to demonstrate practical efficiency, and ranking the fault in the top handful of the most suspicious lines of code (≤ 5) on average is sufficient to demonstrate practical effectiveness. In the remainder of this section we present our experimental setup (where we describe our scoring system and benchmarks), and our results.

6.1   Setup

For the purposes of comparison, we tested the fault localisation potential of *sfo* and sfo_p against a method named *1f*, which performes SBFL when only a single failing test case was generated by CBMC (and thus UUTs covered by the test case were equally suspicious). We used the following scoring method to evaluate the effectiveness of each of the methods for each benchmark. We envisage an engineer who is inspecting each LOC in descending order of suspiciousness using a given strategy (inspecting lines that appear earlier in the code first in the case of ties). We rank alternative techniques by the number of non-faulty LOC that are investigated until the engineer finds a fault. Finally, we report the average of these scores for the benchmarks to give us an overall measure of fault localisation effectiveness.

---

[3] https://github.com/theyoucheng/cbmc.

We now discuss the benchmarks used in our experiments. In order to perform an unbiased experiment to test our techniques on, we imposed that our benchmarks needed to satisfy the following three properties (aside from being a C program which CBMC could be used on):

1. Programs must have been created by an independent source, to prevent any implicit bias caused by creating benchmarks ourselves.
2. Programs must have an explicit, formally stated specification that can be given as an assertion statement in order to apply a model checker.
3. In each program, the faulty code must be clearly identifiable, in order to be able to measure the quality of fault localisation.

Unfortunately, benchmarks satisfying these conditions are rare. In practice, benchmarks exist in verification research that satisfy either the second or third criterion, but rarely both. For instance, the available SIR benchmarks satisfy the third criterion, but not the second[4]. The software verification competition (SV-COMP) benchmarks satisfy the second criterion, but almost never satisfy the third[5]. Furthermore, it is often difficult to obtain benchmarks from authors even when usable benchmarks do in fact exist. Finally, we have been unable to find an instance of a C program that was not artificially developed for the purposes of testing.

The benchmarks are described in Table 1, where we give the benchmark name, the number of faults in the program, and lines of code (LOC). The modified versions of tcas were made available by Alex Groce via personal correspondence and were used with the EXPLAIN tool in [33][6]. The remaining benchmarks were identified as usable by manual investigation and testing in the repositories of SV-COMP 2013 and 2017. We have made our benchmarks available for download directly from the link on footnote 4. Faults in SV-COMP programs were identified by comparing them to an associated fault-free version (in tcas the fault was already identified). A series of continuous lines of code that differed from the fault free version (usually one line, and rarely up to 5 LOC for larger programs) constituted one fault. LOC were counted using the cloc utility.

We give further details about our application of CBMC in this experiment. For all our benchmarks, we used the smallest unwinding number that enables the bounded model checker to find a counterexample. These counterexamples were sliced, which usually results in a large improvement in fault localisation. For details about unwindings and slicing see the CBMC documentation [34]. In each benchmark each executable statement (variable initialisations, assignments, or condition statements) was determined as a UUT.

---

[4] http://sir.unl.edu/portal/index.php.
[5] Benchmarks can be accessed at https://sv-comp.sosy-lab.org/2018/.
[6] For our experiment we activated assertion statement P5a and fault 32c.

6.2 Results and Discussion

In this section we discuss our experimental results. In Table 1, columns $1f/sfo_p/sfo$ give the scores for when the respective method is used. Column t gives the runtime for CBMC and sfo_p respectively (we ignore the runtime for sfo due to negligible difference). $|E|$ and $|\overline{E}|$ give the number of failing and passing test cases generated by sfo_p. The AVG row gives averages column values. We are primarily interested in comparing the scores of sfo_p and $1f$.

Table 1. Experimental results

#	Benchmark	Faults	LOC	$1f$	t	sfo	sfo_p	t	$|E|$	$|\overline{E}|$
1	cdaudio_simpl1	4	2102	24	1.04	22	13	1.10	3	8
2	floppy_simpl3	6	1080	39	0.36	33	8	0.38	3	11
3	s3_clnt_1	1	546	35	3.52	33	3	3.56	2	7
4	kundu2	3	534	63	0.58	63	7	0.60	1	13
5	tcas	1	396	6	0.20	5	5	0.21	2	4
6	rule57_ebda	4	249	9	0.17	9	2	0.18	1	4
7	rule60_list2	1	187	14	0.17	14	8	0.18	1	3
8	merge_sort	1	111	1	2.19	1	1	2.32	1	0
9	byte_add	1	90	17	0.18	15	0	0.18	3	8
10	alternating_list	2	56	1	0.31	1	1	0.32	1	0
11	eureka_01	1	52	7	0.17	7	3	0.26	1	7
12	string	1	43	5	0.17	2	2	0.17	3	3
13	insertion_sort	1	25	3	1.05	3	0	4.28	1	3
AVG		2.08	420.85	17.23	0.78	16.00	4.08	1.06	1.77	5.46

We now discuss the results of the three techniques $1f$, sfo and sfo_p. On average, $1f$ located a fault after investigating 17.23 lines of code (4.09% of the program on average). The results here are perhaps better than expected. We observed that the single failing test case consistently returned good fault localisation potential given the use of slicing by the technique.

We now discuss sfo. On average, sfo located a fault after investigating 16 lines of code (3.8% of the program on average). Thus, the improvement over $1f$ is very small. When only one failing test case was available for sfo (i.e. $|E| = 1$) we emphasise that the SMT solver could not find any other failing traces which covered different parts of the program. In such cases, sfo performed the same as $1f$ (as expected). However, when there was more than one failing test case available (i.e. $|E| > 1$), sfo always made a small improvement. Accordingly, for benchmarks 1, 2, 3, 5, 9, and 12 the improvements in terms fewer LOC examined are 2, 6, 3, 1, 2, and 3, respectively. An improvement in benchmarks where sfo generated more than one test case is to be expected, given there was always a fault covered by all failing test cases in each program (even in programs with multiple faults), thus taking advantage of the property of single fault optimal data. Finally, we conjecture that on programs with more failing test cases available in the population, and on longer faulty programs, that this improvement will be larger.

We now discuss sfo_p. On average, sfo_p located a fault after investigating 4.08 LOC (0.97% of each program on average). Thus, the improvement over the other techniques is quite large (four times as effective as $1f$). Moreover, this effectiveness came at very little expense to runtime – sfo_p had an average runtime of 1.06 s, which is comparable to the runtime of $1f$ of 0.78 s. This is despite the fact that sfo_p generated over 7 executions on average. We consequently conclude that implementations of Algorithm 1 can be used to facilitate efficient and effective fault localisation in practice on small programs.

7 Related Work

The techniques discussed in this paper improve the quality of data usable for SBFL. We divide the research in this field into the following areas; many other methods can be potentially combined with our technique.

Test Suite Expansion. One approach to improving test suites is to add more test cases which satisfy a given criterion. A prominent criterion is that the test suite has sufficient program coverage, where studies suggest that test suites with high coverage improve fault localisation [15–17,20]. Other ways to improve test suites for SBFL are as follows. Li et al. generate test suites for SBFL, considering failing to passing test case ratio to be more important than number [35]. Zhang et al. consider cloning failed test cases to improve SBFL [13]. Perez et al. develop a metric for diagnosing whether a test suite is of sufficient quality for SBFL to take place [14]. Li et al. consider weighing different test cases differently [36]. Aside from coverage criteria, methods have been studied which generate test cases with a minimal distance from a given failed test case [18]. Baudry et al. use a bacteriological approach in order to generate test suites that simultaneously facilitate both testing and fault localisation [19]. Concolic execution methods have been developed to add test cases to a test suite based on their similarity to an initial failing run [20].

Prominent approaches which leverage model checkers for fault localisation are as follows. Groce [33] uses integer linear programming to find a passing test case most similar to a failing one and then compare the difference. Schupman and Bierre [37] generate short counterexamples for use in fault localisation, where a short counterexample will usually mean fewer UUTs for the user to inspect. Griesmayer [38] and Birch et al. [39] use model checkers to find failing executions and then look for whether a given number of changes to values of variables can be made to make the counterexample disappear. Gopinath et al. [40] compute minimal unsatisfiable cores in a given failing test case, where statements in the core will be given a higher suspiciousness level in the spectra ranking. Additionally, when generating a new test, they generate an input whose test case is most similar to the initial run in terms of its coverage of the statements. Fey et al. [41] use SAT solvers to localise faults on hardware with LTL specifications. In general, experimental scale is limited to a small number of programs in these studies, and we think our experimental component provides an improvement in terms of experimental scale (13 programs).

Test Suite Reduction. An alternative approach to expanding a test suite is to use reduction methods. Recently, many approaches have demonstrated that it is not necessary for all test cases in a test suite to be used. Rather, one can select a handful of test cases in order to minimise the number of test cases required for fault localisation [42, 43]. Most approaches are based on a strategy of eliminating redundant test cases relative to some coverage criterion. The effectiveness of applying various coverage criteria in test suite reduction is traditionally based on empirical comparison of two metrics: one which measures the size of the reduction, and the other which measures how much fault detection is preserved.

Slicing. A prominent approach to improving the quality of test suites involves the process of slicing test cases. Here, SBFL proceeds as usual except the program and/or the test cases composing the test suite are sliced (with irrelevant lines of code/parts of the execution removed). For example, Alves et al. [44] combine Tarantula along with dynamic slices, Ju et al. [45] use SBFL in combination with both dynamic and execution slices. Syntactic dynamic slicing is built-in in all our tested approaches by appeal to the functionalities of CBMC.

To our knowledge, no previous methods generate data which exhibit our property of single fault optimality.

8 Conclusion

In this paper, we have presented a method to generate single fault optimal data for use with SBFL. Experimental results on our implementation sfo_p, which integrates single fault optimal data along with passing test cases, demonstrate that small optimized fault localisation data can be generated efficiently in practice (1.06 s on average), and that subsequent fault localization can be performed effectively using this data (investigating 4.06 LOC until a fault is found). We envisage that implementations of the algorithm can be used in two different scenarios. In the first, the test suite generated can be used in standalone fault localisation, providing a small and low cost test suite useful for repeating iterations of simultaneous testing and fault localisation during program development. In the second, the data generated can be added to any pre-existing data associated with a test suite, which may be useful at the final testing stage where we may wish to optimise single fault localisation.

Future work involves finding larger benchmarks to use our implementation on and developing further properties, and methods for use with programs with multiple faults. We would also like to combine our technique with existing test suite generation algorithms in order to experiment how much test suites can be additionally improved for the purposes of fault localization.

References

1. Zhivich, M., Cunningham, R.K.: The real cost of software errors. IEEE Secur. Priv. **7**(2), 87–90 (2009)
2. Collofello, J.S., Woodfield, S.N.: Evaluating the effectiveness of reliability-assurance techniques. J. Syst. Softw. **9**(3), 745–770 (1989)
3. Wong, W.E., Gao, R., Li, Y., Abreu, R., Wotawa, F.: A survey on software fault localization. IEEE Trans. Softw. Eng. **42**(8), 707–740 (2016)
4. Landsberg, D., Chockler, H., Kroening, D., Lewis, M.: Evaluation of measures for statistical fault localisation and an optimising scheme. In: Egyed, A., Schaefer, I. (eds.) FASE 2015. LNCS, vol. 9033, pp. 115–129. Springer, Heidelberg (2015). https://doi.org/10.1007/978-3-662-46675-9_8
5. Landsberg, D., Chockler, H., Kroening, D.: Probabilistic fault localisation. In: Bloem, R., Arbel, E. (eds.) HVC 2016. LNCS, vol. 10028, pp. 65–81. Springer, Cham (2016). https://doi.org/10.1007/978-3-319-49052-6_5
6. Landsberg, D.: Methods and measures for statistical fault localisation. Ph.D. thesis, University of Oxford (2016)
7. Naish, L., Lee, H.J., Ramamohanarao, K.: A model for spectra-based software diagnosis. ACM Trans. Softw. Eng. Methodol. **20**(3), 1–11 (2011)
8. Lucia, L., Lo, D., Jiang, L., Thung, F., Budi, A.: Extended comprehensive study of association measures for fault localization. J. Softw. Evol. Process **26**(2), 172–219 (2014)
9. Wong, W.E., Debroy, V., Gao, R., Li, Y.: The DStar method for effective software fault localization. IEEE Trans. Reliab. **63**(1), 290–308 (2014)
10. Wong, W.E., Debroy, V., Choi, B.: A family of code coverage-based heuristics for effective fault localization. JSS **83**(2), 188–208 (2010)
11. Yoo, S.: Evolving human competitive spectra-based fault localisation techniques. In: Fraser, G., Teixeira de Souza, J. (eds.) SSBSE 2012. LNCS, vol. 7515, pp. 244–258. Springer, Heidelberg (2012). https://doi.org/10.1007/978-3-642-33119-0_18
12. Kim, J., Park, J., Lee, E.: A new hybrid algorithm for software fault localization. In: IMCOM, pp. 50:1–50:8. ACM (2015)
13. Zhang, L., Yan, L., Zhang, Z., Zhang, J., Chan, W.K., Zheng, Z.: A theoretical analysis on cloning the failed test cases to improve spectrum-based fault localization. JSS **129**, 35–57 (2017)
14. Perez, A., Abreu, R., van Deursen, A.: A test-suite diagnosability metric for spectrum-based fault localization approaches. In: ICSE (2017)
15. Jiang, B., Chan, W.K., Tse, T.H.: On practical adequate test suites for integrated test case prioritization and fault localization. In: International Conference on Quality Software, pp. 21–30 (2011)
16. Santelices, R., Jones, J.A., Yu, Y., Harrold, M.J.: Lightweight fault-localization using multiple coverage types. In: ICSE, pp. 56–66 (2009)
17. Feldt, R., Poulding, S., Clark, D., Yoo, S.: Test set diameter: quantifying the diversity of sets of test cases. CoRR, abs/1506.03482 (2015)
18. Jin, W., Orso, A.: F3: fault localization for field failures. In: ISSTA, pp. 213–223 (2013)
19. Baudry, B., Fleurey, F., Le Traon, Y.: Improving test suites for efficient fault localization. In: ICSE, pp. 82–91. ACM (2006)
20. Artzi, S., Dolby, J., Tip, F., Pistoia, M.: Directed test generation for effective fault localization. In: ISSTA, pp. 49–60 (2010)

21. Perez, A., Abreu, R., D'Amorim, M.: Prevalence of single-fault fixes and its impact on fault localization. In: 2017 ICST, pp. 12–22 (2017)
22. Steimann, F., Frenkel, M., Abreu, R.: Threats to the validity and value of empirical assessments of the accuracy of coverage-based fault locators. In: ISSTA, pp. 314–324. ACM (2013)
23. Groce, A.: Error explanation with distance metrics. In: Jensen, K., Podelski, A. (eds.) TACAS 2004. LNCS, vol. 2988, pp. 108–122. Springer, Heidelberg (2004). https://doi.org/10.1007/978-3-540-24730-2_8
24. Steimann, F., Frenkel, M.: Improving coverage-based localization of multiple faults using algorithms from integer linear programming. In: ISSRE, pp. 121–130, 27–30 November 2012
25. Abreu, R., Zoeteweij, P., van Gemund, A.J.: An evaluation of similarity coefficients for software fault localization. In: PRDC, pp. 39–46 (2006)
26. DiGiuseppe, N., Jones, J.A.: On the influence of multiple faults on coverage-based fault localization. In: ISSTA, pp. 210–220. ACM (2011)
27. Jones, J.A., Harrold, M.J., Stasko, J.: Visualization of test information to assist fault localization. In: Proceedings of the 24th International Conference on Software Engineering, ICSE 2002, pp. 467–477. ACM (2002)
28. Wong, W.E., Qi, Y.: Effective program debugging based on execution slices and inter-block data dependency. JSS **79**(7), 891–903 (2006)
29. Liblit, B., Naik, M., Zheng, A.X., Aiken, A., Jordan, M.I.: Scalable statistical bug isolation. SIGPLAN Not. **40**(6), 15–26 (2005)
30. Naish, L., Lee, H.J.: Duals in spectral fault localization. In: Australian Conference on Software Engineering (ASWEC), pp. 51–59. IEEE (2013)
31. Naish, L., Lee, H.J., Ramamohanarao, K.: Spectral debugging: how much better can we do? In: ACSC, pp. 99–106 (2012)
32. Clarke, E., Kroening, D., Lerda, F.: A tool for checking ANSI-C programs. In: Jensen, K., Podelski, A. (eds.) TACAS 2004. LNCS, vol. 2988, pp. 168–176. Springer, Heidelberg (2004). https://doi.org/10.1007/978-3-540-24730-2_15
33. Groce, A.: Error explanation and fault localization with distance metrics. Ph.D. thesis, Carnegie Melon (2005)
34. CBMC. http://www.cprover.org/cbmc/
35. Li, N., Wang, R., Tian, Y., Zheng, W.: An effective strategy to build up a balanced test suite for spectrum-based fault localization. Math. Probl. Eng. **2016**, 13 (2016)
36. Li, Y., Liu, C.: Effective fault localization using weighted test cases. J. Soft. **9**, 08 (2014)
37. Schuppan, V., Biere, A.: Shortest counterexamples for symbolic model checking of LTL with past. In: Halbwachs, N., Zuck, L.D. (eds.) TACAS 2005. LNCS, vol. 3440, pp. 493–509. Springer, Heidelberg (2005). https://doi.org/10.1007/978-3-540-31980-1_32
38. Griesmayer, A., Staber, S., Bloem, R.: Fault localization using a model checker. Softw. Test. Verif. Reliab. **20**(2), 149–173 (2010)
39. Birch, G., Fischer, B., Poppleton, M.: Fast test suite-driven model-based fault localisation with application to pinpointing defects in student programs. Soft. Syst. Model. (2017)
40. Gopinath, D., Zaeem, R.N., Khurshid, S.: Improving the effectiveness of spectra-based fault localization using specifications. In: Proceedings of the 27th IEEE/ACM ASE, pp. 40–49 (2012)
41. Fey, G., Staber, S., Bloem, R., Drechsler, R.: Automatic fault localization for property checking. CAD **27**(6), 1138–1149 (2008)

42. Vidacs, L., Beszedes, A., Tengeri, D., Siket, I., Gyimothy, T.: Test suite reduction for fault detection and localization. In: CSMR-WCRE, pp. 204–213, February 2014
43. Xuan, J., Monperrus, M.: Test case purification for improving fault localization. In: FSE, FSE 2014, pp. 52–63. ACM (2014)
44. Alves, E., Gligoric, M., Jagannath, V., d'Amorim, M.: Fault-localization using dynamic slicing and change impact analysis. In: ASE, pp. 520–523 (2011)
45. Xiaolin, J., Jiang, S., Chen, X., Wang, X., Zhang, Y., Cao, H.: HSFal: effective fault localization using hybrid spectrum of full slices and execution slices. J. Syst. Softw. **90**, 3–17 (2014)

TCM: Test Case Mutation to Improve Crash Detection in Android

Yavuz Koroglu$^{(\boxtimes)}$ and Alper Sen

Department of Computer Engineering, Bogazici University, Istanbul, Turkey
{yavuz.koroglu,alper.sen}@boun.edu.tr

Abstract. GUI testing of mobile applications gradually became a very important topic in the last decade with the growing mobile application market. We propose Test Case Mutation (TCM) which mutates existing test cases to produce richer test cases. These mutated test cases detect crashes that are not previously detected by existing test cases. TCM differs from the well-known Mutation Testing (MT) where mutations are inserted in the source code of an Application Under Test (AUT) to measure the quality of test cases. Whereas in TCM, we modify existing test cases and obtain new ones to increase the number of detected crashes. Android applications take the largest portion of the mobile application market. Hence, we evaluate TCM on Android by replaying mutated test cases of randomly selected 100 AUTs from F-Droid benchmarks. We show that TCM is effective at detecting new crashes in a given time budget.

1 Introduction

As of April 2016, there are over 2.6 billion smartphone users worldwide and this number is expected to go up [1]. There is an increasing focus on mobile application testing starting from the last decade in top testing conferences and journals [2]. Android applications have the largest share in the mobile application market, where 82.8% of all mobile applications are designed for Android [1]. Therefore, we focus on Android GUI Testing in this paper.

The main idea of TCM is to mutate existing test cases to produce richer test cases in order to increase the number of detected crashes. We first identify typical crash patterns that exist in Android applications. Then, we develop mutation operators based on these crash patterns. Typically mutation operators are applied to the source code of applications. However, in our work we apply them to test cases.

Typical crash patterns in Android are Unhandled Exceptions, External Errors, Resource Unavailability, Semantic Errors, and Network-Based Crashes [3]. We describe one case study for each crash pattern. We define six novel mutation operators (Loop-Stressing, Pause-Resume, Change Text, Toggle Contextual State, Remove Delays, and Faster Swipe) and relate them to these five crash patterns.

© The Author(s) 2018
A. Russo and A. Schürr (Eds.): FASE 2018, LNCS 10802, pp. 264–280, 2018.
https://doi.org/10.1007/978-3-319-89363-1_15

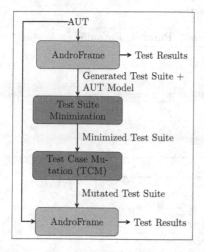

Fig. 1. TCM overview

We implement TCM on top of AndroFrame [4], a fully automated Android GUI testing tool. We give an overview of TCM in Fig. 1. First, we generate a test suite for the Application Under Test (AUT) using AndroFrame. AndroFrame obtains an AUT Model which is represented as an Extended Labeled Transition System (ELTS). We then minimize the Generated Test Suite using the AUT Model in order to reduce test execution costs (Test Suite Minimization). We apply Test Case Mutation (TCM) on the Minimized Test Suite and obtain a Mutated Test Suite. We use AndroFrame to execute the Mutated Test Suite and collect Test Results.

We state our contributions as follows:

1. *Test Case Mutation Operators.* We define six mutation operators on Android test cases to uncover new crashes. Our mutation operators are based on typical Android crash patterns described in the literature [3]. All of the mutation operators are novel with the exception of changing text inputs. To the best of our knowledge, ours is the first work to use mutation-based test case generation to detect different crash patterns in Android.
2. *Test Case Mutation (TCM) Algorithm.* We describe a novel algorithm to generate new test cases from existing ones to detect more crashes.
3. *Test Suite Minimization Algorithm.* We propose a coverage-based minimization algorithm to increase the effectiveness of TCM.
4. *Case Studies.* We relate known Android crash patterns to our mutation operators using case studies from F-Droid benchmarks.
5. *Experiments.* We evaluate TCM for crash detection of 100 AUTs downloaded from F-Droid benchmarks. We investigate how coverage and number of detected crashes change with respect to time.

2   Background

In this section, we first describe the basics of the Android GUI to facilitate the understanding of our paper.

Android GUI is based on *activities*, *events*, and *crashes*. An *activity* is a container for a set of GUI components. These GUI components can be seen on the Android screen. Each GUI component has properties that describe boundaries of the component in pixels (x_1, y_1, x_2, y_2) and how the user can interact with the component (*enabled*, *clickable*, *longclickable*, *scrollable*, *password*). Each GUI component also has a *type* property from which we can understand whether the component accepts text input. A GUI component accepts text input if its *password* property is *true* or its *type* is *EditText*.

Table 1. List of GUI actions

Non-contextual	Param1	Param2	Param3	Param4	Param5
Click	x	y	-	-	-
Longclick	x	y	-	-	-
Text	x	y	string	-	-
Swipe	x1	y1	x2	y2	duration
Menu	-	-	-	-	-
Back	-	-	-	-	-

Contextual	Parameter
Connectivity	on/off/toggle
Bluetooth	on/off/toggle
Location	gps/gps&network/off/toggle
Planemode	on/off/toggle
Doze	on/off/toggle

Special	Param1	Param2	Param3	Param4	Param5
Reinitialize	Package	Activity	-	-	-

The Android system and the user can interact with GUI components using *events*. We divide events in two categories, *system events* and *GUI events (actions)*. We show the list of GUI actions that we use in Table 1, which covers more actions then are typically used in the literature. Note that GUI actions in Table 1 are possible inputs from the user whereas system events are not. We group actions into three categories; non-contextual, contextual, and special. Non-contextual actions correspond to actions that are triggered by user gestures. *Click* and *longclick* take two parameters, x and y coordinates to click on. *Text* takes three parameters, x and y for coordinates and string to describe what to write. *Swipe* takes five parameters. The first four parameters describe the starting and the ending coordinates. The fifth parameter is used to adjust the speed of *swipe*. *Menu* and *back* actions have no parameters. These actions just click to the menu and back buttons of the mobile device, respectively. Contextual actions correspond to the user changing the contextual state of the AUT. Contextual state is the concatenation of the global attributes of the mobile device (internet connectivity, bluetooth, location, planemode, sleeping). The *connectivity* action adjusts the internet connectivity of the mobile device (adjusts wifi or mobile data according to which is available for the mobile device). *Bluetooth*, *location*, and *planemode* are straightforward. The *doze* action taps the power button of the mobile device and puts the device to sleep or wakes it. We use the *doze* action to pause and resume the AUT. Our only special action is *reinitialize*, which reinstalls and starts an AUT. System events are system generated events, e.g. *battery level*, *receiving SMS*, *clock/timer*.

We report a *crash* whenever a fatal exception is recorded in Android logs similar to previous work [3,5]. Crashes often result with the AUT terminating with or without any warning. Some crashes do not visually affect the execution, but the AUT halts as a result.

We use the *Extended Labeled Transition System* (ELTS) [6] as a model for the AUT. Formally, an ELTS $M = (V, v_0, Z, \omega, \lambda)$ is a 5-tuple, where

- V is a set of *states* (vertices),
- $v_0 \in V$ is the *initial state*,
- Z is the set of all *actions* (input alphabet),
- $\omega : V \times V \times Z$ is the *state transition relation*, and
- $\lambda : V \to \wp(Z)$ is a *state labeling function*, where $\forall v \in V, \lambda(v) \subseteq Z$ denotes the set of actions enabled at state v.

We define a GUI state, or simply a *state* v to be the concatenation of the (1) package name (a name representing the AUT), (2) activity name, (3) contextual state, and (4) GUI components.

Each state v has a set of enabled actions $\lambda(v)$, extracted from its set of GUI components. We say that a GUI action, or simply an *action* $z \in \lambda(v)$ *is enabled* at state v iff we can deduce that z interacts with at least one GUI component in v.

A *transition* is a 3-tuple, (start-state, end-state, action), shortly denoted by (v_s, v_e, z). We extend the standard transition and define a *delayed transition* as a 4-tuple, (start-state, end-state, action, delay in seconds), shortly denoted by (v_s, v_e, z, d). We do this to later change the duration of transitions via mutation. We define an execution trace, or simply a *trace* t, as a sequence of delayed transitions. An example trace can be given as $t = (v_1, v_2, z_1, d_1), (v_2, v_3, z_2, d_2), \ldots, (v_n, v_{n+1}, z_n, d_n)$ where n is the *length* of the trace.

We say that a trace t is a *test case* if the first state of the trace is the initial state v_0 (the GUI state when the AUT is started). A *test suite* TS is a set of test cases. AndroFrame generates these test suites. Then, TCM applies minimization and mutation to generate new test suites.

3 Android Crash Patterns and Mutation Operators

In this section, we first describe typical crash patterns for Android applications based on related work in the literature [3]. We give a list of the crash patterns in Table 2 and describe them below.

3.1 Android Crash Patterns

C1. Unhandled Exceptions. An AUT may crash due to misuse of libraries or GUI components, e.g. overuse of a third party library (stressing) may cause the third party library to crash.

C2. External Errors. An AUT may communicate with external applications. This communication requires either permissions or valid Inter Process Communication (IPC) for Android. There are three types of IPC in Android; intents, binders, and shared memory. Intents are used to send messages between applications. These messages are called bundles. Binders are used to invoke methods of other applications. An AUT may crash with an external error due to (1) the AUT attempts to communicate with another application without sufficient permissions, (2) the AUT receives an intent with an invalid bundle from another application, (3) the AUT sends an intent with an invalid bundle and fails to receive an answer due to a crash in the other application, (4) another application uses a binder with illegal arguments, (5) the AUT uses a binder on another application with illegal arguments and fails to receive the return value due to a crash in the other application, or (6) shared memory of the AUT is freed by another application.

Table 2. Relating crash patterns and mutation operators

Crash patterns	Mutation operators
C1. Unhandled Exceptions	M1, M3, M6
C2. External Errors	M1, M4, M5, M6
C3. Resource Unavailability	M2, M5
C4. Semantic Errors	M3
C5. Network-Based Crashes	M4, M5, M6

C3. Resource Unavailability. In Android, an AUT may be paused at any time by executing an *onPause()* method. This method is very brief and does not necessarily afford enough time to perform save operations. The *onPause()* method may terminate prematurely if its operations take too much time, causing a resource unavailability problem that may crash the AUT when it is resumed. Another problem is that an AUT may use one or more system resources such as memory and sensor handlers (e.g. orientation) during execution. When the AUT is paused, it releases system resources. The AUT may crash if it is unable to allocate these resources back when it is resumed.

C4. Semantic Errors. An AUT may crash if it fails to handle certain inputs given by the user. For example, AUT may crash instead of generating a warning if some textbox is left empty, or contains an unexpected text.

C5. Network-Based Crashes. An AUT may connect with remote servers or peers via *bluetooth* or *wifi*. The AUT may crash and terminate if it does not handle the cases where the server is unreachable, the connectivity is disabled, or the communicated data causes an error in the AUT.

3.2 Mutation Operators

We now define the set of Android mutation operators that we developed. We denote these operators by Δ. We describe these mutation operators, then relate them to the crash patterns above, and summarize these relations in Table 2.

Definition 1. *A mutation operator δ is a function which takes a test case t and returns a new test case t'. We denote a mutation as $t' = \delta(t)$.*

M1. Loop-Stressing (δ_{LS}). $t' = \delta_{LS}(t)$ reexecutes all looping actions of a test case t multiple times with d' second delay. An action z_i of a delayed transition $t_i = (v_i, v_{i+1}, z_i, d_i)$ in t is *looping* iff $v_{i+1} = v_i$. Let $t_{j...k}$ denote the subsequence of actions between j^{th} and k^{th} indices of test case t, inclusively. Then,

$$\delta_{LS}(t) = t_1^{ls} \cdot t_2^{ls} \cdot \ldots \cdot t_n^{ls} \text{ where } t_i^{ls} = \begin{cases} t_i & v_i \neq v_{i+1} \\ \underbrace{t_i' \cdot t_i' \cdot \ldots \cdot t_i'}_{m \text{ times}} & v_i = v_{i+1} \end{cases} \quad (1)$$

Here n is the length of test case t and $t_i' = (v_i, v_{i+1}, z_i, d')$. We pick $d' = 1$ to avoid double-click, which may be programmed as a separate action than single click. We pick $m = 9$. We have two motivations for choosing $m = 9$. First, in our case studies, we did not encounter a crash when $m < 9$. Second, although we detect the same crash when $m > 9$, we want to keep m as small as possible to keep test cases small. Loop-stressing may lead to an unhandled exception (C1) due to stressing the third party libraries by invoking them repeatedly. Loop-stressing may also lead to an external error (C2) if it stresses another application until it crashes.

M2. Pause-Resume (δ_{PR}). $t' = \delta_{PR}(t)$ adds two consecutive *doze* actions between all transitions of the test case t. Let $t_i^{pr} = (v_i, doze\ off, 2) \cdot (v_i, doze\ on, 2)$. Then,

$$\delta_{PR}(t) = t_1^{pr} \cdot t_1 \cdot t_2^{pr} \cdot t_2 \cdot \ldots \cdot t_n^{pr} \cdot t_n \quad (2)$$

Pause-resume may trigger a crash due to resource unavailability (C3).

M3. Change Text (δ_{CT}). We assume that existing test cases contain well-behaving text inputs to explore the AUT as much as possible. To increase the number of detected crashes, we modify the contents of the texts.

$t' = \delta_{CT}(t)$ first picks one random abnormal text manipulation operation and applies it to a random *textentry* action of the existing test case t. Abnormal text manipulation operations can be *emptytext*, *dottext*, and *longtext* where *emptytext* deletes the text, *dottext* enters a singe dot character, and *longtext* enters a random string of length >200.

Let z_i^{ct} denote a random abnormal text manipulation action where z_i is a text action and d_i^{ct} denotes the new delay required to completely execute z_i^{ct}. We define $t' = \delta_{CT}(t)$ on test cases as follows:

$$\delta_{CT}(t) = \begin{cases} t & \nexists z_i = textentry \\ t_{1...i-1} \cdot t_i^{ct} \cdot t_{i+1...n} & \text{otherwise} \end{cases} \quad (3)$$

where n is the length of t and $t_i^{ct} = (v_i, v_{i+1}, z_i^{ct}, d_i^{ct})$. An AUT may crash because the corresponding *onTextChange()* method of the AUT throws an unhandled exception (C1). The AUT may also crash if the content of the text is an unexpected kind of input, which causes a semantic error later (C3).

M4. Toggle Contextual State (δ_{TCS}). Existing test suites typically lack contextual actions where the condition of the contextual state is crucial to generate the crash. Therefore, we introduce contextual state toggling with $t' = \delta_{TCS}(t)$ which is defined as follows.

$$\delta_{TCS}(t) = t_1 \cdot t_1^{tcs} \cdot t_2 \cdot t_2^{tcs} \cdot \ldots \cdot t_n \cdot t_n^{tcs} \qquad (4)$$

where n is the length of test case t and t_i^{tcs} is a contextual action transition $(v_{i+1}, v_{i+1}, z^{tcs}, d')$. z^{tcs} corresponds to a random contextual toggle action. We pick $d' = 10\,\text{s}$ for each contextual action since Android may take a long time before it stabilizes after the change of contextual state. Toggling the contextual states of the AUT may result in an external error (C2), or a network-based crash if the connection failures are not handled correctly (C5).

M5. Remove Delays (δ_{RD}). $t' = \delta_{RD}(t)$ takes a test case t and sets all of its delays to 0. When reproduced, the events of t' will be in the same order with t, but sent to the AUT at the earliest possible time.

$$\delta_{RD}(t) = (v_1, v_2, z_1, 0) \cdot (v_2, v_3, z_2, 0) \cdot \ldots \cdot (v_n, v_{n+1}, z_n, 0) \qquad (5)$$

If the AUT is communicating with another application, removing delays may cause the requests to crash the other application. If this case is not handled in the AUT, the AUT crashes due to external errors (C2). If the AUT's background process is affected by the GUI actions, removing delays may cause the background process to crash due to resource unavailability (C3). If the GUI actions trigger network requests, having no delays may cause a network-based crash (C5).

M6. Faster Swipe (δ_{FS}). $t' = \delta_{FS}(t)$ increases the speed of all swipe actions of a test case t. Let z_i^{fs} denote a faster version of z_i, where z_i is a *swipe* action. Then, we define δ_{FS} on test cases with at least one *swipe* action as follows.

$$\delta_{FS}(t) = t_1^{fs} \cdot t_2^{fs} \cdot \ldots \cdot t_n^{fs} \qquad (6)$$

where n is the length of test case t and

$$t_i^{fs} = \begin{cases} (v_i, v_{i+1}, z_i, d_i) & z_i \text{ is NOT a } swipe \\ (v_i, v_{i+1}, z_i^{fs}, d_i) & \text{otherwise} \end{cases}$$

If the information presented by the AUT is downloaded from a network or another application, swiping too fast may cause a network-based crash (C3) due to the network being unable to provide the necessary data or an external error (C2). If the AUT is a game, swiping too fast may cause the AUT to throw an unhandled exception (C1).

Algorithm 1. Test Suite Minimization Algorithm

Require:
  TS : A test suite for the AUT
  M : AUT Model
Ensure:
  TS' : Minimized Test Suite

1: $TS' \leftarrow \emptyset$
2: **for** $t \in \{t : t \in TS \wedge t$ does not crash$\}$ **do**   ▷ Iterate over non-crashing test cases
3:    **if** $\text{cov}_M(TS' \cup \{t\}) > \text{cov}_\omega(TS')$ **then**   ▷ Take only the test cases that increase coverage
4:       $t' \leftarrow \underset{i}{\operatorname{argmin}} \, t_{1...i}$ **s.t.** $\text{cov}_M(TS' \cup \{t_{1...i}\}) = \text{cov}_M(TS' \cup \{t\})$ ▷ Shorten the test case
5:          $TS' \leftarrow TS' \cup \{t'\}$ ▷ Add the shortened test case to the Minimized Test Suite
6:    **end if**
7: **end for**

Algorithm 2. Test Case Mutation (TCM) Algorithm

Require:
  TS : A Test Suite
  X : Timeout of the New Test Suite
  Δ: Set of Mutation Operators
Ensure:
  TS' : New Test Suite

1: $TS' \leftarrow \{\}$
2: $x \leftarrow 0$
3: **repeat**
4:    $t \leftarrow$ random $t \in TS$ ▷ Pick a random test case
5:    $\delta \leftarrow$ random $\delta \in \Delta$ **s.t.** $t \neq \delta(t)$ ▷ Pick a mutation operator that changes the test case
6:    $t' \leftarrow \delta(t)$ ▷ Apply the mutation operator to the test case
7:    $TS' \leftarrow TS' \cup \{t'\}$ ▷ Add the mutated test case to the New Test Suite
8:    $x \leftarrow x + \sum_{(v_s, v_e, z, d) \in t'} d$ ▷ Calculate the total delay
9: **until** $x > X$ ▷ Repeat until the total delay is above the given timeout

---

4   Test Suite Minimization and Test Case Mutation

Before mutating the existing test cases in a test suite TS, we first minimize TS. In order to minimize a test suite TS, we first define an edge coverage function $\text{cov}_\omega(TS)$ over the AUT model M as follows:

$$\text{cov}_M(TS) = \frac{\text{\# of unique transitions covered in the AUT Model } M \text{ by } TS}{\text{\# of all transitions in the AUT Model } M}$$

(7)

We present our Test Suite Minimization approach in Algorithm 1. We iterate over all non-crashing test cases of the original test suite TS in line 2. We use non-crashing test cases in Algorithm 1 because our goal is to generate crashes from non-crashing via mutation. We check if the test case t increases the edge coverage in line 3. If t increases the edge coverage, we shorten the test case t from its end by deleting transitions that are not contributing to the edge coverage and add the shortened test case t' to the minimized test suite.

We present our Test Case Mutation approach in Algorithm 2. We pick a random test case t from given TS in line 4. Then, we pick a random mutation operator δ that changes t in line 5. We mutate t with δ and add the mutated test case t' to TS' until the total delay of TS' exceeds the given timeout X.

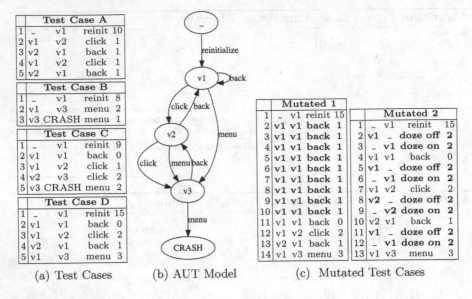

Test Case A			
1	_	v1	reinit 10
2	v1	v2	click 1
3	v2	v1	back 1
4	v1	v2	click 1
5	v2	v1	back 1

Test Case B			
1	_	v1	reinit 8
2	v1	v3	menu 2
3	v3	CRASH	menu 1

Test Case C			
1	_	v1	reinit 9
2	v1	v1	back 0
3	v1	v2	click 1
4	v2	v3	click 2
5	v3	CRASH	menu 2

Test Case D			
1	_	v1	reinit 15
2	v1	v1	back 0
3	v1	v2	click 2
4	v2	v1	back 1
5	v1	v3	menu 3

Mutated 1			
1	_	v1	reinit 15
2	v1	v1	back 1
3	v1	v1	back 1
4	v1	v1	back 1
5	v1	v1	back 1
6	v1	v1	back 1
7	v1	v1	back 1
8	v1	v1	back 1
9	v1	v1	back 1
10	v1	v1	back 1
11	v1	v1	back 0
12	v1	v2	click 2
13	v2	v1	back 1
14	v1	v3	menu 3

Mutated 2			
1	_	v1	reinit 15
2	v1	_	doze off 2
3	_	v1	doze on 2
4	v1	v1	back 0
5	v1	_	doze off 2
6	_	v1	doze on 2
7	v1	v2	click 2
8	v2	_	doze off 2
9	_	v2	doze on 2
10	v2	v1	back 1
11	v1	_	doze off 2
12	_	v1	doze on 2
13	v1	v3	menu 3

(a) Test Cases   (b) AUT Model   (c) Mutated Test Cases

Fig. 2. Motivating example (mutations are denoted as bold)

5   Motivating Example

Figures 2a and b show a test suite and an AUT model, respectively. We generate this test suite and the AUT model by executing AndroFrame for one minute on an example AUT. We execute AndroFrame for just one minute, because that is enough to generate test cases for this example. We limit the maximum number of transitions per test case to five to keep the test cases small in this motivating example for ease of presentation. The test suite has four test cases; A, B, C, and D. Each row of test cases describes a delayed transition. The *click* action has coordinates, but we abstract this information for the sake of simplicity.

Among the four test cases reported by AndroFrame, we take only the non-crashing test cases, A and D. In our example, we include D since it increases the edge coverage and we exclude A since all of A's transitions are also D's transitions, i.e. A is subsumed by D. Then, we attempt to minimize test case D without reducing the edge coverage. In our example, we don't remove any transitions from D because all transitions in D contribute to the edge coverage. We then generate mutated test cases by randomly applying mutation operators to D one by one until we reach one minute timeout. Figure 2c shows an example mutated test suite. Test case Mutated 1 takes D and exercises the back button for multiple times to stress the loop at state v1. Test case Mutated 2 clicks the hardware power button twice (doze off, doze on) between each transition. This operation pauses and resumes the AUT in our test devices. We then execute all mutated test cases on the AUT. Our example AUT in fact crashes when the loop on v_1 is reexecuted more than eight times and also crashes when the AUT is paused in state v_2. When executed, our mutated test cases reveal these crashes both at their ninth transition, doubling the number of detected crashes.

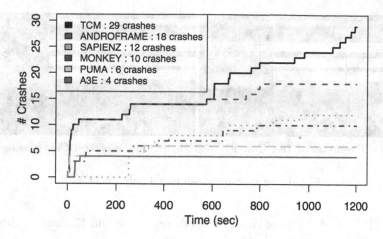

Fig. 3. Number of total distinct crashes detected across time

6   Evaluation

In this section, we evaluate TCM via experiments and case studies. We show that, through experiments, we improve crash detection. We then show, with case studies, how we detect crash patterns.

6.1   Experiments

We selected 100 AUTs (excluding the case studies described later) from F-Droid benchmarks [7] for experiments. To evaluate the improvement in crash detection, we first execute AndroFrame, Sapienz, PUMA, Monkey, and A^3E for 20 min each on these applications with no mutations enabled on test cases. Then we execute TCM with 10 min for AndroFrame to generate test cases and 10 min to mutate the generated test cases and replay them to detect more crashes. AndroFrame requires the maximum length of a test case as a parameter. We used its default parameter, 80 transitions maximum per test case.

Figure 3 shows the number of total distinct crashes detected by each tool across time. Whenever a crash occurs, the Android system logs the resulting stack trace. We say that two crashes are distinct if stack traces of these crashes are different.

Our results show that AndroFrame detects more crashes than any other tool from very early on. TCM detects the same number of crashes with AndroFrame for the first 10 min (600 s). During that time, AndroFrame detects 15 crashes. In the last 10 min, TCM detects 14 more crashes whereas AndroFrame detects only 3 more crashes. As a result TCM detects 29 crashes in total whereas AndroFrame detects 18 crashes in total. As a last note, all other tools including AndroFrame seem to stabilize after 20 min whereas TCM finds many crashes near timeout. This shows us that TCM may find even more crashes when timeout is longer.

   (a) Execution of Test Case t (b) Execution of Test Case $t' = \delta_{\mathrm{CT}}(t)$

Fig. 4. An example crash found only by TCM

Overall, TCM finds 14 more crashes than AndroFrame and 17 more crashes than Sapienz, the best among other tools.

We also investigate how much each mutation operator contributes to the number of detected crashes. Our observations reveal that M1 (δ_{LS}) detects one crash, M2 (δ_{PR}) detects four crashes, M3 (δ_{CT}) detects two crashes, M4 (δ_{TCS}) detects two crashes, M5 (δ_{RD}) detects four crashes, and M6 (δ_{FS}) detects one crash. These crashes add up to 14, which is the number of crashes detected by TCM in the last 10 min. This result shows that while all mutation operators contribute to the crash detection, M2 and M5 have the largest contribution.

We present and explain one crash that is found only by TCM in Fig. 4. Figure 4a shows an instance where AndroFrame generates and executes a test case t on the Yahtzee application. Note that t does not lead to a crash, but only a warning message. Figure 4b shows the instance where TCM mutates t and executes the mutated test case t'. When t' is executed, the application crashes and terminates. We note that this crash was not found by any other tool. Mao et al. [8] also report that Sapienz and Dynodroid did not find any crashes in this application.

6.2 Case Studies

In this section, we verify that the aforementioned crash patterns exist via case studies, one case study for each crash pattern. These studies verify that all of our crash patterns are observable in Android platform. These case studies help us develop and fine-tune our mutation operators.

Case Study 1. Figure 5a shows a crashing activity of the *SoundBoard* application included in F-Droid benchmarks. Basically, the *coin* and *tube* buttons activate a third party library, AudioFlinger, to produce sound when tapped. AndroFrame generates test cases which tap these buttons. These test cases produce no crashes. Then, we mutate the test cases with TCM. When we apply *loop-stressing* (M1) on any of these buttons, AudioFlinger crashes due to overuse. AudioFlinger produces a fatal exception (C1) in Android logs. This crash does not cause an abnormal termination, but it causes the AUT to stop functioning (the AUT stops producing sounds until it is restarted).

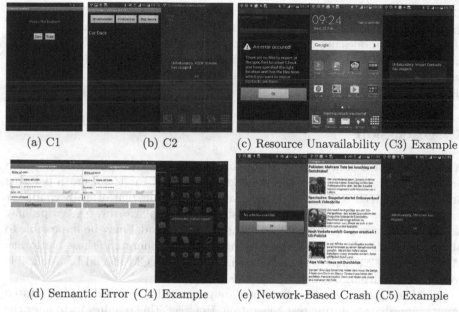

(a) C1   (b) C2   (c) Resource Unavailability (C3) Example

(d) Semantic Error (C4) Example   (e) Network-Based Crash (C5) Example

C1: Unhandled Exception (C1) Example
C2: External Error (C2) Example

Fig. 5. Case studies 1–5

Case Study 2. Figure 5b shows a crashing activity of the *a2dpVol* application included in F-Droid benchmarks, where AndroFrame fails to generate crashing test cases. We mutate these test cases with TCM. When we activate bluetooth (M4), tapping *find devices* button produces a crash in the external *android.bluetooth.IBluetooth* application due to a missing method (C2) and the AUT terminates.

Case Study 3. Figure 5c shows a crashing activity of the *importcontacts* application included in F-Droid benchmarks. The AUT handles the case that it fails to import contacts, as we show in the leftmost screen. Pausing the AUT at this screen causes the background process to abort and free its allocated memory (we show the related screen in the middle). However, the paused activity is not destroyed. If the user tries to resume this activity, the AUT crashes as we show in the rightmost screen, since the memory was freed before. TCM applies a pause-resume mutation (M2) and triggers this resource unavailability crash (C3).

Case Study 4. Figure 5d shows a crashing activity of the *aCal* application included in F-Droid benchmarks. AndroFrame generates test cases with well-behaving text inputs. These test cases produce no crashes. Then, we mutate the test cases with TCM. When we apply *change text* (M3) on the last text box and then tap the *configure* button, this produces a semantic error (C4). The AUT crashes and terminates.

Case Study 5. Figure 5e shows a crashing activity of the *Mirrored* application included in F-Droid benchmarks. When *wifi* is turned off, the AUT goes into offline mode and does not crash as shown in the leftmost screen. When we toggle *wifi* (M4), the AUT retrieves several articles as shown in the middle, but crashes when it fails to retrieve article contents due to a network-based crash (C5) as shown in the rightmost screen.

7   Discussion

Although TCM is conceptually applicable to different GUI platforms, e.g. iOS or a desktop computer, there are three key challenges. First, our crash patterns are not guaranteed to exist or be observable in different platforms. Second, our mutation operators may not be applicable to those platforms, e.g. swipe may not be available as a gesture. Third, either an AUT model may be impossible to obtain or a replayable test case may be impossible to generate in those platforms. When all these challenges are addressed, we believe TCM should be applicable to not just Android, but other platforms as well.

TCM mutates test cases after they are generated. We could apply mutated inputs immediately during test generation. However, this requires us to alter the test generation process which may not be possible if a third party test generation tool is used. Our approach is conceptually applicable to any test generation tool without altering the test generation tool.

We use an edge coverage criterion to minimize a given test suite. Because of this the original test suite covers potentially more paths than the minimized test suite and therefore explores the same edge in different contexts. Without minimization, test cases in the test suite are too many and too large to generate enough mutations to observe crashes in given timeout. Therefore, we argue that by minimizing the test suite we improve the crash detection performance of TCM at the cost of the test suite's completeness in terms of a higher coverage criterion than edge coverage.

Although TCM detects crashes, it does not detect all possible bug patterns. Qin et al. [9] thoroughly classifies all bugs in Android. According to this classification, there are two types of bugs in Android, Bohrbugs and Mandelbugs. A Bohrbug is a bug whose reachability and propagation are simple. A Mandelbug is a bug whose reachability and propagation are complicated. Qin et al. further categorize Mandelbugs as Aging Related Bugs (ARB) and Non-Aging Related Mandelbugs (NAM). Qin et al. also define five subtypes for NAM and six subtypes for ARB. TCM detects only the first two subtypes of NAM, TIM and SEQ. TIM and SEQ are the only kinds of bugs which are triggered by user inputs. If a bug is TIM, the error is caused by the timing of inputs. If a bug is SEQ, the error is caused by the sequencing of inputs.

We note two key points on the crash patterns of TCM. First, testing tools we compare TCM with only detect SEQ bugs. TCM introduces the detection of TIM bugs in addition to SEQ bugs. Second, Azim et al. [3] further divides SEQ and TIM bugs into six crash patterns. We base our crash patterns on these crash patterns. We present both external errors and permission violations as one crash pattern since permission violations occur as attempts to communicate with external applications with insufficient permissions. As a result, we obtain five crash patterns.

We did not encounter any crash patterns other than the five crash patterns that we describe in Sect. 3. However, it is still possible to observe other crash patterns with our mutation operators due to emerging crash patterns caused by the fragmentation and fast development of the Android platform.

Our mutation operators insert multiple transitions to the test case, creating an issue of locating the fault inducing transition. Given that the mutated test case detects a crash, fault localization can be achieved using a variant of *delta debugging* [10].

We use regular expressions on the Android logs to detect crashes. In the experiment, we only detected *FATAL EXCEPTION* labeled errors as done in previous work [3,5], ignoring Application Not Responding (ANR) and other errors described by Carino and Andrews [11]. Although we believe that TCM would still detect more crashes than pure AndroFrame (fatal exception is the most common crash in Android), we will improve our crash detection procedure as a future work to give more accurate results.

We randomly selected 100 Android applications from the well-known F-Droid benchmarks also used by other testing tools [7]. We show that these applications have similar characteristics with the rest of F-Droid applications in our previous work.

8 Related Work

Test Case Mutation (TCM) differs from the well-known Mutation Testing (MT) [12] where mutations are inserted in the source code of an AUT to measure the quality of existing test cases. Whereas in TCM, we update existing test cases to increase the number of detected crashes. Oliveria et al. [13] are the first to suggest using Mutation Testing (MT) for GUIs. Deng et al. [14] define several source code level mutation operators for Android applications to measure the quality of existing test suites.

The concept of Test Case Mutation is not new. In Android GUI Testing, Sapienz [8] and EvoDroid [15] are Android testing tools that use evolutionary algorithms, and therefore mutation operators. Sapienz shuffles the orders of the events, whereas EvoDroid mutates the test case in two ways: (1) EvoDroid transforms text inputs and (2) EvoDroid either injects, swaps, or removes events. TCM mutates not only text inputs, but also introduces 5 more novel mutation operators. Furthermore, Sapienz and EvoDroid use their mutation operators for both exploration and crash detection whereas we specialize TCM's mutation operators for crash detection only. In Standard GUI Testing, MuCRASH [16] uses test case mutation via defining special mutation operators on test cases, where the operators are defined at the source code level. They use TCM for crash reproduction, whereas ours is the first work that uses TCM to discover new crashes. Directed Test Suite Augmentation (DTSA) introduced by

Xu et al. in 2010 [17] also mutates existing test cases but for the goal of achieving a target branch coverage.

We implement TCM on AndroFrame [4]. AndroFrame is one of the state-of-the-art Android GUI Testing tools. AndroFrame finds more crashes than other available alternatives in the literature such as A^3E and Sapienz. These tools generate replayable test cases as well. They provide the necessary utilities to replay their generated test cases. We can mutate these test cases but most of our mutations won't be applicable for two reasons. First, A^3E and Sapienz do not learn a model from which we can extract looping actions. Second, A^3E and Sapienz do not support contextual state toggling. Implementing all of our mutations on top of these tools is possible, but requires a significant amount of engineering effort. Therefore we implement TCM on top of AndroFrame.

Other black-box testing tools in the literature include A^3E [18], SwiftHand [6], PUMA [19], DynoDroid [20], Sapienz [8], EvoDroid [15], CrashScope [5] and MobiGUITAR [21]. From these applications, only EvoDroid, CrashScope, and MobiGUITAR are publicly unavailable.

Monkey is a simple random generation-based fuzz tester for Android. Monkey detects the largest number of crashes among other black-box testing tools. Generation-based fuzz testing is a popular approach in Android GUI Testing, which basically generates random or unexpected inputs. Fuzzing could be completely random as in Monkey, or more intelligent by detecting relevant events as in Dynodroid [20]. TCM can be viewed as a mutation-based fuzz testing tool, where we modify existing test cases rather than generating test cases from scratch. TCM can be implemented on top of Monkey or DynoDroid to improve crash detection of these tools.

Baek and Bae [22] define a comparison criterion for Android GUI states. AndroFrame uses the maximum comparison level described in this work, which makes our models as fine-grained as possible for black-box testing.

9   Conclusion

In this study, we developed a novel test case mutation technique that allows us to increase detection of crashes in Android applications. We defined six mutation operators for GUI test cases and relate them to commonly occurring crash patterns in Android applications. We obtained test cases through a state-of-the-art Android GUI testing tool, called AndroFrame. We showed with several case studies that our mutation operators are able to uncover new crashes.

As a future work, we plan to study a broader set of GUI actions, such as *rotation* and *doubleclick*. We will improve our mutation algorithm by sampling mutation operators from a probability distribution based on crash rates rather than a uniform distribution. We will find the most optimal timings for executing the test generator and TCM, rather than dividing the available time into two equal halves. We will further investigate Android crash patterns.

References

1. Piejko, P.: 16 mobile market statistics you should know in 2016 (2016). https://deviceatlas.com/blog/16-mobile-market-statistics-you-should-know-2016
2. Zein, S., Salleh, N., Grundy, J.: A systematic mapping study of mobile application testing techniques. J. Syst. Softw. **117**, 334–356 (2016)
3. Azim, T., Neamtiu, I., Marvel, L.M.: Towards self-healing smartphone software via automated patching. In: 29th ACM/IEEE International Conference on Automated Software Engineering (ASE), pp. 623–628 (2014)
4. Koroglu, Y., Sen, A., Muslu, O., Mete, Y., Ulker, C., Tanriverdi, T., Donmez, Y.: QBE: QLearning-based exploration of android applications. In: IEEE International Conference on Software Testing, Verification and Validation (ICST) (2018)
5. Moran, K., Vásquez, M.L., Bernal-Cárdenas, C., Vendome, C., Poshyvanyk, D.: Automatically discovering, reporting and reproducing android application crashes. In: IEEE International Conference on Software Testing, Verification and Validation (ICST), pp. 33–44 (2016)
6. Choi, W., Necula, G., Sen, K.: Guided GUI testing of android apps with minimal restart and approximate learning. In: ACM SIGPLAN International Conference on Object Oriented Programming Systems Languages and Applications (OOPSLA), pp. 623–640 (2013)
7. Gultnieks, C.: F-Droid Benchmarks (2010). https://f-droid.org/
8. Mao, K., Harman, M., Jia, Y.: Sapienz: multi-objective automated testing for android applications. In: 25th International Symposium on Software Testing and Analysis (ISSTA), pp. 94–105 (2016)
9. Qin, F., Zheng, Z., Li, X., Qiao, Y., Trivedi, K.S.: An empirical investigation of fault triggers in android operating system. In: IEEE 22nd Pacific Rim International Symposium on Dependable Computing (PRDC), pp. 135–144 (2017)
10. Zeller, A.: Yesterday, my program worked. Today, it does not. Why? In: 7th European Software Engineering Conference Held Jointly with the 7th ACM SIGSOFT International Symposium on Foundations of Software Engineering (ESEC/FSE-7), pp. 253–267 (1999)
11. Carino, S., Andrews, J.H.: Dynamically testing GUIs using ant colony optimization. In: 30th IEEE/ACM International Conference on Automated Software Engineering (ASE), pp. 135–148 (2015)
12. Ammann, P., Offutt, J.: Introduction to Software Testing, 1st edn. Cambridge University Press, Cambridge (2008)
13. Oliveira, R.A.P., Algroth, E., Gao, Z., Memon, A.: Definition and evaluation of mutation operators for GUI-level mutation analysis. In: IEEE Eighth International Conference on Software Testing, Verification and Validation Workshops (ICSTW), pp. 1–10 (2015)
14. Deng, L., Offutt, J., Ammann, P., Mirzaei, N.: Mutation operators for testing android apps. Inf. Softw. Technol. **81**(C), 154–168 (2017)
15. Mahmood, R., Mirzaei, N., Malek, S.: EvoDroid: segmented evolutionary testing of android apps. In: 22nd ACM SIGSOFT International Symposium on Foundations of Software Engineering (FSE), pp. 599–609 (2014)
16. Xuan, J., Xie, X., Monperrus, M.: Crash reproduction via test case mutation: let existing test cases help. In: 10th Joint Meeting on Foundations of Software Engineering (ESEC/FSE), pp. 910–913 (2015)
17. Xu, Z., Kim, Y., Kim, M., Rothermel, G., Cohen, M.B.: Directed test suite augmentation: techniques and tradeoffs. In: 18th ACM SIGSOFT International Symposium on Foundations of Software Engineering (FSE), pp. 257–266 (2010)

18. Azim, T., Neamtiu, I.: Targeted and depth-first exploration for systematic testing of android apps. In: ACM SIGPLAN International Conference on Object Oriented Programming Systems Languages and Applications (OOPSLA), pp. 641–660 (2013)
19. Hao, S., Liu, B., Nath, S., Halfond, W.G., Govindan, R.: PUMA: programmable UI-automation for large-scale dynamic analysis of mobile apps. In: 12th Annual International Conference on Mobile Systems, Applications, and Services (MobiSys), pp. 204–217 (2014)
20. Machiry, A., Tahiliani, R., Naik, M.: Dynodroid: an input generation system for android apps. In: 9th Joint Meeting on Foundations of Software Engineering (ESEC/FSE), pp. 224–234 (2013)
21. Amalfitano, D., Fasolino, A.R., Tramontana, P., Ta, B.D., Memon, A.M.: MobiGUITAR: automated model-based testing of mobile apps. IEEE Softw. **32**(5), 53–59 (2015)
22. Baek, Y.M., Bae, D.H.: Automated model-based android GUI testing using multi-level GUI comparison criteria. In: 31st IEEE/ACM International Conference on Automated Software Engineering (ASE), pp. 238–249 (2016)

CRETE: A Versatile Binary-Level Concolic Testing Framework

Bo Chen[1]([⊠]) , Christopher Havlicek[2] , Zhenkun Yang[2] , Kai Cong[2] ,
Raghudeep Kannavara[2] , and Fei Xie[1]

[1] Portland State University, Portland, OR 97201, USA
{chenbo,xie}@pdx.edu
[2] Intel Corporation, Hillsboro, OR 97124, USA
{christopher.havlicek,zhenkun.yang,kai.cong,
raghudeep.kannavara}@intel.com

Abstract. In this paper, we present CRETE, a versatile binary-level concolic testing framework, which features an open and highly extensible architecture allowing easy integration of concrete execution frontends and symbolic execution engine backends. CRETE's extensibility is rooted in its modular design where concrete and symbolic execution is loosely coupled only through standardized execution traces and test cases. The standardized execution traces are LLVM-based, self-contained, and composable, providing succinct and sufficient information for symbolic execution engines to reproduce the concrete executions. We have implemented CRETE with KLEE as the symbolic execution engine and multiple concrete execution frontends such as QEMU and 8051 Emulator. We have evaluated the effectiveness of CRETE on GNU COREUTILS programs and TianoCore utility programs for UEFI BIOS. The evaluation of COREUTILS programs shows that CRETE achieved comparable code coverage as KLEE directly analyzing the source code of COREUTILS and generally outperformed ANGR. The evaluation of TianoCore utility programs found numerous exploitable bugs that were previously unreported.

1 Introduction

Symbolic execution [1] has become an increasingly important technique for automated software analysis, e.g., generating test cases, finding bugs, and detecting security vulnerabilities [2–11]. There have been many recent approaches to symbolic execution [12–22]. Generally speaking, these approaches can be classified into two categories: online symbolic execution (e.g., BitBlaze [4], KLEE [5], and s^2E [6]), and concolic execution (a.k.a., offline symbolic execution, e.g., CUTE [2], DART [3], and SAGE [7]). Online symbolic execution closely couples Symbolic Execution Engines (SEE) with the System Under Test (SUT) and explore all possible execution paths of SUT online at once. On the other hand, concolic execution decouples SEE from the SUT through traces, which concretely runs a single execution path of a SUT and then symbolically executes it.

A. Russo and A. Schürr (Eds.): FASE 2018, LNCS 10802, pp. 281–298, 2018.
https://doi.org/10.1007/978-3-319-89363-1_16

Both online and offline symbolic execution are facing new challenges, as computer software is experiencing an explosive growth, both in complexities and diversities, ushered in by the proliferation of cloud computing, mobile computing, and Internet of Things. Two major challenges are: (1) the SUT involves many types of software for different hardware platforms and (2) the SUT involves many components distributed on different machines and as a whole the SUT cannot fit in any SEE. In this paper, we focus on how to extend concolic execution to satisfy the needs for analyzing emerging software systems. There are two major observations behind our efforts on extending concolic execution:

- The decoupled architecture of concolic execution provides the flexibility in integrating new trace-captured frontends for emerging platforms.
- The trace-based nature of concolic testing offers opportunities for selectively capturing and synthesizing reduced system-level traces for scalable analysis.

We present CRETE, a versatile binary-level concolic testing framework, which features an open and highly extensible architecture allowing easy integration of concrete execution frontends and symbolic execution backends. CRETE's extensibility is rooted in its modular design where concrete and symbolic execution is loosely coupled only through standardized execution traces and test cases. The standardized execution traces are LLVM-based, self-contained, and composable, providing succinct and sufficient information for SEE to reproduce the concrete executions. The CRETE framework is composed of:

- **A CRETE tracing plugin,** which is embedded in the concrete execution environment, captures binary-level execution traces of the SUT, and stores the traces in a standardized trace format.
- **A CRETE manager,** which archives the captured execution traces and test cases, schedules concrete and symbolic execution, and implements policies for selecting the traces and test cases to be analyzed and explored next.
- **A CRETE replayer,** which is embedded in the symbolic execution environment, performs concolic execution on captured traces for test case generation.

We have implemented the CRETE framework on top of QEMU [23] and KLEE, particularly the tracing plugin for QEMU, the replayer for KLEE, and the manager that coordinates QEMU and KLEE to exchange runtime traces and test cases and manages the policies for prioritizing runtime traces and test cases. To validate CRETE extensibility, we have also implemented a tracing plugin for the 8051 emulator [24]. The trace-based architecture of CRETE has enabled us to integrate such tracing frontends seamlessly. To demonstrate its effectiveness and capability, we evaluated CRETE on GNU COREUTILS programs and TianoCore utility programs for UEFI BIOS, and compared with KLEE and ANGR, which are two state-of-art open-source symbolic executors for automated program analysis at source-level and binary-level.

The CRETE framework makes several key contributions:

- **Versatile concolic testing.** CRETE provides an open and highly extensible architecture allowing easy integration of different concrete and symbolic execution environments, which communicate with each other only by exchanging standardized traces and test cases. This significantly improves applicability and flexibility of concolic execution to emerging platforms and is amenable to leveraging new advancements in symbolic execution.

– **Standardizing runtime traces.** CRETE defines a standard binary-level trace format, which is LLVM based, self-contained and composable. Such a trace is captured during concrete execution, representing an execution path of a SUT. It contains succinct and sufficient information for reproducing the execution path in other program analysis environment, such as for symbolic execution. Having standardized traces minimizes the need of converting traces for different analysis environment and provides a basis for common trace-related optimizations.

– **Implemented a CRETE prototype.** We have implemented CRETE with KLEE as the SEE backend and multiple concrete execution frontends such as QEMU and 8051 Emulator. CRETE achieved comparable code coverage on COREUTILS binaries as KLEE directly analyzing at source-level and generally outperformed ANGR. CRETE also found 84 distinct and previously-unreported crashes on widely-used and extensively-tested utility programs for UEFI BIOS development. We also make CRETE implementation publicly available to the community at github.com/SVL-PSU/crete-dev.

2   Related Work

DART [3] and CUTE [2] are both early representative work on concolic testing. They operate on the source code level. CRETE further extends concolic testing and targets close-source binary programs. SAGE [7] is a Microsoft internal concolic testing tool that particularly targets at X86 binaries on Windows. CRETE is platform agnostic: as long as a trace from concrete execution can be converted into the LLVM-based trace format, it can be analyzed to generate test cases.

KLEE [5] is a source-level symbolic executor built on the LLVM infrastructure [25] and is capable of generating high-coverage test cases for C programs. CRETE adopts KLEE as its SEE, and extends it to perform concolic execution on standardized binary-level traces. S^2E [6] provides a framework for developing tools for analyzing close-source software programs. It augments a Virtual Machine (VM) with a SEE and path analyzers. It features a tight coupling of concrete and symbolic execution. CRETE takes a loosely coupled approach to the interaction of concrete and symbolic execution. CRETE captures complete execution traces of the SUT online and conducts whole trace symbolic analysis off-line.

BitBlaze [4] is an early representative work on binary analysis for computer security. It and its follow-up work Mayhem [8] and MergePoint [12] focus on optimizing the close coupling of concrete and symbolic execution to improve the effectiveness in detecting exploitable software bugs. CRETE has a different focus on providing an open architecture for binary-level concolic testing that enables flexible integration of various concrete and symbolic execution environments.

ANGR [14] is an extensible Python framework for binary analysis using VEX [26] as an intermediate representation (IR). It implemented a number of existing analysis techniques and enabled the comparison of different techniques in a single platform. ANGR needs to load a SUT in its own virtual environment for analysis, so it has to model the real execution environment for the SUT, like system calls and common library functions. CRETE, however, performs in-vivo binary analysis, by analyzing binary-level trace captured from unmodified execution environment of a SUT. Also, ANGR needs to maintain execution states for all paths being explored at once, while CRETE reduces memory usage dramatically by analyzing a SUT path by path and separates symbolic execution from tracing.

Our work is also related to fuzz testing [27]. A popular representative tool for fuzzing is AFL [28]. Fuzzing is fast and quite effective for bug detection; however, it can easily get stuck when a specific input, like magic number, is required to pass a check and explore new paths of a program. Concolic testing guides the generation of test cases by solving constraints from the source code or binary execution traces and is quite effective in generating complicated inputs. Therefore, fuzzing and concolic testing are complementary software testing techniques.

3   Overview

During the design of the CRETE framework for binary-level concolic testing, we have identified the following design goals:

- **Binary-level In-vivo Analysis.** It should require only the binary of the SUT and perform analysis in its real execution environment.
- **Extensibility.** It should allow easy integration of concrete execution frontends and SEE backends.
- **High Coverage.** It should achieve coverage that is not significantly lower than the coverage attainable by source-level analysis.
- **Minimal Changes to Existing Testing Processes.** It should simply provide additional test cases that can be plugged into existing testing processes without major changes to the testing processes.

To achieve the goals above, we adopts an online/offline approach to concolic testing in the design of the CRETE framework:

- **Online Tracing.** As the SUT is concretely executed in a virtual or physical machine, an online tracing plugin captures the binary-level execution trace into a trace file.
- **Offline Test Generation.** An offline SEE takes the trace as input, injects symbolic values and generates test cases. The new test cases are in turn applied to the SUT in the concrete execution.

This online tracing and offline test generation process is iterative: it repeats until all generated test cases are issued or time bounds are reached. We extend this process to satisfy our design goals as follows.

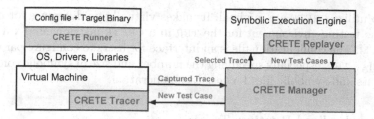

Fig. 1. CRETE architecture

- Execution traces of a SUT are captured in its unmodified execution environment on binary-level. The tracing plugin can be an extension into a VM (Sect. 4.1), a hardware tracing facility, or a dynamic binary instrumentation tool, such as PIN [29], and DynamoRIO [30].
- The concrete and symbolic execution environments are decoupled by standardized traces (Sect. 4.2). As long as they can generate and consume standardized traces, they can work together as a cohesive concolic process.
- Optimization can be explored on both tracing and test case generation, for example, selective binary-level tracing to improve scalability (Sect. 4.3), and concolic test generation to reduce test case redundancy (Sect. 4.4). This makes high-coverage test generation on binary-level possible.
- The tracing plugin is transparent to existing testing processes, as it only collects information. Therefore, no change is made to the testing processes.

4 Design

In this section, we present the design of CRETE with a VM as the concrete execution environment. The reason for selecting a VM is that it allows complete access to the whole system for tracing runtime execution states and is generally accessible as mature open-source projects.

4.1 CRETE Architecture

As shown in Fig. 1, CRETE has four key components: **CRETE Runner**, a tiny helper program executing in the guest OS of the VM, which parses the configuration file and launches the target binary program (TBP) with the configuration and test cases; **CRETE Tracer**, a comprehensive tracing plug-in in the VM, which captures binary-level traces from the concrete execution of the TBP in the VM; **CRETE Replayer**, an extension of the SEE, which enables the SEE to perform concolic execution on the captured traces and to generate test cases; **CRETE Manager**, a coordinator that integrates the VM and SEE, which manages runtime traces captured and test cases generated, coordinates the concrete and symbolic execution in the VM and the SEE, and iteratively explores the TBP.

CRETE takes a TBP and a configuration file as inputs, and outputs generated test cases along with a report of detected bugs. The manual effort and learning curve to utilize CRETE are minimal. It makes virtually no difference for users to setup the testing environment for the TBP in a CRETE instrumented VM than a vanilla VM. The configuration file is an interface for users to configure parameters on testing a TBP, especially specifying the number and size of symbolic command-line inputs and symbolic files for test case generation.

4.2   Standardized Runtime Trace

To enable the modular and plug-and-play design of CRETE, a standardized binary-level runtime trace format is needed. A trace in this format must capture sufficient information from the concrete execution, so the trace can be faithfully replayed within the SEE. In order to integrate a concrete execution environment to the CRETE framework, only a plug-in for the environment needs to be developed, so that the concrete execution trace can be stored in the standard file format. Similarly, in order to integrate a SEE into CRETE, the engine only needs to be adapted to consume trace files in that format.

We define the standardized runtime trace format based on the LLVM assembly language [31]. The reasons for selecting the LLVM instruction sets are: (1) it has become a de-facto standard for compiler design and program analysis [25,32]; (2) there have been many program analysis tools based on LLVM assembly language [5,33–35]. A standardized binary-level runtime trace is packed as a self-contained LLVM module that is directly consumable by a LLVM interpreter. It is composed of (1) a set of assembly-level basic blocks in the format of LLVM functions (2) a set of hardware states in the format of LLVM global variables (3) a set of CRETE-defined helper functions in LLVM assembly (4) a main function in LLVM assembly. The set of assembly-level basic blocks is captured from a concrete execution of a TBP. It is normally translated from another format (such as QEMU-IR) into LLVM assembly, and each basic block is packed as a LLVM function. The set of hardware states are runtime states along the execution of the TBP. It consist of CPU states, memory states and maybe states of other hardware components, which are packed as LLVM global variables. The set of helper functions are provided by CRETE to correlate captured hardware states with captured basic blocks, and open interface to SEE. The main function represents the concrete execution path of the TBP. It contains a sequence of calls to captured basic blocks (LLVM functions), and calls to CRETE-defined helper functions with appropriate hardware states (LLVM global variables).

An example of a standardized runtime trace of CRETE is listed in Fig. 2. The first column of this figure is a complete execution path of a program with given concrete inputs. It is in the format of assembly-level pseudo-code. Assuming the basic blocks BB_1 and BB_3 are of interest and are captured by CRETE Tracer, while other basic blocks are not (see Sect. 4.3 for details). As shown in the second and third column of the figure, hardware states are captured in two categories, initial state and side-effects from basic blocks not being captured. As shown in the forth column of the figure, captured basic blocks are packed as LLVM functions, and captured hardware states are packed as LLVM global variables in

Concrete Execution Path		Initial HW State		HW Side Effects		Standardized Trace as a LLVM Module
		CPU	Memory	CPU	Memory	@init_state = {<r0,r1,...,rn>, <[0x1234]>}
		r0,r1,...,rn				@side_effects = {<r1>,<[0x5678]>}
1	mem_ld r1, [0x1234] BB_1		[0x1234]			define asm_BB_1() {
2	add r1, r0					%1 = load * 0x1234
3	mem_st [0x1234], r1					%2 = getelementptr @init_state, r0_offset
4	Br r1, inst_5, xxx					%3 = load * %2
5	mem_ld r1, [0x5678]			r1		%4 = add %1, %3
6	add r1, r0 BB_2			r1		%5 = getelementptr @init_state, r1_offset
7	mem_st [0x5678], r1				[0x5678]	store %4, * %5
8	Jump inst_9					store %4, * 0x1234
9	mem_ld r0, [0x1234]		[0x1234]			br %4, %.path_true, %.path_false
10	add r1, r0 BB_3					%.path_true:
11	mem_st [0x5678], r1					%.path_false:
12	Br r0, xxx, inst_13					} ;asm_BB_3() is omitted
13	nop BB_4					external sync_state() ;crete helper function
14	nop					define main() {
						call sync_state(@init_state)
						call asm_BB_1()
						call sync_state(@side_effects)
						call asm_BB_3()
						}

Fig. 2. Example of standardized runtime trace

the standardized trace. A main function is also added making the trace a self-contained LLVM module. The main function first invokes CRETE helper functions to initialize hardware states, then it calls into the first basic block LLVM function. Before it calls into the second basic block LLVM function, the main function invokes CRETE helper functions to update hardware states. For example, before calling asm_BB_3, it calls function sync_state to update register r1 and memory location 0x5678, which are the side effects brought by BB_2.

4.3 Selective Binary-Level Tracing

A major part of a standardized trace is assembly-level basic blocks which are essentially binary-level instruction sequences representing a concrete execution of a TBP. It is challenging and also unnecessary to capture the complete execution of a TBP. First, software binaries can be very complex. If we capture the complete execution, the trace file can be prohibitively large and difficult for the SEE to consume and analyze. Second, as the TBP is executing, it is very common to invoke many runtime libraries (such as libc) of no interest to testers. Therefore, an automated way of selecting the code of interest is needed.

CRETE utilizes Dynamic Taint Analysis (DTA) [36] to achieve selective tracing. The DTA algorithm is a part of CRETE Tracer. It tracks the propagation of tainted values, normally specified by users, during the execution of a program. It works on binary-level and in byte-wise granularity. By utilizing the DTA algorithm, CRETE Tracer only captures basic blocks that operate on tainted values, while only capturing side-effects from other basic blocks. For the example trace in Fig. 2, if the tainted value is from user's input to the program and is stored at memory location 0x1234, DTA captures basic block BB_1 and BB_3, because both of them operate on tainted values, while the other two basic blocks do not touch tainted values, and are not captured by DTA.

CRETE Tracer captures the initial state of CPU by capturing a copy of the CPU state before the first interested basic block is executed. The initial CPU state is normally a set of register values. As shown in Fig. 2, the initial CPU state is captured before instruction (1). Näively, the initial memory state can be captured in the same way; however, the typical size of memory makes it impractical to dump entirely. To minimize the trace size, CRETE Tracer only captures the parts of memory that are accessed by the captured read instructions, like instruction (1) and (9). The memory being touched by the captured write instructions, like instruction (3) and (11), can be ignored because the state of this part of the memory has been included in the write instructions and has been captured. As a result, CRETE Tracer monitors every memory read instruction that is of interest, capturing memory as needed on-the-fly. In the example above, there are two memory read instructions. CRETE Tracer monitors both of them, but only keeps the memory state taken from instruction (1) as a part of the initial state of memory, because instruction (1) and (9) access the same address.

The side effects of hardware states are captured by monitoring uncaptured write instructions of hardware states. In the example in Fig. 2, instructions (5) and (6) write CPU registers which cause side effects to the CPU state. CRETE Tracer monitors those instructions and keeps the updated register values as part of the runtime trace. As register r1 is updated twice by two instructions, only the last update is kept in the runtime trace. Similarly, CRETE Tracer captures the side effect of memory at address 0x5678 by monitoring instruction (7).

4.4   Concolic Test Case Generation

While a standardized trace is a self-contained LLVM module and can be directly executed by a LLVM interpreter, it opens interfaces to SEE to inject symbolic values for test case generation. Normally SEE injects symbolic values by making a variable in source code symbolic. From source code level to machine code level, references of variables by names have become memory accesses by addresses. For instance, a reference of a concrete input variable of a program becomes a access of a piece of memory that stores the state of that input variable. CRETE injects self-defined helper function, `crete_make_concolic`, to the captured basic blocks while capturing trace. This helper function provides the address and size of the piece of memory for injecting symbolic values, along with a name to offer better readability for test case generation. By catching this helper function, SEE can introduce symbolic values at the right time and right place.

A standardized trace in CRETE represents only a single path of a TBP as shown in Fig. 3(a). Test case generation on this trace with näive symbolic execution by SEE won't be effective, as it ignores the single path nature of the trace. As illustrated in Fig. 3(b), native symbolic replay of CRETE trace produces execution states and test cases that are exponential to the number of branches within the trace. As shown in Fig. 3(c), with concolic replay of CRETE trace, the SEE in CRETE maintains only one execution state, requiring minimal memory usage, and generates a more compact set of test cases, whose number is linear to the number of branches in that trace. For a branch instruction in a captured basic

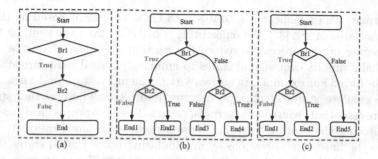

Fig. 3. Execution tree of the example trace from Fig. 2: (a) for concrete execution, (b) for symbolic execution, and (c) for concolic execution.

block, if both of the paths are feasible given the collected constraints so far on the symbolic values, the SEE in CRETE only keeps the execution state of the path that was taken by the original concrete execution in the VM by adding the corresponding constraints of this branch instruction, while generating a test case for the other path by resolving constraints with the negated branch condition. This generated test case can lead the TBP to a different execution path later during the concrete execution in the VM.

4.5 Bug and Runtime Vulnerability Detection

CRETE detects bugs and runtime vulnerabilities in two ways. First, all the native checks embedded in SEE are checked during the symbolic replay over the trace captured from concrete execution. If there is a violation to a check, a bug report is generated and associated with the test case that is used in the VM to generate this trace. Second, since CRETE does not change the native testing process and simply provides additional test cases that can be applied in the native process, all the bugs and vulnerability checks that are used in the native process are effective in detecting bugs and vulnerabilities that can be triggered by the CRETE generated test cases. For instance, Valgrind [26] can be utilized to detect memory related bugs and vulnerabilities along the paths explored by CRETE test cases.

5 Implementation

To demonstrate the practicality of CRETE, we have implemented its complete workflow with QEMU [23] as the frontend and KLEE [5] as the backend respectively. And to demonstrate the extensibility of CRETE, we have also developed the tracing plug-in for the 8051 emulator which readily replaces QEMU.

CRETE Tracer for QEMU: To give CRETE the best potential of supporting various guest platforms supported by QEMU, CRETE Tracer captures the basic blocks in the format of QEMU-IR. To convert captured basic blocks into standardized trace format, we implemented a QEMU-IR to LLVM translator based on the x86-LLVM translator of S^{2}E [37]. We offload this translation from the runtime tracing as a separate offline process to reduce the runtime overhead of CRETE Tracer. QEMU maintains its own virtual states to emulate physical hardware state of a guest platform. For example, it utilizes virtual memory state and virtual CPU state to emulate states of physical memory and CPU. Those virtual states of QEMU are essentially source-level structs. CRETE Tracer captures hardware states by monitoring the runtime values of those structs maintained by QEMU. QEMU emulates the hardware operations by manipulating those virtual states through corresponding helper functions defined in QEMU. CRETE Tracer captures the side effects on those virtual hardware states by monitoring the invocation of those helper functions. As a result, the initial hardware states being captured are the runtime values of these QEMU structs, and the side effects being captured are the side effects on those structs from the uncaptured instructions.

CRETE Replayer for KLEE: KLEE takes as input the LLVM modules compiled from C source code. As the CRETE trace is a self-contained LLVM module, CRETE Replayer mainly injects symbolic values and achieves concolic test generation. To inject symbolic values, CRETE Replayer provides a special function handler for CRETE interface function `crete_make_concolic`. KLEE is an online symbolic executor natively, which forks execution states on each feasible branches and explores all execution paths by maintaining multiple execution states simultaneously. To achieve concolic test generation, CRETE Replayer extends KLEE to generate test cases only for feasible branches while not forking states.

CRETE Tracer for 8051 Emulator: The 8051 emulator executes a 8051 binary directly by interpreting its instructions sequentially. For each type of instruction, the emulator provides a helper function. Interpreting an instruction entails calling this function to compute and change the relevant registers and memory states. The tracing plug-in for the 8051 emulator extends the interpreter. When the interpreter executes an instruction, an LLVM call to its corresponding helper function is put in the runtime trace. The 8051 instruction-processing helper functions are compiled into LLVM and incorporated into the runtime trace serving as the helper functions that map the captured instructions to the captured runtime states. The initial runtime state is captured from the 8051 emulator before the first instruction is executed. The resulting trace is of the same format as that from QEMU and is readily consumable by KLEE.

6   Evaluation

In this section, we present the evaluation results of CRETE from its application to GNU COREUTILS [38] and TianoCore utility programs for UEFI BIOS [39]. Those evaluations demonstrate that CRETE generates effective test cases that are as effective in achieving high code coverage as the state-of-the-art tools for automated test case generation, and can detect serious deeply embedded bugs.

6.1 GNU COREUTILS

Experiment Setup. GNU COREUTILS is a package of utilities widely used in Unix-like systems. The 87 programs from COREUTILS (version 6.10) contain 20,559 lines of code, 988 functions, 14,450 branches according to lcov [40]. The program size ranges from 18 to 1,475 in lines, from 2 to 120 in functions, and from 6 to 1,272 in branches. It is an often-used benchmark for evaluating automated program analysis systems, including KLEE, MergePoint and others [5,12,41]. This is why we chose it as the benchmark to compare with KLEE and ANGR.

CRETE and ANGR generates test cases from program binaries without debug information, while KLEE requires program source code. To measure and compare the effectiveness of test cases generated from different systems, we rerun those tests on the binaries compiled with coverage flag and calculate the code coverage with lcov. Note that we only calculate the coverage of the code in GNU COREUTILS itself, and do not compute code coverage of the library code.

We adopted the configuration parameters for those programs from KLEE's experiment instructions[1]. As specified in the instructions, we ran KLEE on each program for one hour with a memory limit of 1 GB. We increased the memory limit to 8 GB for the experiment on ANGR, while using the same timeout of one hour. CRETE utilizes a different timeout strategy, which is defined by *no new instructions being covered in a given time-bound*. We set the timeout for CRETE as 15 min in this experiment. This timeout strategy was also used by DASE [41] for its evaluation on COREUTILS. We conduct our experiments on an Intel Core i7-3770 3.40 GHz CPU desktop with 16 GB memory running 64-bit Ubuntu 14.04.5. We built KLEE from its release v1.3.0 with LLVM 3.4, which was released on November 30, 2016. We built ANGR from its mainstream on Github at revision e7df250, which was committed on October 11, 2017. CRETE uses Ubuntu 12.04.5 as the guest OS for its VM front-end in our experiments.

Table 1. Comparison of overall and median coverage by KLEE, ANGR, and CRETE on COREUTILS.

Cov.	Line (%)			Function (%)			Branch (%)		
	KLEE	ANGR	CRETE	KLEE	ANGR	CRETE	KLEE	ANGR	CRETE
Overall	70.48	66.79	74.32	78.54	79.05	83.00	58.23	54.26	63.18
Median	88.09	81.62	86.60	100	100	100	79.31	70.59	77.57

Comparison with KLEE and ANGR. As shown in Table 1, our experiments demonstrate that CRETE achieves comparable test coverage to KLEE and generally outperforms ANGR. The major advantage of KLEE over CRETE is that it works on source code with all semantics information available. When the program size is small, symbolic execution is capable of exploring all feasible paths

---

[1] http://klee.github.io/docs/coreutils-experiments/.

Table 2. Distribution comparison of coverage achieved by KLEE, ANGR, and CRETE on COREUTILS.

Cov.	Line			Function			Branch		
	KLEE	ANGR	CRETE	KLEE	ANGR	CRETE	KLEE	ANGR	CRETE
90–100%	40	24	33	65	60	65	15	16	19
80–90%	15	22	25	12	8	10	27	12	17
70–80%	13	14	10	3	7	5	14	16	25
60–70%	9	12	10	2	4	3	9	15	6
50–60%	5	7	4	1	4	1	8	11	9
40–50%	1	2	3	1	1	2	8	7	6
0–40%	4	6	2	3	3	1	6	10	5

with given resources, such as time and memory. This is why KLEE can achieve great code coverage, such as line coverage over 90%, on more programs than CRETE, as shown in Table 2. KLEE requires to maintain execution states for all paths being explored at once. This limitation becomes bigger when size of program gets bigger. What's more, KLEE analyzes programs within its own virtual environment with simplified model of real execution environment. Those models sometimes offer advantages to KLEE by reducing the complexity of the TBP, while sometimes they lead to disadvantages by introducing inaccurate environment. This is why CRETE gradually caught up in general as shown in Table 2. Specifically, CRETE gets higher line coverage on 33 programs, lower on 31 programs, and the same on other 23 programs. Figure 4(a) shows the coverage differences of CRETE over KLEE on all 87 COREUTILS programs. Note that our coverage results for KLEE are different from KLEE's paper. As discussed and reported in previous works [12,41], the coverage differences are mainly due to the major code changes of KLEE, an architecture change from 32-bit to 64-bit, and whether manual system call failures are introduced.

ANGR shares the same limitation as KLEE requiring to maintain multiple states and provide models for execution environment, while it shares the disadvantage of CRETE in having no access to semantics information. Moreover, ANGR provides models of environment at machine level supporting various platforms, which is more challenging compared with KLEE's model. What's more, we found and reported several crashes of ANGR from this evaluation, which also affects the result of ANGR. This is why ANGR performs worse than both KLEE and CRETE in this experiment. Figure 4(b) shows the coverage differences of CRETE over ANGR on all 87 COREUTILS programs. While CRETE outperformed ANGR on majority of the programs, there is one program `printf` that ANGR achieved over 40% better line coverage than CRETE, as shown in the left most column in Fig. 4(b). We found the reason is `printf` uses many string routines from `libc` to parse inputs and ANGR provides effective models for those string routines. Similarly, KLEE works much better on `printf` than CRETE.

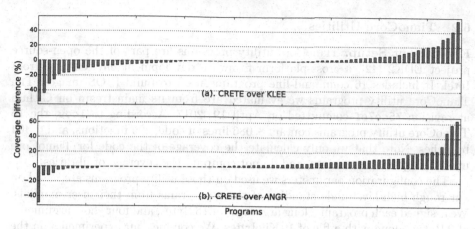

Fig. 4. Line coverage difference on CoREUTILS by CRETE over KLEE and ANGR: positive values mean CRETE is better, and negative values mean CRETE is worse.

Coverage Improvement over Seed Test Case. Since CRETE is a concolic testing framework, it needs an initial seed test case to start the test of a TBP. The goal of this experiment is to show that CRETE can significantly increase the coverage achieved by the seed test case that the user provides. To demonstrate the effectiveness of CRETE, we set the non-file argument, the content of the input file and the stdin to zeros as the seed test case. Of course, well-crafted test cases from the users would be more meaningful and effective to serve as the initial test cases. Figure 5 shows the coverage improvement of each program. On average, the initial seed test case covers 17.61% of lines, 29.55% of functions, and 11.11% of branches. CRETE improves the line coverage by 56.71%, function coverage by 53.44%, and branch coverage by 52.14% respectively. The overall coverage improvement on all 87 CoREUTILS programs is significant.

Fig. 5. Coverage improvement over seed test case by CRETE on GNU CoREUTILS

Bug Detection. In our experiment on CoREUTILS, CRETE was able to detect all three bugs on mkdir, mkfifo, and mknod that were detected by KLEE. This demonstrates that CRETE does not sacrifice bug detection capacity while working directly on binaries without debug and high-level semantic information.

6.2   TianoCore Utilities

Experiment Setup. TianoCore utility programs are part of the open-source project EDK2 [42], a cross-platform firmware development environment from Intel. It includes 16 command-line programs used to build BIOS images. The TianoCore utility programs we evaluated are from its mainstream on Github at revision `75ce7ef` committed on April 19, 2017. According to `lcov`, the 16 TianoCore utility programs contain 8,086 lines of code, 209 functions, and 4,404 branches. Note that we only calculate the coverage of the code for TianoCore utility programs themselves, and do not compute the coverage of libraries.

The configuration parameters we used on those utility programs are based on our rough high-level understanding of these programs from their user manuals. We assigned each program a long argument of 16 Bytes, and four short arguments of 2 Bytes, along with a file of 10 Kilobytes. We conduct our experiments on the same platform with the same host and guest OS as we did for the COREUTILS evaluation, and set the timeout also as 15 min for each program.

High Coverage Test Generation From Scratch. For all the arguments and file contents in the parameter configuration, we set their initial value as binary zeros to serve as the seed test case of CRETE. Figure 6 shows that CRETE delivered high code coverage, above 80% line coverage, on 9 out of 16 programs. On average, the initial seed test case covers 14.56% of lines, 28.71% of functions, and 12.38% of branches. CRETE improves the line coverage by 43.61%, function coverage by 41.63%, and branch coverage by 44.63% respectively. Some programs got lower coverage because of: (1) inadequate configuration parameters; (2) error handling code triggered only by failed system calls; (3) symbolic indices for arrays and files not well handled by CRETE.

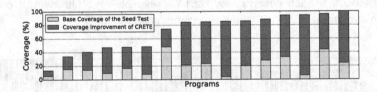

Fig. 6. Coverage improvement over seed test case by CRETE on TianoCore utilities

Bug Detection. To further demonstrate CRETE's capability in detecting deeply embedded bugs, we performed a set of evaluations focusing on concolic file with CRETE on TianoCore utility programs. From the build process of a tutorial image, OvmfPkg, from EDK2, we extracted 509 invocations to TianoCore utility programs and the corresponding intermediate files generated, among which 37 unique invocations cover 6 different programs. By taking parameter configurations from those 37 invocations and using their files as seed files, we ran CRETE with a timeout of 2 h on each setup, in which only files are made symbolic.

Table 3. Classified crashes found by CRETE on Tianocore utilities: 84 unique crashes from 8 programs

Crash type	Count	Severity	Crashed programs
Stack corruption	1	High (Exploitable)	VfrCompile
Heap error	6	High (Exploitable	GenFw
Write access violation	23	High (Exploitable)	EfiLdrImage, GenFw, EfiRom, GenFfs
Abort signal	2	Medium (Signs of exploitable)	GenFw
Read access violation	45	Low (May not exploitable)	GenSec, GenFw, Split, GenCrc32, VfrCompile
Other access violation	7	Mixed	GenFw

Combining experiments on concolic arguments and concolic files, CRETE found 84 distinct crashes (by stack hash) from eight TianoCore utility programs. We used a GDB extension [43] to classify the crashes, which is a popular way of classifying crashes for AFL users [44]. Table 3 shows that CRETE found various kinds of crashes including many exploitable ones, such as stack corruption, heap error, and write access violation. There are 8 crashes that are found with concolic arguments while the other 76 crashes are found with concolic files. We reported all those crashes to the TianoCore development team. So far, most of the crashes have been confirmed as real bugs, and ten of them have been fixed.

We now elaborate on a few sample crashes to demonstrate that the bugs found by CRETE are significant. VfrCompile crashed with a segmentation fault due to stack corruption when the input file name is malformed, e.g., '\\.%*a' as generated by CRETE. This bug is essentially a format string exploit. VfrCompile uses function vsprintf() to compose a new string from a format string and store it in a local array with a fixed size. When the format string is malicious, like '%*a', function vsprintf() will keep reading from the stack and the local buffer will be overflowed, hence causing a stack corruption. Note that CRETE generated a well-formed prefix for the input, '\\.', which is required to pass a preprocessing check from VfrCompile, so that the malicious format string can attack the vulnerable code.

CRETE also exposed several heap errors on GenFw by generating malformed input files. GenFw is used to generate a firmware image from an input file. The input file needs to follow a very precise file format, because GenFw checks the signature bytes to decide the input file type, uses complex nested structs to parse different sections of the file, and conducts many checks to ensure the input file is well-formed. Starting from a seed file of 223 Kilobyte extracted from EDK2's build process, CRETE automatically mutated 29 bytes in the file header. The mutated bytes introduced a particular combination of file signature and sizes and offsets of different sections of the file. This combination passed all checks on file format, and directed GenFw to a vulnerable function which mistakenly replaces the buffer already allocated for storing the input file with a much smaller buffer. Follow-up accesses of this malformed buffer caused overflow and heap corruption.

7   Conclusions and Future Work

In this paper, we have presented CRETE, a versatile binary-level concolic testing framework, which is designed to have an open and highly extensible architecture allowing easy integration of concrete execution frontends and symbolic execution backends. At the core of this architecture is a standardized format for binary-level execution traces, which is LLVM-based, self-contained, and composable. Standardized execution traces are captured by concrete execution frontends, providing succinct and sufficient information for symbolic execution backends to reproduce the concrete executions. We have implemented CRETE with KLEE as the symbolic execution engine and multiple concrete execution frontends such as QEMU and 8051 Emulator. The evaluation of COREUTILS programs shows that CRETE achieved comparable code coverage as KLEE directly analyzing the source code of COREUTILS and generally outperformed ANGR. The evaluation of TianoCore utility programs found numerous exploitable bugs.

We are assembling a suite of 8051 binaries for evaluating CRETE and will report the results in the near future. Also as future work, we will develop new CRETE tracing plugins, e.g., for concrete execution on physical machines based on PIN. With these new plugins, we will focus on synthesizing abstract system-level traces from trace segments captured from binaries executing on various platforms. Another technical challenge that we plan to address is how to handle symbolic indices for arrays and files, so code coverage can be further improved.

Acknowledgment. This research received financial supports from National Science Foundation Grant #: CNS-1422067, Semiconductor Research Corporation Contract #: 2708.001, and gifts from Intel Corporation.

References

1. King, J.C.: Symbolic execution and program testing. Commun. ACM **19**, 385–394 (1976)
2. Sen, K., Marinov, D., Agha, G.: Cute: a concolic unit testing engine for C. In: Proceedings of the 10th European Software Engineering Conference (2005)
3. Godefroid, P., Klarlund, N., Sen, K.: Dart: directed automated random testing. In: Proceedings of the ACM SIGPLAN Conference on Programming Language Design and Implementation (PLDI 2005) (2005)
4. Song, D., et al.: BitBlaze: a new approach to computer security via binary analysis. In: Sekar, R., Pujari, A.K. (eds.) ICISS 2008. LNCS, vol. 5352, pp. 1–25. Springer, Heidelberg (2008). https://doi.org/10.1007/978-3-540-89862-7_1
5. Cadar, C., Dunbar, D., Engler, D.: KLEE: unassisted and automatic generation of high-coverage tests for complex systems programs. In: Proceedings of the 8th USENIX Conference on Operating Systems Design and Implementation (OSDI 2008) (2008)
6. Chipounov, V., Kuznetsov, V., Candea, G.: The s2e platform: design, implementation, and applications. ACM Trans. Comput. Syst. **30**, 1–49 (2012)
7. Godefroid, P., Levin, M.Y., Molnar, D.: Sage: whitebox fuzzing for security testing. Commun. ACM **10**, 1–20 (2012)

8. Cha, S.K., Avgerinos, T., Rebert, A., Brumley, D.: Unleashing Mayhem on binary code. In: Proceedings of the 2012 IEEE Symposium on Security and Privacy (2012)
9. Cadar, C., Sen, K.: Symbolic execution for software testing: three decades later. Commun. ACM **56**, 82–90 (2013)
10. Kuznetsov, V., Kinder, J., Bucur, S., Candea, G.: Efficient state merging in symbolic execution. In: PLDI 2012 (2012)
11. Marinescu, P.D., Cadar, C.: Make test-zesti: a symbolic execution solution for improving regression testing. In: Proceedings of the 34th International Conference on Software Engineering (ICSE 2012) (2012)
12. Avgerinos, T., Rebert, A., Cha, S.K., Brumley, D.: Enhancing symbolic execution with veritesting. In: ICSE 2014 (2014)
13. Avgerinos, T., Cha, S.K., Rebert, A., Schwartz, E.J., Woo, M., Brumley, D.: Automatic exploit generation. Commun. ACM **57**, 74–84 (2014)
14. Shoshitaishvili, Y., Wang, R., Salls, C., Stephens, N., Polino, M., Dutcher, A., et al.: SOK: (state of) the art of war: offensive techniques in binary analysis. In: IEEE Symposium on Security and Privacy (2016)
15. Stephens, N., Grosen, J., Salls, C., et al.: Driller: augmenting fuzzing through selective symbolic execution. In: Proceedings of the Network and Distributed System Security Symposium (2016)
16. Redini, N., Machiry, A., Das, D., Fratantonio, Y., Bianchi, A., Gustafson, E., Shoshitaishvili, Y., Kruegel, C., Vigna, G.: Bootstomp: on the security of bootloaders in mobile devices. In: 26th USENIX Security Symposium (2017)
17. Palikareva, H., Kuchta, T., Cadar, C.: Shadow of a doubt: testing for divergences between software versions. In: ICSE 2016 (2016)
18. Palikareva, H., Cadar, C.: Multi-solver support in symbolic execution. In: Sharygina, N., Veith, H. (eds.) CAV 2013. LNCS, vol. 8044, pp. 53–68. Springer, Heidelberg (2013). https://doi.org/10.1007/978-3-642-39799-8_3
19. Bucur, S., Kinder, J., Candea, G.: Prototyping symbolic execution engines for interpreted languages. In: Proceedings of the 19th International Conference on Architectural Support for Programming Languages and Operating Systems (2014)
20. Kasikci, B., Zamfir, C., Candea, G.: Automated classification of data races under both strong and weak memory models. ACM Trans. Program. Lang. Syst. **37**, 1–44 (2015)
21. Ramos, D.A., Engler, D.: Under-constrained symbolic execution: correctness checking for real code. In: Proceedings of the 24th USENIX Conference on Security Symposium (2015)
22. Zheng, H., Li, D., Liang, B., Zeng, X., Zheng, W., Deng, Y., Lam, W., Yang, W., Xie, T.: Automated test input generation for android: towards getting there in an industrial case. In: Proceedings of the 39th International Conference on Software Engineering: Software Engineering in Practice Track (2017)
23. Bellard, F.: QEMU, a fast and portable dynamic translator. In: Proceedings of the Annual Conference on USENIX Annual Technical Conference (2005)
24. Kasolik, M.: 8051 emulator. http://emu51.sourceforge.net/
25. Lattner, C., Adve, V.: LLVM: a compilation framework for lifelong program analysis & transformation. In: Proceedings of the International Symposium on Code Generation and Optimization: Feedback-directed and Runtime Optimization (2004)
26. Nethercote, N., Seward, J.: Valgrind: a framework for heavyweight dynamic binary instrumentation. In: PLDI 2007 (2007)
27. Godefroid, P.: Random testing for security: blackbox vs. whitebox fuzzing. In: Proceedings of the 2nd International Workshop on Random Testing (2007)

28. AFL: American fuzzy lop. http://lcamtuf.coredump.cx/afl/
29. Luk, C.K., Cohn, R., Muth, R., et al.: Pin: building customized program analysis tools with dynamic instrumentation. In: PLDI 2005 (2005)
30. Bruening, D., Zhao, Q., Amarasinghe, S.: Transparent dynamic instrumentation. In: Proceedings of the 8th ACM SIGPLAN/SIGOPS Conference on Virtual Execution Environments (2012)
31. Lattner, C., Adve, V.: LLVM language reference manual (2006). http://llvm.org/docs/LangRef.html
32. Lattner, C.: LLVM and Clang: next generation compiler technology. In: The BSD Conference (2008)
33. Dhurjati, D., Kowshik, S., Adve, V.: Safecode: enforcing alias analysis for weakly typed languages. In: PLDI 2006 (2006)
34. Geoffray, N., Thomas, G., Lawall, J., Muller, G., Folliot, B.: VMKit: a substrate for managed runtime environments. In: Proceedings of the 6th ACM International Conference on Virtual Execution Environments (2010)
35. Grosser, T., Größlinger, A., Lengauer, C.: Polly-performing polyhedral optimizations on a low-level intermediate representation. Parall. Process. Lett. **22**, 1–28 (2012)
36. Schwartz, E.J., Avgerinos, T., Brumley, D.: All you ever wanted to know about dynamic taint analysis and forward symbolic execution (but might have been afraid to ask). In: Proceedings of the IEEE Symposium on Security and Privacy (2010)
37. Chipounov, V., Candea, G.: Dynamically translating x86 to LLVM using QEMU. Technical report EPFL-TR-149975 (2010)
38. GNU: GNU coreutils - core utilities. https://www.gnu.org/s/coreutils
39. Tianocore: Tianocore. http://www.tianocore.org/
40. Oberparleiter, P.: A graphical front-end for gcc's coverage testing tool gcov. http://ltp.sourceforge.net/coverage/lcov.php
41. Wong, E., Zhang, L., Wang, S., Liu, T., Tan, L.: Dase: document-assisted symbolic execution for improving automated software testing. In: ICSE 2015 (2015)
42. Tianocore: EDK II. https://github.com/tianocore/edk2
43. Foote, J.: The 'exploitable' gdb plugin. https://github.com/jfoote/exploitable
44. AFL-Utils: Utilities for automated crash sample processing/analysis. https://github.com/rc0r/afl-utils

Family-Based Software Development

Abstract Family-Based Model Checking Using Modal Featured Transition Systems: Preservation of CTL*

Aleksandar S. Dimovski$^{(\boxtimes)}$ (ID)

Faculty of Informatics, Mother Teresa University, Skopje, Republic of Macedonia
aleksandar.dimovski@unt.edu.mk

Abstract. Variational systems allow effective building of many custom variants by using features (configuration options) to mark the variable functionality. In many of the applications, their quality assurance and formal verification are of paramount importance. Family-based model checking allows simultaneous verification of all variants of a variational system in a single run by exploiting the commonalities between the variants. Yet, its computational cost still greatly depends on the number of variants (often huge).

In this work, we show how to achieve efficient family-based model checking of CTL* temporal properties using variability abstractions and off-the-shelf (single-system) tools. We use variability abstractions for deriving abstract family-based model checking, where the variability model of a variational system is replaced with an abstract (smaller) version of it, called *modal featured transition system*, which preserves the satisfaction of both universal and existential temporal properties, as expressible in CTL*. Modal featured transition systems contain two kinds of transitions, termed may and must transitions, which are defined by the conservative (over-approximating) abstractions and their dual (under-approximating) abstractions, respectively. The variability abstractions can be combined with different partitionings of the set of variants to infer suitable divide-and-conquer verification plans for the variational system. We illustrate the practicality of this approach for several variational systems.

1 Introduction

Variational systems appear in many application areas and for many reasons. Efficient methods to achieve customization, such as *Software Product Line Engineering* (SPLE) [8], use *features* (configuration options) to control presence and absence of the variable functionality [1]. Family members, called *variants* of a *variational system*, are specified in terms of features selected for that particular variant. The reuse of code common to multiple variants is maximized. The SPLE method is particularly popular in the embedded and critical system domain (e.g. cars, phones). In these domains, a rigorous verification and analysis is very important. Among the methods included in current practices, *model checking* [2]

© The Author(s) 2018
A. Russo and A. Schürr (Eds.): FASE 2018, LNCS 10802, pp. 301–318, 2018.
https://doi.org/10.1007/978-3-319-89363-1_17

is a well-studied technique used to establish that temporal logic properties hold for a system.

Variability and SPLE are major enablers, but also a source of complexity. Obviously, the size of the configuration space (number of variants) is the limiting factor to the feasibility of any verification technique. Exponentially many variants can be derived from few configuration options. This problem is referred to as *the configuration space explosion* problem. A simple "brute-force" application of a single-system model checker to each variant is infeasible for realistic variational systems, due to the sheer number of variants. This is very ineffective also because the same execution behavior is checked multiple times, whenever it is shared by some variants. Another, more efficient, verification technique [5,6] is based on using compact representations for modelling variational systems, which incorporate the commonality within the family. We will call these representations variability models (or featured transition systems). Each behavior in a variability model is associated with the set of variants able to produce it. A specialized family-based model checking algorithm executed on such a model, checks an execution behavior only once regardless of how many variants include it. These algorithms model check all variants simultaneously in a single run and pinpoint the variants that violate properties. Unfortunately, their performance *still* heavily depends on the size and complexity of the configuration space of the analyzed variational system. Moreover, maintaining specialized family-based tools is also an expensive task.

In order to address these challenges, we propose to use standard, single-system model checkers with an alternative, externalized way to combat the configuration space explosion. We apply the so-called *variability abstractions* to a variability model which is too large to handle ("configuration space explosion"), producing a more *abstract model*, which is smaller than the original one. We abstract from certain aspects of the configuration space, so that many of the configurations (variants) become indistinguishable and can be collapsed into a single abstract configuration. The abstract model is constructed in such a way that if some property holds for this abstract model it will also hold for the concrete model. Our technique extends the scope of existing over-approximating variability abstractions [14,19] which currently support the verification of universal properties only (LTL and ∀CTL). Here we construct abstract variability models which can be used to check arbitrary formulae of CTL*, thus including arbitrary nested path quantifiers. We use modal featured transition systems (MFTSs) for representing abstract variability models. MFTSs are featured transition systems (FTSs) with two kinds of transitions, *must* and *may*, expressing behaviours that necessarily occur (must) or possibly occur (may). We use the standard conservative (over-approximating) abstractions to define may transitions, and their dual (under-approximating) abstractions to define must transitions. Therefore, MFTSs perform both over- and under-approximation, admitting both universal and existential properties to be deduced. Since MFTSs preserve all CTL* properties, we can verify any such properties on the concrete variability model (which is given as an FTSs) by verifying these on an abstract MFTS. Any model checking problem on modal transitions systems (resp., MFTSs) can be reduced to two traditional model checking problems on standard transition systems (resp., FTSs). The overall technique relies on partitioning and abstracting concrete FTSs, until the point we obtain models with so limited variability (or, no variability) that it is feasible to complete their model checking in the brute-force fashion using the standard single-system model checkers. Compared to the family-based model checking, experiments show that the proposed technique achieves performance gains.

2   Background

In this section, we present the background used in later developments.

Modal Featured Transition Systems. Let $\mathbb{F} = \{A_1, \ldots, A_n\}$ be a finite set of Boolean variables representing the features available in a variational system. A specific subset of features, $k \subseteq \mathbb{F}$, known as *configuration*, specifies a *variant* (valid product) of a variational system. We assume that only a subset $\mathbb{K} \subseteq 2^{\mathbb{F}}$ of configurations are *valid*. An alternative representation of configurations is based upon propositional formulae. Each configuration $k \in \mathbb{K}$ can be represented by a formula: $k(A_1) \wedge \ldots \wedge k(A_n)$, where $k(A_i) = A_i$ if $A_i \in k$, and $k(A_i) = \neg A_i$ if $A_i \notin k$ for $1 \leq i \leq n$. We will use both representations interchangeably.

We recall the basic definition of a transition system (TS) and a modal transition system (MTS) that we will use to describe behaviors of single-systems.

Definition 1. *A transition system (TS) is a tuple $\mathcal{T} = (S, Act, trans, I, AP, L)$, where S is a set of states; Act is a set of actions; $trans \subseteq S \times Act \times S$ is a transition relation; $I \subseteq S$ is a set of initial states; AP is a set of atomic propositions; and $L : S \to 2^{AP}$ is a labelling function specifying which propositions hold in a state. We write $s_1 \xrightarrow{\lambda} s_2$ whenever $(s_1, \lambda, s_2) \in trans$.*

An *execution* (behaviour) of a TS $\mathcal{T}$ is an *infinite* sequence $\rho = s_0 \lambda_1 s_1 \lambda_2 \ldots$ with $s_0 \in I$ such that $s_i \xrightarrow{\lambda_{i+1}} s_{i+1}$ for all $i \geq 0$. The *semantics* of the TS $\mathcal{T}$, denoted as $[\![\mathcal{T}]\!]_{TS}$, is the set of its executions.

MTSs [26] are a generalization of transition systems that allows describing not just a sum of all behaviors of a system but also an over- and under-approximation of the system's behaviors. An MTS is a TS equipped with two transition relations: *must* and *may*. The former (must) is used to specify the required behavior, while the latter (may) to specify the allowed behavior of a system.

Definition 2. *A modal transition system (MTS) is represented by a tuple $\mathcal{M} = (S, Act, trans^{may}, trans^{must}, I, AP, L)$, where $trans^{may} \subseteq S \times Act \times S$ describe may transitions of $\mathcal{M}$; $trans^{must} \subseteq S \times Act \times S$ describe must transitions of $\mathcal{M}$, such that $trans^{must} \subseteq trans^{may}$.*

The intuition behind the inclusion $trans^{must} \subseteq trans^{may}$ is that transitions that are necessarily true ($trans^{must}$) are also possibly true ($trans^{may}$). A *may-execution* in $\mathcal{M}$ is an execution with all its transitions in $trans^{may}$; whereas a *must-execution* in $\mathcal{M}$ is an execution with all its transitions in $trans^{must}$. We use $[\![\mathcal{M}]\!]_{MTS}^{may}$ to denote the set of all may-executions in $\mathcal{M}$, whereas $[\![\mathcal{M}]\!]_{MTS}^{must}$ to denote the set of all must-executions in $\mathcal{M}$.

An FTS describes behavior of a whole family of systems in a *superimposed* manner. This means that it combines models of many variants in a single monolithic description, where the transitions are guarded by a *presence condition* that identifies the variants they belong to. The presence conditions ψ are drawn from the set of feature expressions, $FeatExp(\mathbb{F})$, which are propositional logic formulae over $\mathbb{F}$: $\psi ::= true \mid A \in \mathbb{F} \mid \neg\psi \mid \psi_1 \wedge \psi_2$. The presence condition ψ of a transition specifies the variants in which the transition is enabled. We write $[\![\psi]\!]$ to denote the set of variants from $\mathbb{K}$ that satisfy ψ, i.e. $k \in [\![\psi]\!]$ iff $k \models \psi$.

Definition 3. *A featured transition system (FTS) represents a tuple $\mathcal{F} = (S, Act, trans, I, AP, L, \mathbb{F}, \mathbb{K}, \delta)$, where $S, Act, trans, I, AP$, and L are defined as in TS; $\mathbb{F}$ is the set of available features; $\mathbb{K}$ is a set of valid configurations; and $\delta : trans \rightarrow FeatExp(\mathbb{F})$ is a total function decorating transitions with presence conditions (feature expressions).*

The *projection* of an FTS $\mathcal{F}$ to a variant $k \in \mathbb{K}$, denoted as $\pi_k(\mathcal{F})$, is the TS $(S, Act, trans', I, AP, L)$, where $trans' = \{t \in trans \mid k \models \delta(t)\}$. We lift the definition of *projection* to sets of configurations $\mathbb{K}' \subseteq \mathbb{K}$, denoted as $\pi_{\mathbb{K}'}(\mathcal{F})$, by keeping the transitions admitted by at least one of the configurations in $\mathbb{K}'$. That is, $\pi_{\mathbb{K}'}(\mathcal{F})$, is the FTS $(S, Act, trans', I, AP, L, \mathbb{F}, \mathbb{K}', \delta)$, where $trans' = \{t \in trans \mid \exists k \in \mathbb{K}'.k \models \delta(t)\}$. The *semantics* of an FTS $\mathcal{F}$, denoted as $[\![\mathcal{F}]\!]_{FTS}$, is the union of behaviours of the projections on all valid variants $k \in \mathbb{K}$, i.e. $[\![\mathcal{F}]\!]_{FTS} = \cup_{k \in \mathbb{K}} [\![\pi_k(\mathcal{F})]\!]_{TS}$.

We will use modal featured transition systems (MFTS) for representing abstractions of FTSs. MFTSs are variability-aware extension of MTSs.

Definition 4. *A modal featured transition system (MFTS) represents a tuple $\mathcal{MF} = (S, Act, trans^{may}, trans^{must}, I, AP, L, \mathbb{F}, \mathbb{K}, \delta^{may}, \delta^{must})$, where $trans^{may}$ and $\delta^{may} : trans^{may} \rightarrow FeatExp(\mathbb{F})$ describe may transitions of $\mathcal{MF}$; $trans^{must}$ and $\delta^{must} : trans^{must} \rightarrow FeatExp(\mathbb{F})$ describe must transitions of $\mathcal{MF}$.*

The *projection* of an MFTS $\mathcal{MF}$ to a variant $k \in \mathbb{K}$, denoted as $\pi_k(\mathcal{MF})$, is the MTS $(S, Act, trans'^{may}, trans'^{must}, I, AP, L)$, where $trans'^{may} = \{t \in trans^{may} \mid k \models \delta^{may}(t)\}$, $trans'^{must} = \{t \in trans^{must} \mid k \models \delta^{must}(t)\}$. We define $[\![\mathcal{MF}]\!]_{MFTS}^{may} = \cup_{k \in \mathbb{K}} [\![\pi_k(\mathcal{MF})]\!]_{MTS}^{may}$, and $[\![\mathcal{MF}]\!]_{MFTS}^{must} = \cup_{k \in \mathbb{K}} [\![\pi_k(\mathcal{MF})]\!]_{MTS}^{must}$.

Example 1. Throughout this paper, we will use a beverage vending machine as a running example [6]. Figure 1 shows the FTS of a VENDINGMACHINE family. It has five features, and each of them is assigned an identifying letter and a color. The features are: VendingMachine (denoted by letter v, in black), the mandatory base feature of purchasing a drink, present in all variants; Tea (t, in red), for

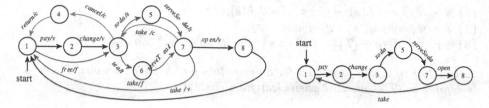

Fig. 1. The FTS for VENDINGMACHINE.
(Color figure online)

Fig. 2. $\pi_{\{v,s\}}$(VENDINGMACHINE)

serving tea; Soda (s, in green), for serving soda, which is a mandatory feature
present in all variants; CancelPurchase (c, in brown), for canceling a purchase
after a coin is entered; and FreeDrinks (f, in blue) for offering free drinks. Each
transition is labeled by an *action* followed by a *feature expression*. For instance,
the transition ① $\xrightarrow{\mathit{free/f}}$ ③ is included in variants where the feature f is enabled.

By combining various features, a number of variants of this VENDINGMA-
CHINE can be obtained. Recall that v and s are mandatory features. The set
of valid configurations is thus: $\mathbb{K}^{VM} = \{\{v,s\}, \{v,s,t\}, \{v,s,c\}, \{v,s,t,c\}, \{v,$
$s,f\}, \{v,s,t,f\}, \{v,s,c,f\}, \{v,s,t,c,f\}\}$. In Fig. 2 is shown the basic version
of VENDINGMACHINE that only serves soda, which is described by the con-
figuration: $\{v,s\}$ (or, as formula $v \wedge s \wedge \neg t \wedge \neg c \wedge \neg f$), that is the projection
$\pi_{\{v,s\}}$(VENDINGMACHINE). It takes a coin, returns change, serves soda, opens a
compartment so that the customer can take the soda, before closing it again.

Figure 3 shows an MTS. Must transitions are denoted by solid lines, while
may transitions by dashed lines. □

CTL* Properties. Computation Tree Logic* (CTL*) [2] is an expressive temporal logic for specifying system properties, which subsumes both CTL and LTL
logics. CTL* state formulae Φ are generated by the following grammar:

$$\Phi ::= \mathit{true} \mid a \in AP \mid \neg a \mid \Phi_1 \wedge \Phi_2 \mid \forall\phi \mid \exists\phi, \qquad \phi ::= \Phi \mid \phi_1 \wedge \phi_2 \mid \bigcirc\phi \mid \phi_1 \mathsf{U} \phi_2$$

where ϕ represent CTL* path formulae. Note that the CTL* state formulae Φ
are given in negation normal form ($\neg$ is applied only to atomic propositions).
Given $\Phi \in$ CTL*, we consider $\neg\Phi$ to be the equivalent CTL* formula given in
negation normal form. Other derived temporal operators (path formulae) can be
defined as well by means of syntactic sugar, for instance: $\Diamond\phi = \mathit{true}\, \mathsf{U}\phi$ (ϕ holds
eventually), and $\Box\phi = \neg\forall\Diamond\neg\phi$ (ϕ always holds). $\forall$CTL* and $\exists$CTL* are subsets
of CTL* where the only allowed path quantifiers are $\forall$ and $\exists$, respectively.

We formalise the semantics of CTL* over a TS $\mathcal{T}$. We write $[\mathcal{T}]^s_{TS}$ for the
set of executions that start in state s; $\rho[i] = s_i$ to denote the i-th state of the
execution ρ; and $\rho_i = s_i\lambda_{i+1}s_{i+1}\ldots$ for the suffix of ρ starting from its i-th state.

Definition 5. *Satisfaction of a state formula Φ in a state s of a TS $\mathcal{T}$, denoted
$\mathcal{T}, s \models \phi$, is defined as ($\mathcal{T}$ is omitted when clear from context):*

(1) $s \models a$ *iff* $a \in L(s)$; $s \models \neg a$ *iff* $a \notin L(s)$,

(2) $s \models \Phi_1 \wedge \Phi_2$ *iff* $s \models \Phi_1$ *and* $s \models \Phi_2$,

(3) $s \models \forall\phi$ *iff* $\forall\rho \in [\![T]\!]^s_{TS}.\, \rho \models \phi$; $s \models \exists\phi$ *iff* $\exists\rho \in [\![T]\!]^s_{TS}.\, \rho \models \phi$

Satisfaction of a path formula ϕ for an execution ρ of a TS T, denoted $T, \rho \models \phi$, is defined as (T is omitted when clear from context):

(4) $\rho \models \Phi$ *iff* $\rho[0] \models \Phi$,

(5) $\rho \models \phi_1 \wedge \phi_2$ *iff* $\rho \models \phi_1$ *and* $\rho \models \phi_2$; $\rho \models \bigcirc\phi$ *iff* $\rho_1 \models \phi$; $\rho \models (\phi_1 U \phi_2)$ *iff* $\exists i \geq 0.\, (\rho_i \models \phi_2 \wedge (\forall 0 \leq j \leq i-1.\, \rho_j \models \phi_1))$

A TS T satisfies a state formula Φ, written $T \models \Phi$, iff $\forall s_0 \in I.\, s_0 \models \Phi$.

Definition 6. *An FTS $\mathcal{F}$ satisfies a CTL* formula Φ, written $\mathcal{F} \models \Phi$, iff all its valid variants satisfy the formula: $\forall k \in \mathbb{K}.\, \pi_k(\mathcal{F}) \models \Phi$.*

The interpretation of CTL* over an MTS $\mathcal{M}$ is defined slightly different from the above Definition 5. In particular, the clause (3) is replaced by:

(3') $s \models \forall\phi$ iff for every may-execution ρ in the state s of $\mathcal{M}$, that is $\forall\rho \in [\![\mathcal{M}]\!]^{may,s}_{MTS}$, it holds $\rho \models \phi$; whereas $s \models \exists\phi$ iff there exists a must-execution ρ in the state s of $\mathcal{M}$, that is $\exists\rho \in [\![\mathcal{M}]\!]^{must,s}_{MTS}$, such that $\rho \models \phi$.

From now on, we implicitly assume this adapted definition when interpreting CTL* formulae over MTSs and MFTSs.

Example 2. Consider the FTS VENDINGMACHINE in Fig. 1. Suppose that the proposition start holds in the initial state ①. An example property Φ_1 is: $\forall\Box\forall\Diamond$start, which states that in every state along every execution all possible continuations will eventually reach the initial state. This formula is in $\forall$CTL*. Note that VENDINGMACHINE $\not\models \Phi_1$. For example, if the feature c (Cancel) is enabled, a counter-example where the state ① is never reached is: ① → ③ → ⑤ → ⑦ → ③ → .... The set of violating products is $[\![c]\!] = \{\{v, s, c\}, \{v, s, t, c\}, \{v, s, c, f\}, \{v, s, t, c, f\}\} \subseteq \mathbb{K}^{VM}$. However, $\pi_{[\![\neg c]\!]}($VENDINGMACHINE$) \models \Phi_1$.

Consider the property Φ_2: $\forall\Box\exists\Diamond$start, which describes a situation where in every state along every execution there exists a possible continuation that will eventually reach the start state. This is a CTL* formula, which is neither in $\forall$CTL* nor in $\exists$CTL*. Note that VENDINGMACHINE $\models \Phi_2$, since even for variants with the feature c there is a continuation from the state ③ back to ①.

Consider the $\exists$CTL* property Φ_3: $\exists\Box\exists\Diamond$start, which states that there exists an execution such that in every state along it there exists a possible continuation that will eventually reach the start state. The witnesses are ① → ② → ③ → ⑤ → ⑦ → ⑧ → ①... for variants that satisfy $\neg c$, and ① → ③ → ⑤ → ⑦ → ③ → ④ → ①... for variants with c. □

3   Abstraction of FTSs

We now introduce the variability abstractions which preserve full CTL and its universal and existential properties. They simplify the configuration space of an FTSs, by reducing the number of configurations and manipulating presence conditions of transitions. We start working with Galois connections[1] between Boolean complete lattices of feature expressions, and then induce a notion of abstraction of FTSs. We define two classes of abstractions. We use the standard conservative abstractions [14,15] as an instrument to eliminate variability from the FTS in an *over-approximating* way, so by adding more executions. We use the dual abstractions, which can also eliminate variability but through *under-approximating* the given FTS, so by dropping executions.

Domains. The Boolean complete lattice of feature expressions (propositional formulae over $\mathbb{F}$) is: $(FeatExp(\mathbb{F})_{/\equiv}, \models, \vee, \wedge, true, false, \neg)$. The elements of the domain $FeatExp(\mathbb{F})_{/\equiv}$ are equivalence classes of propositional formulae $\psi \in FeatExp(\mathbb{F})$ obtained by quotienting by the semantic equivalence $\equiv$. The ordering $\models$ is the standard entailment between propositional logics formulae, whereas the least upper bound and the greatest lower bound are just logical disjunction and conjunction respectively. Finally, the constant *false* is the least, *true* is the greatest element, and negation is the complement operator.

Conservative Abstractions. The *join abstraction*, α^{join}, merges the control-flow of all variants, obtaining a single variant that includes all executions occurring in any variant. The information about which transitions are associated with which variants is lost. Each feature expression ψ is replaced with *true* if there exists at least one configuration from $\mathbb{K}$ that satisfies ψ. The new abstract set of features is empty: $\alpha^{\text{join}}(\mathbb{F}) = \emptyset$, and the abstract set of valid configurations is a singleton: $\alpha^{\text{join}}(\mathbb{K}) = \{true\}$ if $\mathbb{K} \neq \emptyset$. The abstraction and concretization functions between $FeatExp(\mathbb{F})$ and $FeatExp(\emptyset)$, forming a Galois connection [14,15], are defined as:

$$\alpha^{\text{join}}(\psi) = \begin{cases} true & \text{if } \exists k \in \mathbb{K}.k \models \psi \\ false & \text{otherwise} \end{cases} \qquad \gamma^{\text{join}}(\psi) = \begin{cases} true & \text{if } \psi \text{ is } true \\ \bigvee_{k \in 2^{\mathbb{F}} \setminus \mathbb{K}} k & \text{if } \psi \text{ is } false \end{cases}$$

The *feature ignore abstraction*, $\alpha_A^{\text{fignore}}$, introduces an over-approximation by ignoring a single feature $A \in \mathbb{F}$. It merges the control flow paths that only differ with regard to A, but keeps the precision with respect to control flow paths that do not depend on A. The features and configurations of the abstracted model are: $\alpha_A^{\text{fignore}}(\mathbb{F}) = \mathbb{F} \setminus \{A\}$, and $\alpha_A^{\text{fignore}}(\mathbb{K}) = \{k[l_A \mapsto true] \mid k \in \mathbb{K}\}$, where l_A denotes a literal of A (either A or $\neg A$), and $k[l_A \mapsto true]$ is a formula resulting from k by

---

[1] $\langle L, \leq_L \rangle \xrightleftharpoons[\alpha]{\gamma} \langle M, \leq_M \rangle$ is a *Galois connection* between complete lattices L (concrete domain) and M (abstract domain) iff $\alpha : L \to M$ and $\gamma : M \to L$ are total functions that satisfy: $\alpha(l) \leq_M m \iff l \leq_L \gamma(m)$ for all $l \in L, m \in M$. Here $\leq_L$ and $\leq_M$ are the pre-order relations for L and M, respectively. We will often simply write (α, γ) for any such Galois connection.

substituting *true* for l_A. The abstraction and concretization functions between $FeatExp(\mathbb{F})$ and $FeatExp(\alpha_A^{\text{fignore}}(\mathbb{F}))$, forming a Galois connection [14,15], are:

$$\alpha_A^{\text{fignore}}(\psi) = \psi[l_A \mapsto true] \qquad \gamma_A^{\text{fignore}}(\psi') = (\psi' \wedge A) \vee (\psi' \wedge \neg A)$$

where ψ and ψ' need to be in negation normal form before substitution.

Dual Abstractions. Suppose that $\langle FeatExp(\mathbb{F})_{/\equiv}, \models \rangle$, $\langle FeatExp(\alpha(\mathbb{F}))_{/\equiv}, \models \rangle$ are Boolean complete lattices, and $\langle FeatExp(\mathbb{F})_{/\equiv}, \models \rangle \xrightleftharpoons[\alpha]{\gamma} \langle FeatExp(\alpha(\mathbb{F}))_{/\equiv}, \models \rangle$ is a Galois connection. We define [9]: $\widetilde{\alpha} = \neg \circ \alpha \circ \neg$ and $\widetilde{\gamma} = \neg \circ \gamma \circ \neg$ so that $\langle FeatExp(\mathbb{F})_{/\equiv}, \Rrightarrow \rangle \xrightleftharpoons[\widetilde{\alpha}]{\widetilde{\gamma}} \langle FeatExp(\alpha(\mathbb{F}))_{/\equiv}, \Rrightarrow \rangle$ is a Galois connection (or equivalently, $\langle FeatExp(\alpha(\mathbb{F}))_{/\equiv}, \models \rangle \xrightleftharpoons[\widetilde{\gamma}]{\widetilde{\alpha}} \langle FeatExp(\mathbb{F})_{/\equiv}, \models \rangle$). The obtained Galois connections $(\widetilde{\alpha}, \widetilde{\gamma})$ are called dual (under-approximating) abstractions of (α, γ).

The *dual join abstraction*, $\widetilde{\alpha^{\text{join}}}$, merges the control-flow of all variants, obtaining a single variant that includes only those executions that occur in all variants. Each feature expression ψ is replaced with *true* if all configurations from $\mathbb{K}$ satisfy ψ. The abstraction and concretization functions between $FeatExp(\mathbb{F})$ and $FeatExp(\emptyset)$, forming a Galois connection, are defined as: $\widetilde{\alpha^{\text{join}}} = \neg \circ \alpha^{\text{join}} \circ \neg$ and $\widetilde{\gamma^{\text{join}}} = \neg \circ \gamma^{\text{join}} \circ \neg$, that is:

$$\widetilde{\alpha^{\text{join}}}(\psi) = \begin{cases} true & \text{if } \forall k \in \mathbb{K}.k \models \psi \\ false & \text{otherwise} \end{cases} \qquad \widetilde{\gamma^{\text{join}}}(\psi) = \begin{cases} \bigwedge_{k \in 2^{\mathbb{F}} \setminus \mathbb{K}}(\neg k) & \text{if } \psi \text{ is } true \\ false & \text{if } \psi \text{ is } false \end{cases}$$

The *dual feature ignore abstraction*, $\widetilde{\alpha_A^{\text{fignore}}}$, introduces an under-approximation by ignoring the feature $A \in \mathbb{F}$, such that the literals of A (that is, A and $\neg A$) are replaced with *false* in feature expressions (given in negation normal form). The abstraction and concretization functions between $FeatExp(\mathbb{F})$ and $FeatExp(\alpha_A^{\text{fignore}}(\mathbb{F}))$, forming a Galois connection, are defined as: $\widetilde{\alpha_A^{\text{fignore}}} = \neg \circ \alpha_A^{\text{fignore}} \circ \neg$ and $\widetilde{\gamma_A^{\text{fignore}}} = \neg \circ \gamma_A^{\text{fignore}} \circ \neg$, that is:

$$\widetilde{\alpha_A^{\text{fignore}}}(\psi) = \psi[l_A \mapsto false] \qquad \widetilde{\gamma_A^{\text{fignore}}}(\psi') = (\psi' \vee \neg A) \wedge (\psi' \vee A)$$

where ψ and ψ' are in negation normal form.

Abstract MFTS and Preservation of CTL*. Given a Galois connection (α, γ) defined on the level of feature expressions, we now define the abstraction of an FTS as an MFTS with two transition relations: one (may) preserving universal properties, and the other (must) existential properties. The may transitions describe the behaviour that is possible, but not need be realized in the variants of the family; whereas the must transitions describe behaviour that has to be present in any variant of the family.

Definition 7. *Given the FTS $\mathcal{F} = (S, Act, trans, I, AP, L, \mathbb{F}, \mathbb{K}, \delta)$, we define the MFTS $\alpha(\mathcal{F}) = (S, Act, trans^{may}, trans^{must}, I, AP, L, \alpha(\mathbb{F}), \alpha(\mathbb{K}), \delta^{may}, \delta^{must})$ to be its abstraction, where $\delta^{may}(t) = \alpha(\delta(t))$, $\delta^{must}(t) = \widetilde{\alpha}(\delta(t))$, $trans^{may} = \{t \in trans \mid \delta^{may}(t) \neq false\}$, and $trans^{must} = \{t \in trans \mid \delta^{must}(t) \neq false\}$.*

Note that the degree of reduction is determined by the choice of abstraction and may hence be arbitrary large. In the extreme case of join abstraction, we obtain an abstract model with no variability in it, that is $\alpha^{\text{join}}(\mathcal{F})$ is an ordinary MTS.

Example 3. Recall the FTS VENDINGMACHINE of Fig. 1 with the set of valid configurations $\mathbb{K}^{\text{VM}}$ (see Example 1). Figure 3 shows $\alpha^{\text{join}}(\text{VENDINGMACHINE})$, where the allowed (may) part of the behavior includes the transitions that are associated with the optional features c, f, t in VENDINGMACHINE, whereas the required (must) part includes the transitions associated with the mandatory features v and s. Note that $\alpha^{\text{join}}(\text{VENDINGMACHINE})$ is an ordinary MTS with no variability. The MFTS $\alpha^{\text{fignore}}_{\{t,f\}}(\pi_{[\![v \wedge s]\!]}(\text{VENDINGMACHINE}))$ is shown in [12, Appendix B], see Fig. 8. It has the singleton set of features $\mathbb{F} = \{c\}$ and limited variability $\mathbb{K} = \{c, \neg c\}$, where the mandatory features v and s are enabled. □

From the MFTS (resp., MTS) $\mathcal{MF}$, we define two FTSs (resp., TSs) $\mathcal{MF}^{may}$ and $\mathcal{MF}^{must}$ representing the may- and must-components of $\mathcal{MF}$, i.e. its may and must transitions, respectively. Thus, we have $[\![\mathcal{MF}^{may}]\!]_{FTS} = [\![\mathcal{MF}]\!]^{may}_{MFTS}$ and $[\![\mathcal{MF}^{must}]\!]_{FTS} = [\![\mathcal{MF}]\!]^{must}_{MFTS}$.

We now show that the abstraction of an FTS is sound with respect to CTL*. First, we show two helper lemmas stating that: for any variant $k \in \mathbb{K}$ that can execute a behavior, there exists an abstract variant $k' \in \alpha(\mathbb{K})$ that executes the same may-behaviour; and for any abstract variant $k' \in \alpha(\mathbb{K})$ that can execute a must-behavior, there exists a variant $k \in \mathbb{K}$ that executes the same behaviour[2].

Lemma 1. *Let $\psi \in FeatExp(\mathbb{F})$, and $\mathbb{K}$ be a set of valid configurations over $\mathbb{F}$.*

 (i) *Let $k \in \mathbb{K}$ and $k \models \psi$. Then there exists $k' \in \alpha(\mathbb{K})$, such that $k' \models \alpha(\psi)$.*
 (ii) *Let $k' \in \alpha(\mathbb{K})$ and $k' \models \tilde{\alpha}(\psi)$. Then there exists $k \in \mathbb{K}$, such that $k \models \psi$.*

Lemma 2

 (i) *Let $k \in \mathbb{K}$ and $\rho \in [\![\pi_k(\mathcal{F})]\!]_{TS} \subseteq [\![\mathcal{F}]\!]_{FTS}$. Then there exists $k' \in \alpha(\mathbb{K})$, such that $\rho \in [\![\pi_{k'}(\alpha(\mathcal{F}))]\!]^{may}_{MTS} \subseteq [\![\alpha(\mathcal{F})]\!]^{may}_{MFTS}$ is a may-execution in $\alpha(\mathcal{F})$.*
 (ii) *Let $k' \in \alpha(\mathbb{K})$ and $\rho \in [\![\pi_{k'}(\alpha(\mathcal{F}))]\!]^{must}_{MTS} \subseteq [\![\alpha(\mathcal{F})]\!]^{must}_{MFTS}$ be a must-execution in $\alpha(\mathcal{F})$. Then there exists $k \in \mathbb{K}$, such that $\rho \in [\![\pi_k(\mathcal{F})]\!]_{TS} \subseteq [\![\mathcal{F}]\!]_{FTS}$.*

As a result, every $\forall$CTL* (resp., $\exists$CTL*) property true for the may- (resp., must-) component of $\alpha(\mathcal{F})$ is true for $\mathcal{F}$ as well. Moreover, the MFTS $\alpha(\mathcal{F})$ preserves the full CTL*.

Theorem 1 (Preservation results). *For any FTS $\mathcal{F}$ and (α, γ), we have:*

($\forall$**CTL***) *For every $\Phi \in \forall CTL^\star$, $\alpha(\mathcal{F})^{may} \models \Phi \implies \mathcal{F} \models \Phi$.*
($\exists$**CTL***) *For every $\Phi \in \exists CTL^\star$, $\alpha(\mathcal{F})^{must} \models \Phi \implies \mathcal{F} \models \Phi$.*
(**CTL***) *For every $\Phi \in CTL^\star$, $\alpha(\mathcal{F}) \models \Phi \implies \mathcal{F} \models \Phi$.*

---

[2] Proofs of all lemmas and theorems in this section can be found in [12, Appendix A].

Abstract models are designed to be conservative for the satisfaction of properties. However, in case of the refutation of a property, a counter-example is found in the abstract model which may be spurious (introduced due to abstraction) for some variants and genuine for the others. This can be established by checking which variants can execute the found counter-example.

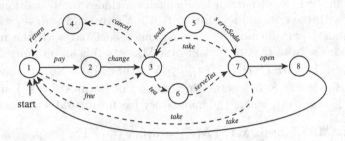

Fig. 3. $\alpha^{\text{join}}(\text{VENDINGMACHINE})$.

Let Φ be a CTL* formula which is not in $\forall$CTL* nor in $\exists$CTL*, and let $\mathcal{MF}$ be an MFTS. We verify $\mathcal{MF} \models \Phi$ by checking Φ on two FTSs $\mathcal{MF}^{may}$ and $\mathcal{MF}^{must}$, and then we combine the obtained results as specified below.

Theorem 2. *For every $\Phi \in CTL^\star$ and MFTS $\mathcal{MF}$, we have:*

$$\mathcal{MF} \models \Phi = \begin{cases} true & if \left(\mathcal{MF}^{may} \models \Phi \wedge \mathcal{MF}^{must} \models \Phi\right) \\ false & if \left(\mathcal{MF}^{may} \not\models \Phi \vee \mathcal{MF}^{must} \not\models \Phi\right) \end{cases}$$

Therefore, we can check a formula Φ which is not in $\forall$CTL* nor in $\exists$CTL* on $\alpha(\mathcal{F})$ by running a model checker twice, once with the may-component of $\alpha(\mathcal{F})$ and once with the must-component of $\alpha(\mathcal{F})$. On the other hand, a formula Φ from $\forall$CTL* (resp., $\exists$CTL*) on $\alpha(\mathcal{F})$ is checked by running a model checker only once with the may-component (resp., must-component) of $\alpha(\mathcal{F})$.

The family-based model checking problem can be reduced to a number of smaller problems by partitioning the set of variants. Let the subsets $\mathbb{K}_1, \mathbb{K}_2, \ldots, \mathbb{K}_n$ form a *partition* of the set $\mathbb{K}$. Then: $\mathcal{F} \models \Phi$ iff $\pi_{\mathbb{K}_i}(\mathcal{F}) \models \Phi$ for all $i = 1, \ldots, n$. By using Theorem 1 (CTL*), we obtain the following result.

Corollary 1. *Let $\mathbb{K}_1, \mathbb{K}_2, \ldots, \mathbb{K}_n$ form a partition of $\mathbb{K}$, and $(\alpha_1, \gamma_1), \ldots, (\alpha_n, \gamma_n)$ be Galois connections. If $\alpha_1(\pi_{\mathbb{K}_1}(\mathcal{F})) \models \Phi, \ldots, \alpha_n(\pi_{\mathbb{K}_n}(\mathcal{F})) \models \Phi$, then $\mathcal{F} \models \Phi$.*

Therefore, in case of suitable partitioning of $\mathbb{K}$ and the aggressive $\boldsymbol{\alpha}^{\text{join}}$ abstraction, all $\boldsymbol{\alpha}^{\text{join}}(\pi_{\mathbb{K}_i}(\mathcal{F}))^{may}$ and $\boldsymbol{\alpha}^{\text{join}}(\pi_{\mathbb{K}_i}(\mathcal{F}))^{must}$ are ordinary TSs, so the family-based model checking problem can be solved using existing single-system model checkers with all the optimizations that these tools may already implement.

Example 4. Consider the properties introduced in Example 2. Using the TS $\alpha^{\text{join}}(\text{VENDINGMACHINE})^{may}$ we can verify $\Phi_1 = \forall\Box\forall\Diamond\text{start}$ (Theorem 1, $(\forall\text{CTL}^{\star})$). We obtain the counter-example $①\rightarrow③\rightarrow⑤\rightarrow⑦\rightarrow③\ldots$, which is genuine for variants satisfying c. Hence, variants from $[\![c]\!]$ violate Φ_1. On the other hand, by verifying that $\alpha^{\text{join}}(\pi_{[\![\neg c]\!]}(\text{VENDINGMACHINE}))^{may}$ satisfies Φ_1, we can conclude by Theorem 1, $(\forall\text{CTL}^{\star})$ that variants from $[\![\neg c]\!]$ satisfy Φ_1.

We can verify $\Phi_2 = \forall\Box\exists\Diamond\text{start}$ by checking may- and must-components of $\alpha^{\text{join}}(\text{VENDINGMACHINE})$. In particular, we have $\alpha^{\text{join}}(\text{VENDINGMACHINE})^{may}$ $\models \Phi_2$ and $\alpha^{\text{join}}(\text{VENDINGMACHINE})^{must} \models \Phi_2$. Thus, using Theorem 1, $(\text{CTL}^{\star})$ and Theorem 2, we have that $\text{VENDINGMACHINE} \models \Phi_2$.

Using $\alpha^{\text{join}}(\text{VENDINGMACHINE})^{must}$ we can verify $\Phi_3 = \exists\Box\exists\Diamond\text{start}$, by finding the witness $①\rightarrow②\rightarrow③\rightarrow⑤\rightarrow⑦\rightarrow⑧\rightarrow①\ldots$. By Theorem 1, $(\exists\text{CTL}^{\star})$, we have that $\text{VENDINGMACHINE} \models \Phi_3$. $\Box$

4   Implementation

We now describe an implementation of our abstraction-based approach for CTL model checking of variational systems in the context of the state-of-the-art NUSMV model checker [3]. Since it is difficult to use FTSs to directly model very large variational systems, we use a high-level modelling language, called fNUSMV. Then, we show how to implement projection and variability abstractions as syntactic transformations of fNUSMV models.

A High-Level Modelling Language. fNUSMV is a feature-oriented extension of the input language of NUSMV, which was introduced by Plath and Ryan [28] and subsequently improved by Classen [4]. A NUSMV model consists of a set of variable declarations and a set of assignments. The variable declarations define the state space and the assignments define the transition relation of the finite state machine described by the given model. For each variable, there are assignments that define its initial value and its value in the next state, which is given as a function of the variable values in the present state. Modules can be used to encapsulate and factor out recurring submodels. Consider a basic NUSMV model shown in Fig. 4a. It consists of a single variable x which is initialized to 0 and does not change its value. The property (marked by the keyword SPEC) is "$\forall\Diamond(x \geq k)$", where k is a meta-variable that can be replaced with various natural numbers. For this model, the property holds when $k = 0$. In all other cases (for $k > 0$), a counterexample is reported where x stays 0.

The fNUSMV language [28] is based on superimposition. *Features* are modelled as self-contained textual units using a new FEATURE construct added to the NUSMV language. A feature describes the changes to be made to the given basic NUSMV model. It can introduce new variables into the system (in a section marked by the keyword INTRODUCE), override the definition of existing variables in the basic model and change the values of those variables when they are read (in a section marked by the keyword CHANGE). For example, Fig. 4b shows a FEATURE construct, called A, which changes the basic model in Fig. 4a. In particular, the feature A defines a new variable nA initialized to 0. The basic system is changed in such a way that when the condition "$nA = 0$" holds then in the next state the basic system's variable x is incremented by 1 and in this case (when x is incremented) nA is set to 1. Otherwise, the basic system is not changed.

Classen [4] shows that fNuSMV and FTS are expressively equivalent. He [4] also proposes a way of composing fNuSMV features with the basic model to create a single model in pure NuSMV which describes all valid variants. The information about the variability and features in the composed model is recorded in the states. This is a slight deviation from the encoding in FTSs, where this information is part of the transition relation. However, this encoding has the advantage of being implementable in NuSMV without drastic changes. In the composed model each feature becomes a Boolean state variable, which is non-deterministically initialised and whose value never changes. Thus, the initial states of the composed model include all possible feature combinations. Every change performed by a feature is guarded by the corresponding feature variable.

For example, the composition of the basic model and the feature A given in Figs. 4a and b results in the model shown in Fig. 4c. First, a module, called *features*, containing all features (in this case, the single one A) is added to the system. To each feature (e.g. A) corresponds one variable in this module (e.g. fA). The *main* module contains a variable named f of type *features*, so that all feature variables can be referenced in it (e.g. $f.fA$). In the next state, the variable x is incremented by 1 when the feature A is enabled (fA is *TRUE*) and nA is 0. Otherwise (*TRUE:* can be read as *else:*), x is not changed. Also, nA is set to 1 when A is enabled and x is incremented by 1. The property $\forall\Diamond(x \geq 0)$ holds for both variants when A is enabled and A is disabled (fA is *FALSE*).

```
1  MODULE main
2  VAR x : 0..1;
3  ASSIGN
4     init(x) := 0;
5     next(x) := x;
6  SPEC AF(x ≥ k);
```
(a) The basic model.

```
1  FEATURE A
2  INTRODUCE
3     VAR nA : 0..1;
4     ASSIGN init(nA) := 0;
5  CHANGE
6     IF (nA = 0) THEN
7     IMPOSE next(x) := x + 1;
8           next(nA) :=
9        next(x) = x+1?1:nA;
```
(b) The feature A.

```
1  MODULE features
2     VAR fA : boolean;
3     ASSIGN
4        init(fA) := {TRUE,FALSE};
5        next(fA) := fA;
6  MODULE main
7     VAR f : features; x : 0..1; nA : 0..1;
8     ASSIGN
9        init(x) := 0; init(nA) := 0;
10       next(x) := case f.fA & nA=0 : x+1;
11             TRUE : x;
12          easc;
13       next(nA) := case
14          f.fA & nA=0 & next(x)=x+1 : 1;
15          TRUE : nA;
16          easc;
```
(c) The composed model $\mathcal{M}$.

Fig. 4. NuSMV models.

Transformations. We present the syntactic transformations of fNuSMV models defined by projection and variability abstractions. Let M represent a model obtained by composing a basic model with a set of features $\mathbb{F}$. Let M contain a set of assignments of the form: $s(v) := \mathsf{case}\ b_1 : e_1; \ldots b_n : e_n;\ \mathsf{esac}$, where v is a variable, b_i is a boolean expression, e_i is an expression (for $1 \leq i \leq n$), and $s(v)$ is one of v, $\mathsf{init}(v)$, or $\mathsf{next}(v)$. We denote by $[\![M]\!]$ the FTS for this model [4].

Let $\mathbb{K}' \subseteq 2^{\mathbb{F}}$ be a set of configurations described by a feature expression ψ', i.e. $[\![\psi']\!] = \mathbb{K}'$. The projection $\pi_{[\![\psi']\!]}([\![M]\!])$ is obtained by adding the constraint ψ' to each b_i in the assignments to the state variables.

Let (α, γ) be a Galois connection from Sect. 3. The abstract $\alpha(M)^{may}$ and $\alpha(M)^{must}$ are obtained by the following rewrites for assignments in M:

$$\alpha\big(s(v):=\mathsf{case}\ b_1:e_1;\ldots b_n:e_n;\ \mathsf{esac}\big)^{may} = s(v):=\mathsf{case}\ \alpha^m(b_1):e_1;\ldots \alpha^m(b_n):e_n;\ \mathsf{esac}$$

$$\alpha\big(s(v):=\mathsf{case}\ b_1:e_1;\ldots b_n:e_n;\ \mathsf{esac}\big)^{must} = s(v):=\mathsf{case}\ \widetilde{\alpha}(b_1):e_1;\ldots \widetilde{\alpha}(b_n):e_n;\ \mathsf{esac}$$

The functions α^m and $\widetilde{\alpha}$ copy all basic boolean expressions other than feature expressions, and recursively calls itself for all sub-expressions of compound expressions. For $\alpha^{join}(M)^{may}$, we have a single Boolean variable rnd which is non-deterministically initialized. Then, $\alpha^m(\psi) = rnd$ if $\alpha(\psi) = true$. We have: $\alpha([\![M]\!])^{may} = [\![\alpha(M)^{may}]\!]$ and $\alpha([\![M]\!])^{must} = [\![\alpha(M)^{must}]\!]$. For example, given the composed model $\mathcal{M}$ in Fig. 4c, the abstractions $\alpha^{join}(\mathcal{M})^{may}$ and $\alpha^{join}(\mathcal{M})^{must}$ are shown in Figs. 5 and 6, respectively. Note that $\widetilde{\alpha^{join}}(f.fA) = false$, so the first branch of case statements in $\mathcal{M}$ is never taken in $\alpha^{join}(\mathcal{M})^{must}$.

```
1  MODULE main
2    VAR x : 0..1; nA : 0..1; rnd : boolean;
3    ASSIGN
4      init(x) := 0; init(nA) := 0;
5      init(rnd) := {TRUE,FALSE};
6      next(x) := case rnd & nA = 0 : x + 1;
7                      TRUE : x; easc;
8      next(nA) := case
9        rnd & nA = 0 & next(x) = x + 1 : 1;
10       TRUE : nA; easc;
```

Fig. 5. $\alpha^{join}(\mathcal{M})^{may}$

```
1  MODULE main
2    VAR x : 0..1; nA : 0..1;
3    ASSIGN
4      init(x) := 0; init(nA) := 0;
5      next(x) := x;
6      next(nA) := nA;
```

Fig. 6. $\alpha^{join}(\mathcal{M})^{must}$

5   Evaluation

We now evaluate our abstraction-based verification technique. First, we show how variability abstractions can turn a previously infeasible analysis of variability model into a feasible one. Second, we show that instead of verifying CTL properties using the family-based version of NuSMV [7], we can use variability abstraction to obtain an abstract variability model (with a low number of variants) that can be subsequently model checked using the standard version of NuSMV.

All experiments were executed on a 64-bit Intel®Core^{TM} i7-4600U CPU running at 2.10 GHz with 8 GB memory. The implementation, benchmarks, and all results obtained from our experiments are available from: https://aleksdimovski. github.io/abstract-ctl.html. For each experiment, we report the time needed to perform the verification task in seconds. The BDD model checker NuSMV is run with the parameter -df -dynamic, which ensures that the BDD package reorders the variables during verification in case the BDD size grows beyond a certain threshold.

Synthetic Example. As an experiment, we have tested limits of family-based model checking with extended NuSMV and "brute-force" single-system model checking with standard NuSMV (where all variants are verified one by one). We have gradually added variability to the variational model in Fig. 4. This was done by adding optional features which increase the basic model's variable x by the number corresponding to the given feature. For example, the CHANGE section for the second feature B is: IF $(nB = 0)$ THEN IMPOSE next$(x) := x + 2$; next$(nB) :=$ next$(x) = x + 2?1{:}nB$, and the domain of x is 0..3.

We check the assertion $\forall\Diamond(x \geq 0)$. For $|\mathbb{F}| = 25$ (for which $|\mathbb{K}| = 2^{25}$ variants, and the state space is 2^{32}) the family-based NuSMV takes around 77 min to verify the assertion, whereas for $|\mathbb{F}| = 26$ it has not finished the task within two hours. The analysis time to check the assertion using "brute force" with standard NuSMV ascends to almost three years for $|\mathbb{F}| = 25$. On the other hand, if we apply the variability abstraction α^{join}, we are able to verify the same assertion by only one call to standard NuSMV on the *abstracted* model in 2.54 s for $|\mathbb{F}| = 25$ and in 2.99 s for $|\mathbb{F}| = 26$.

Elevator. The ELEVATOR, designed by Plath and Ryan [28], contains about 300 LOC and 9 independent features: Antiprunk, Empty, Exec, OpenIfIdle, Overload, Park, QuickClose, Shuttle, and TTFull, thus yielding $2^9 = 512$ variants. The elevator serves a number of floors (which is five in our case) such that there is a single platform button on each floor which calls the elevator. The elevator will always serve all requests in its current direction before it stops and changes direction. When serving a floor, the elevator door opens and closes again. The size of the ELEVATOR model is 2^{28} states. On the other hand, the sizes of $\alpha^{join}(\text{ELEVATOR})^{may}$ and $\alpha^{join}(\text{ELEVATOR})^{must}$ are 2^{20} and 2^{19} states, resp.

We consider five properties. The $\forall$CTL property "$\Phi_1 = \forall\Box\,(floor = 2 \land liftBut5.pressed \land direction = up \Rightarrow \forall[direction = up\,\mathsf{U}floor = 5]$" is that, when the elevator is on the second floor with direction up and the button five is pressed, then the elevator will go up until the fifth floor is reached. This property is violated by variants for which Overload (the elevator will refuse to close its doors when it is overloaded) is satisfied. Given sufficient knowledge of the system and the property, we can tailor

prop. -erty	family-based app.		abstraction-based app.		improvement
	$\|\mathbb{K}\|$	TIME	$\|\alpha(\mathbb{K})\|$	TIME	TIME
Φ_1	512	36.73 s	2	2.59 s	14 ×
Φ_2	512	35.89 s	2	6.95 s	5 ×
Φ_3	512	54.76 s	1	1.67 s	32 ×
Φ_4	512	2.65 s	2	1.04 s	2.5 ×
Φ_5	512	37.76 s	2	2.62 s	15 ×

Fig. 7. Verification of ELEVATOR properties using tailored abstractions. We compare family-based approach vs. abstraction-based approach.

an abstraction for verifying this property more effectively. We call standard NuSMV to check Φ_1 on two models $\alpha^{\text{join}}(\pi_{\llbracket \text{Overload} \rrbracket}(\text{ELEVATOR}))^{may}$ and $\alpha^{\text{join}}(\pi_{\llbracket \neg \text{Overload} \rrbracket}(\text{ELEVATOR}))^{may}$. For the first abstracted projection we obtain an "abstract" counter-example violating Φ_1, whereas the second abstracted projection satisfies Φ_1. Similarly, we can verify that the ∀CTL property "$\Phi_2 = \forall\Box\,(floor = 2 \wedge direction = up \Rightarrow \forall\bigcirc(direction = up))$" is satisfied only by variants with enabled Shuttle (the lift will change direction at the first and last floor). We can successfully verify Φ_2 for $\alpha^{\text{join}}(\pi_{\llbracket \text{Shuttle} \rrbracket}(\text{ELEVATOR}))^{may}$ and obtain a counter-example for $\alpha^{\text{join}}(\pi_{\llbracket \neg \text{Shuttle} \rrbracket}(\text{ELEVATOR}))^{may}$. The ∃CTL property "$\Phi_3 = (\text{OpenIfIdle} \wedge \neg\text{QuickClose}) \implies \exists\Diamond(\exists\Box\,(door = open))$" is that, there exists an execution such that from some state on the door stays open. We can invoke the standard NuSMV to verify that Φ_3 holds for $\alpha^{\text{join}}(\pi_{\llbracket \text{OpenIfIdle} \wedge \neg\text{QuickClose} \rrbracket}(\text{ELEVATOR}))^{must}$. The following two properties are neither in ∀CTL nor in ∃CTL. The property "$\Phi_4 = \forall\Box\,(floor = 1 \wedge idle \wedge door = closed \implies \exists\Box(floor = 1 \wedge door = closed))$" is that, for any execution globally if the elevator is on the first floor, idle, and its door is closed, then there is a continuation where the elevator stays on the first floor with closed door. The satisfaction of Φ_4 can be established by verifying it against both $\alpha^{\text{join}}(\text{ELEVATOR})^{may}$ and $\alpha^{\text{join}}(\text{ELEVATOR})^{must}$ using two calls to standard NuSMV. The property "$\Phi_5 = \text{Park} \implies \forall\Box\,(floor = 1 \wedge idle \implies \exists[idle\,\mathsf{U}\,floor = 1])$" is satisfied by all variants with enabled Park (when idle, the elevator returns to the first floor). We can successfully verify Φ_5 by analyzing $\alpha^{\text{join}}(\pi_{\llbracket \text{Park} \rrbracket}(\text{ELEVATOR}))^{may}$ and $\alpha^{\text{join}}(\pi_{\llbracket \text{Park} \rrbracket}(\text{ELEVATOR}))^{must}$ using two calls to standard NuSMV. We can see in Fig. 7 that abstractions achieve significant speed-ups between 2.5 and 32 times faster than the family-based approach.

6 Related Work and Conclusion

Recently, many family-based techniques that work on the level of variational systems have been proposed. This includes family-based syntax checking [20,25], family-based type checking [24], family-based static program analysis [16,17,27], family-based verification [22,23,29], etc. In the context of family-based model checking, Classen et al. present FTSs [6] and specifically designed family-based model checking algorithms for verifying FTSs against LTL [5]. This approach is extended [4,7] to enable verification of CTL properties using an family-based version of NuSMV. In order to make this family-based approach more scalable, the works [15,21] propose applying conservative variability abstractions on FTSs for deriving abstract family-based model checking of LTL. An automatic abstraction refinement procedure for family-based model checking is then proposed in [19]. The application of variability abstractions for verifying real-time variational systems is described in [18]. The work [11,13] presents an approach for family-based software model checking of #ifdef-based (second-order) program families using symbolic game semantics models [10].

To conclude, we have proposed conservative (over-approximating) and their dual (under-approximating) variability abstractions to derive abstract family-based model checking that preserves the full CTL*. The evaluation confirms that interesting properties can be efficiently verified in this way. In this work, we assume that a suitable abstraction is manually generated before verification. If we want to make the whole verification procedure automatic, we need to develop an abstraction and refinement framework for CTL* properties similar to the one in [19] which is designed for LTL.

References

1. Apel, S., Batory, D.S., Kästner, C., Saake, G.: Feature-Oriented Software Product Lines - Concepts and Implementation. Springer, Heidelberg (2013). https://doi.org/10.1007/978-3-642-37521-7
2. Baier, C., Katoen, J.: Principles of Model Checking. MIT Press, Cambridge, London (2008)
3. Cimatti, A., Clarke, E., Giunchiglia, E., Giunchiglia, F., Pistore, M., Roveri, M., Sebastiani, R., Tacchella, A.: NuSMV 2: an opensource tool for symbolic model checking. In: Brinksma, E., Larsen, K.G. (eds.) CAV 2002. LNCS, vol. 2404, pp. 359–364. Springer, Heidelberg (2002). https://doi.org/10.1007/3-540-45657-0_29
4. Classen, A.: CTL model checking for software product lines in NuSMV. Technical report, P-CS-TR SPLMC-00000002, University of Namur, pp. 1–17 (2011)
5. Classen, A., Cordy, M., Heymans, P., Legay, A., Schobbens, P.: Model checking software product lines with SNIP. STTT **14**(5), 589–612 (2012). https://doi.org/10.1007/s10009-012-0234-1
6. Classen, A., Cordy, M., Schobbens, P., Heymans, P., Legay, A., Raskin, J.: Featured transition systems: foundations for verifying variability-intensive systems and their application to LTL model checking. IEEE Trans. Softw. Eng. **39**(8), 1069–1089 (2013). http://doi.ieeecomputersociety.org/10.1109/TSE.2012.86
7. Classen, A., Heymans, P., Schobbens, P.Y., Legay, A.: Symbolic model checking of software product lines. In: Proceedings of the 33rd International Conference on Software Engineering, ICSE 2011, pp. 321–330. ACM (2011). http://doi.acm.org/10.1145/1985793.1985838
8. Clements, P., Northrop, L.: Software Product Lines: Practices and Patterns. Addison-Wesley, Boston (2001)
9. Cousot, P.: Partial completeness of abstract fixpoint checking. In: Choueiry, B.Y., Walsh, T. (eds.) SARA 2000. LNCS (LNAI), vol. 1864, pp. 1–25. Springer, Heidelberg (2000). https://doi.org/10.1007/3-540-44914-0_1

10. Dimovski, A.S.: Program verification using symbolic game semantics. Theor. Comput. Sci. **560**, 364–379 (2014). https://doi.org/10.1016/j.tcs.2014.01.016
11. Dimovski, A.S.: Symbolic game semantics for model checking program families. In: Bošnački, D., Wijs, A. (eds.) SPIN 2016. LNCS, vol. 9641, pp. 19–37. Springer, Cham (2016). https://doi.org/10.1007/978-3-319-32582-8_2
12. Dimovski, A.S.: Abstract family-based model checking using modal featured transition systems: preservation of CTL* (extended version). CoRR abs/1802.04970 (2018). http://arxiv.org/abs/1802.04970
13. Dimovski, A.S.: Verifying annotated program families using symbolic game semantics. Theor. Comput. Sci. **706**, 35–53 (2018). https://doi.org/10.1016/j.tcs.2017.09.029
14. Dimovski, A.S., Al-Sibahi, A.S., Brabrand, C., Wąsowski, A.: Family-based model checking without a family-based model checker. In: Fischer, B., Geldenhuys, J. (eds.) SPIN 2015. LNCS, vol. 9232, pp. 282–299. Springer, Cham (2015). https://doi.org/10.1007/978-3-319-23404-5_18
15. Dimovski, A.S., Al-Sibahi, A.S., Brabrand, C., Wasowski, A.: Efficient family-based model checking via variability abstractions. STTT **19**(5), 585–603 (2017). https://doi.org/10.1007/s10009-016-0425-2
16. Dimovski, A.S., Brabrand, C., Wasowski, A.: Variability abstractions: trading precision for speed in family-based analyses. In: 29th European Conference on Object-Oriented Programming, ECOOP 2015. LIPIcs, vol. 37, pp. 247–270. Schloss Dagstuhl - Leibniz-Zentrum fuer Informatik (2015). https://doi.org/10.4230/LIPIcs.ECOOP.2015.247
17. Dimovski, A.S., Brabrand, C., Wąsowski, A.: Finding suitable variability abstractions for family-based analysis. In: Fitzgerald, J., Heitmeyer, C., Gnesi, S., Philippou, A. (eds.) FM 2016. LNCS, vol. 9995, pp. 217–234. Springer, Cham (2016). https://doi.org/10.1007/978-3-319-48989-6_14
18. Dimovski, A.S., Wąsowski, A.: From transition systems to variability models and from lifted model checking back to UPPAAL. In: Aceto, L., Bacci, G., Bacci, G., Ingólfsdóttir, A., Legay, A., Mardare, R. (eds.) Models, Algorithms, Logics and Tools. LNCS, vol. 10460, pp. 249–268. Springer, Cham (2017). https://doi.org/10.1007/978-3-319-63121-9_13
19. Dimovski, A.S., Wąsowski, A.: Variability-specific abstraction refinement for family-based model checking. In: Huisman, M., Rubin, J. (eds.) FASE 2017. LNCS, vol. 10202, pp. 406–423. Springer, Heidelberg (2017). https://doi.org/10.1007/978-3-662-54494-5_24
20. Gazzillo, P., Grimm, R.: SuperC: parsing all of C by taming the preprocessor. In: Vitek, J., Lin, H., Tip, F. (eds.) ACM SIGPLAN Conference on Programming Language Design and Implementation, PLDI 2012, Beijing, China, 11–16 June 2012. pp. 323–334. ACM (2012). http://doi.acm.org/10.1145/2254064.2254103
21. Holzmann, G.J.: The SPIN Model Checker - Primer and Reference Manual. Addison-Wesley, Boston (2004)
22. Iosif-Lazar, A.F., Al-Sibahi, A.S., Dimovski, A.S., Savolainen, J.E., Sierszecki, K., Wasowski, A.: Experiences from designing and validating a software modernization transformation (E). In: 30th IEEE/ACM International Conference on Automated Software Engineering, ASE 2015. pp. 597–607 (2015). https://doi.org/10.1109/ASE.2015.84
23. Iosif-Lazar, A.F., Melo, J., Dimovski, A.S., Brabrand, C., Wasowski, A.: Effective analysis of C programs by rewriting variability. Program. J. **1**(1), 1 (2017). https://doi.org/10.22152/programming-journal.org/2017/1/1

318   A. S. Dimovski

24. Kästner, C., Apel, S., Thüm, T., Saake, G.: Type checking annotation-based product lines. ACM Trans. Softw. Eng. Methodol. **21**(3), 14:1–14:39 (2012). http://doi.acm.org/10.1145/2211616.2211617
25. Kästner, C., Giarrusso, P.G., Rendel, T., Erdweg, S., Ostermann, K., Berger, T.: Variability-aware parsing in the presence of lexical macros and conditional compilation. In: Proceedings of the 26th Annual ACM SIGPLAN Conference on Object-Oriented Programming, Systems, Languages, and Applications, OOPSLA 2011, pp. 805–824 (2011). http://doi.acm.org/10.1145/2048066.2048128
26. Larsen, K.G., Thomsen, B.: A modal process logic. In: Proceedings of the Third Annual Symposium on Logic in Computer Science (LICS 1988), pp. 203–210. IEEE Computer Society (1988). https://doi.org/10.1109/LICS.1988.5119
27. Midtgaard, J., Dimovski, A.S., Brabrand, C., Wasowski, A.: Systematic derivation of correct variability-aware program analyses. Sci. Comput. Program. **105**, 145–170 (2015). https://doi.org/10.1016/j.scico.2015.04.005
28. Plath, M., Ryan, M.: Feature integration using a feature construct. Sci. Comput. Program. **41**(1), 53–84 (2001). https://doi.org/10.1016/S0167-6423(00)00018-6
29. von Rhein, A., Thüm, T., Schaefer, I., Liebig, J., Apel, S.: Variability encoding: from compile-time to load-time variability. J. Log. Algebr. Methods Program. **85**(1), 125–145 (2016). https://doi.org/10.1016/j.jlamp.2015.06.007

FPH: Efficient Non-commutativity
Analysis of Feature-Based Systems

Marsha Chechik[1]([⊠]) [iD], Ioanna Stavropoulou[1][iD], Cynthia Disenfeld[1][iD],
and Julia Rubin[2][iD]

[1] University of Toronto, Toronto, Canada
{chechik,ioanna,disenfeld}@cs.toronto.edu
[2] University of British Columbia, Vancouver, Canada
mjulia@ece.ubc.ca

Abstract. *Feature-oriented software development (FOSD)* is a promising approach for developing a collection of similar software products from a shared set of software assets. A well-recognized issue in FOSD is the analysis of *feature interactions*: cases where the integration of multiple features would alter the behavior of one or several of them. Existing approaches to feature interaction detection require a fixed order in which the features are to be composed but do not provide guidance as to how to define this order or how to determine a relative order of a newly-developed feature w.r.t. existing ones. In this paper, we argue that classic feature non-commutativity analysis, i.e., determining when an order of composition of features affects properties of interest, can be used to complement feature interaction detection to help build orders between features and determine many interactions. To this end, we develop and evaluate Mr. Feature Potato Head (FPH) – a modular approach to non-commutativity analysis that does not rely on temporal properties and applies to systems expressed in Java. Our experiments running FPH on 29 examples show its efficiency and effectiveness.

1 Introduction

Feature-oriented software development (FOSD) [3] is a promising approach for developing a collection of similar software products from a shared set of software assets. In this approach, each feature encapsulates a certain unit of functionality of a product; features are developed and tested independently and then integrated with each other; developed features are then combined in a prescribed manner to produce the desired set of products. A well-recognized issue in FOSD is that it is prone to creating *feature interactions* [2,13,22,28]: cases where integrating multiple features alters the behavior of one or several of them. Not all interactions are desirable. E.g., the Night Shift feature of the recent iPhone did not allow the Battery Saver to be enabled (and the interaction was not fixed for over 2 months, potentially affecting millions of iPhone users). More critically, in 2010, Toyota had to recall hundreds of thousands of Prius cars due to an

A. Russo and A. Schürr (Eds.): FASE 2018, LNCS 10802, pp. 319–336, 2018.
https://doi.org/10.1007/978-3-319-89363-1_18

interaction between the regenerative braking system and the hydraulic braking system that caused 62 crashes and 12 injuries.

Existing approaches for identifying feature interactions either require an explicit order in which the features are to be composed [6, 8, 18, 19, 26] or assume presence of a "150%" representation which uses an implicit feature order [12, 15]. Yet they do not provide guidance on how to define this order, or how to determine a relative order of a newly-developed feature w.r.t. existing ones.

A classical approach of feature non-commutativity detection, defined by Plath and Ryan [25], can be used to help build a composition order. The authors defined non-commutativity as "the presence of a property, the value of which is different depending on the order of the composition of the features" and proposed a model-checking approach allowing to check available properties on different composition orders. E.g., consider the Elevator System [14, 25] consisting of five features: *Empty* – to clear the cabin buttons when the elevator is empty; *ExecutiveFloor* – to override the value of the variable stop to give priority to the executive floor (not stopping in the middle); *TwoThirdsFull* – to override the value of stop not allowing people to get into the elevator when it is two-thirds full; *Overloaded* – to disallow closing of the elevator doors while it is overloaded; and *Weight* – to allow the elevator to calculate the weight of the people inside the cabin. Features *TwoThirdsFull* and *ExecutiveFloor* are not commutative (e.g., a property "the elevator does not stop at other floors when there is a call from the executive floor" changes value under different composition orders), whereby *Empty* and *Weight* are. Thus, an order between *Empty* and *Weight* is not required, whereas the user needs to determine which of *TwoThirdsFull* or *ExecutiveFloor* should get priority. Thus, *feature non-commutativity guarantees a feature interaction, whereas feature commutativity means that order of composition does not matter. Both of these outcomes can effectively complement other feature interaction approaches.*

In this paper, we aim to make commutativity analysis practical and applicable to a broad range of modern feature-based systems, so that it can be used as "the first line of defense" before running other feature interaction detections. There are three main issues we need to tackle. First of all, to prove that features commute requires checking their composition against all properties, and capturing the complete behavior of features in the form of formal specifications is an infeasible task. Thus, we aim to make our approach *property-independent*. Second, we need to make commutativity analysis *scalable* and avoid rechecking the entire system every time a single feature is modified or a new one is added. Finally, we need to support analysis of systems expressed in modern programming languages such as Java.

In [25], features execute "atomically" in a state-machine representation of the system, i.e., they make all state changes in one step. However, when systems are represented in conventional programming languages like Java, feature execution may take several steps; furthermore, such features are composed *sequentially*, using *superimposition* [5]. Examining properties defined by researchers studying such systems [6], we note that they do not refer to intermediate states within the feature execution, but only to states before or after running the feature, effectively treating features as atomic. In this paper, we use this notion of atomicity to formalize commutativity. The foundation of our technique is the separation between feature behavior and feature composition and efficiently checking whether different feature compositions orders leave the system in the same internal state. Otherwise, a property distinguishing between the orders can be found, and thus they do not commute. We call the technique and the accompanying tool Mr. Feature Potato Head (*FPH*), named after the kids' toy which can be composed from interchangeable parts.

In this paper, we show that FPH can perform commutativity analysis in an efficient and precise manner. It performs a modular checking of *pairs of features* [17], which makes the analysis very scalable: when a feature is modified, the analysis can focus only on the interactions related to that feature, without needing to consider the entire family. That is, once the initial analysis is completed, a partial order between the features of the given system can be created and used for detecting other types of interactions. Any feature added in the future will be checked against all other features for non-commutativity-related interactions to define its order among the rest of the features, but the existing order would not be affected. In this paper, we only focus on the non-commutativity analysis and consider interaction *resolution* as being out of scope.

Contributions. This paper makes the following contributions: (1) It defines commutativity for features expressed in imperative programming languages and composed via superimposition. (2) It proposes a novel modular representation for features that distinguishes between feature composition and behavior. (3) It defines and implements a modular specification-free feature commutativity analysis that focuses on pairs of features rather than on complete products or product families. (4) It instantiates this analysis on features expressed in Java. (5) It shows that the implemented analysis is effective for detecting instances of non-commutativity as well as proving their absence. (6) It evaluates the efficiency and scalability of the approach.

The rest of the paper is organized as follows. We provide the necessary background, fix the notation and define the notion of commutativity in Sect. 2. In Sect. 3, we describe our iterative tool-supported methodology for detecting feature non-commutativity for systems expressed in Java. We evaluate the effectiveness and scalability of our approach in Sect. 4, compare our approach to related work in Sect. 5 and conclude in Sect. 6[1].

2   Preliminaries

In this section, we present the basic concepts and definitions and define the notion of commutativity used throughout this paper.

---

[1] The complete replication package including the tool binary, case studies used in our experiments and proofs of selected theorems is available at https://github.com/FeaturePotatoHead/FPH.

```
1  package ElevatorSystem;                          7  private boolean stopRequestedInDirection (Direction
2  public class Elevator {                              dir , boolean respectFloorCalls , boolean
3    int executiveFloor = 4;                            respectInLiftCalls ) {
4    public boolean isExecutiveFloor(int floorID)  {...}   8  if ( isExecutiveFloorCalling ()) { ... }
5    public boolean isExecutiveFloorCalling ()  {...}    9  else return original (dir , respectFloorCalls ,
6    private boolean stopRequestedAtCurrentFloor() {...}  10     respectInLiftCalls );
                                                      10  }}
```

Fig. 1. Java code snippet of the feature *ExecutiveFloor*.

Feature-Oriented Software Development (FOSD). In FOSD, *products* are specified by a set of features (*configuration*). A *base system* has no features. While defining the notion of a feature is an active research topic [11], in this paper we assume that a feature is *"a structure that extends and modifies the structure of a given program in order to satisfy a stakeholder's requirement, to implement a design decision and to offer a configuration option"* [5].

Superimposition. *Superimposition* is a feature composition technique that composes software features by merging their corresponding substructures. Based on superimposition, Apel et al. [5] propose a composition technique where different components are represented using a uniform and language independent-structure called a *feature structure tree (FST)*. An *FST* is a tree $T = \langle$(Terminal Node) | (Non Terminal Node) (Tree T)+$\rangle$, where + denotes "one or more". A *Non Terminal Node* is a tuple $\langle name, type \rangle$ which represents a non-leaf element of T with the respective name and type. A *Terminal Node* is a tuple $\langle name, type, body \rangle$ which represents a leaf element of T. In addition to *name* and *type*, each *Terminal Node* has *body* that encapsulates the content of the element, i.e., the corresponding method implementation or field initializer. A *feature* is a tuple $f = \langle name, T \rangle$, where *name* is a string representing f's name and T is an FST abstractly representing f.

Each feature describes the modifications that need to be made to the base system, also represented by an FST, to enable the behavior of the feature. While FSTs are generally language-independent, in this paper we focus on features defined in a Java-based language. For example, consider the Java code snippet in Fig. 1, which shows the *ExecutiveFloor*. This feature makes one of the floors "an executive one". If there is a call to or from this floor, it gets priority over any other call. This feature is written in Java using a special keyword `original` [5] (line 9). Under this composition, a call from the new method to every existing method with the same name is added, in order to preserve the original behavior. Without `original`, new methods replace existing ones.

The feature *ExecutiveFloor* in Fig. 1 is represented by the tuple $\langle executive, T \rangle$, where T is the FST in Fig. 2. `ElevatorSystem` is a Non Terminal Node that represents the `ElevatorSystem` package with the tuple $\langle$`ElevatorSystem`, `package`$\rangle$, and `stopRequestedInDirection` is a Terminal Node represented by $\langle$`stopRequestedInDirection`, `method`, *body*$\rangle$, where *body* is the content of the `stopRequested-InDirection` method in Fig. 1 (lines 8–9). Another Non Terminal Node is `Elevator`, whereas `executiveFloor`, `isExecutiveFloor`, `isExecutiveFloorCalling` and `stopRequestedAtCurrentFloor` are Terminal.

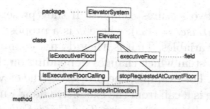

Fig. 2. FST representation for the feature *ExecutiveFloor*.

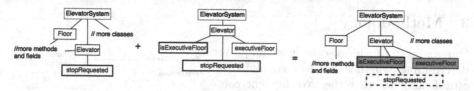

Fig. 3. Simplified composition of *ExecutiveFloor* and the base elevator system.

For Java-specified features, Terminal Nodes represent methods, fields, `import` statements, modifier lists, as well as `extends`, `implements` and `throws` clauses whereas directories, files, packages and classes are represented by Non Terminals.

Superimposition Process. Given two FSTs, starting from the root and proceeding recursively to create a new FST, two nodes are composed when they share the same name and type and when their parent nodes have been composed. For Terminal Nodes which additionally have a body, if a Node A is composed with a Node B, the body of A is replaced by that of B unless the keyword `original` is present in the body of B. In this case, the body of A is replaced by that of B and the keyword is replaced by A's body. Since the `original` keyword is not used for fields, the body of the initial field is always replaced by that of the new one.

Figure 3 gives an example of a composition of a simplified *ExecutiveFloor* feature with the elevator base system. Terminal Nodes that have been overridden by the feature are with dashed outline and new fields and methods added by the feature are shown as shaded nodes. For example, the method `stopRequested`, which is part of the base system, is overridden by the feature, whereas the field `executiveFloor`, which is only part of the feature, is added to the base system.

Commutativity. We define commutativity w.r.t. properties observable before or after features finish their execution (as those in [6]). A *state* of the system after superimposing a feature is the valuation of each variable (or array, object, field, etc. [24]) of the base system and each variable (or array, etc.) introduced by the feature. We also add a new variable *inBase* which is *true* iff this state is not within a method overridden by any feature. In the rest of the paper, we refer to states where *inBase* is *true* as *inBase* states. A *transition* of the system is an execution of a statement, including method calls and return statements [24].

Then we say that two features *commute* if they preserve valuation of properties of the form G(*inBase* $\implies$ ϕ), where ϕ is a propositional formula defined over any system state variables. That is, they do not commute if there is at least one state of the base system which changes depending on the order in which the features are composed. For example, the property "the elevator does not stop at other floors when there is a call from the executive floor", used in Sect. 1 to identify non-commutativity between features *TwoThirdsFull* and *ExecutiveFloor*, is G(*inBase* $\implies$ $\neg$(*isExecutiveFloorCalling* $\wedge$ *stopped* $\wedge$ *floor*$\neq$*executiveFloor*)).

3   Methodology

Our goal is to provide a scalable technique for determining whether features commute by establishing whether the two different composition orders leave the system in the same internal state. The workflow of FPH is shown below. The first step of FPH is to transform each feature from an FST into an FPH representation consisting of a set of fragments. The base is transformed in the same way as the individual features. Each fragment is further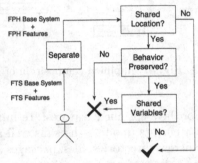
split into feature behavior and feature composition – see Sect. 3.1. Afterwards, we check for non-compositionality. If there do not exist feature fragments that have *shared location* of composition, i.e., whose feature composition components are the same, then the features commute. Otherwise, check the pairs of feature fragments for *behavior preservation*, i.e., when the two features are composed in the same location, the previous behavior is still present and can be executed. If this check succeeds, we perform the *shared variables* check – see Sect. 3.2.

3.1   Separating Feature Behavior and Composition

We now formally define the FPH representation of features that separates the behavior of features and location of their composition and provide transformation operators between the FPH and the FST representations.

Definition 1. *An FPH feature is a tuple ⟨*name*, *fragments*⟩, where* name *is the feature name and* fragments *is the list of feature fragments that comprise the feature. Let a feature f be given. A* Feature Fragment fg *is a tuple ⟨fb, fc⟩, where* fb *is a feature behavior defined in Definition 2 and* fc *is a feature composition defined in Definition 3.*

Definition 2. Feature Behavior fb *of a feature fragment* fg *is a tuple ⟨*name*, *type*,*body*, *bp*, *vars*⟩, where* name, type *and* body *represent the name, type and content, respectively, of the element represented by* fg. bp *is a boolean value which is set to* true *if the feature preserves the original behavior, i.e., when the keyword* original *is present in the body and not within a conditional statement.* vars *is a list of variable names read or written within* fg.

Definition 3. Feature composition fc *of a feature fragment* fg *is represented by* ⟨location⟩ *which is the path leading to the terminal node represented by* fg.

The *Separate* operator (see Fig. 4a) transforms features from the FST to the FPH representation by creating a new fragment for each Terminal Node in the given FST. For the behavior component of the fragment, its *name*, *type* and *body* attributes come from the respective counterparts of the FST Terminal Node. The *bp* field is *true* if every path within *body* contains the keyword `original`; otherwise, it is *false*. For the composition component, the *location* field gets its value from the unique path to the Terminal Node from the root of the FST. *vars* are the parameters of the method and the fields that are used within it.

E.g., consider creating the FPH representation for *ExecutiveFloor* feature in Fig. 2. Since there are five Terminal Nodes, five fragments will be created to represent each node. In the fragment created for the `stopRequestedInDirection` node, the information in *fb* about *name*, *node* and *type* is derived from the information stored in the node, $fb = \langle$`stopRequestedInDirection`, method, [body]$\rangle$, where body consists of lines 8–9 of Fig. 1. *bp* is *false* since the keyword `original` is within an if statement and *vars* consists only of the method parameters since the method does not use any global fields. After separating, the feature composition is $fc = $ ElevatorSystem.Elevator.stopRequested-InDirection.

To transform features from FPH back to FST, we define the *Join* operator. It takes as input a list of feature fragments and returns an FST (see Fig. 4b).

Input: FST Representation of F
Output: Fragments of F {f = (fb, fc)}
1 **begin**
2 | *fragment list* ← []
3 | **forall** *Non Terminal Nodes* n ∈ FST **do**
4 | | f = (fb, fc) ← new Feature Fragment
5 | | fc.location ← n.name
6 | | fb.type ← n.type
7 | | fb.body ← n.body
8 | | fb.vars ← n.get-Variables()
9 | | **if** fb.body contains original in every path **then**
   | | | fb.bp ← true
10 | | **else** fb.bp ← false
11 | | add f to fragment list
12 | **return** *fragment list*

(a)

Input: Set of fragments of F {(fb, fc)}
Output: FST representation of F
1 **begin**
2 | **forall** (fb, fc) ∈ F **do**
3 | | t ← new Terminal Node
4 | | t.name ← fb.name
5 | | t.type ← fb.type
6 | | t.body ← fb.body
7 | | **forall** node ∈ F **do**
8 | | | **if** node ∉ FST **then** add node to FST
9 | | | **else** continue
10 | **return** FST

(b)

Input: Fragments of F_1 and F_2 {$f_j = (fb_j, fc_j)$} with $j \in \{1, 2\}$
Output: Yes if F_1 and F_2 commute, No otherwise
1 **begin**
2 | **forall** $(fb_1, fc_1) \in F_1, (fb_2, fc_2) \in F_2$ **do**
3 | | **if** $(fc_1 = fc_2)$ **then**
4 | | | **if** $(fb_1.bp = false \lor fb_2.bp = false)$ **then**
5 | | | | **return** *No*
6 | | | **if** $(fb_1.vars \cap fb_2.vars) \neq \emptyset$ **then**
7 | | | | **return** *No*
8 | **return** *Yes*

(c)

Fig. 4. Algorithms *Separate*, *Join* and *CheckCommutativity*.

It creates a new Terminal Node to be added to the FST for each feature fragment in the given feature. The *name*, *type* and *body* attributes of the node are filled using the corresponding fields in the feature behavior component of the fragment. Then, starting from the root node, for every node in the *location* path of the feature composition component, if the node does not exist in the FST, it is added; otherwise, the next node of the path is examined. The information about *bp* and *vars* is already contained in the body of the Terminal Node and is no longer considered as a separate field. E.g., joining the *ExecutiveFloor* feature that we previously separated yields the FST in Fig. 2, as expected.

Theorem 1. *Let n be the number of features in a system. For every feature F which can be represented as (fb, fc),* Join *and* Separate *are inverses of each other, i.e.,* Join*(*Separate*(F)) = F and* Separate*(*Join*(fb,fc)) = (fb,fc).*

3.2   Compositional Analysis of Non-commutativity

We now formally present the algorithm *check commutativity*, a sequence of increasingly more precise, and more expensive, static checks to perform non-commutativity analysis. These are called *shared location, behavior preservation* and *shared variables* – see Fig. 4c. Additionally, we prove soundness and correctness of the FPH methodology, i.e., that our checks guarantee feature commutativity as defined in Sect. 2.

Check Shared Location. The first check examines whether F_1 and F_2 have any fragments that can be composed in the same location (line 3). Clearly, when F_1 and F_2 are applied in different places, e.g., they change different methods, *inBase* states are the same independently of their order of composition, and thus the features commute. Otherwise, more precise checks are required. E.g., *ExecutiveFloor* (see Fig. 2) and *Empty* (see Fig. 5a) do not share methods or fields and thus can be applied in either order.

Theorem 2. *If features F_1 and F_2 are not activated in the same location, any* inBase *state resulting from first composing F_1 followed by F_2 (denoted $F_1; F_2$) is the same as for $F_2; F_1$.*

Check Behavior Preservation. Suppose one pair of feature fragments of F_1 and F_2, say, f_1 and f_2, can be composed in the same location. Then we examine whether the original behavior is preserved or overridden (indicated by the *fb*

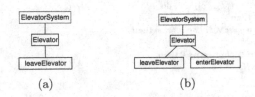

(a)   (b)

Fig. 5. Two features of the elevator system.

field of each fragment). If bp of f_1 and f_2 is *true*, an additional check for shared variables is applied. Otherwise, i.e., when bp of either f_1 or f_2 is *false*, we report an interaction. Clearly, this check can introduce false positives because we do not look at the content of the methods but merely at the presence of the `original` keyword. E.g., two methods may happen to perform the exact same operation and yet not include the `original` keyword. In this case, we would falsely detect an interaction[2].

Check Shared Variables. If F_1 and F_2 are activated at different places and both preserve the original behavior, commutativity of their composition depends on whether they have shared variables that can be both read and written. This check aims to detect that. E.g., both features *Empty* (see Fig. 5a) and *Weight* (see Fig. 5b) modify the `leaveElevator` method and preserve the original behavior. Since no variables between them are shared, the order of composition does not affect the execution of the resulting system.

Extracting shared variable information requires not only identifying which variable is part of each feature behavior, but also running points-to analysis since aliasing is very common in Java. Moreover, a shared variable might not appear in the body of the affected method but instead in the body of a method called by it. Yet existing frameworks for implementing interprocedural points-to analyses [21] may not correctly identify all variables read and written within a method. Moreover, even if two features do write to the same location, this may not manifest a feature interaction. E.g., they may write the same value. For these reasons, our shared variables check may introduce false positives and false negatives. We evaluate its precision in Sect. 4.

Theorem 3. *Let features F_1 and F_2 activated at the same place and preserving the behavior of the base be given. If the variables read and written by each feature are correctly identified and independent of each other ($F_1.vars \cap F_2.vars = \emptyset$), then any* inBase *state resulting from composing $F_1; F_2$ is the same as that of composing $F_2; F_1$.*

When two features merely read the same variable, it does not present an interaction problem. We handle this case in our implementation (see Sect. 4).

Theorem 4 (Soundness). *Given features F_1 and F_2, if variables read and written by them are correctly identified, Algorithm in Fig. 4c is sound: when it outputs Success, F_1 and F_2 commute.*

Complexity. Let $|F|$ be the number of features in the system and let M be the largest number of fragments that each feature can have. For a pair of feature fragments, checking shared location and checking behavior preservation are both done in constant time, so the overall complexity of these steps is $O((|F| \times M)^2)$. In the worst case, all features affect the same set of methods and thus the shared variables check should be run on all of them. Yet, all fragments in a feature are non-overlapping, and thus the number of these checks is at most $|F|^2 \times M$.

---

[2] But this does not happen often – see Sect. 4.

The time to perform a shared variable check, which we denote by SV, can vary depending on an implementation and can be as expensive as PSPACE-hard. Thus, the overall complexity of non-commutativity detection is $O((|F| \times M)^2 + SV \times |F|^2 \times M)$.

4 Evaluation

In this section, we present an experimental evaluation of FPH, aiming to answer the following research questions: **(RQ1)** How effective is FPH in performing non-commutativity analysis of feature-based systems? **(RQ2)** How accurate is FPH's non-commutativity analysis? **(RQ3)** How efficient is FPH compared to state-of-the-art tools for performing non-commutativity analysis? **(RQ4)** How well does FPH scale as the number of fragments increases?

Tool Support. We have implemented our methodology (Sect. 3) as follows. The *Separate* process is implemented on top of FeatureHouse's composition operator in Java. We use the parsing process that was provided in FeatureHouse [4] to separate features to the FPH representation and added about 200 LOC.

The main process to check commutativity is implemented as a Python script in about 250 LOC. The first two parts of the commutativity check are directly implemented in the script. The third one, *Check shared variables*, requires considering possible aliases of feature-based Java programs. For this check, we have implemented a Java program, FPH_varsAnalysis, that calls Soot [21] to build the call graph and analyze each reachable method. FPH_varsAnalysis is an interprocedural context insensitive points-to analysis that, given two feature fragments that superimpose the same method, checks whether a variable of the same type is written by at least one of them and read or written by the other. Since feature fragments cannot be compiled by themselves (and thus Soot cannot be used on them), in order to do alias analysis, our program requires a representation that consists of the base system and all possible features. This representation is readily available for systems from the SPLVerifier repository since it uses a family-based approach to analysis. We generate a similar representation for all other systems used in our experiments.

Models and Methods. We have applied FPH to 29 case studies written in Java. In the first five columns of Table 1, we summarize the information about these systems. The first six have been considered by SPLVerifier [6] – a tool for checking whether a software product line (SPL) satisfies its feature specifications. SPLVerifier includes sample-based, product-based and family-based analyses and assumes that the order in which features should be composed is provided. The SPLVerifier examples came with specifications given by aspects woven at base system points, with an exception thrown if the state violates an expected property. The rest of our case studies are SPLs from the FeatureHouse repository [4].

We were unable to identify other techniques for analyzing feature commutativity of Java programs. Plath and Ryan [25] and Atlee et al. [8] compare different composition orders but handle only state machines. SPLVerifier [6] represents state of the art in verification of feature-based systems expressed in Java, but it is not designed to do non-commutativity analysis. In the absence of alternative tools, we adapted SPLVerifier to the task of finding non-commutativity violations to be able to compare with FPH.

We conducted two experiments to evaluate FPH and to answer our research questions. For the first, we ran SPLVerifier on the first six systems (all properties that came with them satisfied the pattern in Sect. 2 and thus were appropriate for commutativity detection) presented in Table 1 to identify non-commutativity interactions. Since SPLVerifier is designed to check products against a set of specifications, we have to define what a commutativity check means in this context. For a pair of features, SPLVerifier would detect a commutativity violation if, upon composing these features in different orders, the provided property produces different values. During this check, SPLVerifier considers composition of all other features of the system in all possible orders and thus can identify two-way, three-way, etc. feature interactions, if applicable. We measured the time taken by SPLVerifier and the number of interactions found.

For the second experiment, we checked all 29 systems using FPH to identify non-commutativity interactions. We measured the number of feature pairs that required checking for shared variables, the time the analysis took and the precision of FPH in finding interactions. We were unable to establish ground truth for non-commutativity analysis in cases where FPH required the shared variables check due to our tool's reliance on Soot's unsound call graph construction [7]. Thus, we measured precision of our analysis by manually analyzing the validity of every interaction found by FPH. We also calculated SPLVerifier's *relative* recall, i.e., the ratio of non-commutativity-related interactions detected by FPH that were also detected by SPLVerifier. We did not encounter any interactions that were detected by SPLVerifier but not by FPH.

When the shared variables check is not necessary, our technique is sound. In such cases, if we inform the user that two features are commutative, they certainly are, and there is no need to define an order between them. As shown below, soundness was affected only for a small number of feature pairs. Moreover, advances in static analysis techniques may improve our results for those cases in the future. Our experiments were performed on a 2 GB RAM Virtual machine within an Intel Core i5 machine dual-core at 1.3 GHz.

Results. Columns 6–10 of Table 1 summarize results of our experiments, including, for the first six examples, SPLVerifier's precision and (relative) recall. "SV pairs" capture the number of feature pairs for which the shared variables check was required. A dash in the precision columns means that the measurement was not meaningful since no interactions were detected. E.g., SPLVerifier does not detect any non-commutativity interactions for Email, and FPH does not find any non-commutativity interactions for EPL. FPH found a number of instances of non-commutativity such as the one between *ExecutiveFloor* and *TwoThirds-Full* in the Elevator System. Only one SV check was required (while checking *Empty* and *Weight* features). Without our technique, the user would need to

Table 1. Overview of case studies.

System	LOC	# Feat.	# Frag.	Description	# Comm Interactions	SV Pairs	FPH Precision	SPLV Precision	SPLV Rel. Recall
Elevator	799	5	19	Our running example	1	1	1	1	1
Email	938	8	55	Email communication suite	3	9	1	-	0
Minepump	425	6	10	Water pump in mining operation	3	0	1	1	0.67
GPL	2510	17	109	Graph product line	2	38	0.1	-	0
AJStats	15311	19	128	Statistics for AspectJ	26	136	1	-	0
ZipMe	5479	12	229	Zip compression library	5	0	1	-	0
BerkeleyDB	64652	98	2667	Embedded database engine	198	1	1		
ChatSystem/Burke	614	7	51	Network client and server	2	14	0.33		
ChatSystem/Dreiling	938	5	78	Network client and server	3	0	1		
ChatSystem/Becker	651	6	42	Network client and server	5	2	1		
ChatSystem/Weiss	931	9	23	Network client and server	4	5	0.75		
ChatSystem/Schink	873	6	50	Network client and server	4	1	1		
ChatSystem/Rehn	862	6	58	Network client and server	14	2	1		
ChatSystem/Thuem	544	7	34	Network client and server	1	2	1		
EPL	99	10	22	Arithmetic expression evaluator	0	1	-		
GameOfLife	1656	14	154	Computer game	5	0	1		
Graph	467	4	26	Graph library	0	6	-		
Notepad/Quark	1397	11	106	Text editor	20	21	1		
Notepad/Delaware	1654	5	122	Text editor	10	0	1		
Notepad/Wellington	1522	3	38	Text editor	0	0	-		
Notepad/Svetoslav	1627	5	83	Text editor	0	0	-		
Notepad/Wehrman	1716	4	83	Text editor	6	6	1		
Notepad/Guimbarda	1586	14	229	Text editor	91	0	1.		
Notepad/Robison	1404	9	90	Text editor	0	0	-		
PKJab	4994	7	99	Chat network client	2	0	1		
Raroscope	428	4	18	Compression library	0	0	-		
Sudoku	1850	6	103	Computer game	5	4	1		
TankWar	3184	19	213	Computer game	71	27	0.97		
Violet	9789	87	912	UML model editor	35	28	1		

provide order between the five features of the Elevator System, that is, specify 20 (5 × 4) ordering constraints. FPH allows us to conclude that *ExecutiveFloor* and *TwoThirdsFull* do not commute, that *Empty* and *Weight* likely commute but this is not guaranteed, and that all other pairs of features do commute. Thus, only two feature pairs required further analysis by the user.

The Minepump system did not require the shared variable check at all and thus FPH analysis for it is sound, and all three of the found interactions were manually confirmed to be "real" (thus, precision is 1). ChatSystem/Weiss has nine features which would imply needing to define the order between 72 (9 × 8) feature pairs. Four non-commutativity cases were found, all using the shared variables check, but only three were confirmed as "real" via a manual inspection (thus, precision is 0.75). We conclude that FPH is effective in discovering non-commutativity violations and proving their absence (**RQ1**).

We now turn to studying the accuracy of FPH w.r.t. finding non-commutativity violations (**RQ2**). From Table 1, we observe that for the Elevator System, both FPH and SPLVerifier correctly detect a non-commutativity interaction. For the Minepump system, SPLVerifier only finds two out of the three interactions found by FPH (relative recall = 0.67). For the Email system, AJStats, ZipMe, and GPL the specifications available in SPLVerifier do not allow detecting any of the non-commutativity interactions found by FPH (relative recall = 0).

GPL was a problematic case for FPH, affecting its precision. The graph algorithms in this example take a set of vertices and create and maintain an internal

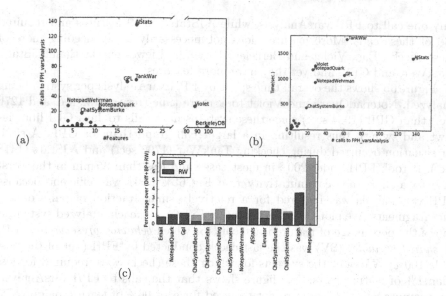

Fig. 6. (a) Number of FPH_varsAnalysis calls per system; (b) Time spent by FPH_varsAnalysis per system; (c) Percentage of non-commutativity checks where BP or SV analyses were applied last. (Color figure online)

data structure (e.g., to calculate the vertices involved in the shortest path or in a strongly connected component). With this data structure, our analysis found a number of possible shared variables and incorrectly deemed several features as non-commutative. E.g., the algorithms to find cycles or the shortest path between two nodes access the same set of vertices but change different fields and thus are commutative. One way of avoiding such false positives would be to implement field-sensitive alias analysis. While more precise, it will be significantly slower than our current shared variables analysis.

For the remaining systems, either FPH's reported interactions were "real", or, in cases where it returned some false positives (ChatSystemBurke, ChatSystemWeiss, and TankWar), it had to do with the precision of the alias analysis. Thus, given SPLVerifier's set of properties, FPH always exhibited the same or better precision and recall than SPLVerifier. Moreover, for all but three of the remaining systems, FPH exhibited perfect precision. We thus conclude that FPH is very accurate (**RQ2**).

We now turn to the efficiency of our analysis (**RQ3**). The time it took to separate features into behavior and composition was usually under 5 s. The outlier was BerkeleyDB, which took about a minute, due to the number of features and especially fragments (BerkeleyDB has 2667 fragments whereas Violet has 912 and the other systems have at most 229). In general, the time taken by FPH's commutativity check was highly influenced by the number of calls to FPH_varsAnalysis. Figure 6a shows the number of calls to FPH_varsAnalysis as the number of features increases. E.g., BerkeleyDB has 98 features and required only one call to FPH_varsAnalysis, while AJStats has 19 features and required 136 of these calls. More features does not necessarily imply needing more of these checks. E.g., Violet and BerkeleyDB required fewer checks than AJStats, TankWar, and GPL, and yet they have more features.

Figure 6b shows the overall time spent by FPH_varAnalysis per system being analyzed. NotepadQuark and Violet took more time (resp., 1192 sec. and 1270 sec.) than GPL (1084 sec.) since these systems have calls to Java GUI libraries (awt and swing), thus resulting in a larger call graph than for GPL. A similar situation occurred during checking TankWar (1790 sec.) and AJStats (1418 sec.). It took FPH under 200 s in most cases and less than 35 min in the worst case to analyze non-commutativity (see Fig. 6b). FPH was efficient because FPH_varAnalysis was required for a relatively small fraction of pairs of feature fragments. We plot this information in Fig. 6c. For each analyzed system, it shows the percentage of feature fragments for which *behavior preservation* (BP) or *shared variables* (SV) was the last check conducted by FPH (out of the possible 100%). We omit the systems for which these checks were required for less than 1% of feature pairs. The figure shows that the calls to FPH_varsAnalysis (to compute SV, in blue) were not required for over 96% of feature pairs.

To check for non-commutativity violations, SPLVerifier needs to check all possible products which is infeasible in practice. So we set the timeout to one hour during which SPLVerifier was able to check 110 products for Elevator, 57 for Email, 151 for Minepump, 3542 for GPL, 2278 for AJStats and 1269 for ZipMe. For each of these systems, a different check is required for every specification, thus the same product is checked more than once if more than one specification exists. Even though GPL, AJStats and ZipMe are larger systems with more features, they have fewer properties associated with them and therefore we were able to check more products within one hour. Thus, to answer **RQ3**, FPH was much more efficient than SPLVerifier in performing non-commutativity analysis. SPLVerifier was only able to analyze products containing the base system and at most three features before reaching a timeout. Moreover, FPH can *guarantee commutativity*, while SPLVerifier cannot because of it being based on the properties given.

Our experiments also allow us to conclude that our technique is highly scalable (**RQ4**). E.g., the percentage of calls to FPH_varsAnalysis is shown to be small and increases only slightly with increase in the number of fragments (see Fig. 6a and b).

Threats to Validity. Our results may not generalize to other feature-based systems expressed in Java. We believe we have mitigated this threat by running our tool on examples provided by FeatureHouse. They include a variety of systems of different sizes which we consider to be representative of typical Java feature-based systems. As mentioned earlier, our use of SPLVerifier was not as intended by its designers. We also had no ground truth when the shared variable check was required. For those few cases, we calculated SPLVerifier's relative instead of actual recall.

5   Related Work

In this section, we survey related work on modular feature definitions, feature interaction detection and commutativity-related feature interactions.

Modular Feature Definitions. A number of approaches to modular feature definitions have been proposed. E.g., the composition language in [8] includes states in which the feature is to be composed (similar to our $fg.location$) and the feature behavior (similar to our $fb.body$). Other work [4,9,10] uses superimposition of FSTs to obtain the composed system. In [14,25], new variables are added or existing ones are changed with particular kind of compositions (either executing a new behavior when a particular variable is read, or adding a check before a particular variable is set). These approaches treat the feature behavior together with its composition specification. Instead, our approach automatically separates feature definition into the behavioral and the composition part, enabling a more scalable and efficient analysis.

Feature Interaction Detection. Calder et al. [13] survey approaches for analyzing feature interactions. Interactions occur because the behavior of one feature is being affected by others, e.g., by adding non-deterministic choices that result in conflicting states, by adding infinite loops that affect termination, or by affecting some assertions that are satisfied by the feature on its own. Checking these properties as well as those discussed in more recent work [8,15,18,19] requires building the entire SPL. Additionally, all these approaches consider state machine representations which are not available for most SPLs, and extracting them from code is non-trivial. SPLLift [12] is a family-based static analysis tool not directly intended to find interactions. Any change in a feature would require building the family-based representation again, whereas we conduct modular checks between features. Spek [26] is a product-based approach that analyzes whether the different products satisfy provided feature specifications. It does not check whether the features commute.

Non-commutativity-Related Feature Interactions. [5,8] also looked at detecting non-commutativity-related feature interactions. [5] presents a feature algebra and shows why composition (by superimposition) is, in general, not commutative. [8] analyzes feature commutativity by checking for bisimulation, and the result of the composition is a state machine representing the product. Neither work reports on a tool or applies to systems expressed in Java.

Aspect-Oriented Approaches. Storzer et al. [27] present a tool prototype for detecting precedence-related interactions in AspectJ. Technically, this approach is very similar to ours: it (a) detects which advice is activated at the same place; (b) checks whether the proceed keyword and exceptions are present; and (c) analyzes read and written variables. Yet, the focus is on aspects, and often many aspects are required to implement a single feature [23]. This implies that for m features with an average of n aspects each, the analysis in [27] needs to make $\mathcal{O}\left((m \cdot n)^2\right)$ checks, while our approach requires $\mathcal{O}\left(m^2\right)$ checks. Therefore, the approach in [27] might be significantly slower than FPH. [1] analyzes interactions of aspects given by composition filters by checking for simulation among all the different orderings in which advice with shared joinpoints can be composed. As the number of advice with shared joinpoints increases, that approach considers every possible ordering, while we keep the analysis pairwise. [16,20] define modular techniques to check properties of aspect-oriented systems. [16] uses assume-guarantee reasoning to verify and detect interactions even when aspects can be activated within other aspects. It does not require an order but does require specifications to detect whether a certain composition order would not satisfy these. [20] uses the explicit CTL model-checking algorithm to distribute global properties into local properties to be checked for each aspect. This yields a modular check. In addition to requiring specifications, this technique assumes AspectJ's ordering of aspects.

6   Conclusion and Future Work

In this paper, we presented a compositional approach for checking non-commutativity of features in systems expressed in Java. The method is based on determining whether pairs of features can write to the same variables and thus the order in which features are composed to the base system may determine their valuation. The method is complementary to other feature interaction detection approaches such as [6,12] in that it helps build an order in which features are to be composed. When two features commute, they can be composed in any order. In addition, this method helps detect a number of feature interactions. The method is implemented in our framework FPH – Mr. Feature Potato Head. FPH does not require specifying properties of features and does not need to consider the entire set of software products every time a feature is modified. By performing an extensive empirical evaluation of FPH, we show that the approach is highly scalable and effective. In the future, we plan to further evaluate our technique, handle languages outside of Java and experiment with more precise methods for determining shared variables.

Acknowledgements. We thank anonymous reviewers for their helpful comments. This research has been supported by NSERC.

References

1. Aksit, M., Rensink, A., Staijen, T.: A graph-transformation-based simulation approach for analysing aspect interference on shared join points. In: Proceedings of AOSD 2009, pp. 39–50 (2009)
2. Apel, S., Atlee, J., Baresi, L., Zave, P.: Feature interactions: the next generation (Dagstuhl Seminar 14281). Dagstuhl Rep. **4**(7), 1–24 (2014)
3. Apel, S., Kästner, C.: An overview of feature-oriented software development. J. Object Technol. **8**(5), 49–84 (2009)
4. Apel, S., Kastner, C., Lengauer, C.: FeatureHouse: language-independent, automated software composition. In: Proceedings of ICSE 2009, pp. 221–231 (2009)

5. Apel, S., Lengauer, C., Möller, B., Kästner, C.: An algebra for features and feature composition. In: Proceedings of AMAST 2008, pp. 36–50 (2008)
6. Apel, S., Von Rhein, A., Wendler, P., Groslinger, A., Beyer, D.: Strategies for product-line verification: case studies and experiments. In: Proceedings of ICSE 2013 (2013)
7. Arzt, S., Rasthofer, S., Fritz, C., Bodden, E., Bartel, A., Klein, J., Le Traon, Y., Octeau, D., McDaniel, P.: Flowdroid: precise context, flow, field, object-sensitive and lifecycle-aware taint analysis for android apps. ACM SIGPLAN Not. **49**(6), 259–269 (2014)
8. Atlee, J., Beidu, S., Fahrenberg, U., Legay, A.: Merging features in featured transition systems. In: Proceedings of MoDeVVa@MODELS 2015, pp. 38–43 (2015)
9. Batory, D., Sarvela, J., Rauschmayer, A.: Scaling step-wise refinement. IEEE TSE **30**(6), 355–371 (2004)
10. Beidu, S., Atlee, J., Shaker, P.: Incremental and commutative composition of state-machine models of features. In: Proceedings of MiSE@ICSE 2015, pp. 13–18 (2015)
11. Berger, T., Lettner, D., Rubin, J., Grünbacher, P., Silva, A., Becker, M., Chechik, M., Czarnecki, K.: What is a feature?: A qualitative study of features in industrial software product lines. In: Proceedings of SPLC 2015, pp. 16–25 (2015)
12. Bodden, E., Tolêdo, T., Ribeiro, M., Brabrand, C., Borba, P., Mezini, M.: SPLLift: Statically analyzing software product lines in minutes instead of years. In: Proceedings of PLDI 2013, pp. 355–364 (2013)
13. Calder, M., Kolberg, M., Magill, E., Reiff-Marganiec, S.: Feature interaction: A critical review and considered forecast. Comput. Netw. **41**(1), 115–141 (2003)
14. Classen, A., Cordy, M., Heymans, P., Legay, A., Schobbens, P.-Y.: Formal semantics, modular specification, and symbolic verification of product-line behaviour. Sci. Comput. Program. **80**, 416–439 (2014)
15. Cordy, M., Classen, A., Schobbens, P.-Y., Heymans, P., Legay, A.: Managing evolution in software product lines: a model-checking perspective. In: Proceedings of VaMoS 2002, pp. 183–191 (2012)
16. Disenfeld, C., Katz, S.: A closer look at aspect interference and cooperation. In: Proceedings of AOSD 2012, pp. 107–118. ACM (2012)
17. Fantechi, A., Gnesi, S., Semini, L.: Optimizing feature interaction detection. In: Petrucci, L., Seceleanu, C., Cavalcanti, A. (eds.) FMICS-AVoCS 2017. LNCS, vol. 10471, pp. 201–216. Springer, Cham (2017). https://doi.org/10.1007/978-3-319-67113-0_13
18. Guelev, D., Ryan, M., Schobbens, P.-Y.: Model-checking the preservation of temporal properties upon feature integration. STTT **9**(1), 53–62 (2007)
19. Jayaraman, P., Whittle, J., Elkhodary, A.M., Gomaa, H.: Model composition in product lines and feature interaction detection using critical pair analysis. In: Engels, G., Opdyke, B., Schmidt, D.C., Weil, F. (eds.) MODELS 2007. LNCS, vol. 4735, pp. 151–165. Springer, Heidelberg (2007). https://doi.org/10.1007/978-3-540-75209-7_11
20. Krishnamurthi, S., Fisler, K., Greenberg, M.: Verifying aspect advice modularly. In: ACM SIGSOFT SEN, vol. 29, pp. 137–146. ACM (2004)
21. Lam, P., Bodden, E., Lhoták, O., Hendren, L.: The soot framework for java program analysis: a retrospective. In: Proceedings of CETUS 2011, vol. 15, p. 35 (2011)
22. Liu, J., Batory, D., Nedunuri, S.: Modeling interactions in feature oriented software designs. In: Proceedings of ICFI 2005 (2005)

23. Lopez-Herrejon, R.E., Batory, D., Cook, W.: Evaluating support for features in advanced modularization technologies. In: Black, A.P. (ed.) ECOOP 2005. LNCS, vol. 3586, pp. 169–194. Springer, Heidelberg (2005). https://doi.org/10.1007/11531142_8
24. Nipkow, T., Von Oheimb, D.: Java$_{light}$ is type-safe - definitely. In: Proceedings of PLDI 1998, pp. 161–170. ACM (1998)
25. Plath, M., Ryan, M.: Feature integration using a feature construct. Sci. Comput. Program. **41**(1), 53–84 (2001)
26. Scholz, W., Thüm, T., Apel, S., Lengauer, C.: Automatic detection of feature interactions using the java modeling language: an experience report. In: Proceedings of SPLC 2011, p. 7 (2011)
27. Storzer, M., Forster, F.: Detecting precedence-related advice interference. In: Proceedings of ASE 2006, pp. 317–322, September 2006
28. Zave, P.: Feature interactions and formal specifications in telecommunications. IEEE Comput. **26**(8), 20–29 (1993)

Taming Multi-Variability of Software Product Line Transformations

Daniel Strüber[1]([✉]) [iD], Sven Peldzsus[1] [iD], and Jan Jürjens[1,2] [iD]

[1] Universität Koblenz-Landau, Koblenz, Germany
{strueber,peldszus,juerjens}@uni-koblenz.de
[2] Fraunhofer Institute for Software and Systems Engineering, Dortmund, Germany

Abstract. Software product lines continuously undergo model transformations, such as refactorings, refinements, and translations. In product line transformations, the dedicated management of variability can help to control complexity and to benefit maintenance and performance. However, since no existing approach is geared for situations in which both the product line *and* the transformation specification are affected by variability, substantial maintenance and performance obstacles remain. In this paper, we introduce a methodology that addresses such *multi-variability* situations. We propose to manage variability in product lines and rule-based transformations consistently by using annotative variability mechanisms. We present a staged rule application technique for applying a variability-intensive transformation to a product line. This technique enables considerable performance benefits, as it avoids enumerating products or rules upfront. We prove the correctness of our technique and show its ability to improve performance in a software engineering scenario.

1 Introduction

Software product line engineering [1] enables systematic reuse of software artifacts through the explicit management of variability. Representing a *software product line* (SPL) in terms of functionality increments called *features*, and mapping these features to development artifacts such as domain models and code allows to generate custom-tailored products on demand, by retrieving the corresponding artifacts for a given feature selection. Companies such as Bosch, Boeing, and Philips use SPLs to deliver tailor-made products to their customers [2].

Despite these benefits, a growing amount of variability leads to combinatorial explosions of the product space and, consequently, to severe challenges. Notably, this applies to software engineering tasks such as refactorings [3], refinements [4], and evolution steps [5], which, to support systematic management, are often expressed as model transformations. When applying a given model transformation to a SPL, a key challenge is to avoid enumerating and considering all possible products individually. To this end, Salay et al. [6] have proposed an algorithm that *"lifts"* regular transformation rules to a whole product line. The algorithm

© The Author(s) 2018
A. Russo and A. Schürr (Eds.): FASE 2018, LNCS 10802, pp. 337–355, 2018.
https://doi.org/10.1007/978-3-319-89363-1_19

transforms the SPL, represented as a variability-annotated domain model, in such way as if each product had been considered individually.

Yet, in complex transformation scenarios as increasingly found in practice [7], not only the considered models include variations: The transformation system can contain variability as well, for example, due to desired optional behavior of rules, or for rule variants arising from the sheer complexity of the involved meta-models. While a number of works [8–10] support systematic reuse to improve maintainability, *variability-based model transformation* (VB) [11,12] also aims to improve the performance when a transformation system with many similar rules is executed. To this end, these rules are represented as a single rule with variability annotations, called *VB rule*. During rule applications, a special *VB rule application* technique [13] saves redundant effort by considering common rule parts only once. In summary, for cases where either the model or the transformation system alone contains variability, solid approaches are available.

However, a more challenging case occurs when a variability-intensive transformation is applied to an SPL. In this *multi-variability* setting, where *both* the input model and the specification of a transformation contain variability, the existing approaches fall short to deal with the resulting complexity: One can either consider all rules, so they can be "lifted" to the product line, or consider all products, so they become amenable to VB model transformation. Both approaches are undesirable, as they require enumerating an exponentially growing number of artifacts and, therefore, threaten the feasibility of the transformation.

In this paper, we introduce a methodology for SPL transformations inspired by the *uniformity principle* [14], a tenet that suggests to handle variability consistently throughout all software artifacts. We propose to capture variability of SPLs and transformations using variability-annotated domain models and rules. Model and rule elements are annotated with *presence conditions*, specifying the conditions under which the annotated elements are present. The presence conditions of model and rule elements are specified over two separate sets of features, representing SPL and rule variability. Annotated domain models and rules can be created manually using available editor support [15,16], or automatically from existing products and rules by using merge-refactoring techniques [17,18].

Given an SPL and a VB rule, as shown in Fig. 1, we provide a *staged* rule application technique (black arrow) for applying a VB rule to a SPL. In contrast to the state of the art (shown in gray), enumerating products or rules upfront is not required. By adopting this technique, existing tools that use transformation technology, such as refactoring engines, may benefit from improved performance.

Specifically, we make the following contributions:

- We introduce a staged technique for applying a VB rule to an SPL. Our technique combines core principles of VB rule applications and lifting, while avoiding their drawbacks w.r.t. enumerating all products or rules upfront.
- We formally prove correctness of this technique by showing its equivalence to the application of each "flattened" product to each "flattened" rule.
- We present an algorithm for implementing the rule application technique.

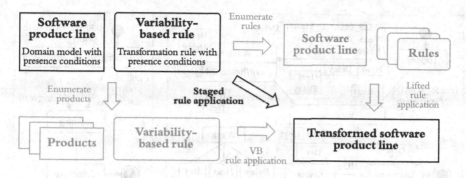

Fig. 1. Overview

– We evaluate the usefulness of our technique by studying its performance in a substantial number of cases within a software engineering scenario.

Our work builds on the underlying framework of algebraic graph transformation (AGT) [19]. AGT is one of the standard model transformation language paradigms [20]; in addition, it has recently gained momentum as an analysis paradigm for other widespread paradigms and languages such as ATL [21]. We focus on the annotative paradigm to variability. Suitable converters to and from alternative paradigms, such as the composition-based one [22], may allow our technique to be used in other cases as well.

The rest of this paper is structured as follows: We motivate and explain our contribution using a running example in Sect. 2. Section 3 revisits the necessary background. Section 4 introduces the formalization of our new rule application technique. The algorithm and its evaluation are presented in Sects. 5 and 6, respectively. In Sect. 7 we discuss related work, before we conclude in Sect. 8.

2   Running Example

In this section, we introduce SPLs and variability-based model transformation by example, and motivate and explain our contribution in the light of this example.

Software Product Lines. An SPL represents a collection of models that are similar, but different to each other. Figure 2 shows a washing machine controller SPL in an annotative representation, comprising an annotated domain model and a feature model. The feature model [23] specifies a root feature *Wash* with three optional children *Heat*, *Delay*, and *Dry*, where *Heat* and *Delay* are mutually exclusive. The domain model is a statechart diagram specifying the behavior of the controller SPL based on states *Locking*, *Waiting*, *Washing*, *Drying*, and *UnLocking* with transitions between them. Presence conditions, shown in gray labels, denote the condition under which an annotated element is present. These conditions are used to specify variations in the execution behavior.

Concrete products can be obtained from *configurations*, in which each optional feature is set to either *true* or *false*. A product arises by removing

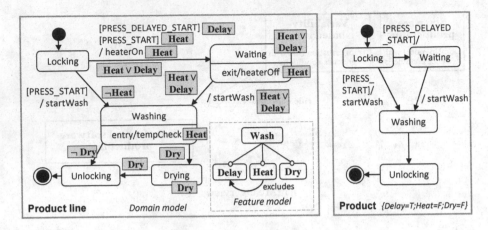

Fig. 2. Washing machine controller product line and product (adapted from [6]).

those elements whose presence condition evaluates to false in the given configuration. For instance, selecting *Delay* and deselecting *Heat* and *Dry* yields the product shown in the right of Fig. 2. The SPL has six configurations and products in total, since *Wash* is non-optional and *Delay* excludes *Heat*.

Variability-Based (VB) Model Transformation. In complex model transformation scenarios, developers often create rules that are similar, but different to each other. As an example, consider two rules *foldEntryActions* and *foldExitActions* (Fig. 3), called *A* and *B* in short. These rules express a "fold" refactoring for statechart diagrams: if a state has two incoming or outgoing transitions with the same action, these actions are to be replaced by an entry or exit action of the state. The rules have a left- and a right-hand side (LHS, RHS). The LHS specifies a pattern to be matched to an input graph, and the difference between the LHS and the RHS specifies a change to be performed for each match, like the removing of transition actions, and the adding of exit and entry actions.

Rules A and B are simple; however, in a realistic transformation system, the number of required rules can grow exponentially with the number of variation points in the rules. To avoid combinatorial explosion, a set of variability-intensive rules can be encoded into a single representation using a *VB rule* [12,18]. A VB rule consist of a LHS, a RHS, a *feature model* specifying a set of interrelated features, and *presence conditions* annotating LHS and RHS elements with a condition under which they are present. Individual "flat" rules are obtained via configuration, i.e., binding each feature to either *true* or *false*. In the VB rule *A + B*, the feature model specifies a root feature *refactor* with alternative child features *foldEntry* and *foldExit*. Since exactly one child feature has to be active at one time, two possible configurations exist. The two rules arising from these configurations are isomorphic to rules *A* and *B*.

Problem Statement. Model transformations such as *foldActions* are usually designed for applications to a concrete software product, represented by a single

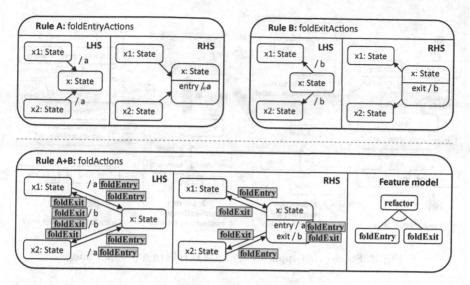

Fig. 3. Two rules and their encoding into a variability-based rule (adapted from [24]).

model. However, in various situations, it is desirable to extend the usage context to a *set* of models collected in an SPL. For example, during the batch refactoring of an SPL, all products should be refactored in a uniform way.

Variability is challenging for model transformation technologies. As illustrated in Table 1, products and rules need to be considered in manifold combinations. In our example, without dedicated variability support, the user needs to specify 6 products and 2 rules individually and trigger a rule application for each of the 12 combinations. A better strategy is enabled by VB model transformation: by applying the VB rule $A+B$, only 6 combinations need to be considered. Another strategy is to apply rules A and B to the SPL by *lifting* [6] them, leading to 2 combinations and the biggest improvement so far. Still, in more complex cases, all of these strategies are insufficient. Since none of them avoids an exponential growth along the number of optional SPL features ($\#F_P$) or optional rule features ($\#F_r$), the feasibility of the transformation is threatened.

Table 1. Approaches for dealing with multi-variability.

Approach	Independent combinations	
	Example	*General case*
Naive	12	$2^{\#F_P} * 2^{\#F_r}$
VB transformation [12]	6	$2^{\#F_P}$
Lifting [6]	2	$2^{\#F_r}$
Staged application (new)	1	1

342   D. Strüber et al.

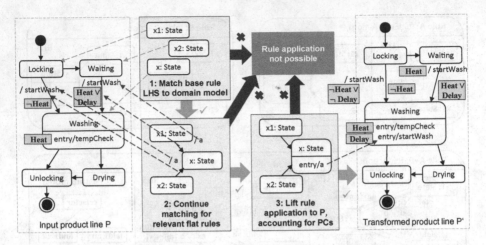

Fig. 4. Staged rule application of a VB rule to a product line.

Solution Overview. To address this situation, we propose a *staged* rule application technique for applying a VB rule to an SPL. As shown in Fig. 4, this technique proceeds in three steps: In step 1, we consider the base rule, that is, the common portion of rules encoded in the VB rule, and match its LHS to the full domain model, temporarily ignoring its presence conditions. For example, considering rule A + B, the LHS of the base rule contains precisely states x1, x2, and x. A match to the domain model is indicated by dashed arrows. Using the presence conditions, we determine if the match can be mapped to any specific product. In step 2, we extend the identified base matches to identify full matches of the rules encoded in the VB rule. In the example, we would derive rules *A* and *B*; in general, to avoid fully flattening all involved rules, one can incrementally consider common subrules. An example match is denoted in terms of dashed lines for the mappings of transitions and actions. In step 3, to perform rule applications based on identified matches, we use *lifting* to apply the rule for which the match was found. Lifting transforms the domain model and its presence condition in such way as if each product was considered individually. In the example, only products for the configuration {*Delay = true; Heat = false*} are amenable to the *foldAction* refactoring. Consequently, the new entry action *startWash* has the presence condition *Delay*, and other presence conditions are adjusted accordingly. Failure to find suitable matches and to fulfill a certain condition during lifting (discussed later) allows early termination of the process.

Performance-wise, the main benefit of this technique is twofold: First, using the termination criteria, we can exit the matching process early without considering specifics of products and rule variants. This is particularly beneficial in situations where none or only few rules of a larger rule set are applicable most of the time, which is typically the case, for example, in translators. Second, even if we have to enumerate some rules in step 2, we do not have to start the matching process from scratch, since we can save redundant effort by extending the available base matches. Consequently, Table 1 gives the number of independent combinations (in the sense that rule applications are started from scratch) as 1.

3 Background

We now introduce the necessary prerequisites of our methodology, starting with the double-pushout approach to algebraic graph transformation [19]. As the underlying structure, we assume the category of graphs with graph morphisms (referred to as *morphisms* from here), although all considerations are likely compatible with additional graph features such as typing and attributes.

Definition 1 (Rules and applications). *A rule* $r = (L \xleftarrow{le} I \xrightarrow{ri} R)$ *consists of graphs* L, I *and* R, *called* left-hand side, interface graph *and* right-hand side, *respectively, and two injective morphisms* le *and* ri.

Given a rule r, a graph G, and a morphism $m : L \to G$, a rule application from G to a graph H, written $G \Rightarrow_{r,m} H$, arises from the diagram to the right, where (1) and (2) are pushouts. G, m and H are called start graph, match, *and* result graph, *respectively.*

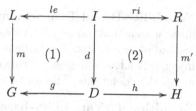

A rule application exists iff the match m fulfills the *gluing condition*, which, in the category of graphs boils down to the *dangling condition*: all adjacent edges of a deleted node in m's image $m[L]$ must have a preimage in L.

Product Lines. Our formalization represents product lines on the semantic level by considering interrelations between the included graphs. The domain model is a "maximal" graph of which all products are sub-graphs. The presence-condition function maps sub-graphs (rather than elements, as done on the syntactic level) to terms in the boolean term algebra over features, written $T_{BOOL}(F_P)$. The set of all sub-graphs of the domain model is written $\mathcal{P}(M_P)$.

Definition 2 (Product line, configuration, product)

- *A product line* $P = (F_P, \Phi_P, M_P, f_P)$ *consists of three parts: a* feature model *that consists of a set* F_P *of* features, *and a set of* feature constraints $\Phi_P \subseteq T_{BOOL}(F_P)$, *a* domain model M_P *given as a graph, and a set of* presence conditions *expressed as a function* $f_P \colon \mathcal{P}(M_P) \to T_{BOOL}(F_P)$.
- *Given a set of features* F, *a* configuration *is a total function* $c : F \to \{true, false\}$. *A configuration* c *satisfies a term* $t \in T_{BOOL}(F)$ *if* t *evaluates to true when each variable* v *in* t *is substituted by* $c(v)$. *A configuration* c *is* valid *w.r.t. a set of constraints* Φ *if* c *satisfies every constraint in* Φ.
- *Given a product line* $P = (F_P, \Phi_P, M_P, f_P)$, *a* product P_c *is derived from* P *under the valid configuration* c *if* P_c *is the union of all those graphs* $M' \subseteq M_P$ *for which* $f_P(M')$ *is satisfied by* c: $P_c = \bigcup\{M' \subseteq M_P | c \text{ satisfies } f_P(M') \text{ and } c \text{ is valid w.r.t. } \Phi_P\}$. *The* flattening *of* P *is the set* Flat(P) *of all products of* P: Flat$(P) = \{P_c | P_c \text{ is a product of } P\}$.

Definition 3 (Lifted rule application). *Given a product line* P, *a rule* r, *and a match* $m : L \to M_P$, *a lifted rule application* $P \Rightarrow_{r,m}^{\uparrow} Q$ *is a construction* that relates P to a product line Q s.t. $F_P = F_Q$, $\Phi_P = \Phi_Q$, and the set of products $\text{Flat}(Q)$ is the same as if r was applied to each product $P_i \in \text{Flat}(P)$ for which an inclusion $j : m[L] \rightarrow P_i$ from the image of m exists.

Salay et al. [6] provide an algorithm for which it is shown that the properties required in Definition 3 apply. The algorithm extends a rule application to the domain model by a check that the match can be mapped to at least one product, and by dedicated presence condition handling during additions and deletions. A more declarative treatment is offered by Taentzer et al. [25]'s product line pushout construction, which is designed to support lifted rule application as a special case.

Variability-Based Transformation. VB rules are defined similarly to product lines, with a "maximal" rule instead of a domain model, and a notion of subrules instead of subgraphs. A subrule is a rule that can be embedded into a larger rule injectively s.t. the actions of rule elements are preserved [12], e.g., deletions are mapped to deletions. The set of all subrules of a rule r is written $\mathcal{P}(r)$.

Definition 4 (Variability-based (VB) rule). *A VB rule $\check{r} = (F_{\check{r}}, \Phi_{\check{r}}, r_{\check{r}}, f_{\check{r}})$ consists of three parts: a feature model that consists of a set $F_{\check{r}}$ of features, and a set of feature constraints $\Phi_{\check{r}} \subseteq T_{BOOL}(F_{\check{r}})$, a maximal rule $r_{\check{r}}$ being a rule, and a set of presence conditions expressed as a function $f_P \colon \mathcal{P}(r_{\check{r}}) \rightarrow T_{BOOL}(F_{\check{r}})$.*

To later consider the *base rule*, that is, a maximal subrule of multiple flat rules, we define the flattening of VB rules in terms of consecutive intersection and union constructions, expressed as multi-pullbacks and -pushouts [12]. The multi-pullback r_0 gives the base rule, over which the flat rule arises by multi-pushout.

Definition 5 (Flat rule). *Given a VB rule $\check{r}$, for a valid configuration c w.r.t. $\Phi_{\check{r}}$, there exists a unique set of n subrules $S_c \subseteq \mathcal{P}(r_{\check{r}})$ s.t. $\forall s \in \mathcal{P}(r_{\check{r}}) : s \in S_c$ iff c satisfies $f_{\check{r}}(s)$. Merging these subrules via multi-pullback and multi-pushout over $r_{\check{r}}$ and r_0, respectively, yields a rule r_c, called flat rule induced by c. The flattening of $\check{r}$ is the set $\text{Flat}(\check{r})$ of all flat rules of $\check{r}$:* $\text{Flat}(\check{r}) = \{r_c | r_c \text{ is a flat rule of } \check{r}\}.$

In the example, $r_{\check{r}}$ is the rule $A + B$, ignoring presence conditions. Given the configuration $c = \{foldEntry = true, foldExit = false\}$, the multi-pullback over each subrule whose presence condition satisfies c yields as the base rule r_0 precisely the part of rule $A + B$ without presence conditions (i.e., only the states). The resulting flat rule r_c is isomorphic to rule A.

As a prerequisite for achieving efficiency during staged application, we revisit VB rule application. The key idea is that matches of a flat rule are composed from matches of all of its subrules. By considering the subrules during matching, we can reuse matches over several rules and identify early-exit opportunities.

Definition 6 (VB match family, VB match, VB rule application)

– *Given a variability-based rule $\check{r}$, a graph G, and a valid configuration c, there exists a unique set of subrules $S_c \subseteq r_{\check{r}}$ s.t. $\forall s \in \mathcal{P}(r_{\check{r}}) : s \in S_c$ iff c satisfies $f_{\check{r}}(s)$. A variability-based match family is a family of morphisms $(m_s : L_s \to G)_{1 \le s \le |S_c|}$ s.t. $\forall m_i, m_j$ with $1 \le i, j \le |S_c|$ the following compatability condition holds: $\forall x \in dom(m_i) \cap dom(m_j) : m_i(x) = m_j(x)$.*

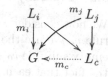

– *Given a variability-based match family (m_s) for $\check{r}$, G, and c, a variability-based match $\check{m}$ is a pair (m_c, c) where the morphism $m_c : L_c \to G$ is obtained by the colimit property of L_c. If m_c is a match, $\check{m}$ is called a variability-based match.*
– *Given a variability-based match $\check{m} = (m_c, c)$ for $\check{r}$ and G, the application of $\check{r}$ at $\check{m}$ is the rule application $G \Rightarrow_{r_c, m_c} H$ of the flat rule r_c to m_c.*

In the example, a VB match family is obtained: Step 1 collects matches of the LHS L_0. Step 2 reuses these matches to match the flat rules: according to the compatibility condition, we may extend the matches rather than start from scratch. The set of VB rule applications for a rule $\check{r}$ to a model G is equivalent to the set of rule applications of all flat rules in Flat($\check{r}$) to G [12, Theorem 2].

4 Multi-variability of Product Line Transformations

A variability-based rule represents a set of similar transformation rules, while a product line represents a set of similar models. We consider the application of a variability-based rule to a product line from a formal perspective. Our idea is to combine two principles of *maximality*, which, up to now, were considered in isolation: First, by applying a rule to a "maximum" of all products, the rule can be lifted efficiently to a product line (Definition 3). Second, by reusing matches of a maximal subrule, several rules can be applied efficiently to a single model (Definition 6).

We study three strategies for applying a variability-based rule $\check{r}$ to a product line P; the third one leads to the notion of *staged rule application* as introduced in Sect. 2. First, we consider the naive case of flattening $\check{r}$ and P and applying each rule to each product. Second, we take the two maximality principles into account to avoid the flattening of $\check{r}$. Third, we use additional aspects from the first principle to avoid the flattening of P as well. We show that all strategies are equivalent in the sense that they change all of P's products in the same way.

4.1 Fully Flattened Application

Definition 7 (Fully flattened application). *Given the flattening of a product line P and the flattening of a rule family $\check{r}$, the set of fully-flattened rule applications $Trans_{FF}(P, \check{r})$ arises from applying each rule to each product:*

$$Trans_{FF}(P, \check{r}) = \{P_i \Rightarrow_{r_c, m_c} Q_i | P_i \in Flat(P), r_c \in Flat(\check{r}), match\ m_c : L_c \to P_i\}$$

In the example, there are two rules and six products; however, only for two products—the ones arising from configurations with *Delay = true* and *Heat = false*—a match, and, therefore, a rule application exists, as we saw in the earlier description of the example. $Trans_{FF}(P, \check{r})$ comprises the resulting two rule applications.

4.2   Partially Flattened Application

We now consider a strategy that aims to avoid unflattening the variability-based rule $\check{r}$. We use the fact that the rules in $\check{r}$ generally share a maximal, possibly empty sub-rule r_0 that can be embedded into all rules in $\check{r}$. Moreover, we exploit the fact that each product has an inclusion into the domain model.

The key idea is as follows: each match of a flat rule to a product includes a match of r_0 into the domain model M_P. Absence of such a match implies that none of the rules in $\check{r}$ has a match, allowing us to stop without considering any flat rule in its entirety. Such exit point is particularly beneficial if the VB rule represents a subset of a larger rule set in which only a few rules can be matched at one time. Conversely, if a match for r_0 exists, a rule application arises if the match can be "rerouted" onto one of the products P_i. In this case, we consider the flat rules, saving redundant matching effort by reusing the matches of r_0.

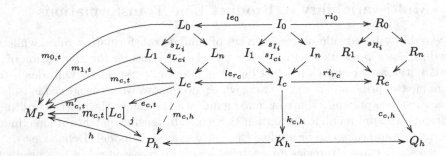

Fig. 5. Partially flattened rule application.

To reuse matches to the domain model for the products, we introduce the rerouting of a morphism from its codomain onto another graph G'. We omit naming the codomain and G' explicitly where they are clear from the context.

Definition 8 (Rerouted morphism). *Let an inclusion $i : G' \rightarrow G$, a morphism $m : L \rightarrow G$ with an epi-mono-factorization (e, m'), and a morphism $j : m[L] \rightarrow G'$ be given, s.t. $m' = i \circ j$. The rerouted morphism $reroute(m, G') : L \rightarrow G'$ arises by composition: $reroute(m, G') = j \circ e$.*

Definition 9 (Rerouted variability-based match). *Given a graph G, a variability-based rule $\check{r}$ with a variability-based match $\check{m} = (m_c, c)$ (Definition 6), and an inclusion $i : G' \to G$. If the epi-mono-factorization of m_c and a suitable morphism j exists, a rerouted morphism onto G' arises (Definition 8). Pairing this morphism with the configuration c induces the rerouted variability-based match of $\check{m}_c$ onto G': $reroute(\check{m}, G') = (reroute(m_c, G'), c)$.*

In Fig. 5, $m_{c,h}$ is the morphism obtained by rerouting a match $m_{c,t}$ from the domain model M_p to product P_h. For example, if $m_{c,t}$ is the match indicated in steps 1 and 2 of Fig. 4, the morphism j and, consequently, $m_{c,h}$ exists only for products in which all images of the mappings exist as well, e.g., the product shown in the right of Fig. 2. Note that $m_{c,t}$ is a variability-based match to M_P: In an earlier explanation, we saw that the family $(m_{i,t})$ forms a variability-based match family. Therefore, per Definition 9, pairing $m_{c,h}$ with the configuration c induces a variability-based match to P_h, which can be used as follows.

Variability-based rule application (Definition 6) allows us to save matching effort by considering shared parts of rules to a graph only once. The following definition allows us to lift this insight from graphs onto product lines. We show that the sets of partially and fully flattened rule applications are equivalent.

Definition 10 (Partially flattened application). *Given a variability-based rule $\check{r}$ and a product line P, the set of partially flattened rule applications $Trans_{PF}(P, \check{r})$ is obtained by rerouting all variability-based matches from the domain model M_P to products in P and collecting all resulting rule applications:*

$$Trans_{PF}(P, \check{r}) = \{P_i \Rightarrow_{\check{r}, \check{m}'} Q_i \mid \check{m} = (m_c, c) \text{ is a VB match of } \check{r} \text{ to } M_P,$$
$$P_i \in Flat(P), \check{m}' = (reroute(m_c, P_i), c) \text{ is a VB match}\}$$

Theorem 1 (Equivalence of fully and partially flattened rule applications). *Given a product line P and a variability-based rule $\check{r}$, $Trans_{FF}(P, \check{r}) = Trans_{PF}(P, \check{r})$.*

Proof idea.[1] For every fully flattened (FF) rule application, we can find a corresponding partially flattened (PF) one, and vice versa: Given a FF rule application at a match m', we compose m' with the product inclusion into the domain model M_P to obtain a match m_c into M_P. Per Theorem 2 in [12], m_c induces a VB match and rule application. From a diagram chase, we see that m' is the morphism arising from rerouting m_c onto the product P_i. Consequently, the rule application is PF. Conversely, a PF variability-based rule application induces a corresponding FF rule application by its definition.

4.3 Staged Application

The final strategy we consider, staged application, aims to avoid unflattening the products as well. This can be achieved by employing lifting (Definition 3): Lifting

---

[1] A full proof is provided in the extended version of this paper: http://danielstrueber. de/publications/SPJ18.pdf.

takes a single rule and applies it to a domain model and its presence conditions in such a way as if the rule had been applied to each product individually. The considered rule in our case is a flat rule with a match to the domain model.

Note that we cannot compare the set of staged applications directly to the set of flattened applications, since it does not live on the product level. We can, however, compare the obtained sets of products from both sets of applications, which happens to be the same, thus showing the correctness of our approach.

Definition 11 (Staged application). *Given a variability-based rule $\check{r}$ and a product line P, the set of* staged applications *$Trans_{St}(P, \check{r})$ is the set of lifted rule applications obtained from VB matches to the domain model M_P:*

$$Trans_{St}(P, \check{r}) = \{P \Rightarrow^{\uparrow}_{r_c, m_c} Q \mid \check{m} = (m_c, c) \text{ is a VB match of } \check{r} \text{ to } M_P\}$$

Corollary 1 (Equivalence of staged and partially flattened rule applications). *Given a product line P and a variability-based rule $\check{r}$, the sets of products obtained from $Trans_{St}(P, \check{r})$ and $Trans_{PF}(P, \check{r})$ are isomorphic.*

Proof. Since both sets are defined over the same set of matches of flat rules, the proof follows straight from the definition of lifting.

5   Algorithm

We present an algorithm for implementing the staged application of a VB rule $\check{r}$ to a product line P. Following the overview in Sect. 2 and the treatment in Sect. 4, the main idea is to proceed in three steps: First, we match the base rule of $\check{r}$ to the domain model, ignoring presence conditions. Second, we consider individual rules as far as necessary to obtain matches to the domain model. Third, based on the matches, we perform the actual rule application by using the lifting algorithm from [6] in a black-box manner.

Algorithm 1. Staged application.

Input   : Product line P, VB rule $\check{r}$
Output: Transformed product line P

1 $BMatches := \text{findMatches}(Model_P, r_0)$;
2 **foreach** m $\in$ BMatches **do**
3 | $\Phi_{pc} := \bigwedge \{\, pc \in pcs_{pre} \,\}$;
4 | **if** $\Phi_P \wedge \Phi_{pc}$ is SAT **then**
5 | | **foreach** c $\in$ configs($\check{r}$) **do**
6 | | | $flatRule := r_{\check{r}}.\text{removeAll}(e \mid c \nvDash pc_e)$;
7 | | | $Matches := \text{findMatches}(Model_P, flatRule, m)$;
8 | | | lift($P, flatRule, Matches$);
9 | | **end**
10 | **end**
11 **end**

Algorithm 1 shows the computation in more detail. In line 1, $\check{r}$'s base rule r_0 is matched to the domain model $Model_P$, leading to a set of base matches. If this set is empty, we have reached the first exit criterion and can stop directly. Otherwise, given a match m, in line 2, we check if at least one product P_i exists that m can be rerouted onto (Definition 8). To this end, in lines 3–4, we use a SAT solver to check if there is a valid configuration of P's feature model for which all

Table 2. Subject rule set.

Category	#Rules	#VBRules
Create/Set	274	171
Delete/Unset	164	121
Change/Move	966	212
Total	1404	504

Table 3. Subject product lines.

SPL	#Elements	#Products
1: InCar	116	54
2: E2E	130	94
3: JSSE	24,077	64
4: Notepad	252	512
5: Mobile	4,069	3,072
6: Lampiro	29,045	5,892

presence conditions of matched elements evaluate to *true*. In this case, we iterate over the valid configurations of $\check{r}$ in line 5 (we may proceed more fine-grainedly by using partial configurations; this optimization is omitted for simplicity). In line 6, a flat rule is obtained by removing all elements from the rule whose presence condition evaluates to *false*. We match this rule to the domain model in line 7; to save redundant effort, we restrict the search to matches that extend the current base match. Absence of such a match is the second stopping criterion. Otherwise, we feed the flat rule and the set of matches to lifting in line 8. Handling dangling conditions is left to lifting; in the positive case, P is transformed afterwards.

For illustration, consider the base match $m_1 = \{Looking, Waiting, Washing\}$ from Fig. 4. First we calculate Φ_{pc}. As none of the states in the domain model has a presence condition, Φ_{pc} is set to *true* and is identified as satisfiable. Two valid configurations exist, $c_1 = \{foldEntry = true, foldExit = false\}$ and $c_2 = \{foldEntry = false, foldExit = true\}$. Considering c_1, the presence condition *foldExit* evaluates to false; removing the corresponding elements yield a rule isomorphic to Rule A in Fig. 3. Match m_1 is now extended using this rule, leading to a match as shown in step 2 of Fig. 4. and then lifted, as discussed in the earlier explanation of the example. Step 2 is repeated for configuration c_2; yet, as no suitable match in c_2 exists, the shown transformation is the only possible one.

This algorithm benefits from the correctness results shown in Sect. 4. Specifically, it computes staged rule applications as per Definition 11: A configuration c is determined in line 5, and values for match m_c are collected in the set *Matches*. Via Corollary 1 and Theorem 1, the effect of the rule application to the products is the same as if each product had been considered individually.

In terms of performance, two limiting factors are the use of a graph matcher and a SAT solver; both of them perform an NP-complete task. Still, we expect practical improvements from our strategy of reusing shared portions of the involved rules and graphs, and from the availability of efficient SAT solvers that scale up to millions of variables [26]. This hypothesis is studied in Sect. 6.

6   Evaluation

To evaluate our technique, we implemented it for Henshin [27, 28], a graph-based model transformation language, and applied it to a transformation scenario with product lines and transformation variability. The goal of our evaluation was to study if our technique indeed produces the expected performance benefits.

Setup. The transformation is concerned with the detection of applied editing operations during model differencing [29]. This setting is particularly interesting for a performance evaluation: Since differencing is a routine software development task, low latency of the used tools is a prerequisite for developer effectiveness. The rule set, called `UmlRecog`, is tailored to the detection of UML edit operations. Each rule detects a specific edit operation, such as "move method to superclass", based on a pair of model versions and a low-level difference trace. `UmlRecog` comprises 1404 rules, which, as shown in Table 2, fall in three main categories: *Create/Set*, *Change/Move*, and *Delete/Unset*. To study the effect of our technique on performance, an encoding of the rules into VB rules was required. We obtained this encoding using RuleMerger [18], a tool for generating VB rules from classic ones based on clustering and clone detection [30]. We obtained 504 VB rules; each of them representing between 1 and 71 classic rules. `UmlRecog` is publicly available as part of a benchmark transformation set [31].

We applied this transformation to the 6 UML-based product lines specified in Table 3. The product lines came from diverse sources and include manually designed ones (1–2), and reverse-engineered ones from open-source projects (3–6). Each product line was available as an UML model annotated with presence conditions over a feature model. To produce the model version pairs used by `UmlRecog`, we automatically simulated development steps by nondeterministically applying rules from a set of edit rules to the product lines, using the lifting algorithm to account for presence conditions during the simulated editing step.

Table 4. Execution times (in seconds) of the lifting and the staged approach.

	Create/Set			Delete/Unset			Change/Move			Total		
	Lift	Stage	Factor	Lift	Stage	Factor	Lift	Stage	Factor	Lift	Stage	Factor
InCar	2.13	0.52	**4.1**	0.23	0.12	**1.9**	7.28	0.86	**8.5**	9.66	1.49	**6.5**
E2E	1.99	0.82	**2.4**	0.35	0.32	**1.1**	7.28	0.95	**7.7**	9.62	2.12	**4.5**
JSSE	2.00	0.51	**3.9**	0.24	0.16	**1.5**	8.40	3.08	**2.7**	10.61	3.79	**2.8**
Notepad	2.05	0.66	**3.1**	0.26	0.14	**1.9**	7.01	1.64	**4.3**	9.38	2.47	**3.8**
Mobile	2.00	0.55	**3.7**	0.24	0.13	**1.9**	8.28	1.62	**5.1**	10.55	2.26	**4.7**
Lampiro	2.05	0.64	**3.2**	0.26	0.15	**1.7**	8.25	2.58	**3.2**	10.55	3.29	**3.2**

As baseline for comparison, we considered the lifted application of each rule in `UmlRecog`. An alternative baseline of applying VB rules to the flattened set of products was not considered: The SPL variability in our setting is much greater than the rule variability, which implies a high performance penalty when enumerating products. Since we currently do not support advanced transformation features, e.g., negative application conditions and amalgamation, we used variants of the flat and the VB rules without these concepts. We used a Ubuntu 17.04 system (Oracle JDK 1.8, Intel Core i5-6200U, 8 GB RAM) for all experiments.

Results. Table 4 gives an overview of the results of our experiments. The total execution times for our technique were between 1.5 and 3.3 s, compared to 9.4 and 10.6 s for lifting, yielding a speedup by factors between 2.8 and 6.5. For both techniques, all execution times are in the same order of magnitude across product lines. A possible explanation is that the amount of applicable rules was small: if the vast majority of rules can be discarded early in the matching process, the execution time is constant with the number of rules.

The greatest speedups were observed for the *Change/Move* category, in which rule variability was the greatest as well, indicated by the ratio between rules and VB rules in Table 2. This observation is in line with our rationale of reusing shared matches between rules. Regarding the number of products, a trend regarding better scalability is not apparent, thus demonstrating that lifting is sufficient for controlling product-line variability. Still, based on the overall results, the hypothesis that our technique improves performance in situations with significant product-line and transformation variability can be confirmed.

Threats to Validity. Regarding external validity, we only considered a limited set of scenarios, based on six product lines and one large-scale transformation. We aim to apply our technique to a broader class of cases in the future. The version pairs were obtained in a synthetic process, arguably one that produces pessimistic cases. Our treatment so far is also limited to a particular transformation paradigm, AGT, and one variability paradigm, the annotative one. Still, AGT and annotative variability are the underlying paradigms of many state-of-the-art tools. Finally, we did not consider the advanced AGT concepts of negative application conditions and amalgamation in our evaluation; extending our technique accordingly is left as future work.

7   Related Work

During an SPL's lifecycle, not only the domain model, but also the feature model evolves [32, 33]. To support the combined transformation of domain and feature models, Taentzer et al. [25] propose a unifying formal framework which generalizes Salay et al.'s notion of lifting [6], yet in a different direction than us: focusing on combined changes, this approach is not geared for internal variability of rules; similar rules are considered separately. Both works could be combined using a rule concept with separate feature models for rule and SPL variability.

Beyond transformations of SPLs, transformations have been used to *implement* SPLs. Feature-oriented development [34] supports the implementation of features as additive changes to a base product. Delta-oriented programming [35] adds flexibility to this approach: changes are specified using *deltas* that support deletions and modifications as well. Impact analysis in an evolving SPL can be performed by transforming deltas using higher-order deltas that encapsulate certain evolution operators [5]. For increased flexibility regarding inter-product reuse, deltas can be combined with traits [36]. Sijtema [8] introduced the concept of variability rules to develop SPLs using ATL. Conversely, SPL techniques have been applied to certain problems in transformation development. Xiao et al. [37] propose to capture variability in the backwards propagation of bidirectional transformations by turning the left-hand-side model into a SPL. Hussein et al. [10] present a notion of rule templates for generating groups of similar rules based on a data provenance model. These works address only one dimension of variability, either of a SPL or a transformation system.

In the domain of graph transformation reuse, rule refinement [9] and amalgamation [38] focus on reuse at the rule level; graph variability is not in their scope. Rensink and Ghamarian propose a solution for rule and graph decomposition based a certain accommodation condition, under which the effect of the original rule application is preserved [39,40]. In our approach, by matching against the full domain model rather than decomposing it, we trade off compositionality for the benefit of imposing fewer restrictions on graphs and rules.

8   Conclusion and Future Work

We propose a methodology for software product line transformations in which not only the input product line, but also the transformation system contains variability. At the heart of our methodology a staged rule application technique exploits reuse potential with regard to shared portions of the involved products and rules. We showed the correctness of our technique and demonstrated its benefit by applying it to a practical software engineering task.

In the future, we aim to explore further variability dimensions, e.g., meta-model variability as considered in [41], and to extend our work to advanced transformation features, such as application conditions. We aim to address additional variability mechanisms and to perform a broader evaluation.

Acknowledgement. We thank Rick Salay and the anonymous reviewers for their constructive feedback. This work was supported by the Deutsche Forschungsgemeinschaft (DFG), project *SecVolution@Run-time*, no. 221328183.

References

1. Pohl, K., Boeckle, G., van der Linden, F.: Software Product Line Engineering: Foundations, Principles, and Techniques. Springer, Heidelberg (2005). https://doi.org/10.1007/3-540-28901-1
2. Apel, S., Batory, D., Kästner, C., Saake, G.: Feature-Oriented Software Product Lines: Concepts and Implementation. Springer, Heidelberg (2013). https://doi.org/10.1007/978-3-642-37521-7
3. Schulze, S., Thüm, T., Kuhlemann, M., Saake, G.: Variant-preserving refactoring in feature-oriented software product lines. In: VaMoS, pp. 73–81 (2012)

4. Borba, P., Teixeira, L., Gheyi, R.: A theory of software product line refinement. Theor. Comput. Sci. **455**, 2–30 (2012)
5. Lity, S., Kowal, M., Schaefer, I.: Higher-order delta modeling for software product line evolution. In: FOSD, pp. 39–48 (2016)
6. Salay, R., Famelis, M., Rubin, J., Sandro, A.D., Chechik, M.: Lifting model transformations to product lines. In: ICSE, pp. 117–128 (2014)
7. Kolovos, D.S., Rose, L.M., Matragkas, N., Paige, R.F., Guerra, E., Cuadrado, J.S., De Lara, J., Ráth, I., Varró, D., Tisi, M., et al.: A research roadmap towards achieving scalability in model driven engineering. In: BigMDE, p. 2. ACM (2013)
8. Sijtema, M.: Introducing variability rules in ATL for managing variability in MDE-based product lines. In: MtATL 2010, pp. 39–49 (2010)
9. Anjorin, A., Saller, K., Lochau, M., Schürr, A.: Modularizing triple graph grammars using rule refinement. In: Gnesi, S., Rensink, A. (eds.) FASE 2014. LNCS, vol. 8411, pp. 340–354. Springer, Heidelberg (2014). https://doi.org/10.1007/978-3-642-54804-8_24
10. Hussein, J., Moreau, L., et al.: A template-based graph transformation system for the PROV data model. In: GCM (2016)
11. Strüber, D.: Model-driven engineering in the large: refactoring techniques for models and model transformation systems. Ph.D. dissertation, Philipps-Universität Marburg (2016)
12. Strüber, D., Rubin, J., Arendt, T., Chechik, M., Taentzer, G., Plöger, J.: Variability-based model transformation: formal foundation and application. Formal Aspects Comput. **30**, 133–162 (2017)
13. Strüber, D., Rubin, J., Chechik, M., Taentzer, G.: A variability-based approach to reusable and efficient model transformations. In: Egyed, A., Schaefer, I. (eds.) FASE 2015. LNCS, vol. 9033, pp. 283–298. Springer, Heidelberg (2015). https://doi.org/10.1007/978-3-662-46675-9_19
14. Kästner, C., Apel, S., Trujillo, S., Kuhlemann, M., Batory, D.: Language-independent safe decomposition of legacy applications into features, vol. 2. Technical report, School of Computer Science, University of Magdeburg, Germany (2008)
15. Di Sandro, A., Salay, R., Famelis, M., Kokaly, S., Chechik, M.: MMINT: a graphical tool for interactive model management. In: P&D@ MoDELS, pp. 16–19 (2015)
16. Strüber, D., Schulz, S.: A tool environment for managing families of model transformation rules. In: Echahed, R., Minas, M. (eds.) ICGT 2016. LNCS, vol. 9761, pp. 89–101. Springer, Cham (2016). https://doi.org/10.1007/978-3-319-40530-8_6
17. Rubin, J., Chechik, M.: Combining related products into product lines. In: de Lara, J., Zisman, A. (eds.) FASE 2012. LNCS, vol. 7212, pp. 285–300. Springer, Heidelberg (2012). https://doi.org/10.1007/978-3-642-28872-2_20
18. Strüber, D., Rubin, J., Arendt, T., Chechik, M., Taentzer, G., Plöger, J.: *Rule-Merger*: automatic construction of variability-based model transformation rules. In: Stevens, P., Wąsowski, A. (eds.) FASE 2016. LNCS, vol. 9633, pp. 122–140. Springer, Heidelberg (2016). https://doi.org/10.1007/978-3-662-49665-7_8
19. Ehrig, H., Ehrig, K., Prange, U., Taentzer, G.: Fundamentals of Algebraic Graph Transformation. MTCSAES. Springer, Heidelberg (2006). https://doi.org/10.1007/3-540-31188-2
20. Czarnecki, K., Helsen, S.: Feature-based survey of model transformation approaches. IBM Syst. J. **45**(3), 621–645 (2006)
21. Richa, E., Borde, E., Pautet, L.: Translation of ATL to AGT and application to a code generator for Simulink. SoSyM, 1–24 (2017). https://link.springer.com/article/10.1007/s10270-017-0607-8

22. Kästner, C., Apel, S., Kuhlemann, M.: Granularity in software product lines. In: ICSE, pp. 311–320 (2008)
23. Kang, K.C., Cohen, S.G., Hess, J.A., Novak, W.E., Peterson, A.S.: Feature-oriented domain analysis (FODA) feasibility study. Technical report, Software Engineering Inst., Carnegie-Mellon Univ., Pittsburgh, PA (1990)
24. Chechik, M., Famelis, M., Salay, R., Strüber, D.: Perspectives of model transformation reuse. In: Ábrahám, E., Huisman, M. (eds.) IFM 2016. LNCS, vol. 9681, pp. 28–44. Springer, Cham (2016). https://doi.org/10.1007/978-3-319-33693-0_3
25. Taentzer, G., Salay, R., Strüber, D., Chechik, M.: Transformations of software product lines: a generalizing framework based on category theory. In: MODELS, pp. 101–111. IEEE (2017)
26. Gomes, C.P., Kautz, H., Sabharwal, A., Selman, B.: Satisfiability solvers. In: Foundations of Artificial Intelligence, vol. 3, pp. 89–134 (2008)
27. Arendt, T., Biermann, E., Jurack, S., Krause, C., Taentzer, G.: Henshin: advanced concepts and tools for in-place EMF model transformations. In: Petriu, D.C., Rouquette, N., Haugen, Ø. (eds.) MODELS 2010. LNCS, vol. 6394, pp. 121–135. Springer, Heidelberg (2010). https://doi.org/10.1007/978-3-642-16145-2_9
28. Strüber, D., Born, K., Gill, K.D., Groner, R., Kehrer, T., Ohrndorf, M., Tichy, M.: Henshin: a usability-focused framework for EMF model transformation development. In: de Lara, J., Plump, D. (eds.) ICGT 2017. LNCS, vol. 10373, pp. 196–208. Springer, Cham (2017). https://doi.org/10.1007/978-3-319-61470-0_12
29. Kehrer, T., Kelter, U., Taentzer, G.: A rule-based approach to the semantic lifting of model differences in the context of model versioning. In: ASE, pp. 163–172. IEEE Computer Society (2011)
30. Strüber, D., Plöger, J., Acreţoaie, V.: Clone detection for graph-based model transformation languages. In: Van Gorp, P., Engels, G. (eds.) ICMT 2016. LNCS, vol. 9765, pp. 191–206. Springer, Cham (2016). https://doi.org/10.1007/978-3-319-42064-6_13
31. Strüber, D., Kehrer, T., Arendt, T., Pietsch, C., Reuling, D.: Scalability of model transformations: position paper and benchmark set. In: Workshop on Scalable Model Driven Engineering, pp. 21–30 (2016)
32. Thüm, T., Batory, D., Kästner, C.: Reasoning about edits to feature models. In: ICSE, pp. 254–264 (2009)
33. Bürdek, J., Kehrer, T., Lochau, M., Reuling, D., Kelter, U., Schürr, A.: Reasoning about product-line evolution using complex feature model differences. Autom. Softw. Eng. 23, 687–733 (2015)
34. Trujillo, S., Batory, D., Diaz, O.: Feature oriented model driven development: a case study for portlets. In: ICSE, pp. 44–53. IEEE Computer Society (2007)
35. Schaefer, I., Bettini, L., Bono, V., Damiani, F., Tanzarella, N.: Delta-oriented programming of software product lines. In: Bosch, J., Lee, J. (eds.) SPLC 2010. LNCS, vol. 6287, pp. 77–91. Springer, Heidelberg (2010). https://doi.org/10.1007/978-3-642-15579-6_6
36. Damiani, F., Hähnle, R., Kamburjan, E., Lienhardt, M.: A unified and formal programming model for deltas and traits. In: Huisman, M., Rubin, J. (eds.) FASE 2017. LNCS, vol. 10202, pp. 424–441. Springer, Heidelberg (2017). https://doi.org/10.1007/978-3-662-54494-5_25
37. He, X., Hu, Z., Liu, Y.: Towards variability management in bidirectional model transformation. In: COMPSAC, vol. 1, pp. 224–233. IEEE (2017)
38. Biermann, E., Ermel, C., Taentzer, G.: Lifting parallel graph transformation concepts to model transformation based on the eclipse modeling framework. Electron. Commun. EASST 26 (2010)

39. Rensink, A.: Compositionality in graph transformation. In: Abramsky, S., Gavoille, C., Kirchner, C., Meyer auf der Heide, F., Spirakis, P.G. (eds.) ICALP 2010. LNCS, vol. 6199, pp. 309–320. Springer, Heidelberg (2010). https://doi.org/10.1007/978-3-642-14162-1_26
40. Ghamarian, A.H., Rensink, A.: Generalised compositionality in graph transformation. In: Ehrig, H., Engels, G., Kreowski, H.-J., Rozenberg, G. (eds.) ICGT 2012. LNCS, vol. 7562, pp. 234–248. Springer, Heidelberg (2012). https://doi.org/10.1007/978-3-642-33654-6_16
41. Perrouin, G., Amrani, M., Acher, M., Combemale, B., Legay, A., Schobbens, P.-Y.: Featured model types: towards systematic reuse in modelling language engineering. In: MiSE, pp. 1–7. IEEE (2016)

Author Index

Printed in the United States
By Bookmasters

Printed in the United States
By Bookmasters